A HISTORY OF THE
UNITED STATES OF AMERICA

Volume One

A HISTORY OF THE
UNITED STATES OF AMERICA

VOLUME ONE
The Search for Liberty
From Origins to Independence

VOLUME TWO
An Empire for Liberty
From Washington to Lincoln

VOLUME THREE
The American Dream
From Reconstruction to Reagan

The Search for Liberty

From Origins to Independence

ESMOND WRIGHT

BLACKWELL
Oxford UK & Cambridge USA

First published 1995

Blackwell Publishers
238 Main Street
Cambridge, Massachusetts 02142
USA

108 Cowley Road
Oxford OX4 1JF
UK

Library of Congress Cataloging-in-Publication Data

Wright, Esmond.
The search for liberty : from origins to independence / Esmond Wright.
p.   cm. — (A History of the United States of America ; v. 1)
Includes bibliographical references and index.
ISBN 1–55786–588–4
1. United States — History — Colonial period, ca.1600–1775.
2. United States — History — Revolution, 1775–1783.   I. Title.
II. Series: Wright, Esmond. History of the United States of America ; v. 1.
E188.W77   1994
973.2–dc20   93–42378
CIP

British Library Cataloguing in Publication Data

A CIP catalogue record for this book is available from the British Library.

Typeset in 11 on 13 pt Sabon Symposia by Apex Products, Singapore
Printed in Great Britain by T. J. Press Ltd, Padstow, Cornwall

This book is printed on acid-free paper

Contents

Maps

Plates

Chronologies

Foreword

This book has taken a lifetime to write; or, at least, an academic lifetime. It began when, after World War II, I left the Middle East and taught British and Near Eastern history at the University of Glasgow. University teaching in Scotland did not – at least in those days – consist of the sherry-laced and gossipy tutorials *à la* Oxford or Cambridge, graced by an occasional (weekly, fortnightly?) paper read out, however inaudibly, by a scholar, from the page proofs of his latest research. The Scottish universities follow American fashion, with students on entrance a year younger than in England and without benefit of the high-pressure training of many English sixth forms; daily one-hour lectures, sometimes from the speaker's own text-book, if he has written one, are designed to provide a factual outline, but, with luck, are occasionally given shape, style, and *brio*. In my day as lecturer (1946–57), the occasional lectures on the history of the United States were given by even more occasional visitors, staying for too short periods. I was asked by the Professor – a term then still used exclusively for the head of the Department – to "become responsible" also for this class, to introduce our visitors to the intricacy of the Greek-letter marking system, to translate their numbers into alpha-beta or whatever, and to fill in the gaps in the lecture course when he – there was never a "she" in my time – wasn't there. In a few years I became Senior Lecturer in American History, mainly because the Professor could lecture, and at one time or another had lectured, on everything else, British, European, Medieval, Modern Imperial, Constitutional History, *et al*. – but confessed that the history of the US was for him *terra incognita*, and he was happy to let it remain so. Accordingly I am in vast debt to the writers on American History

whose surveys, whose specialist studies, and whose articles I have
read and raided over – now – nearly 50 years. This book thus
began in form as a lecturer's notebook, which just might become a
junior college text. It has grown slowly over the years, interrupted
by lecture-and-research forays at home and abroad, and by, among
other things, a term in the House of Commons. It has been revised,
amended, then erased and re-written, and amended again in the light
of or in disagreement with the current fashions; I take note of some
of these in the bibliographical appendices. It is meant to be factual,
descriptive, biographical – but, here and there, with some analysis
of major issues.

My indebtedness is vast: to the legion of American scholars who
have preceded me, as authors of text-books or of monographs, to
a legion of contributors to periodicals, not least the *William &
Mary Quarterly*, to generations of students in Glasgow and London,
asking questions, to librarians in Glasgow and London, Philadelphia
and Yale, to Don Higginbotham of the University of North Carolina
at Chapel Hill, for his kind and careful reading of the text, to
David Burton of St Joseph's University, Philadelphia, for years of
friendship and counsel, to Enid MacDonald for her skill as secretary
and decipherer, and in particular to Alison Cowden of the Senate
House Library in the University of London, formerly Librarian of
the Institute of United States Studies in London, with her encyclo-
pedic knowledge of who wrote what, and when, and where. I owe
even more to those, whether in politics and/or in business or in
academic villages, who reveal how men (and nowadays women) act
in crises, since historians are, I believe, better equipped to describe
the past if they remember that it was once the untidy present, torn
by envy, jealousy, bitterness, and hatred, crowded with rascals and
thugs, crusaders and problem-solvers, wheeler-dealers and media-
distorters, rarely aware of where they or it were going, and before
the tarnish rotted the blade. In understanding the past, it helps not
only to become immersed in contemporary records and diaries, but
to have tasted deep of one's own present. Admiral and Professor
S. E. Morison urged his student-readers to live their lives fully, first
or contemporarily – as he did at sea and on land – and not to be
merely "men of the lamp."

The code-word of the last generation has been "relevance." As
interpreted, this has allowed writers to address themselves primarily
to social or economic issues, or to selected topics deemed by them
to have been minimized or ignored in the past, not least the rights
of women, of blacks, of the inarticulate and illiterate, and of those
who were or thought they were or were said to be or to have been

disadvantaged. It has been history "from the bottom up," wearing its conscience on its sleeve, seeking to find a voice for the voiceless. Too often, given the silence of the illiterate majority, this becomes anonymous history, heavily reliant on mortality and statistical tables, census and shipping returns – history with the individual frequently left out. This is not my style. As my mentor in Virginia, the late Thomas Perkins Abernethy, used to stress, historians should "people the past." At its best this requires the skills of a Freud, or even of a Dostoyevsky, or of Saul Bellow, providing pen portraits of men – and occasionally women – whose emotions were in turmoil; for people in office or wielding influence are rarely simple, and rarely totally honest even with themselves when they talk to themselves in diaries. Perhaps some slight experience of the "real" world can compensate for lack of skill in fiction – although fiction can often etch a portrait more successfully than – allegedly – "straight" history itself.

The main themes in the conventional American story are by this time hallowed. It is an adventure story, of men going – from Asia, Northern Europe, Western Europe, and from Africa – for gold and glory, driven by religion and by hunger, and slowly mastering a near-wilderness. It is a roll-call of discoverers as heroes (and in the anniversary year of 1992 serving both as folk-heroes and folk-villains) according to taste: Columbus and Cortés, Ponce de Leon and Panfilo de Narvaez, Champlain and La Salle, Louis Joliet and Père Marquette, Daniel Boone and Davy Crockett, but also Benedict Arnold and Aaron Burr, Nat Turner and John Brown – heroes in abundance, but sometimes turncoats, madmen and would-be Caesars also, with the normal complement of hesitant men among them. Many who crossed the ocean, however, went under indenture and unwillingly, and in chains. The first Americans of all reached it without realizing it. American history is, moreover, history in which geography is always close. Its existence depended on its overcoming frontier enemies: native and foreign, red and white, including Nature itself. It still does: the story of the American suburb has been called a campaign against the crab-grass frontier. They saw the forest as enemy and destroyed it. For a century and a half its southern frontier, for three centuries its western frontier, were in flux: American maps were ever new. The two most recent states were added less than a century ago, and Puerto Rico is greedily awaiting statehood. The frontier was seen – before Frederick Jackson Turner and since – as America's unique characteristic, western-looking, a safety valve for the removal of restless and ambitious men, a place at once for pioneers and for utopian collectivists, a constant source of optimism and renewal. Change, however, is its only constant, for no "pattern" in it is ever quite the same. It has thus only a limited value for statesmen – the penalty of its uniqueness. "You cannot step twice into the same river," said Heraclitus, "for fresh waters are ever flowing in upon you."

But contemporaries are asking: it is a separate republic, but is it truly unique? Are its social and human problems not those of other societies? Are its ethnic diversities any more complex than those of Africa, India, or Central Europe? Even in its major language and its slang, in its folklore and in its law, in its non-established but numerous churches and in its life-style, the United States of America was, and is still, a republican edition of the mother-country, a mirror England or Scotland or Ireland in the wilderness. Only after 1865 did it become a totally new and independent world. Within the generation after 1865, more in protest against industrial America than against its pre-civil war form, Henry James would lament the price exacted by republicanism and by political separation from the mother-countries. As S. V. Benet wrote:

> They tried to fit you with an English song
> And clip your speech into an English tale
> But even from the first the words went wrong,
> The catbird pecked away the nightingale.[1]

---

[1] S. V. Benet, *John Brown's Body* (New York, Rinehart, 1927).

General Chronology

1492	Columbus's first voyage to the New World
1519–21	Conquest of Mexico
1531–3	Conquest of Peru
1549	Portugal established colonial rule in Brazil
1585–90	Unsuccessful attempt to establish an English colony on Roanoke Island (now North Carolina)
1607	Settlement of Jamestown, Virginia
1608–27	French settlement of St Lawrence Valley
1619	Appearance of first African-Americans, brought to Jamestown in a Dutch ship
1620	Pilgrim Fathers established Plymouth Colony
1630	Puritan settlement of Massachusetts Bay
1634	Settlement of Maryland
1636	Harvard College founded
1640	*Bay Psalm Book*
1661–4	British conquest of New Netherland (New York)
1662	Michael Wigglesworth, *The Day of Doom*
1669–80	Founding of Charleston
1675–6	King Philip's War broke Indian resistance in New England
1680–2	Founding of Pennsylvania
1689–97	King William's War against French
1698– 1702	French settlement of Louisiana
1702	Cotton Mather, *Magnalia Christi Americana*
1702–13	Queen Anne's War against French

Introduction: The Enterprise
of the Indies

1   THE NEW ATLANTIS

Of the locations, time and circumstances of the nation's origins, there are no doubts. The colonial origins are clear. The events of 1607, 1620, 1776, and 1787 are abundantly documented. All the participants in the stormy decade 1774–87 left behind ample accounts of their own roles in the story. Yet is it enough to describe the nation's origins as part of the biographies of Jefferson, Franklin, and John Adams – or, with Samuel Adams's achievement as mob-organizer in mind, with, as sub-title, "How the Green Dragon Tavern caused the War of Independence"? Was the Declaration of 1776 more than another protest, however eloquent? Was a document, even a binding compact, enough? Even before Washington's death, Mason Weems was shamelessly collecting "anecdotes" about him. His *The Life and Memorable Actions of George Washington* (1800) became in its fifth edition (1806) *The Life of Washington the Great* and was enriched with fiction, including the tale of "the little hatchet and the cherry tree" and other "curious anecdotes." Time has to pass, however, memories have to become blurred, and survival has to be assured before legends are born. Certainly by July 4, 1826, it seemed that there was a touch of magic about the events of 50 years before. On that day, and within hours of each other, Jefferson and Adams died. Their warm correspondence during the last decade of their lives fixed in the records the part they had played, and revealed their own characters.

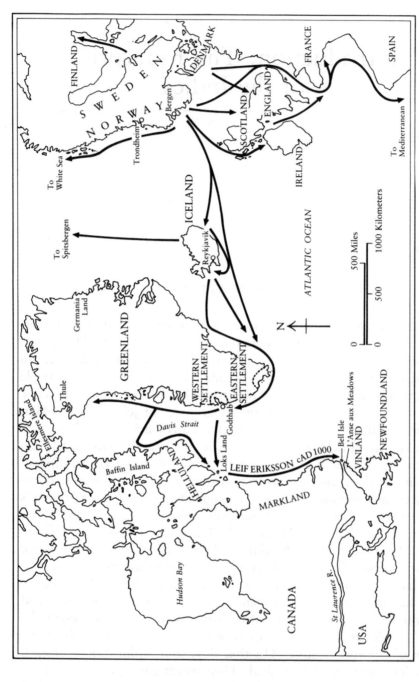

Map 1 The sea-routes of the Norsemen. The Norwegian ship might be 24 meters long, its breadth midships 5 meters, with 30 or 32 oarsmen; its average speed might be 5 knots, or — in good weather — more. Iceland and Greenland were convenient staging posts for voyages to North America — Helluland, Markland, and Vinland.

There was already much here for literary-minded men to ponder on, even to burlesque – witness Washington Irving's Knickerbocker's *History of New York* and his tales of Rip Van Winkle and his legend of Sleepy Hollow. In the same decade James Fenimore Cooper in upstate New York was producing a legend of his own: the activities of a part-saint, part-Daniel Boone in the person of Natty Bumppo. In his idyllic years in Spain, when he set out as tale-teller to outmatch the writings of his friend and model Sir Walter Scott, and when for a year he was privileged to live in the Alhambra, it was natural for Irving to go well beyond the tales of the Hudson Valley, and no longer necessary to raid and adapt German folklore. He drew on the records of the Spanish scholar Navarrete and the resources of his friend the Massachusetts bibliophile Obadiah Rich, with whom he lived, not only for his biography of Columbus (1828), but also for *The Voyages and Discoveries of the Companions of Columbus* (1831), with its other exotic heroes, Balboa and Ponce de Leon, and for his historical romance *The Conquest of Granada* (1829), the story of Boabdil, the last of its Moorish kings, and

Plate 1 Norse flint arrowhead, found in Greenland, but made from Labrador quartzite, ca.1000 AD. Tools, and the relics of them, indicate the presence of the First Americans in what are now Colorado, New Mexico, and Wyoming, perhaps 20,000 years ago or more.
(Reproduced by kind permission of Nationalmuseets Atelier, Copenhagen; photograph: Niels Elswing.)

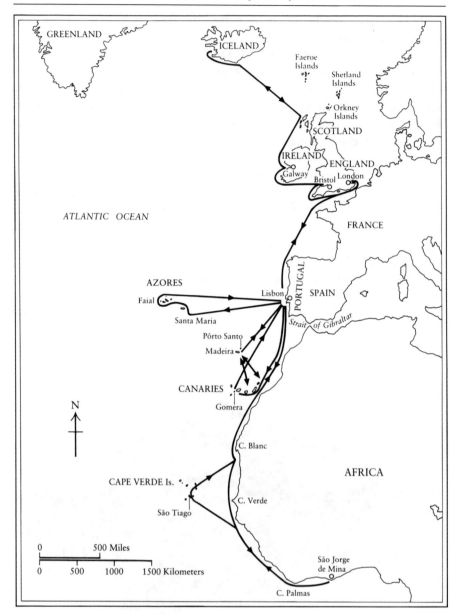

Map 2 The New Atlantis. The chain of volcanic islands that stretches from the Azores via Madeira to the Canaries and to the Cape Verde group — though known to occasional Arab geographers, and some of them spoken of by Plutarch and by Ptolemy as the Fortunate Islands, the Isles of the Blessed — were all being discovered, mapped and settled during the fifteenth century.

The Alhambra (1832). When Washington Irving received a LL D at Oxford, were the students not wise to chant and to challenge "Who discovered Columbus?" Or was Columbus not a wise choice as Romulus, for a country ceasing to be Anglo-American in composition? By the end of the nineteenth century Columbus's origins as Genoese-Portuguese and Spanish, and Catholic by religion, appealed to millions of new immigrants. There was a need for history as legends. The America to which Washington Irving returned in 1832 he found by contrast "all-pervading commonplace."

What then of Leif Eriksson's settlement in the year 1000, and the Norse legends? Now that tale has been confirmed by the work at L'Anse aux Meadows in Newfoundland, at the entrance to the Belle Isle Strait, where Helge and Anne Stine Ingstad did their excavating less than 30 years ago. What then of the tales of Irish monks voyaging west, as recorded in the Brendan *Navigatio*, written three centuries after St Brendan's life (ca.484–577); what of Prince Madoc's journey (ca.1170?), or of those seafarers who may have come by the long-lost Atlantis; what of those Indians in Hispaniola whom Columbus found to be people "almost as white as in Spain?"

In the century before Columbus's voyages even Atlantis was found – and occupied. The chain of volcanic islands that stretch from the Azores via Madeira to the Canaries and to the Cape Verde group – though known to occasional Arab geographers, and some of them spoken of by Plutarch and by Ptolemy as the Fortunate Islands, the Isles of the Blessed – were all being discovered, mapped, and settled during the fifteenth century. Porto Santo in the Madeiras, for a time Columbus's home, was first sighted in 1418 by João Goncalvez Zarco; colonization of the uninhabited Madeira itself was begun in 1420. The Portuguese navigator Gonzalo Velho Cabral discovered Santa Maria in the Azores in 1432, and other islands in the group were discovered over the next quarter-century; it became the main rendezvous of the fleets returning from the Indies, rumor and map center – and site of innumerable raids and battles. The Venetian captain Alvise Cadamosto, in the service of Prince Henry the Navigator, discovered some of the 14 islands in the Cape Verde group in 1456. Prince Henry the Navigator (1394–1460), with the flair of a Leonardo and of a Hakluyt, lived in monastic seclusion at Sagres, training center for navigators and map-makers. He looked firmly south, for stepping stones that would lead down and round the African coast. In 1415 a Portuguese army took Ceuta, in part a crusade, in part a step to the rumored gold of the Niger delta and to trade in slaves. To the Portuguese, it was the brothers Gaspar and Michael de Corte Real who discovered Labrador and Newfoundland, and to whom belongs the credit usually given to Columbus; and each was lost on his return.

The Spanish monarchs Ferdinand and Isabella established sovereignty over the Canary Islands in 1479, and took occupation of Palma in 1491 and of Tenerife in 1495. This sea inside the Ocean, a mini-Caribbean, became familiar to those in service of Portugal and Spain, as did its trade winds, its currents, and its levanters. It was natural to assume there were still more islands to be explored north and west, if luck and the winds held.

Such islands might be rich in gold and silver, for these were Spain's first objectives. But the true wealth of the New World was to be in the land itself, and in those who exploited it. In Mexico and Peru the Indians were quickly put to work. Elsewhere the native population was inadequate to meet the demand, or, as in the Caribbean, proved culturally incapable of adjusting to Spanish needs. The result for the Carib Indians was genocide: in a few decades they perished by the hundreds of thousands. To replace them, African slaves were imported – again in their thousands.

When Columbus established his settlement on Hispaniola (now the Dominican Republic), using for timber the wreck of the *Santa Maria*, and left a remnant of his crew behind in 1493, it has been estimated that there may have been half a million Indians on the island. By 1519 only some 500 remained. It was by no means the legacy only of his and his successors' savagery and greed, and of a clash – and incomprehension – of cultures. There was also what has come to be called the "Columbian Exchange." Part of that was an exchange of diseases. The discoverers carried microbes as part of their invisible and secret weaponry. The death that in the New World walked alongside Spanish – and later French and English – forces was due less to greed and cruelty, weapons and war, than to disease, which unknowingly they transmitted. The New World suffered more from this exchange than the Old, though some historians argue that since syphilis reached Europe after Columbus's voyages it must have come from the Americas. *Post hoc, ergo propter hoc*: whatever the origin, syphilis spread rapidly. After his first voyage, Columbus sailed up the river Guadalqivir to Seville, where his seamen stayed a month, and then disbanded to various parts of Spain. When, in the summer of 1494 Charles VIII of France crossed the Alps, intent on the conquest of Naples, his army of 36,000, mainly mercenaries, was accompanied by several hundred prostitutes. The syphilis that broke out among these troops was so virulent that Charles had to abandon the siege; the troops – and the prostitutes – were dissipated across Europe, and again, the disease went with them. Hence its names: the Neapolitan Itch, the Spanish Disease, the German Disease, the French Pox – and, to the Turks, the Christian Disease. In its early days, it was especially malignant, disfiguring, and often fatal.

Many experts now discount the view that the disease spread from its introduction in 1493. It is now generally believed that syphilis – a term not in use until the nineteenth century – existed in the West long before 1493, although in a different form. Yet another theory is that syphilis is caused by the same microbe that produces the tropical diseases of yaws, bejel, and pinta, which originated in Africa, and then adapted itself to more temperate climes. Not until 1910, when Paul Enreich of Frankfurt discovered Salvarsan, an arsenic-based compound, was it possible to destroy the microbe responsible for syphilis ("the magic bullet"). The campaign against the disease was also helped – by the discovery of penicillin in the course of World War II. Penicillin was more effective, and had fewer side-effects than Salvarsan.

But there was more to the so-called Columbian Exchange than an end to immunity from the foreigners' diseases. Both the New World and the Old were changed beyond recognition by the animals and plants that Columbus and his successors carried across the Atlantic. The horse – which had been missing in the Americas from the end of the Ice Age – transformed the Indians' way of life, and not least their mastery as buffalo-hunters; both in North and South America, cattle would create a cowboy culture; in the end, the extermination of the buffalo would destroy the Indian way of life; and then cattle gave way to wheat. The root crops that the first Europeans barely noticed proved more valuable than the gold and silver they sought; the American potato made possible a boom in Europe's own population; the sugar cane introduced by Columbus to Hispaniola brought both wealth and slavery in its wake, and for efficient organization sugar cane exploitation required vast plantations – as later in Jamaica, Cuba, and other Caribbean islands. From the New World came corn and peppers, pumpkins and cocoa, coffee and peanuts, cane-sugar, tomatoes, and tobacco; from the Old, sheep and pigs, as well as horses and cattle. In the end there was not only a New World but a single integrated Atlantic community, that became the seed-bed and model for a world culture.

2 THE COLUMBUS CONSPIRACY – THE SOURCES

Controversy still surrounds the memory – and the achievement – of Columbus. So it was in 1492. Vessels were abandoned by Columbus during his four voyages: he left behind him ships wrecked during his first and his fourth voyages. As John Dyson stressed in BBC's *Timewatch* programme of 16 October 1991, little is yet known of the actual methods of construction of Columbus's caravels; and there have been, since then, earthquakes and tremors in the Bermuda seas that have themselves given rise to legends of unusual magnetic storms in the Caribbean; Columbus was seeking Atlantis, was he not? Was it the Azores, or the Canaries, or San Salvador? Or some other island now buried? It is only in the last three years that the site has been uncovered of Columbus's first colony, which he called La Isabela, set on a low limestone bluff on Hispaniola, where the 1,500 sailors, soldiers, and settlers who accompanied Columbus on his second expedition in 1493 were planted; the colony was abandoned in less than five years. Today only 40 families occupy the site; it is some 20 miles distant by unpaved road from the nearest town. Yet here was the first attempt at European colonization, the first evidence of house and church building, and the port from which Columbus began his pillaging; from here he loaded 500 Taino Indians into four caravels and shipped them back to Spain as evidence of his "triumph." And on his second voyage, when he arrived at La Navidad (now En Bas Saline, Haiti) in November 1493 to rescue the men he had left behind on his first voyage, he found their stockade burned to the ground, and the Spaniards dead. It was not only the Europeans who behaved as savages.

The story of Columbus is one of great physical courage, unyielding determination, skill in handling ships and men, and mastery of navigation. On this there is no debate. Nor is there debate on the fact that he was not seeking America, and did not know it was there, but that he did find the West Indies. Only during his third voyage, when he found the mouth of the Orinico and realized its width and the freshness and force of its waters, did he sense that there was a vaster land mass than he had ever expected, and that it was not Cipango (Japan). Nor is there any questioning the scale of his savagery and cruelty towards Indians.

There is, however, controversy over Columbus's original intentions: was he seeking Asia, and did he use the term "Indies" and "Indians" to cover his doubts over what he had found; or was he simply looking for new islands in or beyond those of the still-mythical

Plate 2 Christopher Columbus, by an anonymous artist. The Latin inscription, though partially worn, reads: "Columbus the Ligurian [the Latin name for Genoa] Discoverer of the New World." Columbus was born in Genoa. He offered his services to England and to France, where he was rejected, before serving Spain. (Museo Civico, Como; photograph: Scala, Florence.)

Antilles? Was he seeking to do more than the Portuguese had done in discovering Corvo, the most westerly of the Azores, in 1452? Or is there any controversy at all? Or as John Dyson argued, was

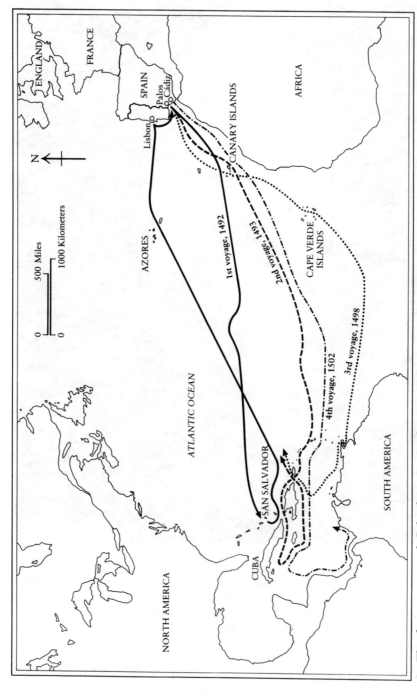

Map 3 The four voyages of Columbus. In April 1492 Columbus was appointed "Admiral of the Ocean Sea" by Ferdinand and Isabella of Spain, and received support and crews for voyages, mainly through fines imposed on Palos, and by loans from Genoese banks.

First Voyage, 1492–3
The *Niña* (captained by Vicente Yanez Pinzón), *Pinta* (captained by Martin Alonzo Pinzón), and the *Santa Maria* (flagship) sailed on August 3, 1492, from Palos in the Bay of Cádiz, with 90 men on board. They reached the Canaries a week later, and on September 8 sailed west. There was near-mutiny three days before first land was sighted (October 12) by Rodrigo de Triana, the lookout on the *Pinta* — who was denied the reward promised by Queen Isabella, which Colombus claimed for himself. They went ashore at Watling Island (or Samona Cay) in the Bahamas, named San Salvador by Columbus. They explored the Bahamas, the coast of Cuba and the northern coast of Hispaniola (Santo Domingo), where they established a port. The *Santa Maria* ran aground and was wrecked. Columbus returned via the Azores on the *Niña* (his favourite vessel), and on March 4, 1493, reached the River Tagus. He was received at the Spanish Court in Barcelona on April 20, 1493.

Second Voyage, 1493–6
Columbus sailed from Cádiz, with 17 ships and 1,200 men. They explored the coasts of Santo Domingo and Cuba, discovered many islands, and established the colony of Isabella on Hispaniola. They found that the post left behind during the first voyage had been destroyed. After the return voyage (March–June 1496), the Treaty of Tordesillas (June 1494) gave to Spain all discoveries west of a line 370° west of the Cape Verde Islands, and to Portugal all discoveries east of that line.

Third Voyage, 1498–1500
With 7 ships, Columbus reached Trinidad on July 31, 1498, and on August 1 sighted the coast of South America. They explored the mouths of the Orinoco, and suppressed a rebellion in the Spanish colony on Santo Domingo. But a new governor replaced him, and Columbus returned in chains because of the continuing unrest in Santo Domingo. The brilliant navigator was an incompetent and unlucky administrator — "a good admiral but not a good viceroy," was Ferdinand of Aragon's verdict.

Fourth Voyage, 1502–4
Columbus sailed along and explored the Central American coast from Honduras south to Panama; he was shipwrecked on Jamaica in the summer of 1503.

Columbus died in Valladolid in northern Spain in 1506, still believing that he had found the coast of Asia.

his false log designed to conceal the duration of his voyage and its southerly course lest he encounter Portuguese ships, and be treated as an interloper in Portuguese waters?

Central to any historical analysis is the fact that all biographers of Columbus are dependent on four contemporary sources. His younger son Ferdinand (Fernando), as a boy of 13, was his father's companion on his fourth voyage; he became a scholar and book collector, and lived a comfortable life in Seville. The original Spanish version of Ferdinand's work was written about 1539, but was never published and has completely disappeared. It is only known to us in an Italian edition first published at Venice in 1571. The only accurate version of it, *The Life of the Admiral Christopher Columbus*, is that edited and translated by Benjamin Keen (Rutgers University Press, New Brunswick, NJ, 1959). It may have been Ferdinand's own writing, or merely attributed to him to give it credence.

About the middle of the sixteenth century, Bishop Las Casas, the bishop of Chiapas in Mexico and the Apostle of the Indies, took up the task of recounting the glorious deeds of the Admiral in his History of the Indies (*Historia de las Indias*), and had access to the various papers that Columbus had left. Las Casas had first gone to Hispaniola as a settler and became a convert while there; in 1510 he was the first priest to be ordained in the New World. He knew Columbus personally. He was biographer and historian, defender of the Indians, conscience of a nation. His book was first published in 1535.

Third, Peter Martyr d'Anghiera, yet another North Italian attracted to Spain (he was born on the shores of Lake Maggiore in 1457), was in attendance at court when Columbus was welcomed on his triumphal return after the first voyage. He published his history *De Orbe Novo* — the first time the term New World had been used — in 1511, though he never visited it himself. He provides more information on the second voyage than any other source. He was the first to describe the equatorial current, the Trade Winds blowing from the Northeast, and the Westerlies for the return, awareness of which was Columbus's secret weapon.

Finally, also in Barcelona when Columbus had his triumph in 1493, was a young 15-year-old hidalgo, El Capitan Gonzalo Fernandez de Oviedo y Valdes, Oviedo for short. In 1513 he went out to the Caribbean as officer-in-charge of the gold diggings, at last discovered and functioning at Darien, and he spent 34 years in Central America. He became official chronicler of the Indies, and the first volume of his *Historia General Natural de las Indias* appeared in 1526, with his own illustrations.

In 1601 there was published the first volume of a great history of the deeds of the Spaniards in the New World by Antonio de Herrera, who took his story of Columbus's discovery from the pages of Ferdinand and Las Casas jointly. Herrera's work consolidated and established the Columbian tradition of the discoverer as a divine instrument of Providence, and upon it most writers, including Washington Irving, have based their story of the discovery.

Moreover, there is no evidence that rebuts the charge that the story of a search for the Indies was invented after the new lands were discovered, and that the scientific reasoning employed to support the practicability of the western route to Asia and the Spice Islands was only assembled in 1493 or 1494, based solely upon such facts as could be culled from one or two works on cosmography published in the earlier years of the fifteenth century. It may have been his brother Bartholomew's contriving, with or without Christopher's knowledge. From this, it is easy to contend that the expedition of 1492 had for its sole object the discovery of new islands in the Atlantic beyond the Cape Verde Islands; and, according to the evidence of a member of the commission to which Columbus's proposals were submitted for examination by Queen Isabella, they dealt only with the discovery of such islands. Columbus himself never mentioned Asia or the Indies before his return, but always stated that he wished to search for islands which he knew existed beyond the Atlantic fringe. Las Casas affirms this, and Columbus's certainty seemed so strange to men at the time that the story went abroad that he had been told of the existence of such lands by a pilot of Huelva, who had once been driven there by a storm; to whom Columbus gave shelter, and who, while a lodger in his home, conveniently died, bequeathing to Columbus the map of his discoveries – circumstances which explain Columbus's certainty on his voyage and (according to John Dyson) his knowledge of what he would find. (The so-called "Unknown Pilot" thesis in Columbiana, about which Columbus's most thorough biographer, S. E. Morison, is scornful). It seems true that to his crew he stated that the lands lay 700 or 750 leagues to the west (some 2200 miles), and when he did not find them there he was exceedingly disappointed, but persisted in his search. The idea of searching for Cipangu came in fact from his partner, Martin Pinzón, and it was he who secured from the Catholic kings letters of credence to the Great Khan who ruled there, as Pinzón had heard tell on his visits to Rome.

Before Columbus's death, a long series of cosmographical reasons had been put together by him and his brother Bartholomew to prove that the new lands to which they had come were the easternmost parts of Asia. When Ferdinand Columbus and Las Casas came to write the life of the Admiral, the general belief was that he had only discovered islands of the existence of which he had known before. His son and the bishop (despite his criticisms of Columbus's attitude to and treatment of the Indians) were determined to show Columbus's heroic stature. They stressed the extent to which he had consulted not accidentally-met pilots but learned cosmographers, including the Italian physician and cosmographer Paolo dal Pozzo Toscanelli. When he learned that Columbus was thinking of an exploring voyage, it is said that Toscanelli supplied him with a copy of his letter of 1474 and a map which proved that the Indies could be reached by the west. Unfortunately Columbus never mentioned Toscanelli, and the astronomer, in those of his works that have been preserved, never speaks of Columbus, nor of dealings with the Portuguese explorers of the route to India. The most that can be said is that Toscanelli had been suggesting voyages west to a friend, Canon Fernao Martins, who was at the Portuguese Court of Afonso V, and from whom Columbus might have acquired (purloined? stolen?) any suggestions or information. Maps and charts were guarded as treasures, as routes to untold wealth. Henry Vignaud, in his *The Letter and Chart of Toscanelli* (New York, Dutton, 1902) and *The Columbian Tradition on the Discovery and of the Part Played therein by the Astronomer Toscanelli* (Oxford University Press, Oxford, 1920), is iconoclastic, and contends that the Toscanelli correspondence and his chart are figments of the biographers' imagination, even with Christopher Columbus's connivance.

These variant views have largely been reduced to order (and the debunkers firmly savaged) by Admiral and Professor S. E. Morison of Harvard, from his personal knowledge of Columbus's route under sail, and from his familiarity with ocean currents and wind charts as well as documents. His 1-volume life, *Christopher Columbus, Mariner* (Boston, Little Brown, 1955), is a masterly story brilliantly told, and it has an even richer 2-volume companion, *Admiral of the Ocean Sea: A life of Christopher Columbus* (Oxford University Press, New York, 1942). Morison's massive writing is clearly the place with which to begin. His strength is his knowledge of what is incontestable: of Columbus as a sailor, at ease and in command in his own element, on the ocean swells when he took the Canaries Current and the Northeast Trades out, and came homeward by the Gulf Stream and the Westerlies.

Alongside S. E. Morison — unsurpassed as a storyteller of Columbus on the seas — now stands *Christopher Columbus, the Grand Design* (London, Orbis, 1985; originally published in Italian) by Paolo Emilio Taviani, himself a Genoese, a professor, a resistance fighter in World War II, and later an Italian senator. His is a massively detailed and passionately admiring account of the man's origins, of the development of the Great Plan, and of "the greatest discovery in history" up to 1492. The story he tells reads like a novel, but is stronger, more complex and more fascinating than most of them. His chapters 25 and 26 are the best description of the forces that drove Columbus west. His bibliographic support is even more meticulous than Morison's. He and Morison are alike in their admiration for the sailor and put beyond all doubt Columbus's mastery as a navigator on the seas, with only a compass, a quadrant and a half-hour glass as his instruments, and praise his skill at dead-reckoning, assessing winds, and ocean currents, and in handling restless crews in stormy waters. Columbus has been lucky in his two great "discoverers."

An anti-establishment view of the Admiral, an indictment of his cruelty towards the Indians, and of his greed, and the ravaging of a continent that began with him, is given by Hans Koning in *Columbus: His enterprise* (New York, Monthly Review Press, 1976), recently republished; while novelist Stephen Marlowe provides a vivid and fictional recreation of his life in *The Memoirs of Christopher Columbus* (London, Jonathan Cape, 1987). Marlowe adds to the canon some unnecessary embroideries, but his readable "1492 and all that" is wrecked by its many anachronisms and by its camp style, by its thinness on the stories of the voyages, and by the absence of a single map. A much superior recreation of the first voyage comes from another novelist, who uses history as raw material for the picturesque and the anecdotal, in C. S. Forester's *The Earthly Paradise*. Or, for still another "story within a story", as told by Mascarenhas Barreto in *The Portuguese Columbus: Secret agent for King John II* (London, Macmillan, 1992), was Columbus not in fact a Portuguese spy, Salvador Fernandez Zarco, who ingratiated himself at the Spanish Court and persuaded Ferdinand and Isabella to invest in this diversion of a western journey, while the Portuguese explored the coasts of Africa west and east, rounded the southern cape and found and exploited for King John II of Portugal the riches of India and the Indian seas?

In this richness, of sources, of rivalry and of ignorance, are any conclusions possible? On the controversy whether Columbus's brother, and son, and the good Bishop Las Casas conspired to develop a myth of their own devising, in order to exaggerate the Discoverer's achievement, perhaps St Augustine (as quoted by Oviedo) should give the verdict: "Melius est dubitare de occultis, quam litigare de incertis – Better to doubt what is obscure than dispute about uncertain things." For surveys of recent literature, see John Larner, "The certainty of Columbus, some recent studies," in *History*, 73 no. 237 (1988), pp. 3–23 and "North American hero? Christopher Columbus 1702–2002," *Proceedings of the American Philosophical Society*, 137 no. 1 (March 1993), pp. 46–23. On the achievement, one could fall back on anecdote: since Columbus or his brother Bartholomew approached Portugal, France, and England before sailing in the employ of Spain, the story is still apt that when Columbus set off he didn't know where he was going, when he got there he didn't know where he was, when he returned he didn't even know where he had been – and he did it all on other people's money. Unfortunately, it is not quite true. The money came not from the Spanish sovereigns but from the Bank of St George in Columbus's native city Genoa, which financed much of Spanish enterprise. What Genoa did not provide, the two brothers Pinzón did: they each went on the first voyage, as captains of the *Niña* and the *Pinta*, and provided the ships and the crews. To the people of Palos today the Pinzóns are the real discoverers of America. Certainly Columbus did not know exactly where his landing was; he called it San Salvador, and for centuries it was identified as Watling Island, with S. E. Morison sailing to it on his own voyage in 1940, and concurring. However, 30 years later the research and the expedition financed by the National Geographic Society established that the landing was on Samana Cay, some 60 miles southeast of Watling Island. What is not in question is that Columbus did discover Hispaniola, i.e. what is now Santo Domingo and Haiti. (In the light of *their* later histories, unhistorically-minded cynics might wonder whether these might not have been best left undiscovered. In 1986 Columbus's statue in Port-au-Prince was thrown into the harbor: for happiest is the country that has no history.)

There were two land masses that Columbus almost discovered, and of whose presence he had an uneasy awareness when in bitter arthritic and malaria-prone retirement in Valladolid he reflected gloomily on what he had done, on the humiliations he had suffered, and on what he saw as his lack of proper recognition. His body did go to the New World, and then was returned to Spain, as the tides of his fame flowed and then ebbed. He was, in Gianni Granzotto's words, "a hero who was buried too many times." Fair enough, Spaniards might say, the man was an alien after all. More than that (would add Salvador de Madariaga), he was probably a *converso*, a Jew whose family had taken refuge in Genoa. It seems unlikely:

but certainly he had little standing at court in Spain as an "alien," and he was ultra-emphatic on being a good Catholic – though in 1492, when Moors and Jews were being expelled, he had every reason to stress it. There are even those who say that, as a man ahead of his time, a Renaissance spirit still in an intensely religious age, he was in fact looking for a safe haven for his people; 500 years too soon he was seeking "a national home for the Jewish people". A man, it seems, for all seasons.

His brother and the good bishop sought to correct the balance and to create the legend. But even that is now being savaged. The navigator? Alpha plus. The man? Greedy in small things as in big, hypocritical, ruthless, and cruel; it seems he was also a loner – gauche, bookish, driven by a great idea.

Yet, paradoxically, he did not give his name to the New World. And the *victor ludorum* was, irony of irony, to be not a Spaniard, nor a Genoese, but a Florentine. For Amerigo Vespucci (1454–1512), the best brief analysis is in S. E. Morison, *The European Discovery of America: the southern voyages 1492–1616* (New York, Oxford University Press, 1974), chapter 12, pp. 272–312. Vespucci, who accompanied Hojeda in his 1499 expedition, which discovered and named Venezuela ("Little Venice"), was neither a practical navigator nor a pilot, though he claimed to be both. He was in fact a Florentine ship-chandler turned banker, sent to Seville by Lorenzo de Medici's affiliate, Juanoto Berardi. To the new world, however, he bequeathed his name. And note, in Morison's bibliography, his delightful reference to the career of Vespucci's collateral descendant in the nineteenth century, Miss America Vespucci, who was active in the Young Italy movement; on being required to quit Florence, she became mistress to the Duc d'Orléans, son of King Louis-Philippe of France, to name only the most distinguished of her friends.

It was Vespucci's self-advertising in his letters to his former employers the Medici, (and Columbus was not slow at self-publicity), his craft in dating the first of his two journeys (he claimed that there were four, however) to two years earlier (1497) than the date on which it occurred (1499), and the academic chance of the discovery of his letter of 1503 by a young German professor in a French College in the Vosges (Saint-Die in Lorraine), that the name given to the vast land masses of the western hemisphere came to be that of a naturalized Spanish citizen of Florentine birth, some of whose sailing was in the service of Portugal. When Columbus was still describing his discovery as eastern Asia, Vespucci called it "a new world ... I have found a continent." The claim – if claim to uniqueness it was – deceived no contemporary in Spain or Portugal.

But the letter, when printed and circulated outside these two countries, did give him fame – though after Columbus's death (1506) and his own (1512). Vespucci did not go to sea until he was nearly 50, at which age a successful businessman does not usually become a professional navigator. He went along either as a cosmographer, or as business sponsor. His lack of experience at sea, and his deliberate exaggeration of the extent of his voyages, did not prevent his being appointed Chief Pilot to the Spanish king, a post that was a combination of Lord High Admiral and Chief of Naval Staff.

The showmanship was in the family genes. Vespucci appears as an angelic boy in Ghirlandaio's *Madonna della Misericordia*, standing next to the Virgin, in a lunette in the Ognissanti church in Florence. His cousin Simonetta (1453–1476) was a beauty queen in a Florentine fête in 1471, and was used as a model for Botticelli's The *Birth of Venus* and *Primavera*. She was married at 15 to Marco Vespucci, with whom she moved from Genoa to Florence. She attracted the attention of Giuliano de Medici, brother of Lorenzo the Magnificent, and she figured prominently in Giuliano's tournament in 1475. She died of TB when she was 28: she was carried to her grave on an open bier so that all could see her beauty.

To which a Bristol footnote should be added. In 1497 and 1498 another Italian, John Cabot, then living in Bristol and trading from it to the Newfoundland Banks, was paid – by order of Henry VII of England – £10, and a pension of £20 for discovering the North American continent. That is, the king told his Customs Officer in Bristol to pay Cabot from the customs receipts, and that official, officially described as "The Customer" and also a merchant, was Richard Amerike or Ap Merrick. He appears – in fun or seriously – to have made to his friends grants of land in his rich vice-royalty. From 1497 on, Cabot's discoveries were described in Bristol as "the land of Amerike" – a more accurate source for the title than Columbus's "Indies" and at least as accurate a source as Amerigo Vespucci.

Only one conclusion seems firm. Whatever the consequences – and can men and women ever foresee what will follow? – the Portuguese and the Spaniards, the men of the Madeiras and of Bristol, of Genoa and Florence, proved – as Robert Thorne of Bristol put it in 1527 – "no land uninhabitable nor sea unnavigable;" sailors, mercenaries, and merchants, in two generations they had discovered and mapped half the world.

3 THE FIRST AMERICANS

In fact, neither the Welsh, nor the Irish, nor the Norsemen, nor the Venetians, nor the Basques got there first. It was not the Chinese either, although a Peking professor, Chu Shien-chi, claims that five Chinese, led by a Buddhist monk, Hoei Shin, sailed from China to Mexico in AD 459. The only certainties are that it was neither the British nor the Spaniards, Norse, French, or Welsh who got there first, but the Indians. Indeed, they arrived millennia ahead of anybody else; and they came by way of an "ocean" of their own. By noting the flint arrow-points discovered in Clovis, New Mexico, and in Wyoming, in Alaska, in the Kurile Islands, and in the Lake Baikal region of Siberia, it seems clear that the ancestors of the Indians in fact followed a route into America from Asia over the land bridge of the Alaskan corridor, or over the narrow Bering Straits, probably in one of the warm spells between ice ages, perhaps 30,000 or more years ago. They came without horses and without wheeled vehicles, carrying what they could, and they spread as nomadic hunters over all America, north and south. They reached the high Andes, southeast of Lima. Those who reached Patagonia may have travelled by sea as well as by land, and the end of the ice age or ages may have swallowed up any evidences they left behind. One estimate puts the drift southward at 17 miles per generation.[1]

When the Spaniards invaded the mainland in the early sixteenth century, they were astonished to find civilizations which compared in many respects with those of Europe itself. In Mexico, the Aztec empire dominated a large number of cultures which were at a similar level of development, while in South America – from its heartland in highland Peru – the Inca empire covered an area of some 350,000 square miles. These powerful states were highly organized theocracies, with great cities of stone and elaborate religious systems, and they produced magnificent works of art in pottery, stone, and precious metals.

Atlantic-oriented, the Spaniards assumed that all this indicated settlements by earlier European ancestors. The Spaniards found it easy to discover the exotic origins of these native Americans. In the late sixteenth century Padre Duran proposed that the Mexicans were Israelites because of their propensity for infant sacrifice: the

---

[1] Richard ("Scotty") McNeish, "Early Man in the Andes", in Nigel Davies, *Voyagers to the New World* (London, Macmillan, 1979), p. 34.

Canaanite god Moloch and the Mexican Rain God, Tláloc, had similar tastes. Fray Juan de Torquemada, writing a generation later, suggested that the Indians' ancestors were Romans and Carthaginians; in the nineteenth century Augustus le Plongeon was convinced that the Maya were part of the lost tribes of Israel, and that their tombs and pyramids, and the presence of elephants and lotus flowers in Mayan reliefs, prove a common Nile Valley origin; and the Abbé Brasseur de Bourbourg and the ex-Napoleonic soldier turned Mayan scholar Jean Frederic de Waldeck were alike convinced that the New World and Near Eastern civilizations had a common origin, that Horus was the Mexican Plumed Serpent who had overthrown Atlantis, and that Atlantis was but a staging post between the two worlds.

From the fifth century the Greeks believed that the world was round. Aristotle, though sceptical of Plato, was aware that voyagers had reached a western ocean, and recognized the possibility that at least one continent lay beyond the pillars of Hercules. Plato thought it likely that it was vast in size. The intercontinental abyss became a great breeder of dreams: and all are interlinked, from the passing of Arthur and the quest for the Holy Grail to the ocean saga of St Brendan, from the belief that the first Americans were the Lost Tribes of Israel uprooted in the eighth century BC, who had trekked through Asia and crossed Beringia, to Joseph Smith's *Book of Mormon*. There are no hard facts, no artifacts that substantiate Atlantis, only legends. Moreover, the incomers made a total break in culture and language with their ancestral homelands, whether in Asia or Europe. And the Mexican legends, mentioning Atslan but not Atlantis, refer frequently to alien and seaborne traders/invaders. There is, however, no hard evidence of settlement of the Americas before Columbus – except for a few years only of Norsemen in northern Newfoundland; there is no evidence of discovery. But legends may contain long-buried truths. Sometimes they may be untrue or unproven, but still be useful – as to Cortés in Mexico and to the Tudors. Whether true or false, they have their own power to shape history. They are the motor-myths; they are, in the Indian phrase, "ideas-that-walk."

If we can be sure that it is fact, not legend, to say that the first Americans were the Indians, uncertainty does not cease at that point. For these Indians were not the nomadic horsemen of the Plains galloping bareback on their mustangs, or the warlike Apache and Comanche of the southwest who form the Hollywood stereotype, and who were themselves in many ways a by-product of European culture. Nor were they akin to the forest Iroquois or Mohicans of

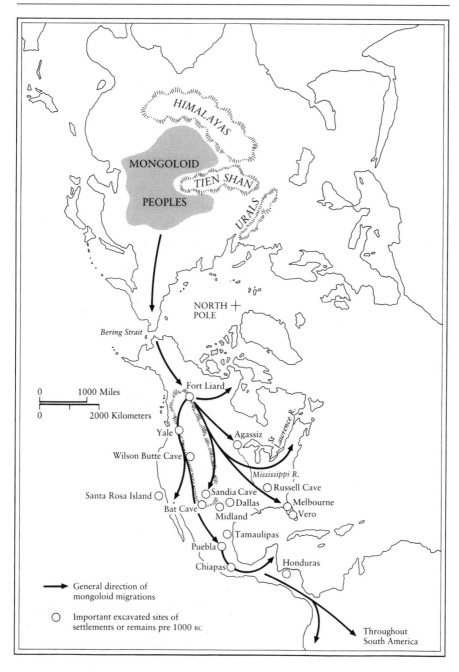

Map 4 The origin of settlement in America, 50,000–1000 BC. The first Americans migrated across the land bridge of Beringia (now the Bering Straits) from Asia during the late Ice Age. They hunted big game and used weapons and tools of chipped stone. Arrowheads used by them, or their successors, have been found near Folsom, Colorado, and Clovis, New Mexico, dating from ca. 9000 BC.

whom Fenimore Cooper wrote. They were a migrating and hunting people, who only slowly became agrarian. They were in appearance of East Mongolian origin, as their ubiquitous blood group O confirmed (other peoples' blood groups were and are immensely varied); but their hooked Roman noses and large almond-shaped eyes are rare in Asia; and not one of their many languages, despite the similarity of a few words, resembles in structure any Asian, Siberian, or Mongolian tongue.

The peoples who migrated from Asia into North America seemingly crossed what is now the Bering Strait from Siberia into Alaska by a land bridge well over 1,000 miles wide, when the climate was much warmer than today; and then moved down through the twin continents, or possibly down the then coastline, east and west. They came from one of history's end-places, far removed from the culture of Europe or of Asia. The prevailing view is that they could not read or write; they were in the hunting-fishing stage of development; they might have used the bow and arrow, but did use flint-headed spears; they did not know the plough, the wheel, or the horse (which was not introduced – or, more accurately, re-introduced – until the Spaniards came, and the Indians called them "mystery dogs"); they were ignorant of livestock and of iron. The wheel does occur on toys, of tiny dogs on wheeled bases; but there is no sign of it in general use. The dog, the llama, and the guinea pig were their only domesticated animals; their tribal organization was the basis of government, economic life was at an elementary level, and religious and ethical ideas were less advanced than those of Christianity. They were in essence a Stone Age people. In North America itself, they were even more insulated than in Siberia, cut off by distance and by new advances of ice: the ice reached as far south as southwestern Wisconsin.

But when did they come? The frequently cited date (based on "big game hunting" digs at Clovis, New Mexico, in the 1930s) is 15,000–12,000 years ago; the last retreat of the ice was ca.10,000–7,000 years ago, but this is now seen as too cautious. The likelihood is that they crossed what was a vast treeless steppe, where the arctic grasses and occasional swamps supported scattered groups of bison, mammoth, and reindeer. Beringia was more a continent than a corridor. The Stone Age hunters, in stalking their prey, moved east into what is now Alaska, gradually finding their line of communication cut behind them as the Wisconsin ice-sheet collapsed. They were not aware, of course, that they left one continent for another, or that they were – if they were – the First Americans. Nor was it a smooth or easy process.

Radiocarbon dating has established that some 26,000–30,000 years ago ice age animals were being hunted in the American southwest, as diggings reveal at Sandia Cave in New Mexico. Ten thousand years ago, hunters in New Mexico and Colorado were living on bison (the Folsom camp-dwellers). When the ice melted, the large mammals, on which the early hunters depended, disappeared.[2] A culture replaced it of small-game hunting, and the use of vegetable foods, fish, and shellfish; in the northwest, there was in essence a salmon-fishing economy, and the people were sea-raiders and totem-pole builders, with sharp distinctions between rich and poor. By 3000 BC, primitive varieties of maize ("Indian corn") are found, as at Bat Cave in New Mexico. And with agriculture came pottery, permanent settlement, the accumulation of property, and, in the end, a more developed social organization with kings, priests, palaces, and temples. Among the Natchez of Mississippi there was a highly developed clan system. The Neolithic period had begun.

By the time Columbus reached what he thought was Asia, the Indians had spread over both North and South America. They had – in some areas – learnt agricultural practices, and knew how to weave, how to work with metals, and how to make pottery. Climatic conditions retarded some, especially those in Canada and in the tropical Amazon Valley. By contrast, the Incas of Peru, probably numbering three million, and the Aztecs and Maya of Mexico and Central America ("Meso-America"), probably numbering four million, had developed an intensive agriculture, good roads, careful methods of irrigation and crop rotation, and even a system of pensions and unemployment insurance that made possible the support of large populations. For their elaborate religious ceremonies they built stone and mortar pyramid temples faced with carved stone. Around them "cities" grew. The Maya had a culture rich in paradox: they had elaborated a remarkable calendar – their culture was obsessed with the idea of time – and a system of writing based on hieroglyphics; their priests were highly trained students of mathematics and astronomy. They kept scroll books, or codices, arranged in almanac form, so that they could anticipate the seasons, plot the movement of heavenly bodies and plan the future. Only one, the Dresden Codex, survives as testament of their knowledge. All the rest were destroyed as pagan by the Europeans. Yet in all their sophistication they failed to invent the wheel, and believed

---

[2] By ca. 6000 BC, the large mammals became extinct: the giant mammoth, the large American camel, the wild pig, the horse.

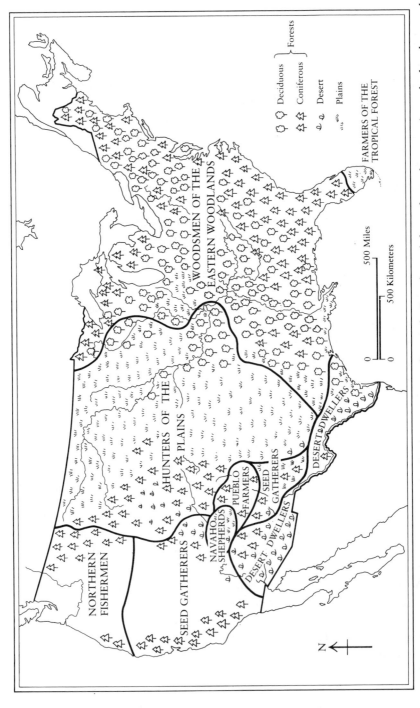

Map 5 Pre-Columbian North America. The land was vast and varied. For the palefaces from the east, it took decades to clear forests and to blaze trails and tracks. The forest and the frontier were the central themes in the American story.

that the world was supported on the backs of two giant alligators. But if the culture of Meso-America was still a Stone Age culture as far as tools were concerned, the work in gold and copper was elaborate, and there were well-organized city states, and even, under Aztecs and Incas, empires, albeit of cruelty and savagery, as evidenced by the horde of human remains at Chichén Itzá in Yucatán. It was a land of kings, priests — and peasant revolts.

The Indians in what is now the United States in the 1600s were much less developed than Aztecs or Incas. There was no one Indian type, no homogeneity. They may have numbered in all little more than 1 million (though some estimates go much higher), thinly spread in some 200 distinct "nations." Today the Bureau of Indian Affairs recognizes 266 American Indian groups, ranging from the 160,000 Navajos in Arizona and New Mexico, the largest Indian nation, to the Chumash of California and the Modoc of Oklahoma, each of which has fewer than 100, and the Osages of Oklahoma, who are hard to distinguish from their white neighbours. This indicates a long history and endless migrations. When the white man came, the Utes probably numbered only 3,600, the Comanche 3,500, the Arapacho 3,000, the Cheyenne 3,500 and the Sioux only 11,000. The tribes were then, as they still are, diverse in character, in historical experience, and particularly in language. There were at least 400 distinct Indian languages (over 100 are still in use today). Even in the same area of settlement, languages were distinct. Apache and Hopi have distinct roots. The tongue of the Zuni in the same geographical area has not been shown to be related to that of a single tribe within more than 1,000 miles; it may have distant connections with the speech of a Mexican tribe far to the south. The Huchi on the Savannah River spoke a language utterly unrelated to any other. Although all their eastern languages belonged to one linguistic family, the Algonkian, the Indian world was nevertheless a veritable Tower of Babel.

By the time of the coming of the palefaces, North America had two distinctive Indian culture patterns. The region from the east coast to the Mississippi depended on maize, beans, and squash; the women cultivated the crops, the men raided the forests for fish or game, and they could be rapidly organized for tribal war. But across the Mississippi, from Canada to Texas, the plains were blackened by buffalo, on which the Indians subsisted, the hides for clothing and for *tipi* covering (the average *tipi* required 25 buffalo skins), the meat for food. Sun-dried, it became "jerky", pounded fine and mixed with berries it became the staple pemmican. When the white man came, there may have been as many as 60 million bison on the plains. When the tribes drove them, it took three days for the buffalo to cross the Missouri. The Indian terrains of mountains and high plains seemed unsuited to farming, and they bred a restless, mobile, yet a totally buffalo-dependent people.

There were many variations, however. The Indian ecologies were as varied as their languages: from the arctic tundra where the Inuit lived (the most recent of the incomers from Siberia) to the Mexican desert, from the mound-builders of the Great Lakes and Mississippi Valley to the peaceful ways of the Hopi and Amasazi cliff-dwellers, who irrigated and worked the land intensively. There was none of the developed stone architecture or the systems of writing and of measuring time of the Maya, Aztec, and Toltec of Central and South America, but there was skilled copper-working and pottery, and delicately carved clay pipes have been found in an area stretching from New York to Kansas; the burial mounds, though less pyramids than great heaps of earth, have sometimes a base area greater than the pyramid of Cheops; they were vastly greater in number and would have required a greater expenditure of labor than the great monuments along the Nile. But it was a basket-weaving, clay-baking culture, bows and arrows its native weapons. And its major limitation was of course the absence of writing (and thus of record, administration, and continuity of ordered government). Teaching, song, legend: all were oral – as in Homer's Greece. Not until 1823 did Sequoia, the crippled son of a Cherokee woman and a white trader, introduce a written language among the Cherokees – with dramatic modernizing effects.

The Indians were appallingly badly treated by the discoverers, and went down in hordes to the white man's weapons – and his diseases. Those of them who survived (settled in some 260 reservations) live primitive lives, and are too often addicts of drink and drugs. But: the Atlantic meant little to their ancestors – except that across it came the enemy. For the First Americans had reached their American hunting and camping grounds by way of an ocean of their own – before the ice melted and it was still Beringia. And they settled it from Alaska to Patagonia.[3]

---

[3] Henry F. Dobyns, *American Historical Demography* (Bloomington, Ind., Indiana University Press, 1976). Given, as he calculates, that there were 40 million Indians in North America (of whom 30 million were in Mexico), the steady decline in the 10 million in what is now the US due to war and disease over the next 300 years, is a horror story of awesome proportions. See also Henry F. Dobyns, *Their Number Became Thinned: Native American population dynamics in eastern North America* (Knoxville, University of Tennessee Press, 1983); Russell Thornton, *American Indian*

4 THE RE-DISCOVERERS AND THEIR ACHIEVEMENTS

What themes run through the stories of the Discoveries, and of those who made them possible?

One, the men themselves. In all their individual differences these men were cast in an heroic mould, as robust in will as in physique, unyielding and patient in seeking their goals, courageous in defying the elements – the Mare Tenebroso of the north, with its giant icebergs and savage storms, the sultry Spanish Main with the challenges of pirates and of avowed enemies as well as of the sea; and – always – in their handling of ill-fed, vitamin-starved, disease-prone, and nervy crews, often on the edge of mutiny. Their experience and their professional skills allowed them to navigate unknown seas, and to survive longer voyages than ever before. Their faith made their swords all but invincible. The anguish and the doubts of latter-day imperialists are missing.

Many of them died or were lost at sea, and usually their ships with them: John Cabot was lost with 4 ships and all hands; both Corte-Reals, with 2 ships and all hands; Richard Grenville on the *Revenge* was killed after fighting alone against 15 Spanish ships for 15 hours; John Hawkins died of a fever at Puerto Rico; Humphrey Gilbert, on his northern journey in his fatal expedition, saw his

Holocaust and Survival: A population history since 1492 (Norman, University of Oklahoma Press, 1987); Ann F. Ramenofsky, *Vectors of Death: The archaeology of European contact* (Albuquerque, University of New Mexico Press, 1987); Daniel T. Reff, *Disease, Depopulation, and Culture Change in Northwestern New Spain 1518–1764* (Salt Lake City, University of Utah Press, 1991); Douglas H. Ubelaker and John W. Verano (eds), *Disease and Demography in the Americas: Changing patterns before and after 1492* (Washington, DC, Smithsonian Institution Press, 1992); J. Axtell, "Moral reflections on the Columbian legacy," in *Beyond 1492*, ch. 10, and his "The ethnohistory of early America, a review history", *William & Mary Quarterly*, 35 (1978), pp. 110–44; John D. Daniels, "The Indian population of North America in 1492," ibid., 49 (1992), pp. 298–332; Carl Wildman (compiler), *Atlas of the North American Indian* (New York, Facts on File Publication, 1985); Francis Paul Prucha, *Atlas of American Indian Affairs* (University of Nebraska Press, 1990); D'Arcy McNickle, *Native American Tribalism: Indian survivals and renewals* (New York, published for the Institute of Race Relations by Oxford University Press, 1973); D'Arcy McNickle and Harold E. Fey, *Indians and other Americans: Two ways of life meet*, rev. edn (New York, Harper and Row, 1970); Stan Steiner, *The New Indians* (New York, Harper and Row, 1968); and D'Arcy McNickle, *They Came Here First* (Harper and Row, Perennial Paperback, 1975).

flagship the *Delight* lost, with all his supplies, his books and charts, and with Hakluyt's room-mate at Oxford, Stephen Parmenius, the geographer, aboard; and, on the return, his tiny pinnace the *Squirrel*, with himself seen reading in the stern, was "devoured and swallowed up by the sea" in a storm off the Azores and within sight of his consorts. The queen was only too much justified in her fear that he was a man "not of good hap by sea." Sir George Peckham, Gilbert's chief backer, lost everything he had put into the venture, and later lost his estate to pay his debt to the Crown. Martin Frobisher, explorer of the Canadian sea-ice, died in 1594 when he lost a leg to a Spanish bullet; Panfilo Narvaez was swept out to sea; Magellan was killed by natives; Francis Drake, who made camp at or near what is now San Francisco, and whose voyage round the world brought a return to his backers of 1,000 percent, died at sea 15 years later off Nombre de Dios, and to the sea he left his bones; and Henry Hudson, who served the Dutch East India Company in quest of "the isles of spicery," discredited the notion of reaching "Cathay" by a strait across North America in low latitudes, sailed up the river named after him as far as Albany in 1609, and, finally, then in English service, made a last attempt to reach the "sea to the westwards," only to be cast adrift, with his son and five others, in an open boat without food by mutineers in 1611, to die in the emptiness of the bay named after him. Not one of them except Drake got adequate recognition: neither Columbus nor Cartier got the patent of nobility or the courtly recognition they craved. They all sailed at high risk. Insurance of such voyages was unusual, but in 1547, in England, insurance policies were issued by Italian bankers. The landsmen had little better fortune: John Dee, the Elizabethan map-maker, died in poverty after selling his books in order to survive; and Thomas Harriot, as a friend of Ralegh and a "magi" of Henry, the "Wizard" earl of Northumberland, went to the Tower along with his patron, on suspicion after the Gunpowder Plot in 1605. The earl stayed there for 16 years.

Their stories are of a harshness and brutality hard to comprehend — until we find them recurring in our own times. To them the Indian natives lived barbarous lives, and were heretics. The cross as much as the sword became the symbol of conquest, religious tenets the justification for plunder, torture, genocide, and slavery. The iniquities perpetrated in the name of religion have always been the bane of theologians; but the sheer demonic relentlessness and ingenuity with which Christianity annihilated the native culture of the Americas still appals, as much as the perverted logic of faith which should dictate that in 1637–145 years after Columbus first made landfall – John Winthrop, the founder of the Massachusetts Bay Puritan colony, should describe smallpox as divine providence, an act of God to oblige the English colonists to occupy lands depopulated by the disease.

The natives seem, on occasion, barely more civilized. The Inca chief, Atahualpa, fed the sons of his brother to vultures, and decapitated the prophet who announced misfortune. The Caete Indians were excommunicated in perpetuity for eating the first Brazilian bishop. But this seems only mildly antisocial behaviour in light of their eventual extermination by the Portuguese. One silently offers up an Amen to the Indian chief who at his burning is promised eternal rest if he recognises Christ. Are there Christians in heaven? he asks. Yes, he is told. He chooses hell.

Almost all the discoverers, too, were scholar-heroes, even if some were also and simultaneously pirate kings. And not all were well-born. Cortés was a courtier, a lover, a poet, an orator, a captain, and a governor. Champlain, who rose from nothing, became an admiral, a mathematician, a theorist of navigation, a skillful painter, and a cartographer; in his old age he had someone at the table read in the morning from a historian and in the evening from the biography of a saint. Captain John Smith of Jamestown fame trained himself for knight-errantry, warred against the Mohammedans, put three Turks' heads on his coat-of-arms, was sufficiently a lover to attract the amorous interest of a lady in Constantinople, was a discoverer, a horseman, a navigator, a statesman, a general, and a scholar so trained in Renaissance ideals as to imitate the classical historians by putting formal speeches into the mouths of Powhatan and himself.[4]

The voyagers, however, were as savage and as thoughtless in their attitudes to white men, whether rival compatriots or white enemies, as to Indians. Many early colonizing plans, or Roanoke rescue missions, were wrecked by the temptations of piracy. Cooperation – as in aiding the Huguenot colonies in Florida – was rare. When Ralph Lane was left behind at Roanoke as acting-governor, he complained less of threats from Indians or of the fear of hurricanes

---

[4] Howard Mumford Jones, *O Strange New World: American Culture, the formative years* (New York, Viking, 1964), p. 117; Karen Ordahl Kupperman (ed.), *Captain John Smith, a Select Edition of his Writings* (Chapel Hill, NC, Institute of Early American History and Culture [hereafter IEAHC], North Carolina University Press, 1988); Leo Lemay, *The American Dream of Captain John Smith* (Charlottesville, University of Virginia Press, 1991).

than from "the wild men of my own nation." Columbus and Ralegh could echo his words.[5]

The discoverers were inheritors too of their own past, living in their own dream world, part medieval, part modern: John Dee more medieval than modern, Ralegh the reverse. In them the Renaissance became extrovert, and gave reality to Atlantis. They inherited the myths of the classical and the medieval worlds, some of them made even more vivid by Marco Polo, with his pictures of the wealth of Cathay and of a Cipangu (Japan), with its temples roofed with pure gold. It was the dream of gold that stimulated the quest for Antillia, believed to be the first home of the Seven Bishops and the Seven Cities, until its location was transferred to the Seven Cities of Cibola – a dream that would lead many to their deaths, and Fray Marcos to the *pueblos* of New Mexico. It was real gold, however, and not the dream, which, within a generation of Columbus's first landing, would put into the coffers of Spain the wealth of the Aztecs and the Incas. The myth took Hernando de Alvarado past the upper reaches of the Pecos in search of Quivira and its kingdom of gold. But the reality of its effect on Spain marked the beginning of the modern world. If the gold Columbus found on Hispaniola was alluvial only, the reality was stupifying: the treasures of the Aztecs and Incas, and in 1545 the discovery at Potosi in Bolivia of the greatest mineral discovery ever made – an actual mountain of silver. By 1558 three mines in Mexico were in regular production.[6]

The Christianity of these men was devout and intense, buttressed by priests and regular masses, by the *auto-da-fé* and the Inquisition. They believed in the purification of the body by fire before its redemption, and in the sinful nature of man; so while they were savage and lustful, they could be also unafraid to suffer martyrdom, qualities that their Indian captive enemies would respect and emulate. And Columbus, the realist, probably the best handler of a ship on the high seas of them all, was also a mystic, and surmised that somewhere within the coast of Venezuela was Paradise, Eden itself.

A second recurring feature is the presence in or near each European capital of a group of geographers, map-makers and planners,

[5] Cf. D. B. Quinn: "The discovery of America was the work of Renaissance Europe rather than of any nation," *England and the Discovery of America*, (London, Allen and Unwin, 1973), p. 40.
[6] For the dominance of gold in the imagery of the day, see A. L. Rowse, *The Elizabethans and America* (New York, Harper, 1959), pp. 191–4, and Mumford Jones, *O Strange New World* pp. 40–50.

under royal patronage — as at Sagres, Mortlake, and Palos. Today's term for them would be "policy centers" or "think tanks." Nations and boundaries, however, were still uncertain, especially for Italians. With no united country as yet — or for another three and a half centuries — and with the trade routes along the Mediterranean blocked, Florentines and Genoese, Padovans and Venetians moved to their own kinship groups in Bristol and London, Lyons, and Lisbon, and later, and not least important, in the Canaries; once the Jews were expelled Portugal was heavily dependent on Genoese and Italian bankers. "The Italians found everything and founded nothing. They were cosmopolitan pioneers." [7]

In particular, from these centers came the maps the seafarers needed. It is no accident that in almost every discoverer's family, one or more prominent member would be in training as a cartographer. The maps were largely the work of Italians, constantly changed in the light of each new discovery, guarded carefully — and illicitly passed on through the mapmakers' mafia, from court to court. The first efforts — those of Henry Martellus in 1485–90, and of Fra Mauro, the printing of Ptolemy's *Geography*, and Martin Behaim of Nuremberg's globe of 1492, which put Cathay at Newfoundland — were still medieval fiction. The Contarini-Roselli manuscript map of 1506 recognized South America as a new continent, but still saw North America as part of Asia; so did the Ruysch map of 1508. Only the international contacts ensured accuracy. Where the map-makers drew only on restricted knowledge, they were of limited value. The first English map, the work of Edward Wright, Richard Hakluyt, and John Davis, published in Hakluyt's *Navigations* in 1599, outlines America well; Africa, however, is a mere outline, India and Persia grotesque. In its narrower range, John White's — drawing on his Roanoke experience, though he had had to abandon most of his sketches — provide a good outline of the Carolina-Virginia Tidewater. The map of Juan de la Cosa begun in 1500 is the first significant record of North American exploration, and includes material on the 1497 voyage of John Cabot. It shows North America as part of Asia, but on it the English flags fly from Newfoundland to Florida. The Oliveriana map of a year or two

---

[7] J. D. Rogers, *Shakespeare's England* (Oxford, Oxford University Press, 1916), p. 168. Cf. the comment of Gianni Granzotto: "The notion of native country as we understand it today, mattered little to him (Columbus) ... Dreams have no native country. To dreams, after all, all countries are irrelevant." Granzotto, *Christopher Columbus, the Dream and the Obsession* (London, Collins Grafton, 1988), pp. 18–19.

later is significant as showing the emergence of some degree of scientific skepticism about the location and definition of discoveries across the Atlantic, since alternative, unfinished coastlines give us indications, not alleged certainties, of what had been discovered. The Cantino map of 1502 is an important political document: under Portuguese influence, it placed the western discoveries of Gaspar Corte Real in 1501 on the Portuguese side of the demarcation line of 1494, agreed between Spain and Portugal by the Treaty of Tordesillas. The land which lay beyond this island discovery on the map is clearly intended as part of Asia, but it terminates in a Horn of Asia which is very like the Florida peninsula. The map and globe published by Martin Waldseemuller at Saint-Die in 1507 were, however, especially important. They reveal a new continent, separated from Asia by an ocean. The name "America" on it was also original, though it was applied only to South America, the northern landmass being labelled "Terra ulterius incognita." The Waldseemuller map was widely influential in presenting an outline of some authority for subsequent makers of world maps. Soon their work began to show the northernmost of the new continents, also carrying the name America. By 1525, Jorge Reinel's Atlas is remarkably detailed and accurate. French maps, after Verrazano's careful probing of the coast from Charleston to Maine and the Cartier-Roberval voyages of 1534–43, are also reliable, as is that of Nicholas Desliens of 1541, in Jean Rotz's Atlas of 1542, and in Giambatista Ramusio's third volume, *Navigationi et viaggi*, published in Venice in 1556. By the second half of the century the Age of the Discoverers was being amply and accurately recorded in maps. Its highlights were the three volumes of Richard Hakluyt's second edition of his *Navigations*, including French and Spanish material as well as English; Abraham Ortelius of Antwerp's *Theatrum orbis terrarum* of 1570; Mercator's map of North America of 1584; and the multilingual series of illus-trated volumes of Theodore de Bry at Frankfurt-am-Main, beginning with his *America* in 1590, and its engravings of Indians. To it, as was the way with scholars, Hakluyt had contributed.[8]

Thirdly, despite the fantastic wealth of New Spain, a contem-porary recorder might have thought it a century of successive failures,

---

[8] See W. P. Cumming, R. A. Skelton, and D. B. Quinn, *The Discovery of North America* (London, Elek, 1971); Henri Harrisse, *Découverte et évolution carto-graphique de Terre-Neuve* (1900); Edmundo O'Gorman, *La idea del descubri-miento de America* (Mexico, 1951), and his shorter book on the same topic, *The Invention of America* (Bloomington, University of Indiana Press, 1961).

A llagatto . *This being but one moneth old was 3 foote 4 . ynches in length . and lyue in water .*

Plate 3 "Allagatto," one of the John White's remarkable watercolors of American flora and fauna. Ralegh's instruction to his captains was to map, to explore, and to discover all they could, including plant and animal life. The plants and animals proved more different than the people.
(Reproduced by courtesy of The Trustees of the British Museum, London.)

if settlement rather than exploration was the purpose. Every first settlement, if left for more than a year, was destroyed by Indians, or simply abandoned by its occupants: Columbus's 39 men left at Navidad on Haiti in 1493; Jean Ribaut's Charlesfort on the coast of South Carolina (1562), and his and Laudonnière's Fort Caroline near Jacksonville in 1564; Ralegh's colony at Roanoke, despite the bungled rescue missions 1507–9, and again in 1602. Only a relief expedition arriving just in time, and a radical reassessment of its purpose, saved Jamestown from extinction during its "starving time" from 1607–9; and its twins, at Martin's Hundred nearby, and at Sagadahoc on the Kennebec in Maine, were each abandoned. As a first venture in exploration and in settlement, Elizabethan America was a failure.

Yet there was other, if less substantial, evidence. Captured Indians, brought to Europe for display, could not help on charts and in intelligence, but – as in spreading the view of the fabled diamonds of Saguenay – they could give substance to legends. John White's sketches of flora and fauna and Thomas Harriot's *Brief and True Report* confirmed the agricultural wealth of Virginia, and confirmed the map-makers in their projections. Despite their lack of success in establishing permanent toeholds on a continent, the map-men were the first colonial departments in each of their governments.

Hakluyt was explicit. He enumerated in detail the manpower requirements of a new American colony: he listed no less than 76 separate occupations from archers to whittawers, in five principal categories. The colony would need the following:

1 "Men ... incident ... to the continue of victual," such as "grafters for fruit trees" and "freshwater fishers," who would be responsible for feeding the rest of the task force. They would also establish cash crops for export.

2 "Men ... Tending to force," including "gunpowder makers" and "harquebusiers of skill," responsible for fortification and defense, who would secure the colony against Indian or Spanish attack.

3 "Men ... incident to the first traffic and trade of merchandize," like blacksmiths, "grubbers and rooters up of trees" and millwrights, whose labour would transform the wilderness into an industrial and commercial complex.

4 "Artisans serving our first planters not in traffic but for buildings," including brickmakers and thatchers, who would construct shelters from local materials.

5 A miscellaneous group including laundry-workers and tailors, shoe-makers and makers of leather bottles.

The early reports spoke repeatedly of a wealth of fir and pine and pitch for ship-building and for masts, of a tree-bark that cured scurvy, and sassafras root to cure syphilis, "so many, so rare and so singular commodities ... as all the kingdoms and states of Christendom joined in one together do not yield either more good or more plentiful, whatsoever for public use is needful or pleasing for delight." Sir Walter Ralegh instructed his pioneers at Roanoke; "with Argus eyes to see what commodity by industry of man you are able to make it yield, that England doth want or desire." A colony of woodcutters and men processing lumber would furnish materials for the greatest navy yet to sail the seas. American wood products, such as turpentine and rosin, would guarantee England's sufficiency in naval stores. American dyestuffs would bring new life to the English textile industry. English leather-workers could specialize in American hides. American furs had a guaranteed European market. European wagon wheels needed "train oil" which the English could now supply from American walruses and whales. A colony would be a defense post (or attack point) against Spanish treasure fleets using the Florida channel, and a supply post for the fishermen on the Banks, providing the wooden barrels and the dry salt for their catches. Although the reality on the Tidewater was of disease, starvation, and murder, the dream in Mortlake, Oxford, and Whitehall was of rich and limitless raw materials, and "merchantable" commodities. For timber and ore as exports from this cornucopia, there could go in reverse silks and English woollens, as the settlements became a market for imports. "We shall not only receive many precious commodities from thence, but also shall in time find ample vent [sale] of hats, bonnets, knives, fish-hooks, copper kettles, beads, looking glasses, bugles, and a thousand kinds of wrought wares, that in short time may be brought to use among the people of that country, to the great relief of our poor people and to the wonderful enriching of this realm. We should not depend upon Spain for oils, sacks [sherry], raisins, oranges, lemons, Spanish skins, etc.; nor upon France for wood, bay salt and Gascoyne wines; nor on Estland [the Baltic] for flax, pitch, tar, masts etc." America, a cornucopia, would "yield to us all the commodities of Europe, Africa and Asia." In other words, Hakluyt and Dee realized the character of the mercantile Atlantic empire as it would become. But not yet. Later their message would be confirmed by peppers and paprika, by potatoes and tomatoes, by timbers galore for navies, by tobacco and cotton, corn, turkeys, and pumpkins, sugar, rice, and indigo, the succulent and sustaining raw materials of empire.[9]

In the Latin use of the word *inverere*, the discoverers and the cartographers invented America: they found it, and they founded it; at least in part, because they had conceived it; putting it – as Atlantis, and the Antillia – on maps before they, any of them, had stood on its soil. It was product as much of their imagining as of their skill as navigators, of their cartographers as well as of their pilots.

Fourthly, they all took their sovereignties as well as their Christianity and their maps with them, as agents of Spain, Portugal, France, Holland, and England. All were Atlantic-oriented, since the Ottoman Turks had cut off the Mediterranean trade to the East, and made of that sea a backwater. They thus entangled the lands they liberated with the problems of their 'Mother' country, with its religious and dynastic conflicts and with its trading patterns, so that a settlement's products went as exports to Madrid or Lisbon, Paris,

[9] D. B. Quinn and R. A. Skelton, *Richard Hakluyt: The Principall Navigations, Voyages and Discoveries of the English Nation* (Hakluyt Society, Cambridge, 1965).

Amsterdam, or London, and to them came its major luxury imports. They shared the language and culture of a European country. The transatlantic links, linguistic, historical, and cultural, were more binding than any local but "unnatural" ultra-American connections, after as well as before a colony won its independence.

Success, as always, fed on success. After a first voyage had survived and been profitable, money became more readily available. Royal treasuries were low, and too much was spent from them on foreign wars. For long, parts of western Europe were trading with posts set up in the New World. The investment, like the ships and the crews, came mainly from groups of merchant adventurers of the trading towns – Bristol as well as London, Palos as well as Seville, Nantes and Dieppe as well as Paris. Joint stock companies enjoyed royal support and monopolies, tariff protection, and subsidies where available – and, gradually, government regulation of wages and prices. The gold and silver from the New World permitted the re-priming of the pump, and remorselessly fed inflation even as it was an immense, unexpected economic stimulus. This commercial revolution steadily destroyed the feudal, static, local, and non-profit system of medieval Europe, and ended too the medieval doctrines of the just price and the ban on usury. Small-scale natural economies producing for consumption gave way to a market economy, in which commodities were produced for profit. And with the profits from the lucrative Atlantic trade, a surplus of capital in turn fed investment, more ships, more docks, more warehouses, newly chartered banks. The ducat of Venice, the florin of Florence, the dollar and pieces of eight, became symbols of value across the world. The European had gone out to find Asia. In fact he had discovered a new and greater Cathay – and more. For, since Greek and Roman times, Europe's purchases of Eastern spices and luxury goods of one kind or another had drained Europe of precious metals. With the discovery of America, Spanish silver became available to pay for the products which the West sought in the East; a world economy was now feasible.

No other continent was as much influenced by the discovery of America as was Europe, its re-discoverer. The impact of the New World on the Old and the Old World on the New, was boundless. Its existence fired the imagination of Europeans from Bacon and More to Shakespeare. Writing of *The Tempest*, A. L. Rowse says:

The whole play sings of the sea; the loveliest songs are of the sea:[10]

---

[10] Rowse, *The Elizabethans and America*, p. 197.

> Come unto these yellow sands,
>   And then take hands:
> Curtsied when you have and kissed,
>   The wild waves whist ...

and the most haunting song, surely, ever written:

> Full fathom five thy father lies
>   Of his bones are coral made;
> Those are pearls that were his eyes:
>   Nothing of him that doth fade,
> But doth suffer a sea-change
> Into something rich and strange.

The poets were involved in their world. Shakespeare, like Drayton, had a number of close friends in the Virginia Company, and Spenser was active in plantations in Ireland; John Locke's library was rich in volumes on the American voyages, and he was interested in devising constitutions for the new colonies. "The discovery of the Americas," said Francisco Lopez de Gomara, historian of the conquest of the Indies, writing in the sixteenth century, was "the greatest event in human history since the creation, except for the incarnation of Christ." It was a place of shadowy dreams of perfection, and of Caliban in clash with Prospero, as to Shakespeare and Montaigne; or a challenge to existing philosophical and political ideas, as to More, who also knew through his brother-in-law the practical problems of getting there. By 1795, when two political revolutions had occurred, and an economic transformation was beginning, the German publicist and statesman, Friedrich Von Gentz, could assess 1492 and its consequences in a long retrospect: "The discovery of America and a new route to the East Indies opened the greatest market, the greatest inducement to human industry, that had ever existed since the human race emerged from barbarism." [11]

And fifthly, for the Indians, the coming of the white men was disastrous. It came to mean the near-certainty of enslavement and of death. When food supplies were found to be inadequate for both white men and red, coolness gave way to conflict. When they met in conflict, bows and arrows were a feeble response to swords, armor, and guns. Firewater was almost as lethal as fire-arms; and the white men's diseases were the most lethal of all, smallpox particularly.

---

[11] Carlos Fuentes, *The Buried Mirror* (London, Deutsch, 1992).

It is usual, but inaccurate, to ascribe the introduction of African slaves to America, for work in the mines or on the sugar plantations, to the proposal of the venerable Bishop Las Casas in 1517. When he reluctantly sanctioned the traffic, it had in fact already been in existence for almost two decades. The original intent was that only blacks would go who had already been Christianized, and who would thus not only relieve the Indians of the heavy work for which they seemed temperamentally as well as physically unsuited, but would also serve as Christian examples to them. However laudable, the pretense was soon abandoned: by 1503 at least one Spanish viceroy pleaded that no more should be sent out – and was ignored. Charles V as Emperor granted licenses to Flemings to run the traffic, and then in turn farmed out the job of transportation to the Genoese. John Quincy Adams was, then, only partly correct when he noted: "The negro slave-trade itself was the child of humanity – the contrivance of Las Casas to mitigate the condition of the American Indians."[12]

Finally, here as elsewhere, chance ruled, even with so driven and so committed a man as Columbus, who felt himself the instrument not of *fortuna* but of destiny. He did not find Cathay, and he did not recognize the America he found. But, realizing the significance of the trade winds, and taking the 28th N latitude due west from the Canaries when almost within sight of his goal, he turned southwest. He made his landing, therefore, on one of a chain of islands, and spent the rest of his days vainly trying to identify them and plot their proximity to India. Had he sailed due west all the way, he would have hit Cape Canaveral on Florida, part of the mainland; and North America, north as well as south, would have become Spanish soil. And its history, and the world's, would have been very different indeed.

5 THE WONDERS OF THE NEW WORLD

The achievement of the Discoverers was remarkable enough: the finding of two new continents and innumerable outlying islands, by men of courage and intelligence, who followed that intelligence to new worlds. They were men of two worlds; men of the Renaissance – but men of Faith too. The discoveries were, they

[12] John Quincy Adams, *Diary*, ed. L. H. Butterfield (Belknap Press of Harvard University Press, Cambridge, MA, 1961), April 29, 1819.

believed, part of a divine plan; in 1500 Columbus wrote that "God made me the messenger." That message included the news that, until 1492, the Church had denied: there were people in the discovered land, who did not come from the seed of Adam and Eve. They were not at all as Marco Polo had supposed them, but a semi-pastoral people, and as such similar to the first to dwell in Zion; and they were brought back to Europe as evidence of the Discoverers' success. The Indians were, as all descendants of Adam, guilty of original sin, but as dwellers in a wilderness paradise they were, Adam-like, innocent of the corruptions of civilization, "most gentle, loving and faithful, void of all guile and treason, and such as live after the manner of the golden age." But why did they act as savages, and why had they been hidden so long?

For centuries, therefore, new questions were debated, theological as well as secular. The Americans – the Indians – had to be incorporated into the genealogy of man as recounted by Genesis. For God had created but one couple, Adam and Eve, and allowed but one family, that of Noah, to survive the Flood. From what son of Noah did the Indians descend? Were they originally Spanish, Carthaginian, Greek, Hebrew, Asian, Norse, even Welsh? Were they – since a Yucatan tribe practiced circumcision – a lost tribe of Israel? And how had they made the journey – and without horses, cows, and sheep? And clearly they were "possessed," as well as pagan. Lopez Vaz, a Portuguese, reported that the natives of Tierra del Fuego were 10 or 11 feet high. Frobisher's crew were sure the Eskimos "are great inchanters, and use many charmes of witchcraft." John Davis found them filled with a "devillish nature." John Hawkins found them "no such kinde of people as wee tooke them to bee, but more devilish a thousand partes and are eaters and devourers of any man they can catch." Francis Drake, when he coasted along Brazil, watched the Indians making fires, "a sacrifice (as we learned) to the devils, about which they use conjurations, making heapes of sande and other ceremonies, that when any ship shall goe about to stay upon their coast ... stormes and tempests may arise to the casting away of ships and men." The chief god they worship, reported Captain John Smith, is the devil: "They say that they haue conference with him, and fashion themselves as neare to his shape as they can imagine." And Father Pierre Biard agreed:

all this region, though capable of the same prosperity as ours, nevertheless through Satan's malevolence, which reigns there, is only a horrible wilderness ... as a people they have bad habits, are extremely lazy, gluttonous,

profane, treacherous, cruel in their revenge, and given up to all kinds
of lewdness, men and women alike ...

And when, against the superior military power and technological
skill of the Europeans, the Indian could oppose only cunning and
his knowledge of the land, he was seen as unreliable and quixotic.[13]

These new perplexities were compounded by the introduction of
another: how were these new worlds to be governed? This was a
question for the Spaniards earlier, and far more worryingly, than
for the English: and the New Spain was awesome in its extent.

The total land surface of North, Central, and South America
is over $15\frac{1}{2}$ million square miles; the total superficial area of the
United States as such is a little over 3 million square miles, or only
one-fifth of the whole. Spanish sovereignty once extended as far
north as the Carolinas on the Atlantic and beyond San Francisco
Bay on the Pacific Coast, and thus embraced at one time or another
the Carolinas, Georgia, Florida, Alabama, Mississippi, Tennessee,
Louisiana, Texas, New Mexico, Arizona, Arkansas, Oklahoma,
Missouri, Kansas, Colorado, Utah, Nevada, Iowa, Nebraska, Wyoming, Idaho, Minnesota, the two Dakotas, and, on the Pacific Coast,
California, or parts of these states. In 1680 a Spanish force hoisted
their flag at or near Saint Joseph, Michigan, and in 1693 a Spanish
expedition reached the Mandan country in North Dakota. The
Spaniards at one time penetrated to Alaska. In the east the Spanish
possession of Georgia was at one time a real threat to the Carolinas;
not until 1702 did the English push the frontier back beyond the
St John's River. About two-thirds of the continental United States
owes something to Spanish culture, if it be no more than the 2,000
thousand Spanish place names on the map.

For this vast imperium – to which only that of Rome can be
compared – Spain devised a vice-regal system which in form gave
the king a greater authority in the Indies than at home. By the mid-
sixteenth century the vice-royal system, backed up by the Council
of the Indies and the Casa de la Contratación in Spain, had sub-
stituted for the original anarchy of slaughter a centralized administration that undoubtedly suffered from delay and disobedience –
"I obey but I do not enforce," ran a famous phrase – but that
also, especially when improved in the eighteenth century, brought
prosperity and progress to Latin America. By 1650 the "Indies"
supported about $10\frac{1}{2}$ million souls, of whom probably about 80

---

[13] Mumford Jones, *O Strange New World* p. 56.

percent were Indians living (at least the majority of them) conformably to the Spanish colonial system. Over a vast area Spain has sometimes done no more than establish vague claims, but it has elsewhere left behind perdurable testimony of its influence – the Spanish language in New Mexico, the missions of California and the southwest, city plans for municipalities, a vocabulary for the cattleman, and lasting fashions in art, music, architecture, and customs and habits.[14]

Indeed, it could be argued that Spain did better for its Indians – despite its cruelty and the savage revolts that marked its story – than did Britain, whose relations with the first Americans were always tense, often warlike, and whose Indian "policy" was simply to draw a line, as in 1763, and say "ne plus ultra." Moreover, given the dramatic inflationary effects of vast quantities of gold and silver on the metropolitan power, it probably was more beneficial in the Indies, in providing order and missionary teaching, than in Madrid or Seville.

Great as was Columbus's personal achievement, it has to be set against its consequences for the Indians. Driven by the quest for gold where there was little, except in the streams of Hispaniola, he had to find a labor force to retrieve it: the result was barbarism and enslavement. Despite Queen Isabella's pious injunctions against the mistreatment of innocent people, and her replacement of the Columbus brothers by a special commissioner, Francisco de Bobadilla, during his third voyage, she was convinced by returning voyagers that many Indians were cannibals – which was true only of the Caribs – and thus heathens outside Christian protection. In any case, she was remote – and she died in 1504.

Bobadilla was replaced as governor by Nicolas de Ovando, who surpassed his predecessors in cruelty. He went out between Columbus's third and fourth voyages, taking the largest contingent yet, 31 ships with 2,500 men. When the Indian chiefs assembled to greet him, 84 in all, he killed every one, setting an example Cortés and Pizarro would follow. Bobadilla himself was killed in the storm that hit his ship on its return home. Even in Columbus's day, what ornaments that natives had were handed over, and enslavement was used to fill the supply ships that began to act as ferries to Spain. Usually almost half of the enslaved failed to survive the voyages.

---

[14] The best survey of the impact of "Renaissance" Spain on the Americas is in Mumford Jones, *O Strange New World*, especially ch. 3, on which I draw for these references.

The Spaniards, invincible by dint of armor, swords, and muskets, horses and dogs, against a people armed only with bows and arrows, enslaved, brutalized, and murdered the Indians. In the two years of the Columbus brothers' administration of Hispaniola during the second voyage (1494–6), an estimated one-half of the entire population was killed – or killed themselves (ca.125,000 people). When it was clear that the gold tribute system had failed, it was changed to that of *repartimentos*, or *encomiendas*: Spaniards simply appropriated native land, and those Indians who chose to remain became laborers or slaves. The inefficient exploitation of land and labor by local bosses was often much more culpable than any grand imperial strategy, all too haphazard. Disease, starvation, and hard labor were as effective as open war. No stable civil society emerged, nor the political institutions that would provide a bedrock for democracy. And despite the work of Dominicans and Jesuits, there is no evidence of a single voluntary conversion to the True Faith. Black slaves were imported from Africa to replace the Indians. The story of Spanish cruelty is a Leyanda Negre, a Black Legend with too much truth in it.

Thus, the achievement of Columbus was not of his planning or contriving: there was a force of destiny in the landings wherever the first were, and in Santo Domingo Columbus did not discover a new world, or even re-discover it, but created it: the world of silver and gold, but even more of potatoes and peanuts, tomatoes and maize (which thrived when exported to Africa and – ironically – helped to ensure a steady supply of well-fed slaves). Indians in countless numbers were starved, diseased, or killed off, as rainforests were uprooted for sugar plantations; slaves, again in countless numbers, were imported to work them. The legacy of Columbus was a hybrid Atlantic and interlinked New World that was at once European, African, and American.

1

The Admiral who Rarely
Put to Sea:
Ralegh and Roanoke

By the time of Columbus's death at Valladolid in 1506, the Portuguese Pedro Alvarez de Cabral, blown off course on his way round the Cape of Good Hope, had landed on the Brazilian coast in 1500, and claimed it for Portugal. By 1502 Vespucci reached Porte de San Giulian in Argentina. To Alonso de Hojeda (and to Vespucci) it was clear that there was at least one New World here, perhaps two. In 1519–22 the Portuguese Fernando Magellan, sailing under a Spanish flag, revealed the extent of the two New Worlds.

Moreover, Columbus had, at least until his third voyage, enjoyed all but a monopoly of Spanish exploration, and that by grace and favor. After 1494, both Spain and Portugal had monopolies of their own in their allotted areas, by grace and favour of Rome. Columbus had put his own limited capital in; and the Pinzóns had found ships and crews; but his voyages were always "official." From 1499 other men, drawing largely from experience on voyages with him, or in his wake, mounted expeditions of their own, and at their own risk, abetted by the merchant adventurers of Seville, Palos, and the Rio Tinto estuary. Thanks largely to him, they already knew the Antilles, and they looked beyond them.

In 1499 the handsome *caballero* Alonso de Hojeda (captain of a caravel on Columbus's second voyage), explored the coast of Venezuela and gave it its name. He landed in what is now French Guiana, discovered the mouth of the Amazon and proceeded as far as Cape St Roque. Whereas Columbus, in all his fascination at the beauty of the Gulf of Paria, obstinately thought it part of an island, Hojeda recognized it as part of a mainland. More pirate and buccaneer than explorer, he was greedy for pearls and gold and slaves. In his expedition, he was accompanied by his own contractor and sponsor, the Florentine ship-chandler turned banker, Amerigo Vespucci, who was living in Seville and had helped to provision Columbus's ships, but was himself neither a practical navigator nor a pilot, although he claimed to be both. He had, in fact, been sent to Seville by Lorenzo de Medici after 15 years' legal and banking experience in Florence to run the Medici affiliate, Juanoto Berardi. After accompanying Hojeda (but not staying long with him), he had been asked by King Manuel of Portugal in 1501 – and again in 1503 – to accompany Goncalo Coelho to reconnoitre the territory in Brazil allotted to Portugal under the Treaty of Tordesillas. His account of his experience of 1499, for him a fresh and exotic one, was written to Lorenzo de Medici, and printed in Florence in 1504–6. Vespucci wrote well – he was a copious letter-writer – and his accounts are vivid both on natural scenery and on native sexual practices. By contrast, Columbus had written his reports for his devout queen, and they were therefore properly restrained. Helpfully, Vespucci omitted Hojeda's name, however, and his account was dated two years (1497) earlier than it actually occurred (1499); it cast its author as himself a discoverer, and not of "the Indies" but of a new mainland – even if to him, as to Columbus, it was but "the end of Asia". As *Mundus Novus*, its appearance coincided with Columbus's miserable reception at a Court now without its queen (who had died in November 1504), and just after Columbus's return from his unhappy fourth and final voyage. It went through 40 editions in six languages in the next few years. Vespucci became a Spanish citizen in the same year, and in 1508, until his death in 1512, he enjoyed the title of *piloto mayor*, Pilot-Major to the Kingdom, with power to license all pilots who sailed the ocean blue under the flag of Spain. His acceptance at Court suggested that he was the new man; as such his fame led to his name being given not to one continent but to two: they became not Atlantis, South and North, but America, South and North.

This might suggest that the future – and at least survival, and certainly fame – lay not with the pioneers but with the provision-merchants, the bankers, and suppliers, who put their own or other people's money to the risk – as indeed it would be, again, on America's own frontier in the West. More of them now went out themselves, like Vespucci himself, or as did Anton of the ship suppliers and hard-biscuit suppliers Guerra Brothers in Triana, across

the river from Seville; Anton exploited the pearls of Margarita, off
the coast of Venezuela. But there were still pioneers: in 1500 Vincente
Yanez Pinzón, the nobler of the brothers and the former captain
of the *Niña*, sailed along the coasts of northern Brazil, and recon-
noitred the mouth of the Amazon and Guyana. And Peralonso Hino
of Moguer, pilot of the first *Santa Maria*, always loud in his praise
of his admiral, was by 1500 using illicit knowledge of the admiral's
charts of the Pearl Coast to acquire a fortune of his own. Profit,
whether disguised as patriotism or piracy, exploitation of natives
and of natural resources, and conquest of territory, rapidly replaced
the idea of discovery.

Columbus, increasingly restricted in his movements by arthritis
or malaria, confined himself to shorelines and to establishing contours. He always felt himself a man under instruction, and he –
usually – obeyed. It was only after the Mexican coastal journeys
of Francisco Hernandez de Córdoba and Juan de Grizalva in 1517
and 1518, that the news of the gold of Yucatán and of the interior
reached the Caribbean and Spain, and a new compulsion took over.
And when Cortés, with a small force of troops, moved inland in
1519 to master huge populations – like the returning white gods of
the Aztecs' own legends – conquest replaced exploration as the
driving force.

1 WEST FROM HISPANIOLA

The island that had been Columbus's first center, Hispaniola, but
from which after his third voyage he was banned, became the base
from which others were explored and settled. By 1508 Cuba was
known to be an island; Puerto Rico was mastered by Don Juan Ponce
de Leon (1509–11), Jamaica was conquered by 1510; in turn, all
three became bases from which lands to the south and north could
be explored. Hernando Cortés, who was to become the leader –
and chief chronicler and tale-teller – of the conquest of Mexico,
was an Estremaduran who had settled in Hispaniola in 1504 and
who, after 1512, became an important personality in Cuba. The drive
for conquest was self-generating, peripheral as well as metropolitan;
and it grew by what it fed on.

By 1512 Hispaniola was sending annually to Spain 1 million
dollars' worth of gold, and was raising crops of sugar cane (introduced from the Canaries) and cotton. Vasco Nuñez de Balboa
captured the Indian town of Darien in Panama, and after a 23-day
march reached the Pacific. His success availed him little. Indeed,

success bred rivalry, and his successor Pedrarias de Avila had Balboa arrested for treason and beheaded. In 1513 Don Juan Ponce de Leon, who had sailed with Columbus on his second voyage as a gentleman volunteer, and used Puerto Rico as base, was in search of gold and supplies of fresh water for his men when he sighted what he called Florida, a flower-decked coast. He sent frequent landing parties ashore for fresh water, and knew the coast at least as far north as Miami. He stayed closest to the Florida Keys, which he named Les Martires because the high rocks at a distance look like men in suffering. There is no evidence of a landing near Saint Augustine, and though he knew of the Fountain of Perpetual Youth, he found that no Indian he met had ever heard of it. (The Fountain of Perpetual Youth, allegedly with erotically stimulating as well as medical restorative powers, has nevertheless been located near St Augustine, and has been charmingly, and profitably, exploited by twentieth-century America.) If he did land here, it was the first Spanish landing in what would become the United States. On his second visit in 1521, when he concluded that that legend was a fable, Ponce de Leon had 200 men, 50 horses, and supplies, and planned to found a colony: this led to the now predictable conflict with the Indians; a cruel and ruthless man, he died in Havana of his wounds. In 1519–21 Hernando Cortés was more fortunate: with 500 men he landed on the coast of Mexico and destroyed the most advanced Indian civilization, that of the Aztecs; the stone palaces of their capital, Tenochtitlán, were razed to the ground.

Alonsón Alvarez de Pineda (and not De Soto or La Salle) was the first to find the mouth of the Mississippi in 1518, and sailed 20 miles upstream; he called it Rio Espiritus Santo, since the season was Pentecost. Pineda was also the first to sail all the way from Florida to Vera Cruz, and his map shows Florida as the end of a long arc running from Yucatán round the Gulf of Mexico to end at the Florida Keys. And in June 1527 the proud Castilian *hidalgo*, Panfilo de Narvaez, set off from Sanlucar de Barrameda on the Guadalquivir, with 5 ships and 600 sailors, soldiers and colonists, a few women negroes, some friars, and with the resounding title of his own devising, "Governor of Florida, Rio de Palmas and the River Espiritu Santo," to conquer and settle Florida and what they could of the Gulf States from the Florida Keys to the Rio de la Palmas, a little to the west of Panuco. Theirs was one of the most horrifying of experiences by sea and by land. The ocean crossing in 1527 had many false starts, and on the Atlantic they hit a succession of hurricanes. Eleven months later on April 14, 1528, 400 survivors landed near Tampa Bay. Narvaez rashly dismissed his ships, and thus had to build (or borrow) boats – and none of his men were trained as boat-builders – and to bridge many rivers. They proceeded on foot, encountering some friendly Indians, but also meeting repeated attacks by the expert bowmen of the Apalachees. Their intention was territory, and they lived off it as they could. They crossed Mobile Bay and the Mississippi River, were frequently wrecked, and were steadily weakening from starvation; they killed their own horses for food. Narvaez himself, sleeping on his boat one night but mooring it insecurely, was swept off to sea when a storm arose, and disappeared. The four survivors, most notable of them Cabezade Vaca, were barefoot and near-naked; they passed themselves off among the Indians as medicine-men, with remarkable success it seems, and were thus, attended by an admiring retinue of hundreds of Indians, befriended and indeed escorted from tribe to tribe; they were quacks and hucksters, healers and holy men in tribe after tribe to whom they were gods – but at least they were survivors.

Their march is one of the great American legends: slowly, almost imperceptibly, they moved across Texas, across the Colorado and the Pecos Rivers in, apparently, 18 months' walking. They reached fellow-Spaniards somewhere on the Rio Sonoro, to find that they were not far from the great western ocean; and to find also that the first thoughts of their "civilized" "rescuers" was that their hundreds of Indian companions should at once be captured and enslaved. For their "liberators" were slave-hunters. Cabeza de Vaca, who saw the abject poverty of the Indians, learned to respect them – more than most of the whites he met; in this he was almost unique. He and his three companions slowly learned again the pleasures of wearing clothes and of sleeping in beds; they reached Mexico City on July 25, 1536, almost eight years from the time when they rashly dismissed their boats. Their endurance and ingenuity are the only redeeming qualities in a tale of near-total folly, arrogance, and greed for gold. One of the four, Estevanico, a giant bearded black, who had been liberated from slavery in Morocco, joined the Franciscan, Fray Marcos de Niza, as a guide on his expedition into the *pueblo* country of western New Mexico, among the Zuni people. He went ahead of the friar, still playing the role of healer and reaping a rich dividend of turquoise and women. He had two months of glory. Before the friar caught up with him, however, the Zuni people killed him.

On returning to Castile in 1537, Cabeza de Vaca's trials had another legacy: they became part of the legend that New Mexico and the "Seven Cities of Cibola" were rich in gold. De Vaca at least had a rich time recounting his adventures, not least at the Court of Charles V. One who heard them was Hernando de Soto, a

brother-in-law of Balboa, who had enriched himself (and the royal
treasury) when serving with Pizarro in Peru (1531–5). Thus re-
stimulated, de Soto persuaded the king to appoint him governor of
Cuba and *adelantado* of Florida, with authority to conquer the
unknown lands north of the Gulf of Mexico. He landed on the
west coast of Florida, either at Tampa Bay or Charlotte Harbor, on
May 28, 1539, from his outfitting base at Havana, Cuba, with 570
men and 223 horses in some 9 ships. He spent four years roaming
the south and the southwest, from the site of Augusta, Georgia,
across to Mobile Bay, from the Blue Ridge to Memphis, to the junction of the Arkansas and Canadian Rivers in what is now Oklahoma.
Somewhere there were the Seven Cities of Cibola, but he would
never find them. He died of fever at the mouth of the Red River,
on May 21, 1542. In September 1543 some 300 survivors, with Luis
Moscoso de Alvarado as their leader, reached Panuco. De Soto was
an infinitely shrewder man, and a better organizer, than Narvaez –
which says little – but no colonies came from his efforts, little gold,
and no vice-royalty like those of Mexico or Peru. Courageous men,
certainly, but they were plunderers as well as blunderers; with the
exception of Cabeza de Vaca, they behaved to the Indians with
inhuman savagery. In the monotonous repetition of their cruelties,
they brutalized themselves. And their writ ran, north and west, only
as far as they could enforce it.[1] Francis Vasquez de Coronado, in
search of the Seven Cities of Cibola, wandered throughout the
American southwest (1540–2), penetrating the continent as far north
as present-day Kansas, discovering the Colorado River, but finding
the fabled cities to be only the *pueblos* of the Zuni Indians – stone
and clay, not gold. His lieutenants, Don García Lopez de Cardenas,
went west to find the Grand Canyon, and Hernando de Alvarado,
going east, reached the Rio Grande near Albuquerque and pushed
into the Texas panhandle in search of Quivira, the mythical Kingdom
of Gold.

Cortés, raised in the Spanish nobility to the elevation of a marquis
in recognition of his services in Mexico – Marqués del Valle de
Oaxaca, after the Mexican valley where he had the largest of his
estates, with thousands of Indian slaves – established a shipyard near
Acapulco and sent exploring parties along the coast. In 1535 he
took possession of the lower part of the Lower California peninsula,

[1] Carl Ortwin Sauer, *Sixteenth Century North America: The land and the people
as seen by Europeans* (Berkeley, University of California Press, 1971); Eduardo
Galeano, *Memory of Fire: Genesis* (London, Quartet, 1984).

Plate 4   The leader of the second voyage to Florida finds the natives honoring a monument bearing the French King's arms, from Theodore de Bry, *Voyages* (Frankfurt, 1590–2).
(John Johnson Collection, The Bodleian Library, Oxford.)

calling it Terra de Santa Cruz, intending it to be another personal vice-royalty. Nuno de Guzman, more rival than colleague, was driving north by land, both of them in quest not only of Cibola but of California itself – the name given to the island-kingdom of that legendary Christian queen, who at the head of her army of formidable black Amazons had helped defend Constantinople against the Turks. Their weapons were of gold; they could tame wild beasts; and their home was in the Indies, close to the terrestrial paradise. The marquis returned again to Spain, from which he did not return; a rich man, spurned by the Court – like Columbus before him – he died in his estate in Seville in December 1547, his only heir a bastard by an Indian mistress; he left behind in quest of his paradise lieutenant Francisco de Ulloa, who journeyed from Acapulco as far north as San Diego, established that Lower California was indeed a peninsula, and sailed into the mouth of the Colorado River, El Puerto de Los Lobos. And in turn, his successor, the Portuguese João Rodrigues Cabrilho, and his pilot (and successor) the Italian-Levantine Bartolomé-Ferrer, both serving Spain, may have reached the great bay of San Francisco in 1542, 37 years ahead of Francis Drake.

In 1565 the first permanent white settlement in the present area of the United States was established not in the West but at St Augustine in Florida. It owed its origins not to the idea of expansion, but to thwart French Huguenot landings in the northern part of Florida and at what the French called Fort Caroline at the mouth of the St John's River. These were wiped out by Pedro Menendez de Avila, who then founded St Augustine. It was sacked by Drake three years later. It supported the missions in Georgia but remained a military outpost until the English acquired the peninsula in 1763 – the fourteenth colony that only lasted 20 years (1763–83). Florida's value was strategic: it offered a route for the Spanish treasure ships, and it could not be allowed to fall into enemy hands.

By 1565 and within two generations the Spaniards had control of the West Indies, Mexico, Central America, and much of South America; they had mapped the courses of the Amazon, the Orinoco, and the Parana; and it is estimated that from Argentina to California, some 200 settlements had been established in which 150,000 white Spaniards lived. By 1600 there were 200,000. They included soldiers and priests, merchants, and not least *encomenderos*, lords of Indian serfs. In the south, it would become a society of the great estate and the big house, and the Church was as important as the State. Spain could claim sovereignty too over what is now California, Arizona, New Mexico, Texas, and Florida; but only the last seemed tempting; the interior was to them, and to many for another two centuries, a great American desert.

In the meantime (1519–22) a Spanish expedition, headed by Portuguese navigator and nobleman Ferdinand Magellan, sailed around the world in an expedition which, for the first time, gave some idea of the extent of the new discoveries, of the size of the Pacific and of the earth. It ended Columbus's theories that the land surfaces of the earth were vastly greater than the seas. Magellan's fleet consisted of five clumsy craft, with 265 men, and sailed without charts, equipped only with compass, astrolabe, and hourglass – capable, that is, of calculating latitude but only able to guess at longitude. He was chased by hostile Portuguese ships, which saw him as a renegade, and was burdened by mutinous, ulcerous, and scurvy-ridden crews. He sought (wisely as it proved) to recruit as many Portuguese – his fellow-countrymen – as he was allowed. The crews included Genoese and Greeks, Cypriots, Sicilians, one Englishman ("Master Andrew of Bristol the chief gunner) and two Irish men ("Irish Bill" and "Irish Johnny"). They died steadily – of scurvy and heat, the drinking of stagnant water, the eating of sawdust and rats – and were thrown overboard; with no stone to weight them, their corpses floated, the Europeans with faces to heaven, the Indians face down. Magellan was killed on April 27, 1521, saving his men on Maeton Island in the Philippines, where almost all his officers were massacred; he lies in an unmarked grave. Only one tiny caravel, the *Victoria*, with 18 survivors now commanded by Juan Sebastian del Cano, made it home to Sanlucar; they were the first circumnavigators of the world, their journey "the greatest single human achievement on the sea". But it brought little commercial benefit to Spain. In the Antarctic sea there are no gold or silver mines, no birds sing, and the sinister grey carnaro picks out the eyes of shipwrecked sailors – though there are no mosquitoes, which cannot stand the wind.[2]

The Spanish exploits in the Americas in the first half of the six-teenth century are unmatched in the annals of exploration. The semi-civilized Indians and many of the less civilized Indians were conquered; the coastlines of North and South America on both the Atlantic and Pacific oceans were explored. They had not explored or remained long in the interior, and their knowledge was hearsay only, and unmapped. But, just as the voyages of Columbus had unleashed many imitators and led to mastery of the Caribbean and of the Gulf of Mexico, so the voyage of Magellan and his discovery of a water passage through the southern part of South America to the Pacific – and the maps that followed from Vespucci's claims – assured to Spain considerable and accurate knowledge of coastal profiles, and direct access to the spice islands. Spain had acquired it by voyaging westwards, and without conflict with her neighbor, sometimes rival and sometimes enemy, Portugal, whose own route and near-monopoly lay by way of the Cape of Good Hope (and which would from 1580 to 1640 be absorbed by Spain anyway). Spain had tapped what seemed the limitless gold and silver of Mexico and Peru, and for two centuries its monopoly of them made it a Great Power in Europe, which its own Iberian resources would never have permitted.

2 NEW SPAIN

The trans-Mississippi West was first discovered, then, not by Jim Bridger and Kit Carson and the scouts of early trans-Mississippi

[2] S. E. Morison, *The European Discovery of America: The southern voyages* AD *1492–1616* (New York, Oxford University Press, 1974), p. 320.

America, but by Spain – and by Portuguese and Italian captains in Spanish employ. The English colonies were to be on the seaward side of the Appalachians, and confined to toeholds only. They came a century later, and as settlements, not journeys of discovery. The West was undiscovered country, known only to the Spanish *conquistadors*, and later to Catholic missionaries, in a long string of *presidios* and Franciscan mission stations with sonorous names still echoing a Spanish past.

By 1616 the Franciscans had established ten permanent missions in what was a missionary colony – The Custody of the Conversion of St Paul. Between 1630 and 1660 a native of the Azores, Fray Alonso de Benavides, founded 10 more, among the Gila Apache, the Piro, and the Jemez. The California missions came a century later. The first of the 21 California missions (San Diego de Alcala, in 1769) was built by one of the greatest of Western Americans, Father Junipero Serra, by birth a Majorcan. A man in frail health, lame, and choosing constantly to be scourged for the good of his soul, he built 9 of the 21 missions that stretched along the elegantly entitled El Camino Real from San Diego to Somona, strategically placed 30 miles apart. Serra was as farsighted as he was dedicated: he brought vegetable seed, flowers, and cattle with him. But this was Church, Inquisition and State in uneasy alliance: without the *presidio* the mission was always vulnerable. Where not Spanish, it was Indian. Santa Fe in New Mexico was the second oldest city in the US proper to be founded by Europeans, by Juan de O'Nate in 1605, on the site of a deserted Indian *pueblo*; four years later, Pedro de Peralta made it a seat of local government.[3] The country that stretches in a diagonal line from West Florida through the Panhandle of Texas to Upper California is still a country with a character of its own, and a non-English character: dry heat and dusty summers, a mission station and a paternalist and priestly ethic, the dominance of the *encomienda* and the absence of towns, gave it a pattern not unlike that of the Old South pre-1865, with the role of the Negro slave played by the Indian *peon*. The Spanish founded San Antonio in Texas as late as 1716, and San Francisco in 1776, when the Declaration of Independence was being produced for another world 3,000 miles away. If the accident of Napoleon's career had not

[3] If the test is not the US today but North America, or where a Canadian or American flag flies, San Juan in Puerto Rico predates all of them (1510); and Annapolis Royal, Nova Scotia (1605), Jamestown, and the Dutch posts on Manhattan Island and near Albany (1614), all predate Plymouth Rock.

intervened, and there had been no Louisiana Purchase in 1803, the Spanish two-thirds of North America might have influenced much more strongly the culture of the continent. It might do so yet, in the next century and beyond. But settlement in the West was long delayed; for good or ill the Americas were "re-discovered" from the Atlantic, not the Pacific. It was the Spaniards who founded a string of mission stations up the Californian coast, stretching, in fact, from Argentina to California. Adventurous European fishing crews, especially from Brittany and Bristol, had for centuries kept summer camps in Newfoundland and Labrador (a Portuguese word) while they fished the Grand Banks for cod and mackerel. The recorded expansion of Europe went a long way and took place over four centuries.

All these men, Spanish, French, and English, and the Italians in the employ of foreign governments, were driven men, and Europeans. Their objectives were gold and silver, and with it the exploitation of the land; native people were for conversion, and "pacification" of the natives meant in practice impressment as laborers and porters. They were *conquistadores*, not farmers; early barter was one-sided: trinkets and baubles were exchanged for furs and minerals; the Indian land was seen as theirs for the taking, and only rarely was it "purchased." Trade came late. As Las Casas testifies, whenever Columbus landed anywhere, he wanted to sail on again, to "exercise the appetite and inclination that God had given him," to satisfy his "divine" restlessness; he was, first and last, the Admiral of the Ocean Sea. He, and for almost a century, his successors, would be lyrical about the beauty of what they saw, but sought a return to Europe to display their triumphs – gold to the Spaniards, furs to the French, and always captive Indians to be slaves, though their "souls" were now "free." The idea of any European settlement left behind was of a European enclave forcing two gospels on reluctant and uncomprehending Indians: the gospel of Faith, and the gospel of Work — for *labor omnia vincit*. Of the heroes themselves, few died peacefully, or with minds at peace.

If the building of an overseas empire can best be accomplished by an absolutist state, politically and religiously unified, Spain was admirably suited for the role. Spain was fired with a proselytizing zeal of which the Inquisition was the weapon; it was soon to be quickened by the Reformation, Indians were destroyed even when their culture was an advanced one, less by guns and mounted troops, which many Indians at first saw as centaurs, but by a total contempt, product of the True Faith, before which all pagan opposition was seen as less than human. The Requerimiento of 1514 that all Indians who met Spanish expeditions should become Christians or be en-slaved, made the Faith of the conquerors a death-dealing sword that destroyed without hesitation or compunction. The autocracy was reinforced by the papal bull of 1493, that divided the New World between the Catholic majesties of Spain and Portugal, and by the consequent secular Treaty of Tordesillas of 1494, before any Spaniard or Portuguese had set foot on American soil, or even knew of its existence. The instruments of this divinely sanctioned autocracy were able and active sovereigns, with the best troops in Europe at their command. Spain's wealth and prestige served to attract to its service skilled seamen of foreign birth (Columbus, Vespucci, Magellan), and magnificent adventurers of its own blood (Cortez, Pizarro, de Soto, de Vasca, Fray Marcos, Coronado).

To take possession of a vast region in the name of Spain or of some other state simply demanded the planting of a flag and cross upon one spot. This did not preclude, of course, equally "legal" titles to the same region as a result of similar ceremonies by the subjects of other countries. It ignored the existing natives and any rights they might have. The business of exploration, however, was one thing, and the explorers of the 1500s penetrated many parts of North and South America which were not to be re-visited until the nineteenth and twentieth centuries. The regular extraction of its minerals and their transportation to Spain, however, required organization, and was characterized by centralization, an intricate check and balance system, and manifold regulations touching practically every phase of human life. Spanish colonies did not suffer the salutary neglect that marked the history of the English colonies.

Spain ruled through the Council of the Indies set up at home by Emperor Charles V in 1517. It had eight members, met twice daily, drafted all laws for the colonies and appointed all civil officers and bishops overseas. On the spot, the Council's visible presence was through vice-royalties, audiences, captain-generalcies, and town governments in the New World.

The title of *adelantado*, or licensed conqueror, conferred total civil as well as military power; he drew his salary by exploiting the natives and their land as he decided, by direct labor services and/or by food tributes. The governor would be flanked by a deputy, an accountant, and a captain-general, all modeled on home-country parallels. As pagans, the native populations were devoid of all rights. To Lopez de Gomara, a companion of Hernan Cortés, they were "stupid, wild, insensate asses," fit only for enslavement as the worst people God ever made. God intended them to be converted and saved; but they fell victim to disease, and thus a great part of their

country was left void for the white man's habitation The administrative system, at least on paper, was simple, even more simple
than twentieth-century organizations like OETAs (Occupied Enemy
Territory Administrations). Non-Catholic foreigners were excluded;
immigration was rigidly controlled; the head-right system was employed; and the royal Inquisition, Index and *auto-de-fé* operated
overseas as vigorously as at home. The Church worked hand in
hand with the State in missionary work, in extension of dominion,
and in rendering the Indian orthodox, useful, and tractable. The
mission was an important instrument of empire, as well as a basic
religious and economic institution. So too were the *repartimiento*
and the *encomienda*. Its by-products, much in the focus of twentieth-
century commentators, were racial intermarriages, the caste system,
the status of the Indian in law, and the substitution of Negro for
Indian slavery.

In practical and economic terms the House of Trade in Seville or
Cádiz was the bureaucratic arm of the Council: it ran a mercantilist
system, with royal and merchant monopolies, bounties, staple towns,
yearly fairs, and the fleet-convoy system. The galleons of the Indian
Guard, which formed a protective squadron, was owned by the
Casa de Contratación and convoyed the Flota of ships which annually
brought to Spain the treasures of the New World. Smuggling was
inevitable, and rival nations, notably the English, well poised in
Devon and the southern ports to harass the trade routes, found rich
prey on the Spanish Main. The extraction of mineral resources was
emphasized, and opportunities for less spectacular but more enduring profits requiring agricultural cultivation were often neglected.
But it is easy now to exaggerate the system's weaknesses. The
wealth of Spain lay not merely in the mineral resources of Mexico
and the Andes – and the inflation that came in their wake; it lay
also in the consequent stimulus in Europe to manufacturers, and
in the production of sugar in the "sugar islands", where Columbus
had looked in vain for gold. Moreover, there was one aspect of the
Spanish system envied by its rival empires. The chief executive of
the Casa was the *piloto mayor*, an office usually filled by a veteran
navigator (though for a time by Amerigo Vespucci, hardly so expert).
He licensed all pilots for overseas voyages, and kept an up-to-date
padrón real, a map of the world, of which all pilots got copies.
Under Philip II, all captains were required to submit copies of
the logs of all their voyages; and from 1552 – on the model of
Sagres – the Casa's official professor of geography gave instruction
to and conducted examinations of pilots. Only Portugal had so
thorough a system of training. Richard Hakluyt was a frank admirer.

This colonial policy served for 300 years or more for an empire 20 times the size of its parent state. As a system, it was far superior to any rival. Of course, it took no account of natives and little of local opinion overseas – any more than did Britain or France. It was not local or self-government, and in these centuries could not be so. Spanish rule in America was not, however, entirely dominated by a spirit of "get rich quick" and "after us the Deluge." There were churches, schools, arts, and the first colleges, hospitals, and printing presses in America. Distinguished scholars taught in Hispanic America, and left noteworthy works of anthropology, linguistics, geography, and history. The revolts against Spanish control were quite distinct from those of 1776 in North America: it was Napoleon Bonaparte who, by his invasion of Madre Patria, made the events of 1810 and 1811 possible. The present party songs of the Liberals in Colombia and of APRA in Peru are set to the tune of *La Marseillaise*. As J. Halcro Ferguson put it, "Up till recently, well-bred Argentine children believed that babies, like everything else Mama bought, came from Paris."[4] Despite a colonial rule apparently far more restrictive than that imposed by England upon her Thirteen Colonies, the bonds today between Spain and her former possessions seem at least as close as, and less politically sensitive than, those between the United States and Great Britain.

The decline of Spain has been attributed to many factors. Among these, some hold that the wealth of the Indies and the consequent inflation was a major cause. Weak kings, corrupt administration, the expulsion of the Moors and Jews, the repression of free thought, initiative, and competition, scorn for manual labor, the failure to develop a strong middle class, profitless European wars, heavy taxes, and failure to achieve command of the sea, are equally compelling as reasons that explain the eventual decline of Spain as a Great Power. And the United States at least grew up in time to share the Spanish-American spoils: the riches of a continent's mineral and agricultural wealth, and the labor of its people.

3   THE BRISTOL VENTURERS

The exploration of the eastern and western seaboards was thus the work of Spaniards and French. The English were not the first to

---

[4] J. Halcro Ferguson, *The Revolution of Latin America* (London, Thames and Hudson, 1963), p. 19.

explore or to settle on the continent of North America, even after
the dawn of an awareness that it was a great land-mass, neither
an outcrop of Asia nor an island that was a barrier *en route* to
Cathay. Although, in the end, the impact of the last-comers was
to be the most pervasive – through language, the idea of the common
law and legal institutions, and, not least, the notion of "the
gentleman" – they came late on the scene; and this despite an insular
location off the coast of Europe that kept England safe from the
recurrent land wars and bitter religious divisions that marked the
history of the French, the Spaniards, the Dutch and the Germans.
Once Elizabeth I provided vigorous encouragement, however, that
location, and England's command of her own seas, would be her
major strength. But it needed a century after John Cabot's first
voyage in 1497 before sustained attempts at English colonization
began.

English colonization of America began in 1578. In that year
Queen Elizabeth I granted to Sir Humphrey Gilbert Letters Patent
"for the inhabiting and planting of our people in America." Although
a number of charters to English trading companies had preceded
this, none had contemplated the permanent planting of English people
beyond the seas. It was because he was armed with these Letters
Patent that Gilbert attempted in 1583–4 the settlement of a colony
on the island of Newfoundland.

Nevertheless, the English interest in the New World began before
that of Columbus. Indeed, thanks to letters to him from one "John
Day" (probably the London merchant Hugh Say, who had Bristol,
London and Spanish connections), Columbus knew of English
journeys in the Atlantic. Some of these were in quest of the Isle of
"Brasil", which in the late Middle Ages was the semi-legendary Irish
"Isle of the Blessed", but could perhaps – by extension – be held
to be another range of volcanic mountain peaks like the Canaries,
or a continent in the south Atlantic. Whether or not one ship or
two from Bristol reached "Brasil" in 1480 or 1481, John Day in
London in 1497 indicated to Columbus that John Cabot' s Newfoundland (found in 1497) was the island already found in times
past by the men of Bristol as, he said, Columbus was aware. Again,
Pedro de Ayala, the Spanish ambassador in London, believed in 1498
that two to four ships a year had been going out from Bristol into
the Atlantic from 1490 or 1491, in search of the Isle of "Brasil" or
the Island of the Seven Cities, as he (or Cabot) believed. What is
fact, not legend, is that after 1490 the Bristol, and North Devon,
fishing fleets – sometimes four a year – knew the north Atlantic,
fished for cod in the Banks off Newfoundland and Iceland, and, when

they could, dried their fish ashore in summer camps shared, for the most part harmoniously, with fellow-fishermen from Brittany, from the Azores, and from the Basque ports. There was intermittent trade as far as Iceland. Until European sovereignties intruded, fishing, and the trading that went with it, involved a community of interest among all those who did their business in deep and treacherous waters, and all of whom traded by courtesy of ice-floes and storms. It all took shape with the age of print and maps, and with the seizure of the English throne by a Welsh and Lancastrian claimant, backed by France.

Henry VII was clever but canny, wise but never prodigal; he was prompt to respond to any proposal that promised easy ways to wealth, by way of new routes to the resources of Asia. But he deemed Bartholomew Columbus's schemes too ambitious and too costly, and sent him away. Instead, he found an overseas mariner to his own taste, who would bear his own "proper costs and charges." Two years after the publication of the Treaty of Tordesillas, the king granted Letters Patent on 3 March 1496 which authorized John Cabot and his sons, Ludovico (Lewis), Sebastiano (Sebastian) and Sancius (Sancio), "to sail to all parts of the world to the east, west and north, and seek out, discover and find whatever isles, countries, regions or provinces of the heathens and infidels ... before this time unknown to all Christians." The treaty, at least in form, was being observed. The quest was still for Cathay.

It is one of the most curious of the Discoveries that "Bristowe," by which name it was then known (and pronounced), should allow a north Italian to outmatch its own merchant-princes – the Canynges, the Jays, the Thornes, the Pynkes, the Elyots, the Spensers and, not least, – sheriff Richard Amerike (A. P. Merrick), believed to be one of Cabot's backers, after whom – as they insist on the Avon – America is named. That such men permitted a Genoese in particular to outdo them shows a rare generosity of spirit: it was, after all, the "Janneys" (Genoese) who had wrecked Bristol ships trading to the Levant. [5]

[5] When Henry VII agreed to reward John Cabot by a grant of £10 and a pension of £20 a year for the discovery of North America, he was making his promise to pay from the kingdom's resources, not his private purse. In practice he instructed that the payments be made from the receipts of Bristol customs, and the Bristol "Customer", or customs officer in 1497, was the merchant Richard Amerike or Ap Merrick. At least locally, in Bristol, Cabot's discoveries were known as "The Land of Amerike" in 1497, and afterwards. Indeed, Cabot seems to have promised generous land grants in his "vice-royalty" to many Bristol friends.

Bristol was strategically well placed: it lay half-way between Newfoundland, the Banks and Iceland to the north, and the Azores and Portugal to the south. It exported the wool of the Cotswolds, and imported dried codfish from the north and, from Spain and Portugal, along with wines, olive oil and that Spanish sherry long known as "Bristol milk". The Iceland trade was in decline in the 1480s, after clashes that became open war with Denmark and the Hanseatic League, who moved into what English traders thought was their preserve. Icelanders worked as labourers in Bristol; one William Yslond was a substantial merchant in 1484; some seem to have been kidnapped and enslaved – or driven out of Iceland by poverty and plague. The Portuguese, too, were active; the merchants and pilots of Terceira in the Portuguese Azores were regular visitors, even settlers.

John Cabot's story is curiously similar to that of Columbus. Indeed, Pedro de Ayala, the Spanish envoy, described him to his master Ferdinand as "Uno come Colón." He too seems to have been born a Genoese (though there is no evidence to support this in the Genoese archives); he may even have been born in the same year as Columbus and have known him as a boy. He had, however, been a resident and became a citizen of Venice, and claimed to have visited Mecca for spices, and to have lived in Portugal and Spain. He, too, had failed to sell his ideas of a western voyage to the Iberian monarchs, after visits to Lisbon and Seville. As Juan Cabota Montecalunya, he was designing harbor works at Valencia in the Aragonese part of the Spanish kingdom in 1491 and 1492. He was evidently still in Spain when Columbus returned in 1493 with news of his discoveries; he might even have met him on his triumphal return to Barcelona in that year. At some point between 1493 and 1495 Cabot came to England, settled not in the Italian colonies in London or Southampton but among the merchant adventurers of Bristol, and began to experiment in Atlantic voyages and to make preliminary contacts with the English Court in order to obtain the backing he had failed to receive in the courts of the Iberian monarchs. He offered to sail "on his own proper charges."

With a crew of 18, Cabot sailed on 22 May 1497 from the Bristol Quayhead in the 60-ton ship *Mathew* (perhaps accompanied by his son Sebastian, as the latter always claimed). He landed at his "land of the Great Khan." Its location may have been Cape Race or Cape Bauld on Newfoundland (S. E. Morison's view), Cape Canso on Nova Scotia, or Cape Breton on Cape Breton Island – to the Portuguese "the English Cape", and in the view of D. B. Quinn, "the least unlikely landfall." Cabot reported that it was empty of people, though with much evidence of their presence; but it was thick with conifers and mosquitoes, and its seas were "swarming with fish." He believed that he was in Asia, and claimed the land for the Crown of England. He took 25 days to go, and was back in 15 on the homeward run; he got £10 as a reward, and a life pension of £20 a year. England had now established a stake in the New World; and in fact, though he did not know it, only a few miles from the same spot as the Norsemen had been, five centuries before. Since the *Mathew* had found "Asia," new Letters Patent were issued within a few months.[6]

For Cabot's second voyage, the king provided and equipped one ship; the Bristol merchants were prepared to find and equip four. This was puny in comparison with Columbus's 17 for his second voyage in 1493, or the 13 Manoel V (king of Portugal, which had only half England's population), equipped for the second Indies voyage after Vasco da Gama's first return in 1499; the more so as Cabot was, it was thought, to find and presumably to acquire large parts of China and Japan. Either on his way to it, or on the return voyage, he and all his ships were lost, with all hands. His pension died with him, despite his son Sebastian's long struggle for compensation – and recognition.

For some years, Bristol merchants continued their trade with Newfoundland and Iceland. Two groups can be identified: one was the Cabot partnership that included Hugh Elyot and Robert, William and Thomas Thorne, which had been active since the 1480s and now included Sebastian Cabot (one of these partners would still, 20 years later, be pressing Henry VIII to back an expedition to the North-West and even to the North Pole). The other consisted of a group from Terceira in the Azores, with a patent from the king of Portugal: João Fernandez, who described himself as a *labrador* or farmer, Francisco Fernandez and João Gonsalves, who saw Bristol as an admirable jumping-off point for exploration across the North Atlantic – or at least as a base for piracy on the side. The Corte

---

[6] D. B. Quinn, *North America from Earliest Discovery to First Settlements* (New York, Harper, 1977), p. 116; S. E. Morison, *The European Discovery of America*, vol. I (New York, Oxford University Press, 1971), pp. 157–211, esp. pp. 170–86. Melvin Jackson, "The Labrador landfall of John Cabot, 1497," *Canadian Historical Review*, 44 (1965), pp. 122–41, brings Cabot to Labrador through the Strait of Belle Isle, western Newfoundland, Cabot Strait, and halfway up the east coast of Newfoundland; and John T. Juricek, "John Cabot's First Voyage," *Smithsonian Journal of History*, 2 (1967–8), pp. 1–22, postulates a landfall at the northern tip of Cape Breton Island.

Real brothers, Gaspar and Miguel, were also regularly using Bristol as a port-of-call and transit point.

By 1505, however, the Company of Bristol Adventurers was bankrupt, and the Atlantic voyages for commerce and exploration were interrupted, though fishing "doggers" went regularly to the Banks for cod. The deep sea fishermen of North Devon had long been active, as the island of Appledore in the Isles of Shoals in southern Maine would seem to testify. The Portuguese had already moved in, as had the French and Spanish. Sebastian Cabot in 1508 sought to find a passage to Asia by the northwest, by sailing with 300 men in six ships well inside the Arctic Circle. The complaints from his men of the twin dangers of icebergs — "great icebergs float-ing in the sea and almost continuous daylight" — and frostbite (and they were near to mutiny), led to the abandonment of the exercise, but he may have been as far northwest as the opening of the Hudson Strait at about 60° North, and have seen Hudson Bay far enough south to worry the Spaniards in the Caribbean. In 1511 he joined the service of Spain at the request of Ferdinand of Aragon to Henry VIII, his son-in-law, because of his knowledge (however acquired) of the North Atlantic. For the English, however, there was no follow-through of what seemed resourceless lands; Henry VII had decided that friendship with Spain was essential; his son's first wife came from Aragon; and Spain seemed to have control of the only rich region of the New World. Sebastian served both England and Spain, and got pensions from each of them. He also described himself as a knight of the Venetian Republic, but of English birth; and as "the first discoverer of Newfoundland." When Philip II of Spain visited England in 1557 to talk to his wife Queen Mary, he ended Sebastian's pension; three days later, Mary restored it. Despite the benevolent-looking twin-bearded portrait he had painted of himself, all that we can be sure of is that he was "a genial and cheerful liar".[7]

What the Devon men did for exploration, and for privateering at Spain's expense, Bristol did for early settlement. Bristol was the Cabots' base. The royal charter of the Bristol Merchant Venturers is dated as early as 1552. Martin Pring was financed from Bristol. His 1603 expedition sailed into Massachusetts Bay and he named his landfall Whitson Harbour after a Bristol alderman. The Pilgrim Fathers, also financed in Bristol, renamed the same spot Plymouth

---

[7] Portrait in the Massachusetts Historical Society: D. B. Quinn, *England and the Discovery of America 1481–1620* (London, Allen and Unwin, 1973), p. 159.

Harbour. While charting Hudson Bay in 1631, seeking the North-west Passage to the east, again financed in Bristol, Captain Thomas James discovered James Bay. Between 1654 and 1679 around 10,000 people sailed to the American colonies from the Avon. And James Logan, Penn's secretary, who became chief justice and governor of Pennsylvania, was a Bristol schoolmaster.

Henry VIII was a gifted Renaissance prince, and a devout Defender of the Faith turned head of his own Church of England, greedy for the profits of church lands when sold to the rising gentry, and in the end a moody Nero. His viewpoint seemed insular, or at best European. A voyage sponsored by Sir Thomas More's brother-in-law, John Rastell, got only to Ireland; in 1527–8 John Rut took two ships to Newfoundland, lost one, and returned home; and in 1536 Richard Dore's Newfoundland exploration had no consequences – even though Rut might have sailed down the North American coast as far as the now Spanish West Indies. The urge to explore seemed to have waned. But the despot's Anglicanism was strong, secular even more than theological. He ended England's dependence on Flemings and the Dutch as exporters of its wool, built 100 ships as great floating artillery batteries that could engage in ship-sinking rather than the man-killing land wars of its European rivals, and established the Woolwich dry-dock and Trinity House as a training school for pilots. Without these, and the expedient of fire-ships, she would never have been able to destroy the Armada.

Once Henry's daughter Mary's five-year reign was over, and with it the prospect of an easy Spanish take-over of England, the royal embargo on voyages west into Spanish territory was over too. Once Elizabeth was publicly denounced by Rome, in 1570, as a bastard, an undeclared war with Spain began; and in the 33 years that followed, England's role was transformed; she became a power on the seas, the cutting edge of Protestantism; and a self-conscious nationalism was born. For three decades, English national security – and the Treasury – depended on "interlopers" and "seadogs" raiding the Spanish argosies – the "golden fleece" that "yearly stuffs old Philip's treasury." Piracy became synonymous with patriotism, and was rewarded with spoils and knighthoods. The "red-headed Welsh harridan" became "Gloriana". All were the by-products of the Atlantic struggle with Spain.[8]

---

[8] Note the *caveat* offered by D. B. Quinn to Hakluyt's attempt to find a pedigree of glory for Ralegh, Drake and Hawkins: he denies that the voyages of Cabot and of the men of Bristol had any consequences for the Elizabethans. Until the

4   MEN OF DEVON

The story of Walter Ralegh — his usual way of spelling his name — is in part the story of a memorable Devon cousinhood. The men of Devon were skillful seamen, and even more efficient pirates; the index of their skill was that in the whole 45-year reign of Elizabeth only two English men-of-war were captured by Spain, and then only after fighting against overwhelming force — the *Jesus of Lubeck*, lost under the command of Sir John Hawkins at San Juan de Ulua in 1568, and Sir Richard Grenville's *Revenge*, off the Azores in 1591. Moreover, with the exception of the tiny *Lion's Whelp*, no dockyard-built ship was lost by stress of weather, by fire or by running aground. At Roanoke many more lives were lost on land than at sea. Many more deaths came at the hands of Indians or other whites than when the seas "rolled up from the depths." In these same years, in addition to her other losses, Spain lost a whole Armada — though she rarely lost a treasure convoy.

Ralegh's ventures in North Carolina were largely inspired by Sir Francis Walsingham, Elizabeth's secretary of state, who sought bases on the American coast from which privateers could strike; by contrast, William Cecil, Lord Burghley (whose son-in-law, as it happens, was Philip Sidney, the *beau sabreur*) did not want an open clash with Spain, or at least not until it was unavoidable. He was more interested in the ships' stores of pine and tar that could be obtained from Newfoundland, in the fur trade, and in the actual settlement of, and the agricultural products that could be got from, the more temperate lands. There was, in other words, a Caribbean (warlike and piratical) strategy not always in harmony with a northern (commercial and colonial) alternative. Piracy was endemic, and indulged in constantly, not least by Drake and Ralegh; when, as often, war broke out, it was then merely legitimized as privateering.

The men of Devon, and the secretary of state, needed an intelligence service, notably in 1588. If England's Plymouth Hoe was comparable to Portugal's Sagres as a starting point for many voyages,

---

defeat of the Armada. English interest in the Atlantic was sporadic, mainly piratical and rarely profitable. Even into the seventeenth century, there were two English empires, the eastern primarily commercial, the western in intent colonial. But he concedes that from the sixteenth century came a navy, a cadre of experienced mariners and a knowledge of distant seas. See D. B. Quinn and A. N. Ryan, *England's Sea Empire 1550–1642* (London, Allen and Unwin, 1983).

Plate 5 Sir Walter Ralegh, attributed to the monogrammist "H", 1588.
Ralegh was one of England's first great entrepreneurs. He founded the ill-fated
Roanoke settlement.
(Reproduced by kind permission of The National Portrait Gallery, London.)

the English were as skillful as the Portuguese and the Spaniards in
compiling charts and plans for an overseas empire, and of the best
routes across the oceans to it; as by-product, there was the strategic
value of a settlement on the Carolina/Virginia coast, athwart the
homeward route of Spanish treasure fleets as they emerged from the
Florida Channel.

There was a think-tank at work too, mainly fed from Cambridge University, and recruited from the West Country and from the Welsh borders. It had three headquarters: the college rooms of the geographer and polymath John Dee, a fellow of the newly-founded Trinity College, Cambridge; his massive private library in Mortlake, where scientists and even the queen came to consult him – and not far from Walsingham's own home; and the rooms of the younger Richard Hakluyt, first in Christ Church, Oxford, then in the prebendary's lodgings in Bristol Cathedral, and later at Westminster.[9] Each of these scholars moved around Europe as members of a scholars' international of geographers and public policy advisers; they knew Gerard Mercator, the map-maker, Pedro Nuñez and Abraham Ortelius of Antwerp, and Gemma Frisius in Germany. And Oxford-educated Humphrey Gilbert could easily keep up with them.

John Dee, a London Welshman with his roots in Radnorshire, was one of those richly talented Renaissance men to whom science had still the trace of magic about it. His reputation was not that of scholar, but of sorcerer. He saw himself as Merlin at the court of Arthur's successor. He had been imprisoned in Mary's reign for allegedly trying to "enchant" the queen. To Elizabeth he became "hyr philosopher." He used the near-legendary story of the Welsh prince Madoc's landing at Mobile Bay in 1170 in order to buttress English claims to have prior rights to North America to those that began only in 1492. He wrote four volumes calling on Elizabeth to establish, or rather to re-establish, a British maritime empire in the northern seas. He supplied both Frobisher and Gilbert with maps for their journeys to find a Northwest Passage. It was to Dee that the ex-Portuguese pilot Simon Fernandez, then in Gilbert's employ, reported, after his first recce in the Carolina sandbanks, and on Roanoke Island. When Sir George Peckham conceived a plan to "evacuate" Catholics to a refuge colony on the American mainland, it was to Dee that he went for approval and advice. It all became part of Dee's campaign for avowed colonization on the North American mainland. Dee's word for America was 'Atlantis'; he was the first to use the words 'Thalassokratia Britannike', "The British Empire." By it he dreamed not only of an empire of the seas, but of one that included Europe, and had about it a supernatural mission.[10]

---

[9] He was an orphan, and was brought up by an older cousin of the same name.
[10] Dee was also a shrewd propagandist: while staying at the court of the Holy Roman Emperor, Rudolf II, in 1584, he used the prophecies appearing in Dutch almanacs foretelling the defeat of a great empire to predict the defeat of the Spanish Armada, and undermine Spanish morale. See Peter French, *John Dee*

Hakluyt, whose reputation was also established in Europe as well as Oxford, was a member of that other cousinhood that stood close to the throne: he came, like the Lewises and Cecils, the Parrys, the Llwyds and the Aubreys, from the Welsh borders. These families were as important as the men of Devon, and some great Elizabethans – Ralegh and Gilbert in particular – moved easily between the two groups. On his journeys abroad, Hakluyt was most at home in the Huguenot circles in France, where, especially with Admiral Gaspard de Coligny, French colonialism was born, and French colonial expeditions to the Floridas in the 1560s were encouraged. He served for a spell as a chaplain to the English ambassador in Paris, primarily to tap French geographers' knowledge; and he inspired De Bry's mapping of America. Humphrey Gilbert knew these Frenchmen too; John Hawkins in 1565 visited the French Fort Caroline in Florida and revictualled them – though to no avail; Ralegh's (and Philip Sidney's) military apprenticeship was in the Huguenot service; Plymouth was, in a measure, a twin town of La Rochelle – Protestant, Atlantic-oriented, tacit allies in a war against Spain. And Hakluyt's fellow-geographer, Richard Eden, was as close to Cecil as Hakluyt himself was to Ralegh.

Given that the Huguenots were until – 1589 – seen as an enemy in Paris and in Madrid, and given that Spain was vigilant to curb her enemies in the Indies and on the seas, and to destroy all heretics, including those of *la religion prétendue réformée*, even geographers moved with hooded eyes. They were close to Walsingham, whose functions as secretary of state included that of the queen's trusted spymaster. Hakluyt published in 1582, in support of Gilbert, his *Divers Voyages Touching the Discoverie of America*. In 1584 he summarized the case for a British colony in the Carolinas/Virginia country in his *Discourse of Western Planting*. It was this that secured the queen's approval for the attempt at a Roanoke colony, thanks mainly to Ralegh's standing at Court. In it he spelt out the cases for a settlement, religious and economic, political and strategic, and urged it as a government, and not merely as a private or corporate, enterprise. It represented jobs for the unemployed and opportunities for the poor and restless. More wealth could be won through sales to the Indians, not least of domestic textiles. At this stage, champions of American colonization designed their discourses to woo investors

(London, Routledge and Kegan Paul, 1972), and Ian Seymour, "The political magic of John Dee," *History Today*, Jan. 1989, pp. 29–35. For the term "British Empire," see *American Historical Review*, 27, p. 485.

Plate 6 Early map of Virginia, as charted by John White, which displays the seal of Ralegh and exaggerated depictions of sea creatures: as the poet Michael Drayton put it, "Virginia, Earth's only Paradise." (Reproduced by courtesy of The Trustees of The British Museum, London.)

and to persuade the government, not to recruit prospective settlers
or encourage emigration. Promoters of an English presence in the
New World pitched America as a development opportunity for
speculators and strategic planners, not yet as a haven for Englishmen
on distant shores. To Hakluyt the main advantage of an English
post on or near Cape Hatteras was as a strategic vantage point
from which to attack and despoil the Spanish treasure fleets, but this
could only be implied, since it would invite retaliation. And in the
old adage of diplomatic exchanges: "never write it if you can say
it – and never say it if you can nod your head." The prospect of
Virginia did *not* attract all. In Massinger's *City Madam*, the unscrupulous Luke suggests shipping his sister-in-law and her daughters
off to America:

> *Lady Frugal*: How! Virginia!
>   High Heaven forbid! Remember, sir, I beseech you,
>   What creatures are shipped thither.
> *Anne*: Condemned wretches, forfeited to the law.
> *Mary*: Strumpets and bawds, for the abomination of their
>   life spewed out of their own country.

And Bacon spoke of the first Virginians as "the scum of people."
In any case, Elizabeth could not countenance direct support by
government, which Spain would see as provocative. But royal ships
were occasionally employed, and there was never any doubts of
the queen's quasi-official approval of the English voyages.

Throughout his life, however, Hakluyt was archivist and editor,
as well as consultant and propagandist; he kept the record of Tudor
discoverers' achievements in his *Principal Navigations, Voyages and
Discoveries of the English Nation* (first in MS, then published a year
after the Armada, then enlarged 1598–1600), which he dedicated
to Sir Francis Walsingham. And in 1585 Ralegh, as part of the
Roanoke exercise, sent over as surveyor and reporter Thomas Harriot,
his Oxford tutor, a mathematician and astronomer who had taught
him the mathematics of navigation, and John White as cartographer
and illustrator. Accurate maps of the land they sought were as indispensable as those of the seas they were learning to master. John
White's evidence is still extant, and enticing, as is Harriot's *Brief
and True Report*. David Quinn calls them "the brain and the eye" of
the 1585 settlement.

Intelligence, however, then as now, was more than a matter of
headquarters' plans and designs; it was part of a war game. Rarely then could any reliable informant come from the land as yet

unmapped. But when Hawkins after his defeat at the hands of Spain put 100 men ashore on the Gulf of Mexico in 1568, one of them survived to tell the story, almost as strange as that of Welsh Indians. David Ingram reported to Sir Francis Walsingham in 1582 that, with two companions (sadly if conveniently dead by the time he told his story), he walked 2,000 miles across the North American continent to Cape Breton, where he was rescued a year later – he said – by a French ship, from the elephants and red sheep that were, he said, his main enemies. Although he had waited 13 years to tell his tale, he was prepared to go with Sir Humphrey Gilbert in 1583 to prove it.[11]

Strategy was as important as knowledge and the prospect of trade. Bermuda was discovered as a by-product of Virginia – Sir George Somers was shipwrecked there *en route* to Jamestown in 1609. It was incorporated into the charter of the Virginia Company in 1612 but, located on the sea routes Spain used, was seen as at least as important. Eight forts were built along its 20-mile stretch of islands and, as the Spanish ambassador in London noted, it was its salted meat and its fruit that kept the beleaguered mainland colony alive. In the second decade of the seventeenth century, more people were sent to Bermuda than to Virginia – by 1622 there were 1,500 people living in Bermuda, compared (in 1624) to Virginia's 1,275. And the impact of the discovery of Prospero's island on the imagination of Elizabethan writers was greater than that of any other colony – except, perhaps, Virginia.

But the real heroes of the age were not the undertakers and entrepreneurs planning, financing and sometimes leading their voyages, but those on the waters, whether masters or men. They sailed on little ships, of some 50 tons, sometimes little more than pinnaces, or the size of modern ocean-racing yachts, with bunks in the superstructure, if such there were, reserved for officers only – "sluttish dens that breed sickness," Ralegh called them. The sailors were lucky if they had one hot meal a day, and that not in stormy weather, when any fire was risky. They slept where they could, and sometimes in shifts. Hammocks had not yet been thought of – an Indian invention of great value to mariners (and subsequently to HM troopships). Ship hygiene was always poor. Luke Fox in 1635 summed up the seaman's lot: "but to endure and suffer: as a hard cabin, cold and salt meat, broken sleeps, mouldy bread, dead beer, wet clothes, want of fire." And on top of that they were subject to

[11] Richart Hakluyt, *Principal Navigations*, I. 557–62.

scurvy; they were also subject to the plague, typhus, malaria, yellow fever, fatal injury in battle or accident, and the all but constant "bloody flux" (dysentery).

To survive was, then, to conquer. This was a heroic age — at all levels of the hierarchy. And not only in courtier-like tribute, but in reality, the great Gloriana became not only the symbol but the source of this achievement of the Elizabethan discoverers. From the beginning of her reign Elizabeth was aware of the value of her portrait, not merely from vanity. Foreign Protestants who had taken refuge in England seem to have pioneered the use of portraits of the queen for explicitly political purposes, composing at the time of Alva's prosecution in the Netherlands such pictures as *Queen Elizabeth and the Three Godesses* and *The Allegory of the Tudor Succession*, in which Elizabeth appeared as the saviour of Protestantism. It was appropriate that Edmund Spenser, who had been a friend of Sir Philip Sidney and was an acquaintance of Ralegh in Ireland, should catch its spirit in *The Faerie Queene*, for throughout Elizabeth's reign people had heard:

> ... daily how through hardy enterprise
> Many great regions are discovered,
> Which to late age were never mentioned.
> Who ever heard of th' Indian Peru?
> Or who in venturous vessel measured
> The Amazon huge river now found true?
> Or fruitfullest Virginia who did ever view?
> Yet all these were when no man did them know,
> Yet have from wisest ages hidden been;
> And later times things more unknown shall show.[12]

The great achievement of Elizabeth I was neither the defeat of her enemies on the seas, notably in the defeat of the Spanish Armada — the achievement of men dressed as sailors but with skills and daring learned as pirates — nor the probings of the coast of Virginia — the work, again, of planners and entrepreneurs, some of whom would go to the Tower for their thanks. Her major achievement was to have brought England 45 years of internal peace — a rare boon in English history. She identified with and embodied a national spirit. The defeat of the Armada, the coming of which had been heralded by a chain of beacons at least along the south coast, and the dispersal of which had been celebrated by the ringing of

[12] Spenser, *The Faerie Queene*, Book II, Introduction.

church bells from the Lizard to the Tweed, had brought – perhaps for the first time – a sense of English nationhood triumphant; and the literary outpourings were of a quality not hitherto (nor perhaps ever) matched. In 1603 England's ships were masters of the Channel, and they had ensured the survival of the Netherlands, and of freedom of navigation on much of the Atlantic. More than any of her predecessors, and outdistancing the majority of all her successors, she put her imprint on her age. It could not have been done before the existence of the printing press, nor before portrait-painting and the making of likenesses became fashionable. Her Court was a manufacturer not only of flatterers but of propagandists. And writers took up the theme *con brio*. In 1596 Edmund Spenser dedicated a new edition of *The Faerie Queene* to "The Most High, Mightie and Magnificent Empress, Renouned for Pietie, Vertue, and all gracious government, Elizabeth, By the grace of God Queen of England, France and Ireland and of Virginia." By Virginia, Spenser – like his contemporaries – meant the North American continent, from St Augustine to Newfoundland. Shakespeare's *The Tempest* recorded for all time the shipwreck of Sir George Somers on his way to Jamestown, and made superb poetic drama out of the tale of Prospero's island. And Hakluyt, collector of records on a voluminous scale, made the historian not only a compiler of records but a propagandist and a prophet.

5   THE OUTER BANKS

The Elizabethan age is, of course, rich in personalities. The most colourful were as often entrepreneurs and privateers as sailors; among them the line between heroism and villainy was often elusive; indeed, sometimes heroes and villains were the same people, in that the heroes – often younger sons of the rising gentry, looking for estates of their own to acquire, abroad if they could not afford them at home – were usually also vindictive, greedy and ruthless men, and almost always ardent Protestants. Through Elizabeth's reign, amid all the factions that surrounded and jostled her, a War Party was in power – even if occasionally the queen as diplomat might pretend that it did not exist; and she could always ask Burghley to testify to her pacifism towards Spain. To use Hakluyt's phrase, they had "fame-thirsty and gold-thirsty mindes ... all perils and mis-adventures seeme tolerable unto them." To them plunder was the sword of Protestantism, and each was synonymous with patriotism. For them patriotism meant the Renaissance cult of "vertue," a militant ideal distinct from Victorian "virtue." "Give me leave without offence," wrote Gilbert, "alwayes to live and die in this mind, that he is not worthie to live at all, that for feare, or daunger of death, shunneth his countrey service, and his owne honour, seeing death is inevitable, and the fame of vertue immortall." It also usually meant piracy.[13]

From 1585 to 1603, the years of open war with Spain, at least 100 privateering expeditions were made each year, openly and proudly. Ralegh made £200,000 from one such venture in the Caribbean. John Hawkins, who followed his father's seapaths in the Guinea trade, instructed his crews "to serve God daily" and "to love one another;" he honored both precepts by kidnapping blacks from Sierra Leone, or preferably by seizing them at sea from Spanish ships, and, exchanged them for hides and whatever seemed portable in the Caribbean, and in Vera Cruz in 1562, 1564 and 1567. The slaving and plundering expeditions of this interloper's intervention into what Spain saw as her own preserve became part of a wider conflict. In 1564–5 Hawkins had tried unsuccessfully to re-victual the French Huguenot colony at Fort Caroline, on the St John's River in Florida; his fleet was destroyed by the Spanish forces at San Juan de Ulua in 1567 – a disaster that led the commander of the third ship in his fleet, the *Judith*, his young kinsman, Francis Drake, to vow revenge on Spain.

In three voyages, in 1576, 1577 and 1578, the tough and unscrupulous ex-slaver, often pirate, Martin Frobisher tried to find a Northwest Passage to Cathay, and thought he had found it in what is now Frobisher Bay in Baffin Island, which he thought the northern counterpart to the Strait of Magellan; the ore he picked up he also thought was gold, and triggered off the first gold rush in North American history. The first hysterical investment in North American mineral "futures," "the Company of Cathay," was at Meta Incognita in 1577. The queen was a major investor, holding 20 percent. Frobisher's reward was to be appointed high admiral, like Columbus before him. The "gold" proved as worthless as the wealth of Saguenay, "les diamants du Canada." However, this did not kill the quest for the Northwest Passage; from 1585 to 1587 John Davis of Dartmouth, the most scientific navigator of them all, explored the

[13] Hakluyt, *Principal Navigations*, I.XLIII; D. B. Quinn, *The Voyages and Colonising Enterprises of Sir Humphrey Gilbert* (Hakluyt Society, 1940) I.102; cf. K. R. Andrews, *Elizabethan Privateering* (Cambridge, Cambridge University Press, 1964), p. 16.

icy wastes: on his first voyage (1585) he discovered Cumberland
Sound off Baffin Island, and on his third (1587) he sailed through
Davis Strait into Baffin Bay at latitude 72. From his unsuccessful
efforts came, as bonus, *The Seaman's Secrets* (1594) and *The Worldes
Hydrographical Description* (1595). George Waymouth and John
Knight, working for the East India and Muscovy Companies, ex-
plored the stormy shores of Newfoundland and Labrador.

Francis Drake, impulsive and imperious, was not satisfied with
winning a fortune by piracy or by selling black slaves. In 1573 he
raided and seized a mule-train carrying bullion on the isthmus of
Panama. In 1577 he embarked on his own war with Spain. He had
five vessels and 150 men, and the objective was the Pacific, where
the west coast of South America would provide a new and untapped
source of plunder. A syndicate backed him, including Hawkins, now
treasurer of the Navy, secretary of state Sir Francis Walsingham, and
the earl of Lincoln, who was lord high admiral, so that this was a
private war with Spain, but with royal endorsement, since the queen
contributed her own ship, the *Swallow*. Drake was thus a privateer,
not a pirate. Plundering Spanish towns and capturing treasure ships
en route, he sailed one of his vessels round the world. In the course
of it, the *Golden Hind* dropped anchor (in June or July 1579) and
had its barnacles scraped and its seams caulked at one of the beaches
near San Francisco, where it stayed a month. To his own embarrass-
ment, Drake was crowned king by the local Indians, but formally
laid claim for England to the possession of what he called Nova
Albion, nailing "a plate of brass" with Elizabeth's name and image
on it to "a great and firm post;" long lost, it was miraculously
unearthed 347 years later and is now displayed at the entrance to
the Bancroft Library in Berkeley. Drake was properly evasive about
its exact location in order to outwit the Spaniards, though in private
he called it "the backe side of Virginia." His evasiveness has baffled
subsequent historians as effectively as it baffled – and angered –
Spaniards.[14] He failed to find there the exit of the much-looked-for
Northwest Passage, and wisely concluded that, if it was there, it
was unnavigable. He found the land running continuously northwest,
however, "as if it went directly to meet with Asia."

Thus, perversely, the English claim to the discovery of the territory that became the USA rests not on explorations from Maine to

[14] Warren Hanna, *Lost Harbor* (Berkeley, University of California Press, 1979)
concludes that what has long been called Drake's Bay, with its white cliffs, is the
real "lost harbor."

Florida, but on Drake's short stay on a Pacific beach. His journey – in a ship of just over 100 tons – was of epic character: one non-stop run of 63 days on the Atlantic, two of 50 and 68 days in the Pacific, and a third of seven weeks' duration in the Indian Ocean and South Atlantic; he lost only 17 men in three years, more to brawls with Indians and Spaniards than to illness.[15] When he returned to Plymouth Sound his first question was: "Is the Queen alive?" It was no mere blunt courtier-style greeting, for his voyage had always been quasi-official, and he had brought much booty home; and Burghley had not backed the venture, so that the queen's survival was, for Drake, a personal insurance policy. Instead of being punished, as the Spanish ambassador properly requested, the pirate was knighted by Queen Elizabeth on his own quarter-deck in 1581. With the booty he brought, and which he stored in the Tower, the queen rewarded him with £10,000. For a man with little original capital, this was wealth, and with it he bought Buckland Abbey, originally a Cistercian foundation, from its new owners, the Grenvilles.

To put an end to what he saw as simple piracy by an undeclared and heretical enemy, as well as to reconquer England for the true faith, Philip of Spain despatched the Armada. It had been delayed for a year by Drake's raid on Cádiz in the spring of 1587, in which he destroyed 24 ships and their stores. When Mary Queen of Scots was executed in 1587, Philip saw himself as the only Catholic claimant to the English throne, since her son, James VI of Scotland, was a heretic. So with the backing, financial and spiritual, of the new pope, Sixtus V, Philip moved. His fleet consisted of 126 ships, with 22,000 seamen and soldiers aboard. It was commanded, as was the custom with ships of war, by a soldier, the duke of Medina Sidonia – a landsman who had never been to sea, and who spent much of his time being seasick. In 1579 Spain had conquered Portugal, added a second empire to its own, and there acquired another ocean-going fleet. It outmatched any English fleet by at least 6 to 1.

---

[15] As a *quid proquo*, it could be contended that if Drake, in *The Golden Hind* in 1579, had found a passage inland from San Francisco or San Pablo Bays, or penetrated the Colorado valley, or followed the Columbia or the Fraser inland, and the Northwest Passage had thus been opened up, and if he had crossed the Sierras and the Rockies, and overcome the buffalo and the Indians of the plains, the Nova Albion Drake proclaimed might have become an earlier New England, with a more salubrious climate and happier race relations, and America West as well as North and South would have been English after all. But 'ifs and buts' and 'perhaps' are not history.

The defeat of the Armada has become a legend too: one of those near-bungles that was miraculously turned into triumph when, as the great fleet hove in sight of the Lizard and the first of the warning beacons flared, God suddenly became a Protestant, and unleashed a storm. It blew the unwieldy galleons away from the Goodwin Sands. When they took what shelter they could find in the Calais Roads, the English sent in fire-ships; the winds changed direction, and the Spanish ships were then blown into the North Sea, missing the rendezvous with the land force of the prince of Parma awaiting their transports to Thanet; they were then driven round the Shetlands and to a final shattering off the west coast of Ireland. Fifty of the original 126 ships never got back home. There was no confrontation at any point between the two fleets as such; part of the time the English ships were busy "salvaging" and doing well by it; Drake himself took the *Rosario*, the richest of them all, as prize. The legends have grown as barnacled as the ships; one marked feature of the Armada was the superiority of England's own "great ships." Her 25 men of war in 1588 were all over 200 tons; they were fast, handier than the Spanish ships, and heavily armed. This was the legacy of Sir John Hawkins, who for a decade and more had been building armed merchantmen, war galleons and dockyards. The warning beacons in fact blazed no farther than the south and south-east coasts — they were not needed further north; wounded English sailors were dumped on the beaches of Margate and left to their own resources; ironically, a number of the English ships had been built by Philip II himself, in the years when he was the consort of Mary, England's Catholic queen; but the vast majority of them were privately owned, and commanded by their owners. If they were in general smaller, and thus at once more weatherly and more manoeuvrable, their smaller cannon were a nightmare to fire in raging seas. "God blew, and they were scattered," certainly; but He was helped by fireships, skill and gallantry too.[16] However, a year or two later, Spain was as strong as ever — and her treasure ships brought in more silver.

The success of the freebooters and the defeat of the Armada provided tangible evidence that the English Channel was not only a

---

[16] In 1988, the 400th anniversary of the defeat of the Spanish Armada, HM Treasury received a claim for Drake's expenses of £917, to cover the payments he had made to the officers and crew of his ship, *Revenge*. Lord Burghley, the treasurer, always examined all such claims meticulously, and had met all Drake's other "outgoings," but queried this. It remains unpaid; allowing for 400 years' inflation, the Central Statistical Office estimate that, were the claim met today, it would cost the Treasury £100,000.

moat but an ocean and one indeed that England could transform into a path to overseas expansion. Humphrey Gilbert and Walter Ralegh vainly attempted to profit from it by founding colonies in America. Gilbert, a favourite of the queen's since his days as a courtier when she was a princess with an uncertain future, and with his own grandiose plans for seizing Spanish treasure ships and territory in the Caribbean, obtained from her a patent to explore and to settle the New World. He planned a fiefdom for himself in "Norumbega" (New England), but he was unlucky: he landed at St John's, Newfoundland, with a colony of 250 masons and carpenters, claimed it for the queen, and made land grants on paper, but he lost his life at sea in his tiny *Squirrel*, just off the Azores in 1583.

Gilbert's half-brother, Walter Ralegh, who had accompanied him in 1578, in 1583 set off on his own expedition, only to be recalled – after the fleet had sailed – by the express command of the queen. He took up the challenge in 1584, with a patent to search for "heathen and barbarous lands ... not actually possessed by any Christian princes, nor inhabited by Christian people." He sent an expedition of two Bideford ships, each under a Devon man; but Philip Amadas and Arthur Barlowe were steered through the sandbars by an experienced pilot, Simon Fernandez of the Azores, who had left the service of his native Portugal to engage in piracy on his own, before selling his services to any buyer. In near-warlike waters – as sometimes in peace – cosmopolitans of no fixed allegiance were worthy of their hire, even if they never could be trusted. The Devon captains explored that long and shifting sandreef off the coast of what is now North Carolina, that runs, pencil-like, for 175 miles (today's "Outer Banks"), and the islands north and south of Cape Hatteras, seeking a site for a settlement. Everywhere they were met in friendship by Algonquian-speaking Indians, who lived on the sandy islands and along the inlets and rivers in palisaded, agriculturally supported villages. As Hakluyt describes, Captain Barlowe found the Roanoke Indians "most gentle, loving and faithful, void of all guile and treason, and such as live after the manner of the golden age." Despite the long sandbar, they felt that they were "in the midst of some delicate garden." The high cedars, cypresses and pines, the grapes and the prospect of Mediterranean-type crops, "the country corn, very white, faire and well-tasted," were attractive. In the tradition of European "discoveries," they claimed formal possession of the area – in language which the natives, if present, would not have understood. After a month's stay they sailed back to England, taking back with them two of the Indians, Manteo and Wanchese, as exhibits, as was the practice.

Plate 7   John White's view of an Indian village in Virginia.
(The Bodleian Library, Oxford.)

The expedition's report satisfied Ralegh, who named the North
American coast in honor of the virgin queen, Elizabeth. It was a
sure touch: the queen returned the courtesy by conferring a knight-
hood. The name had not been his first choice; he ascertained that

the name the Indians used seemed to be Wingandacon, but scholarship gave way to flattery – and propaganda. And Hakluyt wrote his *Discourse of Western Planting* as propaganda, the first manifesto of English imperialism; Walsingham, Grenville and London merchants – and Ralegh himself – provided funds. In 1585, Sir Richard Grenville brought out a fleet of seven ships with 107 male colonists to North Carolina, to erect and maintain a permanent settlement. Among them were two "intelligence" men – Thomas Harriot, Ralegh's mathematics tutor (charged to find out all he could of the Indians), and John White, an experienced artist and mapmaker, charged to survey the natural resources, both human and material. White painted many water colours of the Indians and the area's natural flora. The avowed purposes of the colony, established on Roanoke Island under the governorship of Ralph Lane, were to search for gold, silver and pearls, and to be a waterway to the Pacific Ocean. None of the colony's goals was achieved, although they explored Albemarle Sound and did reach Chesapeake Bay. But there were no obvious resources, either mineral or agricultural, and no good harbor. By the spring of 1586 their supplies were running out and the Indians were less friendly, as both groups competed for scarce resources. By June 1586, the tense atmosphere led the colonists to fear that an attack was being planned against them. Determined to end the threat by striking first, Lane summoned the leading Indians to a meeting, then shot them down. He burned Indian crops and Indian homes. Faced by starvation and the hostility of the victims' kinsmen, the colonists spent several miserable weeks before Sir Francis Drake with the West India fleet arrived in July, after raiding Spanish possessions, and evacuated all of them to England. Robbery on the high seas was more profitable than distant colonial outposts.

A few days after their departure, a relief ship sent by Ralegh reached the island, found the abandoned huts, and returned with its stores intact. Grenville's three ships from North Devon did so too, but left 15 men ("the second colony") to maintain the site; on returning they sacked the Azores towns and their stocks of sugar. The next year, 1587, Ralegh sent and financed another fleet to Roanoke, bearing 116 more colonists, in 14 family groups – 88 men, 17 women and 11 children in all – as well as the friendly Manteo, a Croatan Indian of the island of the same name. They were working people, craftsmen from the lesser City of London Companies, yeomen from the Southwest and South of England – and two Irishmen, who deserted *en route*. All who went got 500 acres of land, and were seen as shareholders. Two of the women were pregnant, one of them Elenor Dare, who was Governor White's daughter. Led by

Cornishman John White, the group discovered that the natives had killed two of the men who had been left at Roanoke the previous year, and had driven the rest away. They were never found.

The new arrivals re-established the colony on Roanoke, and White had Manteo baptized a Christian. Their goal had probably been to move the "base" to Chesapeake Bay, and to plan an agricultural settlement there, living alongside, but not displacing, the natives, but their pilot Fernandez would go no further. He wanted to get back to privateering, where the riches were. In August, John White and Thomas Harriot and the ships sailed back to England for supplies; he instructed the colonists to move "50 miles into the Maine" – i.e. on the Chesapeake. The plans for White's return to Virginia the next year, and Ralegh's supply ships to it, were thwarted by the approach of the Spanish Armada; Grenville and his ships could not be spared; the two pinnaces White despatched, and in which he sailed again, turned yet again to privateering on their own, and never crossed the Atlantic; White blamed not Spain but the "theaverie of our evil disposed mariners." When White finally returned to Roanoke in August 1590, without supplies and as the passenger of John Watts' privateer, which spent the early summer months actively seizing any ship it encountered, every member of the colony, including his granddaughter, Virginia Dare, the first child born of English parents in America, had vanished. There was no sign of violence, but the letters "Croatan" carved on the palisade of their fort indicated that for some reason – perhaps the continued anger of Roanoke Indians – the colony had moved south, possibly to Manteo's people on Croatan, 50 miles away on the Outer Banks, or to the mainland. Since Robert Beverley II wrote his *History* in 1705, the accepted explanation has been that the Indians, seeing the colonists as vulnerable, and lacking in reinforcements, destroyed them. Today's historians, for the most part following D. B. Quinn, believe that they took refuge on the Elizabeth River, near the Chesapeake Indians – only to be destroyed when Powhatan attacked the Chesapeakes just before the Jamestown settlement in 1607. Storms prevented a search at Croatan, and although the present-day descendants of the natives of that island claim the colonists among their ancestors, the mystery of the "Lost Colony" has never been solved. The legacy?: gray eyes among some Croatan Indians; and the record of the natural world and of the native inhabitants produced by John White, and by Thomas Harriot in his *Brief and True Report*, compiled on their first voyage.

The colonists may have been befriended by Manteo's people, or killed by Powhatan and the Indians of the Virginia Tidewater (after a period in which they had been kindly treated by the Chesapeake Indians, then enemies of Powhatan). Their disappearance, however, betrays also the ugly side of Elizabethan enterprise: a badly positioned and vulnerable site, selected too quickly and probably not meant to be permanent, with no adequate harbor; rescue ships diverted as much by the prospect of booty from privateering as by the coming of the Armada and by Drake's Lisbon expedition, and putting the rescue aspect low in the scales; the disappearance of goodwill as the settlers used up the Indians' supplies of corn and beans and their own stocks of trinkets, to give in exchange, dwindled. Caliban again turned on Prospero, but a few may have survived as groups, on Indian sufferance. In any case, as bonuses, there were the records of the natural world of Pamlico Sound and the Outer Banks and of its inhabitants, produced by Harriot and White. When Hakluyt recorded the story, he used the moving prose of captains Barlowe and Amadas:

The second of July we found shoal water, where we smelt so sweet and so strong a smell as if we had been in the midst of some delicate garden abounding with all kind of odoriferous flowers, by which we were assured that the land could not be far distant ... We viewed the land about us, being, whereas we first landed, very sandy and low towards the water's side, but so full of grapes as the very beating and surge of the sea overflowed them; of which we found such plenty, as well on every little shrub as also climbing towards the tops of high cedars that I think in all the world the like abundance is not to be found. Under the bank or hill whereon we stood, we beheld the valleys replenished with goodly cedartrees, and having discharged our arquebus shot, such a flock of cranes arose under us, with such a cry redoubled by many echoes, as if an army of men had shouted all together. [17]

Ralegh used it too, in his later *Book of the Ocean to Cynthia*, and Drayton in his *Ode to the Virginian Voyage*:

> What as the luscious smell
> Of that delicious land
>   Above the sea that flows
>   The clear wind throws
> Your hearts to swell
> Approaching the dear strand.

[17] Hakluyt, *Principal Navigations*, VII. 122–3.

> And the ambitious vine
> Crowns with his purple mass
>   The cedar reaching high
>   To kiss the sky,
> The cypress, pine,
> And useful sassafras.

The failure of the Roanoke enterprise was due neither to internal problems among the settlers nor to trouble with the Indians but rather to the ineffectiveness of the organization and conduct of the expeditions. Ralegh's failure to see the area for himself weakened his planning, while the link between privateering and colonization was damaging. Yet with a little more luck, the venture might have succeeded. What was clear was that a colony had to be regularly victualled until it was large enough to be viable; it had to be able to defend itself meantime, and thereafter to work the land (and to know how), and to feed itself; and, ideally, to be able to produce crops for export. All these required time, luck and masterly management. Ralegh was not responsible for any of this – he was one of those admirals who rarely put to sea. When he was a prisoner in the Tower and wrote his *History*, he was frank in his view, a view that echoes that of Columbus:

We finde it in daily experience that all discourse of magnanimitie, of Nationall Vertue, of Religion, of Libertie, and whatsoever else hath been wont to move and incourage vertuous men, hath no force at all with the common Souldier [and sailor?], in comparison of spoile and riches.[18]

However intelligent and imaginative the planners in London, however accurate the maps were coming to be, the plans were devised 3,000 miles away, and to English assumptions. Thus the strategic consideration behind Ralegh's expeditions (of 1585–7) was the erection of a bulwark against the steady expansion northward of the

---

[18] Ralegh, *Historie of the World* (1614), pt I, ch. 2, sec. 4, p. 178. Cf. D. B. Quinn, *Set Fair for Roanoke: Voyages and colonies 1584–1606* (Chapel Hill, NC, University of North Carolina Press, 1985), and *The Lost Colonists, their Fortune and Probable Fate* (Raleigh, NC, 1984), especially for the "conjectures" of its later chapters. Cf. D. B. Quinn (ed.), *The Roanoke Voyages 1584–90* (2 vols, Cambridge, The Hakluyt Society, 1955). Karen C. Kupperman provides a stronger conceptual framework in *Roanoke: The abandoned colony* (Rownan and Allanheld, Totowa, NJ, 1984). Cf. David Stick for his use of John White's Indian drawings in *Roanoke Island: The beginning of English America* (Chapel Hill, NC, University of North Carolina Press, 1983).

Spaniards from Florida. Using Roanoke Island as a base, the English planned to intercept the Spanish silver fleet as it sailed from the Florida Straits to the Azores and Europe. This dictated that the colony be located precisely at Roanoke, where it would be close enough to reach the fleet and yet not so close as to be vulnerable to Spanish attack. As a result, the new colony was at a place with no natural harbor. Instead of offering a shelter for the English fleet, the site offered only swamps and malaria. Nor could planners, familiar though they were with the visitations of plague at home, fully absorb the impact of starvation, malaria – and, erratically, of Indians. The political needs of England doomed the colony to failure. Another intention was to find land suitable for the crops grown around the Mediterranean Sea. The English calculated they needed only to travel westward along the same latitude (35°) to find such land in the New World. What they failed to calculate was the drastic difference in the climates of North Carolina and the Mediterranean. They failed to realize also that they would need a specialized labor force to grow citrus fruits and olives. It was the demands of England that limited the success of the colony. What would grow on native soil was something quite different: neither tobacco plantations nor elected assemblies were part of the London plan.

Ralegh's own story is now legend: a romantic courtier, who was at once a feverish imperial dreamer and a cynical, calculating schemer. Poet and historian, explorer and ship designer, colonizer and statesman, soldier and sailor – and a strikingly handsome captain of the Queen's Guard. Ralegh touched nothing that he did not adorn – and yet he lost his life to the executioner's axe. He was born in a house which still stands at Hayes Barton, near Sidmouth, Devon, and educated at Oriel College, Oxford. No more than Columbus or Cartier was he born to wealth. He was a younger son of lesser gentry, like the Drakes, who were rooted in the land, and had profited greatly from the dissolution of the monastic estates. He soldiered in the Huguenot cause in France and Ireland, where he showed courage and dash. He was a protégé of Robert Dudley, earl of Leicester, at Court, and became a favourite of the queen. His aunt Kate Ashley had been governess to the queen through her far-from-easy childhood and youth, and his half-brother Humphrey Gilbert had been a page at Court. He was knighted in 1584, and became an MP for Devon in 1585. In the same year, with the queen still smiling on him, he became warden of the Stanneries, controlling the tin mines of Cornwall, lord lieutenant of that county and vice-admiral both of Cornwall and Devon. This meant wealth, and he enjoyed displaying it: pearls in his hatband, rings on his fingers.

The debit list in his character is long: vanity, cynicism, cupidity, the quest for glory, "Machiavel" to some, the great "Raw Lie" to others; in practical terms his only successful piece of action was the capture and sack of Cádiz in 1596. But this was the best educated and most sparkling intelligence at the queen's Court; and he saw through all the sycophancy. He recognized that only his own wealth made a man free, that is truly independent of others. "Poverty is a shame amongst men," he wrote, in the *Instructions to his Son*, which were published after his death, "an imprisonment of the mind, a vexation of every worthy spirit." He admired the maritime drive and the commercial ruthlessness of the Dutch, and yet, rightly, be feared them as dangerous competitors. Above all, he grasped the importance of sea-power: "Whosoever commands the sea, commands the trade," he wrote; "whoever commands the trade of the world, commands the riches of the world, and consequently the world itself." His tutors were daring and controversial; the friend and coadjutor of Drake was also the friend of the poets Spenser and Jonson, and of Thomas Harriot, the greatest of the Tudor scientists. And, not least, he was devoid of illusion, aware that time conquers all:

> Our graves that hide us from the searching Sun,
> Are like drawne curtaynes when the play is done,
> Thus march we playing to our latest rest,
> Onely we dye in earnest, that's no jest.

From the start he mixed thought, display and derring-do. Although he never visited the North American continent himself, he planned and financed the expedition led by his cousin Sir Richard Grenville (of Bideford, Devon) which discovered Roanoke Island in 1584, and the colony he named Virginia in honor of the Virgin Queen. In 1585–7 he fitted out two more expeditions to explore the coast north of Florida; no settlements followed, and the unsuccessful colonists brought back only potatoes and tobacco; then exotic and the first of their kind, Ralegh planted them in his Youghal garden. He planted people too, on his Irish estates. In 1592 he searched for gold in Guiana, explored the coast of Trinidad and sailed 400 miles up the Orinoco in an abortive quest for the gold of El Dorado. He had been preceded here by Antonio de Berreo. In 1596 he published his *Discovery of the Large and Beautiful Empire of Guinea*. It had not yet been occupied by the Spaniards, and there was gold there. It was, he reported, "a better Indies for Her Majesty than the king of Spain hath any." He hoped with it to offset his failure in Virginia, and to regain the queen's favour, for, as he wrote in his long but unfinished poem, *Book of the Ocean to Cynthia*:

> When I was gone she sent her memory
> More strong than were ten thousand ships of war.

He served in expeditions against Cádiz in 1596 and the Azores in 1597. However, his secret marriage to Elizabeth ("Bessie") Throckmorton, one of the queen's maids of honor, angered the queen when she discovered it, and he could never count on her total support thereafter. He was supplanted by Robert Devereux, earl of Essex, and Cecil readily became a critic.

On James's accession in 1603, Ralegh was charged with treason and sent to the Tower. There was no evidence. While awaiting execution, he wrote a moving letter of farewell to his wife: "Your mourning cannot avail me that am but dust." He was then pardoned, but condemned to perpetual imprisonment in the Tower, where he wrote his *History of the World*. Its first and only volume (1,300 folio pages) reaches the second Roman War in Macedonia in 130 BC. Among Puritans, it became a basic text, and the most printed book of the seventeenth century after the Authorized Version (the King James version) of the Bible. Ralegh wrote a number of other books, including a *Discourse on War*. He wrote poetry, melancholic and cynical in tone, and attempted suicide; he felt, he said, like a caged hawk. In 1616 – by which time he was 64 – the king, who was short of money, released him on condition that he lead another expedition to the mines of Guiana, but on condition also that there would be no fighting with the Spaniards – objectives that could not be reconciled, as the king knew and intended. Ralegh sold all his possessions – and most of his wife's – to go. There was no gold, and he did fight the Spaniards, and he lost his only son in the course of it. His second-in-command, Lawrence Keymes, blamed himself and committed suicide. Ralegh returned in his ship *Destiny* to Devon, where he had built Sherborne Castle. He never lived in it. He was re-arrested, and was executed in Old Palace Yard in Westminster, on the continuing, and still unproven, charge of treason. His headless body was interred in St Margaret's, Westminster. His widow had his head embalmed and enclosed in a red leather bag; she carried it with her wherever she went, until she died, aged 82, in 1647. The head may be in the Nicholas Chapel of West Horsley Place, in Surrey. But, in his own words, "What matter how the head lie, so the heart be right?"

Of the Elizabethans Ralegh did not stand alone. His half-brother was Sir Humphrey Gilbert of Compton Castle, who took possession of Newfoundland for the queen, and went down with his last ship. Sir Martin Frobisher, dreamed of a northwest passage to Cathay, fought against the Spanish Armada, and died of wounds in battle. Sir Francis Drake, like his kinsman and fellow-explorer John Hawkins, was to die of yellow fever, at Nombre de Dios on the Spanish Main. And Drake was, like all of them, an adventurer, but with his own not other people's money, a patriot and something of a pirate-king. These Elizabethans were the antitheses of democrats; not utopians or dissenters, not political reformers. Their England was manorial and monarchical, rooted in caste and class. But they were scholars and musicians, they read and wrote, and they tried to balance their account-books. They believed that Englishmen could found new homes on foreign soil, that would be thus forever England. Ralegh foresaw the importance of the New World as a land not of gold but of living men. The age of Elizabeth was rich in scholar-heroes, and it was their courage and their seamanship that kept the island, and "Gloriana" herself, virginal, Protestant and safe.

The title deed of empire was royal, not parliamentary or popular; but its instruments were merchant adventuring, trading, fishing – and pirating – for profit, rather than for glory. The Armada was largely defeated, and the British American colonies largely settled, by private enterprise; the only one of the 13 mainland colonies established by the "State" was New York; Newfoundland, after two centuries of effort, did not receive formal colonial status until 1776; not until 1642 did Parliament intervene with the Navigation Acts, and that only because England was engaged in a trade war with the Dutch.[19]

6 STIRRERS ABROAD

On 23 April 1564, when Shakespeare is believed to have been born, there was not a single European settlement north of Mexico. In 1616 when he died there were no less than six centres of European settlement, all small but some with a great potential: St Augustine, Jamestown, Bermuda, Port Royal, Quebec and Avalon Peninsula in Newfoundland. One was Spanish, two French and three English.[20]

---

[19] Christopher Hill, *Intellectual Origins of the English Revolution* (London, Panther Books, 1972), pp. 167–8; A. L. Rowse, *Ralegh and the Throckmortons* (London, Macmillan, 1962), p. 74; Ralegh, *Poems*, ed. A. Latham (London, Routledge, 1951), pp. 51–2; Angus Calder, *Revolutionary Empire* (New York, Dutton, 1981), pp. 84–5.

[20] Quinn, *England and the Discovery of America*, p. 482.

Before the end of the sixteenth century the Atlantic was crossed regularly, the extent of the Pacific glimpsed; only the interior of the two New Worlds, North and South, remained undiscovered, and their extents only surmised. The next century, however, would become a century of settlement along the coasts, or along the banks of the major rivers. It too would breed legends, no longer of islands in an uncharted sea, but of journeys into unmapped lands filled with strange and wild people, of cities of gold, of lost colonies, of suffering and despair. But now the people live and the adventures occur in a real world, and their records need little exaggeration.

On the motives behind colonization there was little debate among the nations of Europe. Hakluyt had spelled them out at length and eloquently in the 1580s – he was still active in 1606 – and they were even more binding 20 years later:

... as in all former ages, Englishmen have bene men full of activity, stirrers abroad, and searchers of the remote parts of the world, so in this most famous and peerlesse Government of her most excellent Majesty, her subjects through the speciall assistance, and blessing of God, in search-ing the most opposite corners and quarters of the world, and to speake plainly, in compassing the vaste globe of the earth more then once, have excelled all the nations and people of the earth. For, which of the kings of this land before her Majesty, had theyr banners ever beene in the Caspian sea? which of them hath ever dealt with the Emperor of Persia, as her Majesty hath done, and obteined for her merchants large & loving privileges? who ever saw before this regiment, an English Ligier in the stately porch of the Grand Signor at Constantinople? who ever found English Consuls & Agents at Tripolis in Syria, at Aleppo, at Babylon, at Balsara, and which is more, who ever heard of Englishman at Goa before now? what English shippes did heeretofore ever anker in the mighty river of Plate? passe and repasse the unpassable (in former opinion) straight of Magellan, range along the coast of Chili, Peru, and all the backside of Nova Hispania, further than any Christian ever passed, travers the mighty bredth of the South sea, land upon the Luzones in despight of the enemy, enter into alliance, amity, and traffike with the princes of the Moluccaes, & the Isle of Java, double the famous Cape of Bona Speranza, arrive at the Isle of Santa Helena, & last of al returne home most richly laden with the commodities of China, as the subjects of this now flourishing monarchy have done?[21]

As late as the reign of Charles II, the English plantations in the West Indies were esteemed more important than the mainland

---

[21] Hakluyt, *Principal Navigations*, 'Epistle Dedicatorie," I.XX.

colonies because they were better based for intercepting Spanish trade. To intercept the Spanish treasure fleet was seen as creating economic wealth in one's own country; European thinking about trade was strictly mercantilistic. To break the power of Spain it was less necessary that Virginia and New England be settled than it was to take military possession of convenient ports, islands and river mouths. Hence the persistent attempt to establish an English colony in Guiana (1604–6, 1609, 1610–11, 1613, 1617, 1620–3). Bermuda was acquired in 1609; and portions of the West Indies fell into English hands: Saint Christopher in 1624, Nevis in 1628, Montserrat and Antigua in 1632. The colony on Barbados was planted in 1627 and by 1640 had a population of 18,000. From 1631 to 1635 English Puritans attempted to found a Puritan colony on Providence Island, off the Mosquito Coast. [22]

The English motives for colonization went beyond Renaissance values – to rival the heroes of Plutarch, the call to convert the heathen, and the desire to expand the bounds of empire – to include a special concern with the problems of population, and a special appeal for trade. Alarm over social dislocation is one of the commonest notes in Tudor literature. The sixteenth century, it has been said, lived in terror of the tramp; and the appeal of colonial promotion literature was alike to those fearful of being uprooted by the enclosure movement, the sale of the monastery lands, or the shifts in population caused by reason of the wool trade or some other rising industry. Thus Gilbert, among the eight numbered reasons of "commodities" that "would ensue," once he found the Northwest Passage, declares: "Also we might inhabite some part of those countryes, and settle there such needy people of our countrey, which now trouble the common wealth, and through want here at home are inforced to commit outragious offences, whereby they are dayly consumed with the gallowes." Prisons were "pestered and filled with able men to serve their Countrie which for small roberies are dayly hanged up in great numbers ("twentie at a clappe" in Rochester), who ought to be sent to the colonies and there fully employed. Plantations would relieve surplus population, even if

---

[22] The last of these was seen by Puritans as at least as important as Massachusetts Bay, a refuge but a sideshow, whereas the island off the coast of Nicaragua would be the germ of an English empire on the Mosquito Coast, would rival Catholic Spain, and would in the end attract those who had temporarily sought shelter on a bleak and rocky shore. From this idea would grow Cromwell's "Western Design." See Karen Kupperman, "Errand to the Indies," *William & Mary Quarterly*, 45 (1988) pp. 70–99.

they were criminals; John Donne would echo his views 40 years later. [23]

By 1600 England was readier for overseas expansion than ever before. Politically, the Spanish menace had passed with the defeat of the Armada in 1588, but the need to weaken the power of Catholic Spain and France remained. England's government was more centralized and stable after the successful 45-year reign of Elizabeth, and the smooth succession of James VI of Scotland (the son of Mary Queen of Scots) to become James I of England, so the two crowns were now one. James, one of the most learned, most garrulous and most drunken of kings – and he had other vices – proposed, abortively, a union of the parliaments and of the churches. He identified with London, as did his male favourites. He visited the land of his birth only once, in 1617. But at a time of rising prices, the English Crown was poor and needed cash: from shares in commerce and piracy, from sales of licenses and offices; it farmed out its customs service, so that those who ran it lived as much from conniving at smuggling as from legal levies. State grants and privileges allowed *laissez-faire* policies to flourish, with names like monopoly, privateering and piracy. In the country, however, capital was accumulating and joint-stock companies were coming into being, ready to finance enterprise and adventure for the sake of profit. The availability of capital was partly the result of the confiscation of church property, partly of the development of trade and commerce, especially of wool manufacture, and partly the result of the enclosure of agricultural land for sheep raising, which threw thousands of agricultural labourers out of work; and the dissolution of the monasteries, while it freed many for new means of livelihood, if they could be found, allowed a class of gentry to rise to become JPs and MPs, and if they had influence also at Court, they ran not only their counties, but the country. England, like Spain, needed gold and silver, timber, pitch and tar; with these, and, with plantations abroad, she could aim at that self-contained economy that was the objective of every European state; and the overseas areas could absorb the less desirable elements of the population, dissenters in religion, veterans with fewer foreign wars to fight, and "rogues, vagabonds and sturdy beggars," destroyed by enclosure of their land, by the trade slump caused by the Thirty Years' War, and by the rise in prices. Despite the war

---

[23] Hakluyt, *Principal Navigations* VII.186, VIII.112. Cf. also his *Divers Voyages* (Hakluyt Society, 1950), p. 8, and Howard Mumford Jones, *O Strange New World: American culture, the formative years* (New York, Viking, 1964), ch. 5.

against Catholic Spain, in England religious crusading, as distinct from refuge-seeking, never played a prominent part in overseas settlements. The mass of dissenting English, whether Protestant or Catholic, had suffered annoyance and humiliation rather than death at the stake. And – unlike Spain – England did allow those who disagreed with the policies of the day to emigrate. The missionary role had never been strong among the men of Plymouth or Bristol: their minds were set more often on cod than on God. What the London merchants dreamed of was another Mexico. If not minerals, then sugar, hides, dyewoods and other dyestuffs, medicinal substances derived from trees and plants, wines, olives, citrus fruits and perhaps other exotica, fine timber, utility timber for masts, shingles, clapboard and barrel staves (which could be roughly processed on the spot), iron, glass, potash, pitch and tar, all of which used timber for their processing, together with useful minerals of every sort. All these would be produced in latitudes more southerly than England, and yet in climates in which Englishmen might live and work without being riddled with tropical and equatorial fevers. The Orinoco sounded as unpalatable as Newfoundland.

In shaping a colonial policy, no mother-country could escape from its own history. Spain had built its own national unity on the regaining of its homeland from the Moors, and had accompanied that by conversions at the point of a sword; in the New World, by royal grants (*encomiendas*), groups of Indian households were "entrusted" to individual officers, or even footsoldiers, in the conquering Spanish armies, as had happened in Granada; in each case former owners now became tenants – or slaves; and from the tribute that Moor or Indian paid, the Spanish *encomendero* would develop an estate and maintain his family.

England, after centuries of sporadic intervention in Ireland, had planted settlements there – especially of Scots in the Ulster plantations, so that McDonalds (McDonells), Montgomerys, Hamiltons became Ulster as well as Scots names, and the City of London merchants invested as heavily in Derry and Coleraine and Virginia, Ireland, as in Virginia, North America. Almost all the English pioneers in North America had Irish experience: Sir Humphrey Gilbert, Ralegh and Drake, Gorges, Lord De La Warr and the earl of Southampton of the Virginia Company, and Ralph Lane of Roanoke Island, a muster-master in Ireland in 1592. Both in Ireland and America the plantation had to be in form a military structure to survive. Spaniards and British alike saw the North American Indians in terms of their own stereotype of "wild Irish" or "enemies within."

By 1600 both Spain and Portugal had an imperial system in being. Under the Council of the Indies, which appointed senior officials and acted as a final court of appeals, the Casa de Contratación at Seville directed Spain's imperial trade. In 1534 a vice-royalty of New Spain was established, with headquarters in Mexico City; it was responsible for North America, the West Indies and the Philippines. From 1542 a vice-roy of Peru, stationed in HQ Lima, directed the trade to and from South America. The Spanish instrument overseas was the *cabildo* or municipality, a semi-autonomous unit largely medieval in structure, seeking to grow into a city, as some did – Santo Domingo, Havana, Panama and Vera Cruz. To its military, administrative and judicial functions, the *cabildo* added the role of market, of collecting point for royal revenues, and, usually, a bishopric. There was no illusion about natives: they were to be used as labour where possible, backed by Negro slaves. Their land and its resources were to be exploited. And behind the State, as reinforcement, stood the Church and the mission. Spain sent out two fleets per year, one for Vera cruz in Mexico, one for Porto Bello, on the isthmus of Panama. From there in the late spring came the treasure fleets of silver that for a century made Spain the Great Power of Europe. Paradoxically, the very success of Spain, and its own struggle for survival against Spain made a commercial power of Holland, vulnerable to enemies though it seemed. When Spain absorbed Portugal in 1580, she absorbed Portuguese colonies also; and to Holland, France and England these former Portuguese colonies became tempting targets. The objectives now were not discovery but trade with the newly discovered worlds, and a monopoly of it. Each overseas holding had special resources that could be exploited and brought to the metropolitan power: gold and silver to Spain, the mercantilists' dream; furs to the French and Dutch, fish, timber and naval stores to the English (the last especially valuable with the loss of Baltic trade). All pointed to the value of settlement and colonization as well as control over natives.

The instrument of colonization was not (except in Spain and France) a department of the State, and as their histories would reveal, government bureaucracy was not equipped to administer distant territories. Elsewhere the state chose the joint-stock trading company and chartered it to organize colonies and develop trade in a stipulated area. This gave legal form to the groups of "adventurers," who until now had come together to finance individual discoverers, making their own terms on each occasion. When the absorption of Portugal by Spain in 1580 cut off access to Lisbon's distribution centre for the spice trade, an East India Company was set up in

London in 1600 to tap the spice trade at source. Such companies rapidly became *imperia in imperium*, with company forts and garrisons to defend their trade posts, to make treaties with natives, and often to engage in undeclared war. Thus the instrument of British policy in India, both political and military as well as economic, was the East India Company, founded in 1600 and continuing until 1877, when the company was dissolved and the queen became empress of India. So, too, with the Dutch East India Company, founded in 1602, which was the model for the English London Company which founded Jamestown. The Dutch Company sent Henry Hudson to find a passage to Asia other than by way of the Cape of Good Hope, and he explored the North American coast from Maine to Delaware Bay, then sailed up the river that now bears his name, as far as Albany. It sent out colonists in 1624: hence its trading posts at Fort Orange (Albany), Fort Amsterdam (Manhattan) and Fort Nassau on the Delaware River. The settlements grew slowly, since the home government wanted an active fur trade rather than agriculture. But its distinctive feature was the patroon ships along the Hudson River, with the recipients of great estates encouraged to bring over settlers who would become their tenants – an unappealing prospect. By 1650 there were only some 3,000 people in the New Netherlands. But elsewhere the Dutch commercial empire was extensive: they seized Amboyna in 1609, set up the company's capital in Batavia on Java, and captured Ceylon, Sumatra, Borneo and in 1641 Malacca – though the last still retains its Portuguese character, and many of its trading groups still speak a variant of Portuguese. From 1637 to 1661 Brazil too became a Dutch state with its capital at Pernambuco. In the seventeenth century, without in fact ever having spent its puny resources on Discoveries, the Dutch prospered as middlemen, traders and interlopers. They were agricultural reformers, land reclaimers, rich in corn and cattle. But their enterprises were too many, and too scattered, for their resources. No large emigration of Dutch settlers was possible – it depended too much on Walloons, Huguenots and British. Though the Dutch West India Company had absorbed its rival, the new Netherlands Company and its colony on Manhattan Island, New Amsterdam, despite the fur trade of the Hudson valley, offered little resistance in 1664 when an English fleet appeared. But, as with the Portuguese in Malacca, so with the Dutch names along the Hudson: the estates of the patroons still lie alongside each other – Roosevelts, Stuyvesants, Rockefellers, Philippses. The Treaty of Westphalia in 1648 would confirm Holland in possession of all the territories she had won from Portugal, and recognize her as a republic. Surrounded by monarchs, most of whom were

Catholics and tyrants, she was in fact a Puritan oligarchy of some 10,000 wealthy men, living by trade, who saw trade as war by other means. Jan Pieterz Coen of the Dutch East India Company admitted in 1614 that "we cannot carry on trade without war, nor war without trade"; the Jakarta in Java that he captured five years later became, as Batavia, the Dutch GHQ in the Far East. Their rivals saw it differently: "the Dutch have a proverb: Jesus Christ is good, but trade is better." In 1628 it was neither trade nor war, but piracy: Piet Heyn for the Dutch West India Company captured Spain's entire Mexican silver fleet. Holland became – and would remain for three centuries – the dominant trading power in the East, and in much of Africa; and from 1638 to 1854 she was the only European state allowed to trade with Japan. In order to have a half-way house to this wealth, the Cape Colony was founded in South Africa in 1651.

Portugal regained its independence from Spain in 1640. It regained Brazil, but the commerce and the colonies Vasco da Gama had been the first to establish remained permanently lost – though Portugal did retain its way-stations on the African coast (which became Mozambique, Angola and Portuguese Guinea). [24]

For France, Richelieu in 1627 created the Company of New France (the St Lawrence) and the Company of the Isles of America (the West Indies). [25] The French East India Company was distinct from its rivals in England and Holland. Founded by Colbert in 1644, it was virtually a branch of government. Its officials in the East were state officials, usually *aristos*, and not the rough operators or experienced traders of the other companies.

In 1606, when a group of West Country and London merchants petitioned James I to plant a colony in North America, similar arguments held: the Company of Adventurers and Planters of the City of London was chartered by the Crown, and thus seen as *approbetur*. It was the New World equivalent of the East India Company, or the Levant Company, or the Muscovy Company. The objective was still called Virginia, stretching from the 34th Parallel N (Cape Fear River) to the 45th (the line of Passamaquoddy Bay, which today marks the boundary between Maine and New Brunswick). Private investors, the Adventurers and Planters were one group of merchants with two divisions – one group to form the First Colony of Virginia, the other the Second Colony of Plymouth, though in practical operations they

[24] C. R. Boxer, *The Portuguese Seaborne Empire* (London, Hutchinson, 1969), pp. 95, 189.

[25] A. P. Thornton, *West India Policy under the Restoration* (Oxford, Oxford University Press, 1956), p. 23.

became distinct. The First Colony was to plant between the 34th and the 38th N latitude, and was backed financially by London merchants; the second, which came to be known as the Plymouth Company, was supported by investors in Bristol, Plymouth and Exeter. The region between 38° and 41° was open to either, on condition that neither settled within 100 miles of the other. More important than the boundary lines was the clause which provided that the colonists "shall have and enjoy all Liberties, Franchises, and Immunities ... as if they had been abiding and born, within this our Realm of *England*," a clause which provided a precedent for later English policy – including, it was assumed, trial by jury.[26] The power to govern any colonies which might be set up under these charters the king reserved to a royal council in England. Virginia was thus seen as an extension of England – as New France was to be France *d'outre-mer*. Ralegh's objective, after all, had been to see Virginia "an English nation." There was no sense of any special break with the mother country, even as the numbers grew; on the contrary. John White wrote in 1630: "I deny that such as are gone out from the State are cut off from the state: roots that issue out of the trunk of the tree, though they be dispersed, yet they are not severed."[27]

The leading members of the London Company were Robert Cecil, now earl of Salisbury, Sir Thomas Gates of Devon and Sir George Somers of Dorset. There were also, from an earlier Elizabethan world, Ralegh Gilbert, Sir Humphrey's son, and Prebendary Richard Hakluyt; and two distinct personalities, Edward Maria Wingfield, whose second name testified to his loyalty to the old religion, and George Popham of Somerset, whom the Spanish ambassador saw as "a great Puritan." The prospect of profit seemed to swallow contentions over doctrine. They were City merchants, but included peers of the realm, knights of the shire, Members of Parliament – also looking for dividends. The money came from private resources, and if the king came in, or helped by providing a ship or ships, he did so only as another investor. But his support brought in other backers – though it might earn the enterprise the opposition of

---

[26] A similar guarantee had already appeared in the Ralegh and Gilbert charters.

[27] *The Planter's Plea* (1630), p. 37. The "model" followed by the Virginia and East India Company, a joint-stock company with its own capital but chartered by the Crown, and with a governor and council appointed by the Crown, was more the Venetian *fondaco* in the eastern Mediterranean, its trade monopolized by the mother country, its forts, churches and warehouses erected by the founder-state, its laws those of "home". Downtown Singapore still reflects the image.

Spain and France. The runners and the drafters of memos were the indispensable backroom boys, Edward Hayes and Walter Cope: then, as now, "policy" was largely manufactured in practice not by a king, a privy council or – even – a parliament; it came from the permanent official (the fashionable word for him today might be "office-wallah" or "bureaucrat"), using briefs supplied (then as now?) by part-time – and usually academic – advisers. But its most important public personalities and merchants were none of these, but Sir Thomas Smythe, already with East India and Levant Company experience (and indeed any company that would, suitably prompted, invite his willing aid), and Sir Edwin Sandys.

Sandys was as versatile a man as Ralegh, as quixotic, as apt to irritate and to flatter his sovereign: prebendary and lawyer, MP and theologian, an author who in *Europae Speculum* boldly tackled Church–State relations, and contended that there were principles of the constitution neither king nor people could violate with impunity; a member of the committees of the East India Company and of the Somers Islands (i.e. the Bermuda) Company, and in 1617 manager, and in 1619 treasurer, of the Virginia Company, he saved it from bankruptcy. His reward? Like Ralegh, he went to the Tower (in 1621) charged with malversation of funds; in fact he was seen as a dangerous Puritan, even perhaps tinged with republicanism – in either case, unpopular with a king who was the son of a Catholic mother brought up among contentious Scots Presbyterians, and sensitive to threats of unrest in Church as in State, for "no bishop, no King.[28]

The two divisions of the Company looked to distinct regions, and had distinct clienteles. The northern ("The Second Colony") was backed by West Coast and Bristol gentry; it was interested in land speculation, in Irish land values as a model, and in fish and furs and oil – seeking, by setting up a colony, to exploit these year-round, and not just in the short summer season. The City of London's objectives were for the goods that were not so readily obtainable now from the eastern Mediterranean: sugar and raisins, wine and citrus fruits and (later) tobacco and cotton, the beginnings of a closed and complementary economic system. The Treaty of Peace with Spain in 1604 still left England excluded from trade with the Spanish Indies, and there seemed no prospect of a British base in the Caribbean. Virginia was clearly in latitudes that suggested it

---

[28] Sandys was the son of the archbishop of York, in whose diocese was Auster-field; in the manor house there the Pilgrim Father William Bradford was born, and it was regularly in use as a meeting-house of the future Separatists.

as an alternative as a source of sugar and fruit – and *vino*. And from both would come timber, pitch and tar. France seemed clearly to be establishing herself in the St Lawrence, Spain in the Floridas. Between the St Croix River in the north and St Augustine in Florida, however, there was open and inviting country available.

Bristol wanted trade, with or without colonies. London looked for settlements and an agricultural program resting on agriculture, industry, and, where possible, mining. Moreover, with the war with Spain officially over, men were available from Irish or European battlegrounds, cashiered captains and idle other ranks, left there by Spanish or French military responses to English permanence. Privateering, though not dead, was now restricted, since at least officially peace held between London and Madrid; so experienced sailors like Christopher Newport were available as commanders, sailing annually, and in 1608 going out twice. For England, with the Dutch as model and rival, the trading and the indirect empire were always more important than flying the flag.

7 FRENCH NORTH AMERICA

France was not slow to imitate Spain. With a population twice that of the Iberian peninsula, and six times that of England, her ports and slipways from Dieppe and Rouen, round the greedy fangs of Ushant and south as far as La Rochelle and Bordeaux, looked out on the Atlantic, and lived by what it brought them. From them, for a century or more, her fishing fleets sailed each spring to raid the Newfoundland Banks; if they were "wet" fishers, they usually made two trips a year; but at least from 1519 onwards, the men of St Malo were drying and curing their catches on a rocky section of the shore, Le Sillon. The Breton and Norman fishermen were the foundation-builders of New France – and its intelligence service. If France lacked a Sagrès of her own, and if her kings lacked the sustained zeal for discovery of Madrid and Lisbon, in Dieppe, between 1542 and 1560, the cartographers Roze, Desliens, Desceliers and Vallard were producing maps of the French discoveries in North America, drawing their data, like cod and herring, fresh from the quayside, from master pilots – like Cartier – who vividly recounted everything they had seen. Despite its Catholicism, the French Court did not feel curbed by papal sanctions that seemed but to put a religious gloss on the carve-up of the extra-European world between Spain and Portugal, a division of the spoils that seemed arbitrary, unreasonable – and unenforceable. The European Courts echoed to

Francis I's *mot* that he wanted to see Adam's will, to see how he had carved up the world. In any case, any French hesitations in seeking territories for herself in the New World were removed in 1533, when Pope Clement VII (a Medici) met Francis I of France in Marseilles to celebrate the marriage of one of the king's sons, the future Henri II, to the pope's niece, Catherine de Medici. (The bride learned early on how to put a wedding festival to other uses.)

To the Court of France in the early sixteenth century, as to that of Spain, the first objective, again, was "a place in the Indies called Cathay", a route to the East rather than knowledge of new worlds. This view received endorsement from the Florentine colony engaged in the Lyons silk industry, notably the Rucellai and the Guadagni families, keen to tap China as a source of raw silk. Unlike Spain, however, France was handicapped. Normandy and the North had been ravaged in the Hundred Years War. If France was becoming unified, Burgundy, Artois and Provence had been acquired only in 1482; and two kings – Charles VIII (r. 1483–98) and his successor, Louis XII (r. 1498–1515), each married Anne of Brittany to secure that duchy for France. Navarre was as distinct as Catalonia, or Granada; and, unlike Spain, France faced five fronts: in both north and south, the Habsburgs; in the centre, the German Empire; in the south-east Savoy: and in the west, Portugal. She had ambitions of her own in Italy; with the growth in numbers of la réligion prétendue réformée, France would be wracked by internal religious and regional turmoil, with La Rochelle virtually a city-state on its own; for overseas, and it seemed near-irrelevant adventures, France lacked the capital and the drive *d'outre-mer* that marked Spain and Portugal. For whole generations, ambitions in North and South America would be matters for adventurers, pirates or groups of seaport merchants, enjoying royal approval if they succeeded, but equally easy to abandon.

Like their Catholic majesties, Francis I of France turned to another Florentine, Giovanni de Verrazano. Verrazano, linked by marriage to the Guadagni of Lyons, and financed by the Lyons silk syndicate, was a trained master mariner, but had been sent home for education – the family Castello Verrazano still stands in splendor 30 miles south of Florence – and was in style a gentleman, very acceptable to the king. He sailed in a royal ship, *La Dauphiné* (100 tons, and a crew of 50), supported by the syndicates' *La Normande*. The latter, however, returned to France, escorting the prizes captured off the coast of Spain *en route* – for the Breton and Norman ships lived as much from piracy as from "normal" trade. The king was in style a Renaissance prince, like his rival Henry VIII of England,

and was indeed an admirer both of England and of things Italian. He was advised by Italian bankers, ministers – and mistresses. With the return of Magellan's solitary *Victoria*, the South American coasts clearly had provided no obvious route to Cathay. So Verrazano left Dieppe in December 1523 and sailed west – via Madeira on latitude 32° 30 N. He explored the still-undiscovered coast from the Carolinas to Maine, leaving as legacy the dream of a great inland sea. His map of the North Carolina coast, included in his report to Francis I of France, is curious and, in language, exotic: its nomenclature runs from "Dieppe" (in the vicinity of Charleston?) by way of the "Cap d' Alençon" (on the Jersey coast, to honour the king's sister) and the "Fleure Vendôme" to the "Côte St Georges" and "Les Trois Filles de Navarre" (the islands off the coast of Maine). He saw Pamlico Sound beyond its long sandbars as part of the Pacific, so clearly he did not penetrate the Outer Banks. He liked Manhattan Island ("Angoulême", in honour of the queen mother), with its friendly Indians, and "a very wide river deep at the mouth." He stayed longest in Narragansett Bay (Refugio) and explored in the area of Pawtucket. But he approved of almost all he saw (excepting Maine, which was Terra Onde di Mala Gente, the Land of Bad People). He called the Carolinas "Arcadie." He too thought that he had seen "the happy shores of Cathay" (*quelli felici liti del Catay*). His ocean crossing took only two weeks, and he anchored at Dieppe on July 8, 1524. He was sure that he had found a new continent. But his king was preoccupied with his own proposed carve-up of Italy. (He was to be defeated at Pavia in 1525). North American affairs were left entirely in private hands. And Verrazano, on a third voyage, this time in the West Indies, for once went ashore – unfortunately to meet the Caribs, who killed and ate him. In Ramusio's words, it was "a miserable end for a valiant gentleman."

Ten years later, Jacques Cartier followed. As a St Malo man himself, he knew the talk of the fishermen, and their ways, exploiters not explorers, all too prompt to quarrel over harbours with the men of Bristol or Terceira in the Azores, and to trade on the side. St Malo was a privateering base, and looked out on the English Channel and the ocean. After his first voyage in 1534, in search of islands and other countries where there might be gold "and other riches," he dismissed Labrador (whose name, Portuguese for "husbandman", indicated that it had long been a Portuguese fishing settlement used by "part-timers" who called there in the summers): it was "the land God gave to Cain," the natives were "untamed and savage." The icebergs of frozen Labrador might "float spectral in the moonshine," but to a navigator they were menacing. He was

back, however, in six months, and on the second voyage he found
a "goodly great gulfe, full of islands, passages and entrances," which
narrowed "from 300 miles to above 20"; he followed it, to enter
the St Lawrence River (the name Mercator gave it in 1569), "the
great river of Hochelaga" to the Indians; and he followed it 100
miles upstream to the rapids that La Salle would later in irony call
the Lachine Falls — the name the sole legacy of the quest for Cathay
by this route. Cartier heard from friendly Hurons that there were
other falls beyond them. He wintered in Quebec (1535–6). On his
journeys upsteam, he heard of two other Indian kingdoms, that of
Saguenay, based on the river of that name, and that of Canada,
the country around Stadacona, to-days Quebec. It was to find the
treasures that he was told lay in abundance in Saguenay that the
king authorized his third voyage in 1541.

In fact he owed his final opportunity to the Huron chief whom —
along with nine of his tribe — he had brought back as captives, or
as booty, or as evidence of the success of his mission. He promised
them that they would all return; none of them did. The chief was
baptized as a Christian and presented at Court, where he confirmed
the tales of the untold wealth of Saguenay — either from his own
ignorance, or from a wish to flatter his hosts/captors. Whether or
not the stories he told were but "tall tales to fool the French," Francis
believed him, for was he not a Christian who had testified to their
truth under oath? To the king, this was to be the promised land,
the Peru of France in the Laurentian wilderness. To it a colony
would go: of carpenters and blacksmiths, farmers and vine-dressers,
doctors and priests; they would have seeds and domestic animals,
and musketeers to protect them; if numbers were not forthcoming,
50 convicts would be sent. This was now overt colonization, and
no longer exploration; the lieutenant-general and governor of New
France would be Jean-François de la Roque, sieur de Roberval, a
Protestant soldier/adventurer who had never been to sea. When
Cartier set sail — without his Indians, all of whom were by that
time dead, except for a ten-year-old girl on whom history is silent —
Roberval's ships were not ready; few volunteers came forward as
colonists, and when the future governor did sail he interrupted his
tranatlantic crossing to indulge in privateering on his own and his
crew's account, at Portuguese and Spanish expense.

Cartier's last voyage, like that of Colombus, was thus anticlimax.
His men died of scurvy. The Hurons were now hostile. He and
Roberval did not meet until Cartier was returning home, and he dis-
obeyed his superior's orders in returning anyway. The Canadian
winter defeated each of them. And the reports on the diamonds he

had found revealed that they were iron pyrites; "les diamants de Canada" became the Laurentian equivalent for "fools gold." Francis I died in 1547 and with him the dream of Saguenay; Cartier died a decade later, of an epidemic in St Malo; and Roberval was killed on leaving a Protestant service in a religious riot in Paris in 1561. For France, the next 30 years were of religious and civil turmoil, the "wars of religion." Although its major statesman, Gaspard de Coligny tried to establish French colonies on the coast of Brazil in 1555, and on the St John River in Florida in 1562, they were destroyed by the Portuguese and the Spaniards. Coligny was himself murdered in 1572 in the Massacre of St Bartholomew.

Nevertheless, Cartier was a founder of New France. Both as master and pilot of his ship, he had made three voyages and lost, not afloat but ashore, only 30 of his men, mainly from scurvy. He discovered and used 50 harbours – and every halt meant sounding and anchoring; and he mapped accurately the Great Gulf and the estuary of the Great River. He had failed to find the sea route to Cathay, because – as he established, at least to his own satisfaction – it did not exist. He had failed to find the mineral wealth to match that of Pizarro, who a decade ahead of him sent back to Spain as his first loot 13,000 pounds of gold and 26,000 pounds of silver. He failed to convert many pagans – but that instruction had not been high in his, or Francis's, priorities. But if fish and furs did not seem as good as gold, they existed in such profusion that there were enough for natives and invaders alike, and they were not the source of war and vendetta that marked the story of New Spain. There were no mines and no pearl-beds to lead to the enslavement of the Hurons, and – though with exceptions – French-Indian relations were happier and more intimate than those of other European invaders. Moreover, the French ports on the great river of his discovery, on the Lakes beyond it, and in due course on the other great river, the Mississippi – Father of Waters – beyond them, allowed the French to penetrate the continent, and to build thereby an inland not an insular empire. Cartier had made explicit what Francis I had claimed in 1533 to Clement VII: that a monopoly of trade in any area did not depend on papal decree, but could be maintained only by permanent occupation of territory; wherever there were no fixed European establishments, trade must be open to all. Sovereignty was a recognition of occupation, not of a papal bull. The notion, though not the realization of a French colony in North America was born with Cartier.

French exploration of North America, and in particular of the St Lawrence River, was intermittent. It was in essence suspended during the eight civil and religious wars or "the wars of the Three

Henrys", from 1562 until the accession of the Protestant Henry of Navarre (Henri Quatre, the first Bourbon king) in 1589 (who as part of the settlement became a Catholic — "Paris," he is said to have said, "is worth a Mass.").

His conversion ended the war with Spain: the Treaty of Vervins concluded in 1598 ended France's Reformation wars; and weakened the nobility, to whom the religious struggle had often been only a cover for faction-fighting and land-grabbing — as in pre-Tudor England. The Edict of Nantes (1598) gave religious toleration, full civil rights and political recognition to the Huguenots, who were for eight years to have exclusive control of their urban enclaves in the South and West, notably Nîmes, Montauban and La Rochelle. When Henry IV was struck down in 1610 by Ravaillac's dagger, however, the civil struggles resumed intermittently, until 1628, when the Catholic party, now led by Cardinal Richelieu, minister of state to Louis XIII, captured La Rochelle and destroyed Montauban, the last refuge of Huguenot independence. In all, the Huguenots' losses had probably reached 1 million (some 20,000 of them in 1572 in the Massacre of St Bartholomew and the local massacres that followed it.) Although they retained their right to worship, under Richelieu the Huguenot *imperia in imperio* were destroyed, and with them went the castles of Languedoc and the Cevennes. The 200 fortified towns granted them in 1598 were an obvious challenge. As a result, some Huguenots had attempted settlements on the Florida and Carolina coasts, but none survived Spanish attack. Catholic France, unlike England, did not encourage its heretics to migrate — to its permanent loss. But its quest for uniformity and for centralization and its numbers — made France a formidable European power.

Henry IV, moreover, shared all the Huguenots' colonial enthusiasm. In 1598 he re-confirmed the Breton nobleman Mesgouez de La Roche as governor and the king's lieutenant-general of all the lands in North America claimed by France: Canada, Hochelaga (Montréal), Newfoundland, Labrador, the Gulf of St Lawrence and Acadia; he could build forts, make laws, and grant lands; and — to the horror of French fishermen — he was given a trade monopoly. For settlers, he raided the gaols and took 200 men and 50 women. He chose to establish his base on Sable Island, a sandy waste 90 miles off the coast of Nova Scotia, isolated and storm-swept. In 1603 the 11 survivors were repatriated to France. A base at Tadoussac, where the Saguenay joins the St Lawrence from the north, was similarly short-lived: of the 16 who wintered there in 1600, only 5 were still alive in the spring. But the peace with Spain, the financial reforms of Sully, and the evidence that the Dutch and the English were moving in on Spain's outlying bases, led to a clear French policy for expansion *d'outre-mer*. In 1603 one of Henri's staff, M. de Monts, was given a license to settle in the lands between 40° and 46° N, on both sides of the St Lawrence, and as far inland as possible. His powers were seigneurial, and he was to have a 10-year monopoly of the fur trade.

The French empire in North America was thus from the start less insular and coastal than inland. It avoided the south, where Spain was too strong. It avoided Newfoundland and the Banks, where English and other fishing fleets were frequent visitors. And inland there might be a way to Cathay, or even gold; and there certainly were natives for conversion – and furs.

The agent of France was the explorer and cartographer Samuel de Champlain (1567–1635): a devout man, with the unyielding curiosity of the born explorer, and – like all of these founding figures – a dedicated record-keeper and note-taker. The French owed most to the labours of de Champlain. In 1599 and 1600 he had visited the West Indies and Mexico, and knew of Spanish explorations inland; he proposed a canal across the isthmus of Panama, and his accounts excited Henry IV. On arriving, in northern waters he learned from the Indians of the great "gulf of this our sea which overflows in the north into the midst of the continent" (Hudson Bay), and of the traditional route from the St Lawrence to the river which "leads down to the coast" (Hudson River). Like Hudson, Champlain searched for a water route between the Pacific and the Atlantic, but with one crucial difference. Champlain did not think in terms of circumnavigation (he wished to avoid the "inconvenience of the northern icebergs") and devoted his energies to finding the network of lakes and navigable rivers which would unite the oceans. Champlain concentrated upon the coasts, bays and rivers of "Acadia" (New Jersey to Nova Scotia) so as to bypass the ice and rapids of the St Lawrence and reach "the great lake" (Lake Huron), which he decided must be the "South Sea."

For one who, like Columbus, had no standing except his own skill, his courage, his experience and his physical strength and survival power, Champlain's was a remarkable career. He made the first of his 11 voyages to Canada 1603, sponsored by Rouen merchants and commenced that triple role of explorer, fur trader and in the end colonizer, which was to continue until his death as governor in 1635. His first voyage resulted in the founding of Port Royal (now Annapolis), Nova Scotia. Its existence was perilous, especially after the assassination of Henry IV in 1610; and it was destroyed in 1613 when discovered by an English force led by Samuel Argall of

Virginia, probing the northern coasts on the 14-gun HMS *Treasurer*. Each group claimed that *its* charter gave it a right to be there. In 1608 Champlain built a fort on the rocky promontory of Quebec, so named from the Algonquian "Kebec," "where the river narrows; his own name for it was "L'Habitation," for that was what it was — a stockade on a safe perch, with a store at the bottom of the cliffs known as Place Royale. In 1611 he established a trading post at Montreal. Setting out with an Indian war party in the following spring, Champlain discovered the lake which bears his name; and on this same expedition he helped his Huron and Algonquin companions disperse a band of Iroquois, thus incurring for the French the undying hatred of one of the most powerful of Indian groups, controlling the Hudson Valley and New York.

In 1614 missionary work was inaugurated, and Recollet priests (a branch of the Franciscans, and mendicants) came out. For the first 10 years there were never more than four Recollets in New France. From 1625 came Jesuits: the opposition of the Huguenot traders and shippers to them re-activated anti-Huguenot sentiments in Paris. Jesuits pushed into the interior, some of them, like Le Caron, among the Hurons, as much pioneering explorers as Champlain. By 1641 they were as far west as Sault St Marie, among the Algonquins. Significant for the future were rivalry with Britain over Acadia; with the Dutch for furs in the Upper Hudson River Valley (Henry Hudson sailed up his river in 1609 and Fort Nassau was founded five years later); and the near-permanent alliance with the Algonquin and the Huron (themselves an Iroquoian people) against the Mohawks, a member of the Five Nations Iroquois Confederacy that dominated the lands south of Lake Ontario. The rivalry and at times the conflict between the economies of two river systems, the St Lawrence and the Hudson, would later mark North American history. Champlain, however, sought trade with all the tribes.

Etienne Brule, one of Champlain's lieutenants, travelled south in 1615 to move from Lake Ontario down the Susquehanna as far as Chesapeake Bay. This great western arc, from the St Lawrence and the Lakes to, later the Mississippi, became France's major area of penetration, as rich in its strategic possibilities as in its furs and beaver pelts. Nor was his career that of explorer and planner only. In 1628, when he was 62, he was sailing with 400 colonists and provisions to Quebec, when the privateering trio the brothers Kirke struck a blow of long-term significance. In 1628 they captured the French expedition in the Gulf of St Lawrence and went on to seize both Quebec and Port Royal. Sir William Alexander, who had never been able to do anything with his grant of Nova Scotia, promptly asserted his right to the area which the Kirkes' boldness had opened up. An Anglo-Scottish consortium was founded when he did a deal with some London merchants and in 1629 settlers were landed at Port Royal and in "New Galloway" (Cape Breton Island). Charles I encouraged Alexander to export Gaelic Highlanders there – 'deburdening ... our kingdome of that race of people which in former times hade bred soe many troubles ther ..."

If the Kirkes' coup seemed all undone first by the weather – 30 of the colonists in Port Royal were dead within a year – and then by Charles I's readiness (Treaty of St Germain, 1632) to abandon his subjects' conquests in order to secure the payment of his wife's dowry from France, in fact, the Kirkes had done permanent damage. Champlain, a prisoner for three years, did not return to Canada until 1633. With the Company almost ruined and the French Crown unable to give further help, the Society of Jesus became Quebec's most effective supporter, attracting funds which helped its members build up the colony. They were not much interested in farmers, and saw their task as living with the Indians – more specifically with the Hurons, who were the middlemen in the growing commerce in pelts, and whose conversion would send them to France. The fur trade and true religion marched together as the Jesuits (founders of Montreal as a missionary centre in 1643) aimed to maintain New France as what one of them called "a holy and sacred temple built by God." Champlain, who died three years after his return, was perhaps the greatest inland explorer of modern times; with idealist views of empire, he was planner of the fur trade and a superb diplomat among the Indians. He too drew his own maps, sketched animals, flowers and Indian costume.

Behind Champlain – but only in his last years, and 3,000 miles away – was a statesman with the vigour of Henry IV – but an ascetic, whereas the king had been a voluptuary: cardinal and minister of state Richelieu. He set up the Company of New France for the St Lawrence area (familiarly, the Company of a Hundred Associates, nobles, clergy and merchants providing capital) and the Company of the Isles of America for the West Indies. His objective was a large-scale settlement of 4,000 habitants in the St Lawrence Valley by 1642, and under his special patronage the Company became in essence a seigneur for New France, giving land grants, and enjoying a monopoly of all trade except fishing.

In the Caribbean, Guadeloupe, Martinique, Dominica and some of the lesser Antilles were occupied, Caribs were driven out (to Granada and St Vincent), and in 1639 sugar was introduced from Brazil as a staple crop alongside tobacco, cotton and indigo. Sugar required slave labour – 200 slaves were needed to produce 150 tons of sugar a year; and soon slaves became the chief import to the islands.

When the "Father of New France" passed from the scene, the French empire in America still consisted of but a handful of fishing and fur trading posts. Unlike its rivals, Spain and England, whose empires were the results of command of the seas and mastery of sea routes, the French went inland, to the Great Lakes, and the head-waters of yet another river system, the Missouri-Mississippi, and to the river routes north through the forests and muskeg, to Hudson Bay. Moreover, the furs from the colder north were superior in quality; and from the forests of white birch could be made the best canoes. Settlement *d' outre mer* was with them implicit almost from the start.

The generation of Champlain and Richelieu gave permanent shape to New France It had taken over 30 years to establish tiny bases that could (just) survive the winters – and they were still dependent, and would so remain, on the river and the supply ships from home. In 1627 Virginia had 2,000 settlers, New England 301, New Nether-land 200, New France 107. There was now, however, a seigneurial system, though with few seigneurs; a commodity, furs and pelts, that ensured trading profits, if the traders did not fight each other; re-liable native allies, in Huron and Algonquin; and a devoted mis-sionary arm, the Jesuits, stronger than that of any other European Empire. There were also some permanent enemies: the Atlantic, which too often the English controlled; internal rivalries and weak central government in Paris; the Iroquois of the Five Nations; and – inter-mittently, locked in their own world – the Puritans in Massachusetts, who at times erupted. In 1655, at a time of Anglo-French peace, the Bostonians with 500 men attacked Port Royal, and the trading posts on the St John River and the Penobscot. The French traders were removed, while the surrender terms allowed the 500 French settlers to remain on their land and enjoy freedom of worship; the Bostonians none the less pillaged the church, killed the Capuchin father superior, and burned both fort and church. Sir William Phips would try again a few years later. Puritanism, and the merchants behind it, bred a foreign policy all its own.

With Louis XIV came a new and sustained vigor, and a true successor to Richelieu: Colbert, an avowed mercantilist. The in-efficient monopoly companies were replaced by direct royal control, under a trio: governor, bishop and intendant. Given the confusion and murder rate of sixteenth- and seventeenth-century France, auto-cracy was progressive, unifying and enlightened. It rested on cen-tralization and on Paris. And Louis XIV sought to bring the same force to France *d'outre-mer*.

In 1665 a regiment of 1200 men was sent to discipline the Iroquois, the first French regulars to serve. They built roads and forts, and destroyed Iroquois villages. The officers were induced to become colonists and given seigneuries (lordships) along the St Lawrence from Quebec to Montreal; wives were sent out from France, bounties were offered for the birth of children. Under this effective if artificial stimulus, the population rose from 3400 to 6000 in less than a decade (1666–75). Intendants to enforce the law and direct the economy came out also – notably Jean Talon (1665–72). To the French the river was the artery of empire. To it came clothes and food. Down it went the furs that were the major export. And to it as fur traders and fishermen came also the Hurons, the most settled of the Indian tribes. And on its island, where the St Lawrence and Ottawa waters met, Ville Marie, or Montreal, was established as now avowedly a mission station, with troops in support. But French Canada paid a price for its dependence on the river. Each seigneur, who was required to bring settlers from France, had a frontage on the river, and a grant of land running back, sometimes miles deep. The grants varied from a 1,000 square miles to a few acres; and though the seigneur and his settlers rendered *foi et hommage*, he did so to the Company, not the Crown; neither he nor his feoffees bought the land nor paid rent; they paid only nominal feudal dues, *cens et rente, lods et vente*. With each generation, they were split into smaller, narrower patterns, all clinging carefully to a – sometimes minute – river frontage. And as they ran back from the river, which France was careful to control, they were increasingly vulnerable to attack from hostile tribes. Settlers were, or had to become, militia men or irregulars in a all-but-constant and savage war. From 1633 to 1700 French Canada had less than 15 years of peace.

For a generation, the largest single landowner in New France was the Church. So much an *imperium in imperio* did it become that in 1663, when Louis XIV took over the colony, the acquisition of land by the Church was discouraged, and in 1743 it was forbidden altogether. Given the donations that reached it from metropolitan France for its role as missionary, it was also very rich. Its annual account of its work, in the Jesuit *Relations*, was at once historical record and begging-letter-to-*alumni*. Moreover, the settlers who came out were far more carefully chosen than in its rival empires, even if, there as in New England, the stocks were in use for blasphemy, drunkenness and failure to attend Mass. In 1635, a year before Harvard, it established a college. And, at least in form, the Indian converts to the Faith became in name French subjects, with full civil rights. Over the years considerable intermarriage took place; on the frontier, lifestyles were Indian rather than French. But the lack of wealth and of numbers on the French St Lawrence prevented any true assimilation of Indian society, which was in itself far more complex than the settlers realized.

This was a vast colony, unlike the English coastal footholds: it was as thoroughly religious in structure as, if less intense than, New England; but it was feudal in form and law, and dependent on its always vulnerable Atlantic line of communication for its survival. However much at risk, the river and the sea linked the settlements with France. So did the Faith, which, in its liturgy and the consolation of confession, was that of the Old Country. New France did not feel abandoned by, or distinct from, the Old; and there was little of the soul-searching that marked the Puritan experiments.

2

The First English Settlements: Cities on Hills and Seashores

Spain may be seen as the first to settle on North American soil; unsuccessfully in the Luna expedition, destroyed by storms off Pensacola in 1559; in Angel de Villafane's short-lived colony on the Carolina coast, abandoned in 1561; and then with success in the St Augustine settlement of 1565; and from 1612, with a screen of mission stations in the interior, clearly foretelling wider territorial domination. The three major French expeditions of the years 1562 to 1565, when the French Huguenots, led by René de Laudonnière, established Fort Caroline at the mouth of the St John's River, would have created a zone of French occupation on the southeast coast between the St John's and Port Royal Sound; instead, their expulsion by Pedro Menendez de Avila led to permanent Spanish occupation of approximately the same coastal strip (with occasional extensions to north and south), and so produced the first enduring European colony in North America. Spanish control there would not be challenged until 1702 (by the English under John Moore from South Carolina) and 1740 (by James Oglethorpe in Georgia). The French again began thinking of colonies from about 1580 onward, but no major experiments are known to have been made by them until after 1597, with the Protestant Henry IV on the throne in Paris. Those that were made in the period 1598 to 1607 (Sable Island, Tadoussac, St Croix and Port Royal) were inconclusive. English projects for commercial settlements in the northeast (Magdalen Islands, Elizabeth Islands, Georges River) also came to nothing before 1607, as had Roanoke.

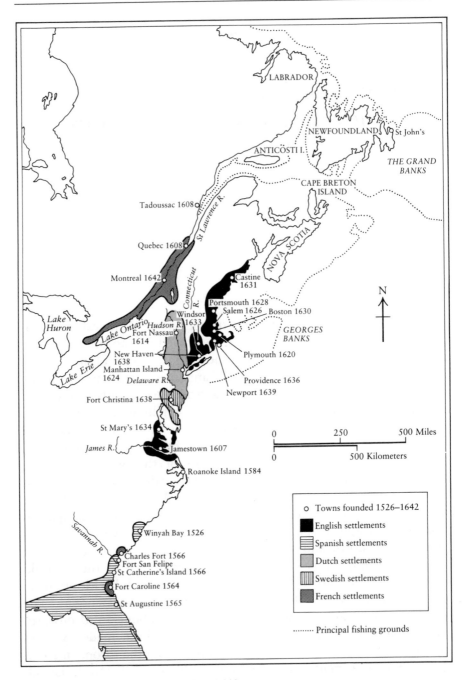

Map 6   European settlements 1526–1642.

1 NEWFOUNDLAND

The century of reconnaissance (from Columbus's landing on St Salvador in 1492 and Cabot's discovery of his "new founde land" in the area of Cape Breton, both distant from the future independent and united states until the death of Elizabeth in 1603), was followed by a century of colonization. The transition from reconnaissance to settlement was, however, taking place from the start, and was almost imperceptible. It began in one sense in Newfoundland, when summer fishermen needed shore-bases for the flakes on which to dry their catches; and what was temporary gradually became permanent. The captain of the first ship on the Banks acted as Admiral for the summer, and to all comers. This was not sovereignty, just convenience. So it was with Columbus's permanent settlements in the Caribbean: a harbour once charted, with its shoals and depths plumbed, became a safe and familiar anchorage. In turn, from Hispaniola mariners moved on to Cuba and Puerto Rico, to the Spanish Main and to Florida. From the start, Spanish exploration was at once imperial and colonial, a quest for gold and for the territory from which regular supplies might come. Spain had a constant resolution of plantation, said Michael Lok, the London merchant, and was building neither fortress nor mission station nor home, but something permanent of each. Cartier in discovering the St Lawrence had wintered at Quebec in 1535–6, and Roberval had planted colonists there (1541–2), who returned or perished. The idea of building far away from the closely guarded Spanish and Portuguese zones was new – and French. When their country was rent by civil war, those who were weaker in number but strong in spirit could seek a New World in which not to fight or to exploit but to live – as did the French Huguenots, abetted by Gaspard de Coligny. The first two settlements, at Rio de Janeiro and Charles Fort on the coast of South Carolina, failed – from Portuguese attack, or from mutiny and Spanish attack. Ralegh was no more successful at Roanoke Island.

Moreover, if "new found land" was vague, as the Cabots knew, so was "Virginia". When Ralegh used the name, in honour of the Virgin Queen, it applied to all North America not under the control of Spain or France, anywhere from Cape Fear to Passamaquoddy Bay. When Thomas Harriot wrote for Queen Elizabeth his *Brief and True Report* in 1582, it was a report of "the newfoundland of Virginia." When Spenser dedicated his *Faerie Queene* to the queen, he described her, *inter aliis*, as queen of Virginia. The term was seen by Hakluyt and Ralegh as synonymous with the unmapped and unknown New World, stretching from Cape Breton and Newfoundland in the north to Florida, already claimed by Spain, in the south. And – to the confusion of the drafters of its first constitution, the Articles of Confederation, in 1777 – it would run from sea to sea. In inception, the Old Dominion was vast indeed. But it was not an easy birth; and it came after at least six miscarriages.

Behind all the color of the Elizabethan adventuring, colonization and discovery had been stories as much of failure as of success. After the abandonment of the lost colony in 1590, later probings had been almost equally without result: the voyages of Captains Bartholomew Gosnold and Bartholomew Gilbert in the *Concord* in 1602 along the coast of Norumbega (New England) in what was seen as the Gilberts' hunting-grounds (and which led at least to the mapping of Cape Cod and Martha's Vineyard, and of Narragansett Bay – all seen as the northern part of Virginia);[1] the voyage of Samuel Mace to the Roanoke coast in the same year; Bartholomew Gilbert's failure in the Chesapeake in 1603, where he was killed by Indians; Martin Pring's voyage from Bristol in 1603, his probing of the Maine coast, and its summer encampment, probably near Plymouth; Geo Waymouth's probings in the *Archangell* in 1605, on behalf of Sir Thomas Arundell seeking a site for a Catholic settlement, and finding it at what is now St George's Island and Allen Island among the Penobscot Indians of Maine. The last was wrecked neither by Indian hostility nor by the cold, for they did not stay more than six weeks; it was the Gunpowder Plot of 1605 that drove Catholics in England into the shadows, or into service in Catholic regiments in the Low Countries. The Jamestown, Sagadahoc and Plymouth expeditions were but the last of many attempts at settlement.

It is thus not easy to draw a clear line between "discovery," "settlement" and "ownership," particularly in the islands, or in the lands nearest to the Grand Banks. Discovery of territory, usually followed by conquest of the native inhabitants, established at least a claim to ownership – or so Spain contended. Not so, replied England: only when the ruler of the discoverer-state then granted the right to colonize, and settlers stayed over a winter, did a claim to territory become effective. Until then there could be freedom of trade for all comers. The Spaniards refused to accept the English

---

[1] For these journeys see D. B. Quinn, *England and the Discovery of America 1481–1620* (London, Allen and Unwin, 1973), pp. 405–90; and Samuel Purchas, *Purchas, his Pilgrims* (1625; published for the Hakluyt Society by Maclehose of Glasgow in 20 vols, 1905–7), XVIII.324–35.

position on freedom of trade and so there continued "war beyond the line," that is the pope's line; buccaneers flying many flags stayed active on the Spanish Main. But however rich the illicit booty it acquired, England could not match the Spanish treasure fleets, nor challenge Spain in South America or openly in the West Indies.

In 1603, indeed, England had established only one colony: in that patch of the grey-green seas least challenged except by fishing fleets, which might be rivals in spirit but in practice were more often allied with one another against the common threats of storms and fogs, and the icebergs that swept down from the Arctic. Its wealth was hard to tap, and its source was invisible – the 40,000 square miles of the continental shelf where feed cod, mackerel, hake, halibut and bluefish. The richest shallows are the Grand Banks off Newfoundland; almost as valuable are those within sailing range of Nantucket. The banks run for some 300 miles southeast towards the central Atlantic, where they drop vertically to the deep. But it was to this, and to Cabot's discovery of what with deliberate imprecision he called his "new Founde land," that Henry VII's successors looked back (and no longer to Madoc the mythical Welshman) for known and recorded evidence on which to base the claim to have an English colony.[2] Newfoundland, then, like Bermuda in 1609, settled by shipwrecked settlers *en route* to Virginia, were part of what John Dee had called – more, then, as a vision than as sober description – "The British Empire." Until 1776, the island colonies of the North and Mid-Atlantic, including by that time Jamaica and its sugar, were as important to England as any mainland colonies – still non-existent in 1603. Whether island or mainland colonies, they came into existence for England's profit, not her glory, and this despite the Arctic cold. Frobisher had told of "the most boisterous Boreal blasts mixt with snow and haile, in the moneths of June and July" ... "great Isles of yce lying on the seas, like mountaines," in "fogge and hidious mist."[3] The Jesuits attributed the extreme cold of Canada to the "wild and primitive condition of the land" never warmed by the sun.

England's first colony, then, was based on cod and on commerce, not on strategy or territorial greed; its much-heralded "gold" had

---

[2] If Cabot did land at Bonavista in 1497, Gaspar Corte-Real discovered and named Conception Bay and Portugal Cove three years later, and was appointed Portuguese governor of Terra Nova.

[3] In Richard Hakluyt, *Principal Navigations, Voyages and Discoveries of the English Nation*, VII.208, 232.

been found to be but quartz. Cod, whale and the furs that contact with Eskimos might bring, seemed inadequate as booty contrasted with gold and silver. In fact they proved to be more constant, in great demand in England and Europe, and infinitely more regular in supply than the "precious" metals – and much less disastrous in the long term to the metropolitan power. "The Newfoundland trade was by far the greatest English enterprise in America up to 1630," says the chronicler of the island.[4] It owed its origin to the discovery not of explorers but of fishermen. Ashore, they set up drying stages and rough cabins; but, summers over, they sailed home, as did Bretons and Basques, Portuguese and men from the Azores. Bristol and the West Country would depend on its dry fish through centuries of winters. For some 70 years it had not been a monopoly, as Hakluyt records. Writing of 1578, there were, he says,

above a hundred sail of Spaniards that come to take cod, who make all wet and do dry it when they come home, besides twenty or thirty more that come from Biscay to kill whale for train [i.e. oil]. These be better appointed for shipping and furniture of munition than any nation saving the Englishmen, who commonly are lords of the harbours where they fish, and do use all strangers' help in fishing if need require, according to an old custom of the country, which thing they do willingly.

The English ships, though fewer in number, were better armed and fought, and the foreigners' submission to them was in return for "protection of them against rovers or other violent intruders, who do often put them from good harbour, etc."[5]

When Sir Humphrey Gilbert formally took possession of Newfoundland in 1583, in the voyage from which he would not return, he found 36 ships there, "over whom the English merchants that were and always be admirals by turns interchangeably ... for our English merchants command all there." Gilbert's plan was for an English proprietor of Newfoundland holding the coastline, and leasing out grounds in the harbours; he would of course favour English fishing crews. Its location would make it a supply base for those using the Northwest Passage, should it ever be found, or the St Lawrence estuary. The Catholic Sir George Peckham, Gilbert's chief "adventurer" (financial backer), who lost everything when the fleet was lost, in his *True Report of the Late Discoveries*, written before Gilbert's fate was known, was lyrical in his description. By

[4] D. W. Prowse, *A History of Newfoundland* (London, 1885), XIV.
[5] Hakluyt, *Principal Navigations*, V.343.

that time the geographical outline of the island had been established, even if its size (it is the tenth largest island in the world) and its mineral wealth had not. But Basques (hunting whale and walrus in the St Lawrence as well as cod), Bretons, Portuguese and Spanish ships were there. On the outbreak of war with Spain in 1585, 600 Spanish fishermen fishing the Banks were made prisoners; and after the Armada, Spanish fishing fleets ceased to go north. By 1603, the British fleets in these waters were well organized, even well insured. The first settlements on the coast were those of winter crews harboring, especially at St John's, to prepare flakes, stages, cellars for the spring fleets. They lived on hard biscuits and salt beef; even their beer froze; and almost all suffered from scurvy, and from drunkenness. However, despite this, the winter settlers did not always welcome more permanent invaders.

At the beginning of the reign of James VI (of Scotland) and I (of England), with fishermen from Brittany and the Basques and Biscayans from St Malo and St Jean de Luz congesting the Banks, a sustained movement began "to animate the English to plant in Newfoundland." The tract came from John Guy of Bristol, and it was with the merchant-princes of Bristol – the Guys and Colstons, Aldworths and Slanys – that Newfoundland remained involved. By 1609 there were 200 English ships in St John's, some of which ("the sack ships") traded direct to the Mediterranean, and then sailed to Bristol as the third leg of a triangular trade. But their role was never uncontested; West Country fishers, even the Welsh, claimed fishing rights of their own, and the French had settlements in Acadia (now Nova Scotia). Indeed, the French had a Jesuit mission further south, in Maine, but it was destroyed in 1613 by an expedition from Jamestown under Samuel Argall. It took more than a century after Cabot's voyages, but Newfoundland can claim to be the oldest permanent British colony on North American soil.[6] Its charter was sealed in 1610: the objective, to establish a colony.

In 1610 a patent was granted to "The Company of Adventurers and Planters of London and Bristol for the colony or plantation of Newfoundland in the southern and eastern parts." The names of a number of grandees were added to grace the document – the earl of Northampton, Sir Francis Bacon, Sir Lawrence Tanfield, Sir John

---

[6] Hakluyt, *Principal Navigations*, V.343 *et seq.*, VI *et seq.* By 1667 the Mediterranean products brought in to Bristol in exchange for Newfoundland fish accounted for £40,000 customs duty at the port. See also D. B. Quinn, *North America from Earliest Discovery to First Settlements: The Norse voyages to 1612* (New York, Harper and Row, 1977), pp. 347–429.

Doddridge; but the work was done by the Guys, Slanys, Aldworths and Colstons. John and Philip Guy, with their brother-in-law William Colston, went out in 1610: three small ships carrying 39 persons, including a few women and children. Their first instruction was to assemble the fishermen and assure them that there was no intent to deprive them of their rights in fishing. On that understanding the fishermen amicably supplied their wants. But Guy was careful to settle out of their way, in a secluded and defensible spot, Cupid's or Cupert's Cove, at the head of an inlet, where he proceeded to build a little fort, with stockade and battery, and to erect cottages, farm buildings, grist and saw-mills. Here they spent an exceptionally mild winter, "small brooks were not the whole winter frozen over so thick as that the ice could bear a dog to go over it, which I found by good proof," Guy wrote home; "for every morning I went to the brook which runneth by our house to wash." All that winter the colony remained in health. But with the spring, Guy as governor gave orders which the fishermen were to follow, and this at once aroused their hostility; they were accustomed to regard the isle as their own and to rule as they pleased. They promptly petitioned the king against the planters, and meanwhile attempted to destroy their mills.

The objective was colonization – but fishermen and pirates were the enemies. In the spring of 1612 Guy took over peasants and artisans, horses, cattle and poultry, and also an aggressively Protestant preacher, the Reverend Erasmus Stourton, who was later banished by Lord Baltimore for his troublesomeness. But for a century and more the land base had an uneasy existence, threatened by fisherfolk, French and Indians alike. As later with Jamestown, there was an abundant and lyrical promotion literature. Richard Eburne, a Somerset clergyman, in *A Plain Pathway to Plantations* (1624), speaks of a house "and one or two hundred acres of ground" for the questing: "Take and reckon that for your Country where you may best live and thrive." And Sir William Vaughan, with Welsh exuberance, stressed that "Ilanders should dwel in Ilands;" Newfoundland was "our Colchos where the Golden Fleece flourisheth on the backes of Neptune's sheepe continuall to be shorne." The climate, in fact, was still the enemy. The first Lord Baltimore, who had visited Newfoundland in 1627 and again in 1628–9, had been granted a large tract called Avalon, which he tried to colonize. He built a mansion at Ferryland, some 40 miles north of Cape Race. After some years he gave up his plans and founded Maryland in its place. He wrote the king:

Your Majesty may please to understand that I have fownd by too deare
bought experience which other men for their private interests always concealed from me, that from the middst of October to the middst of May
there is a sadd face of wynter upon all this land, both sea and land so
frozen for the greatest part of the tyme as they are not penetrable no plant
or vegetable thing appearing out of the earth untill it bee about the beginning of May, nor fish in the sea besides the ayre so intolerable cold as
it is hardly to be endured. Bye meanes whereof, and of much salt water,
my house hath beene an hospitall all this wynter, of 100 persons 50 sick
at a tyme, my self being one and nyne or ten of them dyed.[7]

In 1650, a century and a half after Cabot's discovery, there were
only some 350 families, or 2,000 individuals, on the island, in 15
tiny settlements along the eastern shore. Each summer's fishing fleets
brought a temporary population of several thousands, who sought
an exclusive use of harbors and as much of a monopoly as they could
enforce. The home government sought to satisfy both fishermen and
settlers, banning residence less than six miles from the shore. Fish
got precedence. Nor did France easily abandon her interest. In the
peace treaty of Utrecht in 1713, France was given the right to catch
and dry fish on the western and northern coasts of the island. The
settlers, nevertheless, grew steadily in numbers; by 1763 they were
8,000, with 5,000 more in summer. They got a civil governor in
1728. And in 1763 the coast of Labrador, from Hudson's Strait to
the river St John, opposite the western end of the island of Anticosti,
was attached to the governorship of Newfoundland. It had to wait
until the 20-year-long French Revolutionary wars for its boom-time,
with rival fishing fleets swept from the seas and European markets
greedy for fish, if blockades could be run. For Newfoundland as
for the new United States – and not for the first time – Europe's
discord and distress were the New World's opportunity. But it had
taken 300 years.

2 TRADING COMPANIES

The first permanent English settlement on the North American
mainland was planted by a trading company chartered by the Crown.
These joint-stock trading companies, composed of the big business-
men of the day, had grown up during the sixteenth century for the
purpose of carrying on commerce with various parts of the world.

[7] *Archives of Maryland* (Baltimore, 1885), vol. III, pp. 15–18.

They were ordinarily chartered by the government and given various privileges, including the monopoly of trade in some particular region. In return these companies were expected to protect the political interests of England and assume the expense of governing the colonies. The most famous of all of these companies was the East India Company, which controlled India for almost three centuries; also important were the Muscovy Company, the Eastland Company and the Levant Company. The most important for America was the London Company, which succeeded in establishing the first permanent English settlement in America. The joint-stock device allowed risks and costs – and of course profits – to be shared.

In 1606 James I granted the Virginia charter, which created two companies, one consisting of "certain Knights, Gentlemen, Merchants, and other Adventurers, of our city of London and elsewhere," and the other consisting of a similar group of stockholders centering in Bristol, Exeter and Plymouth. The first was known as the London Company, and the second as the Plymouth Company. Upon them the king bestowed most of the coast of the present United States: to the London Company the region between 34° and 38° north latitude (i.e. today's North Carolina and Virginia), and to the Plymouth, that between 41° and 45° (i.e. New England), with the region between 38° and 41° open to either, on condition that neither settled within 100 miles of the other. More important than the boundary lines was the clause which provided that the colonists "shall have and enjoy all Liberties, Franchises, and Immunities ... as if they had been abiding and born, within this our Realm of *England*," a guarantee that had already appeared in the Ralegh and Gilbert charters, and that provided a precedent for later English policy. The chartered companies became in effect feudal lords in their promised lands, which in all ran from the Cape Fear River to what is now Bangor, Maine. The stated purposes included religion and the proselytizing of Indians; the tacit hopes were to find bullion, to discover a route to the South Seas, to exploit the wine, olive oil and citrus that made England so dependent on the Mediterranean – and to make profits for the shareholders. Those going out did so as company employees. The king reserved the power to govern any colonies which might be set up under these charters to a royal council of Crown nominees in England. This was empowered to issue "Instructions" to each colony, and it alone made grants of land; and it did so without carrying any part of the costs. In Virginia, as in New England, there would be a local governing council, appointed in London, and the names of the members only being known when the sealed orders were opened after the first settlers stepped ashore in the New World. The Virginia

Plate 8   Sidney King, *The Marketplace at Jamestown.*
(Jamestown-Yorktown Education Trust.)

Company of 1606 was thus both more and less than a normal commercial company, and was threefold in character: royal, in that final authority lay with the Crown – with, that is, a royal council resident in London, and its officers royal appointees; proprietorial, in that economic organization and shareholding were matters for the Company's executive; and communist – with duties allocated by the council on the spot, and settlers "slaves" of the company. But conditions in Virginia were appalling, and there were no profits.

Under this authority the Plymouth Company unsuccessfully attempted colonization upon the Kennebec River in Maine, while the London Company sent their colonists farther south. On December 20, 1606, three little ships – the *Susan Constant*, the *Godspeed* and the *Discovery* – carrying 144 men and boys set off from Blackwall on the River Thames for Chesapeake Bay, led by Captain Christopher Newport. Almost half of them were "gentlemen." They began to build a settlement on a peninsula in the James River, easily defensible against Indians, and being 50 miles upriver from the sea, immune (they hoped) from discovery by prowling Spanish ships. The early years of the Jamestown settlement were years of incredible hardships. Many of the newcomers were listed as "gentlemen," some were townsmen, and none were accustomed to manual labor. The site of the settlement proved to be a marshy and malarial region, which doomed many of the settlers to sickness and death. It was impossible to bring sufficient food from England to support life, and the colonists were inadequate to the task of living on the country. Few knew how to hunt or fish. In 1608 fort and storehouse burned

C Smith taketh the King of Pamavnkee prisoner 1608

Plate 9 John Smith captures the king of the Pamaunkees, 1608.
(The Mansell Collection, London.)

down. They were, likewise, unfortunate in their relations with the Indians, and encountered an erratic but unyielding hostility. Of the 105 survivors who went ashore in May 1607, after a harrowing journey by way of the Canaries and the West Indies, only 53 were alive in April of 1608. "Such famine and sickness," said Captain

John Smith, "that the living were scarce able to bury the dead." The bickering among the ineffective leaders led to a decision to abandon the experiment – as the Plymouth Company similarly abandoned Sagadahoc on the Kennebec River after a hard winter and Indian hostility. In January 1608 Captain Newport brought "the first supply" (120 new settlers); but of these, only a dozen were laborers, and the assortment of artisans were intended to refine the gold that was still the goal of the London planners; few were husbandmen – and all had mouths to feed. Hard on them (September 1608) came the "second supply," 70 more, including 2 women. From these difficulties Captain John Smith, aged 26, emerged as the strong man, who would try to induce a sense of order, and among other things, go out and buy maize from the Indians. On one such mission towards the end of the year he was captured. He talked his way out of possible execution, and was, he said later, rescued by the well-timed intervention of Pocahontas, daughter of the Indian ruler, Powhatan; at least he laid foundations for some regular dealings with Powhatan, who seems to have controlled some six Indian "towns," an empire of some 8–9,000 people. He traded with the Indians, and became the most experienced (or indeed the only?) negotiator; he taught the survivors to learn from the Indians, and to work; and he explored to the west and north. Later, to legalize England's claim to ownership of the land, and to make him subject to English rule, Powhatan was solemnly crowned as a vassal of King James. Powhatan, an arch-realist who could have replied that he was already a king of kings as chief *werowance* of his confederacy, refused to be a little king; but he did exchange a mantle and an old pair of shoes for Newport's coronet.

The colonists were the Company's servants, eating at its expense, and so had to work to live. They grew maize and vegetables for themselves, experimented with European crops and tried to produce, economically, potash for soap, glass and iron. Smith explored Chesapeake Bay, buying corn and furs, and finding the Potomac River. With Cathay and the dreams of gold and silver still potent, they explored the James River upstream as far as the falls. But "gentlemen" were inadequate in this thickly forested but potentially fertile wilderness. When the Company, properly preoccupied with balance sheets, asked for evidence of success, particularly in lumps of gold, Smith replied:

When you send againe I entreat you rather send but 30 carpenters, husbandmen, gardeners, fishermen, blacksmiths, masons and diggers up of trees, roots, well provided, than a thousand of such as we have: for except

wee be able both to lodge them and feed them, the most will consume
with want of necessaries before they can be made good for anything.

Drake, when taking the *Golden Hind* through the Straits of Magellan, had made the same point: "I must have the gentleman to haul
and draw with the mariner, and the mariner with the gentleman."

3 VIRGINIA

In 1609, devoid of profits altogether, the company was entirely
reorganized. In that year the king granted a new charter which
conferred upon the London company (now known as the Virginia
Company) the direct management of affairs in the colony.[8] The
Company in effect itself decided on a dictatorship at each end of
the line. In Virginia, the council was abolished and replaced by a
lord governor and captain general: one-man rule. In London, the
Royal Council ceased to function, the gloss of titled nobility no
longer needed as evidence of status; the company's officers (still in
form and at first Crown appointees) were given direct management
of affairs in the colony, and had a new title: "The Treasurer and
Company of Adventurers and Planters of the City of London for
the First Colony in Virginia." The company became in effect the
proprietor of the province of Virginia, and its treasurer became the
chief executive. That treasurer was Sir Thomas Smythe, an official
also of the East India Company. Under his leadership, new sub-
scribers to stock were recruited, prominent among them the City
Livery Companies and those who had subscribed to the "twin"
company, the Plymouth Company, now abandoned as a failure (to
be reconstituted in 1620 as the council for New England). In the
end the shareholders in the London Virginia Company were 659
individuals and 56 London merchant companies, and £18,000 was
raised with which to send out more settlers.

In the summer of 1609, as one of the regular annual relief voyages, Sir Thomas Gates and Sir George Somers sailed from home
with 500 settlers. However, they and their flagship, the *Sea Venture*,
were shipwrecked on Bermuda, notorious for its rocks, shoals and

---

[8] The charter of 1606 had granted land 100 miles inland. The new charter of
1609 granted the region from a point 200 miles north of Point Comfort to a
point 200 miles south, "up into the land throughout from Sea to Sea, West and
Northwest."

hurricanes. The arrival, feeding and dispersal of the 400 survivors of the original nine ships that had left England, and without their leaders, was in fact an appalling burden for Jamestown's tiny "colony," then only of 80 people. Among them were servants, who had agreed to work for the company for seven years in return for their passage. In seven years, in 1616, they would be freed; then profits would be divided up among the shareholders both in England and America, and every shareholder would receive at least 100 acres of land. Smith, now near the limit of his endurance, burnt himself in a gunpowder accident, and was persuaded to go home – persuaded to go by those who detested him, and they were many. When Gates at length arrived in July, he found a shambles – "the palisades torn down, the ports open, the gates from off the hinges, the empty houses rent up and burnt." They were surviving on oysters and game; the rats got the corn. Malaria, scurvy and sheer despair had gone close to destroying the colony completely; and the story of "the starving times," which were also quarrelling times and killing times, reveals that now legends give way to folklore, and are built on savage truths.

In June 1610, Gates took the decision to abandon Jamestown and to sail home by way of Newfoundland. They had reached Mulberry Island, 14 miles downriver, when they encountered a relief fleet under Lord De La Warr (a cousin of Sir Walter Ralegh), happily, with supplies as well as new settlers. So they turned back, and started again. And now they were aggressive. Powhatan demanded in 1610 that "either we should depart his country or confine ourselves to Jamestown only." The settlers responded by destroying Indian villages and by extending their trading net out to Indians beyond his reach, on the Potomac and elsewhere. Eventually Powhatan sought a rapprochement. The colony, he realized, had become stronger. After his daughter Pocahontas, who had earlier saved John Smith from execution (a yarn in no way weakened as legend by the awkward fact that when Pocahontas pled for Smith's life she was only twelve, a tomboy addicted to walking round stark naked among the settlers doing handstands and cartwheels), had been taken as a hostage, he made peace. Pocahontas sealed the bargain in 1612 by turning Christian and marrying an Englishman, John Rolfe. Then the Chicahominy Indians made peace, and thereafter received subsidies from the colony.

After the charters of 1606 and 1609, in 1612 came a third charter. The government of the company was then placed in the whole body of the shareholders assembled in a general court, which would meet four times a year and would elect an executive council and the treasurer, still effectively the chief executive. This was, in other words, a normal trading company charter, on recognizably modern lines, and would be the model for the charters that followed, notably that of Massachusetts Bay in 1629. It was even given permission – after much Christian soul-searching – to hold lotteries as a way of raising funds. Those who emigrated, now described as "planters," were held to hold shares by dint of their labor, and that of their wives and families if they had them. Every worker on the ground was now seen as a shareholder; all were promised maintenance, and at the end of seven years would receive 100 acres of land and a division of the company's assets in proportion to the shares held. All became participants in the enterprise. All worked for the company, in what had passed from being a royal venture to an overtly commercial, but communal, one; they lived in barracks and took orders; and now there was a strong man in charge at either end of a long line of communication.

This combination of communism plus dictatorship was meant to ensure that everyone would work, regardless of ability, and to each would go only the irreducible minimum, since any profits would still return to the Company in London. Until tobacco was exploited commercially, no one was satisfied; once profits came in, communism was no longer necessary – or welcome. But in 1612, John Rolfe discovered that tobacco grew well in Virginia. The Colony's most valuable export turned out to be, not the long-hunted-for gold and silver, the furs and timber of any Atlantic settlement, but what the king called "the stinking weed." By 1617 even the rough streets of Jamestown were planted with it. It proved to be the economic basis of the survival of the colony. John Rolfe's experiments with the high-quality Trinidad tobacco, the milder variety superior to the harsh "Virginian", in 1611–12 led to the first trial exports in 1614. They were well received and over the next few years tobacco, then selling for high prices in England, grew to be a substantial crop, some 19,000 lb reaching England in 1617, and nearly 50,000 lb the following year. This encouraged the expansion of the settled area, and provided an ideal home-grown crop for export.

Rolfe was in fact the first great entrepreneur in American history, and the first to use marriage as a tool of trade and diplomacy. And he rendered another service to Virginia. After wrestling with his Puritan conscience, and after instructing her in Christianity, he married Pocahontas, "for the sake of her soul and for the good of the colony," he said – presumably to enlist Powhatan's benevolence. Mrs Rolfe and her infant son, Thomas, accompanied her husband in 1616 to London, to be treated as a celebrity, to be very confused by all she saw, and, a year later, to catch smallpox and die while awaiting passage home. She is buried at Greenwich. She had been seen and presented at Court as a princess, and had in her retinue:

a Great Man of her own Nation, whose Name was Uttamaccomack. This Man had Orders from Powhatan, to count the People in England, and give him an Account of their Number. Now the Indians having no Letters among them, he at his going ashore provided a Stick, in which he was to make a Notch for every Man he see; but this Accomptant soon grew weary of that tedious Exercise, and threw his Stick away: And at his return, being asked by his King, How many People there were; He desired him to count the Stars in the Sky, the Leaves upon the Trees, and the Sand on the Seashore, for so many People (he said) were in England.

The extent of the "Virginia" that the company controlled was now itself extended to 200 miles north and south of Point Comfort on the Atlantic coast, running indefinitely west and northwest to the sea beyond the American continent, wherever its geographic location – a vague statement in 1612, full of contention in 1781. And the colony's responsibility was in effect extended east also, since it was assumed that its writ would run in the newly found Bermudas, 570 miles east of Cape Hatteras. For this, however, cash was short – plantations were also being established in Ireland, and they were likely to be more profitable; and in 1615 Bermuda got a charter of its own, as "the Company of the Plantation of the Somers Islands."

In 1618 participation went further: under "the greate Charter" of that year the Company authorized both the "headright" system (everyone who paid for a passage, his own or others, got a grant of 50 acres) and the setting up of a general assembly, with burgesses to be popularly elected. A commercial document thus became a constitutional charter – and would be the first of many. This was in large measure the result of a new treasurer in London, Sir Edwin Sandys, and the new governor (from April 1619), Sir George Yeardley. In July 1619 the assembly met in the "quire of the church" at Jamestown; it met again in 1621, 1624 and 1625, and was sanctioned by the king in 1628. It rarely failed to meet at least once a year over the following decades. This was the first democratically elected assembly in America, with two burgesses from each of its then 11 plantations. The first subject of contention, paradoxically for a wilderness, was on the setting up of a school, at Charles City Point, and a university in the city of Henrico, to be supported by the revenues from an iron foundry at Felling Creek. This first step towards democracy had in fact been preceded by continuous debates.

The objective rapidly became to end Company rule altogether, and with it the requirement of making profits for distant adventurers concerned only with balance sheets and dividends. As early as 1621 it faced a challenge; in that year the privy council required the Virginia Company to land all merchandise from Virginia in England, and to pay customs on it before sending it on for sale "in foreign parts" – a requirement renewed in the Navigation Acts of 1651 and 1660. In 1624, with or without the governor's threat of dissolution, the general assembly enacted, and repeatedly re-enacted, the prescription that "the Governor shall not lay any taxes or impositions upon the colony, their lands or commodities, other way than by the authority of the General Assembly to be levied and imployed as the said Assembly shall appoint." Within two decades of its foundation, Virginia's political as well as economic foundations were in place.

Profits disappeared, and the Company went bankrupt. It had been a costly exercise: in Plymouth, ten years later, the Pilgrim Father William Bradford calculated that it had cost 9,000 lives (9 out of 10 of those shipped) and some 100,000 to settle 1,200 people on the coast of Virginia. When men could survive, however – when they could work for themselves, or employ others to work for them – they no longer wanted to work for an anonymous, distant and quixotic master. In 1621 the king added to the Company's burden by withdrawing the right to raise money by holding lotteries, a practice it had followed since 1612. It also lost its tobacco contract: individual planters could make their own arrangements. The Indian attacks of 1622 cost it 400 seasoned lives; its London officials became quarrelsome. The charter was revoked in 1624, and Virginia became a royal colony. A council of trade exercised a very general supervision from London. In 1628 the new king, Charles I, recognized the house of burgesses.

The lesson was clear. To be successful a colony had to have an active population with intelligent and strong leadership, a constant inflow of new blood, a staple product of which the mother-country was in need, and the capacity for self-government. But once the export crop was found and available, the dependence on London for supplies ceased, and made possible the end of colonial status. The early history of Virginia illustrates the inadequacy of continuous direction by a chartered commercial company resident in England. It reveals also how a group of Englishmen in a new environment nevertheless reproduced the institutions with which they were familiar at home; they had their own minute House of Commons, and, from 1624 to the Revolution, they were – except for the short period of the Commonwealth — governed directly by the king, or by his vice-roy on the spot. But its staple crop, the scattered character of its plantations strung along the river, and the absence of towns, would give it its own character, and — along with Maryland — make the culture and economy of the Chesapeake unique.

Moreover, it was a more accurate example of the New World that was to come. It followed the mother-country in its land law and in the law of primogeniture, in its Anglican ecclesiastical organization and in its legislative chamber. It had to rid itself of little that was religious or proprietary to become an independent republic; its people were remarkably homogeneous, and it was little affected by foreign racial influences. But, more than any other colony, for its first two decades Virginia was almost totally dependent on London, looked there for infusions of people, for cattle, and for directions on policy. It would, more than any other colony, retain a close and involved relationship with London, Bristol and (later) Glasgow, with the City of London, and with the Inns of Court. And if Powhatan's "empire" suggested that the Indian tribes were orderly and organized, events would prove the reverse.

With an expanding market in England for tobacco, the settlers pressed the natives for more land on which to grow the crop. Other lands were being acquired greedily, simply as estates by the more wealthy and powerful colonists. As the native hunting-grounds, gardens and cleared village sites were taken by the whites, Indian anger grew. In addition, the increasing white population, much of which was composed of unruly elements from England, subjected individual Indians to indignities, harrassments and injustices. Finally, in 1622, the natives took a stand, determining, under the leadership of Powhatan's elderly half-brother, Opechancanough, to rid the country of the English. On Good Friday of that year, they fell suddenly on outlying English settlements, killing some 300 whites. A 20-year-long and ferociously conducted war ensued, during which Christianized Indians aided the whites. When hostilities finally ended in 1644, Opechancanough and thousands of the Indians were dead, and the Powhatan empire was smashed. Groups of survivors, dispossessed of their lands, were herded onto small reservations and promised protection in their holdings; the rest scattered to live with other tribes. The treaty of 1646 drew a line between Indian and white lands. After Bacon's rebellion came a second treaty, in 1677. By that time the white man was establishing himself in the piedmont, as well as tidewater, and all the Indian tribes had suffered by it.

About Jamestown, more than any of the other memorial parks that now dot the eastern seaboard of the US, there still remains an air of gloom, despite – or because of? – the skill and devotion of archaeologists to the excavations of the tumbled churchyard, with its broken stones for governors' ladies, clergymen and gentlemen alike; and despite, or because of its massive ivy-draped brick tower, probably that of a fourth church begun in 1639 – the church that Charles II proclaimed a cathedral – and its gnarled mulberry trees. Indeed, tourists behave here as in a church, aware that buried deep in the swampy ground is evidence that the first waves of incomers, and those who in trepidation watched them come ashore, included as many villains as heroes, and that only a superhuman effort by a handful ensured that the colony survived. Its buildings were twice destroyed by fire, and in 1676 by the rebels in Bacon's rebellion, to prevent its re-occupation by Governor Berkeley. In 1699 the capital was moved to Williamsburg. As with the sailors on the discoverers' ships, so with the landsmen in Virginia's tidal river valleys: they were prone to disease and starvation; the Virginians were erratically under Indian attack; only the case-hardened, who had built up immunity after recurring fevers and become acclimatized, held on. Now the prospects were of cheap and ample land grants within reach of many rivers, and of a crop that needed few middlemen to sell it. Every settler was entitled to 100 acres, and got as a "head right" 50 acres more for every person he brought over. Westward look, the land is bright.

4 NEW ENGLAND

The Plymouth Company (the Northern Virginia Company, as it was then called) was less fortunate than the Virginia Company in all its difficulties. Various private voyages had been made in the region then known as Norumbega (New England), and ships had returned with reports of the excellence of the fishing, and with cargoes of the drug sassafras, then the universal betany against any and all disease, including witchcraft and other dangerous thoughts. Clearly any colonization would be aided by the facilities available in St John's Newfoundland, England's fishing base for the Banks; indeed England's need to dry her catches ashore, because of her lack of salt – unlike the French and Portuguese who were mainly "wet" fishers, loading their catches directly into their holds and barrelling them with salt – had made her "lords of the harbours." Such primitive camps, however, were menaced by the proximity of the Breton fishing fleet, regularly exploiting "the Great Bay," the broad estuary of the St Lawrence. In 1602 the Devon sailor Bartholomew

Gosnold (1572–1607) had been so impressed by the abundance of fish he found south of a long sandy spit of land that he called it, unromantically, Cape Cod. His landing on May 15, 1602, at what is now New Bedford, Massachusetts (he had sailed on March 26 from Falmouth, England, in the *Concord*), is seen as the first landing by Englishmen in New England. His naming of Martha's Vineyard, off the coast, is at least more romantic. (In 1606, in The *God Speed*, Gosnold took a number of the first settlers to Jamestown, Virginia; he died there of malaria in 1607.)

To develop bases ashore called for more than private adventuring, even if it could secure royal backing. After James's accession to the throne, and the peace with Spain that he brought (the Treaty of London, 1604), a new instrument was needed; the joint-stock company. It became, in East and West, Britain's device for pooling merchants', and shareholders', risks. With it, and with the prospects of larger profits for larger risks, the age of the traders and of the colonizers began.

The Plymouth group consisted of the West Country families associated with Sir Humphrey Gilbert, and two men of importance who advocated emigration as a relief for the growth of crime and pauperism: Sir John Popham, the aged lord chief justice, and Sir Ferdinando Gorges, a well-known soldier. George Popham's the *Gift of God* (which sailed in May 1607) and Ralegh Gilbert's *Mary and John* (which sailed in June), with 100 settlers, only stayed long enough on what is now the Maine coast north of Monhegan (7 August), and then on the lower Kennebec River, to build a fort, Fort St George, with 12 guns, a church and a storehouse; the value of the furs they bought were offset by the hostility of the Indians, by the proximity of foreign fishing fleets off Newfoundland and of the French in the St Lawrence, and, worst of all, by the grim winter, and the rivers that disappeared below the ice; after Sir George's death in 1608, they gave up. They did bring back more accurate maps of the Maine coast than available before, but this part of the "Virginia" project was abandoned, like Roanoke 20 years before. In southern Virginia, as it was first called, the London Company would hold on – just.

The first incorporated city on the thickly forested uncharted continent was Agamentious, renamed in 1642 Georgeana in salute to Sir Ferdinando Gorges (1568–1647) Gorges was cast in the Ralegh mould, a *chevalier sans peur* who never saw his dream-world, but wanted a fiefdom overseas – not for Christian but for commercial motives. Unlike Ralegh, he was well-born: the family was one of the few with a well-authenticated history in France at the time of the Conquest, and came over from Normandy during the reign of Henry III. In its long history it produced 12 English and Irish members of Parliament, 2 admirals, 3 generals, 2 ambassadors, 3 governors, 2 knights of the Bath, 2 peers, 2 baronets and 27 other knights. Gorges had fought against the Spaniards in the Low Countries and in support of Henry of Navarre in France. At the age of 22 he was knighted by the earl of Essex at the siege of Rouen, and was afterwards arrested for involvement in the Essex plot. He escaped the block only because of the intercession of Helena, marchioness of Northampton. After his youthful military adventures abroad he was returned to Parliament as member for Cardigan, and two years later was captain of the fort at Plymouth and deputy lieutenant of Devon.

In 1606 Gorges and Lord Chief Justice Popham successfully petitioned for the Virginia charter, which created the London and Plymouth companies. A year previously, with the earl of Southampton and others, he had dispatched Captain Waymouth to the new world. Waymouth brought back five Red Indians, belonging to the Abenkis tribal confederacy, three of whom stayed in the Gorges household. Inspired by their descriptions of a green and empty land, Gorges and Popham sent two ships under Captain Challons to choose a suitable site for a colony. They were captured by the Spaniards, but, nothing daunted, the two adventurers sponsored another expedition, which settled at Sagadahoc on the estuary of the Kennebec River. This settlement was noteworthy primarily because the first English sermon in New England was preached there, by the Reverend Edward Seymour. A 20-ton ship, the *Virginia*, was also built, but in 1608 the settlement failed. Our hopes, Gorges said bluntly, "were frozen to death." In contrast, Jamestown survived – if only just. The Plymouth Company nevertheless sent several further fishing and trading expeditions across the Atlantic.

Gorges's influence was successful in procuring for members of the old company a revised charter, in which their territory was for the first time called New England. Its privileges were enlarged. The Company's territory was designated as lying between the 40th and 48th parallels, "through-out the mainland from sea to sea," or from the present Philadelphia to North California in the south, and from Newfoundland to Vancouver in the north. Gorges and his associate, Captain John Mason, obtained for themselves a grant of the lands lying between the Kennebec and the Merrimack Rivers. There were settlements at York, Wells, Saco, and Cape Porpoise. His efforts were unsuccessful, however, and the New England charter was surrendered. More company reorganization was attempted, but civil war at home intervened; in 1639 Gorges settled for the province of Maine. His appointment by Charles I as lord proprietor of Maine, with powers of life and death, was meaningless because he could not raise funds to colonize his domain. His 46 years of struggle had put 1,500 people on the coast of Maine. But in 1642, as an incorporated city, Georgeana had an elected mayor, aldermen, and councillors. Blessed by the Protectorate in England, the settlers looked south to the Puritan stronghold of Massachusetts Bay, and Georgeana became York. Eventually, Gorges' grandson Ferdinando Gorges (1630–1718) sold the vast tract to the Commonwealth of Massachusetts for a ridiculous sum; one authority says for £1,250, another for £1,770.

Gorges' career is usually seen as a failure. He died, an unreconstructed royalist, as the king's fortunes were in decline; he never saw New England, he lost four fortunes, and all his ventures failed. But the actual colonization of northern New England, like that of Ralegh in Virginia, owes much to him.

5 BERMUDA

The fascination of the "discovery" of Bermuda in 1609 – or more accurately of its "rediscovery", since it had been found in 1503 and named after Juan Bermudez, a native of Palos, who almost certainly knew Columbus – has been conveyed lyrically in Shakespeare's *The Tempest*, probably the most magical of all his plays. The *Sea Venture*, with Sir Thomas Gates of Devon, Sir George Somers of Dorset, William Strachey, secretary designate of Virginia, and captain of the fleet Christopher Newport aboard, was the flagship of Gates's relief fleet to Virginia in 1609. It met its first storm off the Azores, which scattered the fleet of (then) nine vessels, and then again "the most sharpe and cruell storme", that drove her on to the rocks that were notorious to all mariners as "the still-vexed Bermoothes." One hundred and fifty battered and hungry people got ashore. Sir George had spent three days and nights on the poop, desperately trying to keep the ship afloat and its bearing westward. They found a volcanic and empty island, 20 miles square, and one of some hundred islets, banks and shoals; being volcanic, and rising sheer out of the ocean, and never connected with any continental land-mass, this relict of Atlantis was rich in exotic flora and fauna, and the settlers found it "prodigious and enchanted." One of them, Silvanus Jourdain, was able to set his story down, and it was being sold on the streets of London within a year as *A Discovery of the Bermudas, otherwise called the Ile of Divels*, "by Roger Barnes in St Dunstanes in Fleet Street, under the Diall," as the tract proudly declares.

They stayed nine months, living well on fish and fruit in abundance, on wild hogs and turtles. To two of the castaways – John Rolfe and his wife Dorothea – a baby girl was born, christened Bermuda; but she died after a few months, as did Dorothea when she and her husband reached Jamestown nearly six months later. There were, Jourdain recorded, three mutinies, a murder, a wedding and another birth. And here too a hero emerged: 55-year-old Dorset squire Sir George Somers, "a man inured to extremities," a poor boy who had made a fortune as a buccaneer and bought an estate on it in Dorset, an estate he mortgaged to equip the *Sea Venture*, as was the practice. Somers led the travellers in building two ships, the *Patience*, from the timbers of the shipwrecked *Sea Venture*, and a pinnace, *The Deliverance*," with Cedar ... and with little or no yron worke at all." In them, and leaving two of their number behind, they rejoined the relief fleet (short of the tiniest, the pinnace *Chase*, which had gone down with all hands), reaching Jamestown on May 10, 1610. There they found a crisis equally as challenging; the colony's "starving time;" the decision was taken a month later to abandon the Chesapeake experiment. When this was reversed, with Lord De La Warr's timely arrival, Sir George returned to Bermuda on *Patience* to bring supplies from it, "for the better releefe and comfort of the people in Virginia." He died there on November 19, 1610. His nephew took his body, without its heart, home to Whitchurch Canonicorum in Dorset, leaving the heart in Bermuda. In 1612 Bermuda's own first settlers arrived, 60 in number. The Bermuda Company or Somers Island Company got its own royal charter in 1615, with the ubiquitous Sir Thomas Smythe as governor, and a year later it had 600 settlers – when Jamestown had only 350. The company managed the affairs of the islands until 1684, when the company was dissolved and Bermuda became a royal colony.

Jourdain's account was deposited with Richard Hakluyt; on the latter's death in 1616 all his papers were passed on to his protégé Samuel Purchas, who assumed his role of recorder of travels and travellers in the many volumes of *Hakluytus Posthumus* or *Purchas, his Pilgrims*. It has been called the *Odyssey* to Hakluyt's *Iliad*.[9] Among them is another account by another survivor, William Strachey,

---

[9] *Purchas, his Pilgrims*: see n. 1 above; Howard Mumford Jones, *O Strange New World: American culture, the formative years* (New York, Viking, 1964).

secretary to the governor designate of Virginia, Sir Thomas Gates — which may well have given Shakespeare his inspiration. The most readable account of the origins of what became the Bermuda colony is only part of the vast quantity of writing by its own local historian (though Isle of Wight born), the late Terry Tucker, notably in her *Bermuda Today and Yesterday* (London, Hale, 1975) and *Bermuda's Story* (Bermuda, The Island Press, 1976).

6 JOHN SMITH, JOHN ROLFE AND CHRISTOPHER NEWPORT

The survival of England's first mainland colony was due to the leadership, the energy and the loyalty of three men: John Smith, John Rolfe and Christopher Newport.

John Smith is usually seen as a boastful braggart, whose most striking quality was his skill in self-advertisement. It is a true charge: he was an adept at telling a tale, usually involving vainglory, or even romance — witness Pocahontas. However, behind the braggadoccio, and the patronage of Lord Willoughby and of the good and the great, was a grammar-school boy and an idealist, who fought with the Dutch against Spain, and with the Austrians against the Turks in Hungary. Smith had fought Turks in single combat, he said — he sported the impress of three Turks' heads on his shield — and, he claimed, had been a slave in Istanbul; at 26 Captain Smith had acquired the style of a junior officer, but the experience of people and places of a sergeant-major. The adventurer remained always, however, a scholar and recorder, much taken by the writings of Hakluyt and Harriot, and proud that Hakluyt's successor and protégé Samuel Purchas was his own good friend. Smith wove the writings of others, notably Hakluyt, James Rosier and the Reverend John Breneton's *Relation of the Discoveries* into his own tale, and called it *The Generall Historie of Virginia, New England and the Summer Isles* — the last the current name for Bermuda, or Sir George Somers' island. His was, in a sense, the first original colonial history; it was written in a simple terse and very personal style; and it recommended the ending of company rule ("The multiplicity of opinions here, and Officers there, makes such delaies by questions and formalitie, that as much time is spent in complement as in action ... send Souldiers and all sorts of labourers and necessaries") (vol. II, pp. 326–7). This, however, was not written until 1624; when it appeared, it went through six editions in eight years. A folio of 241 pages, with maps and portraits, it included commendatory verses by, among others, the poet (and his friend) John Donne. Smith tells here how Pocahontas saved his life – probably poetic license to capitalize on the glamour Pocahontas had then acquired in English society and on her early death: he was as skilled a raconteur as an historian.

Within a few months of reaching Jamestown, Smith had sent back by Captain Newport a long lively letter, published as a 44-page tract, without his knowledge or consent, and full of errors – his *The True Relation of such Occurrences and Accidents of Noate as hath Hapned in Virginia*; in 1612 came his *Map of Virginia*, in which he suggested how the settlers might profit from studying Indian agriculture, and tried to follow Harriot's account of the Algonquian Indians by similarly describing the Indians of the Chesapeake Bay region, their adjustment to their environment, their ingenuity and their savagery, and trying to interpret their languages.[10] A few months before his death, in 1631, came his *True Travels*. Indeed, had he not died, he would probably have done for New England what he did for Virginia; after exploring its coasts in 1614, charged to find gold and copper, he returned with a cargo of fish and furs – but no minerals – and wrote *A Description of New England* (1616), which term he was the first to use, and which he made fashionable. He wrote it while a prisoner of the French in 1614, having been captured one day's sail out of Plymouth. Smith's *Sea Grammar* (1627) is in essence a handbook for seamen, shipbuilders and promoters. His most valuable book, however, was his very last, *Advertisements for the Unexperienced Planters of New England, or Anywhere, or, the Pathway to Experience to Erect a Plantation* (1631), in which he stressed the importance of fish as a staple; for 60 years, he said, the Banks had bred the sailors and merchantmen of Holland, France and England. For him the conclusions were clear: for colonization as distinct from conquest, the answer was to exploit the native staple – cod, herring and ling in New England, corn in Virginia. It was no accident that, a year after his death, the Dorchester adventure should be planned: a land settlement in Massachusetts, but designed to exploit the Banks more directly than by undertaking the annual and hazardous voyages from Bristol or the Devon ports.

---

[10] Philip L. Barbour (ed.), *The complete Works of Captain John Smith* (1580–1631), 3 vols (Chapel Hill, NC, IEAHC, 1986), I.86–8; Karen Ordahl Kupperman (ed.), *Captain John Smith: A select edition of his writings* (Chapel Hill, NC, IEAHC, 1988), pp. 202; idem, *Settling with the Indians: The meeting of English and Indian cultures in North America, 1580–1640* (Totowa, NJ, Rowman and Littlefield, 1980), p. 105.

His *Description of New England* is a paean to fish, and to mercantilism. Consider, he says, what the Dutch have done with it.
They "labour in all weathers in the open sea" and so become "hardy
and industrious." Then they sell "this poor commodity" for "wood,
flax, pitch, tar, rosin, cordage, and such like" for their ships. What
is left over they trade again to the French, Spanish, Portuguese and
English, and thus:

> are made so mighty, strong and rich, as no state but Venice, of twice their
> magnitude, is so well furnished with so many fair cities, goodly towns,
> strong fortresses, ... as well of gold, silver, pearls, diamonds, precious
> stones, silks, velvets, and cloth of gold ... What voyages and discoveries,
> East and West, North and South, yea about the world make they? What
> an army by sea and land, have they long maintained in despite of one of
> the greatest princes of the world? And never could the Spaniard with all
> his mines of gold and silver pay his debts, his friends, & army, half so
> truly, as the Hollanders still have done by this contemptible trade of fish.

It was his experiences as soldier, however, not as scholar, that
he called on in order to save the struggling colony: the settlers must
learn from the Indians, and with them alongside as teachers; they
must cultivate the chiefs, but be ready also to overawe by force as
well as by display; they must acquire corn by barter, by ruse and by
force; and they must follow the rule that who would eat must work,
and with their uncalloused hands, whether they be gentlemen-rankers,
or just shirkers, or what he called "tuftaffety humorists." Smith was
explorer and hunter,

> who by his owne example, good words, and faire promises, set some
> to mow, others to binde thatch, some to build houses, others to thatch
> them, himself always bearing the greatest taske for his owne share, so
> that in short time, he provided most of them lodgings, neglecting any for
> himself.[11]

These efforts, he held, would have

> brought that Country to a great happinesse, had they not so much doated
> on their Tabacco, on whose fumish foundation there is small stability: there
> being so many good commodities besides, yet by it they have builded many
> pretty Villages, faire houses, and Chapels.[12]

---

[11] *Generall Historie*, II.244.
[12] *Advertisements*, III.295.

Despite Smith's distaste for its "fumish foundation", and for men grubbing in the ground "like swine" in its cultivation, Virginia's survival was due to tobacco. It had not found the gold and silver hoped for, and had neither the numbers nor the skills to exploit its timber. But tobacco could be raised easily, and with unskilled labor. It replaced the Spanish import, though experiment was required before it caught the sweet-scented flavor of the Caribbean types. Within a decade of the landing at Jamestown, however, John Rolfe's enterprise had made it the new settlement's principal export. To the satisfaction of mercantilists and royal treasurers as well as addicts, by 1618 some 50,000 pounds of tobacco were shipped to England; and in 1619 Virginia got a monopoly of the trade when the planting of tobacco was forbidden in England and Ireland. The land, moreover, seemed theirs for the taking.

Tobacco is one of the recurring themes in all the discoverers' reports on the New World. They noticed smoke inhalation as, apparently, part of Aztec religious ritual. When Columbus landed on San Salvador, the Arawaks offered him some dried leaves as a token of friendship; two of his crew, one of whom was Luis de Torres, the Jew with a knowledge of Oriental languages that would enable him to converse with the Great Khan of Cathay, subsequently saw natives of Cuba smoking leaves rolled up into the shape of a cigar with which "to scent themselves;" it seems to have been a monk, Ramon Pane, who accompanied Columbus on his second voyage in 1493, who brought back tobacco seeds to Spain. Both Amerigo Vespucci (in 1499?) and Fernandez de Oviedo in his history in 1526 report the inhalation of smoke by the natives, the latter calling the Y-shaped tube, the forked end of which was inserted in the nostrils, a *tabaco* (when in fact it was a *taboca*). Others have found its origin in the Mexican province of Tabasco. The Spaniards themselves introduced tobacco to Peru and Chile. In 1535 Jacques Cartier in Hochelaga (Montreal) noticed the habit among the Iroquois. John Florio of Magdalen College, Oxford, turned Cartier's account into English in 1580:

They suck so long that they fill their bodies full of smoke till that it cometh out of their mouth and nostrils even as out of a tunnel or chimney. They say that this doth keep them warm and in health. We ourselves have tried the same smoke and having put it in our mouths it seemed that they had filled it with pepper dust, it is so hot.

Tobacco was introduced to France by the Franciscan André Thevet, on returning to France from Brazil, in 1556, after failing to found a settlement there; he planted the seeds of what he called *petun* in his garden in Angoulême. And Jean Nicot, French ambassador at the Court of Portugal from 1559 to 1561, testified to its proven curative powers and sent seeds to Catherine de Medici, the queen mother, who was to become addicted to snuff. Thereafter the plant was known in France as *nicotiana*. It was grown in royal gardens in Madrid and Lisbon.

When Ralegh's captains Amadas and Barlowe returned from Roanoke in 1584, they brought back with them "two poore wilde barbarous" savages, who "drank tobacco" through clay pipes, and Drake brought a store of tobacco from Dominica back on his Virginia rescue mission in 1586. In 1571, however, writing in Latin, Pierre Pena and Matthias de l'Obel refer to it as growing in England and reaching the height of a man. Smoking became a social habit and fad among those who could afford it, and was associated with Ralegh's name. There was a market for it in England before Rolfe's importation into Virginia of *nicotiana tabacum* from Trinidad, and his ability thus to rival the Spanish weed with his own "sweet" product, against the coarse grain of northern Virginia, and Maryland's Oronoco. King James's *Counterblasts* were due as much to his dislike of Ralegh as to his own fastidiousness – he thought it a "vile, barbarous custom ... loathsome to the eye, hateful to the nose, harmful to the brain and dangerous to the lungs;" "No successful colony could be built upon smoke." He put a severe duty on it, which deferred its use, but greatly stimulated smuggling.

On the other side of the Atlantic, tobacco plantations spread out along the rivers, and then gradually into the interior. By 1662 close to 24 million pounds of tobacco were raised in Virginia and by the end of the colonial period 130 million pounds; it dominated the economic history of Virginia. It promoted large plantations, because it needed new soil every three or four years; it promoted the introduction of slaves; it promoted concentration on one crop, and discouraged industrial development. It delayed the growth of towns, and spread population widely since the hogsheads were rolled to the coast and loaded directly on to ships in the rivers. Virginia was founded, like New Spain in the Caribbean, for gold; but neither in the Caribbean nor in Virginia was gold to be its saviour. The wealth was to come from sugar in the one and from tobacco in the other. The Atlantic's treasure ships of sugar and of tobacco outlasted the gold and silver convoys of Spain.

If Virginia had a debt to John Smith, its soldier-adventurer-turned colonist, and to John Rolfe, its first entrepreneur, its survival in its first years depended equally on Captain Christopher Newport, who brought out its annual relief. In 1608 he came and went twice; in 1609 he was with the *Sea Venture* when it was wrecked on Bermuda. He made five voyages in all to Virginia. An active buccaneer and taker of prizes – renowned in particular for the capture of the *Madre de Dios*, by which he had paid for the outfitting and crews of his earlier journeys, but which had cost him his right arm in 1589 in an attack on the treasure fleet – he now abandoned piracy, not for burglary but to honour a pledge to keep the tiny settlement supplied. (By contrast, one group of colonists went out in a sloop, the *Swallow*, to hunt for corn; having found it, they set off with it for the high seas and for home, preferring piracy and burglary to the welfare of the settlement.) Newport died at sea in 1617, on his third journey for the East India Service. He always brought more settlers than supplies, however, and until the colony grew its own corn, each new shipload was as demanding as it was welcome. [13] But, whatever their deprivations, the new arrivals were new blood, Lord De La Warr in 1610 brought 600 with him. In 1619 no fewer than 1,200 came out. This spelled survival, even as it strained food supplies still further.

Virginia owed its survival also to some, though not all, of its governors. The first, Edward-Maria Wingfield, elected by the council on arrival in Virginia, lasted only four months and was sent home as incompetent. Most of his councillors were little more apt than he was. Almost from the start – before the worst year of "the starving times" – the Company realized the need for military discipline and for "one able and absolute Governor." In the times that try men's wills, it was not summer patriots, shiploads of newcomers or even more investments raised by Sir Thomas Smythe 3,000 miles away, but discipline on the spot that mattered. John Smith (though very much an individualist himself), Sir Thomas Gates, Lord De La Warr – whose code of laws for the colony was modeled on the military code for troops serving in the Netherlands, where he had served – and Sir Thomas Dale (governor 1611–16), an ex-regular soldier, all insisted on good order and obedience, on "The Divine, Moral and Martial Laws." This was a military and communist-style system that remained in force for some eight years.

---

[13] K. R. Andrews, "Christopher Newport of Limehouse, mariner," in *William & Mary Quarterly*, 3rd ser., II (1954), pp. 3–27.

Sir George Yeardley, one of the castaways on Bermuda in 1609, acting governor 1616–17, then governor (1619–21) under the Company, and the first governor of the Royal Province of Virginia, in alliance with Sir Edwin Sandys, the new treasurer in London, brought in more liberal measures. The harsh legal code was repealed. Each settler was allowed a small plot of land of his own to cultivate. The communist period was over. A herd of blooded cattle were introduced and the cultivation of tobacco became scientific. Plantations spread up stream and down. By 1618 there were four incorporations and parishes in Virginia: James City, Henrico (Richmond), Kecoughton and Bermuda County (down river). In them the majority were "free farmers," who had come out, with their families, at their own expense; they got 12 acres apiece, rent-free for the first year. In 1619 a Dutch ship brought "20 and odd Niggers", the first Negroes – but they were, like so many of the white settlers, indentured servants, free after a term of years, and not slaves. And in 1620 the arrival of the good ship *Warwick* brought 38 brave young women, "an excellent choice lot of maids for wives." Whatever the later myths, good breeding was at a discount in the struggle for survival.

John Smith proposed the "placing' of young whites in Indian villages. Robert Beverley thought that the example set by John Rolfe in marrying Pocahontas "might well have been followed by other settlers to the vast improvement of the country." The plans in Virginia for the college in Henrico, as again in the 1693 charter for William and Mary College, included plans for the education of young Indians. They did not like confinement, however, as Governor Dinwiddie reported in 1756 to the Cherokee "Emperor" known as Old Hop, and they should be sent to Williamsburg when less than eight years old. Nevertheless, in the Indian schoolhouse set up at Christanna by the Virginia Indian Company in 1715, and in Brafferton Hall, facing the president's home on the William and Mary campus begun in 1700, Virginia did more to educate the Indians than any other settlement.

There is a bitter irony here. Governor Yeardley had persuaded George Thorpe, a member of the Council of the Virginia Company in London, to come over to direct the project for a college in Henrico. He saw him indeed as his possible successor. Thorpe, a "worthy religious Gentleman", was especially sympathetic to the Indians. He had several fierce mastiffs – the colonists' favourite protection against thieving Indians – killed when the Indians complained. And to cultivate Opechancanough he built him an English-style house, equipped with door with lock and key; the chief, it is reported, was so pleased that he spent a long time each day locking and unlocking the door. As a piece of diplomacy, however, it was unavailing. Thorpe's major legacy is that he is believed to be the first white man to brew a refreshing spirit from Indian corn – though his name has not become as familiar as that of Jack Daniels.

7 WHOSE WAS THE LAND?

Was the land, however, for the incomers to take? "The land was ours before we were the land's," wrote Robert Frost. But what of the First Americans, those who, in all their wandering, also saw it as theirs, or more accurately, theirs to enjoy the use of, without claiming "ownership" as such? Indeed, in the light of the first half-century of white and Indian contact, are any conclusions possible about relations between the races? Only if each episode is seen as unique, with twists and features all its own; and only if a balance can be struck between the conflicting evidence of contemporaries. Thus, on their journey to Roanoke in 1584, Captains Adams and Barlowe refer to their warm reception by the Indian king's brother's wife as she ordered their boat brought ashore, and the oars brought in to prevent theft; they were seated by the fire, women fed them and washed their clothes and bathed their feet. All these early descriptions portray the Indians as a gentle, loving, faithful people, with no traces of guile or treachery. On the west coast, Sir Francis Drake recorded a similar impression in 1579; they were a most gentle people, "like those who live in manner of the Golden age." Henry Hudson, on the site of the future New York City, found its Algonquian-speaking Indians "loving kind." And yet most of the documents of Virginia after 1607 depict the Indians as ruthless savages. It seems clear that the English arrivals after 1584 came after years of Spanish plundering in the wake of the Indian destruction of the Spanish Jesuit mission on the York River in 1572; and the coastal Indians were uneasy at Spanish, and now at English, probing.

From the beginning, conflict was bred by the major difference of attitude to the land: the Indian used the land by hunting and by tilling it, but he did not own it, and never understood the ugly notion of possession of it by an individual and his family in perpetuity. When Myles Standish decided to eliminate fur trade competition from a neighboring white colony in 1625, and to protect his own, he attacked it and killed seven Massachusett Indians; he destroyed both the white settlement, and the Indians. More serious trouble developed in the next decade, when the New England colonists

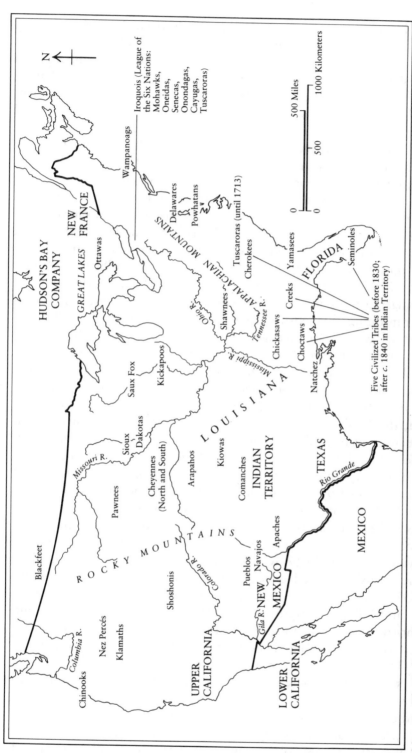

Map 7 The Indian tribes in North America. The many Indian tribes were scattered, speaking many distinct languages and with varying life-styles; few were allies – Powhatan's "empire" or the alliances of the Iroquois or the Five Civilized Tribes were exceptional.

entered trade competition with the Dutch from New Amsterdam. That Dutch settlement, unlike Virginia, had had some 20 years of peace, ever since in 1609 the Dutch West India Company had established its fur trading post on the Hudson, and decreed that all land must be purchased, not stolen, from the Indians. The natives placed a high value on the white men's goods, and land passed quickly into Dutch hands at bargain rates. Adrian Block explored Long Island Sound and reached Narragansett Bay, and Dutch fur traders followed him, meeting the Pequots and Mohegans, who were then united as one people under the *sachem* Wopigwooit.

By the early 1630s, English traders from Plymouth, as well as from the new Puritan-established Massachusetts Bay Colony, were also in the Sound, competing with the Dutch. The latter established a post on the Connecticut River, near present-day Hartford, in 1633, opening trade with local Wappinger groups. When the Pequot leader, Wopigwooit, tried to interfere with Dutch trade with the Wappinger groups in the Connecticut Valley, the Dutch murdered him, ransoming his corpse to his people, inflaming the Pequots against all whites. In revenge, an English trader, John Stone, and nine companions were slain on the Connecticut River. When another English trader, John Oldham (the troublemaker in Plymouth a decade before), and two boys were killed off Block Island three years later, in 1636, this time by aggrieved Manhasset Indians from Long Island, the English in Boston jumped to the wrong conclusion that the Pequots were again responsible. They dispatched a punitive expedition that destroyed the Indian villages on Block Island and — against better advice — went on to burn Pequot settlements in Connecticut. Led by Sassacus the new Pequot leader, the irate Indians struck back at English colonies on the Connecticut River. The colonists in Massachusetts and Connecticut responded, using their own terminology, to see the Pequots as agents of Satan who, according to divine will, should be wiped from the earth. In something close to a religiously inspired crusade, they invaded the Pequots' country in 1637, massacring 600 Indians whom they trapped in one settlement, and killing or capturing hundreds of others in merciless (and un-Christian) actions along the Connecticut coasts. Cotton Mather praised God for helping them send "five hundred heathen souls to hell." This was what is known as the Pequot War; effectively the Pequots were wiped out, or absorbed into other tribes, or sold into slavery.

In the following years, Massachusetts colonists, influenced by the Dutch practice as well as by Roger Williams, paid the Indians for land, and settled new colonies in many parts of New England and eastern Long Island. Meanwhile, local quarrels between the Dutch and the Wappingers erupted into another full-blown war in 1643. Willem Kieft, a hot-headed and fanatically anti-Indian director-general at New Amsterdam, decided to establish authority over the Indians. The Dutch fell suddenly on two peaceful, inoffensive bands of Wappingers, slaying many of them and carrying off their heads as trophies. Outraged bands of all the Wappinger tribes then struck back at all white settlements from Staten Island to the Connecticut River, forcing the English to join with the Dutch in defense. In a series of counter-attacks on native towns, the whites slaughtered hundreds of Indians, reducing the Wappingers to impotence, and thus restored peace in 1645. Shattered remnants of the tribes in southern New York, Connecticut, and Long Island, where great epidemics had all but wiped out the native population, moved inland to join other native peoples; and large areas of their former homelands were now open to white settlement.

Apart from the alliance of the Iroquois in the Hudson River country and Powhatan's empire in southern Virginia, collaboration between Indian tribes was rare. Before the palefaces came, tribe clashed with tribe, usually over claims and counter-claims for hunting rights over territory. Thus, in his "home ground," on the York river bank of the Wetowocomoco Peninsula, Powhatan exercised direct control over six tribes: the Pamunkey (his own), the Mattaponi, Arrohattoc, Appomattoc, Youngtornund and Powhatan, in the area drained by the James, Pamunkey and Mattaponi Rivers. They appear to have been settled there for some 300 years. These tribes aided him in extending his control north to the Potomac River and south of the James River; this area, however, included about 30 other tribes, and his methods of capturing and incorporating them into his "empire" varied. They were all Algonquian-speaking, an unusual feature; and they lived in some 200 settlements.

According to John Smith, Powhatan's empire was the result of careful planning. The conquest of other tribes was characterized by quick strikes and minimum bloodshed. Sometimes only the leaders were killed, and replaced by relatives of Powhatan. Sometimes a whole tribe was wiped out, but in a community where each man was needed for food production this proved economically unsound. A third method of subjugation was to relocate the unloyal tribe closer to the central area, over which Powhatan exercised direct control, and to send a more loyal tribe to live in the distant region.

Powhatan's control over a tribe diminished in direct proportion to its distance from the York River stronghold. The most effective means of unification over large distances was not military control, but rather the benefits of economic welfare and social ties offered by the empire. Its unified structure offered the individual greater security than did the isolation of tribal organization. The imperial system devised better methods of food production, storage, and transferral from one area to another. Systems of trade, exchange and barter soon developed, based on the economic unity of the empire. As Powhatan placed his relatives in positions of leadership throughout the empire, there developed a unity of culture. The social hierarchy was linked by kinship as well as by economic exchange. (The tribal wars of the Indians outside the two great attempts at "empires" was a permanent theme; and those tribes with access to good-quality furs, ensuring trade with the white men – such as the Hurons in Canada – were seen as the most fortunate – and vulnerable.)

At the foundation of the imperial structure were small villages, located along the tidewater where they could not be taken by surprise. The gardens and the houses in these villages reflect their security and sense of permanence. According to Captain John Smith, groups of two or three villages were ruled "absolutely" by a leader appointed by Powhatan. There are many indications that the government of the empire was far from primitive. The English must have been impressed to find a system of capital punishment comparable to their own. To the Indians a capital offense (such as murder) was a crime against the state; as such it was punishable by the state in the person of the public executioner. The population of Powhatan's empire is difficult to determine exactly. Since the economy sustained one person per square mile, and the empire covered about 9,500 square miles, it is estimated that the empire included 9–10,000 persons; this estimate corresponds to that made by John Smith. In light of this, it was not unreasonable for Powhatan to presume that he could absorb 120 Englishmen into his empire. As Powhatan's allies in the power struggle with other tribes, the English were of obvious use to him: they helped him to maintain control over insurgent tribes in his domain, and Powhatan depended on the innate curiosity of the English and their quest for the passage to the South Seas to drive them westward, where they (rather than Powhatan) would have to come to terms with the western Indians, the Manahoac on the Upper Rappahannock and the Monacon along the upper James River, the tribes whom Powhatan feared most. And it was in the West that there were rich supplies of copper. Thus the reasons for Powhatan's befriending the English became clear: they strengthened his empire, and they could be controlled for his purposes – because they needed the Indian's foodstuffs. At any point, he could have destroyed the settlement. He did not want to – until it became clear that they intended to stay, if they could withstand the climate. The arrival of the English, however, was not entirely to Powhatan's advantage. There were many insurgent tribes looking for an ally to upset Powhatan's balance of power. When the English chose to ally themselves with a rebel tribe, they incurred the wrath of Powhatan; when they were allied with Powhatan, they were in danger from all the disloyal tribes. Aged about 60 when the English came, Powhatan played the game of statecraft until he died in 1618. Four years later, his brother came close to the annihilation of the English colony.

The arrival of the English in Virginia was thus not as great an event in Indian development as is usually presumed. Indian tribes, separated by language and cultural differences, found no common reason to fear the English invaders. Each tribe only feared being caught unawares; if the English invaded the settlement of a rival tribe, a tribe tended to give them a warm reception, and even support. The adage that the enemy of my enemy is my friend was as constant a truth among the Indians as to Machiavelli's Florentines; the Pilgrims would find Massasoit, *sagamore* (chief) of the Morattigans, a sect of the Wampanoags, friendly and helpful, but his enemies, the Pequots and Narragansetts, hostile. What was novel was that the English along the coasts – more than the French along the St Lawrence – came to stay, and to expand. In almost every case, the first years of contact, while unpredictable among individuals or small groups, were of curiosity, barter and uneasy peace, land-grabbing or land purchase. Ceremonies of open treaty-making were seen as but indexes of duration of stay: it was this that to the Indians boded ill.

In Virginia, the Indians learned that the Europeans were weak, outnumbered and unable to support themselves on the land from which the Indians knew how to wrest a living, so that some Indians felt very much equal to – if not superior to – the invaders; the English were often treated simply as a rival tribe. In 1607 the English stumbled on Cape Henry when the Indians there were engaged in a great power struggle. Chief Powhatan was trying to extend and to consolidate his rule. His strategy was twofold: the outright conquest of rival tribes and treacherous diplomacy. The arrival of the English presented a possible third method. It was to Powhatan's advantage to befriend the English, to use them as allies in his struggle with other tribes.

The Indians' flourishing culture gave them a sense of strength and accomplishment which blinded them to the threat presented by the English settlers. The iron utensils and weapons imported by the

English were not strange to the Indians, except for the firearms; they had made similar things in wood. Their weapons performed the same functions; the only difference seemed to be the noise. The ships of the English may have been larger and more complex, but the Indian could see how useless they would be in trying to navigate the inland rivers. The literacy of the English was of little use to them in the New World; their mores were irrelevant at best; and their religious beliefs were too intangible and metaphysical to impress the Indian. (In his diary John Smith tells of Powhatan's instructions to his daughter's travelling companion as they left for England: to count all the men he sees, and to find out who the God man is.)

It was the fixed location, and then the steady expansion from it, of the intruders that alarmed the Indians. They had no notion — fortunately for them — of how white numbers would inexorably be sustained from the lands across the seas. They did, however, realize very quickly that, as they acquired the metal tools of the white man, so they had a clear superiority over the Neolithic artifacts of less advantaged tribes. Trade with the white man itself bred tribal wars,though the trading tribe themselves avoided war if they could: the Cree, who were hunters, fought the Sioux who were hunters also; the Chippewa sought to pacify them, for they lived mainly by trade. As William Hubbard of Massachusetts Bay noted: "Whatever honey in the mouth of that beast of trade, there was a deadly sting in the tail." But this is to interpret Powhatan in terms of the European power politics that Smith knew at first hand. Smith said that Powhatan always sought to avoid open war. He recognized also a second feature, one that sharply differentiated English and native, one on which since 1968 scholars have been hesitant, but on which the traditional view is that of Theodore Roosevelt — that the Indians were "squalid savages." Certainly the attacks that Powhatan's brother, Opechancanough, unleashed in 1622 were unsophisticated and ruthless: a drive to destroy the white settlements that came close to wrecking Virginia.[14]

Inter-tribal war, preceding and paralleling the clashes with the whites, was an extension of the family feud, with the added zest of a blood sport. Among the Indians men were raised to be hunters and warriors, and war allowed them to show their prowess and their courage, like medieval knights in tourney. They were trained from childhood to bear pain. When they were prisoners themselves,

[14] Robert Beverley, *The History and Present State of Virginia* (1705), ed. Louis B. Wright (Chapel Hill, NC, IEAHC, University of North Carolina Press, 1947).

or took prisoners, the infliction of searing pain was ceremonial and deliberate, and long-lasting capacity to suffer it without complaint a sign of sound training. It did not always lead to death – fortitude under duress could win reprieve. Equally, inter-tribal wars were usually no more than skirmishes, quick raids, not long campaigns, with scalps as trophies, elaborate torture and sadism serving both as relief and as triumph; casualties were rarely heavy. But all this changed after Opechancanough's massacre of the English in 1622, and the subsequent hostilities that resulted in the dispossession of the tribes.[15]

Along the Atlantic seaboard it was a similar story to that of Virginia. Everywhere, Indians who had welcomed with friendship the first white arrivals were living to regret it. On the New England coast, where Bristol and Devon venturers were busy fishing, trading for furs and charting the shoreline, Captain Thomas Hunt in 1615 kidnapped 24 Indians on Cape Cod, took them to Malaga, Spain, and sold them as slaves. Epidemics, especially of smallpox, introduced by English sea-traders, quickly destroyed nine-tenths of the Massachusetts tribe, and depopulated large parts of the Wampanoag country, including the area of Plymouth – conveniently clearing the way for the Pilgrim Fathers. It did leave one survivor, the interpreter Squanto, who "saved" (and at times imperilled) the Pilgrims. But the Indian-speaking interpreter was far from reliable: could there be total trust in baptized Croatans, or the so-called Don Luis de Velasco, Spanish-educated, who wiped out the Spanish mission on the York in 1572? Yet without Massasoit and Squanto the settlers would not have survived, for they taught them crop rotation and the best hunting and fishing seasons.

8 WHITE AND RED

Although at ease in his surroundings and respectful of Nature, the Native American was not the conservationist and the husbandman we like to think him today. Forests were destroyed by fire, to drive out game or to clear a track. Most of the clearings the paleface found, and in which they could plant crops, were man-made, and

---

[15] For the impact of the massacre of 1622, which ended all illusions of peaceful contacts between white and Indian, ended the life of the Virginia Company and brought in a major change of policy, see Alden T. Vaughan, "Expulsion of the Savages," English policy and the Virginia Massacre of 1622," *William & Mary Quarterly*, 36.1 (Jan. 1978).

sometimes simply abandoned Indian villages. However, the Indians grew corn, beans, potatoes, tobacco, and other crops which would soon be introduced into Europe.

Their food habits were immensely varied. In California they were dependent on fish, acorns, and wild plants, and if the Plains Indians depended on the buffalo for meat and clothing and wigwams, the Indians of the northwest were chiefly fishermen; many in the east were maize-growers, living in long-settled villages; and if those in the southwest included the warlike Apache, then the Hopi and Zuni, not far away, were *pueblo* dwellers, peaceful and settled. On the plains, the Mandan, Arikara and Hidasta lived in stockaded earth-lodge villages and traded their surpluses of maize, beans, squash, and tobacco. They were totally different in language, in life-style, and in their economies of trade from the Sioux and the Cheyenne, the hunters of the northern plains, or the Kiowa and Comanche of the south, horsemen and warlike.[16]

Very rarely could they form alliances against the white man, although the Iroquois, Mohawk, Oneida, Onondaga, Cayuga, Seneca, and later, Tuscarora (with pronounced differences of dialect and speech patterns among them), did so; those who were militant in spirit and considerable in numbers, like the Cherokees in Tennessee and Alabama, were thinly spread. For the Apaches in the southwest, life was a permanent war. Only at rare intervals did a leader emerge to unite them: Hiawatha of the Iroquois, Pontiac and Tecumseh, Powhatan in Virginia, Crazy Horse, and Chief Joseph of the Nez Percés. Indian divisions allowed easy white conquest, abetted by fire-power, by whisky, and in particular by smallpox, the three great killers. This last was the white man's most valuable weapon, even though he was slow to realize its deadly power. Many diseases were endemic around the whole world in the sixteenth and seventeenth centuries, except in America. The prolonged isolation of the American population meant they had no resistance to European disease. Syphilis was the one killer disease which was, it seemed, native to the western hemisphere; but even this, a few historians contend, may have been introduced into North America by Europeans. So many Indians died from the new diseases that it is difficult even to estimate the size of the Indian population on the eve of colonization. Cree, Omaha, Pawnee, Arikara, and Mandan were destroyed by successive invasions of the white men's diseases. In 1849 the cholera

[16] Colin G. Galloway, "The inter-tribal balance of power on the Great Plains 1760–1850," *Journal of American Studies*, 18 no. 1 (April 1982), pp. 25–48.

carried by the immigrants on the Oregon Trail struck the Sioux and the Cheyenne, Blackfoot and Comanche. Squanto, who lived with and helped the Pilgrims at Plymouth, was the last member of his tribe. Modern estimates hold that the Indian population must have declined by somewhere between 75 and 90 percent during the seventeenth century. Thus, in the early 1600s, only some 75,000 Indians lived in the coastal plain from Maine to Georgia. By 1700 the 9 million Indians living in Virginia were no more than 1 million, and mainly west of the fall line.

The effect of the diseases was not only physical, but seemed to the Indians a form of magic. When they died in massive numbers of diseases which appeared to select them and leave the English alone, it was natural for both sides to assume that God or some other controlling force favoured the English and their enterprises over the Indians. Their perception of the diseases as magical was reinforced by the fact that Indians who had been exposed to and were coming down with diseases might go among groups who had never seen the English, and bring the disease with them. The English, it seemed, had the power to make the disease strike by remote control without any physical contact at all. This power possessed by the white man destroyed the grip of the Indian medicine men. Clearly God had forsaken the Indians and favored the white man. And the French? The British trader had one great advantage over the French: rum was easier to get, and cheaper than brandy. And they too, in the end, were destroyers.

Massasoit's death in 1661 brought an end to the era of good relations between the Massachusetts colonists and the Wampanoags. He had faithfully kept the peace for 40 years, since signing the treaty of 1621 with the Pilgrims. Numerous injustices, many having their roots in quarrels over land sales to the expanding settlements, were visited on the Indians, and in 1675 the largest and bloodiest Indian war broke out and spread quickly across eastern Massachusetts and Rhode Island. The new Wampanoag leader, Metacomet, a son of Massasoit known to the English as King Philip, was proud, statesmanlike, and courageous; the war was known as King Philip's War.[17] His initial successes induced other tribes, including the Nipmucs of Massachusetts and the Narragansetts, to join him

---

[17] Douglas Edward Leach's account of the War is still unrivalled: *Flintlock and Tomahawk* (London, Macmillan, 1958). For Indian-white relations, see Karen Ordahl Kupperman, *Settling with the Indians: The meeting of English and Indian cultures in America 1580–1640* (Totowa, NJ, Rowman and Littlefield, 1980).

in a tribal confederation stretching from Maine to Connecticut. The Indian allies enjoyed dramatic victories, attacking 52 of the 90 white settlements in the then West, claiming that they had never granted the land away permanently, but only the use. Deerfield and Northfield, Brookfield and Worcester, Lancaster and Graton, Mendon and Dartmouth, Warwick and Simsbury, were almost totally destroyed. Springfield, Westfield, Middlesbrough, Rehobolt, and Providence were ravaged. Then the tide turned. The Indians, having forgone their plantings for war, began to run out of food. Philip suffered serious defections; and defeatist Indians began to help the colonists track down the warriors. The Narragansetts were caught in a swamp and suffered a crippling defeat, and with the help of an Indian informer Philip himself was found and killed, and his body quartered and exposed; the individual warring bands of Wampanoags and Nipmucks were wiped out one by one; many captives, including Philip's wife and child, were sold into slavery in the West Indies. The natives' power came to an end in New England in 1676. Nevertheless, this little-known frontier war inflicted greater casualties in proportion to population than any other war in American history.

Three alternatives faced the Indians in their dealings with the white settlers: an attempt to destroy the more powerful invaders; removal from their homelands to more remote areas not yet coveted by the whites; or willingess to accept assimilation and disappearance as distinct Indian tribes. On every frontier, the last course was encouraged eagerly by missionaries like John Eliot, "the Apostle of the Indians." Prior to King Philip's War he had converted many New England Indians to Christianity, gathering them into small towns for so-called "praying Indians." He translated the Bible into the Massachusetts tribe's Algonquian tongue, publishing it in 1663. (It was the first Bible printed in America by British authorities.) During the war with Philip, the colonists were fearful of all Indians and treated many of the converted natives as enemies, undoing much of Eliot's work. But with the return of peace and the end of the Indians' power to resist in New England, the forces of acculturation and assimilation worked quickly among the pockets of survivors. Many natives, now leaderless, helpless, impoverished, and sometimes tribeless, became Christians and tried to follow the road of the white man. Among the Massachusetts' leaders, the Providential view still held, and Puritan typology blurs the real contours – as, later, in Canada, it blurs the Jesuit accounts. The War had been long and savage: God was punishing New England for her degeneracy; the hunting down and the killing of King Philip was evidence of God's repledged love for his people. For his chosen people God was always on call, readily available and infinitely adaptable. William Hubbard, the minister in Ipswich who became the first chronicler of King Philip's War (*Narrative of the Troubles with the Indians in New England 1677*), was specific, not moral. The blame for the War, he said, lay with the liquor and fire-arms provided to the Indians by wicked French and Dutch traders, who cared "no more than the Cutler did, to know (as the Tale goes) what the Cutpurse did with the knife he made him." As for the Indians, they were "perfidious, cruel and hellish monsters."

Mobility was equally disruptive during the colonial period; the Shawnee moved from South Carolina to Tennessee, north to Pennsylvania and Ohio, and then crossed the Mississippi to "settle" in Missouri and Indiana. By 1825 they had moved to the area of the headwaters of the Sabine River in Texas, until they were driven out in 1839. The Seminoles do not seem to have existed before 1775, and appear to have been the result of a merger of runaway Creeks, Hitchiti and Yuchi from Alabama and Georgia, and a number of runaway Negro slaves.

The various wars with the Indians created serious consequences for the relationship between the two races during the next 200 years. Indian warfare traditionally had been more in the nature of swift and sudden raids of short duration for prisoners, booty, or revenge, and with comparatively light casualties. Many fights ended in truces or treaties in which one side acknowledged the superiority of the other. The white colonists introduced an all-out, racially and religiously oriented warfare against the natives. The latter, horrified at first by the ferocity of the whites' assaults, which were marked by the wholesale wiping out of villages and cornfields, the cutting off of heads, ears, and scalps as trophies, and the slaughter of whole populations, fought back as fiercely in defense. Among the whites, there were soon created images of Indian "savagery" that would endure from frontier to frontier and would become folklore among the conquerors. From then on, settlers expected the worst from every Indian, often committing violence first and suffering retaliation that might otherwise never have occurred. From this attitude sprang such sayings as "the only good Indian is a dead Indian," reflecting the whites' conviction that "civilized" men and free, unassimilated natives could not live as neighbors. The Indians noted, too, that if all whites were against them, many whites fought each other with equal or greater ferocity – Dutch against Puritans, Puritans against the Chosen People, Catholic French against Protestant English.

The century and a half of colonial settlement by Spain, France, England, Holland and Scotland, was one of near-constant conflict

with the native Americans. Indian-white relations, and the codes
and values of the two races, are the central theme of a vast literature, which was given a new stimulus by the Vietnam War and the
civil rights struggles of the 1960s. A new view of native America
emerges, almost a major school of historiography, comparable with
the new interpretations of American slavery. There have been some
major attempts at generalization, written by men of scholarship —
and conscience. What is clear, however, is the near-impossibility of
generalization about the many episodes that arose along a moving,
restless, and uneasy frontier. H. C. Porter of the University of
Cambridge has summarized the new ethnic view of the British-
Indian relationship, and bravely attributes the adjectives to the appropriate scholars.[18] To this admirable summary it is worth adding the

---

[18] H. C. Porter, "Review essay: reflections on the ethnohistory of early colonial
North America," *Journal of American Studies*, 16.2 (1982), pp. 245 and 246:

> The Indian was peaceable, merciful, less violent than the whites (Jennings and Elizabeth
> John); sober, industrious, disciplined, austere (John); uncomplicated (Nash); generous
> and hospitable (Jennings, John, Axtell, Richard Slotkin); egalitarian (Jennings, Axtell,
> John, Nash, Brandon); kind to animals (Washburn). Indeed the Indian seems to have
> had most of the virtues of small-town Middle America, as portrayed in the Andy
> Hardy films. (Brandon adds a Frank Capra touch: Indians were impractical, bohemian,
> and "Quite a bit of fun"). Washburn praises their medical skill. Wilbur Jacobs thinks
> that modern science could use the medicine man. In their dream therapy for instance —
> Washburn again — Indians were psychologically sophisticated. Jacobs concurs —
> "masters at interpreting the unconscious". Moreover, they had, says Nash, "under-
> standing of many of the basic tenets of modern psychology". They rejoiced in fierce
> independence, a love of liberty, with at the same time a humane communal life-style.
> Sensitive to the supernatural, in harmony with themselves and the cosmos, they were
> (Brandon) "in tune with a presentiment of the eternal". They were also nice to their
> children.
>   Washburn's Indian (1975) seems more Greek than the Greeks (the village a *polis*);
> more Christian than the Christians; and — native trade meetings resembling Business
> Conventions — more American than the Americans. What was the contribution of
> the Indian tradition of hospitality to the "American proclivity for sharing, for
> philanthropy, for generous gifts"? Was Jung correct to claim that there was an Indian
> side to the personality of all his American patients? These questions are raised by
> Jacobs.
>   Ethnohistorians have a duty, it seems, to write exposés of the European way
> of life in America. Axtell, presenting the characteristics of English colonial society
> in North America, stresses social hierarchy, aggressive capitalism, and "exploitative
> attitudes" to natural resources. Thus it is not odd to find ethnohistorians sympathetic
> to the rage of the Sioux Indian Vine Deloria who in 1970 dismissed the way of life
> of the United States as a "monstrosity". We learn that the white world is materialistic,
> dogged by business ethic, the "ideology of getting", the Protestant Ethic of Work as
> Virtue. Jacobs and Brandon are especially lyrical on these themes. Jacobs is also
> obsessive about Ecology. Nature — minerals, waterways, land, timber, wilderness,
> wild life — has been looted, polluted, exploited, raped, and all because of the "Judeo-
> Christian ethic, stressing man's dominance over Nature". Indians were, and are,

qualification, as Karen Kupperman has discerned, that there was a colonial desire for an absolute solution to what seemed to be the Indian menace. Thus the contact, if not at once, soon became conflict: and exploration rapidly became armed invasion. Such was the expectation of John Smith and of Captain Christopher Newport from the start. [19]

No one can approach the story of white contacts with native Americans without being aware that all the sources available are themselves partisan: until our own century they are records kept by white men. One historian of the West writing two centuries later was explicit: Theodore Roosevelt declared that "This great continent could not have been kept as nothing but a game preserve for squalid savages." [20] The Virginian experience with the Powhatan "empire" was epic, in that it established the English-Indian stereotype.

The pictures of the native world drawn even by the first Englishman indicate vast differences in the peoples described. If they usually

---

Ecologists, Environmentalists. (The perspectives, again, of the 1970s: President Carter's "top environmental priority", the Alaska Lands Bill, was signed in December 1980). Jacobs's Indians have a respect for the "ecological balance sheet" which reminds him of St Francis. He is keen, too, on their "communal democracy" and their "dialogues" on peace. "Nowhere do we see Indian ideals more admired than among American young people today" (Santa Barbara 1972).

... President Nixon gave an address to Congress in July 1970 in which he repeated the points made by Kennedy in 1961, and devotedly copying the opinions and terminology of Josephy, promised that the future of the Indian was to be decided by "Indian acts and Indian decision", the federal government supporting the "capacities and insights of the Indian people", famous for their art, spirit, strength, sense of purpose, and feeling for history.

"Acculturation", then, is a great evil. Unless, of course, a white man is acculturated by Indians, like Axtell's "white Indians" (English people who joined Indian society), or like Paul Newman among the Apaches in *Hombre* (1960).

[19] See Kupperman, *Settling with the Indians* ch. 9, esp. her point that "Racism was the product of, not the cause of, the treatment of Indians by colonists," p. 88. John E. Ferling, *A Wilderness of Miseries: War and warrior in early America* (Worport, Conn., 1980); Wilcomb E. Washburn, *Red Man's Land, White Man's Law* (New York, Scribner's, 1971), and his *The Indian in America* (New York, Harper and Row, 1975); Francis Jennings, *The Invasion of America: Indians, colonialism and the cant of conquest* (Chapel Hill, NC, University of North Carolina Press for IEAHC, 1975); Don Higginbotham, "The early American way of war," *William & Mary Quarterly*, 54.2 (Apr. 1987), pp. 230–73.

[20] For the massacre of 1622, which ended all illusions of peaceful contacts between white and Indian, ended the life of the Virginia Company and brought in a major change of policy, see Vaughan, "Expulsion of the savages, English policy and the Virginia Massacre of 1622."

called them simply savages, and did not always appreciate the differences between the tribes, as they moved west they came to grasp that every part of North America was inhabited – the mountains, the plains the deserts, the tropics, the forests, and the tundra. In these widely varied environments different cultures developed at different speeds. If today there are at least 160 Indian languages and over 1,200 dialects, it is likely that at least this number were used by the aborigines, since tribes were wiped out, moved, and in moving merged with others or died out. The diversity was heightened by the mobility of the tribes. The language barrier made most Indians unable to talk to their neighbors; this inability encouraged their isolation into tribal units, each of which viewed all other tribes as aliens; and this alienation of one from another could be exploited. Moreover, whether the Indians were nomadic or settled – and there were many more of the latter than the former – they were tribal and communal in their habits. Their view of land was nobler than that of the white men, more concerned with its conservation and its protection. By contrast, the whites – of all classes – were individualists. Later, Henry Knox, Washington's artillery chief and later his (and the first American) Secretary of War, said that the Indians would not prosper until they developed "a love for exclusive property."

Not only was there the language barrier between native and interloper, which baffled contemporaries, and still baffles students. There was an equal contemporary barrier of communication and understanding between those who reached America – Columbus and Vespucci, Bradford, Smith, Winthrop and Winslow, Verrazano, Cartier and Champlain – and those who read their accounts back home. Even the sophisticated among the stay-at-homes could envisage the New World only in terms of their own natural surroundings. Even in English America, the word "king" (*weroance*) did not mean the same when used of Powhatan as of George II; what was described as an "empire" by Captain Smith became a "confederacy" for Jefferson.

Moreover, as tribes moved, local whites were apt to continue using the old names for newcomers. With the changes came new languages and more, not less, incomprehension. The Huron words Jacques Cartier listed in his *Récit* after his second voyage were little use 70 years later to Champlain, since the Hurons had been destroyed by drought and disease, and displaced by the Iroquois. And the names by which they came to be known in English or French history were, of course, not theirs. Thus the name Hurons (from *hures* or boors) is a slang reference to their fashion of a scalplock dressed in a ridge down the middle of the scalp. They called themselves Wendat or

Ovendat, a name surviving in the Wyandots of the Green Bay area to which their survivors moved, and a reference to their view of their original locale as an "island," since it was surrounded by lakes and waterways. The "emperor's" name seems in fact to have been Wahunsonacock; Powhatan was actually the name of one of his villages at the falls of the James River. And Pocahontas's real name was Motoaka.[21] It is no accident that the best chronicler of the Indian western world is still Francis Parkman, who, Boston Brahmin as he was, went and lived among the Sioux to catch the flavor of the West of his day — even though he has been much criticized recently, notably by Francis Jennings.

There is another characteristic; the Indian did not integrate with the white man. Western experience hitherto had been that invaders and those invaded eventually integrated into a composite of both groups. The invasion of America did not follow this pattern, as the Indians refused to integrate. And this was especially so of the English, more so than with any other people. The French came much closer than the English to assimilating the Indians. They taught prayers to the Indians, married Indian women, and lived among the tribes in the forest. When Alexis de Tocqueville reached Saginaw on his journeys in 1831–2, he was impressed by the Indians, and by the *métis*, the *bois-brulés* as he called them.[22] The Spanish were even more successful in incorporating the Indians into their society. They were dealing with a far more technologically advanced Indian society than were either the French or English. The Spanish imposed a colonial structure on the Indians and reduced many of them to slavery. But the *criollo* or Creole was a feature of Spanish America.

The Indians of the Middle Atlantic colonies fared no better, in the end, than those in Virginia, New York and New England. Maryland settlers showed little patience with the Nanticokes, seizing their lands, killing many of them, and driving the rest inland, where they found refuge with other tribes. For a while, the Swedes and Dutch in Delaware and the Quakers in Pennsylvania got on more amicably with members of the Delaware confederacy. It was the good fortune of the Delawares, temporarily, to have their country-settled upon by the Quakers, for the latter showed more concern for Indian rights than did the other colonists. Several Delawares, including Tamanend,

---

[21] George T. Hunt, *The Wars of the Iroquois* (Madison, University of Wisconsin Press, 1960), p. 59; James Axtell, "The ethnohistory of early America," *William & Mary Quarterly*, 35.1 (Jan. 1978), p. 142.

[22] It was about them that Tocqueville's travelling companion, Gustave de Beaumont, wrote his novel, *Marie*.

whom the English called Tammany (a name later adopted by the New York Democratic organization) made the celebrated treaty with William Penn in 1682, and interracial goodwill lasted for 50 years. Then white expansion in Pennsylvania began in earnest. Cheating, stealing, and murdering, the colonists crowded the Delawares out of their homelands and across the Alleghenies.

The ardent competition for profits from the fur trade had, meanwhile, brought colonists into contact with still other tribes. The Dutch on the Hudson River had met the Mohawks, the easternmost members of the powerful Iroquois Confederacy. United with the Oneidas, Onondagas, Cayugas, and Senecas in the Five Nations' League of the Iroquois, they were rivals of the Hurons and Algonquian tribes farther north who traded, and were allied, with the French on the St Lawrence River. By 1625 the Dutch were supplying guns to the Iroquois for furs. The Iroquois soon depleted their own country of beaver, and then invaded the lands of the northern tribes. The French resisted this diversion of pelts to the Dutch, and for some years machinations between the Dutch and the French kept the Indians stirred up. Beginning in 1649, the Iroquois, determined to establish domination over the fur-supplying tribes, waged wars against the Hurons and many of their neighbors in the eastern Great Lakes country and Pennsylvania. The conflicts, which had repercussions among Indian groups working with the French as far west as the Mississippi River, lasted for three decades and left the Iroquois with unrivalled power, politically and militarily strong, and occupying a geographically strategic position between the English — who had succeeded the Dutch in New York in 1664 — and the French in Canada.

It was white savagery and fire-power that transformed the scene — whole villages and old and very young were killed indiscriminately. The whites came to stay, and were not just raiders or traders; and, later, the alliance of white and Indian against other whites and other Indians produced a new unpredictability of savagery and scalping knives unleashed from the forests alongside murderous flintlocks and muskets — and the fear induced by the former was more worrying than the possible impact of the latter. Within three generations of white settlement, the coast from Maine to Virginia had been more or less cleared of "hostiles." They moved west, and names changed, since they were conferred by whites. It is an ugly story, and the last two decades of rewriting, portraying the Indians as the innocent victims of white greed, is itself false to the violence on both sides, and the mutual incomprehension.

Not that the picture that came from the conflict gives a total view of Indian culture. In the tribes there was a peace-chief alongside the war-chief, and if prestige went to the warriors, there was also another side to the lives of the first Americans. For this, there are two groups of sources, though they offer a conforming rather than dissenting view: the oral legends of the Indians, and the captivity tales of white prisoners of the Indians.

The oral legends of the Indians were not probed by whites until the early nineteenth century, largely under Jefferson's encouragement. In his *Notes on Virginia* (1781), he recounts excavating one of the mounds on his own land; and he sent Meriwether Lewis and William Clark to the West on an avowedly scientific and geological expedition. The legends were mainly the result of research among the Odjibwa nation, then inhabiting the region about Lake Superior, but there is no reason to doubt that they were typical of peoples whose shamans and "old men" became keepers of legends, Homers who, in retelling, embroidered and probably reset familiar incidents in a tribal past. From this there comes a picture of people who were polytheists, believing in thousands of local spirits, some malignant, some benign, and in the personification of inanimate objects. Their spirits require conciliation by repeated sacrifices, so that the misery and fear that marked a daily life of poverty and wandering is offset by occasional bacchanalia, thanks to the sacrificial meat. All conclaves and powwows of colonists and Indians could testify to the importance of securing written agreements before torrents of oratory and before the ritual firewater were handed over, and orgies followed. The Indian tales are old: they make no reference to guns or knives or metallic objects. They appear to go back to the era of flint arrowheads, of earthen pots and skin clothes, to the era, that is, when the First Americans first appeared on what can be called American soil. There were, then, two totally distinct cultures in conflict. "Savages we call them," Benjamin Franklin would say later, "because their Manners differ from ours, which we think the Perfection of Civility: they think the same of theirs."

The contrast in cultures was most evident in war itself. To many Europeans, death in battle could be honorable, even noble: to the Indian it was the reverse — one of the main purposes of any conflict with other tribes was not to take scalps, but to restock their population with captive adoptees at least cost in lives to themselves. Wars were necessary to the Iroquois: the warrior was the ideal. When the white man came and declared his need for furs, and revealed the power of his musket, inter-tribal wars became uglier, but — by European standards — more normal: witness the "Beaver Wars" for territory between the Iroquois and the Hurons and the Eries in the St Lawrence region. And once the English replaced the Dutch in

New York, Sir Edmund Andros used them as diplomatic fodder: the Iroquois were persuaded to fight alongside the English against "King Philip" in the 1675–6 war.

Of the contemporary records, and noting that the Puritans were even more savage than any other colonists, and more grateful to God, in their treatment of Indians, the most curious are the captivity tales. In the *Magnalia Christi Americana*, Cotton Mather tells the story of Hannah Dustin, kidnapped with her infant daughter and the nurse attending her lying-in in 1697. On the forced march of over 150 miles, the Indians "dash'd" out the brains of the infant against a tree; and several of the other captives as they began to tire in their sad journey, were soon sent "unto their long home." Hannah and her nurse survived and were taken into an Indian family of "two stout men, three women, and seven children," which had already "adopted" an English youth. One night,

when the whole crew was in a dead sleep, (reader, see if it prove not so!) one of [the captive] women took up a resolution to imitate the action of Jael upon Sisera; and being where she had not her own life secured by any law unto her, she thought she was not forbidden by any law to take away the life of the murderers by whom her child had been butchered. She heartened the nurse and the youth to assist her in this enterprise; and all furnishing themselves with hatchets for the purpose, they struck such home blows upon the heads of their sleeping oppressors, that e'er they could any of them struggle into any effectual resistance, "at the Feet of those poor prisoners they bow'd, they fell, they lay down; at their feet they bowed, they fell; where they bowed, there they fell down dead". Only one squaw escaped sorely wounded from them in the dark; and one boy.

Few of the captivities ended in such ruddy gore. Nor, if the young were taken sufficiently early, did they always welcome rescue. No more did Indian youths respond to white schools. They found the rooms overheated and the food distasteful. To paraphrase Benjamin Franklin, in his *Conversations between the English and the Six Nations*, with an English education, the Indians could not kill a deer, track and surprise the enemy, or find beaver pelts. When, in Quebec, Indian girls were left for training with Catholic nursing sisters, at the first opportunity they fled back to the forest. Indians in white society were treated as laborers and even as slaves, but were frequently unruly; then they might be sold, and particularly to the West Indies; whereas a white slave in an Indian tribe was an adoptee, trained in their ways and treated as an equal. Nova Scotia even tried to foster intermarriage between Indians and whites, with offers of cash and land, but without success, with or without a formal ceremony, the Englishman adopted the ways of an Indian wife; and children born of Indian wives grew up as Indians. There was much miscegenation, most of it outside the "law," but it did not bridge the racial divide. The Indians seem remarkably free of it. An individual was judged on his merits and his manhood, not by his color, but by severe tests. In the late eighteenth century, Alexander McGillivray, son of a Loyalist Scots father and a Creek mother, was readily accepted as a Creek chief; Osceola of the Seminoles was at least half Negro.

The English failure of assimilation rested on the contrast between two social orders. With the Indians, the tribe was dominant; each tribe had customs that exercised a powerful influence over daily affairs. The chief, or *sachem*, had coercive authority. James Adair lived with New England Indian tribes in the seventeenth century, and his accounts of their government indicate there was no king or emperor, but only a chief who ruled by persuasion and whose only distinction was that of merit. His authority rested on public esteem. Even in battle the chief's coercive powers were limited. Indian warfare, therefore, was without strategy; war parties were small and without leaders. Warfare was carried on to display individual prowess as well as to intimidate the enemy. Not only the chief had a position of dignity; in the absence of coercive government, all men maintained their own dignity and expected the same of others. Modes of punishment in the Indian community reflect the high value placed on individual dignity. When an Indian violated a tribal custom, reform was forced upon him by the chief or by the offended party. Rather, punishment was calculated to shame the offender into reform. The chief weapon used by the community for this purpose was sarcasm. Adair reports that those caught stealing were lauded for honesty and those who deserted a hunting expedition were lauded for courage.

In English society the esteem in which a person was held was commensurate with his material wealth. The Indian could not understand the Englishman's tendency to acquire material goods until he was no better than a beast of burden. To the Indian, wealth was a handicap that stood in the way of achieving stature solely on moral grounds. This indifference to material goods exasperated the white man, who sought to bring the Indian to his value system. To the Indian, material goods were for use and enjoyment, not for social esteem. He took them where he found them, from white men and from red men of other tribes: brandy and rum, guns, and hatchets. In return, he gave what he could: furs and women. "Wickedness" was — or seems to have been — less usual among Indians than whites; "sin" was not a concept among them, since they were happily free from Calvinist virtues. Indeed, it was easier for Catholics than for Protestants to convert. The Indian could more readily respond to colorfulness and to a few rote movements and prayers, than to the sophistications of the many and competitive Protestant creeds. And to one of these — work on six days, rest on the Sabbath — he was especially alien. Governor Winthrop's journal relates the teaching of the Commandments. With regard to the commandment to do no work on the Sabbath, Indians said they would be glad to comply, as they did as little work as possible on any day. For this the Indians were seen as not only lazy but proud of it. The white man's gospel of work, especially of routine labor in one place, was as destructive of the ways of the Indian as his guns, his drink, his diseases, and the rumors of his scientific skills that spread remorselessly through oral societies.

The impact of the continent and its native Americans upon the white incomers went beyond the imagery of Shakespeare and the accurate descriptions of Harriot and John White, of Edward Winslow, and of many captains of ships, or the tales of John Smith. Within a generation of the first settlement, tobacco was Virginia's best known contribution to Europe. There came a legion of others. For his meeting of white men and of red in North and South America was a meeting not only of what are now fashionably called cultures but also of biological systems, of plants, of germs, and of disease. Europeans did not know bison, cougars, armadillos, opossums, sloths, tapirs, anacondas, vampire bats, toucans, Andean condors, humming-birds, or American robins (the size of an English blackbird). Nor did they know the muskrat or the cattail of the bayous. Among the few domesticated animals, they could recognize the dog and the duck, but turkeys and guinea pigs in the northern continent, llamas, vicunas, alpacas, and guanacos in the southern, were all new. Nor did the Indians know of cattle, pigs, sheep, goats, and (maybe) chickens. Spain's greatest gifts to its New World were the Faith, horses, swords and armor, and pigs; England's were swords and armor, muskets, and smallpox.

White men encountered for the first time maize, potatoes (sweet and white), and many kinds of beans (snap, kidney, lima beans, and others); manioc (soon a staple in tropical Africa, consumed in the United States chiefly as tapioca), peanuts, squash, peppers, tomatoes, pumpkins, sassafras, and — the more plentiful the farther south they went — pineapples, papayas, guavas, avocados, cacao (the source of chocolate), and chicle (for chewing gum). Europeans would steadily introduce rice, wheat, barley, oats, the vine, coffee, olives and bananas, "Kentucky bluegrass," daisies and dandelions, plantain and chicory — now from their familiarity thought of as indigenous to America.

Moreover, unlike the meetings of men, there was no conflict here. Indian corn spread quickly throughout the world. Before the end of the 1500s American maize and sweet potatoes were staple crops in China. The "green revolution" exported from the Americas thus helped nourish a worldwide population explosion probably greater than any since the invention of agriculture, something like a fivefold increase from 1630 to 1950, from some 500 million to almost 2.5 billion.

Europeans would adopt many Indian devices: canoes, snowshoes, moccasins, ponchos, dogsleds, toboggans, parkas, and the hammocks that so impressed the first settlers in Virginia. The rubber ball, like the game of lacrosse, had Indian origins. Indian words became familiar: wigwam, teepee, papoose, succotash, hominy, tobacco, moose, skunk, opossum, woodchuck, chipmunk, tomahawk, mackinaw, hickory, pecan, raccoon, and bayou (the Choctaw word for a sluggish stream) — and new terms in translation: warpath, warpaint, paleface, medicine man, firewater.

There were still other New World contributions: a number of drugs, including coca (for cocaine and novocaine), curare (a muscle relaxant), and cinchona bark (for quinine), and one common medical device, the enema tube. In exchange, minor European diseases like measles turned killers in the bodies of Indians who had never encountered them and thus had built no immunity. Smallpox and typhus killed all the more speedily. According to Thomas Harriot's account from the first colony sent by Sir Walter Ralegh to Roanoke Island, within a few days after Englishmen visited the Indian villages of the neighborhood, "people began to die very fast, and many in short space ... The disease also was so strange that they neither knew what it was, nor how to cure it; the like by report of the eldest man in the country never happened before, time out of mind."

The Indian response was syphilis. For syphilis, medical opinion in general holds that it was the New World's revenge on the Old, and came when Columbus's men, with his captive Indians, sailed back to Spain. Las Casas believed it to be endemic in Hispaniola. To a minority, "the French evil" or the "Neapolitan evil" was a variant strain of a disease as old as humanity itself, though both descriptions testify to the invasions and wars of north and central Italy in the early sixteenth century. In any case, by 1586, when Harriot reported after the first expedition to Roanoke on the native commodities available there, he mentioned sassafras, the root that was already being sold by Spaniards as a cure for syphilis. Since it was also being sold as a stimulant and arouser, it was in demand, and stayed so. The disease was the New World's gift to the Old, but the latter could be a steady transmitter. When it was carried by the Portuguese to Brazil it led to that colony, in the words of the late Gilberto Freyre, being "syphilised before being civilized." [23]

23 W. H. McNeill, *Plagues and Peoples* (Harmondsworth Penguin, 1979); J. S. Cummins, "Pox and paranoia in Renaissance Europe," *History Today*, 38 (Aug. 1988), pp. 28–35; and Alfred W. Crosby, Jr, *The Columbian Exchange: Biological and cultural consequences of 1492* (Westport, Conn., Greenwood Press, 1972), pp. 22–30.

3

The Puritan dream

The story of the Pilgrim Fathers, of their hardships on the *May-flower*, of the Compact they signed on board ship before they landed on Plymouth Rock, and of that first grim winter when half of them died of starvation, exhaustion and plague, is for Americans one of their most cherished epics. The first settlements on the continent by white men had been made elsewhere and earlier: Newfoundland (by Leif Eriksson the Norseman, John Cabot the Venetian-Englishman, and Sir Humphrey Gilbert), St Augustine (by Ponce de Leon and other Spaniards), Roanoke (by Amadas and Barlowe), San Francisco Bay (by Sir Francis Drake), Jamestown in 1607, and Quebec (by Champlain). But for religion, for idealism, for yet another attempt at communal living, and for "free" government by men choosing their own rulers, Plymouth Rock is for Americans the most potent symbol of all. And here at last was an – perhaps until the Mormon trek to the Great Salt Lake, the sole? – example of a North American settlement for conscience's sake. When the Pilgrims aboard the *Mayflower* finally sighted land on November 9, 1620, some of them had been at sea for almost three grim months from Leiden via Southampton (leaving in August) and Plymouth (leaving in September). The *Mayflower* was carrying the first contingent of European immigrants to settle permanently in Massachusetts, "the place near the great hill;" 50 Puritans, earning the name "Saints," though they never so called themselves, crowded her deck, as did near 50 others, referred to by their fellow passengers as "Strangers." The latter, a mixed lot of settlers and indentured servants under the military leadership of Captain Myles Standish, had been recruited

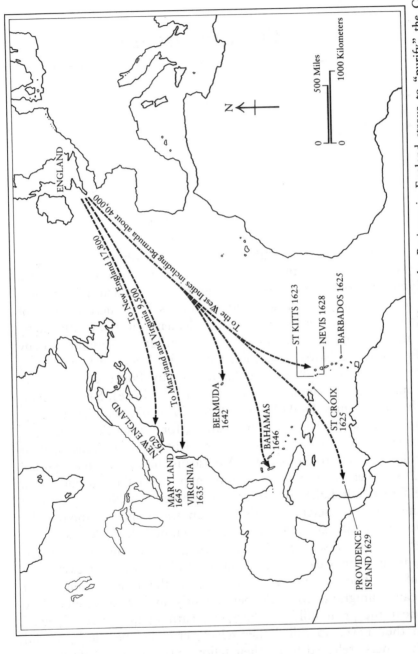

Map 8 Puritan emigration from England 1612–1646. From 1560 on, the Puritans in England strove to "purify" the Church of England of its vestiges of Catholicism. Their religious zeal was combined with social radicalism, and from 1603 they were vocal in opposing the power of the Crown. In 1620 the first Puritan extremists fled to New England.

by the colonial developers to back up their investment in the New World. They had got their land grant from the Virginia Company, largely through the persuasions of Sir Edwin Sandys. The crew and some of the passengers were, throughout, on the edge of mutiny.

The Puritans aboard the *Mayflower* were almost at the end of an odyssey that had begun over a decade before. It had started with their attempts to purify the Church of England of what they termed "popery." They saw in Henry VIII's break with Rome something more fundamental than it was, for his motives were sexual, selfish and secular – not least in acquiring church lands and their rents, or profits from the sale of them. As Separatists, they sought a church of laymen, a simplification of religious services, a renewed emphasis on the reading of the Word without the need for priest or bishop as intercessor, the election of pastors by church members and the organization of each church into a single, self-contained and self-governing congregation – in contrast to the maintenance of church rituals, the liturgical use of the prayer book, and the appointment of the hierarchy, all of which last had the support of Henry's successors, not least of James I. As monarch, he was head of the Church as well as the State. Brought up among Presbyterians in Scotland, he was expected to be tolerant of, even to support, the Puritans. He made his position clear, however, at the Hampton Court Conference in 1604. He saw an attack on the Church and its structure as an attack on the Crown: "no bishops," he said, "no King." James I vowed either to make the would-be reformers conform, or to drive them out of England; and in the case of this small band of Puritans, he succeeded. Those he castigated went through a turmoil of their own. Was emigration, a denial of the State Church, also a denial of God's law? John Rogers insisted that it was

lawful for a minister or any other tied by calling, either when persecution is only or chiefly intended against him ... to go aside, seeing it be best for the rest: Its lawful for any, either when God makes a way for them that seems to call them thereto (whereunto if they should not yield, we are to think they have some extraordinary notion of the spirit of God to the contrary, as its written of some of the martyrs) or find themselves as yet not strong enough to endure their rage; those, I say, may fly to be reserved as a seed to propagate the church afterward.[1]

Perhaps exile, even colonization, was God's way? Perhaps sainthood even required physical as well as theological separation? The State

---

[1] John Rogers, "A Godly & Fruitful Exposition," (London, 1650) p. 7.

itself, in any event, often sought to imprison, or to banish them. Robert Cushman, who agonized most over *Reasons for Removing*, and moved in the end, himself was driven to accept exile as itself a fulfilling —

our dwelling is but a wandering; and our abiding, but as a fleeting; and, in a word, our home is nowhere but in the heavens; in that house not made with hands, whose make and builder is God; and to which all ascend, that love the coming of our Lord Jesus.[2]

And William Bradford, in *Of Plimouth Plantation*, put it similarly:

So they lefte that goodly and pleasante citie, which had been their resting place near 12 years; but they knew they were pilgrimes, and looked not much on those things, but lifted up their eyes to ye heavens, their dearest cuntrie, and quieted their spirits.

Harassed beyond endurance, these "Separatists" ("The Church of England once removed", as they became known, to distinguish them from the vast majority of Puritans, who continued to press for reform from within the Church and within the State), emigrated first to the Dutch University town of Leiden. There, it was confidently expected, they could practice their religion without interference — like-minded Puritans were already in Amsterdam.[3]

Many of the Mayflower Saints had thus been in exile since 1609, driven out of England by threats of, and sometimes the reality of, imprisonment, even losing much of their property *en route* to Holland to thieving officers and crew. Other Separatists had gone to Holland before them, in fact since 1580, when the flock of Robert Browne of Norwich had moved to Amsterdam, denying the authority of the Anglican Church in religious matters and its monopoly of religious truth, but not querying the State's regimen in civil affairs. Efforts had been made, backed by Hakluyt, to plant another Separatist congregation on the Magdalen Islands in the St Lawrence — to no avail except for near-war at sea with Basque and Breton whalers. As

[2] Robert Cushman, "The Lawfulness of Removing Out of England," in E. Arber (ed.), *The Story of the Pilgrim Fathers* (Boston, Houghton Mifflin, 1897), p. 479.
[3] There were those who held that by removing themselves from the State, they could yet remain firmly inside the church: witness John Endicott, John Humfrey and the Rev. John White, who established themselves at Salem in 1628. But it would have to be "Reformed."

with Roanoke and Jamestown, the *Mayflower* had its own precursor, when in 1618 Francis Blackwell and 180 members of the Ancient Church in Amsterdam had sailed for the Chesapeake; but from storms and scurvy, amateur mishandling and incompetence, the expedition had lost 130 people *en route*, including Blackwell, the ship's master and six of his crew. The Saints were afraid of losing their English language and identity if they remained longer in Leiden; as rural folk they disliked its industrialism; they longed for isolation in which to live out their religious faith; and, not least, they were aware of the grimmer prospect of Spanish invasion of the Low Countries. In Bradford's words, "Not out of any new fangledness or other such-like giddy humour," they decided to move on to America. One of their two little ships, the 62-ton *Speedwell* (bought with money raised, and by the sale of property, in Leiden), proved unseaworthy, "open and leakie as a sieve," and on the main journey to the New World would finally turn back at Plymouth. The negotiations for support and for a patent were long and difficult. Not all who wanted to go could find room on one ship. By that time some were ready to stay at home anyway – like Robert Cushman, who, he said, had no wish to become "meate for ye fishes." "Friend," he said, "if ever we make a plantation, God works a miracle". The Separatists – or, to be precise, William Brewster, their ruling elder, and John Carver, merchant and deacon of the Leiden congregation, as their agents – had got only verbal promises of a land grant from Sir Edwyn Sandys. They accepted an offer of Thomas Weston, a London merchant prince, who formed a company to sponsor them. The settlers were to contribute labor, and the merchant adventurers capital. Shares were rated at £10 each, and went to any who contributed that amount in money or supplies, with each settler receiving in addition a share for himself, and a share for every member of his household over 16 years of age, servants included. All profits from "trade, traffic, trucking, working, fishing, or any means" were to go into the common fund from which the settlers were supplied, and from which all shareholders anticipated eventually taking their profit. The incorporation would last only for seven years, a short period in which to make profits from life in a wilderness.

Of the Leiden congregation of 300, 35 had sailed on the *Speedwell* from Delftshaven. Sixty-seven more of their own Church had already boarded the *Mayflower* at Southampton, and found it almost full: for Thomas Weston, who had agreed to finance their crossing, had recruited Strangers, not Saints; he wanted men to work, rather than to pray; they might be basically Anglican, but were not necessarily so, and one of whom would be hanged for murder.

The *Mayflower* was a 180-tonner, sturdy, square-rigged, double-decked, and slow. It was overcrowded, and it suffered 67 storm-tossed days and nights; as always then on shipboard hot meals were rare, and the only toilet facilities were a bucket. One young Saint died (William Butten came from the South Yorkshire village of Austerfield, at whose manor house William Bradford was born); others came close to it; and all suffered agonizingly. They finally anchored off Cape Cod on December 21, 1620. "For sumer being done, all things stand upon them with a weatherbeaten face, and ye whole countrie, full of woods and thickets, represented a wild and savage heiw." Only 17 men went ashore, to build a common house. For more than a month, the rest stayed on board the damp and dirty ship, and many died, sometimes two or three on a single day: juniper was burnt on the ship to dispel the smell of death. By the spring of 1621, of the 102 pilgrims who reached their promised land – 28 of them women, and 24 heads of families – 52 were dead – 15 of them women, and 13 of them heads of families. They went down with scurvy and pneumonia, bad food, short commons, exposure. They endured, in John Smith's word, "a wonderful deal of misery." For them, the killing times came earlier than at Jamestown, encouraged by snow and icy winds. Yet when Captain Jones offered passage home in the spring, not one chose to return.

Once on shore, around them on the rim of the forest, prowled the Indians. Constantly inquisitive, always in quest of food and fire-water, they were almost as much of a menace and an inconvenience when friendly as when hostile. And when, all too slowly, English reinforcements came, they included sinners as well as Saints and Strangers; the frontier did not attract gentle men, and was not tamed by prayer. As Robert Gorges, son of the founder of Maine, put it, the wilderness did not "answer to his quallitie and condition." Survival was difficult – the old burying grounds of New England are filled with stones that tell their own story, not least that of the Pilgrim Mothers worn out by childbirth, and often with five or six infants lying beside them. The land might be reached and won and tilled by courage, but in 1620 the reality was that there were only 21 men and 6 big boys to do the planting; it took four years before the corn grew in any abundance. In 1623 the Pilgrims abandoned the last myth of all, the adventure in common land ownership, in practice the living on common stock produced by the harder-working. As much as faith, it was hunger for land and the hope of owning their own farms without feudal ties and distraints that had driven them to the New World. Freedom of worship, yes; but they sought freedom of land ownership also, and more keenly. The harder workers

Plate 10 Jennie A. Brownscombe, *The First Thanksgiving* (1914). Thanksgiving Day is not a celebration of the landing on Cape Cod, but of the first harvest reaped by the Plymouth Colony in November 1621. (Courtesy of the Pilgrim Society, Plymouth, MA.)

resented the fact that their efforts reaped no extra return; single men did not enjoy working for other men's families; married women, and still more their husbands, resented having to wash and cook for those not in their own family — indeed, the strength of family feeling weakened the communal experiment from the start. Nor did the idea of equality mesh easily with Saints and Sinners, with leaders and led.

To this familiar epic some glosses have to be added. First, origins. In a general sense the Pilgrim Fathers (who like the Puritans a decade later were distinctly English), came from the east, from a region stretching from South Yorkshire southwest to Nottingham and southeast to Lincolnshire and the Fens, from the flat, cold and empty lands looking east and south as far as Essex. The two great Pilgrim leaders, William Brewster and William Bradford, came from neighbouring villages — Scrooby in Nottinghamshire, where there is a prominent pub on the Great North Road called The Pilgrim Fathers, and Austerfield, just inside South Yorkshire. Forty miles east of Scrooby is Boston, from which the very first Pilgrims sought to escape to Holland. And if one adds that strong Pilgrim contingents also came from the southwest of England, it is striking that these two regions were, on the whole, opposed to the king in the Civil War.

Secondly, they landed not at Plymouth Rock, which not one of them ever mentions, but — a few of them anyway — on the long tip of Cape Cod, at what is now Provincetown. The "invention" of Plymouth Rock as an icon was the work of Ephraim Spooner in 1769, addressing the Old Colony Club in Plymouth, a small and exclusive dining club which decided to hold a celebration of the landing, in a town then neglected, and long since bypassed by Boston. Spooner reminded the Club of the efforts of Congregational Elder Thomas Faunce's struggles against the "New Light" evangelists of the previous generation, and of Faunce's use of Plymouth Rock as a symbol of the old covenant theology of the Forefathers against what seemed revivalist unorthodoxy. The Club had many Tories and Loyalists in its ranks, and did not want to mix with the *hoi polloi* in the taverns. To them the Rock was a symbol of their past; they did not want it broken into fragments for sale to tourists, a practice that had already begun. They paraded solemnly to the Rock and dined in style on clams, venison and succotash. Five years later, Boston became famous with her Tea Party, so the local Sons of Liberty in Plymouth, whose natural venues were the public saloons, decided to use the Rock to exploit it for "patriot" and liberal purposes; in doing so — like the Stone of Scone in Westminster Abbey two centuries later, in the course of a Scottish National student "caper" to remove it from the Abbey to its "rightful" place in Perth in Scotland – it was split in twain, and the Rock fell apart. From 1820, with Freedom won, the bicentennial of what was then called Forefathers' Day, the alleged day of the alleged "landing," was saluted at what remained of the Rock by no less a spellbinder than Daniel Webster. And, again by one of those bits of chance that minister to the making of legends, when a Mrs Felicia Dorothea Hemens, a popular and pietistic English versifier, was holidaying in a small town, Rhyllon, in Wales, and came across (on a piece of newspaper in which her shopping happened to be wrapped) a reference to Forefathers' Day in distant Plymouth 3,000 miles away, she pictured not low-lying and soft sand, "dangerous shoals and roting breakers," but wild waves breaking against a rock-bound shore.

> Aye, call it holy ground,
> The soil where first they trod!
> They have left untouched what
>   there they found –
> Freedom to worship God[4]

When the tricentennial came along, the relic, now restored, had been suitably housed in a noble baldachino of Quincy granite, and, whatever the original facts, the venue had itself become a national shrine, which it would, by then, have been a sacrilege to violate, or to impugn. The address was given in 1920 by another, though less gifted, orator: President Warren Gamaliel Harding.

Thirdly, in 1620 their own status was ambiguous. In name, they were sailing for Virginia. But, despite 18 months of debate with the near-bankrupt Virginia Company, and despite the liberalism and the sympathy of Sir Edwin Sandys, in effect its chief executive, who had offered a tempting deal of a seven-year contract, during which they would work for the Company but at the end of which all property would be divided up into private holdings, they had not obtained direct backing from the Company.[5] And they sailed to a region well north of that allotted to that company.

---

[4] Mark L. Sargent, "Plymouth Rock and the Great Awakening," Notes and Comments, *Journal of American Studies* 22.2 (Aug. 1988), pp. 249–55. See also George Willison, *Saint and Strangers* (London, Heinemann, 1966), pp. 258–65.
[5] It is worth noting that the "good" Sir Edwin was a son of the archbishop of York, in whose diocese and among whose land agents (like Brewster) Separatism was born.

The king did not give consent but, a master of ambiguity himself, undertook "to connive at them, and not molest them." Thus permitted, but without funds for a ship, shipping, crew or stores, they had turned to Thomas Weston, who was in turn backed by "some seventy Gentlemen and Merchants", some of whom "adventured great sums, some small, as their estates and affection served", some £7,000 in all. Weston had, of course, to obtain his patent, and from the near-bankrupt Virginia Company. In fact, *that* patent had not been signed when they sailed, and when it was issued it was not to them but to John Wincob (a "religious gentleman" of the household of the influential Countess Dowager of Lincoln), who planned to sail with them, but "God so disposed as he never went." The commitment to Weston was to make profits, not to worship God.

In the end, and largely from mounting desperation, Bradford and Brewster, with as they first thought — two ships, cut the knots of argument, and sailed. In the end, however, only one ship crossed the Atlantic. On the high and stormy seas, the *Mayflower* did not know where it was going, who was financing it, and what lay ahead, and the Pilgrims landed on a shore to which they had no claim, in an area outside the remit of the London Virginia Company. When, on the *Mayflower's* return, Weston heard of their location, he then approached the (new) Council for New England, run by Sir Ferdinando Gorges and his partners. The Council for New England had monopoly rights over the region in which the Pilgrims had landed; and thus the Pilgrims had to reckon not only with Weston but with Sir Ferdinando Gorges of Plymouth, a member of the Plymouth Virginia Company that had made an unsuccessful venture in Maine in 1607–8, and which had passed on its claims to the new Council. The Pilgrims' seven-year partnership with Weston was not long in which to pay their debts. To use the words of Robert Cushman, who stayed behind when the *Speedwell* had been declared unseaworthy, the whole voyage as well as its beginning "had been as full of crosses as ourselves have been of crookedness."

The Pilgrims stayed in the cold and wintry North, because it had no established government and no Anglican church, and no one — except Indians — to interfere with them. Despite their efforts to secure backers in London before they sailed, their leaders had probably planned to stay in the North from the start. They scouted various locations along the coast until deciding to settle at the Bay that John Smith had some years before named Plymouth. He had offered to accompany them, but they had refused his services. They had no taste for his braggadocio. His view of them was scathing: "they would not be knowne to have any knowledge of any but themselves, pretending onely Religion their governour, and frugality their counsell, when indeed it was onely their pride, and singularity, and contempt of authority; because they could not be equals, they would have no superiours..."

Fourthly, but for another accident they might even have founded not New Plymouth but what was to become New York: not a place one usually associates with Puritanism. They chose in fact unwisely. They had been offered generous terms by the New Netherland Company, with supplies of cattle and grain awaiting them on Manhattan Island on their arrival, and warships to accompany them to secure their safety. They chose to move before the Prince of Orange had added his approval. Boston, founded ten years later, was a much superior site; so – as the Dutch kept reminding them afterwards – were the Hudson and the Connecticut Rivers.

So, fifthly, outside all jurisdiction, and outside the boundaries of any patent, they did need a "frame of government." With Cape Cod in sight, and before any had gone ashore, they drew up the Mayflower Compact on November 21, 1620. They pledged themselves to obey "such just and equall laws as shall be thought most meete and convenient for ye generall good of the colonie." This was signed by 41 – Strangers as well as Saints – out of the 65 adult male passengers; since the signatures of the fathers covered the allegiance of the children, for 41 read also 13 children (of these, at least 7 were not children of any passengers but waifs from the Bridewell prison in London). Of the remaining 9, 8 soon died, so that it must be assumed that they were too ill to sign. As agreement, it was thus all but unanimous. It has been called "the first pure democracy in America;" perhaps the first – and only? – example of a group in a state of nature coming together to form a civil government agreeing to abide by laws made by leaders of their own choosing – to be cited with approval by Rousseauists ever since:

We whose names are under-written, the loyall subjects of our dread soveraigne Lord, King James ... doe by these presents solemnly and mutualy in the presence of God, and one of another, covenant and combine ourselves togeather into a civill body politick, for our better ordering and preservation and furtherance of the ends aforesaid; and by vertue hearof to enacte, constitute, and frame such Just and equall lawes, ordinances, acts, constitutions and offices, from time to time, as shall be thought most meete and convenient for the generall good of the Colonie, unto which we promise all due submission and obedience.

In fact, the Mayflower Compact is neither single nor simple. The Pilgrim Fathers were protesting only against the English Church, not the English State; they stayed loyal to its king. In their negotiations with the Virginia Company, they expressly acknowledged the 39 Articles, the Confession of Faith of 1562: "the King's Majesty as Supreme Governor in his Dominions in all causes, and over all person, ... and the authority of the present Bishops in the land ... so far forth as the same is indeed derived from His Majesty ...." They left England to sever relations with the Anglican Church, but they made every effort to maintain their ties with English culture. The Separatists' departure from England was dictated only by their own attitudes; it was not a response to political or social conditions in England at the time. They were not rebels, just exiles – and none of them Cromwellians. They left to keep their religion intact, in rebellion against the dicta of "one doctrine and one discipline, one religion in substance and in ceremony" of the Church of England. In Leiden, the Separatists sought equally to avoid assimilation into the Dutch way of life. The language barrier helped them in this effort; but the young were readily susceptible to the influences of Dutch society, and were drawn into such Dutch occupations as merchant and soldier, which hardly befitted an Englishman of the new Church. Moreover, if they did become urban craftsmen, printers and carpenters, weavers and masons, the Dutch kept them in their place, workmen not masters. The Separatists resolved to leave the Netherlands in order to prevent the total loss of their English identity; the price they had to pay there for religious liberty, the sacrifice of English culture, was too high. On the banks of the Amstel they saw their family system decaying, and their strength as a church being undermined. The threat was equally evident to them on the *Mayflower* itself. They believed that a solemn oath and a signature would ensure their preserving English life, now in a New England.

Before their arrival in the New world, the Pilgrims realized that they were outside the boundaries designated by their patent. Only a few of the men on the ship were unified in a commitment to the new Church: the rest were aboard to represent the Anglican Church or London merchants, or at least as their employees. During the voyage the latter groups had made frequent mutinous speeches, threatening to break away from the young enterprise. The Mayflower Compact was simply a voluntary agreement to establish local self-government on the basis of common consent until a legal patent could be obtained, a reference not to a specific religious dogma, but to a common bond: King James and their political heritage. Their need to define authority forced them to reassert their English identity.

They could be both good Christians and good Englishmen. At a time when the Reformed Religion was dividing Europe on new lines, until the formula of "cuius regio, eius religio" was devised, the Separatists were England's Huguenots.

The Compact was an expression of an English development. It was in fact based on the Scrooby Church covenant – for each Separatist congregation made its own avowal. For a generation, banishment of Protestant nonconformists had been discussed as a penalty between death and imprisonment. In a debate on the proposal in the House of Commons, Sir Walter Ralegh had asked the practical question: "If 2000 or 3000 Brownists meet at the Sea … at whose charge shall they be transported, or whither will ye send them? I am sorry for it. I am afraid ther be 10,000 or 12,000 of them in England. When they be gone, who shall maintain their wives and children?" By 1620 the answer had been found: send them as "planters," with the money raised by the Virginia Company in commercial fashion. Their congregations, which consisted of craftsmen and schoolmasters, could meet overseas as easily as in the Clink or the Fleet or the Bridewell – the London jails – and at less expense.

The Pilgrims, it is often claimed, were classless, products of the cottages not the castles of England. Yet Brewster, like his father before him, was bailiff and postmaster of Scrooby, lived in the manor house and was land agent for the archbishop of York, and had a university education; Bradford, as a youth, a sickly and lonely lad, was the son of a wealthy yeoman family, brought up after his father's death by Brewster; Winslow and Carver ranked as "gentlemen." Small though their numbers were, they were more a microcosm of Old England than a class making a social protest.

The Compact was no cornerstone of a great democracy, but an attempt by the "natural" leaders to organize a tiny society going ashore into the unknown – if "society" it was. Of the 102, 5 were hired men, 4 were sailors and 1 a cooper; two of these died in the first winter, and one of them – John Alden, the cooper, hired in Southampton to look after the beer hogsheads – remained in the colony (which he had doubtless not intended to do), and in the end became a Saint – if Longfellow is to be believed, because of Priscilla Mullens, his companion on the voyage, whom he married. This was a distinctly two-class society that was being shaped, on English lines, and on which English law would be binding. They did not believe in an egalitarian democracy, for some were clearly "leaders," usually the better educated, just as some were "Saints" and of the elect; and the rest, the majority, were reprobate. And their pastor back in Leiden, John Robinson, in his letter of instruction to them, had advised them to choose as leaders those who "entirely love and will promote the common good," and to yield "unto them all due honour and obedience in their lawful administrations." They were directed by a governor, John Carver, until his death in April 1621; then by Governor Bradford; and then by a militia captain and soldier of fortune, the stocky and peppery Myles Standish, to whom in large part they owed their survival, and who was not a Saint in any sense at all.

Of the 102, 15 were servants of the rest; Carver brought 4 servants with him, and Winslow 2. The Compact was a secular, not a religious, bond. There was no notion here of independence, or of republicanism, or of disloyalty; and certainly no evidence of democracy, since it was and was meant to be government by Saints. Of them only a small group, "The Old Comers," would have the exclusive power to allot land in the settlement. In 1643, when there were 634 males "able to bear arms," there were only 233 freemen or voters. They did discover, however, that leadership was no monopoly of the tiny number of "gentlemen" among them. One of Governor Carver's servants, John Howland, was a member of the committee that organized the fur trade, and that paid off the debts to Weston's company; and Thomas Prence, the son of a London coachmaker, who came out on the *Fortune* a year after the *Mayflower* when he was only 21, was the first man in the colony other than Bradford and Carver to be elected governor, in 1634. There was implicit here what Thomas Jefferson would recognize as the only effective form of democracy: a system of government that permits an aristocracy of merit to become the governors.

It was, again, the Revolution and the afterglow of victory in the War of Independence that led John Adams in 1802 to see in the Mayflower Compact a harbinger of 1776 and of men like himself, building afresh a self-governing society, with a promise of "just and equall laws" for all. There is no evidence of this in the reality of 1620 and 1621.

And sixthly — to attempt to follow the structure of a New England sermon — the Separatists drew on experience of two exiles, in Holland and in Plymouth, to refine their creed down to its essence. Three thousand miles away from all the familiar institutions of home, and living almost in a state of nature, authority for them became internalized: a man was governed by his conscience, which was the voice of God; without centuries-old cathedrals and churches, the Almighty did not speak through ceremony and statuary but through the Word, in the Scriptures and in a constant flow of exposition and exegesis from those trained to the task: his vehicles were not superstitions but sermons, not altars but pulpits – when there were pastors to fill them. For long this was not so in New Plymouth; their pastor, John Robinson, stayed behind in Leiden with the bulk of his congregation. For four years Elder Brewster had to carry the burden of being spiritual as well as secular leader. Not being ordained, he had not presumed to administer the Sacraments, so there were no baptisms and no Lord's Suppers. When in 1624 the London Company sent out a pastor, John Lyford, he was a Church of England clergyman who had declared an interest in Puritan principles. His Plymouth flock found him to be a "canting hypocrite."

Problems of creed, and of conscience, remained. Those problems were not now of the mediation of bishop and priest, and the struggle with sin, contrition, the nature of the Trinity or of transsubstantiation, for them now resolved. But agonies remained: predestination – why were some called and some not, and how be sure? How did the unredeemed find salvation? Did baptism have meaning for babes? Must conversion be visible, and be in public? By the middle of the seventeenth century a goodly share of the first generation New England Puritans had passed away, and with their passing a new problem presented itself: namely, how could the Church, made up of regenerated members only, be maintained? The children of the "Saints" were accounted church members, because they shared the covenant with their parents, and were entitled to baptism because they were already church members. The question of maintaining a regenerated Church arose when some of these children of the "saints" who had received baptism grew to maturity and it was found that they could not claim a religious experience which would entitle them to be called "converted." Were they now to be admitted to the Lord's Supper? The question became even more complex with the rise of the third generation: the children of the unconverted second generation. Should they receive baptism as had their parents, and should they also be considered church members on reaching maturity? And, in a wilderness, in a permanent war with Nature and with pagans, how to maintain the faith? And, not least, whose was the land, and was it theirs to take? The years ahead would continue to be years of mental as of physical torment over these and other issues. And in the end, as always, the temptations of this secular world, and its pressures, material success and compromise on doctrine, would erode away the intensity of the Pilgrims' faith.

2 CHRISTIANS AND SURVIVORS

Three men saved the Pilgrims, William Bradford served as governor almost continuously for 30 of his remaining 36 years; for the first 18 of that 30 he was not paid any salary. In about 1630 he began to write his *History of Plimouth Plantation*, and in old age he began to study Hebrew, in order to see "the ancient oracles of God in their native beauty." The delicate orphan, with little education, had grown in physique, endurance – and dedication. The general court consisted of the governor, his assistants and all freemen – those entitled to vote.

Myles Standish's role has been well chronicled: the leading Stranger became the prop of the Pilgrims' security against Indians, and against odd, perverse and even hostile white intruders. Edward Winslow's role, though less chronicled, was the most important of them all: unique to the Pilgrims, but in a distinct way significant of the future Atlantic role of many of the leaders of the Puritan congregations. Of all the Pilgrims, only John Carver – the first governor – and Winslow ranked as gentlemen. Winslow was well travelled and well educated, though not at a university; he had social advantages lacking among the rest. (Only Elder Brewster had been to a university: a few months at Peterhouse, Cambridge.) Edward Winslow's handling of the Indians was masterly. His wife Elizabeth died in the first winter, on March 24, 1621. His marriage in May 1621 to Susannah White, widow of William and mother of Peregrine White, the first English child born in New England, was the first marriage to be celebrated in the New England colonies. In 1623 Winslow visited England, returning in March 1624, bringing, as he recorded, "3 heifers and a bull, the first beginning of any catle of that kind in ye land."

The next year Winslow was back in London, publishing his *Good News from New England*, and defending the settlement against the criticisms sent back by John Oldham – who, on Winslow's return to the colony, was driven out from it, and ended up in his own wilderness, being scalped by Pequot Indians. Winters were severe, Winslow warned, and the summers brought mosquitoes. The Indians were not bloodthirsty savages, but they were not always good neighbours. But in North America, "religion and profit jump together." Winslow was one of the "Undertakers," the finance committee who in 1627 assumed the colony's debts in return for its trading privileges. He was active as explorer as well as trader: he set up posts on Cape Ann, in Maine and, later, on the Connecticut River. He was a skillful negotiator with the Indians, and with the London merchants – but not with Archbishop Laud, who imprisoned him because he had "taught" in a Pilgrim Church. He never returned to Plymouth. As a commissioner for Cromwell, he was a negotiator with the Dutch. He died at sea of fever in 1655, on returning from an attempt to capture the Spanish West Indian colonies, and the conquest of Jamaica. Of all the Pilgrims he alone survives as a face: a portrait of him was painted in London in 1651.

The *Mayflower* story is thus a prototype indeed, but not merely of the Pilgrims' progress through many desponds, of "a hideous and desolate wilderness full of wild beasts and men", as Bradford first described the wintry Cape, of homes mainly dug out of hillsides with walls of rough-hewn pines filled in with clay, and "roofed" with seaweed overlaid with turf; of heroic, hard-toiling Christian men living on ship and shore, among hostile, rough and panicky Strangers; of physical survival after hardship, and starvation; of bad luck, so that after the snow of the first winter, which prevented planting in the frozen ground, came the severe drought of the third summer that all but wrecked their first crops; of the death of half their number, including most of the women, in the first winter, even if it was milder than usual – with, that is, more rain and snow than ice; of the relief ship, the *Paragon*, which sailed in 1622, but did not get far before storms forced her to return. It is even more a story of human perversity. When Thomas Weston, their backer in 1620, glib and plausible as ever, could have joined then in 1622 with his new colony, he directed it instead to Wessagusset (Weymouth) 50 miles away, where it revealed itself as a band of desperadoes, who raided New Plymouth, and took all they could before their own primitive settlement was itself wiped out by Indians.[6] Nor does this catalogue of God's displeasure include the major threat of all, the Indians, ever prowling and apt to stroll in peacefully but uninvited, and at other times to loot or even to kill. Massasoit, sagamore of the Wampanoags, was friendly and helpful, but his enemies, notably the Narragansetts further south, were hostile to him, and thus to them.

They had, it seems, one piece of good fortune, but that too has to be qualified: his name was Squanto, a Patuxet Indian. He had been kidnapped years before by a passing English ship, sold into slavery in Spain, whence, somehow, he made his way to England,

---

[6] Thomas Weston was a man of parts. In 1628 he was elected to the Virginia House of Burgesses, but in 1631 was in the Maryland Assembly. Some years later he died in Bristol, England.

to Newfoundland, and then to England again. He was finally returned by Sir Ferdinando Gorges in 1619 to his native village, only to find all its inhabitants dead of the white man's diseases. He spoke English, and he taught the colonists how to grow corn, snare fish and trap beaver. He became their interpreter and their trusted intermediary – until Governor Bradford suspected him of treachery in negotiations with the Narragansetts. Spy? Inevitably. Traitor – to whom? Egotist – or are they all interchangeable terms? He wielded a power greater than any *sachem*, and may indeed have played all sides to his own greater glory. His death "of an Indian feaver" removed him, but while he lived he rendered immeasurable service. He died a Christian and hoped that he might "goe to ye Englishmen's God in heaven." On earth at least, he and Edward Winslow as negotiator (and even nurse to their chief) gave the Pilgrims a happier experience with the Indians than Virginia had had.

Survival itself was costly. More and more Strangers reached them, with more mouths to feed. In 1621 the ship *Fortune* added to the community more members who failed to share the Separatists' purposes, since they adhered to the Established Church that the Separatists had left. Many people in this second group were destitute, driven across the Atlantic by hopes for a new life. In addition, there were such non-Christians as the Indians, always hungry and usually light-fingered, and such dissidents as Thomas Morton.

The Separatists were in fact religious but not political exiles. They emphasized that they were proud, indeed stubborn, not only in their faith but in their politics, breaking their ties to Old England but going to a New. They went, with commercial backing, like other planters. They sought to retain their identity as a religious and social unit, but in a wider English context. Moreover, they were all indebted to London merchants, and obligated to pay off their debt by sending back to England all their profits from the new land for seven years. Most of the Anglicans with them were indentured servants of London merchants, bound, like the Separatists, to work the land communally for seven years and return the profits to London.

There was another group who might be seen as the proud ones, and were usually known as The Particulars, since they came to the New World on their own "particulars" and with no indebtedness: they had the money to pay for their own outfitting and transportation to the New World. Because of this, they were given land as incentive to go, and owed nothing to the merchants. The Particulars, because of their private land ownership, upset the balance inherent in the London joint-stock company. According to the prevailing system of the joint-stock company those who had money advanced it, and stayed in England waiting for returns on their investment; those who had no money went to the New World and labored in the hope of a better life than they would have had in England. Obviously the system favoured the wealthy entrepreneurs; they owned and controlled everything. Those in Plymouth, New England, owned nothing; they sent all the communal profits back to London. The Particulars, on the other hand, were not indebted to the London entrepreneurs. They had been given free land in the colony by the merchants as an inducement for more people to migrate at less cost to themselves. The effect in the colony was the creation of two classes – the Particular land owners and the communal planters. Once again it was the English heritage – now in the nature of the joint-stock company – that was directly responsible for the course of developments in the new colony.

The communal society at Plymouth devised methods to prevent the Particulars from sharing in the benefits of their community. First, they denied the Particulars political citizenship or any voice in community affairs. Second, they barred the Particulars from participation in the Indian fur trade. Was this discriminatory? The society had a basic economic goal – the communal tilling of the soil – and those who put themselves outside the pursuit of that economic goal also put themselves outside the political affairs of the community. As the planter saw the Particulars enjoying the fruits of their labor, while he shipped his back to England, he began to see himself as the victim of the London merchants. Dissatisfaction with the communal system increased almost before it began, and any uniform approach to economic problems began to dissolve. By 1623, the communal system was on the verge of collapse. Bradford, too, soon realized that the communal ownership of property – even if it was the highest form of society – was untenable in Plymouth. He initiated a system of private ownership in which every man could work his own land and pay a certain percentage to the "Undertakers". The new arrangement was built on common sense by Bradford, Brewster and other Separatist leaders. It produced a solid economic base which drew the Particulars toward the planters. And as with John Smith's and John Rolfe's efforts in Jamestown, it could only be done locally, by the men on the spot. Each colony – like every individual activity – took its own path.

The Separatists sought escape from persecution, but were not crusading for converts, of white men or Indians. They were firm in handling the "Particulars;" they legislated against Quakers and other dissenters. They found biblical texts in plenty for journeys in wildernesses, and discovery of Canaans, and they wrestled with the still-abiding question: whose is the land? One of their master casuists, Deacon Robert Cushman, now emerging more as Founding Forefather than as Pilgrim, saw the place of the Indians clearly, in his *Lawfulness of Plantations*, and was firm in his answer:

Their land is spacious and void, and there are few; and they do but run over the grass as do also the foxes and wild beasts. They are not industrious, neither have art, science, skill or faculty to use either the land or the commodities of it ... so it is Lawful now to take a land which none useth, and to make use of it.[7]

The self-consciousness on this point of the more thoughtful of the Puritan leaders comes through in phrases like "It is the "Lord's waste,"" or, later, at a town meeting in Milford, Connecticut in 1640: "Voted, that the earth is the Lord's and the fulnes thereof. Voted, that the earth is given to the Saints. Voted, that we are the Saints."

And, even more perplexing, even among the Saints, how to ensure in a wilderness that selfishness and greed for land would not "corrupt" the noble dedication of November 1620? If communism in land ownership was abandoned, it was not replaced by overt individualism: wages and prices were regulated; people were punished for idleness as well as for drunkenness and Sabbath-breaking; freedom of movement was restricted: no one could move, buy land or settle elsewhere, except by permission of the Court.

The 14 families dropped in a hostile wilderness did not know of the perils ahead. Those who survived did so from their own determination, and from Myles Standish's combination of skill and bluff in deceiving and overawing the Indians. And, be it emphasized, with no pastor among them through the trying times. When John Lyford arrived in 1624, he was a disruptive force, and his obsequious personal and bombastic "Anglicism" split the Pilgrim Church. But by that time they had a patent in their own right, obtained from the Council for New England (the old but reorganized Plymouth Company), thanks to Edward Winslow's vivid accounts to Lord Sheffield when he visited London in 1623. They were now empowered to build a town and to enact such laws as they saw fit. They had, a year before, abandoned the expedient of communal living. The *Anne* and the *Little James* brought supplies, and new blood; 60 people in August 1623. In 1629, 35 settlers came in, and a year later another 60, on the *Handmaid* from Leiden. They were the last of the Pilgrim

[7] Arber (ed.), *The Story of the Pilgrim Fathers*, pp. 499–500.

Fathers, and for them supplies were waiting. Among them came, inevitably, dissidents, trouble-makers and barrack-room lawyers like John Oldham, who declared on his arrival that he had come to reform the Church and set up a rival body, and whom the Rev. John Lyford would abet. But when Lyford arrived in 1624, argument, which had bred Separatism in the first place, was just as fertile in breeding offshoots and rivals even on now-hallowed ground. With some of them it even meant return to the Anglican fold, though calling itself a Reformed religion. But argument and awkwardness for their own sake became the mark of the Calvinist, and of the Yankee.

Central to the story, the source of endless contention among them, and – for some – a cause of exile and exile again, the creed of the Pilgrims gave them their inner tension, and their strength. Vivid and detailed on their daily anxieties, on the threats from Indians and the constant need for corn, as is Bradford's story, singularly uncharitable as it is to particular individuals, the call to prayer is the refrain that echoes through *Plimouth Plantation*: prayer, and the sanctity of Sundays, in the wilderness as at home. Twice on Sunday and early on Thursday evening ("Lecture Day"), the Saints and their families assembled at the beat of a drum, each man with a musket, at the foot of Fort Hill, then marched up three abreast for worship. "Behind," a Dutch visitor reported, "comes the Governour, in a long robe. Beside him, on the right hand, comes the preacher, with his cloak on, and on the left hand, the Captain, with his sidearms and cloak on, and with a small cane in his hand." It is a society orderly, militant, ceremonial, yet small and intimate. It made a daunting regimen: Sunday services began at 8 a.m., men and women sitting separately; an hour-long opening prayer was observed standing up, since kneeling was an idolatrous Roman practice; and a sermon of at least two hours' duration was then given, not from a pulpit but from a bare wooden table. Psalms were sung without instrumental aid of any kind. The organ – if in Plymouth they had had such – was, in particular, "the Divill's bag-pipes." Readings from the Bible were frequent, chosen by chance, and always with comment and exposition. "Dumb Reading" was a deplorable Anglican practice. Prayers and sermons marked a long Sunday morning. But Sunday afternoons were devoted to "Prophecyings", at best soliloquies, at worst remarks from any member of congregation so moved, regardless of his education or qualifications. It was expected that all such testimony, like prayers and sermons, would be delivered extempore – like speeches in the English House of Commons, where the rule still obtains. Unlike the latter case, where the timetable is tightly controlled, the unlimited time available encouraged verbosity, even incoherence. Thomas Morton singled out this characteristic for savage attack in his "New Canaan."

The Separatists' crusade against ceremony, altars and high style seemed made for observance by simple and illiterate rustic folk, in rocky and barren lands. Nor were these practices curbed by the absence of a pastor, without whom there could be no sacraments: there was no ordained cleric until Lyford came in 1624. The Church, like the tiny and vulnerable community of which it was the essence, was held together alike in spirit as in flesh by William Bradford, the sword arm of Elder William Brewster, in whose home at Scrooby long years ago the orphaned and sickly boy had been brought up.

The regimen was the more striking since, as there was no pastor among them, there could be no baptism by an ordained person, no celebration of communion until an ordained visitor reached them. Nor is the only surviving sermon – Robert Cushman's "On the danger of self-love" – typical.[8] In the light of their experiences over the previous 18 months, the theme sounds perverse, even obtuse. But the good deacon, who had decided not to sail on the *Mayflower*, had come as Thomas Weston's emissary in the *Fortune* in November 1621, to try to persuade the Pilgrims to sign a new agreement with Sir Ferdinando Gorges and the newly established Council of New England, now that it was clear in London that that was where the Pilgrims had landed. His arrival was the occasion for a welcoming party and a feast of "wild turkie" – America's First Thanksgiving. As one of them, he was appealing for unity and for harmony. He was "their right hand with their friends, the adventurers." He was literate, sensible and statemanlike. He steered clear of doctrine, and sought to remind the settlers that they were there virtually indentured as a group to the London merchants who financed their transport. But he also knew the language of the sect, and described himself as "a poor weakling ... a frail man." He was aware that the Separatists were, by calling, an awkward squad, given to dissonance, generating divisiveness, yet in all their prickliness taking pride in their own abasement as unworthy vehicles of Grace; he knew all too well that their way of celebrating and giving thanks was to hold a "solemn day of humiliation." He pleaded – and returned. And he did testify that the care of the Pilgrims had been "to settle religion ... before either profit or popularite." The Pilgrims promised to supply more goods, but protested as explanation of

---

[8] Willison, *Saints and Strangers*, p. 116.

their remissness that "they were yoked with some ill-conditioned people." And the shrewd deacon insured himself on his return by having his sermon printed.[9]

Indeed, when, after 1623, they began to feel more confident of their own survival, they could permit their Puritanism to show. When the secular-spirited Captain Thomas Wollaston and Thomas Morton settled at Quincy in 1625, and did more than trade with the Indians, Governor Bradford condemned "the beastley practicses of the madd Bacchinalians," "drinking and dancing aboute in many dayes together, inviting the Indian women for their consorts, dancing and frisking together like so many fairies or furies."[10] In the end Myles Standish captured the post and deported Morton to England. He returned, and was again expelled. But the zeal was not only religious. "Merrymount" (Quincy) or "the New English Canaan", as Morton lyrically wrote it up, was a trading centre – liquor and arms in exchange for furs that cut into Plymouth's trade. Within five years of the foundation, and in as barren a soil as this, Calvinism was moving close to profit-making.

The encounter of the Rev. John Lyford with the planters is sometimes seen in the framework of a religious struggle – the Anglicans against the Separatists. On the basis of Bradford's account it is more accurate historically to see Lyford as a Particular challenging the rule of the planters, for Lyford was aware of his power as a Particular to upset the Separatists' equilibrium, since Particulars outnumbered Separatists. Morton is even more misused than Lyford by historians wishing to make a case for Anglican-Separatist hostilities. Morton, once an Anglican, abandoned his religious affiliation when he left Plymouth to live his eccentric life at Merrymount. It is true that the Separatists disliked Morton because they found him morally offensive, but the matter was more complex. His gay world at Merrymount attracted those people most dissatisfied with the system at Plymouth. He contributed to the breakdown of the communal system by luring indentured servants away from their work. Furthermore, Morton sought from England more guns to sell to the

---

[9] Cushman's return had been as unhappy as his experiences as negotiator, both in 1619 in London, and in 1624 in New Plymouth; the *Fortune*, with its precious and long-awaited cargo of furs and pelts, as – at last – the Pilgrims' thanks for the adventurers' aid, was captured by French pirates, and its cargo lost. He still planned to settle in the colony, but died suddenly in London in 1625, possibly of plague.

[10] Bradford's *Of Plimouth Plantation*, cited in G. F. Willison, *The Pilgrim Reader* (Garden City, NY, Doubleday, 1953), p. 332.

Indians. It was not the moral fibre of the Separatists that Morton threatened; it was their physical safety. The initiative to eliminate Morton from the Plymouth scene came from the small farmers around Boston whose farms had been invaded by Indians armed by Morton.

The Pilgrim colony was a tiny foothold on a hostile shore. The little community remained a simple, agricultural, inward-looking society, fishing, growing maize and wheat and keeping cattle. (They had only one plough between them as late as 1640.) By 1691 they had been absorbed into their more powerful and successful neighbor, Massachusetts.

The Pilgrims were held together by their Faith, and by a few heroic leaders. One of these was Francis Johnson (he and his brother George, also a Separatist, were Cambridge men, of Christ's College), who had led the Amsterdam Congregation (the Ancient Church) and who was imprisoned, first in England, then in Holland. He died in Amsterdam in 1618. A follower of Johnson, Francis Blackwell, took an overloaded ship to Virginia in the winter of 1618–19, and died with many of the company at sea. Another of their company, Henry Jacob, who like Johnson had been an Anglican clergyman before he became a "Brownist," founded the settlement of Jacobopolis in Virginia in 1622.[11] Pastor Robinson, who never got to Cape Cod, emerges in recent studies as a hero of whom before now we have known little. John Oldham, fighting his own corner, came out to try to win the Pilgrims back to his Established Church, and they drove him out ruthlessly. The hero who got no credit was the *Mayflower's* captain, Christopher Jones, who stayed on his – by that time filthy – ship, to ensure their survival through their first winter; he did not sail home until 5 April 1621. He died shortly after his return, as much a victim of the journeys as any Pilgrim. But dwarfing them all was William Bradford (1590–1657), a Yorkshire yeoman brought up by Brewster after becoming an orphan, who had spent the years in Holland studying Latin, Greek, Dutch, and the Bible. His judgment and integrity during the voyage had impressed his fellow Pilgrims, and when the first governor of Plymouth Plantation died, Bradford succeeded him and was re-elected 31 times; their elected governor was also judge and treasurer, genuine Christian, preacher since there was no other, consummate politician, who, in 1627, with seven leading pilgrims bought out the merchant investors who

[11] For Francis Johnson, see D. B. Quinn, *England and the Discovery of America 1481–1620* ((London, Allen and Unwin, 1973), pp. 337–52.

had staked them; he and "The Old Comers" owned land and houses, cattle and implements, and shared them out to give "all good contents." Now colony and corporation were merged, but Plymouth never received a royal charter. Bradford was at once persuasive and commanding, with, for bonus, a prose style whose writing has a Biblical cadence; happily he became the historian of the enterprise – and thus their advocate. For their story, Bradford's *Of Plimouth Plantation* – his "scribled writings" begun in 1630 and "peaced up at times of leesure afterwards," – is the major, for long the only, source. By 1650 it was 270 folio pages, all in his own hand. He wrote slowly, and stopped at 1646. The manuscript remained unpublished in his family, was stored in Old South church tower in Boston during the Revolution, was lost, and turned up years later in the library of the bishop of London. A final and authoritative version was published only in 1912. His model is that of a biblical exodus; his prose rich with Old Testament phrases. He had his own private cross to carry; his wife threw herself overboard before they all went ashore; and on this he is oddly terse and unforthcoming. Non-clerics all; but then "as long as Governor Bradford lived, no minister ever dared to aspire to lead them." [12]

That they did survive was due to the strength of a few, to the skill of a handful, and – it has to be added – to their muskets. Survival on this bleak and wintry shore depended on food, and firepower. The communal experiment was short-lived. Within three years some families were prosperous, and some not: the former jealously guarding all that they had won by their own labor, the indolent begging for bigger shares from the common reserves of corn. But then it had not really been designed as a communal, but as a Christian, adventure. The Mayflower compact was for the survival of civil government in a wilderness, in which it became clear that the Indians were usually unfriendly, and even when friendly, unreliable. So, equally erratically, were a few of the Strangers who had accompanied the Saints. But the Founding Fathers went for religion's sake, not politics' sake. They were socially conservative, contentious and skilled dialecticians (their Saturday services in Leiden, led by Pastor Robinson, ran from 8 a.m. to noon, and from 2 p.m. to 6; and should children or adults fall asleep, they were struck sharply on the knuckles with a switch by a vigilant deacon); Brewster had been a part-time professor in Leiden University. Of the 102, no less than 15 went as servants to the others. Nor was it escape

---

[12] See Arber, *The Story of the Pilgrim Fathers*, Introduction, p. 30.

to a new political order, or to democracy. The freemen were consulted by the governor and his assistants "only in some weighty
matters, when we thinke good." They acknowledged James I of
England as king. They did not seek independence – indeed they
were pathetically dependent on aid from home. Their rights to the
land were confirmed by a new patent, and at the end of seven years
(by profits obtained chiefly from the fur trade), they purchased
their release for £1,800 from the merchants who had financed them.
They were zealous to do what they did inside the laws of England.

Three thousand miles of ocean might dilute the rule of bishops to the
vanishing point, but they did not dilute the sense that the equality of
men came far short of annihilating distinctions between the wiser and
the simpler, the graver and the more flighty, the advantaged and the disadvantaged ... some were worthy of a special respect and address beyond
others, and society should, as it were, institutionalize this.[13]

Plymouth Rock became legendary largely for false reasons, thanks
to William Bradford the historian, and to Longfellow. Moreover,
the settlement had little direct impact on American colonial history.
Almost from the beginning it was overshadowed by Massachusetts
Bay, into which it was merged in 1691. The Pilgrims and the Puritans
survived as theocracies and as family groups, with outstanding
leaders, and not as rebels. Power rested with those chosen to lead;
and by the second and third generations, they were becoming an
interlinked kinship of cousins and in-laws. In G. P. Gooch's words,
"Modern Democracy is the child of the Reformation, not of the
Reformers."[14]

C. M. Andrews was right, however, to describe the Plymouth
settlement as America's "emblem nation". And its longer-term impact,
if mainly emotional, can be put in statistics. Twenty-three Pilgrims
are known to have produced children. But today there are 16,000
members of the Society of Mayflower Descendants, all of whom to
secure membership have to supply genealogical proof that they are
descended from at least one of those 23 Pilgrims. And no fewer
than four presidents of the United States can make the claim to such
illustrious origins: Zachary Taylor (descendant both of William
Brewster and Isaac Allerton), Ulysses Simpson Grant (descended from

[13] Larzer Ziff, *Puritanism in America, New Culture in a New World* (New York,
Viking, 1973), p. 40.
[14] George P. Gooch, *English Democratic Ideas in the Seventeenth Century* (Cambridge University Press, 1927), p. 7.

Richard Warren), William Howard Taft (from Francis Cooke) and Franklin Delano Roosevelt (claiming descent from no less than six Founding Fathers: Francis Cooke, the Allertons, the Warrens, John Rowland, John Tilley and the De La Noye family).

3 THE PURITANS

In all their humility, the Pilgrims saw only one path to salvation: their own. To those they found to be uncongenial, lewd or ill-disposed, or to those following other dissenting creeds, however similar they might seem, the Pilgrims could be intolerant: they were driven out as Thomas Morton was from Quincy. On this wild frontier, expulsion was a severe sentence. But the settlers could not be lax. The exile of dissenters was as much a matter of survival as of conviction: supplies of corn were low; winters brutal; and the Indians at best unreliable. Another exile was Roger Conant, who had come out "on his particular" on the *Anne* in 1623, and moved on within a year to Nantasket (Hull). Within another year he became governor of the Pilgrims' rival settlement (the work of the Reverend John White's Dorchester Company), up the coast at Gloucester on rocky Cape Ann, designed to bring a Christian message as well as to serve as a base for fishermen; and when that failed, within the year, he moved again, down the North Shore to found Naumkeag in 1626. Two years later, he was joined there by John Endicott with a commission as governor; quarrels arose over who acted for whom and over who owned what; in adjusting these claims, and as a pledge that the future would be different from the past, the town was given a new name, Salem or Shalom (peace). Peace brought among other things the persecution of Quakers; and the flight of Pastor Roger Williams before he faced banishment himself. Conant moved out yet again, to found Beverly in 1636; and for the record, and as evidence of kin seeking kin, one of his nine children married the daughter of Thomas Weston, the merchant who had financed the Pilgrim Fathers' crossing, and Conant gave it all up and returned to London. Dreams, even enterprise, were not enough; but they made for restlessness.

There were others, with other ambitions, some lordly, some not of this world. The post at Wessagusset, now Weymouth, when abandoned by Thomas Weston's unruly agent, was taken over by Captain Robert Gorges, son of Sir Ferdinando, chairman of the so-called Council for New England. Under its imposing title, the Council was in fact an ambitious but yet another public company, in which the

king, two dukes, four earls and 34 other lords and gentry had
shares and claims for land, and with a charter (granted July 23, 1620)
that gave it, on paper, the whole of the New England coast between
the 40th and 48th parallels, extending "throughout the mainland,
from sea to sea." Gorges the son had full powers from the Council,
"civil, military and ecclesiastical;" his father had a vast monopoly
that included all goods on the seas "in going to and from the said
colony." He gave himself also a grant of all the region lying between
the Kennebec and Merrimack Rivers. Later he took all land north of
the Piscataqua River, which he called the Province of Maine. He
clearly hoped for at least a palatinate, if not a kingdom, and intended
to absorb all the unconsidered sectaries that were springing up in his
dominion. But the plans and lotteries for land among the nobles in
Greenwich, on June 29, 1623, did not take accord of weather and
wilderness, or of the qualities needed to resist them. Earlier – after
the failure of his Plymouth settlement on the Sagahadoc River in
1607–8 – Sir Ferdinando had admitted that his hopes had been
"frozen to death." But he went on dreaming. The son returned to
the comfort of England in the spring of 1624, "not having found
the state of things near to answer his qualitie and condition." But
from the remnants of his colony came the solitary plantations that
are now within the metropolitan area of Boston, at Hull and Mount
Wollaston; the militant churchman Thomas Walford trekked to
Mishawum, now Charlestown. Samuel Maverick, gentleman trader,
established himself on Noddles Island, now East Boston; and David
Thompson, Gent, an attorney for Gorges, settled on the island in
Boston Harbor that still bears his name.

One of the restless was the rebel Anglican churchman, Reverend
William Blaxton or Blackstone, yet another Cambridge (Emmanuel)
man, and still in name an Anglican; he sought solitude with his 180
books in a house on Beacon Hill, with an orchard below him on
the Common. The first settler in what would become Boston, he
developed the first named variety of apple in America, "Blaxton's
Yellow Sweeting." The first Bostonian was also its first eccentric:
when not tending his orchard, he rode about the three-hilled peninsula on a saddled bull he had trained. When the Puritans reached
Charlestown and wanted – as ever – to expand across the river to
the more inviting prospect of what the Indians called the Shawmut
peninsula, with its three hills promising freedom from mosquitoes,
they promised him 50 acres. This was, it seemed, no bargain for
him, since it had all been his anyway, before his rash offer of hospitality. But the eccentric had a shrewdness all his own. He accepted
their generosity, and then sold them back their 50 acres for $150,

a princely sum for what, after all, was not originally his at all. In England, he said, he didn't like the Lords Bishops; he would not now be under the Lords Brethren. He preferred Indians, and rum, he said, to Puritans, who did not like either. So he uprooted himself and moved to Rhode Island, where he lived in happy isolation, with only books, rum and Indians for solace, until he was 80. William Hilton founded Cocheco, later Dublin, New Hampshire, on the Piscataqua River, ten miles above its mouth. In Maine, York (1624), Wells (1640), Cape Porpoise, and Saco (1631) followed. By 1628 a number of small fishing villages had been founded along the New England coast, all with licenses to fish granted by the (new) Council of New England. In the light of the accession of Charles I in 1625, less tolerant than his father to the "heretics," all these could be seen as advance posts for a much greater migration. Of this the Massachusetts Bay Company became the vehicle.

The Massachusetts Bay Company, originally organized for the business of fishing and fur trading, and having absorbed the defunct group, the Dorchester Adventurers, which in 1623 had tried to plant the settlement on Cape Ann, secured in 1628 a patent for the region stretching from three miles south of the Charles to three miles north of the Merrimac, and extending from the Atlantic to the Pacific. There remains a mystery here, since this was part of the area under the authority of the Council for New England, whose charter was still in effect. In the following year the Company was enlarged and came under the control of the Puritans, who determined to use it as a means of founding a Puritan commonwealth. The charter of March 1629 granted the company self-government, with the power to make laws not contrary to those of England, and directed that the freemen of the company meet four times a year to elect officers and transact business. Again, what began as a commercial charter became the constitution of a new state. As the charter failed to specify where these meetings should take place, the leaders took their charter with them – an act of doubtful legality – and established the seat of the government in America. It now seems clear that the Endicott mission to Salem had been a preliminary reconnoitre, and that a fishing and merchant company was the cover for a colony of refugees who planned to create a virtually independent state.

In August 1629, 12 of the Puritan group, independent-minded and prouder than the Pilgrims, wealthier, drawn mainly from London and the eastern counties, held a secret conference in Cambridge (which some of them knew from student days), where their plans were made. The Congregational system was made for just such a journey into exile: each individual – in their words, "particular" – congregation was self-governing, choosing its own pastors and officers, run by those who had made a public confession and had a conversion, the "visible saints." It involved an organized movement of families and resources, in total contrast to the chapter of accidents and misfortunes that had bedevilled the migration to Plymouth. It was no less than a transfer of a people, a government, and a Church. For its first year at least, Church and State in New England were one and the same. The planners were men of means, responsible country gentlemen and merchants, who took yeomen and artisans with them. And they signed their agreement before they sailed. Their elected leader was John Winthrop, with John Humfry his deputy; Isaac Johnson and John Endicott, already "on station," would become his assistants on reaching Salem.

In terms of doctrine, these families were Congregationalists, not Separatist. In fact, by 1630 there was in their eyes much to warrant total exile. Until then, they had sought to reform the Church of England, their "dear mother," from within, which meant in fact making it Calvinist, on the model of Calvin's system in Geneva. The alternative model was that of the Church of Scotland, in which the hierarchy of archbishops, bishops and priests would be replaced by another hierarchy of governing bodies, from the national General Assembly – presided over by a moderator elected annually, who would take precedence over any state representative attending it – to the parish presbytery of minister and elders. This Presbyterianism was, however, still too hierarchical for the Congregationalists. To them each congregation was its own sovereign, with its own covenant of grace; it "called" a minister, and, when it could, the "teacher" also, and they would expound and elaborate the message, not merely read the Good Book. It emerged also as less fatalist than Calvin's "Institutes;" a man could be saved, nothing was written; its cosmic optimism was a stronger weapon than was predestination for a journey into and survival in a wilderness. William Ames, the English theologian, and John Cotton were almost as important as Calvin in this formulation.

By 1630, however, the earl of Strafford was at the head of the army in England; and by 1633, William Laud, the High Anglican bishop of London and vigorous opponent of the Puritans, had been appointed archbishop of Canterbury – both with the declared objective of making their master the most absolute prince in Christendom. With ship money, illegal taxes, and forced loans imposed by royal decree, and, a week after they got their charter, with the king beginning to rule without Parliament altogether, the struggle for change from within in England seemed to have been totally lost. What they sought, in Winthrop's words, was "a shelter and a hidinge place for us and others;" "the church hath noe place lefte to flie into but the wildernesse." This now was exile from both Church and State, and permanently. The first Puritans went to Massachusetts for the sake of their Faith. On the *Arbella* Winthrop addressed his fellow passengers in "A Modell of Christian Charity": "Wee are a Company professing our selves fellow members of Christ, wee ought to account ourselves knitt by this bond of love, and live in the experience of it ... for wee must Consider that wee shall be as a Citty upon a Hill, the eies of all people are uppon us ..." He saw Old England as corrupt and dissolute: "this lande growes wearye of her Inhabitantes." He would sell all he had, and take family and flock to a New Canaan. He would be a Moses to his people. To the task he brought his own talents: not as warm a man as Bradford, but with matching dedication.

Born in the year of the Armada, Winthrop was the son of a wealthy cloth merchant, whose own father had acquired Groton Manor in Suffolk, part of the dissolved monastery of Bury St Edmunds in East Anglia. He was yet another Cambridge man (Trinity College), and a lawyer of the Inner Temple – but on the abrogation of Parliament by the king, he lost his attorneyship. Succeeding his father in 1618, and inheriting Groton Manor, he lived well, but his debts grew and his family was large, and he saw the future of the country in gloomy terms: inflation, mounting taxes, the depression in cloth manufacturing in eastern counties, religious tyranny, and what he saw as the "generall calamitie" of its people. To "My dear wife," he wrote in May 1629, "I am verily perswaded God will bringe some heavye Affliction upon this lande, and that speedylye." His own conversion to the Puritan cause was slow, in part the result of his awareness of the sins of the flesh. So too with the decision to go into exile. He was all too aware of the failure of earlier expeditions. In 1623 he thought of emigration to Ireland. As he was deliberate, so was he determined. He put his fortune where his heart and mind were: he sold it to finance the project. He was the wealthiest man in Massachusetts Bay, with an annual income of £600 to £700. So, of course, was William Bradford the wealthiest man in New Plymouth – although his total estate at his death was worth only £900. In spirit Winthrop was more a man of books than of the market place, a Puritan cast in the Milton mould. Like Bradford and like John Smith, he kept a journal. All three were zealous to leave their mark on their times and on history.

The care and planning in the Puritan expedition emphasizes its significance. This was no small group of *dévots*. The first swarming of the English, in the two decades before the civil war, in which between 1,000 and 3,000 colonists migrated each year – as many to Virginia as to Massachusetts – points to a social and economic malaise as well as a theological debate; and Catholics as well as Protestants sought refuge overseas. America would relieve England of its excess and unemployed population – for "the people ... doe swarme in the land, as yong bees in a hive in June;" the country was "pestered with multitude." Prices were higher and real wages lower than they had been for almost a century; lords of manors reduced whole townships to "a shepheard and his dog'; traditional jobs were being denied to people of "the middling sort;" university men found opportunities in the Church closed to them, thanks to the doctrinal vigilance of Laud and his supporters: in its first decade, Massachusetts Bay had a higher proportion of university graduates (130 in all, 92 of them clerics) than any society in the history of the world. The great migration was a brain-drain of highly talented men. [15]

In 1623, Winthrop had drawn up 23 "Common Grievances Groaninge for Reformation." But redress now seemed less and less likely. In March 1629 Charles I dissolved Parliament and began his personal rule. And from a small group of like-minded men came the ideal of "a new colony upon the old foundation": Winthrop, the Dorchester group (Master John White, a lawyer, and the bishop of Bath and Wells, who had as students been contemporaries at New College, Oxford), Reverend Hugh Peter, and John Humfry, (as students, contemporaries at Trinity College, Cambridge); Humfry was married to a sister of the earl of Lincoln, and resided near Dorchester. Thus what had been tried on Cape Ann became "the New England business;" but until the ships sailed, it would be a business "which the world sees nothing of."

On Easter Monday 1630, off the Isle of Wight in the English Channel, Winthrop and a group of settlers boarded the *Jewel*, the *Ambrose*, the *Talbot*, and the fleet's flagship, the *Arbella*. The *Arbella* was named after (or, in "American", for) the daughter of the Puritan earl of Lincoln, who was Isaac Johnson's wife; they would name

---

[15] S. E. Morison et al. (eds), *Winthrop Papers*, 5 vols (Boston, Massachusetts Historical Society, 1929), vol. II, p. 114. Cf. Edmund S. Morgan, *The Puritan Dilemma: The story of John Winthrop* (Boston, Little Brown, 1958); Carl Bridenbaugh, *Vexed and Troubled Englishmen* (New York, Oxford University Press, 1968), p. 327.

their settlement Boston because she, and not they, came from Boston, England. Seven other ships, including the *Mayflower*, were to follow these four as soon as the necessary preparations were completed. In all the fleet took 1,000 colonists to a New World. Many middle-class among them paid their own way. And their numbers at least ensured a firm foothold, and security against the Indians.

According to Winthrop's journal, the Atlantic crossing was both relatively pleasant and appropriately pious. There were morning and evening prayers, and two sermons preached every Sabbath. The watches were changed with the singing of a psalm, and a prayer which, Winthrop emphasized, was not read out of a book. Three of the four ships were usually within sight of each other, and on one occasion the *Arbella* borrowed a midwife from the *Jewel*. On June 8, two months out of port, the coast of Maine was sighted; a few days later Endicott came aboard and was informed that he had been succeeded as governor by Winthrop. It had been a 76-day voyage. Some rowed to Salem for dinner, while others feasted on the wild strawberries growing along the coast. They did not stay long in Salem, and moved to Charlestown in September 1630. Lack of water then drove them to cross the Charles and, with the agreement of the Reverend William Blackstone, in 1631 they moved to the three-hilled peninsula which the Indians called Shawmut. Isaac Johnson and Lady Arbella died in Charlestown in the first grim winter; so did one of Winthrop's children, when his wife and family joined him in November 1631; the baby daughter his wife brought, whom the father had not seen, died on the voyage. By the end of the summer almost 2,000 immigrants from England had arrived, bringing with them about 200 cattle.

John Smith, on his voyage in 1614, had been lyrical about New England:

I did not think that in all the knowne world it could be paralleled ... for so many goodly groves of trees ... Dainty fine round-raising hillocks ... Delicate fair plaines, sweet crystal fountaines and cleare running streames ... Fowle in abundance, Fish in multitude, and besides, millions of Turtle doves on the green boughs, which sate pecking in the full, ripe grapes. Here and there dispersed, you might see Lillies, which made the Land to me seem paradise. In mine eye, 'twas Nature's masterpiece, her chiefest magazine of all where lives her store ... If this land be not rich, then is the whole world poore ...[16]

---

[16] *A Description of New England* (1616).

Boston was a good location, said William Wood. Being "a necke and bare of wood," it was free also from "the three great annoyances of woolves, rattle-snakes and Musketoes."[17] Once the invaders came it acquired a hazard all its own. The Common, now deemed unsafe for solitary strollers in the evening, soon had a set of stocks, at Governor Winthrop's order.

The Bay colony's first winter, like Jamestown's and like New Plymouth's, was grim. The settlers had arrived too late to plant, and the provisions which they had brought with them proved to be inadequate, as were the supplies acquired from the Indians. They lived on "clams and muscles, groundnuts and acorns." One dejected woman exclaimed: "The air of the country is sharp, the rocks many, the trees innumerable, the grass little, the winter cold, the summer hot, the gnats in summer biting, the wolves at midnight howling &c."[18] Finally a relief ship appeared, bringing grain, pease, barrelled beef, and, fortuitously, lemons — which helped cure an outbreak of scurvy, although this property of citrus fruits was not then known.

Only a few hundred settlers arrived in Massachusetts Bay in 1631 and 1632, but the following year what became known as the "Great Migration" began. Within a year the Bay was ringed with settlements: Dorchester, Roxbury, Watertown, Newton, Cambridge, Charlestown and Boston. In 1631 the Company was transformed from a trading organization to a commonwealth. In England the "freeman" was a voting member of a trading company or of an incorporated city or borough. In Massachusetts, when company and colony became identical, the freemen of the company, who had crossed the ocean, became the freemen of the colony, with a right to vote for representatives in the colonial assembly. And all were Congregationalists or Puritans. During the next decade as many as a dozen ships were sometimes anchored in Boston Harbor at one time. In the ten years before England again had a Parliament, some 20,000 English men and women, in some 4,000 families, would follow Winthrop to the shores of Massachusetts Bay. Over 100 of them were university-trained ministers of religion: and the best of them — John Cotton, Thomas Shepherd, and Peter Hobart of Hingham — brought their congregations with them. As, under Laud's vigilance, Puritan tracts were suppressed, Puritan parsons and lecturers silenced, and chaplains

---

[17] William Wood, *New England Prospects*, ed. Boynton (Boston, 1898), p. 39, quoted in Walter M. Whitehill, *Boston, A Topographical History* (Cambridge, MA, Harvard University Press, 1976 edn), p. 3.
[18] Bridenbaugh, *Vexed and Troubled Englishmen*, p. 11.

to the gentry forbidden, whole congregations pooled resources and moved to New England.

As movements of local congregations, not of individuals, the earliest settlers represented a cross-section of English society, rather than any one distinct class. This cross-section was practically a miniature England and unusually homogeneous in character; some were gentry, while the majority were tradesmen, small landowners, and artisans. These first settlers were men and women of substance and ability, of energy and independent thought. The migration was halted only by the outbreak of war in England between king and Parliament in 1642, and the growing prospect of a Puritan parliament's success. Although drawn from different regions, four-fifths of the Puritan company came from south of a line drawn from Bristol to the Wash; they were homogeneous, their leaders known to each other and highly experienced: merchants like John Cradock and Richard Saltonstall, lawyers like Winthrop, Humfry and John White, country gentlemen like Isaac Johnson and John Pelham. Abetting and encouraging them were Puritan-minded nobility, the earls of Lincoln and Warwick, Lord Saye and Sele, and Lord Brooke. Either in themselves or through their many contacts they commanded large amounts of capital. And they sought to leave nothing to chance. If the movement had an "intellectual headquarters," it was in Cambridge, at Emmanuel College, founded by Sir Walter Mildmay in 1584 to propagate Puritan doctrine, which sent 35 of its graduates to Puritan New England, including John Harvard and John Cotton (one of its Fellows, and as dean preacher and theologian, the most influential force of all); at Peterhouse College, where William Brewster, the Pilgrim leader, matriculated; and at Caius and Christ's Colleges, at the latter of which both John Robinson of Leiden and Francis Johnson were Fellows. Roger Williams was at Pembroke College; John Winthrop the elder, and John Cotton as student, at Trinity College. Only one member of the first Harvard Board of Overseers went to Oxford: John Davenport, who went to Merton College. Almost all the rest of the Puritan leaders were Cambridge men.

Everyday life in Massachusetts Bay was austere and harsh, and there were few amenities. The Sabbath Day, which began at six in the evening on Saturday, was set aside for religious devotion. The whole family participated, including any servants and apprentices. Sunday was spent at the meeting house, where the congregation listened to sermons, which would sometimes last for four hours, and to prayers which could last for an hour or longer. This was varied only by the singing of an occasional psalm, without instrumental accompaniment; to the Puritans, instrumental music was papist. The meeting house, totally devoid of warmth, was uncomfortable at best, and in the bitterly cold New England winter attendance was a physical ordeal. Children, like adults, sat through it all in utter silence, or at least were enjoined to. And to it all paraded.

The Puritans who founded the Massachusetts Bay Colony had no intention of establishing an open society of religious or civil freedom; they had come to the New World to practice their own kind of Puritanism; those who did not conform to it would not be allowed to practice variants of their own. They were as intolerant as Laud himself. Those who had fled from a persecuting Church for conscience' sake became a persecuting Church in their own commonwealth. So it was that self-righteousness and intolerance, the forces that had called the Bay Colony into existence, led inexorably to the establishment of yet other colonies, founded by exiles from Massachusetts.

Roger Williams, who had settled at Salem in 1631, wanted no autocracy, and could raid the Bible for quotations too. He was young — only 27 in 1631 — and well-educated (Charterhouse, and Pembroke College, Cambridge), where he went to study law and left as a Puritan, intense and idealistic. He suffered only from an excess of virtue; he asserted that the authority of the magistrates "extended only to the bodies, and goods, and outward estates of men," and not to their consciences, recalling the biblical injunction that Caesar and God were not synonymous. He accepted the doctrine of predestination, and the distinction between saint and sinner: but these were for religious worship. In civil rights, the sinner was not inferior to the saint; and for him Christ was Shepherd as well as King. For him his conscience was his guide. The Indians had rights too. He thought that land on which Indians swarmed should not be taken from them by force. In June 1636, "with at least three persons," Williams went out into the wilderness, bought land from the Indians and established a settlement he called Providence. He believed in tolerance and gave refuge to all seekers, to Quakers, to the followers of Anne Hutchinson, and those of Samuel Gorton, the believer in the priesthood of all men. The first Baptist Church was set up in 1639. In 1644, ever the good legalist, he sailed back to England, and obtained a charter for his little colony around Narragansett Bay, and it was named Rhode Island. It was to have a representative assembly, for which the suffrage — unlike Massachusetts — was not confined only to church members. Williams visited England again in 1651–4 to secure Cromwell's endorsement.

While Williams's stress on the individual's direct relationship to God, and on the complete separation of Church and State, were anathema in Massachusetts, his concept of land ownership was even more heretical. The land, he held, belonged not to the king but to the Indians. The royal charter granted to liberal Rhode Island by a returned Charles II in 1663 expressly guaranteed it full liberty of conscience, and united Portsmouth and Newport with Williams's own Providence Plantations. The charter served the colony and the state as a constitution until 1842. Rhode Island continued for long a refuge for dissenters of all kinds from the other states. Massachusetts, it was said, had law but not liberty; Rhode Island liberty but not law. Williams would not have seen them as antitheses: for him the law should ensure total liberty of thought, expression, – and worship. He was zealous in ensuring the state's endorsement of all he did. He was the supreme total Puritan individualist, his writings vividly autobiographical: *The Bloudy Tenent [sic] of Persecution for Causes of Conscience* (1644); the indictment of the intolerance of Boston, *A Key into the Language of America* (1643); a warm picture of life among the Narrangansetts designed for the missionary-trader, but a revelation also of one man's imaginative skill in leaping the racial fence and his view of all men as brothers, irrespective of rank, caste or race, in his *Experiments of Spiritual Life and Health* (1652). He managed, too, to survive through stormy times and die, indeed, in obscurity, aged 80, in 1683.

As a model for the American Constitution of 1787, Rhode Island, with its distinction between Church and State, was to be an apter model than Massachusetts, Williams's ethic of Christian love a nobler model than Winthrop's theocracy. At least with Williams, the exile was not bitter: John Haynes, the governor who pronounced his banishment from Massachusetts, became a cooperative and amiable governor of Connecticut. But here too in the practical world, secularism crept in. Rhode Island retained, until after the Revolution, a reputation for trading in rum and slaves, a reputation not only for liberty but for license.

In the Bay State, "the Bible Commonwealth," neither good works nor seniority were guarantees against the continuous inquisition. Mrs Anne Hutchinson, wife of William and mother of 15 children, admired the preaching of John Cotton when he moved from Cambridge to become vicar of St Botolph's in Boston, Lincolnshire; so much so that she followed him with her family to Boston, Massachusetts, in 1634, after his move there the year before. She was the daughter of a spirited English divine, Francis Marbury, himself a Puritan, and her husband was a wealthy merchant – a frequent alliance. Her family was indeed the first to settle on a site that is now historic in downtown Boston, The Old Corner Bookstore, on Washington

Street. She was active in good works ("a nimble wit ... and a very
voluble tongue, more bold than a man"), and visited sick neighbors,
of whom there were many. But she also held religious meetings
("two public lectures every week in her house, where to 60 or 80
persons did usually resort"); she was a dedicated commentator on
all she heard on Sundays from the preacher. She urged her friends
to seek salvation through a spiritual surrender to inner promptings,
as well as by good works and good conduct. To Winthrop this
Antinomian heresy connoted the abandonment of an individual's
moral responsibility; to follow "inner voices" could produce ethical –
and in the end – social anarchy. The Church he led held to a
"covenant of works," a religion of obedience to the laws of Church
and State. If good conduct was held to be meaningless, why be
good at all? Doctrine was not to become a topic for female chit-chat.
Theology, and pronouncements on it, were for men only. Winthrop's
own view was made plain:

That though women might meet (some few together) to pray and edify
together; yet such a set assembly (as was then in practice at Boston) where
sixty or more did meet every week, and one woman (in a prophetical way,
by resolving questions of doctrine, and expounding scripture) took upon
her the whole exercise, was agreed to be disorderly and without rule.

Moreover, intellectual pursuits, he believed, overtaxed women's
minds. Mrs Hutchinson was sentenced to be banished in 1637, a
verdict in which John Cotton now acquiesced; she, her husband,
and her large brood emigrated yet again, this time "as a leper," to
Rhode Island. After her husband's death, she moved in 1642 with
her family to New Rochelle, New York, to be safe among the
Huguenots; a year later they were all butchered by Indians, except
for her youngest daughter, Susanna, aged ten, who was ransomed
by the Dutch in New York. To Winthrop and the General Court
the massacre was but divine confirmation of their own diagnosis
and of their own judgment. "God's hand," he said, "is seen herein."
But her great-great-grandson would become a royal governor of the
colony of Massachusetts Bay from 1771 to 1774, and would, as a
Loyalist, go into exile himself, to die of a broken heart in London
in 1780.[19]

John Cotton, the Cambridge guru of a devoted flock, moved
towards more stringent orthodoxy; his code of laws, drawn up at

[19] John Winthrop, *Journal: History of New England 1630–1649*, ed. J. K.
Hosmer, 2 vols (New York, Scribner's), I. 234, II.225.

the request of the Massachusetts General Court in 1636, was seen as a Bible ("the Mosaic Code"); his *Milk for Babes* (1646) was its standard catechism; and in particular his *The Keyes of the Kingdom of Heaven* (1643), a declaration of anathema on Roger Williams as Leveller, was an insistence on the authority of the magistrate in Church as in State. Democracy, he declared, was not "a fitt government either for church or Commonwealth."

An offshoot of the Antinomian excitement was that Rev. John Davenport of St Stephen's church in London, an original stockholder in the Bay Company, who had escaped from Laudian heretic-hunting and followed his friends John Cotton and Thomas Hooker to Boston with his flock of 250, stayed only two months, and in 1636 moved on to found New Haven. Though modeled on Massachusetts, with a government similarly based on a church-membership suffrage, and with a similar ministerial leadership, New Haven developed into a loose confederation of towns held together by a central court, until its amalgamation with Connecticut in 1665.

Davenport's story is symbolic. In the Bay Colony as in New Plymouth, it was expected of the individual that he or she would testify to his worthiness for membership of these very select communities by declaring to his fellows that God had "sanctified" him, and that he would describe and make plain, even dramatic, his conversion experience. Never easy, this process was more familiar to older than younger people; for the young it was difficult, even strange. By the third generation, Church differed from Church in the intensity of the experiences of its members. Moreover, as time passed, fewer and fewer people had such experiences. In 1662 a Massachusetts synod agreed that, for all churches, a "half-way" membership would be recognized: adults who had been baptized as children, but who had not themselves experienced the conversation necessary for full membership, could have their own children baptized. The solution finally adopted has been nicknamed by its critics the Half-Way Covenant, a compromise reached by the Ministerial Convention of 1657 and later confirmed by the Synod of 1662. It was there agreed that the unregenerate members of the Church were entitled to transmit church membership and baptism to their children, but as unregenerate members they could not be partakers of the Lord's Supper, nor could they have a part in church elections. They were to be considered members of the Church, but not in full communion. Such was the plan by which the Puritans' Church attempted to keep within the sphere of its influence a large and growing class of people, who otherwise would have been lost to it. This half-way church membership was not to be automatically secured, for it was required that

those receiving it must give a public profession of willingness to
be guided by Christian principles, and to promise to bring up their
children by the Church's highest standards of moral conduct, and
in the fear of the Lord.

The controversy over the Half-Way Covenant divided the Churches.
John Davenport, a Founding Father and now 70 years of age, left
his New Haven congregation to accept a call to the First Church
in Boston, where a majority of the members shared his opposition
to the Covenant. A number of those who supported it – mainly
well-to-do merchants and tradesmen – in turn broke away to found
a new Church, the Third (familiarly "The Old South") Church.
Divisive though it was, and a stimulus to controversy for decades
ahead, the Half-Way Covenant was supported by the majority of
New England churches. Youthfulness, tolerance, and secularism were
now creeping in.[20]

4 THE NEW ENGLAND CONFEDERATION

Like John Davenport, Rev. Thomas Hooker – also of Emmanuel
College (where he had been a Fellow), who had been driven out by
Laud from his charge in Chelmsford, Essex, *via* Holland (Amsterdam,
Rotterdam and Delft) Hooker became disenchanted with autocratic
rule. He had sailed to Boston with Cotton in 1633, and they were
seen as at once friends and rivals – almost competitors, had there
been a contest to be hailed as best preacher. As the years passed,
however, Cotton, the unmitred pope, grew increasingly narrow and
more a friend of authority, wherever it was located. But Hooker held
that all the people should have a say in choosing their public magistrates, rather than, as was the practice in Massachusetts Bay Colony,
having them selected by church members only. He thus sought permission from the general court to move to the Connecticut River
valley, arguing that his Newtown (later re-named Cambridge) congregation needed more land, and had better move before the Dutch
moved there; moreover, he said, his flock felt strongly inclined "to
move hither." They were, he might almost have said, not merely
against Laud, but for land. The Connecticut valley was fertile, fed
by a broad navigable stream, and land was available not for the

---

[20] Ziff, *Puritanism in America* ch. 7; *Letters of John Davenport*, ed. Isabel M.
Calder (New Haven, Yale University Press, 1937); Robert G. Pope, *The Half-Way
Covenant: Church membership in Puritan New England* (Princeton, NJ, Princeton
University Press, 1969).

taking but for the purchasing. Despite the opposition of the general court, led by Cotton, Hooker and the majority of his congregation made the first westward migration in 1636, moving along the Indian path westward to what later became Hartford. He and the lawyer Roger Ludlow were largely responsible for drawing up and issuing, on January 14 1639, what became the colony's constitution, the Fundamental Orders of Connecticut, incorporating the enlargement of the franchise. And from Hooker came the first hint of a new order: "The foundation of all authority is laid ... in the free consent of the people." Impressive claims have been made for the Fundamental Orders as the world's first constitution, the prototype of the Federal Constitution.

Contentions marked the history of the Bay Colony, and so did the banishment of critics. The Rev. John Wheelwright, brother-in-law of Anne Hutchinson, was convicted of sedition and banished to Exeter, New Hampshire. In 1645 Doctor Robert Child presented his "Remonstrance and Humble Petition" for religious tolerance, for a Presbyterian form of government, and for the rights of those who were not church members. He even challenged the right of the general court to legislate without Parliament's consent. He was fined, imprisoned, and in the end sent back to England in 1647. For the first 30 years of its history the Bay Colony was committed to a crusade to preserve its own faith, and its own form of worship, and to wipe out heresy. To disagree was not merely to be wrong, but to be evil. As Nathaniel Ward put it in 1645, "poly-piety is the greatest impiety in the world." To be tolerant of other faiths was to be untrue to your own. The Bay Colony was, in Perry Miller's words, "deliberately, vigorously and consistently intolerant." [21] This was a society that depended on its own vigilance against its own members. The central malaise of the human condition was man's self-seeking will. "The very names of *Self* and *Own* should sound in the watchful Christian's ear as very terrible, wakening words that are next to the names of sin and Satan." Since every man carried with him a capacity to sin, the Holy Commonwealth existed to punish vice and reward virtue, said Richard Baxter, student of witchcraft and other sins. Submission to the brotherly watch of fellow members was part of one's commitment. "The Lord must work in me that which I must do on my own;" but He could be assisted. Parents spied on children, children on parents; all sexual irregularity, all suspicion of it, was

[21] "Errand into the wilderness," *William & Mary Quarterly*, 10 (Jan. 1953), p. 6.

taboo. The religious communities and the new towns indistinguishable from them, were keepers of morals as well as of the peace.[22]

The vigilance went beyond doctrine. Robert Keayne, the self-made man who from being a butcher's boy in London became one of the wealthiest men in New England, became suspect because of that success itself. The Puritans approved of material success, but when Keaynes went beyond the "just price" and the "fair reward" and overcharged mercilessly, he was called before the general court, and there "did, with tears, acknowledge and bewail his covetous and corrupt heart." He was fined and reprimanded. Winthrop's God was a Big Brother, an all-seeing Eye. There would be no escape for the unworthy. There was no privacy: everyone had to be a member of a family; there were rules regulating sexual practices, the use of alcohol, and recreation on the Sabbath. What freedom and what "democracy" there was in the Bay Colony began as a protest against Boston's absolutism.

As the Puritanism of the Bay Colony was dogmatic and intolerant, so was its government. Indeed, civil and religious authority were hard to distinguish. What was said from the pulpit became the law of the land: sovereignty lay with God not the people. And God spoke through and from the pulpit. One of the first ministers of the church at Stratford, Samuel Stone, commenting on the trust "the people" put in the competence of their ministers to interpret the will of God, saw a Congregational church as "a speaking aristocracy in the face of a silent democracy." The "freemen" had no legislative authority; all they could do was elect the Assistants, who formed in effect the governor's executive council.

Maine and New Hampshire had slow beginnings, although there were settlements in both even before the establishment of the Bay Colony. In 1641 the New Hampshire towns of Portsmouth, Dover, Exeter, and Hampton put themselves under the jurisdiction of Massachusetts Bay, and remained a part of the colony for 38 years, until New Hampshire became a separate royal province. The Puritan colonies of Massachusetts Bay, New Plymouth, Connecticut, and New Haven agreed in 1643, largely under Winthrop's urging, to form the New England Confederation, of which he became the first president. It was primarily for defense, but also for "the mutual

---

[22] Sacvan Bercovitch, *The Puritan Origins of the American Self* (New Haven, Yale University Press, 1975), p. 17; William Carey MacWilliams, *The Idea of Fraternity in America* (Berkeley, University of California Press, 1973), p. 121; Edmund Morgan, *The Puritan Family* (New York, Harper and Row, 1944), p. 10.

advice and succor upon all occasions, both for preserving and pro-
pagating the truth and liberties of the gospel, and for their own
mutual safety and welfare." Rhode Island, Maine, and New Hampshire
were pointedly excluded: Massachusetts Bay hoped to extend its
territory and influence by annexing them.

A brief quarter of a century after the Pilgrim landing, therefore,
New England had taken on a political shape that is still in a sense
recognizable today, and which had in it the precursor of the Albany
Plan for Confederation of 1754, and even of the ultimate constitution of 1787. As the Boston community expanded, similarly each
new settlement was as much a congregation as a town. As the colony
developed, the town, and in due course the town-meeting, became
the characteristic unit of government. Each town was also a church
congregation, and from them in due course would come representatives to a central assembly. As Winthrop had said in his "City on
the Hill" speech on the *Arbella*, the body politic was founded on
a social compact, a "covenant" among the members, bound in
Christian love – even if that love, as charity of mind and mercy
towards others, was often conspicuous by its absence.

Church and Commonwealth were hard to distinguish, and were
run by the same few. But, in recognition of the reality of secular
pressure, by the mid-1640s, the council became distinct from the
assembly in a two-house legislature; and the "Massachusetts Body
of Liberties" was adopted, derived in part from English common
law, from measures already passed by the general court, and in part
from the Bible. This was but to put into constitutional form what,
again, Winthrop had heralded on the *Arbella*, that God had "soe
disposed The Condicion of Mankinde, as in all times some must
be rich some poore, some highe and eminent in power and dignitie,
others meane and in subjeccion." Authority was vested in magistrates,
"high and eminent in power and dignitie;" and once elected, they
were empowered to rule – until re-elected.[23]

Humor did not come easily to Winthrop, yet his entries in the
Journal which he called his *History of New England*, which he kept
methodically from the voyage in 1630 until his death in 1649, and
in which he speaks of himself throughout in the third person, even

[23] Contrast the views of one who was his kin by marriage, Colonel Rains-
borough, one of the leaders of the Levellers, in the ferment of debate in civil war
England: "The poorest he that is in England hath a life to live as the greatest
he" (Address to fellow officers, August 1647, *Clarke Papers*, Camden Society,
1891, cited by G. M. Trevelyan, *England under the Stuarts* (London, Methuen,
1904), p. 282).

when recording (laconically) his third wife's death, have touches
that might easily occur in Franklin's *Poor Richard*.

(13 April 1641) fire in the house of a godly woman of the church of Boston
which destroyed "a parcel of very fine linen of great value, which she set
her heart too much upon". But it pleased God, that the loss of this linen
did her much good, both in taking off her heart from worldly comforts,
and in preparing her for a far greater affliction by the untimely death of
her husband, who was slain not long after.

(13 April 1645) The wars in England kept servants from coming to us,
so as those we had could not be hired, when their times were out, but
upon unreasonable terms, and we found it very difficult to pay their wages
to their content (for money was very scarce). I may upon this occasion
report a passage between one Rowley and his servant. The master, being
forced to sell a pair of his oxen to pay his servant his wages, told his
servant he could keep him no longer, not knowing how to pay him the
next year. The servant answered, he would serve him for more of his cattle.
"But how shall I do", saith the master, "when all my cattle are gone?" The
servant replied, "You shall then serve me, and so you may have your cattle
again."

Although, lest the reader should have doubts, he wrote in the margin
of his record of the servant's reply the word "Insolent."
   Winthrop's third wife, the mother of eight of his children, died
in June 1647, when he was 59. In December he married his fourth
wife, herself a widow – widows and widowers were rare in colonial society; marriage, remarriage and many children, usually in-
extricably interlinked, were colonial America's devices for welfare
provision, and tribal kinship in North as well as South was striking.
In Winthrop's Boston, an individual was required to live in a family,
if necessary as a servant. Of his fourth marriage, a son was born,
his sixteenth child, but died in early childhood. Winthrop himself
died 18 months later, aged 61. Seven weeks before, Charles I had
been executed, and England had also become a Protestant republic.
It seemed that his dream had come true: he had never, in form,
"separated"; the Anglican Church at home and abroad could now
be reformed. Winthrop's letters suggest a tender, even an affectionate,
man. Kinship mattered, and easily became nepotism: a father must
look after his own, in New England as in Virginia. It brought jobs,
profits and status and it rendered the fragile state some service.
   Connecticut does not owe its origins only to the religious intolerance of Massachusetts. The fertile soil, the pressure of population
around Boston, the determination to thwart the Dutch, the prospects

of the fur trade, were as important as religious dissent. Indeed it was due as much to heredity and empire-building. Late in 1635, John Winthrop Jr brought a commission from Lord Saye and Sele, Lord Brooke, and others to start a settlement there, with himself as governor. John, Governor Winthrop's eldest son (1605–1676), born when his father was 18, was, like his father, a barrister, and well travelled (all countries were, he said, so many inns); he had stayed behind in England to sell their estates, and sailed in 1631 to become an assistant to his father. He had been educated at Trinity College, Dublin, where his uncle by marriage, Emmanuel Downing, then living in Ireland, could watch over him. In 1634 he had founded Ipswich, where his wife and infant daughter died. In London in 1635, he was invited by his father's friends Lord Saye and Sele and Lord Brooke to found a plantation in Connecticut and be its governer; they would supply men, money and equipment. In 1635 he was back in Boston, equipped with a second wife, and accompanied for counsel by her stepfather, Reverend Hugh Peter. From his energy came the fort at Saybrook at the mouth of the Connecticut River, schemes for the manufacture of salt and the mining of graphite, iron furnaces at Lynn and Braintree, and estates for his family at New London and on Fisher's Island on Long Island Sound.

After his father's death John identified himself with Connecticut and moved to Hartford. From 1659 until his death in 1676, he was annually elected governor. Winning the new king's friendship on a visit "home" in 1661–3, he obtained from him the most liberal charter yet granted to any colony, making Connecticut virtually an independent state, and including within its boundaries the former colony of New Haven, founded by John Davenport in 1636. He had considerable land holdings in Connecticut, Massachusetts, and New York, but his scientific ventures were unsuccessful, and – like his father – he was always worried over money. But he indicated the changing mood of the next generation. Unlike his father, his tastes were scientific, not theological. He was the first American to become a Fellow of the Royal Society, in 1663, and he predicted the discovery of a fifth satellite to Jupiter. He believed that New England's future lay in manufacture and commerce, rather than in agriculture. He was versatile, and tolerant – notably to Roger Williams and the Quakers. In turn, so it was through the troubled times of 1688–92 with John Jr's own son, known as Fitz-John (1638–1707), who left Harvard to serve in the Parliamentary army in England, served also in war in America (against the Indians, 1675–6) and against the French and Indians in 1690), was also an FRS, and served as governor of Connecticut from 1689 until his death in 1707.

What of John Winthrop Sr's achievement? Plainly, he was one of the handful who founded the Massachusetts Bay Colony, and – in part by expulsions – the rest of New England. Of its economic development there can be no question. Boston and Salem became shipping ports, and prospered by raiding the Banks for the cod that could be cured, salted, and dried for export south to Catholic Europe, the West Indies and England itself, as well as for its own use. For that, it could be supplemented by salmon and shad from its rivers. With fish came shipbuilding, lumber, and timber, and horses to Barbados for use in the sugar mills. Whaling became lucrative, since whale oil was needed for lamps, and New Bedford and Nantucket (ceded to Massachusetts in 1692) became its headquarters. Before the Revolution, Nantucket claimed that its whaling fleet consisted of 125 vessels, and by that time one in every six Boston males was part-owner of a merchant vessel. The settlements grew steadily, in part because land could be obtained freely by any group of town proprietors who were church members; and now they were moving westward as well as north, marking the beginning of that American feature of a mobile belt of people steadily moving to the land of the setting sun, the frontier.

Farming was still the biggest business. If cleared land was valuable, the work involved in clearing it, chopping down trees and digging up stumps, was strenuous, time-consuming – and dangerous. But it was essential if hostile Indians were to be denied cover. Since labor was scarce, the farms were small, and designed for self-sufficient, if very large, families. And, again, the prospect of a farm in freehold, rent-free, and devoid of manorial controls and taxes, became another of America's realizable dreams. The pattern became recurrent through-out New England: houses clustered together around the common, graced by the meeting house (which from the mid-eighteenth century began to acquire a steeple), and increasingly by a separate little red schoolhouse. The clergyman often doubled as lawyer, doctor, and schoolteacher. But prosperity brought its challenges: "an insatiable desire after Land, and worldly Accommodations, yea, so as to forsake Churches and Ordinances, and to live like Heathen, only that so they might have elbow-room enough in the world. Farms and mer-chandising have been preferred before things of God."

Whereas the Old Faith conveyed its message in altar, ornament, and sculpture, and told its story in stained glass for the masses who could not read, the Calvinist Church was for the literate; it was essential for everyone to read the Bible. Schools were therefore as basic as homes, and for such well-schooled parishioners, colleges for the training of pastors were equally essential. It is one of the most striking features of Winthrop's settlers that within six years of their arrival in the wilderness they should found Boston Grammar School and Harvard College. In the "Great Migration," 35 men of Emmanuel College, Cambridge, had reached Massachusetts. When they looked for a site for a college, they found a plain "smooth as a bowling green" on a quiet river, and the Charles River recalled their *alma mater.* So the new town became Cambridge, and when one of the Emmanuel men, John Harvard at Charlestown, gave it his library of 400 volumes and half his estate, the college became Harvard, set down as it was *hic in silvestribus et incultis locis,* to cite the words over the stage in Sanders Theater. Every household was required to contribute a quarter-bushel of wheat a year, or a shilling in money, or the equivalent in wampum, to provide teaching fellowships; the president – Henry Dunster, a Magdalene man, followed the first of them, Nathanael Eaton, who stayed only a few months after flogging too many, and when he disappeared took what he could of the colleges funds with him – was paid in beef and mutton, butter and eggs and cheese. Every building extension could be financed only by tithes, or by public appeals, or by special chasing of alumni – the last happily a continuing tradition. Harvard is the oldest corporation in the US.

In Massachusetts in 1647 every town of 50 families was required to establish an elementary school, and towns of twice that size a secondary school; and for each of them education meant the basics: grammar and numbers, Latin and Greek. Connecticut in 1650 required every town of 50 households to have a teacher supported by the community. While the purpose was theological, these were not divinity schools, but, as the college charter of 1650 put it, the purpose was "advancement and education of youth in all manner of good literature, Artes and Sciences." It was the teaching of reading and writing that was preeminent, "it being one chief project of that old deluder Satan, to keep men from the knowledge of the Scriptures." By contrast, Virginia did not found William and Mary College until 1693; Massachusetts' first press began operating (in Harvard Yard) in 1639, Virginia's not until 1729.

Training was practical, as well as theological. The most common route to a business career or the acquisition of a skill was, in the colonies as at home, an apprenticeship; a master would agree to take in a young lad who would have the privilege of learning the master's craft, and sometimes even marry the master's daughter. But the purpose was to train artisans, and to secure cheap child labor, not – as in Britain, and in Europe – a legal requirement for practicing a trade. Guilds did not develop, with their control

of quality and their programes of mutual aid; and, like Benjamin
Franklin at 17, the apprentice whose skills were not perceived could
simply run away and find a better opportunity elsewhere without
curb.

Boston enjoyed tremendous growth during the seventeenth century, although almost half the inhabitants of 1687 were gone by
1695, having moved into the interior, back across the Atlantic, or
down the coast to New York and beyond. By 1700 only Bristol and
London were greater ports, and Boston was unique to New England
in her social complexity, diversity of occupational structures, and
outwardness. By 1700 the population of New England was to reach
150,000, and most could expect to live to a ripe old age; half the
first settlers of Andover, Massachusetts, lived to be 70 years old.
And as trade flourished along its seashore, so it ceased to be an
intense and lower middle-class edition of Old England. Non-English
merchants' names appeared: the Devereux, Delano, Faneuil, and
Bowdoin families of French Huguenots; Caspar Crowninshield from
Germany; John Wendell from Holland; and Patrick Tracy from
Ireland.

5 THE PURITAN INTERNATIONAL

The twenty years of the English civil war and the Protectorate
(1640–1660) were decisive for the new commonwealths. By 1641,
70,000 English people had migrated to the mainland colonies. As
would occur again in 1789 for a generation the New World was
now left alone, and immigration dropped. Indeed, a number of the
leaders returned home to continue the greater struggle there, since at
last the chance seemed to have come to reform England, in Church
and now in State. As many as one in six returned to England, often
for good; a phenomenon that began shortly after the arrival of Winthrop's fleet in 1630. For, the Separatists in Plymouth colony apart,
the Atlantic did not divide: the experiment in New England was,
after all, but part of a great Puritan International stretching from
Geneva to Holland, England, Scotland, Huguenot France, the White
Mountains of Bohemia and the Waldensian Piedmont. In Perry
Miller's phrase, New England was but a Puritan "laboratory experiment."[24] The peoples in New England were on the Puritan periphery.

[24] Perry Miller, *The New England Mind: From colony to province* (Cambridge,
MA, Harvard University Press, 1953), Foreword.

This is an issue that runs through contemporary writing: America was the promised land, "giving the Kingdom of God a local habitation and a name," [25] and, in practice if not in name, there was a single Puritan Atlantic, with two (or more?) Israels. Certainly this was true in theological terms. The themes that were debated in New England recur in Geneva, in Saumur and Sedan, in Leiden and in Westminster, in Glasgow and Edinburgh. They were the problems of the relation between grace and works, between knowledge and faith, of infant baptism and the Half-Way Covenant. They were the themes of Saint-Cyran and Pascal as well as of the Cambridge tutors of the founders of New England. The schools of Port-Royal were one institutional answer, as Harvard College was another. It was no obscure, provincial, eccentric movement that provided the ideology of early Massachusetts. The aim of the New England Puritans was, again in Perry Miller's words, "to vindicate the most rigorous ideal of the Reformation." [26] But was it Reformation, or Renaissance? Or neither? [27]

The beginnings of the story of white men in America are certainly the legacy of Europe's Renaissance and Reformation. The discoveries were the result of compass and astrolabe, maps and charts – and the stimulus that went with them. And, just as South America was intensely Catholic, a product of the Counter-Reformation and of crusading, so English North America was the distant legacy of Calvin and Luther, and of the turmoil in politics and in religion that followed their teaching. And, at least in intention, its crusading was by the Word, not the Sword.

Calvinism was certainly an activist creed, seeking "the sanctification of the world by strife and labour." From the start, it was a system of government as well as a creed – Calvin was a lawyer, whereas Luther was a monk. It saw the state as its good right arm. Calvinism took root where there was literacy (one of the clichés of the day was that, to Catholics, "ignorance was the mother of devotion"), where there were intelligent and skilled craftsmen in market towns, in the cloth industry of East Anglia and the southwest

[25] Sacvan Bercovitch, *The American Jeremiad* (Madison, University of Wisconsin Press, 1978), p. 40.
[26] Miller, "Errand into the wilderness," p. 10.
[27] David Grayson Allen, "Both Englands," in David D. Hall and D. G. Allen (eds), *Seventeenth-Century New England* (Colonial Society of Massachusetts, *Publications LXII*, Boston, 1984), pp. 76–8; David Cressy, *Coming Over: Migration and communication between England and New England in the seventeenth century* (Cambridge, Cambridge University Press, 1987).

of England, in cities and in ports concerned with overseas trade, where there were universities, and among Scots, Scotch-Irish, French Huguenots and Dutchmen. Thomas Hobbes likened the coming of universities and of literacy to the arrival of the wooden horse among the Trojans. John Foxe, in his *Book of Martyrs*, which became second only to the Bible as a text among the Puritans, countered with: "How many printing presses there be in the world, so many block-houses there be against the high castle of St Angelo, so that either the Pope must abolish knowledge and printing or printing at length will root him out."[28] Less attached to the soil than were villagers (and English Cavaliers, and French Royalists), townsmen moved abroad more easily, and took their models with them. By contrast, when Cavaliers took refuge abroad, after 1640 it was usually to sit out the crisis in Europe before returning, rather than to plan organized Anglican settlements in America or the Caribbean. Even the English Catholics did not emigrate in great numbers to the Catholic refuge planned for them in Maryland. Again, John Knox as well as John Winthrop wanted – and largely got – a school, often an academy, in every parish.

They were family people. In New England they bred fast and often. It was rare for widow and widower to stay long in single blessedness. "An old maid or an old bachelor are as scarce among us, and reckoned as ominous, as a blazing star," wrote William Byrd in Virginia. Wives were exhausted by the constant child-bearing. The Puritan code was strict: that aspect of it most scrupulously honoured was the adage: "Increase and multiply." John Winthrop Sr had 16 children. Benjamin Franklin, born in Boston in 1706, was one of 17. Franklin's pastor in the Old South, Doctor Willard, had 20 children by two wives; Adam Winthrop had 18, all by one wife. Increase Mather had 10 children, Cotton his son 15 – of whom all but 6 died in childhood. Rev. John Sherman, of Emmanuel College, Cambridge, and later a Fellow of Harvard, had 26 – and at least one of his distant descendants left a savage mark on his times. Sir William Phips was also one of 26. Samuel Sewall, the Salem witch-craft judge, had 14. Easy come, easy go. Death was a frequent visitor and brought a morbid pleasure. Judge Sewall, the Puritan Pepys, records Christmas Day 1696 with the note that he buried his little daughter Sarah, the sixth of his 14 children to die, and went and sat in the south burying ground, contemplating the coffins of

---

[28] *Foxe's Book of Martyrs and the Elect Nation*, ed. William Haller (London, 1963), p. 110.

his departed family. "Twas an awfull yet pleasing treat ... Having said, the Lord knows who shall be brought hether next, I came away." Five months later, he was back, the one "brought hether next" being a stillborn son.[29] During the 20-year Interregnum in England, when the tide of immigration not only ceased but actually reversed itself, the New England population increased by internal generation; it began and long remained remarkably homogeneous in racial composition, and it had an unusually high literacy, with one university man for approximately every 40 families.

There was, moreover, a remarkable traffic in people to and fro across the Atlantic. John Winthrop Jr did the journey five times; Sir Harry Vane – like Cromwell, from the eastern shores, but an Oxford man (Magdalen Hall) in this Cambridge gallery – went over in 1635, and served for a year as governor of Massachusetts; it was during his chairmanship that the decision was taken to establish Harvard College. He sympathized both with Mrs Hutchinson and Roger Williams, whom he helped to obtain his charter for Rhode Island. With Williams, he also helped to prevent the Narragansetts joining in the Pequot wars in the revolt of 1636. He returned to England in 1637, was knighted by Charles I for his services as treasurer of the Navy, was a member both of the Short and the Long Parliaments, and secured the condemnation of Strafford and Laud. He had no part, however, in the trial and execution of the king and was not a supporter of the Protectorate. He retired from public life, and fathered 13 children. He paid the price paid by many a Sir-Facing-Both-Ways, however, and was executed for treason by Charles II on that king's return; he proclaimed his faith in liberty to the last. Governor Winthrop, no friend in his lifetime, paid tribute to "a true friend to New England, and a man of noble and generous mind;" Milton's sonnet honors his memory.

Seven other New Englanders sat alongside Vane in the House of Commons, one of them that adept turner-of-coats, George Downing. "Fitz-John" Winthrop, the first governor's grandson, as noted earlier, fought with the Parliamentary army. Edward Winslow left the Plymouth Colony to die at sea in the West Indies in the service of the Cromwellians. More East Anglian ministers returned than any other group, Giles Firmin and Hugh Peter among them, seeking a more tolerant creed than Winthrop's version of Congregationalism, but Peter too was executed by Charles II for complicity in and

---

[29] *The Diary of Samuel Sewall* (Boston, Massachusetts Historical Society, 1878–82), I.443–4.

presence at the execution of Charles I. Of Harvard College's first 20 graduates up to 1646, 11 emigrated to England and never returned. One who did, Leonard Hoar, became the College's third president, and a very very unhappy one, quarreling with colleagues and with students before his early death. Increase Mather went over to London in 1658, when he was 19, was tempted to stay, but returned after the Restoration. He was back again 30 years later and involved in its politics. And George Downing, one of Harvard's first graduating class, the Irish-born nephew of Winthrop senior, became no less than a commissioner to the Dutch for both Cromwell and Charles II, and betrayed some of his earlier friends to their deaths in changing sides himself; not only did he avoid the executioner's axe, but won a fortune and a title and gave his name to Downing Street, London, and, thanks to his grandson's bequest, to Downing College, Cambridge. Was his success due to Puritanism, or to a native dexterity? (George Downing's mother, Lucy, the sister of John Winthrop Senior, had married Emmanuel Downing as his second wife, for the Winthrops had interests in Ireland as well as Sussex). Oliver Cromwell himself had considered emigration, once in 1635, when he sold his land to raise the money, and his friends Pym and Hampden became interested in Connecticut; and, again in 1641, when the Grand Remonstrance was in danger of rejection by the Commons.[30]

Indeed, Cromwell was England's Winthrop; Winthrop, had he not moved in 1630, could have been England's Lord Protector. Winthrop drew up a social compact; but in his view, once government was established, it drew its inspiration from and was responsible only to God, not to the people. His government, like Cromwell's, might plan to be benevolent, but it was certainly absolute: each congregation might be separate from another, but all were intolerant, and sometimes not only of their neighbors but also of their pastors. If Cromwell was also a benevolent despot, his Independent creed at least professed tolerance towards other creeds — provided they

---

[30] James W. Jones, *The Shattered Synthesis: New England — Puritanism before the Great Awakening* (New Haven, Yale University Press, 1973). In the 1670s William of Orange (the future William III of England) had, in the gloomy periods of his struggle for survival against Louis XIV, talked of continuing the struggle from the other side of the Atlantic. Cf. S. E. Morison, *The Intellectual Life of Colonial New England* (Ithaca, Cornell University Press 1965), 17–19; William L. Sachse, "The Migration of New Englanders to England 1640–60," in *American Historical Review*, 53 (Jan. 1948)), pp. 251–78; and Harry S. Stout, "The morphology of remigration," *Journal of American Studies*, 10 (Aug, 1976), pp. 151–72.

denounced the King, the Pope and the Devil, and did not threaten the State ("This realm of England is an Empire.") Winthrop and Cromwell did not in fact speak the same language. Henry Vane and Roger Williams, with their codes of liberty of conscience, were welcomed home to England, to a land that was then freer in doctrine, and the home of those brave enough to oppose a royal army, and to kill a tyrant. Like all Internationals, this too was torn by dissension. The gulf that emerged during the Protectorate between the Independent and the Presbyterian and the Congregational wings was almost as significant as the original division in the True Faith caused by Calvin and Luther, Zwingli and Knox. The New England model, designed to be a model for Old England, simply proved unserviceable there.

Perry Miller's comment is apt:

New England did not lie, did not falter; it made good everything Winthrop demanded — wonderfully good — and then found that its lesson was rejected by those choice spirits for whom the exertion had been made. By casting out Williams, Anne Hutchinson, and the Antinomians, along with an assortment of Gortonists and Anabaptists, into that cesspool then becoming known as Rhode Island, Winthrop, Dudley, and the clerical leaders showed Oliver Cromwell how he should go about governing England. Instead, he developed the utterly absurd theory that so long as a man made a good soldier in the New Model Army, it did not matter whether he was a Calvinist, an Antinomian, an Arminian, an Anabaptist or even a Socinian ... Out of the New Model Army came the fantastic notion that a party struggling for power should proclaim that, once it captured the state, it would recognize the right of dissenters to disagree and to have their own worship, to hold their own opinions. Oliver Cromwell was so far gone in this idiocy as to become a dictator, in order to impose toleration by force! Amid this shambles, the errand of New England collapsed. There was nobody left at headquarters to whom reports could be sent.[31]

There were always those for whom emigration was no mere escape to a land of isolationist promise, whose millenarianism required an activist political struggle, for whom indeed, in Edmund Morgan's phrase, "emigration offered a substitute for revolution," precursors of Cromwell: Henry Vane, Hansard Knollys, Thomas Tillam, Christopher Blackwood and — eventually — William Hook, for whom pacifism would turn to militance when he became Cromwell's chaplain.

[31] Miller, "Errand into the wilderness," 7–18; see also his book of the same title (Cambridge, MA, Belknap Press of Harvard University Press, 1956), pp. 14–15.

The Puritan International, however, was no simple transatlantic duality; it was triangular, since to the Puritans in England, and not least their wealthy backers, the West Indies were more important than cold and inhospitable New England. To Winthrop, the latter might have been simply an escape, "a rock and a shelter for the righteous ones." John Cotton, who preached the valedictory when they sailed in 1630, and followed them later, was conscious that they might appear to flee from England "like mice from a crumbling house, anticipating its ruin, prudently looking to their own safety, and treacherously giving up the defence of the common cause of this Reformation." Unlike the German Forty-Eighters of two centuries later, there was little talk of a return or a rescue mission. One of Thomas Hooker's sermons in 1631 was *The Danger of Desertion*. Conspicuous as were some of the leaders, in fact not many foot-soldiers returned to fight the good fight when open war erupted in England in 1642.

That this was not seen in such sharp terms was because of the third leg in the triangle. In 1630 the Puritan *aristos* – the earl of Warwick and his cousin Sir Nathanael Rich, Lord Brooke, Lord Saye and Sele, Sir Thomas Barrington and John Pym – founded another Puritan colony, the island in the Spanish West Indies off the coast of Nicaragua that they called Providence (the Providence Island Company, 1630). As its location implied, it was to sponsor other colonies on the Mosquito Coast of Central America, and to serve as privateering base to thwart the Spanish treasure fleets that assembled at Cartagena and Porto Bello, and their flow of gold and silver to Europe that fueled the Counter-Reformation. Compared with this, New England was seen by many as but a sideshow. It was indeed expected that after their seasoning in the bleak and rocky North, New Englanders would be glad to move to the tropics, and some of their ministers – like Hugh Peter, who for a time served as Cromwell's private chaplain – were open advocates of the move. These settlements would be strategically placed to weaken Spain; they would be Protestant; they would produce the drugs and dyes, the tobacco and cotton that England needed – and that by a slave labor force that formed half of the island's population, and was kept totally distinct from the congregations and the governing hierarchy of the island. If this was a Utopia, it was so only for the elect.

Elizabethan statecraft thus became Puritan foreign policy, and in it was the seedbed of Cromwell's own Western Design. The Puritan aristocracy had forgotten little, and learnt nothing. The company was limited to 20 wealthy backers. The colonists sent out went as tenants, not freemen. Only one minister, Hope Sherrard, stayed for long, and he quarreled constantly with the other leaders. Almost everyone quarreled with the London Company; the civil versus the military role was never reconciled. It took longer than any of the planners expected for the tiny island to become self-supporting; no commodity of any value came from it. From 1640 to 1641 London was trying hard to persuade New Englanders to move south, to no avail. The plantation was overpowered by the Spanish Plate Fleet in May 1641.

It left a legacy, however: to Cromwell. He was not an investor in the Providence Company, but he knew, or was related to, many who were. The goals of a West Indian empire saved from Spain, its products coming to England, became the core of his Atlantic foreign policy. Fulke Greville, the first Lord Brooke, and uncle of the Providence Island company member, published his *The Life of Sir Philip Sidney* (1554–1586) in 1653 as a salute to "the perfect hero knight of militant Christianity;" his program for attacking Spain in the West Indies became the core of Cromwell's Western Design. Cromwell was confirmed in it after discussions with Roger Williams of Rhode Island and Hugh Peter, and after correspondence with John Cotton. He saw the struggle against Charles as part of an Atlantic-wide struggle against Spain as well as Rome, and found it hard to distinguish between Jesuits and Quakers – a view shared by the Rev. John Davenport of New Haven. His hopes may have included the conquest for Protestantism of Hispaniola and Cuba and the invasion of Mexico. As Roger Williams told Winthrop, "I looke to heare of an invitation at least to these parts for remoovall from his Highness, who looks on N.E. only with an eye of pitie, as poore, cold and useless."

After his great fleet had conquered the islands, the Lord Protector expected massive New England migration to the West Indies. The fleet was led by Admiral William Penn and Robert Venables; Edward Winslow, the pilgrim, was with them as a commissioner, as was Robert Sedgwick, one of Boston's chief merchants, who was always unsympathetic to the intolerance of the Bay Colony. The attempt on Hispaniola, however, proved a failure, and disease mowed down the invaders after their capture of Jamaica. Edward Winslow died before reaching Jamaica, and the other leaders either died or abandoned the cause. And now, with more than 30 years of experience in a wilderness of their own, the New Englanders could tell Cromwell that the reason for the failure was, in Robert Sedgwick's phrase, that God is angry. "It was," he held, not "honourable, that your highnes's fleet should follow this old trade of West-India cruisers and privateers, to ruin and plunder poor towns, and so leave them."

A godly experiment would need slaves as a labor force; and was being erected by a military expedition. The Protector himself called for days of fasting and humiliation, to determine in what ways the nation had sinned. He saw the defeat at Hispaniola as a divine rebuke, and lost confidence in himself about it. One who believed that he had been brought to power to secure the triumph of Protestanism no longer knew what "the mind of God was."

Hugh Peter (1598–1660) is almost the model of the Anglo-Americanism of the founding generation. A Cornishman, who took the name Peter, he was a Master of Arts of Trinity College, Cambridge. He left England when Laud became bishop of London in 1628, and, after some years in Delft and Rotterdam, where he was an associate of the theologian William Ames and of John Davenport, he moved to Massachusetts Bay in 1635. He travelled on the same ship as Henry Vane and John Winthrop Jr, who married (as his second wife) Hugh Peter's stepdaughter, Elizabeth Reade. Peter succeeded Roger Williams in Salem a year later, and stressed that the function of Congregationalism was non-Separatist – the "New England Way." He tried, with Henry Vane, another "internationalist," to mediate between Winthrop and Dudley in their differences in 1636, then rebuked Vane for the extent of his interference in church affairs. He was one of the first overseers of Harvard, and one of the founders of the Saybrook settlement. In 1641, however, he returned to England, as one of the three agents sent by the New England Churches to help the Reformation of the Church in England. He planned to return to New England, but at each opportunity pleaded ill health. Vigorous in his criticism of Catholicism, he became a chaplain in Cromwell's forces, and campaigned alongside him in Ireland, his sermons vehemently propagandist in tone. In 1648 he was equally vehement in his denunciations of Charles I, and was in the escorting party that brought the monarch back from Windsor to stand trial; and after the execution – in a letter to Queen Christina of Sweden – he explained the reasons for it. (His letter may well have hastened her own decision to abdicate her throne at 28 in favor of her cousin, Charles Gustavus, her departure for Rome and her conversion to Catholicism. Her own title was "king," not queen; and kingship was a perilous profession.) On the Restoration, Peter was arrested in June, 1660 as a leading regicide, and executed at Charing Cross on October 16, 1660.

Victims of one persecution could make themselves agents of another, and call their new version freedom. For 11 years, from the king's execution in 1649 until 1660, England was a republic with Cromwell as Lord Protector, for whom the government of "free" men became in practice but the old tyranny writ large, with no dancing around maypoles and much harrying of opponents. One who was harried was the Rev. Lawrence Washington, "a Scandalous, Malignant Priest," "a common frequenter of ale-houses"; so his son John emigrated, not as Puritan but as Cavalier, and went in 1657 as mate on the *Sea Horse of London*; he went not to Puritan Boston but to the Northern Neck of Virginia, to become the great-grandfather of the first president of the US.

The Cromwellian interregnum might appear to justify the Puritan experiment in New England. In fact the curb on immigration was almost disastrous for its economy. Plymouth was practically a ghost town in 1646 when, most ironically, it was relieved by the arrival of a pirate (one Captain Cromwell or Crumwell), driven in by a storm with three shiploads of Spanish loot. His 80 crewmen "did so distemper them with drinke as they became like madd-men," Governor Bradford observed in his *Historie*, but he also noted that in their stay of some weeks, "they spente and scattered a greate deale of money among the people." Massachusetts responded to the crisis with an ambitious attempt to establish a self-sufficient economy. But despite John Winthrop Jr's various schemes, the one field in which real advance was made was shipbuilding. A 300-ton ship – large for the day – was made at Salem as early as 1641. As civil war at home disrupted normal traffic, as sailors, fishermen, and their ships were swept into service, with fewer West country vessels visiting New England fisheries, the New Englanders began a foreign trade of their own. By 1660 they were masters in their own fisheries, and a fleet of locally owned ships were plying to Iberia and the Wine Islands. There they found a demand for foodstuffs and timber. After calling at the Canaries they proceeded to the Cape Verde Islands for slaves, took these on to Barbados and exchanged them there for tobacco. This was the small beginning of a trade with the Caribbean which within a few years was vital both to New England and to the islands.

6 MARYLAND

The dream of a city on a hill that would be a beacon for all men was no Puritan monopoly. There were three other notable experiments: Maryland, Pennsylvania, and French Quebec. The first two, however, were not exercises in self-government, but proprietaries; the third was a colony of France, and stayed so until 1763.

The first proprietary (1623) was distinct from all of them: it enjoyed for its brief History the name "The Province of Avalon, though located in a non-idyllic waste of seas. So with the grant in 1628 to the earl of Carlisle, referring to "Barbadas alias Barbades alias Barbudos alias Barbadus." In 1629 Sir Robert Heath was granted "Carolana" to the south of Virginia, and Sir Ferdinando Gorges got Maine. The form was that the new colonies should be established under individual owners, on whom feudal powers were conferred. All land was to be held directly or indirectly from the proprietor, who was himself tenant-in-chief under the king. He could set up courts and appoint officers for the enforcement of laws, which he endorsed himself. He might grant pardon to offenders and make war against native Indians. These were in form feudal seignories in a New World setting. And in all the motivation was Catholic.

The effect of the Elizabethan settlement in England had been to outlaw Roman Catholics from public office, and severe anti-Catholic laws made it impossible in law to follow Catholic worship. Catholic gentry paid their fines for not attending the Anglican church, from whose buildings they had been dispossessed; they were forbidden to hear their own Mass, and resorted where they could to secret services of their own. Those who still adhered to the Old Religion were in a small minority: for the most part they were landed gentry, less interested in trade than in the land, conservative in State as in Church, and suspicious of projects of a new social order to be created in some remote Utopia. They played a minute part, therefore, in the colonization of America. Their families, however, had had centuries of public service, and were concerned for the welfare of their co-religionists.

As early as 1569 Sir Thomas Gerard planned a Catholic settlement in Ireland, to render service against the Irish, as a reward for which they were to be allowed freely to practice their religion, but the plan fell through. So in 1582 did the more ambitious plan of Gerard and Sir George Peckham to set up a Catholic colony on the shores of Narrangansett Bay. The architect was no less than Sir Humphrey Gilbert but this plan too fell through when Sir Humphrey was lost at sea in September 1583. By the 1590s the motives were no longer generous. The Armada, and the war with Spain, led to Catholics and "counterfeit Protestants" being seen as dangerous enemies. The Gunpowder Plot in 1605 seemed but to prove the point. As Puritan tempers rose, some Catholic leaders began seriously to consider exile themselves. They were landed, and for the most part gentry. They were dependent for their incomes on the rents of their tenancies and on the agricultural profits of their soil, and were suffering from the changes accompanying the transition from an agricultural to a mercantile economy. Tenants could not pay their rents and were leaving the manors for the towns and seaports. Prices were rising and the values of land were falling. New lands were obtained with difficulty at home by draining the marshes and fens, and in Ireland by the escheating of conquered territories to the Crown. Woods and forests were being laboriously turned into arable and sheep pastures. Feudalism and all that it stood for as an agricultural form of social and economic life was passing away.

Sir George Calvert had been a Yorkshire MP, a private secretary to and friend of Elizabeth's greatest secretary of state, Sir Robert Cecil; he himself became in 1619 secretary of state and privy councillor to James I, and he was knighted for his public services. He had a reputation for prudence, and for integrity. When he became a convert to Catholicism, he resigned his public offices, as the law required. He seems to have been greatly impressed, and probably converted, by Father Henry More, who was the Provincial of the English Jesuits, and great-grandson of the author of the *Utopia*. The king, in acknowledgement of service rendered, raised him to the peerage in 1625, as the first baron of Baltimore, in the peerage of Ireland. He retired to his Irish estates.

Calvert had long been interested in colonization, as attested by his membership both of the Virginia and of the New England Companies, and by his settlement in Ireland. In 1620 he had purchased land in Newfoundland, where he had established a small colony. Then in 1623 he had acquired a royal patent, enlarging the grant and erecting it into the 'Province of Avalon', so named after the traditional birthplace of Christianity in England. He visited it himself in 1627 and 1629.

Calvert did not live to carry out his project of a settlement for fellow Catholics in a warmer clime, but his son Cecilius, second Lord Baltimore, was granted a charter in 1632, conferring on him the land between the Potomac and the 40th latitude on either side of Chesapeake Bay; he named it Maryland after Henrietta Maria, French wife of Charles I. His own wife, Lady Anne Arundel, daughter of the earl of Arundel, tied him firmly in to the Howard clan, who in Arundel in Sussex, Castle Howard in Yorkshire, and in Carlisle, reigned over vast estates and provided the hereditary Earls Marshal, the heads of the English Catholic nobility. Here again, capitalism marched alongside faith, and sometimes at its expense. Lord Baltimore was given with the land the powers of a county palatine. Since one of his sources of revenue was to be feudal inheritance taxes, monasteries were forbidden, since the land would then have belonged to a single group in perpetuity and would have been exempt from taxation. To add to the exotic, there would be landed gentry, serfs and feudal dues. The model, paradoxically, was that of the Bishop of Durham, who in the fourteenth century exercised secular jurisdiction over his northern marches, and maintained his castle alongside his cathedral on the Wear as a fortress against the Scots: "What the King was without, the Bishop was within." Maryland was seen as a similar buffer between Virginia and the Dutch in New Amsterdam.

The idea of handing a difficult frontier over to a single vice-roy had long been obsolete in England, but no other precedent existed to give legal shape to so large a grant as James made to Calvert. It would be a model for a number of other proprietories in America. No other, however, would be required to pay as its sole annual tribute two Indian arrows to Windsor Castle. The proprietor in Maryland was thus free to grant baronies and manors as he pleased, "to be held only of himself in as ample a manner as any king in England granted and held them." Furthermore, Baltimore controlled all branches of the government in his colony, executive, judicial, and even legislative, in that under the charter he had full right to initiate legislation, and in all other respects exercised the equivalent of that regal and imperial power "which is granted in all things of sovereignty, saving only allegiance to the king's majestie." Thus he owned all the land, received all the profits from it, controlled the government in all its branches, and owed the king only a nominal payment. The king even gave up his peculiarly sovereign right of pardoning criminals, reserving no right of appeal from justice to his own royal person, and relinquished even the right of disallowing laws as long as they were consonant to reason or not contrary to the laws of England. Baltimore became the absolute lord, vice-roy, seigneur, and proprietor of the province of Maryland.

Unlike other proprietors, but like Smith and Bradford and Winthrop, Sir George Calvert had planned to go in person. In contrast with icy "Avalon," he looked with favor on a settlement where "the winters be shorter and less vigorous." His sons Cecilius and Leonard took up the challenge, though with a very different view than that of Bradford or Winthrop. They planned to build a feudal estate on the medieval English model, and they enlisted the aid of the Jesuits as propagandists. Father Andrew White proclaimed Baltimore's main aim to be "not to think so much of planting fruits and trees in a land so fruitful," as of sowing the seeds of religion and piety. "Surely a design worthy of Christians, worthy of angels, worthy of Englishmen. The English nation, renowned for so many ancient victories, never undertook anything more noble or glorious than this." [32]

However well-meant the plan, few Catholics could be induced to go, since all who went into exile for their Faith's sake were required to take an oath denying papal authority in England. Of the more than 200 who sailed on the *Ark* and the *Dove*, on November 22, 1633, only 128 took the oath. They were, for the most part, the craftsmen, the laborers and the servants, Protestants presumably or those to whom oaths came easily. Most of the Catholics, including the two Jesuit Fathers White and Atham, avoided the oath by going on board later at the Isle of Wight. Probably all of the 16 gentlemen-adventurers who sailed with wives and families were Catholics, but most of the 200 laborers and servants were Protestants. Although it was planned as a haven for them, Catholics would always be a minority of the population in Maryland.

Arriving in the Chesapeake in February 1634, the colonists, led by Leonard Calvert, Cecilius's younger brother, as governor, chose to settle on "St Mary's", a site on the broad Potomac which even that patriot Father White conceded was "the sweetest and greatest river I have seene, so that the Thames is but a little finger to it." The local Indians were friendly, and unlike Virginia or Plymouth, no famine confronted the 200–300 settlers. An exotic attempt was indeed made to transplant English feudalism. Some 60 manors were set up with grants of 1,000 to 3,000 acres; but freeholders, with plots up to 1,000 acres, were much more numerous than the manor lords; and those few lords who bothered to exercise their jurisdictive prerogatives, in manorial courts, courts baron for civil cases and courts leet for criminal, soon gave them up. As in Virginia, the county court became the important judicial unit in the colony. What for a time was significant – and unique to Maryland – was the smaller unit, the hundred, with its constable, who served as military officer and tax collector. Soon, however, he too would be overshadowed by the justice of the peace. As in Virginia, the elite did not stay long, replaced by planters of humble origins who had come out, for the most part, with no more than one or two servants, even by some who had been servants themselves. They were "tough, unsentimental, quick-tempered, crudely ambitious men", as Bernard Bailyn describes them, "concerned with profits and increased landholdings, not the graces of life." [33] They

---

[32] Clayton C. Hall, *Narratives of Early Maryland 1633–1684* (New York, Barnes and Noble, 1953), p. 7.
[33] Bernard Bailyn, "Politics and Social structure in Virginia," cited on p. 95 of James M. Smith (ed.), *Seventeenth-Century America* (Chapel Hill, NC, IEAHC, 1959).

wanted aggressive expansion at the expense of Indians, and unrestricted access to land. As a Catholic experiment, however, Maryland failed. By the 1630s, the English Catholic community, approximately 50,000 strong, did not want to move: conservative and
tradition-minded, lay Catholics in England had made the necessary
adjustments, and could not be tempted by promises of greater freedom of worship, or of possible economic advantage.

As in Virginia, so in Maryland, a representative assembly was
established in 1635, however alien to the original paper plan of a
Catholic feudal palatinate. As early as 1638 the proprietor surrendered his claim to the sole right of legislation. By 1650 the assembly had been divided into two houses; and one of these, the
consent of which was necessary before a bill might become law,
was composed entirely of the representatives of the freemen; annual
sessions as well as triennial elections were becoming usual. Indeed,
Leonard Calvert summoned an assembly within a year of his arrival,
although his elder brother back in England refused to recognize its
laws. Until his death in 1647, Leonard himself spent more time in
Virginia than in Maryland, in exile from a feudal dominion in which
the Protestants were in rebellion, reflecting England's civil war. The
leader of the rebellion, Richard Ingle, was a tobacco trader and
pirate, who rejected the legitimacy of Charles I's kingship, and
proclaimed himself governor in "the plundering year" (1645), as
index of his loyalty to the cause of the Protectorate. Alongside the
civil strife of Catholic *versus* Protestant was a third war, over
Virginia-Maryland boundaries: from Kent Island in Chesapeake Bay
came rival leaders William Claiborne of Virginia – surveyor, fur
trader and Indian fighter – and notably (1643–4) Giles Brent, with
the self-proclaimed title of "Lieutenant General, Chancellor, Admiral,
Chief Captain, Magistrate and Commander of Maryland," who
buttressed his title by marriage to the elder daughter of the "Emporer"
of the Piscataway Indians. Anglican Virginia, especially its Secretary
William Claiborne, looked askance at the Jesuit accumulation of
landed property. To protect the Catholic minority, who after a
decade were less than a quarter of the population, toleration of
worship was extended to all comers in the Toleration Act of 1649.
Since the Act excluded non-Christians, however, it represented something less than full religious freedom. Indeed, anyone denying that
Jesus was the son of God or the unity of the Godhead was subject
to the death penalty. This major restriction was not of Lord Baltimore's devising, but was added to the original text by the Puritan
group in the Maryland Assembly, to accord with the views of the
Long Parliament on the punishing of heresies. To counter their

pressures, the proprietor appointed a Protestant, William Stone, as governor in 1648, and he invited some 500 Puritans from the James River settlements in Virginia to move to what is now Annapolis.

During the Protectorate, Maryland's feudal regime was overthrown, and despite the Toleration Act harsh laws were enacted against Catholics. Governor Stone, in an attempt to uphold the proprietor's rights, resorted to arms, and a petty civil war ensued, in which Claiborne and the Puritans won a complete victory and savage vengeance was meted out upon Catholics. Four were hanged, others were fined and their property confiscated. In 1654 a Puritan parliamentary commission repealed the Toleration Act and forced Governor Stone from office. The Jesuit priests fled to Virginia and their houses were plundered. Not until 1658 did Lord Baltimore regain control of his colony.

From 1661 until 1684 Charles Calvert, son of Cecilius, was governor, except for two short intervals when he visited England. He became the third Lord Baltimore in 1675. He had played a shrewd game in England, and managed to keep the friendship both of Cromwell and of the exiled king. He regained control of his province in 1660 and restored religious toleration, but to maintain his claims to his lands and his rents required three visits to England. In 1670 he tried to thwart opposition (mainly Protestant) in his province by disfranchising all freemen who did not have a freehold of 50 acres or a visible estate of £40 sterling. What is now the state of Delaware, but which was known then as the "Lower Counties" – though within the limits, the 40° N parallel, of Maryland – was transferred by the duke of York (three years later to become James II) to William Penn's new province, whose charter also specified the 40° North as its southern limit. The problem would await a final solution for a century; not until 1763–7 did the English mathematicians Charles Mason and Jeremiah Dixon establish the boundary at 39° 43' 26.3".

Maryland, in other words, had its own civil war whenever the home country was in turmoil, and sometimes without that stimulus; it had a number of anti-proprietorial agitators, notably Josiah Fendall and John Coode, who used their seats in the Assembly as a platform for trouble-making, as is the way in democratic assemblies. Fendall was banished in 1681. And in the presence of the Jesuits it had its own special problem child.

The Jesuits claimed the right to accept for their Society gifts of land directly from the Indians: under canon law, they held, they were in any case exempt from lay jurisdiction, and not bound by the terms of any royal charter. The proprietor sent as intermediary his own secretary, John Lewger, another convert who later became a priest. The Jesuits called on some of the planters as their allies, notably Thomas Cornwallis, the military leader of the Province. The proprietor, however, won a double victory: Lewger persuaded the Maryland Assembly to pass laws that removed Catholic juris- diction over marriages and wills. Father More, the Jesuit Provincial, made a renunciation by the Jesuits of all claims, past and present, to Indian lands, and to exemption from the laws of the Province. For a time the Jesuit mission in Maryland was withdrawn.

In essence, this conflict of jurisdictions has echoes of medieval Europe; in the claims and counter-claims of the papacy (and the Catholic orders who vowed allegiance to it) against the secular kings and emperors. It echoes also Puritan Massachusetts: no more than the Puritans did Catholics favor religious freedom for others; each in principle was intolerant. The proprietor was unusual: he was both a good liberal and a devout Catholic, two positions hard to reconcile. To live with his contradictions, to survive personally, and to help his colony survive also, were achievements indeed through these years of torments. In 1669 the proprietor complained that there were but two priests in Maryland to minister to the 2,000 Catholics in the colony. This complaint was reported to the Con- gregation de Propaganda Fide at Rome, with the result that two Franciscans were sent out in 1673. By the time of the proprietor's death in 1675, there were 5 Jesuit priests and 5 Franciscans to minister to some 2,000 Catholics, and a Catholic school was es- tablished. The Catholics in Maryland in the 1680s numbered some 25 percent in a colony of 25,000, mainly settled in the western shore provinces of Charles and St Mary's; they were small land- holders living lives no different from their Protestant neighbors, but held together by the missions and the handful of priests. They were headed, however, by the small but wealthy elite of their faith, bound by blood and marriage to the proprietor.

This political achievement did not last. Come the next turn of the tide with the accession of William and Mary to the throne in England, in 1691 the province was taken from the proprietors, and put under a royal governor. Locally, this was the result of John Coode's "risinge in armes," that was as much the product of envy of what seemed a Catholic monopoly of provincial power – or of envy compounded by intolerance. It could masquerade as a struggle for freedom, as in London – and in Boston. John Coode (himself once a preacher) and his Protestant Association set up in 1689, like John Waugh's use of his pulpit in Virginia's Stafford County, exploited anti-Catholic sentiment for their own purposes. Once the Glorious Revolution (so called) had taken place in London, the

Anglican Church became the Established Church in Maryland, and the capital was moved from St Mary's, the Catholic centre, to Annapolis, the Protestant settlement from Virginia of a decade before. Once again Catholics were deprived of their political rights, and not only in Maryland: in Baptist Rhode Island and Quaker Pennsylvania, Catholics were disfranchised, and unable to hold office. They were barred from all colleges except the College of Rhode Island and the College of Philadelphia. When Charles Carroll the settler, "Marylando-Hibernus," died in Maryland in 1720, he was its wealthiest inhabitant and largest landowner, banker, and merchant, but he had been, as a Catholic, disfranchised within a year of his arrival in 1688.

In form, however, Maryland stayed feudal. There were 60 manors, and also some 6,000 tracts, which had been set aside for the proprietor and his relatives. The manors were from 1,000 to 3,000 acres in extent, and their owners had all the rights and privileges belonging to a lord of the manor in England, subject of course to the quitrent due the proprietor of the province. This system of large estates created distinct social classes, the manor holders and the plantation owners constituting an upper class, the tenants and the servants the lower classes. Roman Catholicism was the prevailing religion among the upper class; on many of the large estates, chapels and priests were maintained and regular services of the Catholic Church conducted. The third Lord Baltimore had lost political control, but retained his ownership of land and rights to specific revenues – and Charles Carroll as his agent, and attorney, prospered with him. Carroll prospered also by marrying well: first, as her third husband, a wealthy and well-endowed lady (who had married her first husband when serving him as an indentured servant); and second, on the first wife's convenient death within a year, the 15-year-old daughter of Colonel Henry Darnall, Calvert's cousin and, next to the proprietor, the colony's wealthiest man. In all its fluidity, and with all its opportunities for men of talent, a class system based on land ownership emerged in both Chesapeake colonies, marked not by democracy but by deference. In Maryland, however, the coterie of Catholic office holders did not produce what Ronald Hoffman has called "an intergenerational ruling elite," and they held power only briefly. The proprietor was restored to his colony on the Hanoverian succession – because in 1715 the fourth Lord Baltimore had, for himself and his sons, become an Anglican. It seemed that the Calverts had purloined the Carroll family motto: for Charles Carroll on arriving in Maryland in 1688 had changed his family crest from "In fide et in bello forte" (Strong in faith and war) to "Ubicunque cum libertate" (Anywhere so long as there is freedom.)[34]

Nor should the missionary role of the Jesuits be minimized. The Patuxets and Piscataways were exposed to the inroads of the fierce Susquehannas, and, as was generally true of the weaker tribes, welcomed Christian teaching. Father White for a time was a resident among the Patuxets, and reported many conversions among them. Later he resided among the Piscataways, where he was successful in converting one of the chiefs, Chilomacon, who was baptized in the presence of the officials of the colony. As a result, Maryland was spared the Indian wars so common in the New England colonies. In 1651 Lord Baltimore set aside 10,000 acres on the Wicomico River as an Indian reservation for the remnants of the Maryland tribes and Catholic work was carried on among them. Here the Indians developed a settled life, and after a few generations, through intermarriage with the whites, and still more because of their sus-ceptibility to the diseases the Europeans brought with them, they gradually but steadily disappeared.

More significant than the Catholic scheme of colonization, even more significant than John Rolfe's marriage of the Trinidad weed to Virginia's red clay soil to breed the "sweet-scented" leaf, was the coincidence of the ease of exportation of tobacco in so well-watered a country as the Chesapeake Tidewater. As Dr Charles Carroll put it, "the great Bay of Chesapeak and the many Rivers falling therein and the many Creeks Coves and Branches thereof affords Carriage Commodious and Easie for Tobacco ... were it not for this Con-venience it would be impracticable or at least very Expensive to Carry on the making of Tobacco." The navigability of the more than 100 rivers and creeks that reached it, and its 4,500-mile-long shoreline, made it possible to adopt as a staple a bulky commodity like tobacco that could not stand overland transportation. The two together account for the rapid growth of the tobacco colonies in wealth and numbers, and explain their preeminence among the American colonies. As, again, Carroll put it, "tis the Blessing of this Country ... and fits it extremely for the Trade it carries on, that the Planters can deliver their Commodities at their own Back doors, as the whole Colony is interflow'd by the most navigable Rivers in the World."[35] As a result, in Maryland as in Virginia, the people "lived dispersed;" Jamestown and St Mary's never developed into

---

[34] Ronald Hoffman, "Charles Carroll the Settler," *William & Mary Quarterly*, 45 (Apr. 1988), pp. 215, 227.
[35] *Maryland Historical Magazine*, 25 (1950), p. 62.

centres of residence for planters; ports were slow to develop, and towns grew up only along the fall line of the rivers, at the heads of navigation; social and intellectual life thus lost the stimulus that Philadelphia, New York, and Boston provided further north.

Tobacco itself grew apace. Half an ounce of tobacco seeds would produce 20,000 to 25,000 plants ready for harvesting in four to six months. It grew to 4–6 ft high, and exhausted the soil: so land, and yet more land, was needed. Immigration was reinforced by the "headright" principle: new land for each man who paid the cost of importing a fresh laborer. By 1635, Virginia had nearly 5,000 people: by 1640, 8,000: by 1660, 33,000. Eight counties were drawn in 1634, three new ones in 1648–51, and by 1660 Virginia had expanded into the Pamunkey Valley and along the Chesapeake coastline from the Potomac to Hampton Roads: while settlements were approaching, in various places, the "fall line", which interrupted river navigation and seemed to impose a natural limit to expansion. In Maryland, from the original St Mary's on the west of the Chesapeake and Isle of Kent on the Eastern shore, settlements spread to both sides of the Potomac, and north along both banks of the Patuxent.

Inevitably, there were spells when there came a glut, and prices fell. In 1630, for instance, Virginia tobacco sold at less than 1d a pound. But planters would not be deterred. The English government helped them, imposing an adverse duty on Spanish imports – 2s a pound in 1631, as compared to 9d on Virginian; and the colonists through their Assembly tried to regulate the crop – for instance, a code of 1633 laid down that no one might grow more than 1,500 plants. Tight controls were kept on the quality and the packing of the leaf. In 1640 the Assembly accepted a proposal from the English merchants and made the draconian ruling that not only all the bad but also half the good tobacco in that year's crop should be destroyed, while a production limit of 170 lb per head was set for the next two years. The annual tobacco fleet and dependence on its safe arrival for imports in return, kept the Chesapeake dependent on, and a mirror of, London and the British tobacco ports, despite the efforts of colonial officials to stimulate the production of corn and hops, flax and wine. For a century or more, it was to little effect.

In Maryland as in Virginia, society was governed by St James's fashions. The *Tatler* and the *Spectator* were read avidly. Cloth and fabrics, clothes and furniture, china and linen, tools and hardware were imported from England in a vast mail order business; if not English in manufacture, they came through London or Bristol, Liverpool or later Glasgow as entrepots. As in its taste, so in economics:

as the St Lawrence tied Canada to Paris, so the Chesapeake was dependent on the British merchant fleet, and on insurance against storm, against enemy men-of-war and pirates lurking outside, or just inside, the Capes, and often finding shelter on the Eastern shore. The Chesapeake colonies were more dependent on Great Britain for naval protection than were the other continental colonies.

Maryland's economy could safely imitate Virginia, and grow with tobacco. Market conditions shaped the pace of economic development. After an initial boom as a highly profitable staple, the cultivation of tobacco stagnated; when it later resumed growth it was within a diversified agriculture, and by 1760 the balance of the region's economic activity had shifted towards supplying food for other colonies and southern Europe. Market forces also shaped immigration, initially by encouraging the rapid development of a male immigrant society; after 1680 the failure of tobacco to grow temporarily discouraged new white immigration, and slavery expanded to replace servant labor. Slavery notwithstanding, the social structure over which the ruling merchant planters presided was closer in kind to rural England than to other colonial settlements in New England and the Caribbean. Of the 300 "gentlemen" in the colony, not all were necessarily of that rank in England, but reached it in the colony thanks to attachment to the Calverts, or to ease of land purchase, or to office-holding as surveyors, sheriffs, and militia officers, or to native talent, or to that "shipboard mobility" that allowed them to claim a higher rank as they came down the gangplank. Vertical mobility was as striking in colonial society as movement westwards. Even indentured servants rose in step with them. Stitt Robinson calculates that, again in the first 40 years, some 50 percent of those who came under indenture became landholders in Maryland, 14 of them with over 1,000 acres and one acquiring over 4,000 acres. Sixteen of them became justices of the peace, 7 became sheriffs, 12 burgesses, and 2 members of the governor's council. The newer the county, the more it was run by men to whom indeed Virginia and Maryland were "the best poor men's country in the world."[36]

[36] W. Stitt Robinson, *The Southern Colonial Frontier, 1607–1763* (Albuquerque, University of New Mexico Press, 1979), pp. 52–3; cf. Lois G. Carr and David W. Jordan, *Maryland's Revolution of Government 1689–92* (Ithaca, NY, Cornell University Press, 1974); Lorena S. Walsh, "Servitude and opportunity in Charles County, Maryland, 1658–1705," in Aubrey C. Land, Lois G. Carr, and Edward C. Papenfuse (eds), *Law, Society and Politics in Early Maryland* (Baltimore, Johns Hopkins University Press, 1977), pp. 111–33; Russell R. Menard, "From servant to freeholder: status mobility and property accumulation in seventeenth-century Maryland," *William & Mary Quarterly*, 30 (Jan. 1973), pp. 40–1.

7 "THE CITY ON THE HILL"

The sermon which Winthrop wrote and possibly delivered on board the flagship *Arbella* was double-edged. The godly society that he and his shipmates were going to build was also going to represent a model for a reformed England: "Wee shall bee as a Citty upon a hill, the eyes of all people ... upon us." Later, the image would become a symbol of American republicanism, of its Puritan mission, and of its exceptionalism.

The six "cities on hills" were: Virginia, a commercial enterprise that became a royal colony in less than 20 years; two experiments in communal and Puritan life, one of which absorbed the other and which survived as a theocracy – Massachusetts Bay and Plymouth; and three others: Maryland, a refuge for Catholics that survived as tolerant and non-Catholic; Pennsylvania, a Quaker commonwealth that became the most liberal of the proprietaries; and a French imperial stronghold that alone of them all was a Catholic missionary base – Quebec.

They were equally varied in their economies and social structure. Virginia developed by the extension of its county system, run by landed gentry and JPs on familiar English lines. Its House of Burgesses was a representative assembly of the counties, peopled by ambitious county squires with parallels to the landed aristos of the mother-country. Land and its products were not only the source of wealth but the index of success. Religious worship there was Anglican, conservative, social and rather casual. The colony flourished by the production and export of tobacco – a system that held true also for Maryland, its neighbor on the Chesapeake. By contrast, the northern colonies were organized in their townships, and with local decisions taken after vigorous debate in town meetings, where the issues and the language in which they were voiced were as often theological as secular. Status was measured by urban and Puritan standards: by trade and turnover, trust – and visible and regular church-going. Their economies too were still sea-based: ships and the timber with which to build them, furs for export, and – as it had been since the first explorers went out from Bristol, Brittany, or the Bay of Biscay – fish. The first tribute to fish in American literature came from that founder of Virginia, John Smith, in his *Description of New England*, written in 1616 after his explorations of its coast. From personal trial on his voyage to New England Smith learned of the value of fish, and his pamphlet like Benjamin Franklin's on his first travels to New York from Boston, is almost rhapsodical in praise of fish. Fisheries may be worth more than all the gold and jewels of the Spaniards, he asserted, and the Spaniards are less able to pay their debts than the Hollanders, who depend chiefly upon "this contemptible trade of fish," which "is their mine, and the sea the source of those silvered streams of all their virtue."[37]

Some cities on hills did not prosper, however. The British, not the Spanish or the French, were the real founders of Texas. The remains of their settlement were unearthed in 1987 at Buffalo Bayou, now the Houston ship canal in downtown Houston, with evidence of a small church, and of pottery identical with that of Jamestown. It would seem to have been part of that province of "Carolana," conferred in 1629 on Sir Robert Heath, Charles I's attorney-general, that lay between the 30th and the 36th parallel of latitude, and which, in name, ran from the Atlantic to the Pacific. The burial site is dug so thoroughly that the excavator, Kenneth Brown, of the University of Houston, has concluded that the settlers died either of plague or smallpox; and that their burial in shrouds, with the graves then covered with heavy black earth, complied with the English law of 1563 that required that to avoid the spread of the contagion from the earth covering the bodies, that earth itself should be thoroughly buried. The intention was to destroy the disease effectively by composting bodies and earth alike, to hasten decomposition. The English were thus the first to plant a settlement in Texas, but they were wiped out more effectively than by any native Americans.

[37] Philip L. Barbour (ed.), *The Complete Works of Capt. John Smith (1580–1631)*, 3 vols (Chapel Hill, NC, IEAHC, 1986), vol. II, p. 194.

4

The Restoration

1 THE RETURN OF THE EXILES

In 1660, Charles II was restored to the English throne, a restoration
by consent and not by conquest. Perhaps it was less a restoration
than a revulsion – against Paul Prys, against government by the
redcoats and the blacks, and against near bankruptcy. But in exile
the king had learned much, and the kingship restored was totally
distinct from that overthrown in Whitehall only 11 years before.
As Lawrence Stone has put it: "After the Restoration the clergy and
the Tory gentry spoke incessantly of their devotion to the principles
of Divine Right and Non-Resistance to a lawful king, but the very
stridency of their professions betrays an inner insecurity."[1] If dedicated idealists such as Sir Harry Vane, the high-minded Cromwellian, or zealous Presbyterian leaders such as the 8th earl of Argyll,
were executed, and Baptists, Quakers, and Covenanters were harried,
there was less savagery than in most restorations. More vengeance
was visited on the dead than on the living. Cromwell's body was
dug up and hanged at Tyburn (near what is now Marble Arch);
buried at the gallow's foot, it has now been trodden over for more
than three centuries. Only a dozen of the regicides were executed.
The Cromwellian regiments received their arrears of pay, were disbanded, and happily remained so – only the regiment of foot of
General Monk, the king maker, the Coldstream Guards stayed intact,

[1] Lawrence Stone, *The Causes of the English Revolution 1529–1642* (London,
Routledge and Kegan Paul, 1972), p. 91. Cf. Christopher Hill, *The Century of
Revolution* (London, Sphere, 1969 edn), and especially for his estimate of Claren-
don, idem, *Puritanism and Revolution* (London, Secker and Warburg, 1958).

as they still do. Monk got a dukedom, and did not ask for more. Scotland got its independence, but on Episcopalian terms; if the men at the head of state there "were almost perpetually drunk," at least they were Scots drunks. Ireland was secured for the Protestant cause, and for fortune-making. An Act of Indemnity and Oblivion was passed to wipe the slate clean; from it those who had served the king in exile in Paris, then in Cologne and then in Brussels, got compensation; but many Cavaliers complained that the Act meant Indemnity for the king's enemies and Oblivion for his friends. Some 700 Royalists had lost their lands, and the lands stayed lost. The majority of the new owners had been Presbyterians, but they rapidly turned Anglican for security's sake. And there were many Vicars of Bray. The efforts aimed at securing the tenure of copyholders had been vanquished along with the attempt to protect common rights to common land.

As the French ambassador, De Cominges, reported to Louis XIV, England had the constitution of 1641: the king would rule with the Lords and Commons in Parliament; he would be a well-paid ceremonial servant, as Pym had then suggested; there would be no standing army; local gentry and justices of the peace as well as the king had "come into their own" again. Anglicans all, they legislated against Puritans and sectaries of all denominations, in what has come to be known as the Clarendon Code, after its architect, Chancellor Hyde, later earl of Clarendon. They made religion a matter of class, as well as of creed, and drove Dissent into the middle and lower classes, without a place in government. And with them, as after all wars, came the trimmers and survivors, the "mutable and slippery men," "the Catholics of the court," who would shape the king's colonial policy as they had shaped the lord protector's: notably Clarendon himself, now the king's major aide, who stressed the importance of shipping, the fisheries, the plantations, and "the infinite importance of the improvement of trade;" Viscount Saye and Sele ("Old Subtlety"), Anthony Ashley Cooper (Lord Shaftesbury), and that distinguished nephew of the first John Winthrop, George Downing, who was to leave his name to London's most distinguished street but who was at once an Irishman, a Cromwellian – and the second man to graduate from Harvard College. If the Navigation Acts that formed the most striking feature of the Old Colonial System – itself a product that was both Cromwellian and Caroline – has a single author, it is George Downing. Behind the aristos, as always, were the "men of business," "the men of affairs:" Charles Davenant, William Blathwayt (Increase Mather's chief adversary in the Massachusetts charter negotiations in 1689/90), James Drax,

Martin Noell, Maurice Thompson, Thomas Povey (both of them West Indies merchants), and the office-holders such as Joseph Williamson, Francis Nicholson, Richard Nicolls, John Werden, Edward Randolph, Robert Southwell – and George Downing again. They were more than the hands and servants of power. All pressed for a reduction of the number of governments in America, and for the greater independence of governors from their assemblies (though, without paying their salaries from England, this was impossible); one of them, Samuel Maverick, may, by his *Account of New England* (published in 1660), have led to the seizure of New York in 1664. But the king's views were less sophisticated; he was careless as well as calculating, more pragmatist than policy-maker; he would reward the loyalists, and would do so by outright grants of proprietaries to them, as to his own family, and to those who had been true through the dog days. As with all men of power, he would find himself surrounded by zealots; they would, in the king's name, line their own pockets, and do more damage to his cause than any avowed enemy.

2 THE REWARDS

It is usual to categorize the "English" colonies as either commercial ("charter colonies") or as proprietaries. This may be true of their formal character at origin, but says nothing of their sharp individuality, any more than does the word "royal." Of the mainland colonies established before 1660 that in the end became part of England's "Thirteen Colonies," Virginia was founded by a commercial company, but when that company failed, and the settlement was all but destroyed by the Indian massacre of 1622, it became royal – within 20 years of its foundation; Massachusetts too was founded as a commercial exercise, but since it took its charter with it, had from the start a remarkable degree of freedom; and in 1691, as part of its own imperialism, it absorbed its predecessor at Plymouth. Of necessity, the Pilgrims had virtually indentured themselves as a group to an English business concern, which gained a London Company patent and provided ships and equipment for the venture. Because the colony was outside the London Company grant, a patent was secured from the New England Council, but, lacking a charter, the Pilgrims had no legal rights to government until their union with Massachusetts Bay in 1691. As soon as possible the settlers purchased a release from their obligations to the company in England. In a constitutional sense the freest of them all, Plymouth was soon governed by an elected governor and a bicameral representative assembly. If the colony of Plymouth was never rich, strong, nor especially distinguished, it was through its efforts that Congregationalism and the notion of self-government first came to America.

Of the colonies established by other countries, New York, originally the New Netherlands, had been founded by the Dutch West India Company in 1623; Delaware was founded by a Swedish company in 1638 (and it was the Swedes who introduced the log cabin); and, though in the heart of the Spanish Main, the Scots established their short-lived colony in Darien, and had their own settlements in New Jersey from 1683 to 1702 — the work of proprietors from the east and north-east of Scotland, mainly Quakers and Episcopalians and agricultural "improvers," representing in fact the most anglicized elements in Scottish society. Except in Plymouth and Boston, the religious drive was much less intense than in the Spanish colonies, and it was a religion of personal salvation, not of missionary zeal. Moreover, as commercial exercises all were unsuccessful. After the Restoration, the number of colonies more than doubled; and all were to be founded as proprietaries.[2]

The proprietary colonies were to be seven in number. Maryland had been founded by Sir George Calvert, Lord Baltimore, in 1634, and New Hampshire by Captain John Mason in 1635. New Jersey was awarded to Sir William Berkeley and Sir George Carteret in 1663; the Carolinas to a group of royal favorites, including the earl of Shaftesbury, in 1663; Pennsylvania to William Penn in 1682; and Georgia to philanthropists, of whom the chief was James Oglethorpe, in 1732. The grant to Sir Ferdinando Gorges in Maine was also a proprietary.

There were proprietaries within colonies, as in Virginia, and sometimes proprietaries within proprietaries, as in the Jerseys. Shortly after being proclaimed king after his father's execution, and when he was still in exile at St Germain-en-Laye, near Paris, Charles II allotted the "Northern Neck" — unoccupied and unmapped land in Virginia lying between the Potomac and the Rappahannock Rivers, covering at least 1 million acres — to seven of his companions in exile, in recognition of their loyalty, and the sufferings and losses that loyalty brought them. Among them was the plausible, ambitious and never-fully-trusted Lord John Culpeper, who had ridden with Prince Rupert at Edgehill, and owned what was and still is perhaps the most

---

[2] Ned C. Landeman, *Scotland and its First American Colony 1683–1765* (Princeton, NJ, Princeton University Press, 1985).

attractive ancient "pile" in England, Leeds Castle in Kent. The grants were lavish in extent, and, being feudal, bestowed all but unlimited powers, including the right to divide the land into manors, to collect tolls, customs, and quit-rents. The feudal principle was *nulle terre sans seigneur*: the new proprietors foresaw a small legion of tenants owing and paying homage to them, and from whom at least quit-rents would be due, in perpetuity unless the benefactor gave his grants free from all such dues. Potential settlers could be persuaded to migrate, especially as the "headright" system further rewarded those who brought people to Virginia with 50 acres per person. Five hundred and seventy-six grants of "headright" lands had been made in the Northern Neck in the king's name by 1661.

When the Northern Neck grant was made in 1649, Virginia was a loyalist colony; in 1652, on the appearance of parliamentary commissioners and a parliamentary fleet, it changed its allegiance; all earlier royal largesse was confiscated, and its royal governor, Sir William Berkeley, was retired. Thus after the Restoration the land-grants, and who owned what, became a rich field for controversy and litigation. Much of it was by that time already claimed, settled, and planted. The patents were renewed in 1669, but not all the old loyalists still survived. Among the next wave of beneficiaries of royal bounty was Thomas, Lord Culpeper, heir to his father's claim in the Northern Neck. He was also a member of the Committee for Trade and Plantations, and was himself busy buying up the rights of the other proprietors of the Northern Neck; he was brother-in-law to Governor Berkeley, and he was named to be Berkeley's successor when that worthy governor was retired; he also had a cousin, Alexander Culpeper, who in 1661 was appointed surveyor general of Virginia, vigilant to protect the Culpeper interests everywhere. In 1673, to add to the confusion, and to emphasize the Culpeper power, the king allotted all land in the colony not previously patented to Lord Culpeper and to Henry, earl of Arlington, for a term of 31 years. Culpeper was appointed governor of the colony in 1677, took the oath of office and the salary (twice that paid his predecessor), but was reluctant to visit it in person until ordered to do so by Charles II in 1680. By that year he had bought out Arlington's own rights and was thus, as well as governor, in name sole proprietor of southern Virginia and owner of five-sixths of the Northern Neck. Yet he stayed only four months in 1680; on being ordered out again by the king in 1682 after the tobacco riots of that year, he stayed in Virginia less than a year, and on returning without appointing a deputy, he was arrested and replaced. In his last year he had sought to collect the quit-rents he saw as his due, and dissolved the House of Burgesses when it protested. For settlers already cultivating the land they thought their own, this was a Johnny-come-very-lately, and a very greedy one too. They believed him to have constituted the main opposition to their plans for a charter which would guarantee them "the same liberties and privileges of Englishmen in England", which their agents had negotiated in 1675–6, but which was annulled by the Privy Council in May 1676. Culpeper was "one of the most cunning and covetous men in England." He stayed unrepentant: "what the wit of men can expect from a Governor beyond peace and quiet and a large crop of tobacco, I know not." [3]

It was not quite the end of the story. Culpeper sold to the Crown his rights in southern Virginia, but secured from James II a renewal of the grant to the Northern Neck, now extended to the land between the two rivers as far inland as their "first heads or springs." He got his grant, moreover, from a ruler whom he was conspiring to replace. When James II fled the country in December 1688, Culpeper became a member of the commission that governed the country until Parliament tendered the crown to William of Orange and Mary, Protestant son-in-law and daughter of the king now over the water. Neither the new ruler nor his loyal subject were graced by strength of family feeling. Culpeper in fact died in January 1689 at the home of his mistress, who, with her two daughters, received all his carefully acquired estate — except the Northern Neck of Virginia, which passed to Catherine Culpeper, his legitimate daughter, aged 19. A year later she married Thomas Lord Fairfax, grandson of Cromwell's officer. Thus arose the "Fairfax" grant which was really misnamed, and arose from a more devious and less honorable pedigree than its name implied. Unlike Lord Culpeper, the Fairfaxes were as devoted to Virginia as to Britain. The last of the proprietors, the 6th Lord Fairfax (1693–1781), best known as the patron and benefactor of the young George Washington, would, though a peer of the realm and a Loyalist, stay in the Valley of Virginia throughout the War of Independence, a sojourn utterly unmolested. The family lost its proprietary rights four years after his death.

After a Hundred Years' War of clashes between territorial magnates, and another century and a half of religious turmoil, Old England was tired of persecution, and wanted no more executions of kings. By executing "the murderer, Charles Stuart," a memory was

---

[3] Robert Beverley, *The History and Present State of Virginia* (1705; ed. Louis B. Wright, Chapel Hill, NC, University of North Carolina Press, 1947), p. 32.

left less of Tyrant than of Martyr. And England – whether or not it loved coalitions – learned not to love republics. Charles II revealed his Catholicism only as he lay dying; when James II made his conspicuous, and yet another civil war became a reality in Ulster, and seemed imminent on the mainland, the nobles – with whom leadership lay – had had enough. The merit of William of Orange was not his marriage to his cousin Mary, James's elder daughter, and thus his hereditary claim, but his experience of 15 years of war against Louis XIV, his skill in survival, his lack of interest in domestic religious controversy, and his personal distaste for persecution and intolerance. If Paris for Henry of Navarre was worth a Mass, London was well worth the recognition of a Parliament. Growing trade now eroded divisions – of language, nation, and religion; the Bible now had a rival in the balance sheet. Moreover, the Toleration Act of 1689 ensured parliamentary toleration for Congregationalists and Presbyterians, but still did not apply to Catholics or to Jews; the Act of Settlement of 1701 required that the sovereign be a Protestant; and Dissenters were still excluded from the ancient universities. The "Revolution of 1688" did ensure freedom of speech, freedom of elections and jury trial, and at least ended many decades of turmoil. Political liberty in England, wrote J. N Figgis, was "the residuary legatee of ecclesiastical animosities." [4] And, outside New England, America was also a haven of refuge open to the dissidents and the tempest-tossed of Europe: for Huguenots in South Carolina, after the Revocation of the Edict of Nantes in 1685; and in the Middle Colonies for Palatines and Rhinelanders after Louis XIV's drive north, for Mennonites, Salzburgers, and Anabaptists from Germany.

The 20-year period of the English Civil War and the Protectorate was, for the mainland colonies, a long Interregnum. The restored king was no admirer of the Puritan experiment, and repeatedly sought the recovery of the Bay charter, but his first and central determination was not to go on his travels again. This allowed distance, and the passage of time, to confer on the New World a real measure of independence. The religious drive that had triggered the great migration firmed now into doctrine, creed, and establishment. A New England way of life developed, with its own trading patterns, a distinct economy, and leading citizens with their own special idiosyncrasies. New England had now a "foreign" threat of its own to face: the Indians.

[4] F. N. Figgis, *Studies in Political Thought from Gerson to Grotius* (Cambridge, Cambridge University Press, 1967), pp. 6, 131.

3 THE DOCTRINE: CALVINISM

As the Westminster Confession of Faith of 1642–3 became the basic creed of English Puritanism, so the Cambridge (Massachusetts) Platform of 1648 was accepted as the essence of the Reformed Faith as seen by the Congregational Church in the four New England colonies. And each in its own way was as much a piece of theological contrivance, even of word-spinning, as Elizabeth's own compromise called the Anglican Church. The government of the Church, the Cambridge Platform said, "is a mixed Government: in respect of Christ the Head and King of the Church, and the sovereign power residing in Him, it is a Monarchy; in respect of the Body of Brotherhood of the Church, and Power from Christ granted unto them, it resembles a Democracy; in respect of the Presbytery, and Power committed unto them, it is an Aristocracy." But it also adopted the Westminster Confession; it could still be seen, in form, as an Anglican variant. What was not Anglican was the precise definition of the power of the clergy, and the statement that the duty of the common people was to obey their elders and to submit themselves to the Lord; Church and State were united by law, and the rule of the clergy was made absolute.

Ironically, the original draft of the Cambridge Platform was the work of a recent immigrant, Richard Mather, the first of the dynasty. He was – let it be written – an Oxford man (Brasenose College), though only for a few months; forbidden to preach in his native Lancashire, he emigrated in 1635, and until his death in 1669 was teacher of the Word in Dorchester. He translated the Psalms in meters suitable for singing in meeting houses (*The Bay Psalter*), but his taste was for "Conscience rather then Elegance, fidelity rather than poetry." He became the great expositor of Congregational doctrine. He drew up also the Half-Way Covenant of 1657, adopted by a synod in Boston in 1662 as a means of ensuring that "the Rising Generation in this Country" would be "brought under the Government of Christ in his Church." The baptized members of a community, even though they had not experienced conversion, and thus could be seen by the "unco' guid" as devoid of personal religious faith, were still held by this compromise to be bound to God. For buttress, since every step had to find support in Holy Writ, they cited Genesis 17:7 and Jehovah's Covenant with Abraham. Those granted baptism by virtue of their parents' church membership could not take communion or participate in the business meetings of the church; but they could vote. Of Richard Mather's six sons, four became ministers, and two of them, after graduating at Harvard, returned and stayed to preach in the England of their father's birth: one of these has the unusual academic distinction of being the first Fellow of Harvard, who was also chaplain of Magdalen, Oxford, and then a Senior Fellow of Trinity College, Dublin. The youngest son, Increase, who planned a career in England, was driven back by the Restoration of Charles II and England's return to Anglicanism. He returned first to Dorchester as a colleague of his father, and then to Boston and its Second Church.

In England, the ties with the Cromwellian Church were broken only with the coming of Charles II; the tyranny might be relaxed once the regicides were removed, but strict conformity to the Book of Common Prayer was demanded. When Cranmer's liturgy was restored, a new General Thanksgiving was added to mark "the end of the Great Rebellion," and prayers for the royal family were promoted from the appendices to be included in Matins and Evensong. Rarely said now, amid the plethora of less sonorous revisions that have marked and weakened the twentieth-century rites, all seeking to evoke an image of a soft deity, the General Thanksgiving reminds monarch and people, wherever placed, of the overriding authority of God: "O Lord, our heavenly father, high and mighty, King of Kings, Lord of lords, the only Ruler of princes, who dost from thy throne behold all the dwellers upon earth...". And, abroad as at home, the franchise could no longer be confined to Church members. It was this more than any other feature that drove Increase to leave England. Thereafter the Congregational Churches were on their own, in practice a theocracy, which charged its secular magistrates to act as its arm, and to restrain and punish not only civil crimes but idolatry and blasphemy, heresy and schism. This power of the magistracy was not removed until the American Revolution. And thus, as new towns spread along and beyond Massachusetts Bay, with their Old English names – Barnstable and Yarmouth, Ipswich, Salisbury, Braintree, and Sudbury – each had its meeting house and usually a school (sometimes the same building) and a Minister of God who would act as lawyer, doctor, and often as schoolmaster, compelling Sunday observance, banning frivolities like maypoles or holidays at Christmas, enforcing the "blue laws' that forbade work on the Sabbath and expelling the shiftless. Farming was small-scale on a thin and rocky soil, a family affair; the freehold in the land treasured as much as the Good Book, with its lists of births and deaths. In practice, New England became an island theocracy, ruled by its priests, notably by the Mathers, Increase and his son Cotton, who called his father simply "Creasy."

Being isolated, New England was no longer part of the Puritan mainland. It devised its own defense policy against Indians and the Dutch in New York, and in 1643 formed the New England Confederation. Its own trading pattern emerged also. However thin its soil, its rich supplies of lumber made it not just a seapower, but North America's major carrier, shipping Virginia's tobacco and Caribbean sugar across the Atlantic, and bringing manufactured goods in return. There was here a minute empire on its own, importing sugar and molasses, wine and slaves, in return for lard, pine, salt beef, and salt pork – and cod. Trade between New England, the West Indies, and Africa was channeled through Boston, and the city drew a rich dividend. There was a problem for the future here. One item of its own manufacture – rum – was at once solace and currency up and down the seaboard.

4 THE DOMINION OF NEW ENGLAND

When, after the Restoration, imperial control tightened, the Bay Colony refused to grant liberty of conscience or citizenship to members of the Church of England, and snubbed royal commissions or agents. In 1684 its charter was revoked, and a new government, the Dominion of New England, provided, and not only for Massachusetts. The Bay Colony, Rhode Island, Connecticut, New Hampshire, and Maine, and later New York and New Jersey, were united into a single unit of government under the control of Sir Edmund Andros. The purpose was defense against the French in Canada, but three of their colonies – Massachusetts, Connecticut, and Rhode Island – claimed that their charters were sacrosanct, and opposed all change, even though they had previously had discussions among themselves on the dangers that threatened, and Winthrop had set up a defense union as early as 1643.

Sir Edmund Andros was arguably not the wisest choice as head of the new Dominion. He was one of the few true aristocrats ever to serve as a colonial governor: a member of the feudal aristocracy of Guernsey and, thanks to the earl of Craven, who was a relative of his wife, a landgrave in Carolina in 1672 under that most aristocratic of colonial schemes, the Fundamental Constitutions. He was "the duke's man," and governor of New York from 1674 to 1681, when the duke of York had his New York propriety returned by the Dutch. In 1685 the duke, his patron, became king as James II.

It was not Andros's fault that the government devised for the new and extensive province excluded a representative assembly. Essex

County, Massachusetts, was prompt to refuse to pay the tax levied for defence, citing charter privileges. Andros quickly and smoothly suppressed the revolt that followed in Ipswich. The policies and the setting were not of Andros's choosing. But he was ill at ease in handling merchants, who resented his enforcement of the Navigation Acts and his attempts to thwart the piracy and smuggling which were among their major activities; and even more was he restless with the Puritan theocrats: for him they spoke a contentious, verbose language which, when translated, invariably spelled Dissent: "Thou, oh Lord, are stronger than I, and in thy Infinite Wisdom, say Nay." His English ideas on landholding, and his opposition to what he saw as schemes of land speculation, lost him what should have been his natural allies. He failed to avert the – temporary – collapse, but it was hardly his doing.

But Andros was seen as an instrument of a new royal tyranny – the enduring shibboleth of America's colonial history. Increase Mather, then serving as Harvard's president, was sent to England to protest to James II at the attack on charters that this new dominion posed. When William and Mary replaced James in England, opportunity seemed ripe in New England for the Dominion of New England to be overthrown, a movement discreetly but warmly encouraged by Increase in London, playing the role now of a Yankee Cardinal Mazarin. In April 1689, when news arrived from England that James II had fled, rebellion broke out in Boston. At noon on 18 April, an influential Puritan group met and issued a "Declaration." They justified the revolt as an act of loyalty to the new monarchs, William and Mary, and as the overthrow of an illegal and unjust regime. At the end of the day, the governor, most high officials, and the fort were in insurgent hands. The Dominion of New England disappeared.

Personalities apart, the Dominion of New England was England's first attempt as a state – as distinct from the sponsor of commercial or private enterprise – to devise a plan for colonial mother-country relations. It was an effort to consolidate the small, quarrelsome, and independent-minded colonies, whose laws and whose attitudes were not always in conformity with those of the mother-country, into a few large units capable of being defended against foreign attacks. Had it been successful, had it been followed by similar developments in the Middle colonies and in the South, in each of which foreign or foreign-plus-Indian threats were also a reality, there might have been no need for the Stamp Act, the Boston Tea Party ... or 1776?[5]

[5] The best and fullest 1-volume treatment is Viola Florence Barnes, *Dominion of New England* (New Haven, Yale University Press, 1923 and 1960). For source

Massachusetts revealed an imperialism all its own; led in zeal by Increase's son Cotton, it annexed Maine and New Hampshire. All the other colonies resumed charter government; Andros and other dominion agents were seized.

The new charter which Increase brought back ended such ambitions, as it ended the dominion dream. Indeed, it ended Massachusetts' 60 years of republican theocracy: the colony became royal, like the other colonies, its governor appointed by the Crown, though advised by a council elected by the assembly, which paid the governor's salary. After an interregnum, Andros as a royal governor of Massachusetts would be replaced by Sir William Phips, who was in fact Increase Mather's own recommendation. Brusque where Sir Edmund was smooth, greedy where Sir Edmund was strikingly clean, Sir William would also find the task of "ruling" the theological cauldron beyond his meagre resources of tact and diplomacy. The colony now absorbed the Plymouth of the Pilgrims; and, not least, it lost its theological vestment, that brigantine that had protected its pastors from secular criticism: church membership was abolished as a prerequisite for voting, as Charles II had ordered but been incapable of enforcing. The Bible Commonwealth now became a civil state. If it was no longer an oligarchy of the spiritually elect, it was not a democracy either, since it had a sharp property qualification for the suffrage.

Theocracy's enemy, however, was not across the Atlantic but at home: not only in rising commercialism, but in the rebellion of the next generation against the harshness of their fathers' and grandfathers' regimes. They had won their first concession in 1657 with the adoption of the Half-Way Covenant; but Quakers were still driven out as public enemies, after savage tortures – ears lopped off and holes burnt in tongues by hot irons; and sometimes executed. Highly respected men could lose their jobs over what would now seem mere differences of opinion, as did Henry Dunster, the second president of Harvard. The lords brethren were at least as ruthless as the lords bishops. Since there was a God, there was equally certainly a Devil.

---

material, see E. B. O'Callaghan (ed.) *Documents Relating to the Colonial History of New York*, vol. III (1853), and Robert Toppan (ed.) "Andros records," in *Proceedings of the American Antiquarian Society*, n.s. 13, pp. 237–68, 463–9. For a favorable picture of Increase Mather as diplomat, see S. E. Morison, *Harvard College in the Seventeenth Century* (Cambridge, MA, Harvard University Press, 1935).

5 WITCHCRAFT

In 1689 Cotton Mather published his *Memorable Providence Relating to Witchcrafts and Possessions*. If a leading churchman, one with a reputation as prodigy and scholar, could so testify, it is not surprising that so many followed, even into hysteria. In 1692 in Salem, in the Massachusetts Bay colony, 19 people were hanged on Gallows Hill for witchcraft, at least 2 others died in prison, and 1, who refused to plead guilty or not guilty, was pressed to death with heavy rocks in accordance with an Old English law. What probably began as voodoo tales told by the West Indian slave Tituba to frighten the young charges of the Reverend Samuel Parris, were blown up into the devil's work, and exploited from hellfire pulpits. The legends had echoes in lonely and isolated hamlets, as on Cape Ann, and any widow – especially if old, eccentric, or friendless – was vulnerable to the spite and malice of others. The craze could be said to be over when in 1697 Judge Samuel Sewall stood up in the Old South Church to hear the reading of his confession of contrition for his share in a delusion. Sewall was the only judge to admit that he had been in error.[6]

The witchcraft trials have been seen as exotic, as the last outbreak of mass superstition before rationalism, as material for drama. There are, however, some non-hysterical explanations for the trials of 1692. Larzer Ziff sees the craze that swept through Salem Village as the consequence of its decline when Salem itself was expanding as a port town. The accusers were frail and lowly and oppressed.

The old charter had gone under, the dignity of rural labour had gone under, the unopposed superiority of the Congregational Church had gone under, and the legal protection of the agricultural producer through fair-price and fixed-wage laws in opposition to his being an involuntary victim of international market conditions had gone under ... But the Lord had other ways of manifesting His special interest in His folk.[7]

This was, of course, a masculine society, and one whose preachers were stronger on the wickedness of sin than on brotherly love.

---

[6] Thomas J. Holmes, *Increase Mather*, a bibliography, 2 vols (Cambridge, MA, Harvard University Press, 1931), and *Cotton Mather*, a bibliography of his work, 3 vols (Cambridge, MA, Harvard University Press, 1940); see also Perry Miller, *The New England Mind, from Colony to Province* (Cambridge, MA, Harvard University Press, 1953), esp. chs 2 and 3.

[7] Larzer Ziff, *Puritanism in America: New culture in a new world* (New York, Viking, 1973), pp. 242–3.

Indeed, brotherly love was apt to rouse fears of sin in itself. Every six weeks came training day: all men spent a day drilling, shooting, and vying in physical challenges, rounding off with heavy drinking. The folk heroes were the Indian-killers. Women's place was the home, and the family. And the language of preachers and would-be authors was vitriolic, notably against Catholics, Quakers, Jews – and homosexuals, though they would not seem to have been numerous. Against Rome, and there were few Catholics in New England, Roger Williams, the prophet of tolerance, could be as vehement as Winthrop and the Mathers: a celibate clergy was seen as a nursery for homosexual practices; one Catholic was accused of sodomy, one of bestiality, another of witchcraft. The Mathers and Michael Wigglesworth were outmatched in the rhetoric of terror by Thomas Shepard, who described the heart of the sinner as "a stinking sinkhole of all Atheisime, Sodomie and Buggery." [8]

The Devil was put to rout in Salem, but not in Cambridge; despite the grip of the Mathers, Harvard weakened the grip of the Church remorselessly: the school and the college that were the core of Calvinist training in the end were captured by "willfulle heresie," by disbelief, by the classics, and finally by an anaemic liberalism that pointed towards Unitarianism. Governor Winthrop had warned against "the reading and learning heathen authors," aware that the Renaissance and the Reformation had also come from minds trained in logic, mathematics, and philosophy. The curriculum established in 1640, though religious in purpose, was secular in content. As early as 1663 the Senior Fellow of the College proposed to establish chairs of law, medicine and history.

In 1698 the liberal Brattle Street Church had been organized by Thomas Brattle, son of the wealthiest of Boston merchants. More Anglican than Calvinist in form, it dispensed with "the relation of experiences" as a qualification for membership, and deviated – to the Mathers' horror – from the principles of the Cambridge Platform. Thomas Brattle even offered his church an organ, but its discretion outdid its valor, and the offer was declined. Ethics rather than Calvinism was stressed: God's delight was in mercy, and Christ's mission was to save sinners. In the train of profits, Calvinism seemed to be at risk.

[8] David Leverenz, *The Language of Puritan Feeling* (New Brunswick, NJ, 1980), pp. 22, 119, 128; Philip Greven, *The Protestant Temperament* (New York, 1980), pp. 124–40; Sacvan Bercovitch (ed.) *The American Puritan Imagination* (Cambridge, MA, Harvard University Press, 1974), pp. 19–33.

The advance of science did not, then or later, preclude religious faith. The same Thomas Brattle also condemned the witchcraft proceedings as "ignorance and folly," and made observations of the comet of 1682 that won praise from Sir Isaac Newton. The changing character of the Bay Colony is probably best evidenced, however, in the careers of the first governor's descendants.

6 THE WINTHROPS

John Winthrop, the eldest son of the governor, and himself governor of Connecticut, who obtained for his colony the most liberal charter until then granted to any colony, and included within it the former colony of New Haven, was scientist not theologian, and saw New England's future in manufacturing and trade rather than in agriculture. He set up iron, lead, and salt works, predicted the discovery of a fifth satellite to Jupiter, and contributed papers to the Royal Society on trade, banking, new methods in manufacture, and astronomy, which led to his election to a fellowship – the first Fellow to be resident in America.

The third John, known as Fitz-John, left Harvard without a degree in order to serve in the Parliamentary Army, as we saw earlier. He entered London in Monk's army at the time of the Restoration, but returned to New England to lead troops against the Indians in 1675–6, and against the French in 1690; after the accession of William III he returned to England to secure a renewal of the Connecticut charter, and from 1698 until his death in 1707 himself served as governor of Connecticut.

Professor John Winthrop, faithful communicant of his Congregational Church, great-great-grandnephew of the first John Winthrop and himself one of 16 children, became a leading scientist, friend of Franklin and teacher of Count Rumford of the Holy Roman Empire; in 1759 he predicted the return of Halley's comet of 1682; in 1761 he sent a Harvard expedition to St John's, Newfoundland, during the transit of Venus, to study the parallax of the sun; he established at Harvard the first laboratory of experimental physics in America. He was elected a Fellow of the Royal Society, as were a cousin of his and his great-grand-uncle, all proud bearers of the first governor's name. But when examined in 1738, when he was 24, for the appointment to the chair of mathematics and natural philosophy at Harvard, the Overseers deliberately did not question his theological views, lest they prove too broad for the College to accept. The first Winthrop cast a long shadow over his clan, though they asked their questions not of the purposes of God, but of the properties and the nature of matter.

By 1700, however, the buildings around Harvard Yard were dilapidated, the number of students declining. And Josiah Franklin, a visible saint in the Old South congregation, did not send his gifted son Benjamin there, in part because he could not afford it, but also because he believed that he could learn much more elsewhere; indeed, one of Benjamin Franklin's early (and anonymous) satires, Number Four of the *Letters of Silence Dogood*, did not need to exaggerate much in its scorn for the poor quality of the College. The Gate was kept by "two sturdy Porters, named Riches and Poverty, and the latter obstinately refused to give Entrance to any who had not first gain'd the Favour of the former, so that I observed many who came even to the very Gate were obliged to travel back again as ignorant as they came." The good widow also noticed that many who left Harvard were "unable to dig and ashamed to beg, and to live by their Wits it was impossible."[9]

7 THE MATHERS

The best illustration of all of these years of transition is in the career of Cotton Mather (1663–1728). The minister of Boston's Second Church from 1685 until his death (for all but the last three as colleague to his father) saw himself as a member of a priesthood, a champion of Congregationalism. In his father's absence in London securing the new charter, he dominated State as well as Church – including Harvard, where he became a Fellow, where his father was president until 1701, and where he expected to follow him. His disappointment at being passed over led him to look not to Harvard but to the Collegiate School then at Saybrook, in 1718 transferred to New Haven as the true keeper of the flame.

For some years stricter conservatives had become critics of the growing latitudinarianism of Harvard, and the contamination of the moral atmosphere of Boston. Although (or because) he had been a student there himself, the Rev. Thomas Shepard Jr warned his freshman son: "There are and will be such in even scholastic society, for the most part, as will teach you how to be filthy." An election sermon preached at Boston in 1703 by the Rev. Solomon Stoddard

---

[9] *Papers of Benjamin Franklin*, May 14, 1722, vol, I.15 (New Haven, Yale University Press, 1960).

of Northampton indicates the worries of the conservatives. Places of learning, Stoddard asserts, should not be places of riot and pride ... 'Tis not worth the while for persons to be sent to the College to learn to compliment men and court women. They should be sent thither to prepare them for public service, and had need to be under the oversight of wise and holy men." Stoddard believed that he and his brethren could provide an institution with all of the good qualities that Harvard had possessed in its Puritan prime – or when Stoddard was an undergraduate there – and be free from the distractions of a city like Boston. In fact, all of the promoters of the new college were Harvard men and Harvard not only raised no objection but even prayed for the success of the venture.

In 1716 the Collegiate School moved to New Haven. Mather wrote to a rich East India merchant in London, Elihu Yale, who had been born in New England, suggesting that the college might take his name if Yale would contribute to its welfare. Moved by the letter and by pleas from Jeremiah Dummer, agent in London for the colony of Connecticut, Yale sent over three bales of Indian goods, a parcel of books, and a portrait of King George I. The goods brought £500 at a sale, and the college was named Yale. Rarely has so small a sum bought so much immortality. In his final years it was of Yale, not Harvard, that Cotton Mather became president (1721–7).

In the dedicated patriarch, "called" to be "a prophet among us," vanity and ambition for renown and for power can thus be seen as but determination to preserve orthodoxy against the encroaching, looser ways of a new generation. Cotton Mather was, however, hot-tempered and dogmatic in controversy; despite many hard knocks, he never quite recovered from his reputation as a prodigy, won too early; he was admitted to Harvard aged 11. But he wrote some 470 volumes, in a baroque and highly allusive style; he was immensely erudite; his attitude to the witchcraft cases was in part clinical, and as cures he urged fasting, prayer, and tolerance. Yet he did justify some, though not all, of the executions, and he was flattered to be invited to write the official version of the trials in his *Wonders of the Invisible World* (1693). It is factual, but with omissions, and in its tone it allies him with the witch-hunters. Again, he could be remarkably courageous: when smallpox broke out in Boston in 1721, he interested Dr Zabdiel Boylston in inoculation, and strongly defended the practice against an all-but-unanimous chorus of clergy and physicians and irreverent young journalists opposed to it. He became a Fellow of the Royal Society in 1713. As he grew older, he became more tolerant, more interested in science, more questioning. But he never lost his total certainty of his own rectitude. As a politician he was supremely unskilled: compromise was the devil's whispering.

Cotton's son, Samuel (1706–85), one of his 16 children (six of whom died young), was the last of the dynasty to occupy his father's and grandfather's Second (or Old North) church. Indeed, with him we come full circle. For he married the sister of the Loyalist governor Thomas Hutchinson, and their son, a Loyalist, would leave Boston before the British withdrew. From Richard's coming in 1635 to Samuel's death in 1785 had been five generations, fecund, and touched by greatness. All were as much men of affairs as doctrinaires. Perhaps Benjamin Franklin did penetrate to the inner essence at least of Cotton's character. In 1784, six years before his own death he told Samuel, Cotton's son, that one of the books that had most influenced him was Cotton's *Essay to do Good*. And he added that he had never forgotten his father's advice to him, when he bumped his head going through a low doorway – for "he never missed the occasion to give instruction" – "Stoop as you go ... and you will miss many hard bumps."[10]

In fact Increase and Cotton were, or sought to be, Worldly Wisemen. In seeking the restoration of old charter rule in London in 1688–90, Increase had discreetly abetted the revolt against the Dominion of New England, and had suggested as first royal governor of Massachusetts Sir William Phips. It seemed an inspired choice. Like many another royal governor, Sir William was no hereditary knight born to the purple. At first glance he seemed biddable, and he was certainly native to the soil, and the sea. A humble boy on the Maine frontier and apprenticed to a ship's carpenter, he was "converted" by a sermon Increase had preached in 1674; he married a wealthy widow, built ships, hunted for (and found) buried treasure (for which he was knighted), was a member of the Andros government, led the expedition that captured Port Royal in Nova Scotia from the French, and thus won popularity with all sides (and much booty for himself). The self-made man had done well: his religion did seem evidence that God looked after those that looked after themselves and prospered. So that when King William was prepared to abandon the dominion, and to grant a revised charter but with his own man for governor, why not Sir William? It was, however, as events would reveal, an unwise choice, for Sir William added quarter-deck manners and language, and acceptance by the lower deck, to

[10] *The Writings of Benjamin Franklin*, ed. A. H. Smyth (New York, Macmillan, 1905–7), IX.208.

a pompous style, and connivance in piracy as a fact of commercial life on the seafront; and he lacked finesse in handling the intractable pastors of Massachusetts, as well as their witches. He was eventually ordered home to face charges that included illegal trading, but died before his case was concluded.

The theocrats, in other words, were Calvinists, not Lutherans; they were not prepared merely to preach, or to act as *gurus* to secular, even to merchant, princes. The Church-State they sought so hard to maintain was, however, being bypassed; whether it won or lost its own war, it was, paradoxically, becoming the prisoner of its own isolation. The world, instead of following the lead of Massachusetts, had not so much rejected its solution as ceased to be interested in its involved theological controversies. Not that the conservative leaders in Massachusetts were necessarily out of sympathy with the new scientific renaissance. Cotton Mather was a Fellow of the Royal Society and a Doctor of Divinity of Glasgow University; he wrote the earliest account of plant hybridization then known, and held that "he who contributes to the welfare of mankind glorifies God." But the philosophy of the Royal Society was fatal to the philosophy of the founders of New England, and the Glasgow that gratified Mather with a doctorate was already the university of Francis Hutcheson, and about to be the university of Adam Smith. The New England light was not so much hidden under a bushel, as shining like a totally neglected good deed in an almost totally indifferent world – the world now of Bayle, not the world of Pascal or Milton.

But it was not only that Europe did not imitate or revere the colony of the Saints, the colony was undermined from within. Harvard College, by the turn of the century, had turned from orthodoxy, and was in decline. The great Dissenting divines and great Dissenting schools of England were on the way to Unitarianism, to mere morality. The children of the Saints were giving scandal in more ways than one. The founding of Brattle Street Church, the envenomed critics of the Salem witch-hunt, the acceptance of usury, the greed of the rich and the reluctance of the poor to pay their pastors, the vigorous, open, and argumentative character of town meetings that challenged the pastor's lead – these were signs of the times, signs that generations of learned preachers had not created a Christian Commonwealth.

The battle was lost. Both the Mathers made great concessions to the spirit of the age, and it was a lame and bitter revenge for Cotton Mather to persuade Elihu Yale to endow the infant college in Connecticut rather than add to the wealth of backsliding Harvard.

John Higginson's attestation to Cotton Mather, printed in the *Magnalia*, saluted him as "Phosphorus est aliis." Morning star or not, his light did not shine far beyond New England. And young Benjamin Franklin's tutors on the *Courant*, whose editorial line was to outrage the pious in Boston and Cambridge, thought him a "mad enthusiast, thirsting after fame":

> My belly's full of your Magnalia Christi
> Your crude Divinity, and History
> Will not with a censorious age agree.

They were lucky: they got off with a fine.

But if the Puritan empire was small, it was intense and persistent. By 1776 there were 11 Congregational Churches in Boston against only five non-Congregational. Of the five, one was Baptist, one a Quaker meeting house and three were Anglican – the first, King's Chapel in Tremont Street, established in 1688, being the only practical result of Governor Andros having been there at all. Governor though he was, he had been denied the right to hold an Anglican service in any of the then three meeting houses, so he defiantly worshipped in the Town House on Christmas Day – which to Puritans was to go halfway to Rome.

The Puritans were now under threat also from the secular world around them: on the seafront and its taverns. "Rum alias Kill Devil, is as much ador'd by the American English, as a dram of Brandy is by an old Billingsgate", wrote Edward Word. "They can neither drive a bargain, nor make a jest, without a text of Scripture at the end on't". Trade and smuggling developed, with the West Indies, and gradually with Africa. There was a considerable trade in pornographic books: Cotton Mather's tastes were not always scholarly. There was contention in State as in Church, and claims and counterclaims among merchants that rapidly transformed petty disputes into lawsuits; Calvinist skill in dispute over doctrine was good training ground for courtrooms, and "Yankee" soon became synonymous with "litigious." Lawyers became as important a profession as doctors and preachers. Militia days were occasions for orgies, and whatever the condemnations visited on the errant ones on Sundays, bastardy flourish. Reputedly afraid of water, because of its impurities – the most frequent uses to which it was put, it has been said, were for transport and for drowning – Bostonians lavishly consumed beer, ale, applejack, and rum, not least on Guy Fawkes' Day, or Pope's Day, and in the rowdy clashes of North End with South End. On Pope's Day, when the North End and South End mobs clashed, each with its effigies of Pope, Devil and Pretender, shrewd leaders could see in them instruments to use for political clashes. And wealth grew. As the early struggles simply became legends to later generations, and as harvests now regularly filled the garner-floor, the greed for land meant prosperity for some, albeit often the most industrious; it meant land speculation, the growth of classes, the steady dispersion of people, and the beginnings both of the frontier movement – and of wars with the Indians on it. And, with biblical texts resonant, and with their own special affinity for the sufferings of Job, their literature became not merely sermons but jeremiads. The Puritans cast long shadows far beyond Massachusetts Bay, even if their city on a hill and beacon to mankind had degenerated into another Sodom, or "a modern Gomorrah" – to borrow a phrase from a later age and another place. [11]

Puritanism dominated the Bay Colony for a century. Increase Mather died in 1723, Cotton in 1728, and their only rival, Solomon Stoddart, in his outpost in the Connecticut Valley, died in 1730. He had been pastor in Northampton, Massachusetts, from 1673 until his death 57 years later.

The Mathers' scientific interests always made them split personalities. Not so with Stoddard, the unmitred pope of the then-frontier, the valley from Northampton down to New Haven; he was preacher and Puritan fundamentalist; but also – like all of them – a realistic politician. He wanted the clergy to have more power, not less, and not to be answerable to the laity; there should be, he held, a national church, governed by a synod. He too was part of a great cousinhood: the son of one of the richest of pioneer merchants, his mother, Mary Downing, was niece to Governor Winthrop and sister to George Downing, the most crafty politician of them all. At his death in 1729 Stoddard's library of books and pamphlets was greater than John Harvard's – and his will was careful to inventory also his 10 knives and 9 forks. Less the scholar than the Mathers, he had

---

[11] Edward Ward, *A Trip to New England* (London, 1699) pp. 10–11; Roger Thompson, "The Puritans and prurience," in H. C. Allen and Roger Thompson (eds), *Contrast and Connection* (London, Bell, 1976); Sacvan Bercovitch, *The American Jeremiad* (Madison, University of Wisconsin Press, 1978); David Thomas Konig, *Law and Society in Puritan Massachusetts: Essex County 1629–1692* (Chapel Hill, NC, University of North Carolina Press, 1979). "The modern Gomorrah" were the words used by the Rev. Dewitt Talmage, crusading against Boss Tweed in New York City in the 1880s. By it he meant not the Boston seafront but the Tenderloin district of New York, south of 42nd Street, where in the 1880s one-half of all the buildings in the district were believed to cater to vice.

more influence – said Timothy Dwight, grandson of his grandson –
than any other clergyman in the Bay State or in Connecticut. His
sermons were vehement, not least against the Indians: he believed
that big dogs should be trained to hunt them down – "they act
like wolves and are to be dealt with all as wolves." Moreover, he
held to the Puritan faith that preachers addressed their flocks from
mind and heart, not by a lame reading from a script.

> He preach'd with strength
> of Voice and Memory,
> Near sixty years, and not
> a Note at's Eye.

His daughter became the mother of Jonathan Edwards, who was
his associate pastor in Northampton in his last two years. Of his
writing, Perry Miller has claimed that "since the founders and before
Edwards, he alone makes any constructive contribution to New
England theology" [12]

The best contemporary portrayal of the years of transition from
theocracy to royal and secular province is not a sermon, however,
but the *Diary* of Samuel Sewall, the special commissioner in Salem's
witch trials and the hounder of Quakers, who made money from
real estate and by operating Boston's sole printing press. He did well
also, be it added, by marriage to the daughter of the prosperous
merchant-prince John Hull, who was mint-master, fur-trader, and
silversmith in the colony. Sewall became judge, church leader in the
Franklins' church, the Old South Church, and, with the Bible as his
only lawbook, chief justice of Massachusetts. Although he made plain
his scorn for dancing-masters, "naked breasts and arms and superstitious ribbons," his *Diary* is at once vivid and sober reading: the
journal of a morbid, introspective, mercenary man, who was also
kind and honest, a family man recording the births and marriages
and lamenting the deaths of his large brood of children, brothers,
sisters-in-law and cousins, and who records the regularity of his visits
to the Old Granary burying ground, where, alongside his clan, he
was himself to lie. It recounts too his courtship in his old age of
widow Winthrop: in all its frequency in colonial America, marriage,
like everything else, had always to take note of balance sheets. She
would have been his third wife. He married his second nine days
after the death of his first, but she lived only eight months after the

---

[12] Perry Miller, *The New England Mind: From colony to province* (Cambridge,
MA, Harvard University Press, 1953) p. 233.

marriage. He courted La Winthrop with gifts of sermons, ginger-bread and sugar almonds (at three shillings a pound, he notes, and his gift was of half a-pound). The suit proved unsuccessful: the lady insisted on wearing a wig, and keeping a coach, and agreement could not be reached on the financial arrangements. He was luckier when he approached Mary Gibbs, whom he married on his 70th birthday.

The *Diary* of one who has been seen as the Last Puritan is not quite the racy stuff of Samuel Pepys's, but the testimony of one of the most human of New England's first generation of native sons: courageous, devout, opposed to slavery, prosperous and – almost always – prudent.[13]

One whose visits to Boston Samuel Sewall especially noted was Timothy Cutler, the leader of the Connecticut Apostasy. That event was described by Carl Bridenbaugh as "possibly the most dramatic event in the ecclesiastical history of the American colonies." It might even be seen as the beginning of the end of the New England Way, and of New England's special brand of Puritanism. In the early fall of 1722, seven Congregational ministers confessed their doubts about the New England Way and four of them actually defected and were ordained in the Church of England. Their leader, Timothy Cutler (1684–1765), who had graduated from Harvard in 1701, had been called in 1709/10 to quell the Episcopal tendencies of the Stratford, Connecticut, Congregational Church, where he remained until 1719 when he had left to become rector (i.e. president) of Yale College. He had delivered the Connecticut election sermon in 1717 and was among Connecticut's leading ministers. After his apostasy, he journeyed to London, took Anglican orders, and received honorary doctorates from Oxford and Cambridge. Returning to Boston, he was installed at Christ Church, Boston's new Episcopal meeting, as its first minister, on December 29, 1723.[14]

---

[13] Samuel Sewall, *The Diary of Samuel Sewall*, ed. Thomas M. Halsey, 2 vols (New York, Farrar, Straus and Giroux, 1973).

[14] Carl Bridenbaugh, *Mitre and Sceptre: Transatlantic faiths, ideas, personalities, and politics, 1689–1775* (New York, Oxford University Press, 1962), p. 69; Sewall, *Diary* pp. 764, 929, 958, 960, 962, 995, 996, 1008, 1059; Clifford K. Shipton, *Biographical Sketches of Those Who Graduated from Harvard College ... 1701–1712*, (Boston, Massachusetts Historical Society, 1937), pp. 45–67; J. A. Leo Lemay, "Benjamin Franklin and the Connecticut Apostasy," in L. Sampietro and C. Balestra (eds), *Benjamin Franklin, an American Genius* (Rome, Bulzoni, 1993).

8   ROYAL BOUNTY

A century before the Restoration of Charles II, England did not even possess a toehold on the North Atlantic shore. Its Bristol and Devon fishermen sailed West, for cod; only occasionally did they seek a convenient shore on which to dry their fish. Ralegh was talking of and planning a base in what he would call Virginia, in part as enquiring scientist, in part as pirate against Spain, in part as entrepreneur. And Virginia for him was extensive.

Twenty-five years after the return of the exiles in 1660, a vast new geography was unveiled. The main reasons were pecuniary, rather than political or scientific. They looked across the Atlantic, to where the Puritans were already ensconced. South of New England, the Swedes and then the Dutch had tiny settlements. By displacing them and then by parceling out the acquisitions, Charles II not only discharged some of the Crown's debts, but also attached a number of leading gentlemen to his cause.

The New England colonies in America raised similar produce to that of Old England, were a poor market for English manufactures, and had added insult to these injuries by entering into competition with the home country in their trade to the West Indies and to Europe. Their reputation was low. By contrast, and despite their reliance on the tobacco staple, the southern colonies were regarded much more favorably, and, since 1624 – with the Protectorate as interregnum – Virginia had been royal.

Between 1664 and 1682, four proprietary colonies were carved from the territory stretching from the Hudson River to the Delaware and south along the Atlantic Coast to Chesapeake Bay, to which the Swedes and then the Dutch had claims. The entire region was initially granted to the king's brother, James, duke of York and Albany. The Dutch reconquered New York in 1673, only to surrender it again the following year. When the duke ascended the throne as King James II in 1685, New York was automatically converted from a proprietary to a royal colony.

New Jersey was granted to a series of proprietors, among whose leaders were John, Lord Berkeley; Sir George Carteret; and William Penn. One-half of the colony, West Jersey, was purchased by Quakers in the 1670s. The other half, East Jersey, came under the control by 1682 of 24 proprietors, with Quakers, Scots, and Anglicans prominent among their number.

William Penn, whose father had aided the Stuart cause generously, had decided to form his own colony to provide a haven for Quakers and, as it turned out, other persecuted sects attracted by his policy of religious toleration. The proprietary charter he received from the Crown in 1681 designated Penn, or his deputy, as governor. The next year Penn was granted the three lower Delaware counties of Newcastle, Kent, and Sussex. Throughout the colonial era, these "Lower Counties" retained a separate legislature; in 1773 they broke off from Pennsylvania to form the colony of Delaware.

This fragmented and desultory beginning, as well as a late-seventeenth-century drop in English emigration, produced a complex middle-colony society composed of, among others, Dutch Calvinists, Scandinavian Lutherans, German Baptists, Swiss Pietists, Welsh Quakers, French Huguenots, Scots Presbyterians, and a large black slave population. In contrast to New England and the Chesapeake colonies, Englishmen and women composed the least part of early Mid-Atlantic society.

Because the seventeenth century was not a tolerant age, newcomers to the Middle Colonies tended to settle with their own kind in exclusive enclaves, a pattern facilitated by geography and the availability of land. Thus New York's Dutch Calvinists concentrated in King's County and the upper Hudson valley, New England Puritans in eastern Long Island and Westchester County, French Huguenots at New Rochelle, and the later-arriving German Lutherans and Reformed in the Mohawk valley. The English first congregated in Manhattan, later spreading out to nearby Queens and Westchester counties. With the middle-colony landscape dotted by clannish communities of the like-minded — their national origins still visible today in town names — the region came to be characterized by a cultural localism that from the earliest years was and remained a political characteristic.

Each colony had a governor, either proprietary or royal, a council to advise him, and an assembly to represent the people — the last being the only elected part of provincial government. Owing to the diverse origins of the population, assemblymen were closely tied to and were expected to reflect their constituents' cultural, religious, and economic concerns. Yet these local interests often clashed with the governors' imperial objectives, leading to a contentious politics that manifested itself in endemic factional strife. From New York's Leisler's Rebellion in 1689 to Pennsylvania's march of the Paxton Boys in 1764, middle-colony politics typically displayed an ethno-religious edge.

In contrast to the atomized culture of the countryside stood the rising port cities of Philadelphia and New York, whose bustling commercial character became increasingly apparent. Once the seventeenth-century fur trade declined, local farmers turned their labor to the production of wheat, rye, fruits, beef, and the like. By the eighteenth century a strong market had developed for these staple products, which flowed from the hinterlands down the Hudson and Delaware Rivers toward those ports' crowded roadways, there to be loaded on to ships for distribution throughout the Atlantic world. The more metropolitan culture of New York and Philadelphia could be seen in the rising number of newspapers, large churches, libraries, and fraternal organizations. In the mid-eighteenth century each city chartered a college, Kings College (Columbia) in 1751 and the College of Philadelphia (University of Pennsylvania) the next year.

5

The Empire of the North Atlantic
in the Seventeenth Century

When Charles II was restored to the throne in 1660, England's settlements in North America extended from Maine to Long Island and from Maryland to Virginia. Although the English claimed all the Atlantic seaboard, and called it all Virginia, its middle section – present-day New York, New Jersey, Pennsylvania, and Delaware – either fell under Dutch occupation or remained free of Europeans, though Spain looked longingly to it. By early 1685, the date of Charles's death, the framework of English colonization in middle America was secure. And by 1700 a total of almost 50,000 people, mainly from the British Isles, had settled in the Middle Colonies. The Restoration was as important as the decade of the 1620s in the founding of British North America.

1 CONNECTICUT AND RHODE ISLAND

Connecticut ("the long river place" in Algonquin) developed as an isolated Puritan agricultural community of self-contained rural communities in the wide and fertile meadows of its river valleys. It developed around its small towns, sites of Hartford, Windsor, and Wethersfield (now a virtual suburb of the former), plus later New Haven and New London – none of them growing into commercial centers like Boston, Newport, or Philadelphia. Its roads were poor. Despite its long coastline, no single harbor developed. However, it was an open, egalitarian society devoid of the tensions of Massachusetts, with few very rich and few very poor. Apart from copper

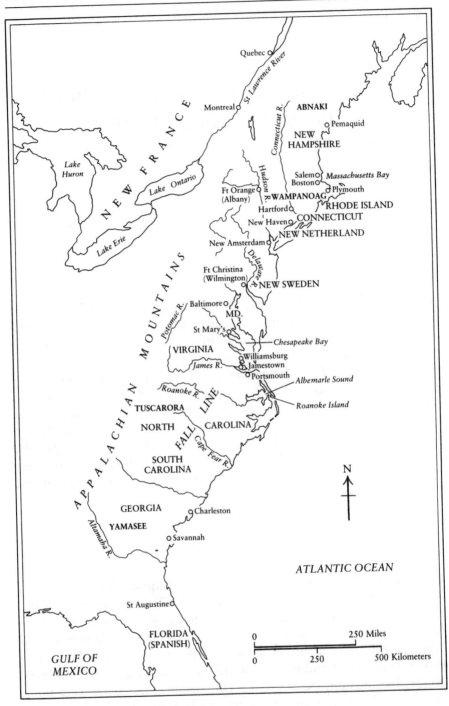

Map 9 The English Tidewater: the North American colonies of settlement
from the Bay of Fundy to Savannah, 1735.

at Newgate and iron in the Salisbury hills, it was poor in mineral resources. With no Anglican church in its midst, such as Massachusetts had after the coming of Governor Andros to the Dominion of New England in 1687, it remained the home of a simple unaffected Puritanism – a land "of steady habits" – at a time when Episcopal and Unitarian Churches were emerging in Boston. The Fundamental Orders of Connecticut of Hooker's and Ludlow's devising in 1639, by which a "General Court" exercised both judicial and legislative power, became the basis of the charter of 1662. The charter was so liberal that Andros tried to seize it, but without success: it was hidden in the hollowed-out Charter Oak in Hartford, which, perhaps because thus weakened, was blown down in 1856 – by which time it had served its purpose. As a charter colony, Connecticut elected its governor through the colonial period; and thus Jonathan Trumbull was similarly elected (in his case re-elected) after the outbreak of the War of Independence.

There were clearly parallels with Roger Williams's ideas in Rhode Island; there were restrictions too. This was a Congregational countryside – the oath of fidelity excluded Jews, Quakers, and atheists. It was a paternalist country, too; since governors were banned from serving consecutive terms, its two founders, John Haynes and Edward Hopkins, took alternate terms through the colony's formative years. Thereafter governors usually served for life; in the eighteenth century only two were defeated when their re-election was due (Roger Wolcott, 1750–4, and Jonathan Trumbull, 1769–84; though the latter had lived through stormy times, and died a year later).

The governors were drawn from the oldest families in one or other of the leading towns, chosen by the other leading men, sitting as "delegates" in the general court. The "twin pillars of the Puritan system," in C. M. Andrews's words, were "heredity and orthodoxy."[1] If there was an opposition base in Connecticut it lay not in urban commerce or manufacture but in the south and southwest of the colony. And it was to be from this region that in 1765 would come the Sons of Liberty and Opposition to the Stamp Act.

Rhode Island was much the smallest of the colonies, only some 40 miles square, and with some one-seventh of that water; its soil was thin and salt. It has been called a spangle instead of a star. It had not attracted the first Puritans, but was in essence – like Connecticut – a squatter colony, the outflow of the more dedicated and thoughtful of the Puritan dissidents, unable to accept the tyranny

[1] C. M. Andrews, *Our Earliest Colonial Settlements* (New York, New York University Press. 1933) p. 132.

of God's elect: Roger Williams in Providence, Anne Hutchinson (who moved on to New York), Samuel Gorton of Warwick, and William Coddington, founder of Newport. Intellectually, its settlers were absolutists: each parish church should be totally independent; Church and State should be totally distinct; each Church should enjoy not merely freedom of worship but should be unmolested by civil authority and exempt from all taxation for the support of other men's faiths; and recognizing the rights of the Indians to their own lands, wherever they might be. There was much truth in the Rhode Island settlers' descriptions of themselves as "poor despised peasants that lived remote in the woods." For, in all their advanced and liberal theologies, they were outcasts, a heterogeneous collection of men and women who held many and diverse religious and social opinions, and who had made life difficult for themselves elsewhere.

Massachusetts, it was said, had law but not liberty; Rhode Island liberty but not law. Quakers and Jews, "Papists and Turks", found a refuge here denied them elsewhere; Quakers moved in in 1657; 15 Jewish families from Holland in 1658. To its neighbors it was "the sink of New England." It was excluded from the New England Confederation, of four then distinct colonies (Massachusetts, Plymouth, Connecticut, and New Haven), that in 1643 came into being as a defensive alliance after the Pequot War, in which military action had been individualist and uncoordinated. The Bay Colony's remarkable story has to include the awkward fact, in C. M. Andrew's words, that:

instead of becoming the protector of New England and the guardian of her weaker neighbors, she surrounded herself with a group of hostile or at least unfriendly settlements, a condition that made rather for disunity and ill will than for unity and co-operation. No one outside her own boundaries really liked her or approached her with sentiments of affection and sympathy. Except during the rule of the Puritan minority in England, the authorities abroad viewed her with misgiving and a rising dissatisfaction that culminated in the loss of her charter and the ending of her career as an independent Puritan commonwealth. But nowhere, whether in England or New England, was the bitterness against her so poignant or prolonged as it was in Rhode Island.[2]

Roger Williams had established his colony at Seekonk on Narragansett Bay in 1636 after buying it from the Indians. Another Boston exile, William Coddington, with Williams's help, bought the island

[2] Ibid., p. 88.

of Aquidneck from the Indians in 1639, and established first what became Portsmouth. Within months he had founded Newport and united his two towns into America's first Union, which lasted only seven years. Samuel Gorton established a fifth settlement at Shawomet, renamed Warwick (now essentially a suburb of Providence), in 1643. These five, then four, communities, with Roger Williams as their ambassador, secured a parliamentary patent in 1644 to organize the Providence Plantations, the name to recognize "God's Providence to him in his distress." Its streets still bear the names he gave: Benefit, Benevolent, Friendship, Hope. Largely by the intermediation of Dr John Clarke, the physician and preacher of Newport, it secured its charter from Charles II in 1663. On it it still rests its statehood, and it is still visible in its state house. Its first governor under the charter was Benedict Arnold, great-grandfather of the Revolutionary War hero-turned-traitor. Its first newspaper, the *Rhode Island Gazette*, appeared in September 1732, founded by Benjamin Franklin's brother James. But its liberal Indian policy and the matching favorable land and trade policies of the Narragansett Indian chiefs did not save the four tiny communities from suffering acutely in King Philip's War, and from absorption into the Dominion of New England.

The significance, and the survival, of Rhode Island, lie in the views and careers of two of its founding fathers, Samuel Gorton of Warwick and William Coddington of Newport; each in his own way represented two distinct aspects of the Puritan ethic. Samuel Gorton (ca.1592–1677) who founded Warwick, was the ultimate Puritan. He had been exiled by both Boston and Plymouth, and then sent back to England. He formulated his own theological ideas, which were highly personal. Like Roger Williams he stood for liberty of conscience and the denial of the power of the civil government to interfere with spiritual things, and was vehemently opposed to the formalities and perfunctory character of church worship. He saw all institutions as a threat to individual freedom and would have nothing to do with schools and universities. He preferred "the universitie of human reason and the reading of the great volume of visible creation." He denied a belief in the Trinity, since it constituted simply three aspects of Christ, and denied the existence of Heaven and Hell. Every man, he said, was his own priest. His theology was close to the antinomianism of Mrs Hutchinson, but he disagreed with her, as he did with the Quakers since appeals to "an inner light" seemed to involve emotionalism. He was, however, a firm believer in the binding force of the common law of England and in the authority of the English government, and refused to recognize the validity of the magistracy in Boston, Plymouth, and Portsmouth or to acknowledge the legality of the New England courts. Unlike Williams, he was a true believer in the efficacy of charters.

William Coddington (1601–1678) was a man of wealth, education, and shrewd business sense. An official of the Bay Colony, he had supported Mrs Hutchinson and the doctrines of justification by faith, and of the inner light, as the supreme revelation. But he was a secular, not a spiritual, Puritan. He hoped to make of his island Aquidneck a feudal proprietory, with tenants, as did the Calverts in Maryland. Over this there was a bitter quarrel with Roger Williams. When, thanks to Williams's standing with the Cromwellians, this plan failed, he moved with John Clarke to Narragansett Bay, and in fact made Newport, which he founded in 1639, the starting point in Rhode Island's great commercial development, so that for more than a century Newport *was* Rhode Island, and with its ships ploughed the sea until it became the richest and most progressive of all the towns in the colony. Coddington made a fortune by shipping tobacco to the West Indies. Later in life he turned Quaker, and exchanged the garb of a man of the world for the drab costume of the Society of Friends. Newport after 1670 became a Quaker center, and as such it flourished, despite (or because of?) its neutrality, and its pacifism in King Philip's War. By 1690 half of its population was Quaker. Coddington was the first governor of a united Rhode Island in 1674–6, and again from August 1678 until his death in November. Feudal landowner, trader, pacifist Quaker: at least the profit motive was common to them all? Newport, and with it Providence, continued to flourish from the profits of maritime trade in the eighteenth century.

2 NEW YORK

The first English arrivals in the lands bordering the Hudson River preceded the formal establishment of English colonies. Families from Puritan Connecticut crossed the Sound to Long Island as early as the 1640s. By the 1660s some land-hungry New Englanders were poised ready to settle on the west bank of the Hudson.

While the French were establishing control of the best route from the ocean to the interior of North America, the Dutch West India Company, created in 1602 for political gain and private profit with a hemisphere as its field of operation, had been exploiting the fur trade along the North (Hudson) and South (Delaware) river valleys. Closely involved with the States-General of the Netherlands, the Company was not unlike the Hundred Associates of France. In 1609 Henry Hudson, as a Dutch employee, had sailed up the North River, giving it his name, and claiming the region for the Dutch; in the *Half-Moon* he had got as far as the site of Fort Nassau in the same year that Champlain found the lake that bears his name. By 1624 there was a permanent site at Albany (Fort Nassau, later Fort Orange) and several fur trading posts on Manhattan Island; the Dutch West India Company absorbed the New Netherland Company and its fur posts, and renamed the settlement on the rocky finger of land not Fort Amsterdam but New Amsterdam. Legal form was given in 1626 when Peter Minuit, director (governor) of the new settlement, "bought" the island from the Manhattoes of the Wappinger Confederacy for cloth and trinkets valued at 60 gulden, once estimated as worth about 24 (gold standard) dollars. Adrian Block explored Long Island Sound as far as Narragansett Bay, and Dutch fur traders followed him to do business among the Connecticut River tribes, including the Pequots and Mohicans.

The most striking feature of the Dutch settlements were the creation of patroonships, still discernible along the banks of the Tappan Zee in Westchester County, and bearing names like Philipse, Van Cortlandt, Van Rensselaer, and (later) Roosevelt; with another downtown at 15th Street in Stuyvesant Square, still staid in its vastly changed landscape. The area from what is now 60th to 135th Streets was once Bloomingdale or Bloemendael (vale of flowers), after the town of that name in the old country, with a fertile tract of rich farm land – Washington Irving's *Knickerbocker's History of New York* ... saw it as "a sweet rural valley ... enlivened here and there by a delectable little Dutch cottage ... sheltered under some sloping hill, and almost buried in embowering trees." The patroonships, begun in 1629, were to be vast land grants given freely and in perpetuity to members of the Company, on condition that they brought 50 settlers over in four years; the fee for their transit was fixed, and agricultural provisions and cattle were to travel free. Each was also to provide for a minister and a schoolmaster. This state-aided entrepreneureship was comparable to that on the St Lawrence; it would counter the small numbers of Dutch settlers thus far moving there voluntarily. But their remoteness and the proximity of the Indians were handicaps. Only one of the first five grants, Rensselaerwyck, became a success. Indeed, in 1664 New Amsterdam, despite the strategic value of its site, was tiny, and only a small part of the population was Dutch. Holland's overseas enterprises were too many and too scattered, draining its slender resources. The Dutch Company depended for settlers on Walloons, Huguenots, and refugee Puritans, who were moving from Massachusetts into Long Island – and occasional Englishmen, going there directly. By 1633 the Dutch had reached the post that is now Hartford, where open war with the Pequots ensued in which Puritan traders such as John Stone and his companions were killed; and in 1636 John Oldham, trader and voluntary exile, and two boys were also killed. The Pequots, like the Wappingers a decade later, paid a heavy price for being in the no-man's-land between English and Dutch. As the tribes were reduced – by smallpox as much as by war – they moved away, or merged with other tribes; and their former villages and cleared grounds lay open to white settlement.[3]

The fur trade, however, was for Old Amsterdam a source of great profit. When the *Arms* docked in 1626 in Old Amsterdam its cargo was of 7,246 beavers, 675 otter skins, 48 minx, 36 wild cat, "and various other sorts; several pieces of oak timber and hickory." The fur boom attracted English and French, Swedes and Jews – a French traveller counted 19 languages in a settlement of some 500 people. In 1655 the town absorbed the Swedish settlements on the Delaware that had been there for 20 years.

The autocratic rule of the Dutch West India Company in the New Netherlands was never welcome to the people over whom it was exercised. The Company viewed the colony as one of the least important of its many ventures, and by 1645 the corporation itself was bankrupt. The Dutch, moreover, cut athwart a coastline which England regarded as its own. They cut across what were English lines of communication, and were potential commercial rivals all over the globe. Under these circumstances it was inevitable that the New Netherlands should be one of the first objects of attack by the English in their wars with the Dutch during the early Restoration period. Influenced by virulent propaganda against Dutch commercial success, and aware of the incongruity of Dutch settlement between the English on the Chesapeake and in New England, Charles II made his brother, James, duke of York, absolute proprietor of a great swathe of territory between the Delaware and the Connecticut Rivers, that included what are now New York State and New Jersey. James, an able soldier and administrator, moved quickly after the chartering of his proprietary in March 1664. The Dutch governor (director-general was their title) was "Old Peg-Leg," Peter Stuyvesant, whom locals thought behaved "like a peacock," "a Czar of Muscovy."

[3] Ada van Gestel, "Van der Donck's description of the Indians," *William & Mary Quarterly*, 47.3 (July 1990), p. 411.

The fleet that he saw sailing through the Narrows was of four ships, with 400 soldiers under the command of Richard Nicolls, the duke's deputy; he surrendered to it promptly, on September 24, 1664. Only ten years before, Stuyvesant had built a protective barrier across the island at its northern limit; its name survives: Wall Street. Beyond it, the Bowery ("Bouwery" farm) was the governor's own farm. After surrendering to Britain, he lived there until his death, aged 80, in 1672, interrupted only by a visit home. He was buried beneath the chapel he had built on his farm – now St Mark's Episcopal Church. Charles Hoyt's popular song "The Bowery" refers, however, not to old "Peg-Leg," but to a place of unspeakable corruption – "The Bowery, the Bowery, I'll never go there any more." And beyond that lay a no-man's-land for traders prepared to risk their lives. North of what is now 125th Street lay the hostiles.

In all his vanity, Peg-Leg ruled as an efficient autocrat. Behind his wall, this son and son-in-law of ministers curbed the hours when liquor could be sold – on his arrival, he found one house in five in New Amsterdam an alehouse – and requested church attendance on afternoons as well as mornings of each Sabbath. He planted churches on Long Island, in Harlem, and in Bergen, New Jersey. Six Dutch ministers were active when the English came. The charter of the Dutch colony of New Netherlands granted (not that "Old Peg-Leg' was a tolerant man) freedom of worship to all citizens. Stuyvesant had, however, refused to extend this right to Jews and Quakers. A Quaker in Flushing was arrested for holding services in his home, and 24-citizens of Flushing, who were not themselves Quakers, protested this arbitrary action of the governor and refused to ban Quakers from the town, in the Flushing Remonstrance. When word of the incident reached Holland, the Dutch West India Company reprimanded Stuyvesant and ordered him to free the persons arrested and to extend to every citizen freedom of worship, as required by the charter. In New York, as in the Old Country, religious liberty was sacrosanct. Two years later, the government of Massachusetts hanged Quakers.

The presence of these varied settlers was welcome to James and his advisers. They intended less to stimulate migration from England to America, as earlier colonial promoters had done, than to build on what existed, while encouraging more New Englanders to trek to the duke's proprietary. So, after the conquest of New Amsterdam, the Dutch were allowed their own local laws, government, religion, and, for the time being, commercial privileges; the inhabitants were probably happier than under the rule of the Dutch West India Company. The Puritans were to be attracted by religious freedom, and by limited forms of local government – excluding, however, town meetings and representative assemblies. Local elections were hardly contested, even though all over 21, whether property owners or not, could vote; there were few divergences on political lines, and, as elsewhere in the colonies, proper deference was shown to those with land, status, and money. Political leaders, with or without elections, did not consider themselves responsible to their "constituents". With democracy – in Church or State – James had no sympathy.

The transition for the Dutch was remarkably smooth. Toleration of worship was but part of the Charter of Liberties, which included commercial privileges and local self-government. Many prominent Dutch residents continued to hold important political offices. There are many non-English names among the City's import merchants long after 1664. Dutch residents in 1677 "accounted for 83% of the ethnically identifiable families on the most fashionable street ... but only 75% of the residents ... on the poorer streets bore Dutch names." By contrast, however, the poorest streets in 1703 housed more Dutch residents than warranted by their proportion of the city's population, then at 60 percent. Proportionately more English, on the other hand, concentrated along Dock Street on the southeastern tip of the island, center of the wealthiest ward in the city. The English – and the Huguenots – dominated the most important professions and were especially strong among the merchants. The Huguenots, though some were very poor, were also among the wealthiest. There was, however, a steady migration of New Yorkers to New Jersey across the river, and on to Pennsylvania. No more then than now can New York City be seen as unrelated to its neighbor states. True to form, the English New Yorkers kept up a refrain to have an elected assembly. But they prospered from the wider trading connection that England brought. Beginning as the West India Company's carpenter in New Amsterdam but marrying a wealthy widow well-endowed with a fleet of merchant ships, Frederick Philipse (Vrydrich Flypsen) became master of a trading empire that ranged from the West Indies to Hamburg, from the North American Atlantic shore to the Madeiras, both coasts of Africa and the Indian Ocean.[4]

New York thus differed from earlier English foundations, since it already had a settled European population. In New York City, Dutch mingled with German, French with Flemish, Jews with Portuguese

[4] Thomas J. Archdeacon, *New York City 1664–1710, Conquest and Change* (New York, Cornell University Press, 1976), p. 79, and his "The age of Leisler," in Jacob Judd and Irwin H. Poleshook (eds), *Aspects of Early New York Society and Politics* (Tarrytown, NY, Sleepy Hollow Restoration, 1974), p. 67.

and with the survivors of the Swedish colony on the Delaware, itself mainly Finnish, that had been taken over by Holland in 1655, making this the most cosmopolitan American town. The visiting Jesuit Father Jogues was told in 1644 that 18 languages were spoken in the province. Along the Hudson River, up to the fortified village of Albany, lived Dutch farmers and fur traders, the latter receiving pelts from as far away as the St Lawrence. Albany, where Henry Hudson had ended the voyage of the *Half-Moon* in 1609, had been settled by French-speaking Walloons, Danes, Norwegians, Germans, and Scots during the patroonship of Kiliaen Van Rensselaer. It got its new name in 1664 in salute to the duke of York and Albany. It was a fur-trading center in peace and war. In 1682 the Philipse family settled where the river widens into the Tappan Zee. In 1686 a grant of a manor on the Hudson to Robert Livingston saw the beginning of a talented clan who also made a distinctive contribution, providing the first governor of the State of New Jersey, a Revolutionary War profiteer, a clergyman of the Dutch Reformed Church, and Robert Cambridge Livingston (1742–1794), who continued his trade with England during and after the War of Independence. On the banks of the Delaware were sprinkled tiny communities of Swedes, Finns, and others. On Long Island the Puritan New Englanders, entrenched in their rural townships, looked toward Westchester and beyond the Hudson, seeing themselves all the time as the southern extension of a Puritan empire rather than as subjects of New York's government. In language and character New York was still Dutch.

New York's early history was to be troubled and stormy. For its first English governor, Richard Nicolls, the troubles came soon. Convinced that New York's hinterland, lying across the Hudson, "is best capable of receiving twenty times more people than Long Island and all the remaining Tracts [in the duke's proprietary]," he began to allocate lands between the Passaic and Raritan Rivers to Puritan settlers. Almost simultaneously, in June 1664, his master in England ceded away to Lord John Berkeley and Sir George Carteret the very region on which Nicolls placed such generous hopes. Like many other Restoration colonial grants, this was a cheap royal gratuity to faithful servants, sufferers in the Stuart exile, now anxious to regain the spoils of power.

Carteret named New Jersey after the Channel Island where he was born. Despite this paternal gesture, neither Sir George nor his partner showed close or consistent interest in their new possession. For them it mainly represented a speculation in distant lands. Like the duke of York, they had no intention of spending money (if they had money to spend, which is doubtful) on shipping English migrants to

America. Like Governor Nicolls of New York, New Jersey's first governor, Philip Carteret, advertised the charms of his province in Boston rather than in London or Bristol, in a leaflet produced for distribution throughout New England.

Here was the first stirring of what became an unsettling rivalry between New York and New Jersey. The terms of New Jersey's original constitution, issued in the "Concessions and Agreements" of 1665, also promised more than New York's laws. While allowing the religious freedoms available to New Yorkers, they gave as well a generous measure of political representation. For years to come New York's officials looked jealously on New Jersey as more attractive to settlers and therefore more profitable than their own province. But Jerseymen resented the commercial supremacy of New York, with its established port on Manhattan. Competition rather than cooperation marked the two provinces' relations.

Internally, too, discord rather than harmony marked their development. The New Englanders, so much courted by the proprietors, proved the main source of their difficulties. In New Jersey, the tiny Dutch village of Bergen apart, transplanted Puritans, Baptists, and Quakers made up the early population. Their townships of Woodbridge, Piscataway, Elizabethtown, Middletown, and Shrewsbury had been founded, or arose from grants made, while New Jersey was under James's government. Their inhabitants quickly used this fact to challenge Governor Carteret's right to collect rents and taxes. The town of Newark, established under Carteret, sheltered dogged and strict Congregationalists from New Haven, suspicious of their rights and fearful that even New England had become too corrupt for the truly godly.

Inevitably, the New Englanders pursued wide political and economic privileges. Accustomed to complete mastery over their own government and lands, they refused to register their properties and attacked the proprietors' authority. In 1672 an illegal convention of the towns' representatives deposed Governor Carteret, forcing him to return to England. Although the quarrel was patched up, these incidents foreshadowed the constant bickerings, controversies, and riots that were to mark New Jersey's early history. Disputes over land-titles and rents lay at the root of this turbulence; its unfolding promoted the rise of the New Jersey assembly, and a hostility to executive power typical of early American politics. To complicate matters, in 1674 Lord Berkeley sold his half-interest (West Jersey) to two Quakers, John Fenwick and Edward Byllynge; when the latter went bankrupt, English Quakers moved in and three trustees were invited to manage its affairs, one of them William Penn. Carteret's area (East Jersey) – the division was formalized in 1676 – still attracted New Englanders looking for a Presbyterian rather than a Congregational regime and seeking to establish townships; but they were irked by the demand for quit-rents and by proprietors' land controls, and still more so when East Jersey was itself in 1682 bought by 12 Quakers, one of them again William Penn, another Robert Barclay of Urie, and the rest mainly Scots. (East and West Jersey were reunited as New Jersey in 1702, when it became a royal colony, with a Scot, Andrew Hamilton, as governor.)

New Jersey's history was marked by the land-title disputes that arose from its complex origins. No social or political group was able to maintain an easy authority least of all proprietors or their officials. From 1702 to 1736 it would share its governor with New York, and a straight carve-up between New York and Pennsylvania was always a possibility. But economically it was a bread colony that grew into a garden state endowed with iron and copper – and strikingly free from memorable Indian massacres. With a population of 8,000 in 1702, by 1776 it had reached 130,000, mainly provincial middle-class and prosperous farmers. Here, as elsewhere, its assembly dealt skillfully with governors, then with the Crown, for control of the public purse.

In New York, the more restrictive political system denied both full town meetings and an assembly. These deprivations in themselves primed the complaints of the New England settlers against James's government. Governor Nicolls, recognizing that New York's laws were "not contrived soe Democratically as the Rest," nevertheless "hoped to lure many New Englanders well affected to Monarchy" – an unrealistic dream. In fact, the Puritan towns on Long Island quickly refused to pay quit-rents, since the grants to the Dutch pre-1664 had always been made free of quit-rent; cries arose of "taxation without consent," and "inslaved under an arbitrary government." At the same time, the Dutch still resented the English victory, welcoming the brief recapture of New York by Netherlands' forces in 1673–4 which betrayed the uncertainty of the duke's control. After the province was returned to James in 1674, his officials thereafter undertook a policy of anglicization. This split the Dutch into co-operating and resisting groups, pushing the ambitious merchants, anxious for commercial benefits, toward the English. Unstable and divided, the first foundations of the English in the middle colonies rested on quicksands of resentment and hostility.

In the conflicts of English and Dutch and Puritan settlers, and amid the claims of settlers against the Crown, the royal generosity included freedom of worship for Catholics and, via the proprietary for the Penns, a matching freedom for Quakers. With the coming of Charles II to the throne, Lord Baltimore's prerogatives in Maryland were once more fully recognized and the Puritan opposition was reduced to a minimum. Likewise the liberal religious policy was restored, and Maryland became the home of an increasing number of religious groups. Catholics remained socially and politically prominent, but on the whole Catholics and Protestants lived together in an atmosphere of amity and tolerance.

In 1669 the duke of York had publicly announced his conversion to Roman Catholicism, and from that time on, both in England and America, he vigorously promoted the interests of Catholicism. As the proprietor of New York and New Jersey he promulgated the Duke's Laws (1665) in the interests of his coreligionists. He gave important colonial offices to Catholics, among them Anthony Brockhome, second in authority under Governor Andros, and Thomas Dongan, an Irish Catholic whom he appointed governor of New York in 1682. Dongan was accompanied to his post by a Jesuit priest, Father Harvey. Under Dongan's rule the first legislative assembly of New York (October 17, 1683) enacted a measure providing that "no person or persons which profess faith in God by Jesus Christ shall at any time be anyway molested, punished, disquieted or called in question for any difference of opinions or matter of religious concernment, who do not actually disturb the civil peace of the province."

In 1703, New York City had 2,732 people, of whom over 900 were children. As Governor Dongan noted in 1687, it was immensely cosmopolitan. "Here bee not many of the Church of England, few Roman Catholicks, abundance of Quakers preachers men and women especially, singing Quakers, Ranting Quakers, Sabbatarians, Antisabbatarians, some Anabaptists, some independents, some Jews; in short of all sorts of opinions there are some and the most part of none at all."[5]

The involved problem of the Jerseys, and the ultimate emergence of a royal colony there, removed them from New York's political — but not its economic — orbit. With James's accession to the English throne in 1685, New York too became a royal, and no longer a proprietary, colony. Its own attractions of location and its steadily increasing population, many of them Yankees, bred their own tensions. They had no town meetings, and no assembly. Governor Nicolls recognized that its laws were "not contrived soe Democratically as

---

[5] Edmund B. O'Callaghan (ed.), *Documents Relative to the Colonial History of the State of New York* (Albany, 1853–7), III.415.

the rest." English settlers established on Long Island for 30 years or more, whose land grants from the Dutch had been given without restrictions, resented having to "renew" their patents and to pay quit-rents when their own royal duke became proprietor. They resented too the payment of taxes for the defence of an exposed and extensive frontier, taxes imposed without their consent, and thus demonstrating the lack of the liberties of Englishmen, a cry that would become the constant refrain of American colonial history. When they did in 1683 win the concession of an assembly, the creation of the Dominion of New England led to its elimination in 1686. And if the Dominion was essential for their, and New England's defence, against the French, in turn it became a target.

When the news reached New York of New England's seizure of Sir Edmund Andros, governor of the Dominion, thus imperilling the tenure of Francis Nicholson, his deputy in New York, six militia captains echoed the *coup* by staging one of their own, and seized the New York fort. One of them was Jacob Leisler, who had reached New York in 1660 as a poor German 20-year-old from the Palatinate, the son of a Calvinist pastor. After marriage to a wealthy widow, Elsje Tymens, widow of the merchant Pieter Cornelisen Van der Veen and thus an in-law of the foremost Dutch families of Loockermans, Bayards, and Van Cortlandts, Leisler prospered as merchant and trader in furs, tobacco and wines. In timing, and as type, Leisler compares with Sir William Phips of Maine. But he had no Mather to guide him through the turmoils of New York's edition of the Glorious Revolution. Less by his own self-seeking than by the choice of his peers, he became the leader of a revolt. It has been seen as a rainbow coalition: the protest of the Dutch as they were slowly replaced, though not of Bayards, of Philipses, or of Van Cortlandts, most of whom resented an upstart; of Long Island towns against Manhattan; of artisans, but also of merchants; or − as the echo of England's own revolution − of Protestant King Billy of Holland and of England, a leader by invitation and proclaiming tolerance and the rights of freemen, against a Catholic who ruled by divine right, who was the ally (perhaps the tool?) of the France that threatened their fur trade, and survival, in the north, and had for a century or more threatened the survival of the Dutch in the Old Country. Nicholas Bayard, Leisler's main critic, saw him and his group, quite a few of whom were relatives by marriage, as a "parcel of ignorant and innocent people, almost none but of the Dutch Nation." It was a New York City affair, and had small impact elsewhere; it arose in the uncertainties after the collapse of the Dominion of New England and took the form of attacks on property, whether English or Dutch.

After ruling for two years and suggesting an ugly belligerence, Leisler surrendered to the new governor, Henry Sloughter, representing the parliamentary sovereigns, William and Mary. He was charged with treason, and hanged in May 1691.

New York was distinctive in one other way: it had more slaves than an other northern colony, and visited more violence on them than any other. In 1712, 19 blacks were executed for firing a building and killing 5 whites; and in 1741, after reprisals and counter-reprisals, 18 were hanged, 13 burned at the stake, and 71 deported.[6]

One family epitomizes the history of colonial New York. Robert Livingston (1654–1729), the founder of a distinguished clan, had been educated in Rotterdam when his father John, born in the Scottish borders and a preacher of the word, took refuge there after the Restoration, which saw the return not only of the Stuarts but of Episcopacy. Robert, as fluent in Dutch as in Lallans and English, reached Albany in 1674, the year of the Treaty of Westminster, when New York was returned to the British. Appointed town clerk of Albany, he became a commissioner for Indian affairs, bought from the Indians tracts of land on the Hudson and, not least, married Alida Van Rensselaer, widow of Domme Nicholas Van Rensselaer, a wealthy Dutch patroon, and sister of Peter Schuyler. He was thus a Scot turned Dutchman turned New Yorker, and trebly a Calvinist. In 1686 his holdings were patented as the manor and lordship of Livingston; when George I confirmed his holdings by charter they covered 160,000 acres in the present Dutchess and Columbia counties. Robert Livingston was never afraid of exploiting public office for private gain; he traded readily with Indians and French, whether friend or foe, and was a formidable combination of genial and courtly Scot, courageous Covenanter, and shrewd trader: in the old Glasgow phrase, you can do anything with a Scotsman if you catch him young. He moved easily between London and his Hudson manor, and was Assemblyman and Speaker, and was one to whom governors had to listen.

One grandson, Philip (1716–1778), was his antithesis, in his generosity but also in his reticence of manner; a Franklinesque figure, he was philanthropist, founder of King's College (later Columbia), of the New York Society Library, of the New York Hospital, and of the St Andrew's Society. But along with his cousin, the second Robert R. Livingston (1718–1775), he was a patriot leader, and like him a member of the New York Congress and the Second Continental

---

[6] Winthrop D. Jordan, *White over Black* (Chapel Hill, NC, University of North Carolina Press, 1968), pp. 115–18.

Congress; he was critical of the Stamp Act, but was no radical; he deplored any interference with trade and deplored still more the appearance of mobs, he signed the Declaration of Independence, though without enthusiasm.

Robert R. Livingston died six months before the outbreak of the War of Independence. But he too was wealthy by marriage (to Margaret Beekman), and by inheritance, and his four sons and five daughters all became Revolutionary leaders. His eldest son, another Robert R. (1746–1813), was a law partner of John Jay, a member of the Continental Congress, and helped to draft the Declaration of Independence. He was the first secretary of the Department of Foreign Affairs. He was the chancellor of New York (1777–1801) who administered the oath of office to the first president on the balcony of Federal Hall near Wall Street in April 1790, and thus inaugurated the new and independent republic of the United States. It was the same Robert R., a Jeffersonian rather than Franklinesque figure, jurist, scholar, agricultural experimenter (with the importing of merino sheep, and the use of gypsum as a fertilizer) and backer of Robert Fulton's steam navigation, who seized the opportunity given him by Napoleon when he was ambassador to France (despite acute deafness and an inadequate command of French) to buy for 60 million francs the Louisiana Territory, thus doubling the extent of the continental United States – a *coup* described by Henry Adams as "the greatest diplomatic success in American history".[7]

Another grandson, William (1723–1790), the younger brother of the second Philip, was the most dedicated Calvinist of them all; worsened in the clan's rivalry with their political rivals, the De Lanceys, he set up an estate near Elizabethtown, New Jersey, flourished there, and fathered 13 children. He was a delegate from New Jersey to the First and Second continental Congresses, commanded the East Jersey militia in the first year of the War of Independence, and became the first governor of the independent state of New Jersey from the adoption of that state's first Constitution (July 1776) until his death. He replaced William Franklin, the Loyalist, who was jailed. A Yale-trained lawyer, he helped draft the Federal Constitution in 1787. He had the literary gifts of his family; one of Princeton's (then the College of New Jersey) undergraduate literacy societies was named after his pseudonym, "The American Whig." He described himself as "a long-nosed, ugly-looking fellow," but he had the skills of his clan, and the legerdemain of a Whig

---

[7] Henry Adams, *History of the United States*, ed. Earl Harbert, 9 vols (New York, The Library of America, 1889–91).

lawyer. His daughter Sally, a beautiful if rather shallow girl with a striking resemblance to Marie Antoinette, married another skillful lawyer and clever pen-man, John Jay – a marriage that took place just after New York City's "Mohawks" imitated Boston and dumped tea into the harbor.[8]

Another clan, as colorful as it was distinguished, was that of the Morrises. Richard Morris, the founder (d.1672), was a Cromwellian veteran who became a merchant in Barbados, and by marrying the wealthy Sarah Pole was able to buy 500 acres in New York just north of the Harlem River, in what was then known as Bronck's land (now the Bronx). On his and his wife's death, two years after the purchase, his brother Lewis took over the estate. Further purchases brought 2,000 acres in the Bronx and 3,500 acres across the Hudson in Monmouth County, New Jersey. From 1697 this became the manor of Morrisania.

Richard's son Lewis (1671–1746) became first lord of the manor, and Lewis's grandson, the third and last lord of the manor, was Lewis the Signer (1726–1789), patriot and general of militia – though he was very much the leader of a minority group in Westchester County, and almost all the other leading families (Pells, Philipses, and De Lanceys) were opposed to him; and in fact he was on leave of absence from Congress when the Declaration of Independence was discussed. New York Patriots had doubts about brother Richard, and his failure to make sufficiently loud patriot noises; his was a conspicuous and "equivocal neutrality." Richard's brother, Staats Long Morris (1728–1800), married the duchess of Gordon as her second husband, and served as a British Major-General (later full General) and a British MP. As such, he married a woman 17 years older than himself, and became step-father to one who was himself an oddity. Lord George Gordon (1751–93), himself an MP, became leader of the Protestant Association which protested against the relief measures for Roman Catholics and was responsible for the so-called Gordon Riots in London in 1780, in which some 50,000 were out destroying Catholic chapels, private houses and Newgate Prison. It was in fact in the rebuilt prison that he died of gaol fever – though by that time he had become a Jew, as Israel Abraham George Gordon.

Another half-brother, Gouverneur Morris (1752–1816), inheriting his mother's Huguenot blood and with it the style, cynicism, affabi-

[8] For William Livingston of New Jersey, see Carl E. Prince *et al. The Papers of William Livingston*, 5 vols (Trenton, NJ, New Jersey Historical Commission, 1979–88).

lity, and grace of an aristo, remained (only just) a patriot, and never hid his misgivings about mobs and revolutionaries in America and in Paris: "Give the votes to the people who have no property and they will sell them to the rich;" this sentiment did not endear Gouverneur to electorates. Speaking fluent French – unlike his predecessors, Franklin and Jefferson – he spent a decade in Europe, three years of them as American ambassador to France. He was, indeed, the only foreign minister to remain in Paris during the Terror. There are those who see the origins of Baroness Orczy's Scarlet Pimpernel in the lame and colorful Gouverneur Morris, who was himself involved in an unsuccessful plot to organize Louis XVI's escape from Paris. He had lost a leg in a fall from a carriage in Philadelphia in 1780, and when a Paris mob threatened his carriage with cries of "aristo," he shook his wooden leg from the window, and in his excellent French replied: "Moi, aristo! La jambe, c'etait perdu dans la guerre de l'independence Americaine!" – and rode away in triumph. He restored Morrisania, no longer a manor, and lived there with his wife, a Randolph from Virginia. He was handsome and dashing. The sculptor Houdon used him as a model for his bust of Washington. He did not greatly enjoy the prospects of the republic's future – but he did draw up the first plans for the Erie Canal.

There was, though, in these years, in the northwest, a power greater than Dutch, French, or English: the Iroquois Confederacy of the Five Nations, formed about 1570 by the Cayuga, Mohawk, Oneida, Onondaga and Seneca tribes – whom the Tuscarora joined in the second decade of the eighteenth century. Legend ascribes the founding of one of the few Indian federations to the meeting in Buffalo of Hiawatha and Deganawida. Unified and formidable in war, they were the most powerful force the whites met, stronger than the only comparable Indian group, Powhatan's in Virginia; and they roamed over, hunted and effectively controlled not only the Mohawk valley and the Great Lakes country, but the water routes to the coast, effectively monopolizing the fur trade. At its peak, ca.1700, after the Dutch colony had gone, the Iroquois determined the balance of power between French and English.[9]

[9] The creation of this Confederacy is now a matter of legend, and of poetry. For Hiawatha, Longfellow's poem is the best and now the only source. It stands in contrast to the view of Rev. Jonas Michaelius, the first Dutch minister of the gospel to stand on American soil. He found the Indians "entirely savages, wild, strangers to all decency ... uncivil and stupid as garden poles, proficient in all wickedness and godlessness."

3 PENNSYLVANIA

The story of Pennsylvania is the best known of all, thanks to the *Autobiography* of its adopted son, Benjamin Franklin.

I was in my working dress, my best clothes being to come round by sea. I was dirty from my journey; my pockets were stuff'd out with shirts and stockings, and I knew no soul nor where to look for lodging. I was fatigued with travelling, rowing, and want of rest, I was very hungry; and my whole stock of cash consisted of a Dutch dollar, and about a shilling in copper. The latter I gave the people of the boat for my passage, who at first refus'd it, on account of my rowing, but I insisted on their taking it. A man being sometimes more generous when he has but a little money than when he has plenty, perhaps thro' fear of being thought to have but little.

Then I walked up the street, gazing about till near the market-house I met a boy with bread. I had many a meal on bread, and, inquiring where he got it, I went immediately to the baker's he directed me to, in Second-street, and ask'd for biscuit, intending such as we had in Boston; but they, it seems, were not made in Philadelphia. Then I asked for a three-penny loaf, and was told they had none such. So not considering or knowing the difference of money, and the great cheapness nor the names of his bread, I bad him give me threepenny worth of any sort. He gave me, accordingly, three great puffy rolls. I was surpriz'd at the quantity but took it, and, having no room in my pockets, walk'd off with a roll under each arm, and eating the other. Thus I went up Market-street as far as Fourth-street, passing by the door of Mr. Read, my future wife's father, when she, standing at the door, saw me, and thought I made, as I certainly did, a most awkward, ridiculous appearance.[10]

The Quaker city on the tongue of land between the Delaware and the Schuylkill was less than half a century old on Franklin's arrival in 1723, but it almost matched Boston in population. The "greene countrie towne" of William Penn's planning had grown fast. From the first, Penn was as good a salesman as he was an organizer of governments: his pamphlets in German and English, not to mention those of his Welsh lieutenants, encouraged many immigrants. His Frame of Government was attractive, providing for free education, the promotion of arts and sciences, full toleration in religion, free election of representatives, and trial by jury in open court. He sought to bring in the wealthy: 5,000 acres for £100, plus an extra 50 acres

---

[10] *The Autobiography of Benjamin Franklin*, ed. L. W. Labaree (New Haven, Yale University Press, 1964), p. 75.

for every indentured servant. He also attracted the poor but enterprising; families could buy 500 acres and pay for them in install-
ments over a period of years, as did Thomas Paschall, the Bristol
pewterer. Of 275 homes in the Middle Ward (bounded by Arch,
Walnut, Front, and Seventh Streets), 47 belonged to shopkeepers
and almost all the rest to artisans, including coopers, carpenters,
cordwainers, merchants, a boatbuilder, and a ropemaker. As Gottlieb
Mittelberger reported in 1754, "Pennsylvania is heaven for farmers,
paradise for artisans and hell for officials and preachers." The city
of brotherly love was from the first a city for tradesmen, craftsmen,
and family homesteaders, for leather-apron men, for men of thrift,
enterprise, and prudence – for men, in fact, like Benjamin Franklin.
Despite being the last proprietary colony, it was strongly liberal in
spirit, particularly in relations with the Indians (until 1764), with an
assembly with executive and legislative powers, and skilled in attracting Welsh and Palatinate German immigrants ("The Pennsylvanian
Dutch"), many of them from strict pietist sects – Mennonites,
Dunkers, and Amish.

In 1683 the learned and public-spirited Lutheran, Francis Daniel
Pastorius, as much a founder as Penn himself, led to Pennsylvania
the Mennonites from Frankfurt and Krefeld who were to make
German-town noted for its flax and its handicrafts. His group included a doctor of medicine with eight children, an apothecary, a
mason, a glassblower, a wheelwright, a cabinet-maker, a cooper, a
cobbler, and a tailor, as well as farmers and seamstresses. And they
came to work. "His opus," Pastorius said, "hic labor est." The first
settlers lived in dugouts gouged from the banks of the Delaware.
"Better a dug-out than a dungeon," they said; "better a cave than a
loathsome prison." But within a year 600 houses had been built, and
Samuel Powel had laid the basis of a fortune in housebuilding. He
also built, in 1709, the first brick-covered market; a second market
was built in 1720. By 1723 Philadelphia was thriving, with a bustling mile-long waterfront and crowded wharves.

The proprietary colony was austere in manner and Quaker-
dominated, but, though it was only a generation old, the waves
of Germans, Welsh, Scots, and Irish were already changing its character. It was all but classless, but already polyglot, with clear ethnic
communities. Even its Germans were mixed: Mennonites and Moravians, Lutherans and Catholics, Schwenkfelders from Silesia and
Dunkers from Westphalia. All, however, spoke Deutsch, and thus
became to all the rest "Pennsylvania Dutch."

4 VIRGINIA

The Glorious Revolution – so-called – of 1688 in England and Scotland had consequences for each of the colonies: consequences, or mere repercussions? It clearly was echoed both in Massachusetts and in New York, but occurred when each was already in constitutional turmoil. William Penn handled it skillfully, and its impact on Philadelphia was small. In Virginia, the rebellion had come a decade earlier: in 1677, in what has become known as Bacon's Rebellion, the major upheaval in Virginian history between the Indian massacre of 1622 and Patrick Henry's seizure of the arsenal at Williamsburg in 1775.

Sixty years after John Rolfe's discovery of its importance, Virginia's was a tobacco economy almost pure and simple. But tobacco quickly exhausted the soil; after the third crop, planters replaced it with maize or wheat. Cultivation became reckless and wasteful simply because so much land was available The natural tendency to expand into virgin territory was restrained only by the equally natural need for access to the sea over which the crop must be transported; and the many rivers branching off the Chesapeake offered easy transport. But the land-hunger was never satisfied. After suppressing the second Opechancanough rising of 1644 and signing a treaty in 1646 with the Indians, promising them land and hunting rights north of the York River, the treaty was ignored. In 1671 two men exploring on behalf of Abraham Wood made the first recorded passage by whites over the Appalachians into the Ohio basin. Two years later another pair of Wood's people reached the land of the Cherokees. This land-hunger itself bred a second product: furs, to benefit those with the resources to equip expeditions, such as Wood, the Byrd family, and Governor Sir William Berkeley, who planned his own expedition across the Blue Ridge. As a result, by the 1670s the population of Virginia, though little more than that of the London parish of Stepney, owned plantations spreading over an area equal to that of the whole of England.

Both in Virginia and Maryland the economic unit remained the small plantation, the labor force provided by the annual supply of indentured servants from home, usually some 1,500 or so. In all, Virginia then had approximately only 3,000 blacks. The days of the large plantation were still to come. As the forests were cleared and trees were girdled only, the tobacco was planted amid the stumps: by the time the stumps had rotted, the soil was exhausted and abandoned. So it was a simple economy too: cattle and pigs, a few sheep and horses, and a staple diet of succotash, hog, and hominy grits. Tobacco was the usual currency, too; debts would be paid when the crop was harvested and in its hogsheads. Virginia was land-rich and cash-poor from the start.

Historians have long debated the causes of Bacon's Rebellion of 1676. It might seem a natural response to the selfish and involved scheming of the Culpeper family after the restoration of Charles II. With that restoration, Sir William Berkeley was restored to the governorship which he had held since 1642, except for the Cromwellian interregnum of 1652–9 when he had retired to his plantation; he would serve until his death in 1677 – the longest and most experienced governorship in Virginia's history. With him returned that Royalist coterie who, though English-born, were loyal to Virginia as a place of permanent residence. The governor's own loyalism increased in intensity as the years passed.

Nathaniel Bacon (1647–1676), a 29-year-old London-trained lawyer "of an inviting aspect," now a planter at Curle's Neck on the James River, and a newcomer to the colony, had the skill of a demagogue in exploiting discontent against a group of "corrupt" aristos, and against increased taxes. He was a member of the Governor's Council, however, and an "aristo" himself – but "of a turbulent spirit." [11] At the core of the unrest was the scale of royal grants of land to favorites, and the consequent uncertainty over land ownership; the extent of the governor's own holdings and of his involvement with the fur traders; the depression in the tobacco market; the unwillingness of the governing councils and governors both of Virginia and Maryland to permit a temporary cessation of tobacco production to stimulate price, since tobacco was to England an important source of customs revenue and to Virginia its export duty was a valuable addition to the poll tax (with, as a result, a number of desultory raids on growing crops by organized gangs of "cutters"); the invasion of the James River in 1673 by a Dutch squadron, which burnt six tobacco-laden ships and took prizes of five more; the restriction of suffrage to property holders only after 1670; the misfortune of the savage winter of 1674–5, and the loss of cattle as a result of it; increased taxes for a defense against Indians and Dutch that was in fact no defense at all; and, not least, the laxity of the government in combating Indian (as well as Dutch) attacks, and the counter-encroachment of white frontiersmen on Indian lands. Moreover, behind the anti-Indian front, and its panic, lay a political

[11] H. Hartwell, S. Blair, and E. Chilton, *The Present State of Virginia, and the College* (1697; ed. H. D. Farish for Colonial Williamsburg, 1940).

protest: a protest of West against East that was echoed in Massachusetts and upstate New York, and which would recur throughout colonial and American history.

These are the "causes" of the rebellion usually cited. Yet, as is usually the case with "causes" of turmoil, most of them were there after the rebellion as before it, for they were the major problems of all the new settlements — whether producing tobacco and sugar, or wheat, corn, timber, furs, or cod — on a wilderness frontier. "Causes" are for propaganda, and serve only as historical shorthand. Other facts have also to be entered into the balance-sheet: that Bacon was more aristo than democrat, and was a cousin of the governor by marriage; that he did not try to distinguish between friendly and unfriendly Indians, and permanently imperilled the difficult task of maintaining frontier peace; add to this the near-panic views of Indians held by whites, the speed with which rumors spread, the ease of arousing mobs and their fickleness — then and now. It has to be recalled that these were also the years of King Philip's Indian war in New England, of Maryland's war with the Susquehannock Indians north of the Potomac, and of the near-hysteria of the Popish Plot in England. Robert Beverley's near-idyllic description of the scattered Tidewater Indians in *The History and Present State of Virginia* (1705) is totally at odds with that of Bacon and of the frontier; Beverley, a governor's man, like his father before him, saw the rioters as "a giddy and unthinking multitude."

Bacon led popular but unauthorized "punitive" expeditions against the Indians, which had the support of many small farmers in exposed regions. The governor, whom Beverley described as the "Darling of the People," saw the expeditions as a challenge to his own authority, and declared Bacon a rebel. On two occasions he was driven to take refuge from his capital across the Chesapeake on Virginia's eastern shore; Jamestown was captured and burned, and a number of plantations sacked by Bacon's men — one of them that of George Washington's grandfather John. Bacon gained control of the Assembly, and passed legislation ("Bacon's Laws") which provided for a widening of the franchise and a more democratic method of electing officials. The governor had the support of the large estates and summoned a warship and troops to suppress the rebellion. Bacon's sudden death — from "the bloody flux and lousy disease" (typhus?) — came six months after the beginning of the campaign and brought a quick end to the rebellion. The rebel forces melted away. The governor's prompt (and over-savage) reprisals and the execution of 40 of Bacon's followers earned a royal comment: "That old fool has taken away more lives in that naked country than I did here for the murder of my father." "Bacon's Laws" were revoked by the king, but some of them were eventually restored. The governor was recalled to England, where he died in July 1677, before he could present his case to the king. Perhaps the verdict can be left to a judge, the Virginian cousin of Thomas Jefferson, Chief Justice John Marshall: "Whatever may have been his object, the insurrection produced much misery, and no good to Virginia."[12]

Nevertheless, the rebellion pointed to the economic, social, and defense problems of the colony. Clearly there were elements of a democratic uprising against a representative of the English Crown, and also of a revolt of the frontiersmen and small farmers against the Tidewater grandees. Before the outbreak of the Rebellion, Governor Berkeley had protested against the "disorder" caused by the greed of the proprietors' agents. "Virginians," he pleaded, ought to "have something out of their sweat and labor to supply their necessities." He had himself repeatedly urged a halt in tobacco production, in order to keep the price up. In 1682 the continuing tobacco surplus and the low prices again led to groups of "cutters" destroying plants in the fields – but, on that occasion, the acting governor, Sir Henry Chicheley, of the Culpeper family, who had been a long-term resident, pardoned the offenders – even including Robert Beverley, clerk of the House of Burgesses, whom many saw as the instigator of the "cutters." Beverley in his *History* is scornful of Chicheley, and condemned his high-handed methods as liable to destroy the liberties of Virginians. He saw little good in the next titled Englishman, Francis, Lord Howard of Effingham, who came to preside over the colony. "This noble lord", he remarks in the *History*, "had as great an affection for money as his predecessor, and made it his business to equip himself with as much of it as he could without respect either to the laws of the plantation or the dignity of his office."

Before Charles II's death, and through the reign of James, the issues between the burgesses and the Crown stayed unresolved. In 1689 there was no eruption in Virginia, as there was in Boston and New York. In fact, the colony was spared any aftermath of the Glorious Revolution in England by the absence on leave of Governor

[12] Robert Beverley, *The History and Present State of Virginia* (1705); ed. Louis B. Wright (Chapel Hill, NC, IEAHC, University of North Carolina Press, 1947), p. 74. Contrast the views of Bernard Bailyn's characterization of the colony's leaders in the post-Company era as coarse, grasping individuals ("Politics and social structure in Virginia," in J. M. Smith (ed.), *Seventeenth Century America: Essays in colonial history*, Chapel Hill, NC, IEAHC, University of North Carolina Press, 1959) with Jon Kukla's picture of a genteel and stable commercially-minded social order modeled on that of the Old Country (*Political Institutions in Virginia 1619–1660*, New York, Garland Publishing, 1989).

Lord Howard. It was a fortunate absence, since he was a devout Catholic in a colony of Protestants. The succession of the Catholic James II to the throne a year after Lord Howard's appointment was a source of mistrust, while the overthrow of James by William of Orange undermined the governor's authority. As luck had it, the acting governor, Nathaniel Bacon, a 40-year resident and a long-time councillor, was a cousin of the rebel. His skill and that of his successor, Francis Nicholson, one of the growing class of professional colonial administrators (in his 37 years of colonial experience he served as chief executive in five different colonies) averted further discord, and killed the rumors of a "Catholic conspiracy" among frontier administrators.

Virginia in 1693, alike in its college, its tobacco mainstay, and its elite recruited from the younger sons of families torn by the English/Scottish Civil War, was a distinctive society. The turmoil of the Civil War helped among much else to breed the Virginia gentry. There was a great overturning, questioning, and revaluing of everything in England. Old institutions, old beliefs, old values came into question. London was the axis from which radical ideas spun outward. From this turmoil conspicuous figures emerged, who would resurface in Virginia's elite – but on the strength of their own resources, and often by happy marriages to the daughters of their future Virginian sponsors, patrons and in-laws; witness John Washington, Nicholas Spenser, Thomas Chamberlain. They came as mariners or merchants working the tobacco trade, often settling in the colony only after making several voyages. In the course of a transaction they might meet an older planter-merchant who was eager to engage a promising young prospect as a business associate or son-in-law. Equipped with some cash, probably an education superior to that possessed by indentured immigrants or natives, and, not least, a firsthand knowledge of the mercantile scene in London or Bristol, they were attractive candidates for elite recruitment. Family connections did not play a direct role in the establishment of these immigrants. Instead, their success resulted from personal enterprise, including their ability to attract their own patrons. Some succeeded even without a local sponsor. William Fitzhugh, for example, described his rise in the colony as unassisted: "I have a long time in a strange land, struggled hard with fortune's adverse hand, but thank God in the end, by God Almighty's blessing upon my mean endeavors, (having no friend or relation to lend a supporting hand) have overcome."[13]

---

[13] Richard Beale Davis (ed.), *William Fitzhugh and his Chesapeake World 1676–1701* (Chapel Hill, NC, University of North Carolina Press, 1963) pp. 169–170.

5 THE CAROLINAS NORTH AND SOUTH

The long stretch of coast from Virginia to Florida was *terra* almost *incognita*, claimed by both Spain and England. Verrazano had seen the Outer Banks and been so impressed by the Pamlico and Albemarle Sounds as to assume them to be the "Western Ocean;" but he sailed on. In 1526 Lucas Vázquez de Ayllon, sailing from Hispaniola, had planted a colony of 500, including Negroes and wives, on the lower Cape Fear River, but it lasted only a year. Ralegh's Roanoke experiment became the "lost colony." When in 1624 the Virginia Company failed and Virginia became a royal colony, Charles I granted the province of "Carolana" (between 31° and 36° north latitude) to his attorney-general Sir Robert Heath, who failed to colonize it and passed it on in 1638 to a number of London merchants; but nothing was done and the grant was itself replaced by Charles II's generosity on his return from exile.

Charles II had many debts to pay. Even before he made his grant (the charters of 1663 and 1665) of semi-royal powers over this area to eight favorites, only one of whom, Sir William Berkeley,[14] moved to America, Virginians and New Englanders had been seeking homes in its northern reaches. To accommodate these settlements the boundaries were extended to 36.30° and 29° respectively, taking in Albemarle Sound and extending "to the west as far as the South Seas." The proprietors expected their settlements to develop into a number of colonies, each with an appointed governor and council and an elected assembly. They did not plan to colonize from England, an elaborate and expensive exercise, but to attract colonists from older settlements by the promise of generous land grants and by liberal concessions of religious and political freedom. The colonists would

[14] The eight were a cross-section of the entrepreneurs of Restoration England: Sir William Berkeley and his brother the earl of Berkeley, a close friend of the duke of York; the earl of Clarendon (the king's first minister); Sir George Carteret (treasurer of the Navy); Anthony Ashley Cooper, later earl of Shaftesbury; William, earl of Craven; the duke of Albemarle (alias General Monk); and — the leading spirit of them all — Sir John Colleton, who after the execution of Charles I became a planter in Barbados, and returned home in 1660. It was Colleton who recruited the others, and through them — Albemarle was his cousin — secured the Carolina Charter. Five of them were members of the Council of Trade, and six were members of the Committee for Trade and Plantations. They were interested also in the Bahamas, the African, and the Hudson's Bay Companies. If the group around Ralegh in the age of the first Elizabeth were England's first imperial think-tank, this group of ex-Cromwellians-turned-king's men were its second.

thus meet the costs themselves, and pay rents, which could be in commodities rather than in silver, to their generous but absentee benefactors. They would, however, be exempt from customs duties for seven years in their export trade into England on all "Mediterranean-style" products (wines, oil, olives, silks, raisins, and currants); sadly, they had no need to invoke this exemption. And each proprietor was to receive 20,000 acres in each settlement.

The beginnings were disappointing. The New England settlers on Cape Fear stayed only a few months (1664), and the Adventurers from Barbados, whom Sir John Colleton recruited, abandoned their enterprise three years later. Colleton died, Albemarle's poor health led him to retire, and Clarendon fell from grace and went into exile in 1667. The Carolinas were saved by the man who has left his name to both of Charleston's rivers, and who in 1672 became earl of Shaftesbury and lord high chancellor: Anthony Ashley Cooper. Moreover, he was the country's ablest (and most agile) politician, one — it seemed — of nature's survivors: he had held office under Charles I and Cromwell and Charles II; and after 1672 he was a member of all the committees dealing with trade and plantations. Under his urging in 1669, the proprietors agreed to bear much more of the costs of settlement, and to be more generous with headrights.[15]

Thus it was that, along with Barbadian and other settlers already over the water, over 100 prospective settlers were recruited in England: under Captain West, they sailed for Port Royal south of Cape Fear in August 1669 in three ships — but only one, with some survivors and some Bermudan recruits, would reach it. The first, the *Albemarle*, went down in a gale at Barbados. Sir John Yeamans, who had already put Barbadians ashore in a settlement on the Cape Fear, took command, with the prospect of becoming the first governor, but the *Port Royal* went down in the Bahamas, the *Three Brothers* (which he rented in Bermuda) was blown to Virginia, and the *Carolina*, the sole survivor of the original fleet, was blown away to Bermuda; Yeamans returned to Barbados. Not until March 1670 did 100 survivors — many of them Bermudans — reach Port Royal.

---

[15] His skill, or luck, failed him in the end. In 1681 he was imprisoned in the Tower for treason; allowed to escape, he took refuge in Holland in 1682, and there, a year later, he died. For years he had suffered acute pain from an ulcer that required regular draining. But in his last years, as plotter in the "Popish Plot," and backer of the duke of Monmouth, Charles II's illegitimate son, in his bid for the succession, Shaftesbury played an inglorious part. He is savaged by John Dryden as "the false Achitophel" in his satire *Absalom and Achitophel* (1681).

However, Captain West (though he lost command of the fleet) had taken with him his document, the *Fundamental Constitution* drawn up by Shaftesbury's doctor – who was also tutor to his children and, as it happened, was both secretary to the Committee for Trade and Plantations and secretary to the Carolina proprietors – the philosopher John Locke. To him, power lay with property, which alone bred responsibility. To avoid the danger of "erecting a numerous Democracy," a balanced government was necessary.

It is as bad as a state of Warr for men that are in want to have the makeing of Laws over Men that have Estate ... Each province shall be divided into countyes, each county shall consist of eight seignioryes, eight barronyes, & four precincts, each precinct shall consist of six collonyes ... To every county there shall be three as ye hereditary nobility of this pallatinate, who shall be called ye one a landgrave & ye other two cassiques, & shall have the place in the Parliament there, ye landgrave shall have four barronyes, and ye two cassiques each of them two a piece hereditaryly & unalterably annexed & settled upon the said dignity.[16]

The intention was to create a landed gentry with a feudal sense of *noblesse oblige*: the charter of 1665 empowered the proprietors to grant titles of nobility; the *Fundamental Constitutions* named the orders of nobility (the senior proprietor a "palatine," whose court was the highest court; landgraves, caciques, and barons, each with manorial courts), and they alone would administer the law. For law was "a base and vile thing," and lawyers flourished by verbosity and perplexity; all laws would be simple, and would automatically become void 60 years after enactment. And slavery was seen as a fact of life. But, to ensure balance, jury trial, religious liberty, and freedom from double jeopardy were also prescribed; freemen owning 50 acres had the vote; and the local parliament would be a unicameral assembly, with voters able to elect as a delegate anyone owning 500 acres. Any freeman acquiring 3000 or more acres could petition for his estate to become a manor, when he would acquire manorial rights. Though the assembly would have no executive power and the palatine court had a veto, Locke and Shaftesbury believed that men who were not equal were to be guaranteed their life, liberty, and property. The intention was not, however, to impose an elaborate

[16] *Collections of the South Carolina Historical Society*, V (Charleston, South Carolina Historical Society, 1897), pp 94–5; K. G. Davies, *The North Atlantic World in the Seventeenth Century* (Minneapolis, University of Minnesota Press, 1974), p. 205.

feudal plan on virgin soil, at once, and in all its exoticism; nor did it include those features of vassalage, of military service, and of oaths of homage that had become synonymous with English and Norman feudalism; it was a "Grand Model" only, the "compass," in Shaftesbury's words, "we are to steere by." Nevertheless, between the feudal dream and the frontier realities of early days lay Indian, Spanish, and piratical incursions, hurricanes and earthquakes, religious clashes, factionalism, and the steady growth of representative and argumentative assemblies: so this "city on a hill" was not reached either. But, as legacy of the document, there was at least a tradition of religious freedom that attracted dissenters; and there was a tradition also of large land grants and of a local aristocracy.

The home government had its own motives, alongside the rewarding of Loyalists. It was not intended that these southern colonies should compete with those already established on the mainland, or in the islands, as producers of tobacco and sugar. The hope was that they would be sources of those other commodities needed in Britain, and which could then only be obtained from the Mediterranean — silks, fruits, and oils; and that they would serve as a shield against Spanish incursions from the south or Indian attacks.

When the remnants of Captain West's prospective settlers finally arrived in 1670, they made their main settlement at Goose Creek, a tributary of the Cooper; they were Bermudans and Anglicans, intolerant of incomers and of dissenters and of any fanciful plans devised in London. For the first 40 years the Goose Creek men were the disloyal opposition, land-hungry, traders with pirates and Indians, a very awkward squad on a restless frontier.

North Carolina, as distinct from South Carolina (although the differentiation between them was unrecognized in law until 1712), originated as Albemarle County (until 1690), or Virginia's "southern plantation;" it then became Carolina north and east of the Cape Fear River, until formal recognition in 1712. Despite its wealth of inland waterways, the reefs, sandbars, and treacherous currents of its coast impeded commerce, and, unlike Virginia, its rivers are shallow and were unusable by transatlantic shipping; only the Cape Fear River empties directly into the Atlantic. Of its immigrants, only the Highland Scots landed directly on the coast; the rest, in the beginnings, were mainly Scots-Irish or Germans, who came down the valley of Virginia, or north from South Carolina. Though protected by the Appalachians, the mountains gave little cover against the frontier Indians, the Tuscaroras, who were almost constant enemies. Settlers were given the same rights as those who stayed at home;

they were entitled to representation in the making of laws; and, like their neighbors in Virginia, they were given the right to take lands on the basis of a 50-acre headright, with one farthing per acre quit-rent. In 1660, however, by the *Fundamental Constitutions* of 1669, binding on North as on South Carolina, the proprietors planned their feudal scheme, with a local nobility and a complex court system: one-fifth of the land should be owned by the lords proprietors, one fifth by exotically titled local nobles, and the rest by the people. Although only a few of such seigniories were actually laid out, the idea of masters and of serfs lingered on; so did the headright system. The first settlers were entitled to 150 acres of land for himself and for each adult male he brought with him, and 100 for each female and each male under 16. Later, the headright grant would be of 50 acres for each settler brought over, including slaves. Families soon became lords of vast acres. In 1677 the settlers rose in rebellion in what has since been called "Culpeper's Rebellion."

The rebellion took the form of a rising against Thomas Miller, who had assumed power as chief executive under questionable author-ity. He was ousted, and the rebels were in control for 18 months. In fact John Culpeper was not among the rebel leaders, and was never governor The settlers' anxieties were economic as much as political: the tobacco crop could be wrecked, as it was in the hurri-cane of 1670; and Parliament could impose high duties on the crop, just as the settlers could respond by sometimes trying to enact a law to maintain the price, as they did in 1667–8 in collaboration with Virginia and Maryland.

There were clashes too with Presbyterians and with Quakers, who – whatever their creed – took to arms in 1701 when the colony passed a Vestry Act requiring the payment of a poll tax for the sup-port of Anglican clergy, and again in 1703 when it passed a further Act requiring the members of the assembly to take an oath of alle-giance to Queen Anne and to pledge that they were communicants of the Church of England. Nor were the governors either deft or dedicated men. They governed through deputies, who came and went (and changed sides) frequently; indeed, the first of these, William Drummond, a Scottish attorney from Virginia, returned there after three years' service in Albemarle, supported Nathaniel Bacon in his uprising against Governor Berkeley, and was executed for his role in the rebellion; others were also apt to turn coat, or to be over-thrown, or to die of yellow fever. Then between 1711 and 1715 came the Tuscarora War, when the Tuscaroras struck at the settlers, many of them Germans and Swiss, in New Bern. The largest town in the colony had a story of origins as hazardous as any of its predecessors: half of the emigrants were lost on the journey, they were plundered by a French privateer off the coast, and arrived too late to plant and harvest crops. North Carolina from the start was seen as a valley of humiliation (between two mountains of conceit?), and certainly of crisis and conflict. It gained a notoriety similar to that of Rhode Island: according to their critics, and with some justice, its democratic frontiersmen were seen as unruly, godless, ignorant, and indolent, sheltering pirates (like "Blackbeard") and conniving with New England shipmasters to violate the Navigation Acts. North Carolina became a royal province in 1729 when the proprietors surrendered all their governmental powers to George II.

South Carolina had some of the disadvantages of its northern twin: rivers that flowed sluggishly to the sea and sea islands that were a barrier to ships. But some of its waterways, red with the clay they brought down from the piedmont – the Savannah, the Congaree and the Wateree that form the Santee and the Pee Dee, the Ashley and the Cooper – became part of its lifestream. Spanish explorers, notably Hernando de Soto, had reached it, and from St Augustine came regular mission-probes along the coast. The Spaniards had, in 1562 and in 1565, destroyed the short-lived French Huguenot settlements at Port Royal and Fort Caroline.

A few months after the first landing in 1670 of the survivors of Captain West's voyage, another settlement was begun to the north at Albemarle Point, and in 1680 another on the peninsula where the Ashley and Cooper Rivers meet, the site of "Charles Town," modern Charleston; by 1704 it had fortified walls and bastions. In 1685, after the Revocation of the Edict of Nantes in France, Huguenots came in some numbers to settle on the south side of the Santee River, especially in Craven County, as merchants and rice planters. Religious toleration encouraged settlers. In 1690 Congregationalists and Presbyterians merged; by 1701 the Baptists had built a church. There were, however, intermittent French and Spanish attacks (and in 1702 a reprisal expedition against St Augustine, led by Governor James Moore in person), raids by Yamasee Indians and incursions by pirates, with whom some leading merchants and the Goose Creek men sometimes conspired. And by 1708 slaves outnumbered British and French alike, once it was clear that rice would be the major staple.

South Carolina's first 40 years were a story of starvation, of internal religious discord, of feeble short-lived governors who as often as not led rebellions against their successors, and of constant Indian threats. For a decade, from 1700 to 1710, they even abandoned toleration and supported Anglicanism. Only two governors, John Archdale in 1696 (who in Archdale's Laws included special

Plate 11 A view of "Charles Town", the capital of South Carolina. (Gibbes Museum of Art/CAA Collection.)

regulations for Negro slaves, and savage punishments to take account of "their barbarous, wild and savage natures"), and Charles Craven (1712–16) secured harmony among the contentious religious and economic factions and the interests of the proprietors. Perversely, after Craven left office, local anger over the alleged indifference of the proprietaries to Indian attacks on the more remote settlements led to the rebellion of 1719, which brought the end of proprietary government. Thus, South Carolina too became a royal province.

When the campaign against the proprietors was clearly won – a campaign fought on the grounds of proprietarial neglect, of indifference to the need for colonial defences, and of meanness with funds – themes which would recur in Pennsylvania in the 1750s and 1760s – John Norris gave it an academic form. (This pattern too would recur: the gloss, and the justification, are usually written in retrospect when the mist has cleared, to explain the turmoil, or retroactively to justify the cause that has "triumphed" – as, again, in 1776?) In 1726 Norris wrote *The Liberty and Property of British Subjects*, and invoked the political writings of John Locke to contend that the proprietors had broken a contract with the colonists, the charter of 1665. By endangering their subjects' property, the old government had failed to honor its commitment, and the people were thus allowed to create a new regime. Ironically, Locke's contract notion was invoked to overthrow the government that Locke himself had designed. And before casting Norris, an assemblyman, as a Wilkes or as Jefferson, it is worth recalling that he had firmly asserted ten years before that slaves were part of a man's property: an owner of slaves was as entitled to them as to his horse or his ox. [17]

But Charleston steadily grew. In its first generation it built wharves along East Bay Street, from which deer skins, lumber and sea stores, and later rice and indigo, would cross the Atlantic. Its harbor was the best in North America south of Chesapeake Bay. In granting the charter to the Carolina proprietors, Charles II had hoped that a feudal colony would supply England with silk, wines, and olive oil, or at least that its long-leaf pines would provide tar and turpentine. But the feudal plan of government and its exotic titles had had to give way to a representative government with a bicameral system, a governor's council and an elected assembly; to the establishment of the Anglican Church; and to measures of defense against the Spanish and Indians. However, from 1700, after a quarter-century

[17] M. Eugene Sirmans, *Colonial South Carolina: A political history 1663–1763* (Chapel Hill, NC, IEAHC, University of North Carolina Press, 1966), pp. 66, 128.

of experiment, the colony had found a staple crop when it culti-vated and marketed rice successfully. Surrounded by territory be-longing to nomadic Indians on many fronts and threatened by slave uprisings, South Carolina developed a militaristic and strongly pater-nalistic tradition that reflected something of its origins. Consider climate, and the isolation of Charleston, and it is easier to see how it became a unique city state, a military as well as a commercial-minded enclave, the hub of a plantation society, resting on slave labor.

6 NEW FRANCE

If democracy is now seen as the major characteristic of American politics and society, it is totally missing in the Stuart years, the first century of discovery and settlement: missing from Spanish, French, and Dutch settlements as well as English. No group landing on an unknown and probably hostile continent, preoccupied with defense and survival, could be governed by a committee; even the Pilgrims needed Myles Standish; and the Puritans were the most authoritarian and ruthless of all, in private life as in the punishments inflicted on those they saw as offenders: idolatry and blasphemy, adultery and witchcraft, the Quaker faith, as well as treason and murder, all got the death sentence. The first European posts in West Africa and India (and Hudson's Bay) were called "forts." Indeed, in each crisis the settlements needed military leadership: Smith, Gates, and Dale in Jamestown, Nolling in New York in 1664, Andros with his 100 grenadiers as bodyguard in New England, to put through an attempt at unification ... as again in 1754, and again in 1776.

New France was avowedly seigneurial. The Compagnie des Cent Associés founded in 1627, created 60 seigniories in New France, and by 1760 there were 250, covering eight million acres, one-quarter of them held by the Catholic Church, mainly the Jesuit Order. They occupied the waterfronts on the St Lawrence, so that New France grew as a ribbon along a river. The river, moreover, made possible the administration of New France as a single colony. The administration of a single colony was much easier than that of the diverse English colonies; not only was the direction from the center unchallenged after Louis XIV took control of New France in 1664, with Colbert as his intendant, but the St Lawrence was always the unifying thread, and Quebec controlled it: "Whoever commands the country below will always rule the country above." As it expanded, there was a separate governorship for Acadia (Nova Scotia); Three

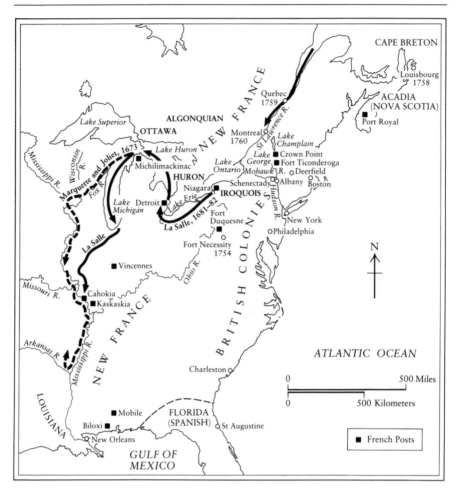

Map 10 New France in the seventeenth and eighteenth centuries: the French settlements on the St Lawrence and in Louisiana, where the French and Indian Wars were fought.

Rivers, Montreal and, later, Detroit stayed clearly subordinate to Quebec. The seigneurs made grants of land to vassals, who paid modest dues in return, and whose position was greatly superior to that of the heavily taxed peasantry of metropolitan France. What was missing was an elective assembly on English lines. But it was not necessary; the only taxes levied in the colony were an import duty on wines, spirits, and tobacco, an occasional tax for local improvements (more easily agreed to than collected), and – until 1717 – an export duty on beaver pelts and moose hides. The seigneurs continued, too, the tradition of military leadership: they led

Indian war parties in raiding New England's frontiers, and led privateers to sea.

The territorial extent of New France, however, was always a major problem; the departments of Labrador and Hudson Bay, of Terre Haute and Acadia and of Up Country (the Great Lakes), were widely spread and thinly settled. La Salle's descent of the Mississippi and the settlement of New Orleans made control from Quebec still more distant; a Conseil Supérieur was set up for Louisiana in 1714. Moreover, the English were in Hudson's Bay, the Dutch were pushing north and east from Albany, and the Puritan colonists were probing and fishing from Maine towards Acadia.

In 1660 New France was remarkably conservative and stable. It was composed of agricultural settlements and two commercial centers, Montreal and Quebec. Each agricultural settlement was relatively small and independent, identified with its own *pays*. The self-sufficiency was afforded by the fertility of the land; the limited size was dictated by the absolutist system in France, under which each settlement was an addition to the feudal domains of the king. In contrast to the English colonies in North America, few immigrants were attracted to New France in the period from 1660 to 1760. The French population of New France did not exceed 10,000 by 1700, and 60,000 when Canada was won by Britain in 1763. By contrast, there were already 75,000 English by 1660, and 2,600,000 by 1763. In the absence of the population explosion that marked the British colonies, homogeneity of the population of New France was never threatened; newcomers were easily absorbed into the existing society. But bounties were given to those with large families – just as subsidies were given to encourage local crafts and industries, such as weaving, leather-work, and welding. The land tenure system was a rigid and self-perpetuating one; it established a fixed role for all members of society, and ruled out land speculation. The geography of New France also facilitated the development of an enduring agricultural settlement. Though once uncleared frontier, the land offered a climate and soil conducive to farming, rivers for transport, and ideal locations for trade centers (Quebec and Montreal). The government militia was a vital force in the establishment of a secure settlement. By 1670 the Carigan-Salières regiment had eliminated the threat of attack from the Iroquois tribes; the regiment had pushed them south to Lake Ontario to ensure the physical safety of the settlement. External institutions and situations reinforced this stability. The constant threat of Indian attack bound the settlers together, and made every Canadian male an irregular soldier. Cooperation and unity afforded protection; venturing out on one's own meant insecurity. Moreover, New France had very strict criminal laws to control the population. These laws also served to keep out adventurers of dubious character, who might have upset the stability of the social or the economic situation. Those who did not fit in could become trappers and traders.

The first Frenchmen to push inland were priests. Father Jacques Marquette, a Jesuit missionary barely 30 when he reached New France in 1666, where he was charged to convert the Ottawa Indians, was sent two years later to the upper lakes of the St Lawrence; and with Louis Joliet he was ordered in 1673 from the Jesuit mission station of St Ignatius at Michilimakinac to follow the Wisconsin River to the Mississippi, and to descend its length; they reached as far as the mouth of the Arkansas (July 1673) before they returned. The only monsters they found were large whale-like fish; there were cattle and deer in plenty, and the Indians were friendly. Their achievements are told quickly but with vividness and effect in the volumes of *The Jesuit Relations*.[18] Their records testify not only to courage but to nobility — and to a near-superhuman patience and restraint. New France could not but echo the statecraft of the old Country; indeed, clashes with England along a long and little-mapped frontier regularly blew into wars between governments — and, as the empires grew, to wars extending over seven seas. Moreover, the Company of Hundred Associates, the colonial arm of French policy, paid the price of dependence on Paris — a Paris that benefited from the rule of strong men like Cardinals Richelieu and Mazarin at home, and Champlain in New France, but was at the mercy of social unrest and civil war, as in the Fronde, or at risk when the ruler was a minor, as was Louis XIV from 1643 to 1660. Its superiority to Spain, nevertheless, lay in the fact that even when in these years there was no freedom for or attention to foreign enterprise in Paris, Montreal was founded, the missionaries and the *coureurs de bois* (fur traders) reached the Great Lakes and Wisconsin, and the population went on growing inexorably. In this same 20 years French numbers grew tenfold, from some 300 to some 3,500. But they, too, were outnumbered tenfold by the English on the east coast, although now they ringed them round.

Four competent men (five, since the king cannot well be excluded) worked a revolution in French colonial policy. The genius of Colbert, the governorship between 1672–82 and 1689–98 of Frontenac, the

---

[18] *The Jesuit Relations and Allied Documents*, ed. Reuben G. Thwaites, 73 vols (Cleveland, Ohio, Burrows, 1896–1901).

intendancy of Talon (1665–72), and the statesmanlike vision and daring of La Salle, gave color and brilliance to the story of New France between 1660 and 1689. Inefficient company control ended, and responsible, centralized administration began. Although the form was that of a chartered company, until its demise in 1674 the Compagnie de l'Occident was no more than an agency of the Crown. After that, it was royal. On three occasions in the 1680s and 1690s D'Iberville attacked the Hudson's Bay Company forts. The Iroquois were curbed for two decades by the ruthlessness of the Carignan-Salières regiment of regulars, which destroyed their villages and their supplies, and greatly impressed New France's own Indian allies, the Hurons and the Susquehannocks. Agriculture and fishing were expanded, with self-sufficiency the objective; a subsistence economy, with furs as its only export, was converted into a diversified industrial community capable of supporting a large population. Livestock and settlers were imported, and, not least, marriageable girls, carefully checked to ensure that they were morally as well as physically healthy. They were to stay there permanently, as were army officers when they retired.

The government of New France was made up of the governor-general, the intendant, and the superior council. The governor-general had real power, being in complete charge of foreign affairs and the army. The intendant was virtually a spy of the king. He had exclusive jurisdiction over cases affecting the king. He also issued ordinances having the force of law. The superior council was composed of the governor-general, the intendant, the bishop, and five councillors appointed by the king. It issued decrees for governing the colony and served as the highest court.

The greatest of the French explorers was René Robert Cavelier, Sieur de La Salle, who explored the Mississippi Valley in 1682, occupied it for France, and named it Louisiana. He was as shrewd as he was bold. He claimed a monopoly of the fur trade in his vast domain, which would have destroyed his rival traders in the east. Indeed, his objective was to set up a government independent of Quebec, and to secure it he returned to France in 1684, and emerged as governor of Illinois. It was on his return in 1685 that he lost his way, and landed on the coast of Texas at Matargordo Bay; he was murdered by his own rebellious men on the banks of the Brazos in 1687. The first permanent French settlement in this new province was at Biloxi in 1699. By the mid-eighteenth century, the French empire was represented by a string of forts and trading posts running from the mouth of the St Lawrence along the lakes, and south by the Illinois and Mississippi Rivers to New Orleans. New

France could encircle New England, New York, Pennsylvania, and Virginia.

Grandiose as was the scheme of empire, and brilliant as was the work of individual explorers and Jesuit missionaries, the great dream of La Salle was to dissolve before simple demography. The French were a nation of peasants, not of farmers; when they moved, it was rarely far. Though independent-minded and acquisitive, and envious of their neighbors, they were not entrepreneurs, but *petit-bourgeois*. To go abroad was a rare experience. Indeed, in the whole period of French colonial rule, fewer than 30,000 Frenchmen migrated to Canada. Not enough Frenchmen ever moved to New France to hold it against the aggression of the more numerous English to the east and south. Inducements of various kinds were made to entice emigrants to Canada, but the French were reluctant to try their fortunes in the New World. Louisiana was settled mainly by vagrants and long had the reputation of being only a penal colony.

Religion was as much weakness as strength. The industrious Huguenots, persecuted at home, would have made good settlers – as did the Puritans – but were denied admittance, just as Spain excluded non-Catholics. Moreover, some governors, like Louis de Buade, Comte de Frontenac (governor 1672–82) favored the Recollect missionaries (allied in France with the king) against the Jesuits, agents of Rome. Frontenac encouraged the fur traders and thus the steady acquisition of new territory, whereas Paris wanted to consolidate the existing settlements and retain the *habitants* there. The climate was severe and the soil stubborn, and it was a long time before the colonists established prosperous communities. Agriculture, furthermore, was always in competition with the more lucrative fur trade, which was the primary economic interest of New France, and which occupied the attention of a third of the colonial population. The government, by offering titles of nobility and land grants, attempted to establish an agricultural feudalism based on the seigneurial system of France, a system of feudal land tenancy and of feudal dues. The seigneur acted as the local squire, magistrate, perhaps militia leader. Sometimes he was prosperous, but generally his rents were small and his economic condition little better than that of his tenants; often he worked in the fields with them. The tenants were assured of the full possession of land so long as they paid small dues and contributed minor labor, and they were free to sell their tenancies at will. Neither tenants nor seigneur had any political power – all this was invested in the council in Quebec. Instead of the compact feudal village of Europe, however, the *habitants* preferred to set up their farms in long strips with a few rods' frontage along the rivers and lakes, so that their villages sometimes stretched for miles along the shore.

What were prerogatives in the Old Country were burdens in the New. The more energetic and venturesome quickly turned to the fur trade. As eastern Canada was not rich in peltries, and as the farmers ploughed the land and cleared forests, the traders had to push further and further into the recesses of the wilderness in search of furs, which accounts in part for the rapidity of the upstream movement, and the vast region over which the French exercised what was often only a nominal control. The furs were largely obtained by the Indians and collected by the French fur men, the *coureurs de bois*, who loaded their imported French commodities in canoes and traveled far inland as traders. Wherever they went, their brandy was specially welcome. Some of them had squaws, it seems, in almost every tribe, to the horror of the Church. Indeed, the intimate relations between Frenchmen and Indians allowed the former to compete successfully with English traders, even if the latter often had cheaper and superior products (and rotgut rum) for barter.

Moreover, New France's ordered plan ran up against human nature. Not all the *habitants* sent out accepted the system. Strong-willed or reckless individualists moved on to become *coureurs de bois*. Among them were adventurers like Pierre Radison and his brother-in-law Médart, Sieur de Groseilliers; the former was a captive of the Hurons for a number of years, the latter a farmer attracted by the fur trade. They went north into Hudson Bay, against official instructions. They then persuaded a group of wealthy Englishmen to back them. In 1670 the Hudson's Bay Company came into existence, to become New France's greatest rival in the fur trade.

Despite the competition of the fur trade, the artificial restraints of feudalism, and the lack of agricultural markets, life in New France was not devoid of reasonable comforts in the eighteenth century. One traveller (La Hontin) remarked that the "boors of the manours" lived with greater comfort "than an infinity of the gentry in France," while the Swedish traveller, Peter Kalm, testified to the general contentment.

New France was, however, riddled with problems: furs versus agriculture; a vast inland empire with too few settlers, that, as it grew, provoked clashes with Indians and, ultimately, with the British as they advanced from the coast; governor, intendant and bishop, designed to be a harmonious trinity, more often found their interests in conflict. The most famous of the many such controversies was between Frontenac, the formidable governor who wished to extend the fur trade as rapidly as possible, and Laval, the greatest of the bishops, who was appalled at the way brandy debauched the Indians and brutalized life in the colony in general. It was inevitable that it should have been Frontenac's point of view that ultimately carried the day.

Moreover, each of these functions was imposed from Paris. The *habitants* were too few in number and too thinly spread to become effective politically. Nor did their seigneurial system have many of the irritating feudal practices of Europe: the seigneur received formal deference, but in practice worked on the land as but the first among equals. There were no representative assemblies, no elections, few towns to breed town meetings and vocal expressions of grievances or of claims to "rights." In the localities alongside seigneur and *curé* was the militia captain, who grew from security officer to become the agent of the intendant, and his eyes and ears.

Compared to Massachusetts Bay, Quebec and Montreal were almost cultural deserts. For the century after 1660, French immigrants were disturbingly few to generate the dynamic growth that New England bred. New France paid the price of its own splendidly rational planning, its central state direction, and its own uniformity, so laboriously won at home. Paris might be worth a Mass but — given its strategical and logistical weakness — it could not develop an empire by decree.

Nevertheless, New France emerged as remarkably stable. It was ringed round by forests and icy wastes, and unreliable Indians; it looked in on itself, and on the river, its link with home. Criminal laws were strict and discouraged adventurers — those so motivated could go to the frontier. Even more than in New England, its strength was in the family, on which the *curés* kept a vigilant eye. Perhaps its most striking feature was the low rate of illegitimate births. From 1621 to 1661 only one out of 674 children born in New France was born out of wedlock. Few prostitutes got through the tight immigration controls (whereas England positively encouraged their emigration). Moreover, in 1663 Louis XIV brought all New France's commercial enterprises under his strict control, thus ending the independent merchants' capitalism that had existed since 1608, when Champlain established his trading post.

Without secure communications, French possessions in North America were bound to be hostages of the British navy, which after the Battle of La Hogue in 1692 gradually achieved an overall command of the seas. Determined to maintain her European hegemony, and at the same time to build a great overseas empire, France fell between the two stools of imperial dreams and continental attachments. Yet, at the end of the seventeenth century, France and her

Indian allies dominated North America from the St Lawrence to the Rockies, from the beaver country and the Great Lakes almost as far south as the Gulf of Mexico. The French in the New Country were better off than in the Old; and the bishop and the *curé* were not the lords and masters that they were in the Old.

In North America, the issue was fundamentally one of manpower, but only the most constant support in terms of men and supplies from Europe could have made the grand project feasible. Had 50,000 Huguenots been forced, like the Puritans, to take refuge in Canada (instead of being barred from that country), French ambitions might have stood a chance of fulfillment. Had a mere half of 1 percent of the French population of some 18,000,000 been persuaded to emigrate to Canada at the beginning of the eighteenth century, the colony would have gained the numerical strength which alone could justify imperial policies of expansion. Against the weight of more than two million British settlers, hemmed within the Atlantic coastal strip east of the Appalachian Mountains, a French colony of under 60,000 in 1755 could scarcely fulfill the designs of its explorers and governors. That New France was able to endure as long as it did was principally owing to professional troops and good organization. Although unrecognized at the time, the beginnings of the "Second Hundred Years' War for Empire", a worldwide war, lay ahead.

That the form of government of New France, in all its extent of geography, was as absolutist as the Old, with intendants, royal agents, and seigneurs, holding land grants from a permanently absentee king, and that it was buttressed by one common Faith, marks the profound gap of New France from the English colonies, each distinct from its neighbor, rarely feudal in origin, and if so, not staying so for long, and where land ownership and freedom of religious worship were the prized objectives of every family.

7 IN THE KING'S NAME

For the British, the King was the source of authority: whether it was exercised at home or abroad. All that was done was done "in the King's name." He never acted alone, however, but with advisers, the members of his Privy Council – just as in the twentieth century the sovereign acts with the advice of a party Cabinet selected from an elected House of Commons. One of Charles II's cynical courtiers spoke of him as a pretty witty king, "Whose word no man relies on, Who never said a foolish thing, And never did a wise one" – only to earn the royal comment: "Quite right!' My words are my own, but my acts are my ministers'." The interests and power of the Privy Council were all but unlimited. It reviewed colonial laws and listened to appeals. In practice it was a registering and not a deliberative body, often little more than a post office. Its detailed work was done in committee, even if as a committee of the whole, as still obtains in the House of Commons. In this capacity it could call in and cross-examine witnesses, hear plaintiffs and defendants, and request information – as Franklin discovered, and suffered from, in 1774.

The Thirteen Colonies were founded either with the permission of the king in Council, or, as in the case of Rhode Island and Connecticut, with a subsequent legalization of their existence by the grant of a royal charter. Parliament played little part in early overseas expansion; the colonies were the king's, and the colonists believed it to be to their advantage to keep them so. In the eighteenth century, those that were not royal sought to become so. Nevertheless, in 1649 and 1689, Parliament asserted its supreme authority over the dominions, as in England, and whether it would exercise its power was deemed by many to be a question of expediency rather than of right.

By 1750, Parliament had on numerous occasions enacted statutes vitally touching the interests of each colony, both in its world relationships and in its internal affairs. Trade, manufacturing, coinage, banking, and the post office were some of the subjects that were affected by this legislation. Several of these laws were distinctly advantageous to the colonies; none of them was passed with an intent to injure, while the measures deemed harmful by the colonists were questionably so, and were not (probably could not be) rigidly enforced.

Beginning in 1660, but drawing on Cromwellian experience, the Crown inaugurated a policy of closer supervision of the empire, including the creation of a bureaucracy at home and abroad for colonial administration (witness the short-lived Andros consolidation in New England); less liberal grants of authority to, and more interference with, the proprietors; a tendency to make all colonies royal; the strengthening of the army and navy on the Atlantic coast, and the exercise of disallowance and appeal.

The prevailing economic theory – shared by all the empires represented in the New World – was built on two assumptions: the importance of bullion (and, therefore, restrictions on the export of coin and bullion, and close supervision of foreign trade), and of mercantilism. Taken together they formed the "mercantile system" – the phrase is Adam Smith's, coined in his *The Wealth of Nations*

(1776), and he used it to attack the system as ultra-protectionist, exclusive and nationalist, and based on a false view that a nation's wealth lay only in its mountains of cash and coin. Since England had no gold or silver mines, it was argued that it must attract coin by exporting more commodities than it imported, and thus in exchange for them receive coin from abroad – what later centuries would call a favorable balance of trade. Thus for the Stuarts and their advisers, wealth meant the accumulation of gold and silver; Spain was model as well as enemy. If there was a handbook that they followed, it was the East India merchant turned analyst Thomas Mun's (1571–1641) *England's Treasure by Forraign Trade*, written ca.1630, but not published until 1664, with its maxim: "the ordinary means therefore to encrease our wealth and treasure is by *forraign trade*, wherein wee must ever observe this rule: to sell more to strangers yearly than wee consume of theirs in value."

Hence the proliferation of controls: tariff walls, import and export duties, prohibitions of import of foreign manufactured goods or of the export of raw wool, regulations of quality and of measure, and monopolies (in domestic manufactures as in foreign trade). They were made easier to enforce, in the centuries of small and inadequate state bureaucracies and unstable foreign governments, by the use of companies given near-royal authority abroad (including the erection of forts and the use of locally recruited troops): the Muscovy Company, the Africa Company, the Levant Company, the East India Company, the Eastland Company (the Baltic), and the Virginia Company. Power had to be delegated to a company, and it acted as a national agency. But monopolies – however much needed in foreign trade – were never uniformly popular; as early as 1604 the House of Commons held that monopolies in restraint of the trade of others were against the laws of England and that merchants should have full liberty to trade with all countries, including Spain, Portugal, and France.

The commercial system was designed as imperial and not merely as English. The navigation laws were the main feature in relations with the colonies, but they were planned to encourage shipping and shipbuilding, colonial as well as English – for the term "English" included the colonists. Nor were they designed with the mainland colonies in mind; the idea of a strong unified state long predated 1607, and the sugar islands mattered more than the landmass, much of which seemed bleak and barren, or hostile. The Navigation Acts were designed to promote the economic welfare of the colonies as well as the mother-country, on the basis of a crude division of functions between the Old Country and the New. Exports from the

colonies were controlled; certain "enumerated commodities" were
to be shipped to England. Of these the Act of 1660 listed sugar,
tobacco, raw cotton, indigo, ginger, and dyewoods; in Queen Anne's
time rice and naval stores were added. Among these, the greater
part were products of the Caribbean region; sugar was regularly 70
percent of England's annual imports from across the north Atlantic;
only tobacco and naval stores came in important quantities from the
North American mainland. The colonists could take their other
products where they liked. Their imports were controlled, too. All
commodities that were the result of the growth, production, or
manufacture of Europe were to be laden in England. (There were
certain exceptions, such as Portuguese salt and wines and Irish and
Scottish provisions and horses.) This was intended to build up a
staple trade in England (the Act of 1663). The carriage of goods to
or from the colonies was prohibited except in British-built ships
owned by Englishmen (including colonists), and having Englishmen
to the proportion of not less than three-quarters of their crews. No
colonial produce from any part of the world was to be imported
into England except in such ships (the Act of 1651). Both shipbuilding and commerce flourished along the seaboard of North America.
Lastly, England began to restrict the freedom of the colonies to
engage in manufactures: 1699 their woolen manufactures were
restrained.

Seventeenth-century English colonial government thus had distinctive characteristics. One was that each colony was linked to
England by trade and/or by trade regulations. Another was the failure
of all the schemes of union, whether domestic to New England, or
imposed from London by Andros. Jacob Leisler's summons to New
York in May 1690 of a meeting of colonial representatives to plan
an attack on the French in Canada was ignored by all the southern
colonies and attended only by representatives from New York, Massachusetts, Plymouth, Connecticut, and Maryland. It produced only
a small expedition whose disastrous outcome ended the attempt at
union. William Penn's plans of 1697 and 1700 for an annual congress with two representatives from each colony, to regulate inter-
colonial disputes and to make contributions for joint defense, all
under a royal commissioner as president, also proved to be abortive,
as were his schemes for a similar federation of the states of Europe.
As the Albany conference in 1754 would again reveal, even neighboring colonies would not form effective unions unless the external
threat was a visible and present danger — as it was, it seemed, in
1776. Each colony's ties, commercial and political, with London,
with Bristol or (later) with Glasgow, were much closer than those

with its neighbors. No king after James VII and II showed any interest in any plan for colonial federation; nor did any minister until the elder Pitt.

A third feature was that within the first century of settlement, each colony had penetrated inland only approximately 100 miles. This was a seabound empire, dependent, like that of France, on ties with home. The Indians, and in particular the Iroquois Confederacy, in alliance with the Appalachians and the wild and thickly forested frontier, delayed further discovery. It was easier to expand north or south along the coast, even to confront and war with French plus Indians, or Spanish plus Indians, than to challenge the unknown, and unmapped, interior.

Fourthly, it was no longer seen as adequate to leave trade to monopolistic trading companies. Thanks to the Navigation Acts and the efforts to enforce them, and to the rivalries with Spain, France, and Holland, a vast and complex bureaucracy grew up. It lacked the clarity of the centralized systems of Spain and France; it was rich in complexity and it fathered confusion. Among the boards and officials in England handling colonial affairs and answerable to the king in Council were the lords commissioners for Trade and Plantations, commonly known as the Board of Trade (set up by William III in 1696 and the key body), the secretary of state for the Southern Department, and the Lords of the Admiralty, whose Vice-Admiralty Courts, set up in 1696, were charged to investigate all offenses against the Navigation Acts, and to empower customs officers to seize smuggled goods by the use of general search warrants (writs of assistance); the commissioners of the customs, the surveyor general, the postmaster general, the chief naval officer, the crown lawyers, and the bishop of London. Each was scattered across London, further handicapping contact and decision-making; the Admiralty Board in Whitehall, as it still is, the Navy Office in Seething Lane, the Victualling Office in East Smithfield, the Ordnance at the Tower. In the colonies, busy with details of the same work, were the royal governors and their councils – to whom went royal instructions, which they must obey, and naval officers, customs collectors, admiralty judges, deputy surveyors, deputy postmaster generals, commissaries, et al. Instructions, commissions, reports, the army and navy, the colonial agents, and disallowance and appeal, formed connecting links between these two sets of officials.

Fifthly, there is little validity in the frequently repeated charge that colonial governors were a collection of greedy incompetents, and that America was "the hospital of Great Britain for her decayed courtiers and abandoned worn-out dependents." It was rarely so. In fact, Virginia apart, the salaries paid the mainland governors were lower than those paid the governors of the larger West Indian islands – Jamaica, Barbados, or the Leeward Islands. Of the 321 governors or their deputies appointed by the Crown between 1624 and 1783, one in four was a peer or a peer's son, including two dukes and nine earls, 45 had experience as members of Parliament before their appointments, and 9 of them on their return; 48 were university graduates, more than a score had been admitted to one or other of the Inns of Court, and 15 were Fellows of the Royal Society. They are thus as a group at least not inferior to those of their contemporaries elected to Parliament; and in New England (after the revocation of the Massachusets Charter) almost half of the governors were natives.[19] On the other hand a balance sheet has to recognize that some were singularly tactless (Sloughter, Belcher, Shute, Cranfield, Reynolds) and five were conspicuously greedy (Fletcher, Cornbury, Parke, Cosby, and Crowe). They were, however, outnumbered by the honorable and able men who did their duty in difficult situations, such as Nicholson, Spotswood, and Gooch, Shirley, Pownal, and Bellomont, Eden, Wright, and the Wentworths, Hunter, Tryon, and Moore. They all depended on patrons, whom they knew – and kept in with. They all obeyed the First Commandment of statecraft: Protect Thyself. And here, as everywhere, there was a destiny that shaped their ends: four died before sailing, 13 did not sail; one was drowned in the Thames, one died *en route*, and two committed suicide in office (one of them after three days' experience of New York). There were enough of these for Junius in his *Letters* to thunder: "It was not Virginia that wanted a Governor, but a court favourite that wanted the salary."[20]

The majority of them faced trying tasks, the challenge of persuading reluctant and contentious colonial assemblies to carry out royal instructions. It was a contest of will, and wits. As Jonathan Belcher put it to Sir Peter Warren, his duty was "to steer between Scylla and Charybdis: to please the King's ministers at home, and a touchy people here; to luff for one and bear away from another."

The patronage system had, however, one serious disadvantage, apart from the quality or otherwise of the personnel who benefited. Both in the Old Country and the New, standards of political

---

[19] L. W. Labaree in his *Royal Government in America* (New Haven, Yale University Press, 1930), p. 43, goes further, and says that "the governors appointed by the crown compare not unfavorably in honesty and ability with the men now elected by the people of the several states of the Union."

[20] Junius, *Letters*, ed. J. M. Good (1812), p. 111.

morality and of political competence were low. But, by centering control of patronage in London, the home government's colonial agents were denied the opportunity to build up effective political support in their own bailiwicks, to recruit their own loyalists and to enjoy the prestige that "influence" brought. As it was, maneuver and machination turned always on who pulled the strings, not in Boston or Philadelphia, New York or Williamsburg, but in Whitehall or Westminster.

Sixth, there was another strand, the one whose puppet-masters were American-based: the colonial agents. These were the lobbyists sent to London by the colonial assemblies, the "American interest," comparable to the sugar interest of Barbados and Jamaica, and the East India Company itself. They failed to avert the passing of the Stamp Act in 1765, but they – or their "star" agent, Benjamin Franklin – did secure its repeal in 1766. Their influence declined with the failure to avert its passing, and still more with the creation in 1768 of a distinct American Department of State, with the earl of Hillsborough, an Irish landowner, at its head, and John Pownall as his under-secretary.

The final characteristic was at once complement and contradiction. The colonial legislatures, checked by the royal or proprietary governors, exercised wide jurisdiction over internal affairs. There was slowly being worked out a most significant distribution of powers between the center and the segments of the empire. While England was attempting to exercise more supervision over her empire, the colonial legislatures were winning more power for themselves. They enjoyed the right to initiate legislation, levy taxes and, most important of all, control appropriations – including in some cases those for the governor's own salary. The governor was poorly placed to withstand legislative pressure or to insist upon obedience to royal instructions. So the assemblies steadily gained power at the expense of the governors. Those assemblies voiced local concerns, in local accents. Perhaps, indeed, it was in the increasing vigor of local debate, by men who – unlike those voiceless at home – were property-holders, that one can detect the first step towards a distinct American identity. The executive and legislative branches of the government in the royal and proprietary colonies regularly quarreled: over the governor's salary; control of the Treasurer and Speaker of the House; quit-rents; appropriations for defense; paper money; control of money bills by the Lower House; specific *vs.* blanket appropriation bills; enforcement of English statute and common law; tenure of judges; size and number of electoral districts; frequency of elections; disposal of the Crown or proprietary lands; evasion of the Crown's exercise of disallowance; the fur trade; the Established Church; and the importation of slaves and convicts.

The governor's position was usually a difficult one, and sometimes he had neither ability nor integrity. If he were shrewd, he might gain his ends by playing the merchant class against the landed gentry, or the back country against the tidewater. Due to the distance from his source of authority, the slowness of communication, and the exasperating procrastination of his superiors in London, he often found that his instructions were inapplicable by the time that they reached him. He was very much left on his own.

Even in the corporate colonies, there was not a single democratic government. An office-holding class monopolized the most desirable posts. Political parties of the modern type were unknown, but loosely knit factions battled for the spoils. Moreover, then even more than now, human nature was fallible and corruptible. The chief posts in the colonial customs service came to be sinecures, and the officials sent to America were rarely men of great ability and integrity. Wretchedly ill-paid, those charged with the enforcement of the law found it hard to resist bribes from colonial merchants to connive at smuggling and other infractions. Few scandals disgraced public life, although then, as now, legislation favored the group that was in office. But in almost all the colonies there was a discontented back country. Religious and property qualifications for voting and office-holding were the rule, and many who were eligible to exercise the suffrage neglected to do so.

As early as 1714, English statesmen and colonial leaders were drifting apart in their viewpoint upon many problems of government. There was contrariety of opinion concerning the constitutional framework of the empire, the tenure of judges, the executive veto, the written constitution, the power of Parliament, the separation of powers, the separation of Church and State, the residence qualification for office-holding, nominal and actual representation, land inheritance and tenure, freedom of the press, etc. But if the political bond between the colonies and the mother-country was tenuous, emphasis must equally be given to trade, protection, race, and language, church, fear of the French, education, literature, etc., as empire-saving factors. In Benjamin Franklin's phrase of 1776 – and he called himself, until he was 70, "an Old England man" – the empire was indeed a "fine and noble china vase."

8 COLONIAL POLICY

Although the form of the land grant from the Crown was in each case similar, the circumstances of the various colonies differed. Pennsylvania and Georgia were founded as social experiments, the former tolerant in religion and liberal in politics, the latter as a place of refuge for debtors. In the Carolinas and in Georgia, as later in Nova Scotia, Maine, and Florida, the motives were as much defensive as commercial – or, in the word of a later century, geopolitical. These were buffer colonies against France or Spain. Massachusetts Bay similarly extended its control over settlements in New Hampshire and Maine. The conflict with the Mason and Gorges heirs over this control was ended in 1679, when New Hampshire became a royal province, and in 1691 when Maine was placed under the jurisdiction of Massachusetts. Each of the southern colonies settled after the Restoration was seen as a barrier, until succeeded by the next. Their proprietors saw them as trade outposts, great estates from which they drew rents; few visited them, and if they did, they did not stay long. Maryland, Pennsylvania, and Georgia had religious and philanthropic motivations too, but settlement as such, indeed as almost always, was incidental to trade and to profit. It was not trade that followed the flag, but the flag that followed trade. Indeed, these images are themselves false; for throughout history, trade was usually with your own folk, who flew your own flag anyway – as Phoenicia founded Carthage, and in turn Carthage founded Gadir (Cádiz), Maluca (Malaga), and Carthago Nova, as Crete founded Troy ... (Later, the French economist and reformer Turgot, writing in 1772, said bluntly: "The fruit clings to the tree only until it ripens; in due season, the English colonies in North America will do what Carthage did.")

To this generalization (as valid for medieval Venice, with its own enclaves in the eastern Mediterranean, as for the French, Dutch, and British empires across the seven seas) there was a major exception. The motive for the founding of Plymouth, and then of Massachusetts Bay, was religious; the Puritans went overseas not for trade, not for freedom (since they drove out any who disagreed with them on creed) but to follow their own faith. And in Maryland as in Georgia the freedom to practise Catholicism and philanthropy marched with profit and patriotism in the motivation of the devout Calverts and the ex-Jacobite James Oglethorpe, with a good landlord's concern for his tenants and for the disadvantaged.

However varied the intentions of the founders, their locations or their resources, their situation, their remoteness from home and their

Anglo-Saxon origin gave all the mainland colonies a common political character, although each was entirely independent of the rest. By 1700 it was hard to distinguish, where the form of government was concerned, between one colony and another. Each had a governor, whether he was a royal or a proprietory or a company appointment sometimes he was a deputy or an agent dressed up for the role; each had an assembly, elected by those with some property stake in the colony; and each was developing its own system of local self-government, through parish, vestry or town meetings, or through the justices of the peace and the county courts. The grants to the Calverts and to William Penn, to the Carolina proprietors and New Jersey proprietors, specified that legislation should be with "the consent of the freemen." In only two cases was the self-government provision omitted: in New York, and in Georgia, which was granted to a group of "Trustees." In both cases, however, the colonial demand for legislative representation was so insistent that it had quickly to be conceded.

Moreover, until the Restoration, England – unlike Spain – had not attempted any extensive control of her American colonies. To English governments, colonists were still Englishmen entitled to the same privileges as those enjoyed by Englishmen in England. This attitude on the part of the mother-country greatly fostered the development of self-government in the various colonies. In 1619, the first representative assembly in the colonies was called in Virginia. It became a model for the assemblies formed later in other colonies. Hence, most of the colonial assemblies were composed of a governor and an assembly, with the assembly divided into two houses, the House of Burgesses, made up of members appointed by the governor, and the lower house, the members of which were elected by the settlers themselves. These assemblies sought to become colonial counterparts of the British Parliament. Autonomous government was probably most successfully maintained in Massachusetts during the Restoration, in spite of Charles II's continued attempts to control the colony. When the Crown attempted to replace the elected governor with one appointed by the king, the colonists refused to receive the king's man. When ordered to cease minting their own money, the colonists continued the coinage, dating each coin prior to the ordinance against minting. In order to frustrate an attempt of the British government to permit the right of appeal from Massachusetts courts to courts in England, the Puritans ceased to persecute the Quakers and other groups which might make use of such a right.

Profiting from this experience with Massachusetts and its sister colonies in New England, after the Restoration the British government exercised more care in the wording of charters. Thus, the right of appeal to English courts was incorporated in the charter for Pennsylvania, together with other clauses, such as one permitting Parliament to levy taxes on Pennsylvania and another requiring Pennsylvania to send to England an agent to represent and be responsible for the colony.

The English approach to colonial governmental problems, however, differed radically from that of the settlers themselves. The former was elaborate, and complex, reflecting the attitude of a mature civilization. This was exemplified in the elaborate constitution drawn up for the Carolinas by John Locke at the request of Sir Anthony Ashley Cooper, the proprietor. The colony discarded this complex feudal system and gradually evolved one more suited to the actual situation. In contrast, the Mayflower Compact offers an example of the direct simplicity of the frontier approach; it provided simply that the heads of the Pilgrim families commit themselves to abide by majority rule.

The near-casualness of the drafting of colonial charters, and the inadequacy of contemporary maps, led to overlapping boundaries, as on the Chesapeake. The regular addition to each charter, except Maryland's, of the sea-to-sea clause, giving each colony jurisdiction over land stretching from the Atlantic to the Pacific, would become, after the outbreak of the War of Independence, a source of bitter debate: for four years, from 1777 to 1781, Maryland would not accept the Articles of Confederation until the other republics surrendered their western claims.

In devising a colonial policy, Charles II recognized that the first chartered colonies had been unsuccessful. Virginia had become a royal colony, the first in English history, as early as 1624. Massachusetts had been a constant irritant, and during the Protectorate a supplier of experienced leaders to the Cromwellian cause. The Council of New England had become moribund. The answer seemed to be proprietaries – like the royal grant to the Baltimores (1632) which saw Maryland as a feudal colony, or the grant to his brother James of New Amsterdam. Future settlements would be proprietories, such as that of the Penns, or attempts at consolidation, such as the Dominion of New England.

The Restoration was more, however, than grants of land to zealots and to loyalists – and of the patronage, "perks," and rents that went with them. Behind them was a group of officials preoccupied by expansion abroad and stability at home, most of whom had been there during the Protectorate, and were continuing its policy. Among them were William Blathwayt, secretary to the Committee for Trade and Plantations, and Samuel Pepys, the ablest man on the Naval Board. Both were friends of Sir William Petty (1623–1687), a poor boy educated in Jesuit schools abroad, who became professor of anatomy in Oxford (and of music in London), and then surveyor general and landowner in Ireland. He was a research assistant to Thomas Hobbes, a founder member of the Royal Society, and his *Treatise on Taxes* (1662) and *Political Arithmetic* made him not only England's leading economist but its first to appreciate the value of comparative statistics. He was the Benjamin Franklin of his age, and his great-grandson, the second earl of Shelburne, would become one of Franklin's English friends and would as prime minister put Franklin's Treaty of Peace through Parliament in 1783.

Close to these men were the city merchants, notably Sir Josiah Child, who became the largest shareholder in the East India Company, and came to rule it absolutely as its governor in the 1680s. When he died in 1699, his estate was well over £200,000. His brother-in-law became duke of Chandos, one granddaughter a duchess of Bedford, and a grandson duke of Beaufort. Farsighted and domineering, he once remarked that all trade was "a kind of warfare."

The Restoration was marked also by awareness of the power of France as the largest country in Europe and now united, a major threat to English security in Europe (and of his Catholic Majesty's role as Charles II's benefactor and paymaster); and of the Dutch as commercial rivals on the seas – and as occasional enemy, in 1665 raiding and destroying English shipping in the Medway and in the James River in Virginia; and first surrendering, then regaining, and then losing again to England in Manhattan. The overseas carrying trade and the prosperity of the tiny confederation of seven united but vulnerable provinces were greatly envied, not least its two great monopolistic chartered companies, the East India Company and the West India Company, models for England's Africa Company, Muscovy Company, East India Company and Hudson's Bay Company. Fish and ships seemed more durable bases of economic strength than gold and silver. Thomas Mun, in his *England's Treasure by Foreign Trade*, envied the Dutch "those multitudes of Ships which unto them are as our Ploughs to us, the which except they stir, the people starve ... such a small Countrey, not fully so big as two of our best Shires." The Dutch became the model of the empire of trade, in the recognition that fish from the Banks of Newfoundland required not only ships but the mariners of England, the oak and timber on which a naval empire would rest. And England had in the North Atlantic its own "nursery of seamen." But trade would no longer be controlled by the grant of area monopolies to particular companies (as in the East India and Muscovy Policy, which all would observe). And successful trades-men, often investing in plantations or in land back at home, could become gentlemen – investors-turned-nobility that were uniquely English.

Before 1763 there was no particular magic about the "original" thirteen colonies. As seen from London, they were only part of a British empire in North America that included the West Indian islands and for which a common policy was devised. In the West Indies, Bermuda, settled in 1612, Barbados, settled in 1627, and Jamaica, conquered from Spain in 1655, became, along with Guiana, St Christopher, Antigua, and Providence, the Sugar Islands. They were the wealthiest part of the British empire, and indeed a single French sugar island like Guadeloupe was thought by many at the time of the Treaty of Paris in 1763 to be more valuable than the whole of Canada. Barbados was seen as the jewel in the imperial crown, its trade turnover greater than that of all the mainland colonies put together.

The colonies were established, whether by company or by pro-prietor, as part of a long-term policy of the home government. The policy was not peculiar to England, for Spain, Portugal, Holland, and France also shared the mercantilist belief that a nation's pros-perity could be measured by its accumulation of gold and silver, and its ability to sell abroad more than it bought. The mercantilists believed that national greatness could be achieved only through economic independence and massive protection of home industries. The state, it was held, should regulate all economic activity within its borders, subordinating private profit to public good and aiming particularly at preserving and increasing the nation's gold supply. This could best be done by planting colonies. Those colonies were most valuable which provided both raw materials needed in the mother-country and a market for its finished goods. The aim was a complementary and closed economic system. The colonies were founded for England's profit, not her glory. This view was rein-forced by the injunctions of Richard Hakluyt, the first propagandist of empire, who saw the colonies as outlets for "sturdy beggars" and those who threatened the social fabric.

Although by 1700 the British government disapproved of indis-criminate emigration it remained ready to speed the departure of undesirables. The practice of using the American colonies as a dump-ing ground for convicts had started before the Virginia colony was a decade old, but it was not until the eighteenth century that the traffic reached its height. In 1717 Parliament created the new legal punishment of "transportation" and contractors began to take out regular shipments from the jails. At least 30,000 felons were transported to America in the course of the eighteenth century, most of them to Virginia and Maryland. Some had admittedly been convicted only of minor offences, but many had been guilty of serious crimes.

At the Restoration, therefore, there were many colonies in many diverse locations, subject to foreign threats, and groups of very interested, and very greedy, entrepreneurs. Behind them there were also trade experts, secretaries and back-room boys, some of whom, like William Blathwayt, would now be called permanent secretaries in Whitehall. Behind them were merchant lobby groups, brains trusts equipped with knowledge of commerce and exports. Some of them had worked for Cromwell's secretariat and continued to work for Charles II: imperial policy now transcended differences of regime or of the "connexions" built up by rival politicians. They were the originators of the Navigation Acts of 1651–73, which remained during the succeeding century the basis of the English colonial system. Subsequent changes took the form of additions to the list of enumerated commodities. By 1763 these additions included practically every colonial product except fish and grain. As manufacturing developed in the mother-country and the colonies in the eighteenth century, the same policy held: new legislation was passed to ensure that the colonial economy would complement, rather than compete with, that of Britain. The most obvious example was the Hat Act of 1732, passed in deference to complaints about colonial competition by London feltmakers, which prohibited the export of beaver hats from the colonies. Much the same motives prompted the passage of the Woolens Act of 1699, and the Iron Act of 1750, which forbade the erection in the colonies of new slitting mills and plating forges and prohibited the export of colonial iron outside the empire.

It is clear that this restrictive legislation hindered the growth of colonial manufactures, that colonial products were tied to English demands, and that the cost of freight and of its insurance was high. But there were many advantages to the system. Particular commodities, like tobacco and later rice, enjoyed a monopoly of the British market. Cromwell used troops to try to destroy the home-grown tobacco crop at Winchcombe in Gloucester, and at Cheltenham; it was destroyed in the 1690s by the better quality and lower prices of the virginian product. Bounties were given to help colonial products like indigo and naval stores, and colonial shipping and shipbuilding were fostered. Foreign-built and foreign-owned ships were banned from its ports. By the time of the Revolution, one-third of the British merchant fleet had been built in the colonies. English regiments defended the colonists. The majority of the colonists, who were subsistence farmers, were little affected by "the laws of trade" that were matters of international trade or – later – manufacturing. Specialization in the production and exchange of crops for "finished" goods was wise. Indeed, the "system" was so unsystematic, the restrictions so difficult to enforce along a coastline of indented bays, inlets, shoals, and sandbars, that it could hardly be called coercive – until British regulars were stationed in unruly towns like Boston in 1774. It was not until 1695 that an enduring body at last assumed the prime responsibility for the colonies: the Board of Trade and Plantations. So many agencies were concerned with administering colonial affairs, with no clear lines of demarcation between their responsibilities, that they weakened rather than strengthened England's hold upon the colonies. However, such weakness reflected, as much as anything else, the long period of "salutary neglect" – the unwillingness of the British government to enforce very strenuously the Navigation Acts.

In 1687, when New England was the major part of James II's Dominion of New England, 136 of the 249 vessels that sailed from its ports went to the West Indian islands; in 1688, 129 out of 229: fish and lumber, horses and European goods, were traded illegally for sugar, molasses, and rum, cotton, ginger, and logwood. And the Puritan merchants could sell at lower rates than could the British. They traded too, especially in fish, with a Catholic Europe greedy for it. Indeed, in the late 1600s, of the more than 200 vessels that left Massachusetts ports annually, only 10 went to England.

Yet where the Navigation Acts bred special resentment with New England's mounting illicit trade with the French as well as British West Indies, they were often evaded, and piracy carried prestige rather than social stigma. Indeed, as later with Walpole's Molasses Act of 1733, they were sometimes not even enforced. Britain met difficulties after 1765 because Walpole's policy of wise and salutary neglect was abandoned, because it began to enforce laws through a vigilant customs service to stamp out smuggling, and because it held that the colonists must contribute to their own defense. The Revolution of 1776 was not a revolution against the mercantile system itself, which on the whole brought prosperity to the colonies. It certainly brought prosperity to the home country, by whom and for whom it was designed. And from its benefits all foreigners were excluded: Dutch, French, and Spanish, and also Ireland and Scotland (except when either of the last two were united with England: Glasgow and Leith had intervened in the English trade as interlopers until 1707; thereafter the Clyde, the Forth, and the Solway flourished.)

The ties of mother-country and colonies went far beyond commerce, and the plans for new colonies in the west, to be backed by British and American merchants (with names like Ohio and Vandalia), far beyond a formal constitutional framework: Britain provided much more than Eton or lesser schools, the Inns of Court and the Edinburgh Medical School. Samuel Mather, "Creasy's" son, accompanied his father on his diplomatic mission in 1688, returned to England a few years later, and, after an inheritance and a "good" marriage, became the first Congregational minister in Witney. Rowland Cotton, without completing his Harvard course, served both as pastor and as doctor to the dissenting flock at Warminster. Benjamin Colman, John Barnard, and Thomas Prince identified in the end with America, but preached in England at Cambridge, Ipswich and Bath. Alongside these were merchants who returned to Cromwellian England in its trials, and whose Puritanism proved prosperous in civil war in London – Richard Hutchinson, Christopher Kilby, and Nathaniel Whitfield.

Colonial agents were more than politicians; they were solicitors for a legion of causes charitable and educational. Within a decade of their foundation, Harvard and Yale had emissaries raising funds in England, notably John Knowles in Twickenham. According to Henry Newman of the Harvard class of 1687, and its librarian, Harvard owed 95 percent of her books to the liberalism of Englishmen. Long before William and Mary College was founded in 1693, James I commanded that four collections be made throughout English parishes to finance the establishment of a college in Virginia. Similarly with the Quakers, the Society for the Propagation of the Gospel (SPG), the Society for the Propagation of the Christian Knowledge (SPCK), and the Associates of Dr Bray (who were concerned with the education of slaves), and with the early days of King's College (Columbia), the College of New Jersey (Princeton), and Rhode Island College; and with William Smith's journeys to Britain in the 1760s to solicit for the University of Pennsylvania (probably the best "beggar" of them all).

By the mid-eighteenth century, the Lees of Virginia were as prominent in the City of London as in the Tidewater. Many New York merchants became, in essence, Londoners: Dirck van der Heyden, the Franks brothers (with Moses and Naphtali in London and David in Philadelphia); and Stephen Sayre, described as the handsomest man in England, who married an heiress, (and on her death in 1789, another), became a member of the firm of Dennis De Berdt, the colonial agent, and became the first American to be elected sheriff of London. He was promptly supported as co-sheriff by the election of William Lee. On the eve of the Revolution, both of London's sheriffs were not only Americans but "known and approved friends of liberty." In fact, they owed their election to the friendship of John Wilkes, for whom the London mobs swarmed the streets shouting "Wilkes and Liberty;" in Virginia another Lee – Richard Henry – was dressing his slaves in "Jack Wilkes" costumes, consisting of high boots, cocked hats, and scarlet coats. In October 1775, however, Sayre spent five days as a prisoner in the Tower; and his banking enterprises, like his later European missions, failed.

Fleet Street and the coffee-house world, as well as Whitehall and Westminster, were noticeable in these same years for their Americans, not least Benjamin Franklin active in the press (133 pieces of his journalism appeared in the London press in his 17 years as agent) and as a scientist of standing in the Royal Society, in devising lightning rods to protect St Bride's and St Paul's, and in persuading the House in 1766 to repeal the Stamp Act. He was abetted in London in the years between 1763 and his departure in 1775 by the presence as MPs of four who were native North Americans: John Huske of Portsmouth, New Hampshire, the Boston merchant elected MP for Malden in 1763 ("a wild absurd man," said Horace Walpole); the New Yorkers Henry Cruger (Burke's colleague as MP for Bristol in 1774) and Staats Long Morris (for the Elgin Burghs in 1774), and former lord mayor Barlow Trecothick, who did most to organize the repeal of the Stamp Act, but was ailing after 1770 and died before Franklin reached Philadelphia. Of these Cruger alone was pro-American, though not consistently so; and he would in 1792 become a member of the New York State Senate – the only American to sit both in the British and one of the American elected assemblies. In the years just before the War of Independence began, there were more Americans in the House of Commons than ever before, though they were but a few. There were not enough of them, however, and in themselves they were divided in allegiance; and they were never strong enough to offset Jamaica or the "nabobs" of India House, or the military and landed blocs of MPs.

The names indicate the range, and the involvement, of family ties. They testify to American fascination with British culture, as witness Franklin's effusive letter to his landlady's daughter, Polly Stevenson, after his first return to Philadelphia (March 25, 1763):

Of all the enviable things England has, I envy it most its people. Why should that petty island, which compar'd to America is but like a stepping-stone in a brook, scarce enough of it above water to keep one's shoes dry; why I say, should that little island enjoy in almost every neighborhood, more sensible virtuous and elegant minds than we can collect in ranging 100 leagues of our vast forests?

Commission-merchant and sheriff William Lee, who like his colleague Stephen Sayre lived by selling his own reputation, put it another way: "It seems to me that because I am a Virginian they have the same expectations from me that the Jews had from a Messiah – that is, I am to make them all rich and Princes over the Earth." [21]

[21] William Lee to Richard Henry Lee, October 4, 1771: Lee–Ludwell *Papers* (Virginia Historical Society); *Franklin Papers* (Yale ed. 1966), vol. X, pp. 232–3; William Sachse, *The Colonial American in Britain* (Madison, University of Wisconsin Press, 1956); Michael Kammen, *A Rope of Sand* (Ithaca, NY, Cornell University Press, 1968); Whitfield Bell, "Philadelphia medical student in Europe," *Pennsylvania Magazine of History and Biography*, 67 (1943), pp. 1–29.

6

The Eighteenth Century:
From the St Lawrence to Savannah

1 A MIDDLING AND A BRITISH PEOPLE

In 1713 some 357,000 colonists were living along the North American littoral, from the St Lawrence to the Carolinas. The mass of the colonists were far from being aristocratic; there was considerable social mobility, and the widespread ownership of property weakened the sense of class division. Yet the social structure was almost as aristocratic as that in contemporary Britain, which it reflected. Few talked about democracy, at least not with approval. Power was usually centered in the governor's council of about a dozen men. Except in Massachusetts, Connecticut, and Rhode Island, councillors were appointed by royal or proprietary authority, and even in New England the general rule applied that the wealthier families were always represented. The governor had to struggle against local men with a good conceit of themselves, and with useful connections in London, while colonists themselves accepted the idea that prevailed in all European societies that, as John Winthrop put it on the *Arbella* and as the Virginian House of Burgesses put it in 1706, some must be 'highe and eminent in power and dignitie; others meane and in subieccion.'

By the mid-eighteenth century there was a distinct upper class, composed of the large landowners, the wealthy merchants and lawyers, the governors and lieutenant-governors, the revenue officers, and "the friends of government." The basis of their prestige was land and, to a lesser but increasing degree, trade. The Granville tract in North Carolina covered one-third of the colony; the Fairfax grant in Virginia ran from the Tidewater to the headwaters of the Potomac, wherever they might be; Maine was almost a private holding of Sir William Pepperell, the conqueror of Louisburg; much of Georgia was owned by Sir James Wright.

If New England was by contrast an area of small, self-sufficient farms and compact settlements, due to the system of townships, and if the Massachusetts 1691 charter gave it the forty-shilling freehold franchise and thus all but universal male suffrage, there were, in the traditions of the Bible Commonwealth and of Yankee thrift, forces making for similar social distinctions. They were seen in the seating of church members by "property, virtue and intelligence," from the brave coat lace-embroidered to the gray coat shading down, and in the listing of Harvard and Yale students by a "class" that sought to reflect social rank rather than merit. Virginia's merchant-planter pioneers of the seventeenth century – the Byrds, Carters, Harrisons, Randolphs, and Lees – were now the colony's upper class. These men of property were "gentlemen" and "esquires," their property sometimes buttressed by laws of primogeniture and entail. They were matched by the merchant-traders of New England – the Browns of Providence, the Cabots and Hancocks, Faneuils and Amorys of Boston, Sir William Pepperell and Sir William Phips of Maine; and by the merchant-financiers and fur traders of New York – the Phillipses and De Pyesters, Morrises and Franks. Newport was ruled by "twenty genteel families," not a few of whom prospered from the rum and slave trades, and by trading regularly with the French West Indies, both in peace and war.

Of all the ports, Boston was the most active in shipbuilding and trading. It prospered not only from smuggling but from the constancy of war. Between 1674 and 1714 New England, mainly Boston, built 2,300 ocean-going vessels, and sold 240 of them abroad. In an age when sea charts were crudely drawn, and lighthouses all but non-existent along the Atlantic coast, losses of ships were high, and the demand for replacements constant. The demand for sloops to fish the Banks, and for whalers for Nantucket, brought steady orders and steady profit. In 1750, 400 vessels were employed fishing the Banks, and 200 inshore. Whaling was beginning to count at Gloucester and Marblehead too: New Englanders traded with the French in Acadia, and with all the West Indies. But for the future it was in a uniquely disadvantageous position, as agricultural productivity steadily declined, making it more and more difficult for the Bay colony merchants to make returns to Britain sufficient to maintain a favorable balance of payments.[1] The hard-scrabble, stony

---

[1] Gary B. Nash, *The Urban Crucible* (Cambridge, MA, Harvard University Press, 1979), p. 128.

soil needed toil and skill; the farms were small, and family-worked; the winters were cold and long. There was no single staple like tobacco. The export trade was varied: wheat, corn, peas, pork, beef – dried, cured, or pickled – ship stores, timber and pine, staves and hoops for barrels for the sugar and molasses of the West Indies, horses and furs, and always fish, salted and dried or fresh or rancid. By the eighteenth century the most prominent imports were slaves.

In 1680 Rhode Island reported to the Board of Trade that there was not a single merchant in the colony, and that their settlers were busy "improving the wilderness." In 1708 its citizens owned 29 vessels; by 1739, the number had reached 100; and by the middle of the century the number of vessels of over 60 tons had grown to 300.

Even Quaker Pennsylvania was dominated till 1756 by an oligarchy of wealthy Quakers, of whom Penn himself, an authentic English gentleman, wrote sarcastically;

There is an excess of vanity that is apt to creep in upon the people in power in America, who, having got out of the crowd in which they were lost here, upon every little eminency there, think nothing taller than themselves but the trees, and as if there were no after superior judgment to which they should be accountable; so that I have sometimes thought that if there was a law to oblige the people in power, in their respective colonies, to take turns in coming over for England, that they might lose themselves again amongst the crowds of so much more considerable people at the custom-house, exchange, and Westminster Hall, they would exceedingly amend in their conduct at their return, and be much more discreet and tractable, and fit for government.[2]

In some colonies these family groups were seeking to be exclusive, but they never were completely so. They could include an enterprising planter like George Washington, himself largely a self-made man and a protégé of the 6th Lord Fairfax; an enterprising privateer like John MacPherson of Philadelphia; a merchant-smuggler like John Hancock; a theater owner like David Douglass; or an enterprising painter like J. S. Copley, who owed his status as much to his choice of a wife as to his skill as artist.

Below the gentry was a large and fluid middle class, embracing clergymen, teachers, lesser merchants and lawyers, yeomen farmers, town craftsmen and shopkeepers, minor officials in government,

---

[2] William W. Comfort, *William Penn 1644–1718* (Philadelphia, University of Pennsylvania, 1944).

plantation overseers, and skilled artisans, "the middling sort." This was a working middle class far more than a professional one, particularly strong in New England. Many a "goodman" and his "goodwife" claimed inclusion in it.

Below them in turn was a laboring force of mainly propertyless and therefore voteless workers, unskilled laborers, journeymen, or poor frontiersmen, many of them German or Scots-Irish. Originally many of these, like many above them in the social scale, had been indentured servants working under a labor contract for a term of years, or convicts. Maryland alone received more than 9,000 convict servants between 1748 and 1775. The expression "convict," of course, covered a multitude of sins, and some virtues: rogues, cut-throats and whores, Covenanters, Jacobites, and Quakers.

In the eighteenth century a new type of indentured servant appeared: the redemptioner. In the South, artisans and craftsmen were hard to discover. By 1763 the Negro slave had almost entirely replaced the indentured servant as the South's labor force, although elsewhere white workers under contract continued to arrive. George Washington's first schoolmaster came under this system; one of the most interesting diaries of the Revolutionary period was that kept by an indentured servant, John Harrower; and one of the most fascinating studies of early Maryland was a "dish of discourse" by an indentured servant, George Alsop. According to tradition, at least one signer of the Declaration of Independence, Matthew Thornton of New Hampshire, had been an indentured servant; so were William Buckland, who built Gunston Hall, and Charles Thomson, secretary of the Continental Congress.

Indentured servants served for limited periods of time. They owed absolute obedience to their owners during their term of service, but indenture also guaranteed them certain rights. Thirteen-year-old Catherine Potts was to get her keep for the term of five years and also to be taught the "art and mystery of Housewifery," and to have 20 dollars in cash as well as two sets of clothing when her time was up. A servant could sue in court to enforce these rights, as well as to protest at cruelty by the master.

Recent research has been more concerned with the poor and disadvantaged than with colonial elites. It is now clear that more than 20,000 immigrants crossed the Atlantic and began a new life between 1607 and 1776 by selling their labor for a period of years. These formed between 5 and 7 percent of the total servant population, which in turn formed at least one-half (perhaps as many as three-quarters) of all white immigrants to North America in the colonial period. It was by the device of indenture that the bulk of the labor force was supplied for the West Indian plantations and for the southern mainland colonies before they turned to black slavery.

By the late seventeenth century came the steady shift to black slaves, and the proportion of white indentured servants to the steadily growing total population began to decline. Slaves were, bluntly, cheaper: in the 1690s the price of a permanent slave with a low yearly upkeep was only two or three times higher than the cost of one who served for only a few years. But the size of the black labor force produced a stronger sense of solidarity among all whites, and color could give solace and even a sense of superiority to the lowest class of white workers. Indentured servants were, of course, predominantly male, and heavily concentrated in the age group from 15 to 25. Very few were in any sense "gentlemen." A large number were farmers, both yeomen and husbandmen; many were skilled, however, notably in building or in textile crafts, and there were not just those whom William Bullock in 1694 called the mother-country's "idle, lazie, simple people." This skilled element increased strikingly among the London indentured servants who emigrated in the eighteenth century. By that time, too, almost all were going to the American mainland, and not to the West Indies. By the 1770s, 79 percent of immigrants, both male and female, were going to Chesapeake Bay. By the time of the Revolution, indentured servitude had almost completely disappeared from the British West Indies: of 3,359 indentured servants registered on leaving England during 1773–5, only 12 were bound for the West Indies. By contrast, in 1770, blacks made up 84 percent of the population of Barbados.

The less literate classes clearly left less evidence, and few reached public office. But other than the indentured – from whom after a term of years came steady supplies of now free men – and other than slaves, town records reveal a considerable wage-earning class, white, free, and poor. Not all acquired land. The headright system of 50 acres for every servant brought in, inhered in the person who imported the servant and not in the servant himself. All he could rely on was a supply of clothes, ready money, and an axe. Thus in Newbury, Massachusetts, of 269 heads of families, 27 had no land, and of these 24 had no property of any kind. While all contemporary observers agree that, in comparison with Europe, there was little desperate poverty, the occasional laws for the relief of debtors, the frequent legislation on poor relief, and the fear lest the poor become a permanent charge on urban communities, all point to misery in the midst of optimism, and to the conclusion that the New World was no place for the weak, the sick, the improvident, the idle – or the unlucky.

It is too easy to lyricize over the rise of the convict or the indentured servant to his own freedom, once he reached American shores. A convict served for a set term of years, usually 7 or 14. For the indentured, conditions varied greatly. By the end of the seventeenth century, a 5-year term for indentured servants over a certain age was laid down by law in Virginia and Maryland and a similar law was made in South Carolina by 1717. Maryland ceased to offer free land at the end of indentures from 1683; New York never promised any; the Carolinas continued to give it until well into the eighteenth century. But since wages were so high, a freed servant might soon be able to buy land – if, that is, he had survived physically. Clearing virgin forests under duress was punishing. Runaways in Virginia had to serve double or more the time of their absence; Maryland exacted ten days for one, Pennsylvania five, and South Carolina seven for one day, a year for a week. Some servants in fact did well. Up to 1666, a third or more of landholders in Virginia had come in under indentures. In Maryland only 1 servant in 25 emerged as a landowner. A. E. Smith has calculated that over the whole colonial period in North America, out of 10 servants, 8 either died during their time, returned to England afterwards, or became "poor-whites."[3] A tiny minority of indentured servants became important men or founded famous families. For most, however, America was a land of toil as much as a land of opportunity.

The massive European immigration altered Nature itself. Forests were valuable and carefully preserved and tended. But the centuries from first contact between Indians and Europeans to the cotton boom after 1793 dramatically increased the amounts of cleared land and the numbers of human residents in the South. Nature acquired a change of face, and was tamed and commercialized: wild animals and trees were replaced by domesticated animals, fences, and farms; Indians died in alarming numbers, more from disease than conflict; whites grew in equally alarming number, thanks mainly to pork and ham, corn and yams. And fire, not always of human instigation, was ally as well as enemy, destroying game and timber. But this process did not begin with the coming of the Europeans; the Indians might appreciate and feel in tune with his habitat; but he too had been a ruthless destroyer.[4]

---

[3] Abbot Emerson Smith, *Colonists in Bondage: White servitude and convict labor in colonial America: an economic analysis* (Chapel Hill, NC, IEAHC, 1947; repr. Cambridge University Press, Cambridge, 1981).
[4] Timothy Silver, *A New Face in the Countryside: Indians, colonists and slaves in South Carolina forests 1500–1800* (Cambridge, Cambridge University Press, 1990).

Despite David Hackett Fischer's arguments that Albion's blood was dominant,[5] English institutions and cultural patterns, and London fashions, were modified in the colonies by new factors. What was English in 1607 and 1620, 1660 and 1688, became distinctive and "American" as new generations came. The Old World family rigidity and the father's standing was softened by New World economic conditions. America offered cheap land and many new occupations to lure children away from their parents' roofs. Status, like parental domination, became less binding. An indentured servant might become a landlord. The son of a blacksmith might become an iron-master. A penniless Franklin might become a man of means. A backcountry farmer's boy like Thomas Jefferson might marry a wealthy man's daughter, who was also a wealthy widow.

This colonial society was increasing its numbers by its own fertility as well as by immigration: high birth rates and large families were the rule – the average number of children per colonial family was 7.5, and wives were exhausted by the constant childbearing. The Puritan code was strict. That aspect of it most scrupulously honored was the adage: increase and multiply. Children were seen as an economic asset as workers, and a form of insurance in old age. Population was in fact doubling every generation, although more slowly in New England than elsewhere. Of the 246 men who were graduated from Harvard College in the classes of 1659 through 1699, 15 among them had a total of 123 children, the most prolific being the Franklins' pastor, Dr Willard, who had 20 children by two wives – a record approached, but not equalled by, Adam Winthrop, with 18; all of them, however, by one wife. Increase Mather had 10 children, and Cotton, his son, had 15. The Rev. John Sherman, a product of Emanuel College, Cambridge, who came to Boston in 1634 and became a fellow of Harvard College, had 26 children. The Puritans were a hardy breed, robust in their eating, vigorous in their drinking, and lusty in their sexual activity. New England was healthier than the Chesapeake, people lived longer and family life was more stable; their contemporaries in Old England married later, and those in the Chesapeake had higher, especially male, mortality. But the reasons for large families were largely economic and actuarial. Children were an economic necessity to the artisan or tradesman; and a succession of sons was sought to provide a renewable source of labor over a whole span of years. Moreover, New England had

[5] *Albion's Seed: Four British folkways in America* (New York, Oxford University Press, 1989).

no headright system, farms were fewer than in the South, the soil rocky. They needed servants less, and slaves hardly at all, so they could make a virtue of necessity.

With the high rate of birth came also high mortality among families. Many women died at a tragically young age, the victims of frequent childbearing, and infant mortality may have averaged as high as 40 percent. Infant mortality and the high death rate among adults in America, as in Europe, were largely due to existing superstition and to ignorance of hygiene and proper medical care. Notable amid this medical ignorance was a campaign for smallpox inoculation in Massachusetts under the leadership of Cotton Mather (d.1728), who had read about the use of this process among the Turks. In 1721–2, Dr Zabdiel Boylston introduced this innovation, and it was gradually adopted despite strong opposition, much of it led by the Franklin brothers' waspish press. Boylston's contribution saved many lives, for smallpox had previously taken a savage toll in New England.

As the human populations of three continents mingled, diseases endemic to Europe, Africa, and America spread, and entirely new diseases developed. Yellow fever and pernicious malaria, for instance, were new to the European colonists, and they had no immunity. Both scarlet fever and diphtheria were in a process of evolution in the eighteenth century; diphtheria had been a mild disease before 1735, when it suddenly assumed a fatal form in an outbreak in Kingston, New Hampshire. Not a single one of the first 40 victims recovered. Measles, whooping cough, and dysentery attacked the white, black, and red populations alike, while the blacks seemed particularly susceptible to pulmonary diseases – influenza, tuberculosis, and pleurisy – and the Indians were defenseless against smallpox.

Smallpox was the most dreaded disease of the eighteenth century. One of the most highly contagious of all diseases, it spread alarmingly wherever there were large numbers of unvaccinated people. Once it appeared, nearly every exposed person who had not been vaccinated or had not had the disease before was virtually certain to contract it. The mortality rate varied, but in the white population of colonial America 1 victim in every 7 or 8 died. Among the blacks, the proportion was slightly lower, since the disease had been endemic in Africa even longer than in Europe, but among the Indians it was much higher. The death rate in eastern tribes was rarely as low as 50 percent, and some groups were entirely destroyed by the disease. In both England and America surgeons were considered craftsmen, not professionals. The men and women who practiced as barbers worked as surgeons as well – setting bones, performing amputations, cutting ulcers and boils, and treating wounds with neither anesthetics nor any interest in cleanliness. It has been estimated that of approximately 3,500 men who practiced medicine in America at the time of the Revolution, only 400 had an MD degree. Patients often died of the cure rather than the disease – especially of bleeding, since it was common to take 40 ounces of blood or even more.

2 AND A RESTLESS PEOPLE

After the Peace of Utrecht, which in 1713 marked the end of the War of the Spanish Succession and France's defeat in Europe and *d'outre mer*, British territory on the North American continent reached from Hudson's Bay to Savannah. From a coastline roughly 1,000 miles long, it extended 100 miles inland – though many colonial charters spoke of their limits as being "from sea to sea," and they had claims to an indefinite frontier inland. The accession of George I was welcomed in the Plantations as a guarantee of the continuance of their political and religious liberties. The Jacobite minorities, whether in Barbados or New York, could not challenge the *fait accompli*, and the colonies settled down to enjoy an era of comparative political calm and rapid economic development.

The common thread of colonial policy for the next 50 years was *quieta non movere* – "let sleeping dogs lie." Peace at home and in Europe, and rising opulence, were the targets, and to attain them required capable ministries, despite the disintegration of parties. The mercantile system begun in the wars against the Dutch in 1651 and 1660, and re-enacted in the Navigation Act of 1696, remained, of course, in operation; indeed, the Committee on Trade and Plantations aimed at stricter control over the trade and development of the colonies, authorized customs officers to search for and to seize smuggled goods, set up ten Vice-Admiralty Courts, serving without juries, and sought to establish a homogeneous system of administration by converting all proprietary and chartered governments into royal provinces, governed directly by the Crown. Between 1700 and 1720 seven bills for the resumption of the charters were introduced into the House of Commons. They were rejected. The charters of Carolina and New Jersey were subsequently resumed, but those of Connecticut and Rhode Island (each of which chose its own governor), of Massachusetts Bay, Pennsylvania, and Maryland were allowed to stand. Maryland provided an early instance of the new policy: there, the new Lord Baltimore was allowed to resume proprietary government, from which, as a Catholic, his grandfather had been suspended. William Penn died without signing the surrender of his proprietorship of Pennsylvania (1718); his successors passed into the position of absentee landlords without his prestige, and of governors acting through deputy-governors. The South Carolina charter was resumed after the failure of the proprietors to defend the settlers in the Yamassee War of 1715, and the threat of a Spanish invasion in 1719.

Along the Atlantic shore from Maine to Cape Fear the constitutional pattern was clear. Each colony had a governor, whether a royal or a company appointment, each an appointed council usually of the wealthiest citizens, each an assembly, elected by those with some property stake in the colony, and claiming a right to initiate legislation and levy taxes; and each was developing its own system of local self-government through parish vestry or town meetings, or through the justices of the peace and the county courts.

A noble prospect greeted the visitor as his ship reached the shoreline: "The air at 12 leagues' distance smelt as sweet as a new-blown garden." "The air is sweet and clear," wrote William Penn, "the heavens serene." As inviting as the climate were the native foods. The sea abounded in oysters and crabs, cod and lobster; and in the woods, there were turkeys "fat and incredible of weight," and quail, squirrels, pheasants, elk, geese, and so many deer that in places "venison is accounted a tiresome meat." Fruits, nuts, and berries grew wild everywhere, and it was soon discovered that more substantial fare like peas and beans and corn and pumpkins could be easily cultivated. Soon the newcomers found that grain would grow and that transplanted fruit trees flourished. And sheep, goats, swine, and cows bred as readily as humans. This was a richly forested land; as travellers constantly noted, the whole country seemed one vast wood. It meant abundant fuel and lumber, the raw material for houses and ships, for dyes, potash, and naval stores, ending the home country's reliance on Baltic timber. Nature was exotic, rich and tempting in its abundance, but also an enemy. The beaver were steadily massacred. In the north, the great fur-trading center was Albany, on the Hudson, with lodges outside its gates for Indians bringing in furs, where town officials jealously strove to guard a monopoly of commerce with the Iroquois. In the south, the lead in the trade in furs and skins was passing from Virginia to Charles Town, Carolina, which was nearer to the hunting grounds of the Catawba and the Cherokee. As the valuable beasts were wiped out, so Indians would become redundant and their lands would attract planters and farmers who had worn out their old holdings by their own greed. Where land had been cleared by Indians there was relatively little underbrush, since the Indians burnt over large areas to make hunting easier. And since the supply of virgin land seemed inexhaustible, it was recklessly exploited.[6]

The shoreline was marked by indented coastal plains – at Massachusetts Bay and Narragansett Bay, around the approaches to the Hudson, and around Chesapeake Bay – and by many broad-sweeping and tidal rivers, reaching far inland, their English names registering the extent of the paleface probing: in Virginia, the James and the York; in South Carolina the Charles, the Ashley, and the Cooper. Their tributaries, and a few others beyond them, bore Indian names; in Virginia the Chickahominy, Rappahannock, the Pamunkey, the Potomac, the Manassas, the Appomattox, and the Shenandoah; in Pennsylvania, the Susquehanna and the Delaware; or in the north, the Mohawk, the Connecticut, and the Kennebec in Maine. None penetrated as far inland as the St Lawrence, but they nevertheless allowed easy access to the interior, as far as the fall line of the rivers, the first frontier.

But any similarities among the colonies were misleading. The several colonies were independent communities, with their own outlets to the sea. Their separateness, together with the distances between the settlements, prevented development of a centralized and unified government. Each colony instead became a separate entity, marked by a strong individuality, which in the later history of the United States became the basis of the concept of "states rights." Each was "run," if not always "governed", by a coterie of oligarchs, largely self-selected, the "big men" locally. But despite this trend to individualism, even from the earliest days the problems of commerce, navigation, manufacturing, and currency cut across colonial boundaries and necessitated common regulations. There were still large gaps in effective settlement, notably the several hundred miles between the North Carolina and Charles Town colonies; and two areas lacked harbors for ocean-going ships: North Carolina and southern New Jersey. Most people still clung to the shorelines and navigable rivers which gave a direct link with Europe. Virginia and Maryland had perhaps 90,000 colonists, New England about the same number, the "middle colonies" something above 50,000, and the Carolinas perhaps 16,000; altogether, about a quarter of a million – far fewer

[6] Despite epidemics, the survival of the Catawba nation is vividly described in James H. Merrell, *The Indians' New World: Catawbas and their neighbors, from European contact through the era of removal* (Chapel Hill, NC, IEAHC, 1989).

than the population of London. However, numbers – as in New France – had doubled, perhaps trebled, since 1660. In temperate regions the New World was healthier and more evenly prosperous than the old. There were no ill years for food. The abundance of land and the lack of economic constraints meant that colonists married younger than people in England. Families on average were twice as large, and more children survived infancy. At the beginning of the eighteenth century, the 12 original states (Georgia's charter was not granted until 1732) fell naturally into four regions, each of which was dominated by a city: Boston, New York, Philadelphia, and a just-emerging Charles Town. And each region had its own character.

A fresh and vivid view of the diversity of the British empire at mid-eighteenth century is provided by the contributors to Bernard Bailyn and Philip D. Morgan's *Strangers within the Realm*, originally assembled at a conference in Williamsburg in 1985.[7] They see the empire less as a London-centered but liberal regime than as a congeries of distinct ethnic groups of ordinary folk as well as elites – Native Americans and Afro-Americans, but also peoples from "marginal kingdoms", Scots-Irish, Dutch, and Germans, and the "Reluctant Creoles" of the West Indies. By the use of a vast archive, a register of emigrants compiled by British officials for the years 1773–6, Bailyn elsewhere traces the movement of peoples not only from the UK, but also from Europe, across a vast terrain. The settlement of North America he sees as only "the ragged outer margin of a central world,"[8] the legacy of a vast surge of movement inside Europe and Britain – from the Shetlands and the Hebrides to London, and via London to Ulster, New York, and the pine-barrens of the Carolinas; from Prussia south to the Danube and west to the Rhineland, and then to the banks of the Hudson and the Delaware Rivers; from the Elbe to the Mississippi.

Impressive as was the Puritan migration to New England, Scotland itself sent almost half the same number to Ulster in two short years in the 1630s. The whole Atlantic world was in restless motion. Bailyn notes that in the 15 years before the outbreak of what he calls the American Revolution (by which, presumably, he means the War for American Independence), there moved to the mainland colonies no less than 55,000 Protestant Irish, 40,000 Scots, 30,000

---

[7] Bernard Bailyn and Philip D. Morgan (eds), *Strangers within the Realm* (Williamsburg, Institute of Early American History and Culture, 1991).
[8] Bernard Bailyn, *The Peopling of British North America* (New York, Knopf, 1986), p. 113.

Englishmen, at least 12,000 Germans (mainly to Pennsylvania), and some 84,000 Africans as slaves. In the eighteenth century the courts sent an estimated 50,000 convicted felons, mainly to Maryland and Virginia – almost one quarter of all British emigrants to North America in that century. The Transportation Act of 1718 decreed that banishment was to be for seven years to life. It was designed not for dangerous criminals, who were hanged, nor for petty thieves, beggars, or prostitutes, but for the virile, however wicked. For those who acquired them, the felons were cheaper than slaves or indentured servants. Unsurprisingly, most of them were young males in their early twenties. Unsurprisingly again, most of them were from the lowest in society. But not all; in 1736 a barrister of the Middle Temple was sentenced for transportation for stealing rare books from the library of Trinity College, Cambridge, and from the main University library.[9]

All of this swirl of peoples was but a spillover of the surging domestic mobility in the countries of origin, across the Atlantic as in America itself. Bailyn calls it "multitudinous and complex ... mysterious and chaotic" – but it is surely not in itself unusual? Witness the invasion of Goths and Vandals into Europe 12 centuries earlier, of Islam into the Mediterranean world in the seventh and eighth centuries, even of the Great Trek in South Africa in the early nineteenth century. In the seventeenth century, this folk-wandering was clearly product of widespread servitude, of extended kin networks and of the perennial pulling power of the big city, whether near or far, whether Norwich or London, New York or Philadelphia. "London devoured people. Disease devastated the slums," but as people died (and in Virginia they would "die like flies") so were they replaced. The Atlantic, in all its hazards, was just another highway – and one without the 40 toll barriers that the traveler met on the Rhine. Nor did it stop at the Atlantic shore. On arrival, Philadelphia became entrepôt for the valley of Virginia and the Carolinas, New York but a staging post for the Mohawk and the northern frontiers.

And those who traveled? Overwhelmingly, the mass of whites were workers escaping one or other form of servitude. They often went under indenture, many of them to be for four years or more still in practice slaves, as were of course all Africans. Overwhelmingly too they were dissidents and Quakers, not just Puritans but

---

[9] A. Roger Ekirch, *Bound for America: The transportation of British convicts to the colonies 1718–75* (Oxford, Clarendon Press, 1987).

Anabaptists – and millenarians, socinians and seekers with all (or no) creeds. America was clearly, in William Allen of Philadelphia's words, "the best poor man's country in the world." It would be so for two centuries. It still is. In 1750 in Pennsylvania there were 48 Amish and Mennonite settlements, 10 Dunkard and the beginnings of several Schwenkfelder, as Ephrata and Lancaster County still remind us.[10]

The majority of English emigrants were indentured servants. On the indentured laborer there is a considerable literature; David W. Galenson's[11] *White servitude in Colonial America* is the first thorough analysis of this important and intriguing phenomenon since Abbot Emerson Smith's pioneering *Colonists in Bondage* appeared in 1947,[11] and if it does not in any major way alter Smith's findings, it brings a formidable quantity of research and statistical evidence to bear on a subject which, compared to slavery, has received little attention. These formed between 5 and 7 percent of the total servant population, which in turn formed at least one-half (perhaps as much as three-quarters) of all white immigrants to North America in the colonial period. It was by the device of indenture that the bulk of the labor force was supplied for the West Indian plantations and for the southern mainland colonies before they turned to black slavery. Galenson argues that the system of indenture was an adaptation to American and West Indian conditions of an institution basic to the English agricultural economy. "Almost all of them," Bailyn concluded of the immigrants whom he studied, "came from southern England".[12] To this view a substantial qualification has been added by David Hackett Fischer, in his *Albion's Seed: Four British folkways in America*.[13]

Fischer's volume, the first in a cultural history, argues that from 1629 to 1775 North America was settled in four great waves of English-speaking immigrants: first, the Puritans coming from eastern England to Massachusetts (1629–40); second, the Royalists and their servants from the south of England to Virginia (1640–75); third, the Quakers from the North Midlands and Wales to the

[10] Bailyn, *The Peopling of British North America*; idem, *Voyagers to the West: A passage in the peopling of America on the eve of the Revolution* (New York, Knopf, 1986).

[11] David W. Galenson, *White servitude in Colonial America, an Economic History* (Cambridge, Cambridge University Press, 1981); idem, *Traders, Planters and Slaves: Market behavior in early English America* (Cambridge, Cambridge University Press, 1986).

[12] Bailyn, *British North America*, p. 61.

[13] see n.5 above.

Delaware valley (1675–1725); and fourth, the Northcountrymen, Scots and Scots-Irish, to the American back country (1717–75). These groups differed not only in religion and place of origin, but in traditions and family habits, in food customs and dialects, in architecture and modes of settlement, in attitudes to childhood, old age, and death. What at first seems a conventional view is revived, but with a difference: a vast supportive bibliography, including research in speech and dress patterns, takes the thesis beyond convention. American history, in this telling and thus far, is a history not only of cultural transmission, but of the interaction of these four distinctive British subcultures. Fischer's portrayal of a regional identity that smoothly crossed the sea is, however, over-tidy. The East Anglian character of New England is familiar, but is already being challenged.[14] David Cressy covers well-trodden ground and confines himself to the Bay Colony, but at least he sees the so-called Puritan migration as multifaceted. If there were over 20,000 migrants, no one motive explains them. "The eloquent, insistent and self-serving assertions of American Puritan authors," writing after the events, overstressed the religious interpretation. Men's own accounts of their actions often carry their own gloss, even when they tell it to themselves at the time. And, Cressy stresses, the migration was a transatlantic phenomenon; to contemporaries, New England was a detached English province rather than the seed-bed of a new nation.

The social characteristics of eighteenth-century North America were less cultural divergence, says Jack Greene, but rather *creolization* – adaptation to local conditions – and metropolitanization – successful cultivation of the principal values and forms of the parent culture. Only if there had been a considerable convergence could the loose political confederation of 1775 have come into being.[15]

[14] By David Cressy in *Coming Over: Migration and communication between England and New England in the seventeenth century* (Cambridge, Cambridge University Press, 1987); David Grayson Allen, *In English Ways: The movement of societies and the transferal of English local law and custom in Massachusetts Bay in the seventeenth century* (Chapel Hill, NC, IEAHC, University of North Carolina Press, 1981); Frank Thistlethwaite, *Dorset Pilgrims: The story of Westcountry Pilgrims who went to New England in the seventeenth century* (London, Barrie and Jenkins, 1989).

[15] Jack Greene, "Interpretative frameworks in American history," *William & Mary Quarterly*, 48 (Oct. 1991), pp. 528–9.

3 THE TIDEWATER

On January 2, 1775, in *Dunlop's Pennsylvania Packet or the General Advertiser* (no. 167), "Rusticus" wrote that the peace and security that the colonists had enjoyed before 1764 under the British connection "must make us look back with regret to those happy days whose loss we mourn, and which every rational man must consider as the golden age of America." Three and a half months later, when British redcoats marched on Lexington and Concord, a few miles from their base in Boston, in order to capture and destroy rebel arms, they were fired on from behind walls and hedges by the embattled farmers and minutemen; and in Emerson's phrase, carved on the memorial at Concord Bridge, the shot was heard round the world. Of 800 British "lobsterbacks" who set out, 244 were casualties by the time the column returned. The Golden Age was violently − and suddenly − at an end.

It is not too difficult to catch the flavor in Virginia of the age from the Glorious Revolution of 1688 to the Declaration of Independence in 1776, for some of its splendid products still survive; in the Tidewater, history is still visible. There have been 500 battles on Virginia's soil, more than twice as many as in any other state, leaving her rich in Civil War memories, and in historical markers. (Not that the War is there called Civil: to all Virginians it is *the* War, the War between the States.) The Golden Age is best seen on the banks of the James River. Here on a lawn sloping down to the slow-moving river is Shirley, still owned and worked by the Hill-Carter family. It was built between 1720 and 1740, a high, square three-story red-brick building in a setting of gnarled poplars and weeping willow. In the large central hall is the famous "hanging stair," which seems to have no support as it swings out on its way up a great central well three stories high; and there hangs near it the oil painting of Robert Carter of Corotoman, known for his pride, for his 300,000 acres and his 1,000 slaves as "King" Carter, elegant in his bright scarlet coat. His great-granddaughter Ann Hill Carter was married here to "Light Horse Harry" Lee, Washington's impulsive cavalry officer; their son was Robert E. Lee.

Four miles farther on is Berkeley, part of that Berkeley Hundred that was first reached on December 4, 1619: "The day of our ship's arrival ... shall be yearly and perpetually kept as a day of thanksgiving." So the first settlers were instructed. The *Margaret* from Bristol, under Captain Woodlet, landed her passengers 1 year and 17 days before the Pilgrims arrived and established their own Thanksgiving, on the bleaker shores of Cape Cod. In 1726 Benjamin Harrison began the building of the warm red-brick house, which stands at the head of low terraced gardens above the river. His son of the same name installed the handsome interior woodwork; this was the same Benjamin – son of Anne Carter, daughter of "King" Carter – who signed the Declaration of Independence, and was in turn a father and great-grandfather of presidents.

Two miles farther on is one of the most splendid of all, Westover, once the home of the Byrd family. The house rises in red brick, with two stories and a lofty attic; it replaced the wooden buildings of one of the first William Byrd's three homes. It is heralded at the head of the drive by massive wrought-iron gates made in England, which frame a prospect of the river across a lawn protected by great tulip poplars, and rich in season with crape myrtle dogwood. It was built by the second William Byrd (1674–1744), who had 4,000 books, the largest library in the colonies (except perhaps for Cotton Mather's?). He was himself an author as well as a collector – *History of the Dividing Line*, *A Journey to the Land of Eden*, *A Progress to the Mines*. The library was a man's room – Byrd records in his diary that he refused to allow his wife to borrow a book; he also had a billiard table, and billiards was considered a proper indulgence for ladies as well as gentlemen. Like many planters' sons, he had been schooled in England (as had four of the five sons of Robert Carter, and Arthur Lee, and George Washington's father and his adored half-brother). In fact from the age of seven, with only one intervening year in Virginia, he was shaped by his next 23 in London; he was in London again from the age of 44 to 52, with only one year in Virginia. But he had 100,000 acres in the West, and had determined the dividing line between Virginia and North Carolina. To recruit settlers for the West, he sought German-speaking Swiss; he wanted, he said, no Scots-Irish or "mixed people from Pennsylvania," whom he saw "like the Goths and Vandals of old." This dream foundered in 1739 when the German-Swiss he had recruited went down with their ship when it was wrecked in Lynnhaven Bay. He ran a saw-mill and a grist-mill, prospected for coal, iron, and copper, traded with Indians and in slaves, "dosed" his friends, his family, and his slaves, and laid out the town of Richmond, until then an Indian trading post, foreseeing its key position at the falls of the James, as indeed his father had. William Byrd I (1652–1704) had made it his first home in Virginia, as well as his store; from it he sent tobacco and furs to England, wheat, corn, and pipe staves to Barbados and Madeira; William Byrd II was born at the Falls. Commuting, almost regularly, to London, William Byrd II astonished its

citizens with the elegance he brought from "the new wilderness."
He was the first great American Anglophile, and an aesthete, who
spent his mornings reading Greek, Latin and Hebrew, Lucian and
Homer; and he was a Fellow of the Royal Society. He was also
burgess, councillor, and for long president of the General Court.
He wanted to exploit his London connections in order to become
governor – to supplant William Gooch, probably the most popular
governor (1727–49) in Virginian history – in which he was unsuccessful. So too with his careful and sustained quest after his
first wife's death for a wealthy English heiress, his "Sabrina," his
"Zenobia," his "Charmonte," his "Minionet," of his passionate effu-
sions to each of whom he kept copies. His last campaign was successful, perhaps because, to show his versatility, he wrote to Maria
Taylor of Kensington, who was half his age, in Greek. She seems
to have brought no fortune with her: but four children were born of
the marriage. The children of his two marriages married well, to
become part of the "closed corporation" of Tidewater society. He
kept a secret diary, to recount his hunger for women of all degrees.
His son, William Byrd III (1728–1777), was a great gambler, dissipated the family fortune, and – passionate Loyalist – shot himself
on New Year's Day 1777. One of his sons, Captain Thomas Taylor
Byrd, served in the British Army, though he never fought against
Americans; after the war he returned to Virginia and settled con-
tentedly in the Shenandoah valley. His brother Otway joined the
rebels, that is the Patriots, and was disinherited by his father before
his death. He stayed disinherited. It was a story not of rags to riches
and back again, but of rise and fall, and in three generations. William
Byrd III's grandfather, son of a London goldsmith, had made his
fortune as an Indian trader and had made his money from furs,
tobacco, and slave-dealing, from land speculation and merchant-
dealing. His widow lived on in Westover until 1814, when the house
was sold and the money distributed among the children – except
the disinherited Otway, who was by that time in Ohio. Much of
the house was destroyed by federal troops in the War between the
States, although it has been, in part, restored.

   Si monumentum requiris circumspice. It is proper to invoke Sir
Christopher Wren, for the models were English. He himself was
said to have designed the Wren Building for the College of William
and Mary, but it was "adapted to the Nature of the Country by the
Gentlemen there." The Williamsburg buildings of the late seventeenth
century – notably the Capitol of the Governor's Palace – became
the models. Almost everywhere in the Tidewater there still stand
the Georgian homes that, however derivative, serve as reminders of

a unique eighteenth-century society. Because of climate, low land, slave labor and limited raw materials (except for wood and sand), the designs imported from England underwent a subtle transformation. In English-named counties (Surry and Westmoreland – so spelled, York and New Kent, Northampton and Northumberland, Essex and Gloucester – where Mann Page's Rosewell was the largest residence ever built in a British American colony) arose English-styled mansions, with porticos and verandahs and ample green lawns, but, unlike those in the mother-country, with high external chimneys, for fire was the great hazard in an age of candles and open hearths – Westover was twice burnt in its first decade); set in a rich red-clay soil, with slave quarters and kitchens discreetly placed at a distance, and with the privy – "the necessary house" it was then obliquely called – at some remove. They had parquet floors and molded ceilings, marble fireplaces and grand staircases. Opulence was the mark of economic success, the buildings the sign that every gentleman was also architect and classical scholar. The Carters, the Byrds, the Lees, the Lewises, the Harrisons, the Randolphs, the Fitzhughs, the Wormeleys, were the grand squirearchy, the "FFVs," the First Families of Virginia. They had vast estates, more akin to small principalities than to farms. William Byrd II at his death owned 179,000 acres; "King" Carter had his 300,000 acres and 1,000 slaves: "an honourable man," said the epitaph on his tomb, amended by an irreverent and no doubt envious scribbler:

> Here lies Robin, but not Robin Hood
> Here lies Robin that never was good
> Here lies Robin that God has forsaken
> Here lies Robin the Devil has taken

The FFVs were long-tailed and intertwined. In the 96 years from 1680 to the Revolution, 23 families held 60 percent of the places on the Virginia Council, and one in six of all Virginia councillors could speak of a single grandmother, "Grandmother Lucy" Higginson. In 1657 there were seven Lees in the Virginia Assembly; in 1720 Thomas Lee, planter, burgess, founder of the Ohio Company and acting governor of Virginia, built Stratford Hall in Westmoreland county; two of his sons signed the Declaration of Independence.[16]

---

[16] One genealogist, in studying the origins of the Carter family, concluded that the Carters were related to everyone in Virginia. He even thought that the most privileged branch of all, the "Shirley" branch, could go back to Adam and Eve. Cf. Moncure Conway, *Barons of the Potomac and the Rappahannock* (New York, The Grolier Club, 1892), p. 34.

The Washingtons were of the lesser gentry: George Washington (b.1732), a poor lad left fatherless at nine, acquired his home, Mount Vernon on the Potomac, from a half-brother; his manners and style (and in the end his wealth) he owed to careful study of the ways of his first employer, and his patron, the 6th Lord Fairfax, who owned 5,000,000 acres in the Northern Neck, the peninsula between the Potomac and the Rappahannock and stretching to the Blue Ridge.

To younger sons and in-laws the models passed. A generation later Thomas Jefferson, born 1743 on the frontier in Albemarle County, but with a mother who was a Randolph of Tuckahoe, built in 1770 Monticello on his little mountain, for his bride and to his own design: red brick, with snow-white trim, porticoed in Roman Doric style and set in a green frame of trees. Sunken and terrace-covered passages lead away to service and slave quarters set in the leveled hillside. Inside it are his gadgets, dumb-waiters and a disappearing bed, a duplicating writing machine and a clock operated by a series of weights and pulleys. This was an inventor, naturalist, architect, lawyer, politician, and polymath; and Monticello for grace is un-rivaled in North America. Matching it, on its bluff on the Potomac stood the house Lawrence Washington built and named in tribute to the admiral under whom he had served at Cartagena in 1740: Mount Vernon.

This Chesapeake society had its parallels on the other side of the Bay. In Maryland, all landowners held land, at least in form, as tenants of the proprietors, the Calverts. This did not preclude the Catholic Carrolls of Carrollton from owning 40,000 acres and 285 slaves, and two town houses in Annapolis; and the Bennetts, the Lloyds, and the Dulanys almost matched them – notably the last, three Protestant brothers from Queen's County, Ireland, who arrived in 1703 as indentured servants, to prosper as planters, lawyers, speculators, and politicians. Though Maryland echoed Virginia as a tobacco colony on the Chesapeake, the Germans in Frederick County produced grain and livestock, and the port of Baltimore was a place for merchants and traders more akin to Boston – though much smaller – than to Williamsburg.

To the north on the Hudson River in New York, the Dutch patroons, the Schuylers and Van Cortlandts, the Van Rensellaers and the Phillipses – one of whom, Mary, Washington almost married – built homes almost as grand as those of the Virginians at the point where their creeks met their river, the Hudson. There too they built saw-mills and flour-mills, for these were also hard-headed and well-heeled working aristos. To drive today from the Bronx north through

Westchester County, past the Gould estates (acquired by a different ladder of fortune, and in a later age), past Tarrytown and Philipsburg, Croton and Hyde Park, is to see a matching world to that of Tidewater Virginia. Stephanus Van Cortlandt owned 200 square miles in the Croton valley; Caleb Heathcote, under letters patent from William III, acquired the manor of Scarsdale in 1702; by 1714 there were 16 baronial manors granted in the colony of New York, 6 of them in Westchester County. Influential though they were, New York was too complex to permit the growth of a paternalistic aristocracy on Virginian lines: they were primarily traders, lawyers, and investors in land rather than agrarians. Some of these – Dutch and English – patroons became Patriots in the Revolution (notably the Livingstons from Scotland), and two families of them have, like those in Tidewater Virginia, produced presidents and vice-presidents. (One of them, the Rockefellers, has restored both colonial Williamsburg and Philipsburg; into the first they put, in 1926 and at 1926 values, $60 million, with which 450 buildings and a great archive have been restored in meticulous and loving detail.) Some stayed Loyalist, as did Frederick Philipse III, who had 270 tenants on his estate in Westchester. He was big and broad: so fat that there was no room for his wife when he was in his English-imported coach. But he died poor, lonely and blind, and was buried in Chester, England, in 1781.

Extensive landholding was not a Southern nor a New York monopoly, however: witness the estates of Simeon Stoddard or of Major James Fitch in Windham County, Connecticut; or, even more striking, that of John Reed, preacher turned jurist turned landowner, extending to 100,000 acres in the "Equivalent Lands" transfered by Massachusetts to Connecticut.

The FFVs, however unique, were not alone in their taste for things English. Peter Harrison, a prosperous New England merchant, a dealer in rum and molasses, and from 1775 Collector of Customs for New Haven, "in point of family second perhaps to very few in America," filled his house at Newport, Rhode Island, with fine English furniture and furnishings, and had a large and elegant library of books, containing between 600 and 700 volumes, along with manuscripts and a large collection of drawings. Like Jefferson, he was a polymath and not least an architect, witness the Redwood Library and the Jewish synagogue in Newport, the King's Chapel in Boston, and Christ Church in Cambridge. Among his most prized books – and they were for use – were the first volume of Colen Campbell's *Vitruvius Britannicus* (1715), James Gibbs's *Book of Architecture* (1728), William Kent's *Designs of Inigo Jones* (1727), and the numerous treatises that poured from the pen of William Halfpenny: *Practical Architecture* (1724), *The Art of Building* (1735), *Useful Architecture* (1751), *Rural Architecture* (1752), *The Modern Builder's Assistant* (1732), and *New Designs of Chinese Temples* (1750–2).

Moreover, American Georgian was the product of amateur gentleman designers, working hand in hand with master-builders. Until the close of the eighteenth century, there were no professionally paid trained architects; and the men who presently became the first professionals were recruited from the ranks of these self-trained amateurs. Nor, it seems, were the plans for buildings brought from England, though they knew at first hand the work of Christopher Wren, and from books the designs of Palladio.

With rising profits, the number of patrons of fine buildings showed a steady increase. The prosperous merchants of New England joined the Tidewater aristocracy of the South. St Martin-in-the-Fields exercised an almost magnetic spell over the church builders of New England. St Michael's and St Philip's, Charleston, South Carolina, both have steeples that are simpler adaptations of its tower and spire; and, in New York City, St Paul's chapel of 1760 has a spire and interior both very similar to St Martin's.

Perhaps the English architect who had most – and most persistent – influence was James Gibbs. His *Book of Architecture* was the source book too for Christ Church, Philadelphia, and for the First Baptist Meeting House at Providence, Rhode Island. The other major "English" influence was William Adam. His designs were published in 1750 and later issued as *Vitruvius Scoticus*, an apt name for one who, along with his sons James and Robert, made Palladio's designs fashionable in England and in the "Old Dominion." Many of the plans and elevations of the country houses in the Rappahannock River valley were derived from Adam, and especially based on Hamilton Hill House in Edinburgh, built by Adam and illustrated in his book; John Ariss's house, Locust Hill in Westmoreland County, Virginia, is modeled on Milton House, another of Adam's Edinburgh houses. Colonel John Tayloe's Mount Airy, near Warsaw, Virginia, began before 1750, owed much also to Adam's designs as it took shape.

The greatest gentleman-designer-builder of all was the third president, Thomas Jefferson. Even before his embassy to France in 1784 he possessed Leoni's *Palladio*, Kent's *Inigo Jones*, and Gibbs's *Book of Architecture*. When he came to design his own house, Monticello, he both executed the preliminary studies himself and produced working drawings, with full-size details and specifications. He supervised its erection with the utmost care, even personally training his stone-masons, since in Virginia experienced artisans, comparable to those of New England, were still rare. Monticello contained elements drawn almost entirely from Palladio, with additional help from Gibbs and Robert Morris for the octagons that he added to the main buildings. Jefferson also built smaller houses, such as Brandon and Battersea in the James River country, and the Randolph-Semple house in Williamsburg. In the 1740s James Logan's Stenton, near Wingohocking Creek, and Graeme Park, 20 miles outside Philadelphia (the home of Elizabeth Graeme who, rejected by William Franklin, became a poet and a bluestocking), match the James River homes, with their ample gardens and lakes and deer-parks. Similarly, John McPherson's Mount Pleasant, and the Norris estate at Fairhill, also match the Georgian homes on the James, and are more truly domestic English as not being the "big house" of a slave economy. And matching Jefferson and Peter Harrison as architect is the Scots Quaker Robert Smith from Glasgow, whose Nassau Hall in Princeton became the model for Dartmouth at Hanover, and for Carpenter's Hall in Philadelphia. Abetted by Dr John Kearsley, the most distinguished of Philadelphia's medical fraternity, they planned the building of Christ Church, and of St Peter's.

The Georgian age in North America was marked by superb building, all the work of gentlemen-architects who in the truest sense of the word were "amateurs," not only of good building but of the classics. The special pride of the planter was a home built with English and imported bricks. Such, however, were rare. Brickworks became important, and increased use of brick in dwelling-houses marked Virginia and Maryland. Since more brick than wooden houses have survived, their number and quality do give a false impression. Wood remained the most popular material for the houses even of the wealthier planters. In the Carolinas, even in closely-packed Charleston, wooden houses were more common than brick. And in Pennsylvania, there was a wide use of stone.

Given the variety of native woods — oak, walnut, ash, hickory, maple, birch, and cherry — and notably stimulated by the appearance in 1754 of Thomas Chippendale's *The Gentleman and Cabinet-Makers Directory*, a group of American interior craftsmen also emerged. They were most conspicuous in Philadelphia — with James Gillingham, Thomas Affleck, Jonathan Gostelowe, Benjamin Randolph, William Savery, and the members of the Junto who gathered round Franklin — and in Newport with John Goddard. Almost all became a mobile workforce. In Virginia, the historian Robert Beverley, writing in 1705, took pride that his own furniture was made on his own plantation, whereas many planters were "ill-husbands have all their wooden ware from England ... to the eternal reproach of their laziness." [17]

4 THE CHESAPEAKE ECONOMY

Basic to Virginian affluence and to its gracious living was an economy as distinctive as the surviving domestic architecture: few poor (except the slaves) and few conspicuously rich, but a middle class of industrious professional men, some of whom sought to cultivate culture as well as land. Almost all of them were planters. As such, they kept careful accounts: their books, strong in law and agriculture, were for use as well as ornament. They lived on a wide coastal plain stretching for 100 miles to the Fall Line of the rivers, the Potomac, the Rappahannock, (to the Indians "the stream that comes and goes"), the York, the James, the Roanoke, whose tidal channels formed great peninsulas, with deep bays and long intervening necks of arable land which made ports and even towns for long unnecessary. The basis of the economy was threefold: cheap land; slave labor; and, within a decade of the founding of Jamestown, broad-leafed tobacco, loaded direct at their own wharves for the British market. James VI and I detested "the Imperial weed," "the stinking custom," and wrote his *Counterblaste* against it, chiefly because its popularity drained specie from Britain to Spain; but it became the mainstay of the colony. Tobacco needed new soil every three or four years, so large plantations grew; it needed labor in semi-tropical conditions, hence slavery. By 1776, of a population of more than two million, 300,000 were black, and almost all of them in the South. When in 1693 Aberdeen-born James Blair, commissary of the Episcopal Church in Virginia, appealed to the Lords of the Treasury for a grant to found a college which would train ministers for the saving of souls in newly established Williamsburg, he received from Sir Edward Seymour, a Treasury official, the answer: "Damn their souls, make tobacco!" Many planters — among them William Byrd — wanted the abolition of the slave trade and the eventual emancipation of the slaves. Many, like Washington and Jefferson, willed freedom to some of their own slaves when they died. But, despite its qualms, the South took no legal action against slavery; nor was such action feasible. For without a large labor force, capable of working

[17] Robert Beverley, *The History and Present State of Virginia* [1705], ed. Louis B. Wright (Chapel Hill, NC, IEAHC, 1947), p. 295.

long hours in a hot sun, the plantation itself was worthless. Tobacco was both exportable wealth and currency in the colony; the plantation was an economic unit, with factories and saw-mills, and the "big house" was the office as well as a social center.

Virginia's economy was distinct, almost unique; it developed along its slow-moving wide-mouthed tidal rivers along novel lines. Here as elsewhere the majority of free men were small farmers, and many of them earned a living by producing grain, fruit, and pork. But the tone of society was set by the plantation. John Rolfe's "discovery" of tobacco made it, despite the fulminations of King James, the staple crop of the Chesapeake Bay region; in South Carolina and Georgia the basis was rice and indigo; in both, the plantation quickly evolved. During the eighteenth century the price of tobacco became steady, but the costs of production inexorably increased, partly because of the heavy charges imposed by transporting it to Britain — for which factors and agents were often blamed, but still more because of soil exhaustion. The reliefs sought by planters — crop restriction, lower import duties, curtailment of the slave trade — were opposed by British interests. There were in 1750 only eight towns in the Chesapeake country, and most of them were "little better than inconsiderable villages." The population of the two largest, Norfolk and Baltimore, just reached 5,000, and they were each involved in the West Indies, not the tobacco, trade. Poor roads and slow travel put a premium on hospitality. Governor Spotswood "showed small concern in reporting that upon an official occasion he had entertained four hundred guests at supper." Stories were told of remote planters haunting the nearest road to watch for the weekly stage, hoping to find a traveler who could be persuaded to stop over for a day or a week to keep them company and pass on the gossip of the day. Colonel James Gordon of Lancaster County noted one day in his diary: "No company, which is surprising." Even as president, half a century later, riding the 100 miles from Monticello to Washington, or the "Federal City" as it was called, Jefferson regularly acted as postman for friends and neighbors on the road. Isolation and poor weather made family burial plots necessary. Jefferson provided space in his mausoleum in case a guest should die while visiting him. Early death, frequent re-marriage and large families made kinship as important as it was involved; life was abundant, varied, busy, and gracious in the Tidewater.[18]

[18] For Virginian hospitality, see Louis B. Wright, *The First Gentlemen of Virginia* (Huntington Library, San Marino, CA, 1940), *passim*.

They were planters first, but much else besides; lawyers and architects, doctors and vets, militia colonels and JPs, horsemen and gamblers, vestrymen and legislators, and managers and traders always. For their labor force, white and black, they had to have a feudal concern: slaves were property, not to be treated lightly, and there was no National Health Service. So this was paradoxically at once a self-sufficient and a dependent world. Thus wrote George Mason of Gunston Hall, a near neighbor of George Washington on the Potomac, living in his own mansion designed for him by William Buckland (who had come to Virginia under indenture);

My father had among his slaves carpenters, coopers, sawyers, blacksmiths, tanners, curriers, shoemakers, spinners, weavers and knitters, and even a distiller. His woods furnished timber and plank for the carpenters and coopers, and charcoal for the blacksmith; his cattle killed for his own consumption and for sale supplied skins for the tanners, curriers and shoemakers, and his sheep gave wool and his fields produced cotton and flax for the weavers and spinners, and his orchards fruit for the distiller. His carpenters and sawyers built and kept in repair all the dwelling-houses, barns, stables, ploughs, harrows, gates, etc., on the plantations and the outhouses at the home house. His coopers made the hogsheads the tobacco was prized in and the tight casks to hold the cider and other liquors. The tanners and curries with the proper vats, etc., tanned and dressed the skins as well for upper as for lower leather to the full amount of the consumption of the estate, and the shoemakers made them into shoes for the negroes. A professional shoemaker was hired for three or four months in the year to come and make up the shoes for the white part of the family. The blacksmiths did all the iron work required by the establishment, as making and repairing ploughs, harrows, teeth chains, bolts, etc., etc. The spinners, weavers and knitters made all the coarse cloths and stockings used by the negroes, and some of finer texture worn by the white family, nearly all worn by the children of it. The distiller made every fall a good deal of apple, peach and persimmon brandy. The art of distilling from grain was not then among us, and but few public distilleries. All these operations were carried on at the home house, and their results distributed as occasion required to the different plantations. Moreover all the beeves and hogs for consumption or sale were driven up and slaughtered there at the proper seasons, and whatever was to be preserved was salted and packed away for after distribution.[19]

A study of Robert Carter of Nomini Hall tells a similar story. He was master of 70,000 acres and over 500 slaves. He produced

[19] Edmund Morgan, *Virginians at Home* (Colonial Williamsburg 1952), pp. 53–4.

tobacco, but he had to supply numerous other staples and the foodstuffs essential to the operation of his plantations, and to supplement the dwindling profits of tobacco culture through the development of other money crops. The economy of Carter's plantations, moreover, was by no means so exclusively agrarian as has been generally believed true of plantations of the Old Dominion. He operated foundries, textile factories, and grain mills, traded with other planters, sent his ships regularly up and down the Chesapeake and the Virginia rivers, and provided his neighbors with credit facilities. Nor did the laborers on Carter's plantations consist solely of white overseers and Negro slaves. The white workers ranged from the chief steward, who managed a number of plantations, to the humble artisans, who laid brick or ground corn. Of the Negroes, some were domestics, many were proficient craftsmen, and others worked in factories. And, in all this, and like most of his fellow planters, he was cultivated, interested in music, science and religion, and, as a member of the Governor's Council, visited Williamsburg "in the public times," and kept a town house there.[20]

To grow tobacco and to make a profit by it was no easy task. Every planter in Virginia cultivated it, and the small man, with on average 10–15 acres in corn and other crops, contrived to have three or four acres in tobacco. Judging both the plant and the weather at the several critical stages of growing, curing, and packing was a matter of great skill, from planning the work of the slaves and clearing new land to the delivery of the hogsheads at the inspection warehouses below the Fall Line, where they were checked by officials selected by the justices. The receipts issued by these inspectors, the tobacco-notes, were the paper money of the colony. Most of the hogsheads were consigned after inspection directly to the ships bound for Britain, which had a monopoly of trade. A fleet of about 120 vessels went annually to Chesapeake Bay, and moved on the average 90,000 hogsheads (each about 1,000 lbs) from Virginia and Maryland. The planter had then to watch the prices his tobacco brought on the British market, and against his tobacco credits order the farm equipment and tools, hardware and textiles, the luxuries and the necessities, not for a family only but for a community often the size of a village. From Britain came the manufactured goods, the cambrics and linens, the coaches and the weapons, sent in exchange for tobacco. London and Bristol, and after 1707, Glasgow, were the market towns of the Chesapeake. Most of the trade was of

[20] Louis Morton, *Robert Carter of Nomini Hall, a Virginia Tobacco Planter of the Eighteenth Century* (Colonial Williamsburg, 1945).

a large planter consigning his crop, plus sometimes the crops of his neighbors, to a British merchant; and there was a measure of specialization in the product, the Yorktown and Rappahannock areas producing a sweeter-scented leaf than the cheaper and stronger-tasting Orinoco of the James and the Potomac – which, diluted and flavored, often went on as snuff to the French market.

Writing in 1786, Jefferson estimated that Virginia owed 2 million sterling to Britain, "as much as all the rest of the states put together;" these debts had become hereditary for many generations, "so that the planters were a species of property annexed to certain mercantile houses in London." [21] Indeed, part of George Washington's strength lay not only in his wealth of land (in the West, as in the Tidewater from marriage), but in the fact that he saw that tobacco was no longer a reliable source of wealth to Virginia. By 1763 he was beginning to experiment; by 1768 he had ceased to grow tobacco on his Potomac farms, and wheat had become the main crop; by 1770 he was planning a new and larger mill to grind his own and his neighbors' wheat into flour. This meant not only self-sufficiency as a farmer but independence of the British market. By 1769 fishing in the Potomac was sufficient to allow a small shipment to Antigua. By 1772 Washington was shipping 270 barrels of flour to the West Indies, too; rather "musty" flour, he confessed, but it would permit the buying of slaves, if "choice ones" could be got for less than £40 a head. In the South as in the North a considerable American coastal traffic grew up, and bred a merchant marine in contrast to colonial France or colonial Spanish America – which would prove invaluable in the War of Independence.

[21] Jefferson to M. de Meusnier, author of the *Encyclopédie Politique*, January 24, 1786, in *The Complete Jefferson*, arranged and assembled by Saul K. Padover (New York, Duell, Sloan and Pearce, 1943), pp. 51–2.

Virginia certainly owed two millions sterling to Great Britain at the conclusion of the war. Some have conjectured the debt as high as three millions – probably nearly as much as all the other states put together. This is to be ascribed to peculiarities in the tobacco trade. The advantages made by the British merchants on the tobaccos consigned to them were so enormous that they spared no means of increasing those consignments. A powerful engine for this purpose was the giving of good prices and credit to the planter until they got him more immersed in debt than he could pay without selling his lands or slaves. They then reduced the prices given for his tobacco, so that let his shipments be ever so great, and his demand of necessaries ever so economical, they never permitted him to clear off his debts. These debts had become hereditary from father to son for many generations, and thus the planters became a species of property, annexed to certain mercantile houses in London.

The same story – of the shift from tobacco to grain – can be told elsewhere in Virginia, and in particular of Maryland's eastern shore. It reflected the early industrialization and hunger for food of Europe, the size of the Caribbean market, and the demand for corn that came from all of them – to the profit of the granaries of New York and Pennsylvania, and, as the eighteenth century wore on, even of Virginia.

It is natural to write of this stately world in terms that would now be called those of "class." But it was not aristocratic as that term was understood in Britain. Nicholas Cresswell, the English traveller, described Washington as "the second son of a creditable Virginia tobacco Planter (which I suppose, may, in point of rank be equal to the better sort of yeomanry in England." [22] It is easy to forget that life could be crude and short: the death rate for children was appalling; the average artisan had little schooling; women had few legal rights and blacks none at all; indentured servants lived in a state of virtual slavery. As slave numbers grew, the colony attracted fewer indentured servants. It was, however, a world of economic opportunity, and Williamsburg's restoration after Bacon's rebellion proves the considerable size of the group of men "of the middling sort," conducting sound businesses, tradesmen, apothecaries, and blacksmiths, cabinetmakers and coopers, clockmakers and silversmiths. Washington himself had no background of wealth or education; one of his first pieces of writing as a schoolboy was a laboriously written Rules of Civility:

When in Company, put not your Hands to any Part of the Body not usually Discovered.

Shake not the head, Feet or Legs, rowl not the Eyes, lift not eyebrow higher than the other, wry not the mouth, and bedew not man's face with your Spittle, by approaching too near him when you speak.

Being to advise or reprehend any one, consider whether it ought to be in publick or in Private; presently, or at some other time in what terms to do it and in reproving Shew no Signs of Cholar but do it with all Sweetness and Mildness.

Play not the peacock.

If Jefferson's mother was a Randolph, his father Peter was an energetic surveyor who settled in the hill country and bought the

---

[22] *The Journal of Nicholas Cresswell 1774–1777* (New York, Lincoln McVeagh, Dial, 1924), p. 75.

400 acres of Shadwell for a bowl of punch. Land was cheap; anyone with a little capital, or a large family, for each of whom he could claim 50 acres as headright, could become a landowner; and land was the key to social status. Density of population was 23 per square mile; there was a perennial labor shortage, and progress up the ladder for what the Scot would call the "lad o' pairts" was easy and rapid. This might be a society run by a cousinhood in which kinship counted, but it was fluid and open and easy to enter, always provided the entrant was industrious – and white. In politics there were property qualifications for voting, but the almost universal ownership of land gave the colony a broad white electorate. The majority were plain farmers, working from 50 to a few hundred acres, and with their own hands, and those of their family. Thomas J. Wertenbaker calculated that only one Virginian in 15 owned more than 1,000 acres of land. Tenants and small farmers, ex-apprentices and freed servants could all vote. They usually voted for the gentry – as they did also in contemporary Britain. But there was less deference, and government was all too visible.[23]

The operation of a plantation was a most public activity, and success in it was as efficient a method of indicating capacity for public service as any of the more democratic devices of later centuries. It was from the planter class that the 12 members of the governor's council were chosen, and the same class provided most of the 104 members of the House of Burgesses (two members for each county, one for the College of William and Mary, and one each for Jamestown, Williamsburg, and Norfolk). Every free adult male possessing 25 acres of land with a house or plantation, or 100 acres of unsettled land, had the suffrage. Elections were public and lively, voting oral, and "refreshments" – of rum punch – abundant. It was the practice "to go merry to the Court House." Only once did James Madison try to win office without "swilling the planters with bumbo;" he was defeated, and he concluded that "the old habits are too deeply rooted to be suddenly reformed." It was his sole defeat, and his sole effort at prohibition. Neither Jefferson nor Washington seemed to lose respect by treating their many friends on election day with generous and frequent hospitality.

From 1699, when the capital was transferred from marshy and malarial Jamestown, until 1779, when it was moved to Richmond, Williamsburg – named after William III – was twice or thrice a year, when the Burgesses met, the political center of Tidewater society.

---

[23] Thomas J. Wertenbaker, *The Planters of Colonial Virginia* (Princeton, NJ, Princeton University Press, 1992), pp. 183–247.

These were "the Publick Times" in the leafy small town, with its elegantly proportioned brick Capitol, with its slender white cupola bearing the arms of Queen Anne, and the Union Flag still flying above, marking the Union of England and Scotland of 1707 (and not to be confused with the Union Jack marking the later Union, of 1800, with Ireland). It was first built in 1701–5, burnt down in 1747, and restored in 1753. Equally striking was the Governor's Palace, begun in 1705 and completed in 1720 at the urging of Governor Spotswood, and its College with its coat of arms, the only coat of arms granted by the British College of Heralds to an American college. With its frame houses, white-painted and weatherboarded, with horse races on a track east of Waller Street, and greased pig races down "the noble great street six poles wide," named after the Duke of Gloucester, and in "Assembly times" with much drinking of apple-toddy, mint sling, and pumpkin flip, it is not difficult to romanticize the Old South; where, two generations before, their ancestors had hacked their path through all-but-impenetrable wilderness, and with muskets at the ready, now foxhunting was fashionable. And in Maryland "the eleven of Prince George's County" regularly met "the eleven South River gentlemen" at cricket.

The Chesapeake society was unique. More than half of its total production – foodstuffs and staples – went into exports. The large planter carried his own risks throughout the growing, the transport, and the marketing; the tobacco merchants came in only at the English end, handling an enumerated commodity, most of which was re-exported, when its import duty was repaid, in a major book-keeping transaction. The grower was tied into the consignment system. Only after the 1740s, with Glasgow traders establishing themselves in the Tidewater and in the piedmont, and their cash offers eliminating risks and attracting many smaller planters, did the pattern change. By the time of the Revolution, the biggest profits in the Chesapeake trade were in fact being earned in the sales of English and European goods in the stores in the Tidewater, largely run by Scots factors learning the tobacco trade before returning to the family merchants' houses in Virginia Street, Glasgow.

The South preserved the class distinctions, the Episcopalian Church, the parish and county government, and the mores of an older England. From Britain it was largely recruited; to Britain it sent its crops and from it bought its goods; and to Britain also came its sons for education – although as often to Edinburgh and the Inns of Court as to the older universities.

The south was rural. The big house of the plantation was work-shop and mill, tannery and hotel, as well as home, and it could occasionally be a cultural center, like Westover on the James, Robert Carter's Nomini Hall, or Bermuda Hundred. But so sympathetic an observer as the Marquis de Chastellux found Virginians in general "ignorant of the comfort of reading and writing." There was only one college in the colonial South, William and Mary. The leisure of the planter was active rather than contemplative: he turned to horses and hunting, cockfights and cotillions, gossip and hospitality, rather than books. His ways were gregarious, not solitary. "He who rides his horse alone can catch his horse alone."[24]

The traditions of the Tidewater South were as well established as those of New England or Philadelphia, but very different. This was a society warm and convivial, quick to anger, sensitive to injury, open, unshrewd and feckless. Yankees found it not to their taste: South Carolina was, to Josiah Quincy, the Harvard liberal, a land of "opulent and lordly planters, poor and spiritless peasants and vile slaves." Samuel Bownas, the Quaker preacher who visited Virginia in 1727, thought that "the intemperance of the people was shortening their days." John Woolman, another Quaker, found "a Dark Gloominess hanging over the land." For, tied to the soil, the inefficient colored labor force was almost completely without initiative, and the plantation economy was draining the land of its vitality. The indebtedness of the South to England was not only social but also economic.[25]

The First Families of Virginia had emerged as the leading Virginian names – Carters, Lees, Digges, Burwells, Beverleys, Ludwells, Byrds; originally, the younger sons of substantial families who had benefited from a Restoration that had given a hierarchical role to the men around Governor Berkeley. Only two of the first families of Virginia, the Fairfaxes and the Wests, were related to or members of the English peerage; dukes don't emigrate. Most of the others were descended from tradesmen in the London area. In all their admiration of England they still felt themselves to be cultural provincials; but they were hard-working managers, gentry who got their hands dirty. What mattered to them, as to their English models, was, in L. B. Namier's words, "blood, name and estate."[26] The

[24] Chastellux, *Travels in North America in the Years 1780, 1781 and 1782*, ed. Howard C. Rice, Jr (Chapel Hill, NC, University of North Carolina, 1963), p. 18.

[25] Josiah Quincy, Jr, *Journal of a Journey to South Carolina, Pennsylvania and New York in 1773* (Massachusetts Historical Society, *Proceedings*, XLIX, Boston, 1916), p. 424; Philip P. Moulton (ed.), *The Journal and Major Essays of John Woolman* (New York, Oxford University Press, 1971), p. 54.

[26] Lewis P. Namier, *England in the Age of the American Revolution* (2nd edn, London, Macmillan, 1961), Introduction.

basis of their power was the extent and wealth of their landholdings. But much was needed, since that under cultivation was worked out quickly, and it needed slaves. As in the home country, primogeniture and entail were part of the law: but they mattered less in Virginia. The eldest son got the home plantation only, and there was land in plenty for the younger; one son of "King" Carter, Robert, became Carter of "Nomini"; Charles (who married Anne, one of William Byrd II's daughters) became Carter of "Cleve"; and Landon (who married Maria, Anne's sister) of "Sabine Hall" and four other plantations; John, the eldest, became Carter of "Corotoman" and "Shirley." Moreover, all the estates were all increasing all the time – profits, and continual supplies of incomers, and the headrights they brought, ensured that. No one son was predestined for leadership. The First Families of Virginia were a tangled cousinry of leaders, or of potential leaders.

In the 50 years from 1722, almost half of all the burgesses who served in Williamsburg came from less than a dozen families, and of these three were preeminent: Randolphs, Carters, and Beverleys. Of the rest, six had married into the Carter line, five into the Randolph, and four into the Beverley. The economy depended on the large estates. Only those with wealth and armies of dependents could afford the time or the means for government. Except for a small number of artisans and traders, every freeholder – an enfranchised citizen because he held land – was a planter, large or small. Those who went to Williamsburg to govern, in acting for themselves, acted also for all citizens. Political parties in a modern sense were nonexistent, because irrelevant; and there was only one annual wooing of the "electorate." Legislation was designed to protect the planter population, usually against the English merchant class which dominated the administration of colonial affairs. So to be born an heir to a large planter was to be born (and to be raised) in the expectation of political office. Indeed membership of the Governor's Council was itself practically hereditary, and held for life.

Yet politically they could not be sure that they would lead, or even be consulted. For their situation was colonial: there was frequent and erratic interruption by an English authority, Crown or City or Parliament; by the mid-eighteenth century in Virginia the local had become distinct from "the State." The governor came and went, almost always an outsider. The most successful, like William Gooch, were so because they rarely disagreed with the Assembly, and turned a blind eye to smuggling, and to the manufacture of cheap linens. Yet position and power in the hierarchy depended on the governor and on cultivating him, or of countering his proposals by rival intrigues in Whitehall and Westminster. Political power and influence could become divorced from social standing: this was a dangerous gap.

Moreover, when the tobacco plantations extended inland beyond the Fall Line, which ocean-going vessels could not pass, tobacco was usually sold to local merchants, usually themselves large planters, so that there arose a domestic market in tobacco: by 1776 some three-quarters of the crop was sold in this way within the colonies.

The role of the large planter was thus an economic determinant in the Upper South. He shipped his tobacco direct, and with the proceeds or credit imported goods for his own stores. The small farmer, with the produce only of a few acres, could not afford to ship direct and had to sell to the large planter or to local buyers. He had in turn to buy his English goods not at English prices but from local merchants; the absence of towns precluded small retail shops and competition. A few English merchant houses appeared in Maryland, in the Cunliffes and Hydes, Hunts and Gildarts. But it was the Yankee hucksters whom the Virginians feared, as they sailed in to bargain with the smaller planters or even with slaves. "Some of these banditti anchor near my estate, for the advantage of traffiquing with my slaves, from whom they are sure to have good pennyworths ...," wrote William Byrd II to his friend Benjamin Lynde in Salem, Massachusetts. "I wish you would be so kind as to hang up all your felons at home, and not send them abroad to discredit their country."[27] The good colonel was equally severe on the "Saints" for "engrossing" the trade of North Carolina: there was a considerable traffic in naval stores and tobacco to Boston from the coves and thinly-settled shores of the Cape Fear country — where the cheapest imported goods were 50 percent dearer than at Philadelphia.

Historians have puzzled over the question why land-rich if cash-starved planters, masters of great acres with many dependents, should ever have gone to war with a mother country from which they drew their furniture, their books, and their gossip, and which ruled them on a loose rein. But there was a gap between the governor and his councillors which could not be bridged by blarney, or by surrender. Moreover, by the 1750s there was an economic problem similar to but lesser in scale than Boston's. There was mounting irritation

---

[27] Louis B. Wright and Marion Tinling, (eds), *William Byrd of Virginia: The London Diary (1717–1721) and Other Writings* (New York, Oxford University Press, 1958), p. 221.

with dependence on the British market for the finished goods they got in return for their tobacco; too often they claimed that the coaches and linens, cambrics and furniture, were of inferior quality. They began to diversify, and to look to other markets, outside the mercantilist system, and thus to break the law. As numbers and estates grew, some (the large and slave-holding plantations) were very rich, some just surviving. Envy grew too. The less fortunate moved into towns or to the West: scouts and rangers, vagrants and feckless. When there were grievances, injustice became a matter for lawyers to use, on which bitterness grew. And the next generation, with their own land-hunger, looked across the Valley and the Alleghenies; individually or in the land companies, in which old Virginian families formed alliances with English merchant-bankers and with Philadelphian traders, they planned new colonies in the West. One Virginian, Treasurer and Speaker of the House, John Robinson – who gave loans from the public purse to his friends, who were often his relatives, in the oligarchy – had anticipated them. With the permission of the council and a patent from the governor, he obtained 100,000 acres on the Greenbrier River in what is now West Virginia. It became the Greenbrier Company on the river of that name. Alongside it were the Ohio Company, set up in 1748 (Lees, Fairfaxes, Washingtons), which had the consent of the Board of Trade to a 200,000 acre settlement, and a fort at what is now Pittsburgh, where 200 families settled; and in the foothills of the Blue Ridge, now well inland from the Fall Line, was the Loyal Company (grant signed 1749), whose two key members, both surveyors, were the friends Peter Jefferson and Dr Thomas Walker. On a single day, in July 1749, the Virginia Council issued grants of more than a million acres. They carried the plantation system westwards with them; and the gap widened between rich and poor, white and black.

5 BEYOND THE FALL LINE

Gracious and entrepreneurial, eighteenth-century Virginia was thus also expansionist. West of the Fall Line lay the rolling piedmont, a frontier still in process of settlement, and still farther west a world that was mountainous and marginal, legendary and little explored, the land of the "Western Waters." There was great uncertainty about its resources, its geography, and its ownership. There was controversy with other colonies – North Carolina, Maryland, and Pennsylvania – over mutual boundaries, and the dream died hard of a short-cut through it to the Indian sea, with a wealth of furs and precious stones *en route*. Yet even at the time Robert Beverley wrote his history, in 1705, one dream was being replaced by another; of virgin land to be occupied by those with the resources to reach it, and those endowed with energy and courage. Beverley described his fellow Virginians as "not minding anything but to be masters of great tracts of land — lords of vast territory." The exotic cavalcade led in 1716 by Lieutenant-Governor Spotswood over the Blue Ridge into the fertile and lovely valley of Virginia, the "knights of the Golden Horseshoe," was recruited largely from Tidewater planters. Robert Beverley was with them, and a Huguenot diarist, John Fontaine. When they reached the summit of the Blue Ridge Mountains on September 5, they stopped to drink healths to King George I and all the royal family — as many as they could remember. On the next day, when they crossed the "Euphrates" — as they called the Shenandoah — and claimed the land beyond in the king's name, they again celebrated:

We had a good dinner, and after it we got the men together, and loaded all their arms, and we drank the King's health in champagne, and fired a volley: the Princess's health in burgundy, and fired a volley; and all the rest of the royal family in claret, and a volley. We have several sorts of liquors, viz. Virginia red wine and white wine, Irish usquebaugh, brandy, shrub, two sorts of rum, champagne, canary, cherry, punch, water, cider, etc.

The 1716 traveller might see the valley of Virginia dimly through a rosy haze of liquor and optimism. But this was a different world, even if in the end Mr Jefferson's Albemarle County, or Augusta County across the Rockfish Gap in the valley, came to resemble Hanover and New Kent counties back in the Tidewater. The county that Spotswood organized and to which he gave his name was Virginia's 28th, and the first beyond the Tidewater. By 1750 there were 16 more. Into the Shenandoah valley from Pennsylvania and the North, and on, through it, into the valleys of the French Broad, the Holston, the Clinch, into the Smoky Mountain Country and the pine-barrens of the Carolinas, moved "new men", mostly Scots and Scots-Irish and German. The tobacco traders here were mobile Scottish factors, usually operating out of Norfolk, setting up stores and buying tobacco on the spot from the newer smaller farmers. By 1776 Charles Lee spoke of them as a "Macocracy." William Byrd II deplored the coming of Scots-Irish to the country on the dividing line between Virginia and North Carolina. He much preferred the more peaceful Germans. The first German group settled at Massanut-ten, near the present Luray. By 1770 the Scots-Irish were at the Cumberland Gap, which the surveyor Dr Thomas Walker – an Englishman, be it noted – had discovered 20 years before, and which stands at the junction where today's Virginia, Kentucky, and North Carolina meet. There are both an Edinburgh and a Glasgow in the valley. By 1776 the Scots-Irish were to give a new character to the Appalachian frontier; democratic, strongly religious, industrious, self-reliant, prone to dissent in Church and State, they were to be "the cutting edge of the frontier."

The frontiersmen were pugnacious and contentious, short sighted and clannish, hard-drinking and independent-minded; they were re-sourceful, quick to take offence, prone to sudden emotion in poli-tics and religion. They were good with a horse and with a rifle; they needed to be. A rifleman of Pennsylvania, when accused in the War of Independence of fighting by non-European rules of etiquette and "picking off the officers first," replied, "Well, if you are trained to shoot squirrels, you can hardly miss men." They were no more generous to the Indians than those in the Tidewater were to blacks. It is doubtful if they were more "democratic" by nature than those back East, but few among them could trace their ancestry far back or be proud of what they found when they did. They were hostile to Establishments, especially eastern, and especially to those they thought snobbish and living off their fat in Charleston or Williamsburg. They bred natural aristocrats, or at least natural leaders, of their own: like Judge Henderson, who had in his own words "A Rapturous idea of property;" John Sevier, blond and handsome; Daniel Boone, the long hunter; William Blount, the first senator from the new state of Tennessee, who in 1797 had impeachment proceedings begun against him – and dropped; and Andrew Jackson. None of these was especially tolerant or peaceful by nature. The last of them, who saw action as a boy aged 12 against the British at Hanging Rock, lived to personify the most profound political change in American history, in giving leadership to that Democratic Party that put him into the White House in 1828, and was closer in style to today's Democratic Party than it was to Thomas Jefferson's "natural aristo-cracy of merit and virtue." The frontier did not breed democrats. It bred men who thought and said that they were as good as their neighbors, and privately were sure that, having tamed a wilderness, they were a great deal better.

The Scottish tobacco factors here produced their own trans-atlantic connection: after the Act of Union, Glasgow became more important than London and Bristol to the frontier farmers, for some of whom it was home. Some of the factors after an apprenticeship in Virginia would return to become Glasgow's "tobacco lords" – Cunninghames, Glassfords, Buchanans, and Spiers traded usually with the French rather than the English, and the French Farmers-General bought four times more tobacco from Scottish factors than they did from England. The Buchanans were wrecked by the coming of the War of Independence; James Buchanan went bankrupt, and was driven to get a job as a Commissioner of Customs in Edinburgh – the same Buchanan who had planned Glasgow's main shopping street on the four acres of land behind his own mansion. His brother George had built his house on the estate known until then as Windy-edge, but which he renamed Mount Vernon in salute to his friend George Washington, whose plantations adjoined his own on the banks of the Potomac. To Glaswegians Mount Vernon is still best known as a district in the city's West End. The Cuninghames were cleverer – or luckier. The War ended the regular supply of tobacco; so as prices soared they sold the tobacco that they had shrewdly stored in their warehouses downriver, in Glasgow and Greenock, and made a fortune. With it they built the Virginia Mansion, now embedded in Glasgow's handsome Royal Exchange.

Paradoxically, they put more Loyalists into action in 1776 than most other areas. Somewhere between 500 and 1,000 Scots High-landers assembled at Cross Creek (now Fayetteville, NC) in 1776, ready to fight for George III as keenly as, 30 years earlier, they had fought against his grandfather's cause, and for Bonnie Prince Charlie at Culloden. Their loyalty to Britain was less striking than their emnity towards Britain's critics in the Tidewater, who fixed the rating and tax systems to hurt them. So on the principle that the enemy of your enemy is your friend, they were for the king. They were indeed inspected and addressed in Gaelic by a woman aged 54 riding a white charger, the same Flora MacDonald who had helped to save the Prince and got him away from Scotland after Culloden, and had emigrated to North Carolina with her husband and four children. Then, as earlier, she was on the losing side. Her husband was captured at Moore's Creek Bridge and his property confiscated; and, penniless, she and the family sailed back to Skye in 1778. Not all frontier stories are of success; but all of them are starred by courage.

Nor does paradox nor courage end there. In 1745 the Rev. John Witherspoon, Edinburgh graduate and minister in the parish of Beith, raised volunteers to fight against the Pretender, and was a prisoner after the battle of Falkirk. Thirty-one years later he had crossed the ocean and changed his allegiance. As president of Princeton and delegate to the Second Continental Congress, he signed the Declaration of Independence.

6 BOSTON

The Bay Colony, like Virginia, had been reached from the sea, and depended on it; township settlements were grouped around the rock-bound coast, and from Gloucester and Marblehead, Boston and Salem, the fleets went out to the Grand Banks for cod, and inshore, along the coast, for mackerel. A line of church steeples pricked the skyline – there were some 20 churches in 1760 – nestling cheek by jowl with warehouses and stores, close to the wharves which carried the owner's name: Griffin's, Hutchinson's, Clarke's, Scarlett's, Grant and Greenwoods' Wharf and Shipyard, Belcher's, Oliver's, Wentworth's – names that are a bead-roll of Boston history. If Virginia's society was of the planter class, Boston's came from trade: Faneuil and Amory, Hancock and Boylston. So it was also with the Browns of Providence and the Wartons of Newport, with New York's Crugers and Lows, and Philadelphia's Whartons, Willings, and Morrises. Jutting out to sea was the Long Wharf, believed to be in its day a wonder of the world, a Ponte Vecchio, but 2,000 feet in length, and lined with handsome warehouses. At the foot of it ran King Street, the main street, with an amphitheatre of houses rising one above the other from the water's edge. In 1760 Boston had 160 warehouses and about 25,000 inhabitants, and was probably then the largest town in North America – not yet, though soon to be, surpassed by Philadelphia.

Much of Boston's history has been swamped by changing contours. Old wharf areas have been filled in and built over. If Faneuil Hall still stands, the Tea Party site lies where today the John F. Fitzgerald Expressway dives under the Congress Street overpass. The inner harbor has been transformed. Castle Island, to which, when troubles arose in 1770, the British garrisons were withdrawn and which then was two miles offshore, is now part of the city mainland and is a cargo-holding area; but for the Tea Party Museum in 1973 one of the 340 tea chests was providentially discovered and put on display. History still lurks, however, around Beacon Hill, with houses famous for the small-paned windows of "blue glass". The Old South Church – originally built in 1729 as the Old South Meeting House – remains: it was from here that the Tea Party began their march to the harbor. The Old State House, built in 1713, still has above its doors the Lion and the Unicorn that it had until 1776.

And the Old North Church survives, even if the steeple from which the lantern was hung — "One if by land, Two if by sea" — to start Paul Revere on his ride, has been replaced. Indeed, if one building has to be selected that speaks of the eighteenth century it is the work of the builder of Blenheim, Peter Harrison's superb King's Chapel, completed in 1754. It was the first Episcopal Church in New England and later the first Unitarian Church in America; in its day it was strongly disapproved of by the more strict Puritans. That it was splendid and 'Piscy' indicates that by 1754 in Boston comfort was threatening Godliness.

In the eighteenth century the mark of the Puritan, however, was still the hallmark of Boston. Not for it a landed aristocracy — but an aristocracy of the Saints. Offenders still "stood up in meeting" and revealed, to the delight of their less afflicted or more reticent brethren, the errors of their ways. But by the opening of the eighteenth century Boston was ceasing to be the tidy and planned city of the Saints of John Winthrop's noble vision. It was the largest town in North America and certainly — not least in its own eyes — the most important. Andrew Burnaby, visiting it in 1760, likened it to a thriving English town. In his map of 1722, Captain John Bonner already claimed for it "near 12,000" people, with "42 streets, 36 lanes and 22 alleys," and "houses near 3,000, 1,000 brick, the rest Timber." The streets were crooked and irregular, paved with cobblestones, with open gutters in the middle; pigs served as collectors of garbage, and geese wandered off the Common. The houses were a maze of crowded, timbered tenements, all tiny, most of them firetraps; Boston had had eight great fires in the previous 80-years, and six outbreaks of smallpox. Families were large and lived public lives; privacy was impossible, so much so that it was rarely mentioned. Everyone knew everyone else's business.

The city was all but an island, linked to the mainland by a mile-long neck of scrub and mudflats over which, in high tides or winter storms, the sea swept. North Boston, north of the Long Wharf and cut off by the Mill Creek (now Blackstone Street), was doubly a peninsula. The Common gave the city grace, and around it stood noble brick houses. Approached from the sea and guarded by Governor's Island and Castle Island, Boston rose like an amphitheater crowned with its three hills — Fort, Beacon, and Copp's — and 11 steeples. A Revere engraving dated 1770 shows it to advantage, with eight big ships riding at anchor. The Long Wharf ran out to sea for half a mile, and the largest ship afloat could berth there whatever the tide. Around the wharves were the ropewalks and cordwainers' shops, the taverns and tenements of a thriving community. The city lived by trade with the West Indies and by building ships. It exported codfish and barrel staves, salt pork, salt beef, and hard pine; it imported sugar and molasses, wine and slaves. One item of its own manufacture – rum – was at once solace and currency up and down the seaboard. Trade between New England, the West Indies, and Africa was funneled through Boston, and the city drew a rich dividend.

By 1706 Boston was moving out of its early generations of high Puritanism. Ten years earlier, Judge Samuel Sewall had stood in his pew in the meeting house to hear the reading of his confession of contrition for his share in the witchcraft delusion of 1692. The liberal Brattle Street Church, with its striking deviations from the principles of the Cambridge Platform, had been organized in 1699 by a group of wealthy and broadminded Boston merchants. It was the church of Whig leaders like John Hancock, James Bowdoin, Dr Joseph Warren, and from time to time of John Adams, but also of some who later became Loyalists, such as the merchant Richard Clarke. For its first 47 years, its minister Benjamin Colman steered clear of controversy. His associate and successor William Cooper, son-in-law of Judge Sewall, and in 1743 William's son Samuel, preached that the poor "should and must give way to the rich," that "The Gospel condemns only an ill-proportioned and vicious self-love," and that Religion is a friend to outward Prosperity. Of the 100 Bostonians with the highest real estate assessments, 27 attended Brattle Street. They were urged to be men of Christian benevolence in a logic and a language that pointed less to Calvin's theology than to the economics and the invisible hand of Adam Smith. Morality rather than piety was being stressed, and in the train of prosperity secularism was creeping in. In the charter granted in 1691, after the overthrow of Governor Andros, the non-conformist elements were no longer disfranchised. Although undemocratic and hierarchical, and insisting on a sharp property qualification for the suffrage, Massachusetts was in social, as in political, character no longer an oligarchy of the spiritually elect. The Puritan code became hard to enforce when population reached 10,000. The state of morals in the Bible Commonwealth of the late 1690s was impishly reported by an English visitor, the satirist Edward Ward. Of the progeny of the visible Saints and those that settled after them, he wrote;

Rum, alias Kill Devil, is as much ador'd by the American English, as a dram of Brandy is by an old Billingsgate. Tis held as the Comforter of their Souls, the Preserver of their Bodys, the Remover of their Cares, and Promoter of their Mirth; and is a Soveraign Remedy against Grumblings of the Guts, a Kibe-heel (sore heel), or a Wounded Conscience, which are three Epidemical Distempers that afflict the Country ...

Notwithstanding their Sanctity, they are very Prophane in their common Dialect. They can neither drive a Bargain, nor make a Jest, without a Text of Scripture at the end on't ...

Their Lecture-Days are call'd by some amongst them, Whore Fair, from the Levity and Wanton Frollicks of the Young People, who when their Devotion's over, have recourse to the Ordinaries, where they plentifully wash away the remembrance of their Old Sins, and drink down the fear of a Fine, or the dread of a whipping-post. Then Up-tails-all and the Devil's as busy under the Petticoat, as a Juggler at a Faire, or a whore at a Carnival. Husking of Indian-Corn, is as good sport for the Amorous Wag-tailies in New England, as Maying amongst us is for our forward Youths and Wenches. For 'tis observ'd, there are more Bastards got in that Season, than in all the Year beside; which occasions some of the looser Saints to call it Rutting Time.[28]

Despite its small size, Boston in 1706 was the largest city and business port in the colonies. Nothing so much became part of the bone and sinew of Benjamin Franklin as the conviction that trade was a virtue, a source of wealth and power and prestige. Commerce and trade and the Puritan gospel of work were effectively destroying whatever class barriers a new world and its expanding and demanding frontier had ever permitted. John Hull, the goldsmith, started life as a blacksmith's son; his widow, Mary, married William Phips, a ship's carpenter who became wealthy in shipbuilding and trade (and the discovery and re-capture of sunken treasure), to end up as Sir William and a rather unskillful royal governor of Massachusetts. Nathaniel Hancock, the shoemaker of Cambridge, was the grandfather of the Thomas Hancock who so prospered by trade, naval contracts, and smuggling that he could build the family home on Beacon Hill and fill it with furniture and a good library of volumes, "well bound with gilt edges," bought in London. Thomas's nephew and heir was to be the first signer of the Declaration of Independence.

Puritans no longer dominated New England society; the great John Winthrop's grandsons were more devoted to real estate than to

---

[28] Edward Ward, *A Trip to New-England with a Character of the Country and People* (London, 1699), pp. 10–11; Charles W. Akers, "Religion and the American Revolution: Samuel Cooper and the Brattle St Church," *William & Mary Quarterly*, 35 (July 1980), pp. 98–477.

godliness, and were "always exceedingly anxious to hear about the latest London fashions in waistcoats and wigs." The Puritan was turning into the Yankee. From early days, the indented coastline and numerous harbors of New England encouraged maritime industries: the short but rapid rivers were a source of water power; cedar, spruce, oak, and pine for ships were abundant. The Maine fishermen fell into the Boston orbit. They bought cloth from them at three times the price it commanded in England, and relied on them wholly for cables and cordage, anchors, lines, hooks, nets and canvas. The farmers of Rhode Island were also resentful; the colony's General Court complained in 1658 that the Bostoners could "make the prices, both of our commodities, and their own also, because wee have not English coyne, but only that which passeth amonge these barbarians [i.e. the Indians], and such comodities as are raised by the labour of our hands, as corne, cattell, tobbacco, and the like, to make payment in, which they will have at their own rate, or else not deal with us."

This same shortage of currency meant that Bostonians anxious to expand could only do so by getting increasing control over valuable natural resources. They looked for timber inland, and established saw-mills. They raised horses and sheep themselves, instead of relying on small farmers. They built ships for themselves to save freight charges and to earn carriage fees. By 1770 New England had almost 1,000 vessels engaged in the cod and mackerel fisheries or in whaling; she built twice as many vessels as all other areas combined. And with shipyards went saw-mills and wagons, barrels, furniture, and household goods, whale oil and spermaceti. Agriculture was important here as elsewhere. It was diversified, and free from the price fluctuations and overproduction that beset the South, but it was handicapped by rock and mountain, by short summers and long winters. This was a soil and climate unsuitable for tobacco, for plantations, or for slave labor; its farms were small and compact, tilled by an independent class of yeomen. Even these looked to the sea – Washington's "marines" and "commandos" were recruited from the fishermen-farmers of Gloucester and Marblehead, New Bedford and Nantucket. Captain John Smith, in his *Present Estate of New Plimouth* (1624), had said: "Let not the meannesse of the word Fish distaste you, for it will afford as good gold as the Mines of Guiana and Potassie with lesse hazard and charge, and more certainty and facility." New England's prosperity came from the sea; it is still symbolized in the gilded codfish on the Speaker's desk in the State House in Boston. There was a ready market for surplus fish in the West Indies and in Catholic southern Europe. And there flourished the triangular trade in rum, molasses, and slaves between the West Indies, New England, and Africa. With wealth they speculated in land, acquiring blocks of wilderness in New Hampshire, Maine or western Massachusetts for the sake of more timber or possible furs, or in the hope that it would increase in value as settlement expanded. The Faneuils and Belchers, Lillies and Gallops of Boston lived in fine houses on Garden Court Street or Beacon Street, and rode in costly coaches. The old four-square meeting house, with the roof rising on four sides to the belfry, gave way to more graceful structures in the style of the Old South, with an octagonal arched superstructure crowned by a spire. Harvard moved erratically towards liberalism, and endowed chairs in Mathematics and Natural Philosophy. Its students in 1758 put on plays (*Cato*, *The Recruiting Officer*, *The Orphan*), despite the law forbidding acting. In the silvercraft of Paul Revere and Samuel Minott, Samuel Edwards and the three Burts, as in the painting of John Singleton Copley, Boston was becoming more than a provincial town, and breaking free from its Puritan traditions. Cotton Mather, that believer in witchcraft, became a Fellow of the Royal Society, a student of fauna who, like Franklin, kept records of the weather, and advocated the most advanced treatment of yellow fever.

What was striking about New England was its homogeneity in race and religion, and the dominance of the English and the Puritan strains in Church and State. There were few Negroes, and almost all of them domestic servants or town workers. Here as elsewhere fundamentalism and deism were making inroads, but as yet they had not got far. To a South Carolinian like Edward Rutledge, New England was peopled by men of "low cunning and levelling principles." It was nourished by a strong current of argument and debate in congregation and in town meeting, fed by a well-organized system of education, evidenced in Harvard (1636) and Yale (1701), Brown (1764) and Dartmouth (1769), and by compulsory education laws, grammar schools such as Boston Latin School, and the Cambridge printing press. Moreover, the Yankee virtues of industry and thrift, caution and esteem for learning, were to move west with the New England settlers into the Ohio and Upper Mississippi valleys. There, as well as in New Haven and Boston, were to rise the little red schoolhouse and the tall white spire.

Learning was seen as basic as worship. Indeed, the legacy of Cambridge (England) to Cambridge (Massachusetts), and of the 100 Oxford graduates in early Boston and the new towns that dotted the shores of the Bay, was that this was probably the best-educated community the world had ever known. "In its inception," wrote Moses

Coit Tyler in his history of American colonial literature, "New England was not an agricultural community, nor a manufacturing community, nor a trading community: it was a thinking community; an arena and mart for ideas; its characteristic organ being not the hand, nor the heart or the pocket, but the brain." [29]

Of the signers of the Declaration of Independence, 8 were Harvard men, 4 from Yale, and 4 from William and Mary, 2 from the University of Pennsylvania, and 3 from Princeton, one of them its president, the Scot John Witherspoon.

7 NEW YORK

Recent writing has thoroughly revised Carl Becker's picture of New York as a mercantile and landed aristocracy, divided into feudal personal factions, that dominated the tenant farmers and kept the franchise tighly restricted. [30] Becker described the Revolution in New York in a phrase that is now a cliché, even if it is also a classic: the struggle for home rule, he said, was a struggle over who should rule at home. He saw it as a class war, even before that phrase, and that interpretation, had also become clichés. The reality is far more confusing than such stereotypes. However, Patricia Bonomi stresses that most of the large manors granted by the governors did not survive long, and were sold to the public in small parcels; manorial privileges had in part to go too, in order to attract tenants. [31] For most of the eighteenth century there were good relations between landlord and tenant – until Yankee incomers reached the Hudson valley. Nor, until the years just before the outbreak of the War of Independence, were New York politics dominated by the feud between the Patriot Livingstons and the Tory De Lanceys; that is another short-hand view. New York City and colony were run by an aristocracy, of wealth and talent, but long before 1776 it included the names of "new men" as well as "patroons". Moreover, New York City and Albany were chartered cities; if mayor and recorder were appointed by the governor, the electors annually chose

[29] Moses Coit Tyler, *A History of American Literature 1607–1765* (Ithaca, NY, Cornell University Press 1949), pp. 85–7; S. E. Morison, *Three Centuries of Harvard 1636–1936* (Cambridge, MA, Harvard University Press, 1963), p. 4.
[30] Carl Becker, *The History of Political Parties in the Province of New York 1760–1776* (Madison, University of Wisconsin, 1909).
[31] Patricia U. Bonomi, *A Factious People: Politics and society in colonial New York* (New York, Columbia University Press, 1971).

an alderman and an assistant from each ward, and assessors, collectors and constables as needed. Freemanship carried the franchise with it, and was available to almost all free white adult males. From 1731 onwards, the citizens of New York City elected 14 aldermen, 7 assessors and 16 constables each year. Residents of manors had similar rights, even if they showed deference to the "big men" in their localities – no manorial family ever lost an election for the assembly seat of its estate. Moreover, in New York's ten counties, five around New York City and along the seaboard, and five in the Hudson valley bordering the river, there developed not English-style justices of the peace sitting in county courts, but county boards of supervisors, elected annually from the townships or from the precincts: Long Island had nearly 20-such precincts by the 1730, Westchester County 8, and Dutchess County, on the east bank of the river, 7; Orange and Ulster Counties, on the west bank, each had 5. If deference was, there as elsewhere, the form, there was much participation also; and the popular protests in New York City against the conspicuous display of the wealthy led in the 1760s to disruptions of fashionable concerts and the destruction of the Chapel Street Theater.

Milton Klein, in his *The Politics of Diversity*, and in numerous essays, stresses the heterogeneity of New York as a clue to its politics. [32] Work habits, reliability, capacity to "muck in" mattered as much as rank or status or ownership of land. It bred bosses and "boodle" and campaign chests, patronage, newspaper propaganda, and appeals to popular support on the grounds of "principle." Trenchard and Gordon's writings were re-printed here, voicing the language and the vocabulary of the English Civil War. *The Independent Reflector*, William Livingston's weekly journal of the 1750s, [33] showed the influence both of Trenchard and Gordon's *Independent Whig*, and of Addison and Steele's *Reflector*. Political parties were seen as guardians of public liberty; and New York brought its own ingredients to its politics: strong trading links with England, offering opportunities for political maneuvering on an imperial scale; [34] Germans *vs* Dutch in the Mohawk valley; Presbyterians *vs* Anglicans in

[32] Milton Klein, *The Politics of Diversity* (New York, Port Washington, Kennikat Press, 1974).

[33] Milton Klein (ed.), William Livingston, et al., *The Independent Reflector* (Cambridge, MA, Harvard University Press, 1963).

[34] Alison Gilbert Olson, *Anglo-American Politics 1660–1775: The relationship between parties in England and colonial America* (New York, Oxford University Press, 1973).

Manhattan; patrician *vs* plebeian over currency devaluation and flour exports; conflicting sectional, ethnic, religious, and economic interests. Rivalries between New York City, Albany, and eastern Long Island generated intense local loyalties, as did commerce *vs* land along the long line of settlement on the Hudson. With a representative assembly in being after 1691, there was a vitality in New York politics more akin to Philadelphia than to Boston, or, more accurately, to New York City in the late nineteenth or in the twentieth century? For New York, in Klein's word, was "prototypical." As he has put it, a trifle lyrically –

Political factions reflected the heterogeneity of the colony's economy, its ethnic and religious composition, its geographic sectionalism, and its social structure. Parties were broad coalitions, and programs were necessarily diffuse enough to appeal to the colony's cosmopolitan population, often in a variety of languages. If there was deference, there was also democracy. If there was aristocracy, there was also public accountability. If there were family rivalries, there were also popular issues. If there were local concerns, there were also Anglo-American interests. If there was social stratification and monopoly of officeholding, there was also mobility and considerable rotation in office. If there was Whig ideology imported from England, there was also the uniquely American idiom in which it was couched by provincial politicians to suit the colony's special political dynamic. If the articulate were spokesmen of conservatism and status, there were also inarticulate believers in liberty and equality. [35]

More recently, historians who try to see history from the bottom up have used material from New York and the other cities, often relying on statistics and demography. To them the British connections of the colonies are all but irrelevant. [36] Some of these writers,

---

[35] Klein, in J. Judd and J. Polishook (eds), *Early New York Society and Politics* (New York, Sleepy Hollow Press, 1974), p. 27. See also Becker, *Political Parties in New York*; Bonomi, *A Factious People*; George Dangerfield, *Chancellor Robert R. Livingston of New York, 1746–1813* (New York, Columbia University Press, 1971); Stanley N. Katz, *Newcastle's New York: Anglo-American politics 1732–1753* (Cambridge, MA, Harvard University Press, 1968); Lawrence H. Leder, *Robert Livingston and the Politics of Colonial New York* (Chapel Hill, NC, IEAHC, 1961).

[36] Among them are those whose essays have been edited by Alfred F. Young in his *The American Revolution: Explorations in the history of American radicalism* (De Kalb, Illinois, Northern Illinois University Press, 1976), prominent among them Dick Hoerder ("Boston leaders and Boston crowds, 1765–1766"), Gary Nash ("Pre-revolutionary urban radicaliam"), Francis Jennings ("The Indians' Revolution"), and Edward Countryman ("Northern land rioters in the eighteenth

stimulated in part by studies of contemporary Britain, by George Rude and others, focus on crowds and mobs.[37] Paul Gilje sees the crowd as an unofficial enforcement agency of traditional standards. Colonial crowds, though composed largely of the lowest orders of society, seamen, laborers, and apprentices, were occasionally joined by young gentry. Revolutionary mobs, too, included members of the elite who shared in the anger toward British policy. During the Revolution, artisans moved from street activity to government by committee. Did this change represent a major shift or maturation of at least one element of the mob, a change that would largely separate the Revolutionary mob from earlier (or later?) crowd actions? And can there be firm reliance on an interpretation of history that rests on so elusive an institution as a "crowd"?

One of the most important of this group of historians is Edward Countryman. In his essay in Young's volume his viewpoint was of a class warrior. In his more scholarly and more ambitious *A People in Revolution: The American Revolution and Political Society in New York 1760–1790*,[38] he sees New York as a more "complicated and tangled place". When he traces the waning of the old order, 1760–75, he discovers that if landlordism was unpopular in some regions, especially in Dutchess, Westchester and Albany Counties, in others – Orange and Ulster – there seemed no special tension between landlord and tenant. But there was a steady, even normal, propensity to riot – as in contemporary Britain; and Countryman draws an interesting distinction between urban discontent, turning on political social and imperial issues, and rural discontent, springing primarily from problems of landownership and the local dominion that went with it. But up the ladder of riot and protest rose the new men, "men on the make, the successful children of oyster-catchers, milkmen and indentured servants." The consequence was a political system in decay because out of touch and closed to change, a vigorous and critical Opposition press, and a deep "contradiction

---

century.") See also Young's article, "English plebeian culture and eighteenth-century American radicalism," in Margaret Jacob and James Jacob (eds), *The Origins of Anglo-American Radicalism* (London, Allen and Unwin, 1984), pp. 185–212; Pauline Maier, *From Resistance to Revolution* (New York, Knopf, 1972); and Gary B. Nash, *The Urban Crucible* (Cambridge, MA, Harvard University Press, 1979).
[37] Thus Paul Q. Weinbaum, *Mobs and Demagogues* (Ann Arbor, University of Michigan Press, 1979), and Paul A. Gilje, *The Road to Mobocracy: Popular disorder in New York City, 1763–1834* (Chapel Hill, University of North Carolina Press for IEAHC, 1987).
[38] New York, Hill and Wang, 1985.

between a rhetoric of involvement, virtue and public liberty and a reality of exclusion, corruption and class interests." Countryman testifies also to a vigorous colonial New York history of pamphleteering, rooted in an Atlantic republican tradition; an interpretation that is now, thanks to Bernard Bailyn, seen as the current orthodoxy.

In his analysis of the impact of the struggle for Independence, Countryman's strong sense of localism leads him to a novel interpretation. There were counties of consensus, whether the consensus was royalist (as in Kings, Queens and Richmond) or of resistance (like Ulster and Orange). In all of these the rate of population growth was well below that of the state as a whole; they were relatively tranquil, with few extremes of wealth and poverty, and the royalist areas were conspicuously more foreign and immigrant in character. By contrast, Westchester and Tryon, Cumberland, Dutchess and New York City had patterns of dynamic growth; they were much more commercial in character, and had conspicuous differences between merchants in their coaches and periwigs and the "leather-apron men." Countryman admits that this pattern is immensely varied, and that many Loyalists were poor men, so that it can never be thoroughly proved that the line between Loyalist and Patriot was simply that between rich and poor. But in the counties that were increasing in population the revolutionary committees played a key role, and power went to those who could seize it. In a sentence, the Revolution in New York State came in the City of New York, and in the "landlord counties" on the Hudson. And in them the crowds marched to different drummers: in the counties, the enemies were sheriffs and court houses, landlords – and their dependents; urban folk rioted over stamps and the presence of British troops, and sacked houses, theatres and personal property. And more than one Son of Liberty could, via mobs and committees, end by becoming a prosperous merchant and banker: witness Isaac Sears and Alexander McDougall.

In all this pattern of restlessness, in all the rivalries of Livingstons on their manor in Albany County *vs* DeLanceys, Cortlandts *vs* Philipses and Robinsons on the Hudson, in all their struggles with their tenants, and their many rent riots, in the confusions caused also by intermarriage between the clans, the stubborn fact remains that New York was the most loyal of all the colonies; and it was loyal in the real sense – it put men into action for the king. Two of every three of the New York Loyalists who claimed compensation from the British relief commissioners after the War said that they had served in the army – some 23,500 men in all: in DeLancey's Brigade (the so-called "Cowboys"), in the King's Royal Regiment of New York (or "Johnson's Greens"), in the Loyal American Regiment (Robinson's Regiment), in Richard Rogers's Queen's Rangers, in Jessup's Corps, or the King's Orange Rangers (John Bayard's.) Indeed, their number and their early establishment may have been responsible for Secretary of War Lord George Germain's faith in ever-flowing Loyalist military support. It proved to be an over-sanguine view.

One must distinguish sharply between the city and the colony. New York City's Loyalism was largely a consequence of its location. It was the natural base for any campaign to cut off New England from the Middle Colonies: once smoothly occupied by Sir William Howe in 1776, it became a Fortress Britannica, part refuge, part port, part supply base for the British Army in the Jerseys, in Pennsylvania, and in the South, with Halifax in Nova Scotia acting as a rear HQ and a strategic reserve. There had never been much affection shown by the farmer hinterland for those who lived by trade in the seaports or in the Tidewater. Too many on the seaboard were Scots who did not usually stay long, and most of whom proved to be Tories. Once occupied by the British and Hessian troops, New York's churches become hospitals, warehouses were cleared to become arsenals, empty buildings in the harbor became prisons. Despite inflation and shortages, and despite the ever-mounting columns of refugees, New York City was peaceful and prosperous, thanks to the skill and patience of its British commander – General James Robertson – and of Andrew Eliot, superintendent of the port and head of the police.

The war drove hesitant merchants to conservatism or exile. Isaac Heron, a Brooklyn watchmaker, said that the rebels had plundered his property but that the Hessians "complet'd his ruin." Of the 104 members of the New York Chamber of Commerce in 1775, 57 became Loyalists, 21 called themselves neutral, and 26 became Patriots. In October 1776, 704 New York City Loyalists petitioned General Howe asking for a restoration of civil law and attesting their loyalty to the Crown, in what was dubbed the Declaration of Dependence. So many merchants were Loyalist that their exile in 1783 was impossible; many were quietly reabsorbed. Even Jemmy Rivington's printing press survived – though not for long: the Tory sympathizer of his *New York Gazetteer* had been too outspoken. But Samuel Fraunces's tavern near Wall Street did well: it served the British HQ until 1783; when Washington moved back, it served him – and Fraunces in the end became the general's chef at Mount Vernon. He called himself a West Indian; he was probably a free slave and certainly a prosperous one. And he may have been through the seven years of British occupation an American spy, funneling out all the information he could glean, and getting it to the rebels across the No Man's Land of Lower Westchester County.[39]

8 THE MIDDLE COLONIES

The Middle Colonies — New York, Pennsylvania, New Jersey and Delaware — were very different. In the three great river valleys, the Hudson-Mohawk, the Susquehanna, and the Delaware, there was abundant and fertile soil, and the Middle Colonies were the granaries for the rest. The governor of Pennsylvania estimated in 1755 that the colony could export enough food each year to feed 100,000 people. Navigation inland was much easier than to north or south, and the West was first reached along the Mohawk. This was Iroquois country, and it was dominated by the Superintendent to the Northern Indians, Sir William Johnson, whose home was a market-cum-debating chamber for Mohawk chiefs, fur traders, company agents, and soldiers. The fur trade was still important and the Mohawk-Hudson junction at Albany was its pivot.

Both in New York and Pennsylvania, population was unusually mixed. New York City was already cosmopolitan, with layers of New Englanders and Scots-Irish, French Huguenots, Negroes, and Rhineland Germans. Politics here was already coming to be a matter of fine calculation among Germans, Dutch, and Irish. With cosmopolitanism of population went a certain culture, a college (King's, now Columbia, founded 1754), a theater and two newspapers, and a tradition, thanks to the German-born journalist John Peter Zenger, of free and frank comment. (When Zenger was arrested for his criticisms of the provincial government he was freed, since truth, it was argued, was always a full defense against charges of libel.) Dutch influence had left its mark on the Hudson valley in a distinguished upper class of Vans and velts: government was distinctly less democratic on the Hudson than in Manhattan; the Van Rensselaer manor covered an area two-thirds the size of Rhode Island; this was a region of tenants rather than freeholders. The upper Hudson River settlements stayed Dutch in language, custom and law for many decades. But New York, colony and city, lived

[39] Esmond Wright, "The New York Loyalists," in Robert East and Jacob Judd (eds), *The Loyalist Americans; A focus on Greater New York* (Tarrytown, NY, Sleepy Hollow Press, 1975).

also by trade. The city was freer and more materialist than Boston, a place of *nouveaux riches*. "With all the opulence and splendor of this city, there is little good breeding to be found ... in their entertainments, there is no conversation that is agreeable; there is no modesty, no attention to one another. They talk very loud, very fast and altogether." But John Adams was a prejudiced observer.[40]

Pennsylvania, with which were linked the "lower counties" of Delaware and west New Jersey, was the most tolerant, and in many ways politically the freest, of all the colonies. To it after 1700 had migrated many Rhinelanders and many Scots-Irish; by 1776, at least a third of its population was German, and Franklin had fears that German would become its principal language. The rest of the population tended to be either Quaker or Scots-Irish.

Picture a stake driven into the ground at the waterfront of Philadelphia. A 25-mile radius from this peg would encompass the area of Pennsylvania settled mainly by English immigrants between 1680 and 1710. Extend the radius to the length of 75 miles, and the outer 50 miles would correspond roughly to the "Dutch" country from Northampton to York counties. Here, from 1710 to 1750, the German-speaking immigrants to colonial Pennsylvania made their homes. Again extend the radius to 150 miles, and in the outermost circumference, corresponding roughly to the arc of the Allegheny Mountains and valley, the Scotch-Irish settled from 1717 to the Revolutionary War.[41]

The Germans were pietist, industrious, and frugal. They made good husbandmen, and they were also among the leaders in all the colonies in glass, brick, and iron production. Even in its own first generation, in men like James Logan (Penn's secretary and deputy in his long absences) and in William Allen — both to become patrons of the immigrant Ben Franklin — and in Andrew Hamilton and Francis Daniel Pastorius, the Quaker colony had remarkable, and scholarly, leaders, not all of them Quakers themselves, Peter Kalm, the Swedish traveller, was lyrical in his praise in 1749:

Again and again as we traveled through the forests of Pennsylvania we saw at moderate distances little fields which had been cleared of wood. Each of these was a farm. These farms were commonly very pretty, and a walk

[40] John Adams, *Diary and Autobiography*, ed. Butterfield (Cambridge, MA, Harvard University Press, 1961), vol. III, p. 109, August 23, 1774.
[41] Philip S. Klein and Ari Hoogenboom, *A History of Pennsylvania* (New York, McGraw-Hill, 1973), p. 3.

of trees frequently led from them to the highroad. The houses were all built of brick or of stone which is found here everywhere. Every country-man, even the poorest, had an orchard with apples, peaches, chestnuts, walnuts, cherries, quinces and such fruits, and sometimes we saw vines climbing in them. The valleys were frequently blessed with little brooks of crystal water. The fields by the sides of the road were almost all mown.

By 1763, however, the Quaker and pietist elements were a source of weakness as well as strength. They were both conservative and pacifist. They had consistently refused appropriations for the colony's defense, and Pennsylvania was saved in Braddock's day only by British regulars – and by Franklin's exertions. The Scots-Irish frontier, menaced by Indians, became hostile both to Quakers and to proprietors; their easy affluence, business acumen, and, it seemed, inveterate meanness seemed to imperil the existence of the colony. This clash between west and east was to store up problems for the future, as it had in the past. Meanwhile, the colony prospered. Its best index was its metropolis, Philadelphia. By 1763 it had 23,000 people and was the largest city in North America, with the first circulating library and the first fire company, a flourishing theater, a secular university, a gazette, and a distinguished "first citizen" and "man of business" – his own and other people's – in Benjamin Franklin. The Scots traveler Dr Alexander Hamilton found the City of Brotherly Love much to his taste in 1744:

They have that accomplishment peculiar to all our American colonys, viz., subtilty and craft in their dealings. They apply themselves strenuously to business, having little or no turn towards gaiety (and I know not indeed how they should since there are few people here of independent fortunes or of high luxurious taste). Drinking here is not att all in vogue, and in the place there is pretty good company and conversation to be had. It is a degree politer than New York tho in its fabrick not so urban, but Boston excells both for politeness and urbanity tho only a town.[42]

Benjamin Franklin has been seen as Philadelphia's most versatile product: printer, author, editor and publisher, deviser of lightning rods for its buildings and of fire insurance companies, of its library company, its philosophical society, and the academy from which grew America's first native university, with curricula designed for a New World in which knowledge was to be put to use. If Franklin

---

[42] *Gentlemen's Progress: The itinerarium of Dr Alexander Hamilton 1744*, ed. Carl Bridenbaugh (Chapel Hill, University of North Carolina Press, 1948), p. 193.

was, as they say on the banks of the Schuylkill, born in Philadelphia at the age of 17, he brought his skepticism and his curiosity, his interest in the religious as well as the secular "Why," and the resonance of his Biblical prose and Bunyanesque style with him from Boston; and there was little except experience that life in Market Street could add to what a boyhood in Milk Street, the Old South Church, and the Boston waterfront had already given him. As Gottlich Mittelberger reported in 1754, "Pennsylvania is heaven for farmers, paradise for artisans, and hell for officials and preachers." The City of Brotherly Love was from the first a city for tradesmen, craftsmen, and family homesteaders, for leather-apron men, for men of thrift, enterprise, and prudence – for men, in fact, like Benjamin Franklin.

Philadelphia, still heavily Quaker in spirit, was, like Boston, coming to be irked by the paternal restraints of its founding fathers, and in its case by the persistent absence of its proprietors, now turned remote, autocratic, and High Anglican. For full tolerance in creed did not mean full liberty in conduct; although there was no civil ban on extravagance and frivolity, the Quaker Yearly Meeting tried to be an effective censor of laxity in morals or behavior – witness its catalog in its *Book of Discipline* of 1704. Alexander Hamilton in 1744 said he had never visited "a place so populous where the gout for public gay diversions prevailed so little.' They were, he thought, "an obstinate, stiff-necked generation, and a perpetuall plague to their governors."[43] The City of Brotherly Love claimed to have no need for lawyers – these were few on the ground in the first generations; nor for printing presses, for scholarship, the Quakers held, bred contention. But if rude, and riotous sports, including gambling, bull-baiting, cock-fighting, and the theater, were banned, the city was already strong in the number of its clubs, taverns, and grogshops, and appropriately convivial. In the October 1728 election it consumed 4,500 gallons of beer; and the rum importation for that year, as Franklin was to reveal in a "surprising tho' authentick" account in the *Gazette*, totaled 212,450 gallons, worth £25,000. "Cyder Royal", new cider fermented with applejack, was a favourite tipple in the Red Lion in Elbow Lane, the Pewter Platter of Market Street, or the Crooked Billet by Chestnut Street Wharf. By 1752 it was estimated that there were at least 120 taverns, 14 rum distilleries – and only 12 churches.

---

[43] Ibid., p. 22.

In exchange for its major imports of rum and molasses and a vast quantity of manufactured goods, Philadelphia exported grain and lumber, beef, pork and horses, furs, tobacco to other colonies, the West Indies, and Britain. Its merchants, like those all along the seaboard, flouted the Navigation Acts; they too needed the currency or bills of exchange from the West Indies that they could spend in England. But what was unique to Philadelphia was its diverse stock of carpenters, smiths and masons, largely recruited from the Quaker north country in England: within a decade of its foundation 22 shopkeepers and 119 craftsmen were practicing 35 different trades and businesses; many of the early merchant traders – Samuel Carpenter, Isaac Norris, Jonathan Dickinson – came, not direct from London or Quaker Bristol, but from Barbados or Jamaica, and with knowledge of other markets. As many as 100 merchantmen with barges and shallops might crowd the river. By 1723 the houses on Front Street had balconies overlooking the Delaware, and were coming to be furnished with imported luxuries. It would be another four years before the new and ornate Christ Church was begun, and another decade and much argument before the State House, birthplace of a nation, was slowly to rise. "The dear old folks, most of whom are dead, may have spoken to their children a good deal about plainness," wrote Christopher Sauer, the German Quietist leader, in 1724. "It is still noticeable in the clothes, except that the material is very costly, or is even velvet." Homemade leather and homespun were still general, but there was rich color in women's dress, and powdered wigs, broadcloth coats, and knee breeches were coming to be the fashion for men. If Quakers were levelers, it was authority that they sought to level, not wealth. The city had its hazards: streets were unpaved and ill-lit; disease and epidemics – yellow fever, "the billious plague," "the epidemic pleurisy" – were regular levelers regardless of sect; and flies, mosquitoes, and roaches were a legend. The only public edifice of note was the court house on the High (now Market) Street. Life revolved round Market Street and the 20 wharves on the river. When in 1723 the Assembly approved Andrew Hamilton's plans for the State House, they located it on Chestnut Street between Fifth and Sixth Streets. Half a mile from the river, it was seen as on the city's outskirts.

Philadelphia was the transit point for a steady immigrant traffic moving through to the West, to the mountains and the forks of the Ohio, or southwest into the Shenandoah and the valleys and the piedmont country of Virginia and the Carolinas. The Great Philadelphia Wagon Road to Lancaster and York Counties was a major artery, not only for Germans, Amish and Moravians and Mennonites, but also for Scots-Irish. The vast majority of these came in as indentured servants, or — the Germans particularly — as "redemptioners", who undertook to repay the cost of passage within a week or two of arrival. The indentured were promised 50 acres of land at the end of their service, with another 50 — "head land" — to the master. And, as with black slaves, they were seen as property. Until 1700 there was no clear line between servitude and slavery; thereafter there were separate courts and stricter punishments for slaves. Pennsylvania was also the breadbasket colony, rich in wheat and corn, hemp and flax, cattle and hogs, timber and bar-iron, almost able to be self-supporting, trading favorably with a New England that lacked almost all these products. It was beginning to turn also to manufacture. Iron and steel were made, although the latter product was not developed; shipbuilding and textiles were becoming important.

Important as was immigration, even more striking was the natural increase of population. Thus Hannah Milner, who died near Philadelphia in 1769 at the ripe age of 100 years and 10 months, had 14 children, 82 grandchildren, and 110 great-grandchildren. A table of births and deaths of a Lutheran congregation of Philadelphia, covering the period between 1774 and 1787, showed the proportion of births to deaths as 2.15 to 1.

That Philadelphia developed so quickly was in part due to the Quaker tradition. Penn's colony was tolerant, as Boston was not. It was set up as a "holy experiment," an asylum for the persecuted. The Philadelphia tax list of 1769 reveals that although the Quakers constituted only one in seven of the population, they formed half of those who paid taxes in excess of £100. Of the 17 wealthiest citizens, only 5 were non-Quakers, and one of these, William Shippen, owed the basis of his fortune to his Quaker grandfathers. As they prospered, some residents moved from the Quaker Meeting to the fashionable Christ Church and the Anglican Establishment, as did the Penns themselves. "One might be a Christian in any Church," it was said, "but one could not be a gentleman outside the Church of England." By 1750 there were 11 Catholic congregations too. But the Friends never quite abandoned the Quaker spirit: diligence and thrift, plain and frugal living, discreet pride in business success, enterprise, and faith in freedom. The conspicuous enjoyment of wealth and of leisure were never quite respectable. Respectability counted almost as much as reward to the Quakers, and Godfearing seemed to be synonymous with moneymaking.

Quakers in Pennsylvania, unlike those in Britain, were free to play a part in politics. In the 50 years before the coming of Independence, the political struggle was of the Quaker party, led from 1750 by Benjamin Franklin, never himself one of them, and with a majority in the legislative assembly, *versus* the Proprietorial party, led first by James Logan and then by William Allen. The two main issues were the taxing of the proprietors' estates and the defense of the province against French and Indian attacks on its frontier, and – in 1747 – the raids of French and Spanish ships into the Delaware River itself. The pacifism of the Society of Friends, though a recurring theme of conscience in their Yearly Meetings, did not prevent the Assembly granting money "for the king's use," a pseudonym for defense; and one source of Franklin's popularity was his campaign for the organizing of a volunteer militia for the defense of the colony. This was a free society – much more so than Massachusetts – but not remotely a democracy. The leaders of each party were drawn from the wealthier families of the eastern counties, and of the City of Philadelphia. Political control was divided between absentee proprietors, the Penn family, and the local oligarchy of merchants and landowners who dominated the council. As a printer, Franklin would need these as patrons. They were prompt to recognize talent, and this was a world in which talent could rise quickly. Sir William Keith spotted Franklin early. So did James Logan, mathematician and classical scholar as well as a Founder and an Establishment figure, who as a local Maecenas gave Franklin and his friends the use of his library, and who described Franklin to an English friend in 1750 as "an extraordinary man in most respects – one of singular good judgement but of equal modesty."

9　THE CAROLINAS

A matching portrait could be drawn of steamy low-country South Carolina, with plantation homes along the Ashley and Cooper Rivers, notably Middleton Place, or Drayton Hall, ten miles upstream from Charleston, with its columns of Portland marble and with bricks specially imported from England, and the Joseph Manigault house in Charleston. This was a slave economy, more Caribbean than mainland in style, working fields of rice and indigo in humid swampy lowlands; and with a similar gentry class. They traded also in naval stores – rosin, turpentine and ship spars from the long-leaf pine forests – and in slaves. They were familiar with the slave trade, since many of the more substantial settlers had come in the first place from Barbados with capital, slaves, and experience of adapting themselves to a new society. They preferred slaves from the Gambia, since it was a rice-producing region. Rice, moreover, needed levées and watergates – that is, money and planning, as well as labor. The slave traffic began early in South Carolina; it has been estimated that by 1700 there were 5,000 Negro slaves in the colony. Being a seacoast town, Charleston was continuously interested in maritime pursuits – trading directly with England and with the New England ports, offering bounties for shipbuilders to break the New England monopoly in that craft. The city became the social center for the rice and indigo planters of the colony, and an escape from the heat and the humidity, the mosquitoes and malaria of the swamplands. Its social seasons – one lasting from May to November, the other beginning in January – featured horse racing, balls and concerts. Like Williamsburg in Virginia, Charleston was the social, governmental, and educational center for the surrounding region.

After Louis XIV's revocation of the Edict of Nantes in 1685, Charleston was reinforced by Huguenot immigrants, many of them skilled craftsmen, not least in gold, and silver, and as jewelers. Some of them – Manigaults and Laurens, Légarés and Mazycks – became Charleston dynasties as important as (or more so than?) Brewtons and Rutledges, Pinckneys and Pringles: merchants, planters, slave-traders all. At the end of the eighteenth century, this tiny city-state of some 15,000 people (half of them slaves) had the greatest per capita wealth of any city in North America. Since its staples were "enumerated," it was closely tied to Britain. Its western frontiersmen had less influence than anywhere else. It boasted libraries and a theatre, a racecourse, and milliners who kept in touch with Paris fashion. By 1750 it had a Scots Presbyterian Church, with a St Andrew's Society "to assist all people in distress," and which elected Occonnastoteh, the Cherokee chief, to membership to show its goodwill; and its Jewish congregation was influential. This could claim to be the Athens of the South. But Gideon Johnston thought even the South Carolina people "the Vilest race of Men upon the Earth ... a perfect Medley or Hotch potch made up of Bankrupts, pirates, decayed Libertines, Sectaries and Enthusiasts of all Sorts ... the most factious and seditious people in the whole World."[44] Well might James Otis predict in 1765: "Were these colonies left to themselves tomorrow, America would be a mere shambles of blood and confusion."

By contrast, North Carolina, lacking ports and towns, roads and specie, did not fit the Southern stereotype. Its chief product was

---

[44] In John Adams, *Diary and Autobiography*, vol. III, p. 109.

naval stores, not tobacco like Virginia or rice like South Carolina. Its social character reflected this. The absence of a staple crop, the inhospitable coastline and poor ports precluded an external stimulus for surplus production. Around 1770 the per capita value of North Carolina's exports (based on its white population) was less than half of Virginia's and only about one-tenth of South Carolina's. Partly because of environmental limitations, a native elite did not emerge. Political leaders were newcomers without substantial property. Between 1754 and 1775, almost 70 percent of the house leaders whose origins can be "approximated" were first-generation immigrants. In contrast, nearly four-fifths of Virginia's assembly leaders between 1720 and 1776 came from families that had settled the colony before the end of the seventeenth century. In 1764–5 only 38 percent of North Carolina representatives owned more than 20 slaves. In 1763 it had just under 100,000 inhabitants, only 16,000 of whom were Negroes. Its scattered lumbermen, planters, and Indian traders were a turbulent community; one visitor called it bluntly "a hell of a hole." Like sentiments, a little more decorously expressed, recur in William Byrd's *History of the Dividing Line*, and *A Journey to the Land of Eden*: "To speak the Truth, tis a thorough Aversion to Labor that makes People file off to N. Carolina, where Plenty and a warm Sun confirm them in their Disposition to Laziness for their whole Lives." To him it was "Lubberland." In 1771 there was an ugly civil war between western and eastern North Carolina. The westerners or the Regulator movement, were disturbed by bad economic conditions, unfamiliar poll taxes, boundary disputes and widespread corruption. At first, westerners rose in opposition to local rulers, who were even newer, less distinguished, and more corrupt than the eastern legislators who set the tone for the colony. The Regulator movement was not at first antilawyer and antimerchant, and, most important, it was not a radical democratic movement. Rather, the Regulators were "Country" advocates who sought to promote their economic independence and personal liberty. The dominant factor was the eastern leaders' own inherent dishonesty. They could not comprehend the Regulators' "anguish over corruption." Unlike Virginia's old aristocracy, North Carolina's rulers were not morally outraged by public wrongdoing. They could see westerners only as selfish rioters threatening their power.

As a result of such contradictory estimates, one of the foremost students of the South in the colonial period, Carl Bridenbaugh, distinguishes three Souths; Chesapeake society, Carolina society, and the back settlements. And if we add this same writer's insistence on the growing importance of craft skills and urban life in North and

South, it is clear that there was little uniformity inside either section or state. When the Revolution came, it took a different form in each section; indeed, in each colony. There were, in a sense, 13 revolutions rather than a single "national" movement.

10 GEORGIA

Like the Carolinas before it, Georgia, the last, the largest and the least populous of the mainland colonies, came into being as an outpost, to hold the frontier against Spaniards, French, and Indians. It had first been explored by Spaniards from the south, Francisco Gordillo and Esteban Gomez, probing along its island-fringed coast, and by Hernando de Soto, who went inland in 1540 and reached the piedmont before moving on west into what is now Alabama. Georgia's lack of gold was its protection. In 1566 the founder of St Augustine on the Florida coast, Pedro Menendes de Avila, landed on Santa Catalina island and conferred there with the Indian chief, Guale, after whom the area was thereafter named; in the next decades, with *presidios* and missions always close, in customary Spanish style, Jesuit and Franciscan missionaries followed, exploring and crusading from their Florida base. They stayed for the most part on the islands, and were never numerous – usually two per mission. But they were good diplomats among the Indians, especially the Apalachee. As English settlers moved into South Carolina, and they and the pirates they sheltered raided the missions, the priests fell back on St Augustine; Yuchi, Creek, and Cherokee Indians allied with the English. By 1686 the missionaries had retreated beyond the St Mary's River, thereafter seen as Georgia's southern boundary; Guale was disputed between Spain, France, and England – and Yamasees, Creeks, Choctaws, and Seminoles.

This was the site of the last piece of feudal experiment. In 1717, to set up a buffer against Spain and the Yamasees, Sir Robert Montgomery obtained a grant from the lords proprietors of Carolina to set up a utopia between the Altamaha and Savannah rivers. It would be called Azilia, he would be margrave, and he would have a palace; and he would graciously protect the existing land rights of the Carolina proprietors. The plantation would live on its wealth, and export tea and coffee, silk and wines, rice, fruits, and nuts, and would use white labor only. He published in London in 1717 *A Discourse Concerning ... the Most Delightful Country in the Universe*, and in 1720 *A Description of the Golden Islands*. But they remained paper-plans and promotional booklets only; the end of proprietary rule, and the harsh reality of Spanish and Indian attacks, ended such pipe-dreams. Had he been successful, the English settlements might have extended not from the prosaically named Bay of Fundy to Savannah, but from Avalon to Azilia. Another plan, which got beyond paper, was that for a Swiss settlement on the northern bank of the Savannah; but Purrysburg did not survive after the death of its founder Jean Pierre Purry in 1736.

The actual founding of Georgia was marked by a matching, but more realistic, idealism. Seeking a barrier to protect the now-royal colony, especially against the Yamassees, South Carolinians allied with merchants, members of parliament, and philanthropists, with a new colony as their objective. The principal founders were Sir John Percival (earl of Egmont in 1733), James Vernon, and James Edward Oglethorpe (1696–1785), who was chairman of a parliamentary committee enquiring into conditions in English jails, and a member of the British African Company. An American colony could be a place, in his view, not for criminals, but for that worthier and disturbingly large group, released debtors, who would become citizen-soldiers; their motives for leaving their country should not be crimes but misfortunes. He saw it as a colony of white yeomen-farmers. In 1732 his report on conditions in prisons for debtors, especially the Fleet, led to the release of some 10,000 prisoners. A royal charter was granted to 21 trustees by George II, after whom the colony was named. Its limits were to be the Altamaha and the Savannah Rivers, and to the west it would run to the western sea. Liberty of conscience was guaranteed to all who worshiped God, and freedom of worship to all except Roman Catholics. The power of the trust would lapse after 21 years, when government would revert to the Crown. Moreover, and unique among all the proprietary colonies, the trustees could not own land, hold any office, or draw any income from their efforts in the colony. There was one omission, striking since it had by that date become a necessity in every other colony: there was no provision for the creation of a legislative assembly.

The colony had a further good fortune: Oglethorpe led the colonists in person as resident trustee. The *Ann*, a 200-ton frigate, with Oglethorpe and 114 passengers aboard, sailed from Gravesend on November 17, 1732, and reached the Yamacraw Bluff, the first high ground on the Savannah River, 17 miles from its mouth, on February 1, 1733: a smooth journey. They had called at Charleston, which provided cattle, scout boats, and rangers for them, and then at Port Royal *en route*. The site was high and swamp-free, with forests for timber and firewood, and the Savannah River, which formed the boundary with South Carolina, gave access to the sea. The Indian nation nearby, the Yamacraws, an outlawed group of Creeks were few in number, and friendly.

Savannah was founded in 1733: its wide streets, its house lots, wards, and tithings focusing on public squares and placed at regular intervals, still show the marks of a splendid urban plan. It clearly owed much to Montgomery's plan for Azilia, and to Governor Robert Johnson's plan for the Carolina frontier. By that time Jamestown, more than a century old, was a ruin; Boston was growing like the proverbial green bay tree; Philadelphia, only 50 years old, and also a planner's toy, was outgrowing them all in numbers and in trade.

Oglethorpe met and made an alliance with chief Tomochichi of the Yamacraws, and, later, with the Creeks, the Cherokees, the Chickasaws, and even the distant Choctaws. He founded Frederica on the Altamaha as a southern bastion against Spain; it had a palisade, a guardhouse, and two blockhouses. He introduced a system of military training, for a settlement that was also to be a frontier outpost. Oglethorpe defended Georgia against the Spaniards during the War of Jenkins' Ear in 1739; although he failed in 1740 and 1743 in his attacks on St Augustine, he defeated the Spaniards on St Simon's Island in 1742, and thereafter Spanish efforts to regain their old mission country ceased. In 1734, its security attracted Salzburger Lutherans, who settled at Ebenezer, 22 miles upriver from Savannah; in the same year came 100 Lowland Scots and, in 1736, 200 Highland Scots, who founded New Inverness (Darien) on the Altamaha River. Three bands of Moravians (in 1735, 1736, and 1738), and Jews also arrived – uninvited, but were invaluable in coping with the wave of disease that hit the settlement in its first summers.

Oglethorpe secured from his fellow trustees three Acts that would enshrine Georgia's special character: Negro slavery was banned, since the redemptive value of hard labor would be lost if slaves tilled the soil; the demon rum was outlawed; and, inside the chartered limits of the colony, Indian trade was to be carefully regulated and licensed. The founder's concern was with "white virtue, white manners and white morals." In its inception, at least, Georgia had something of the idealism of Massachusetts Bay; the idea of a city on a hill was still there, even in Walpole's England. But, unlike Boston, where it was some 60 years before the dream died, in Georgia the prescriptions were honored in the breach within a decade, even before the founder finally sailed home in 1743.

The restriction of rum was impossible to enforce, despite Oglethorpe's conviction that it was the cause of the illnesses and deaths of the first years. South Carolinians took to the courts to overrule the licensing of Indian trade, which deprived them of a lucrative traffic; and despite the support of Salzburgers and Scots, Negroes were — and increasingly — used as slaves. Benevolence was unwelcome, perhaps too visionary for a rough frontier; and rectitude could irritate. The discontent with the prohibitory laws bred opposition to the paternalism of the founder; the Moravians, unwilling to bear arms, moved to Pennsylvania; and in 1743 Oglethorpe returned home to meet overt criticisms — even though they were, in the end, dismissed as "frivolous ... and without foundation." The trustees voted to repeal the prohibitions in 1750.

Oglethorpe's career reflects his idealism and his nobility. He saw military service against the Turks in 1717 under Eugène of Savoy. In 1719 he returned to England and followed his father and his two elder brothers in Parliament, and was an MP for 33 years. As a High Tory, he was an opponent of Sir Robert Walpole, and of what he saw as the extravagance and corruption of his administration; he was an advocate of colonial trade and a humanitarian; vehemently opposing (and pamphleteering against) impressment in the navy, Negro slavery, and conditions in debtors' prisons. He cared for the sick on the *Ann,* and for the first years was seen as "the father" of his people. He supported John Wesley and George Whitefield, who accompanied him to Georgia on his second visit (1735). In 1745, however, after his return, when he served against the Young Pretender, he was charged with indecisiveness, and acquitted; yet, on losing his parliamentary seat in 1754, he sought redemption by serving on the continent under a pseudonym in the Seven Years' War, was wounded, and did not return to England until 1760. He married late, and as a full general spent his old age in the congenial company of Boswell and Johnson, Edmund Burke and Horace Walpole. He was, as Alexander Pope said of him, "driven by strong benevolence of soul." As much as William Penn, and far more than William Pitt, he was an imperial philosopher and philanthropist.

Even this cursory summary of Oglethorpe's career omits the debtors, for whom the plans were originally made. In fact, Georgia never was a haven for debtors, and no more than a dozen came. Those who did come were the "worthy poor": indentured servants, small tradesmen, continental Europeans, and immigrants from the Carolinas. Even before the charter was surrendered, defense, the promotion of the fur trade, Indian relations, and experiments in viticulture and in silk production in the search for a staple, all steadily transformed the planner's vision into the "norm" of a southern frontier settlement.

In its first quarter-century Georgia became a land of small farmers, frontiersmen, and plantation-owners, with slavery as its labor force, rice as its major product, and paternalism breeding a gentry class, but also an opposition, which before long would seek a representative assembly as their platform.

Within the second generation, Georgia developed a plantation empire and a ruling class. This is exemplified by the career of Jonathan Bryan, in its way much more significant than Oglethorpe's. From 1736 until his death in 1788 Bryan acquired over 32,000 acres in Georgia and South Carolina by grant and purchase; he employed over 250 slaves in rice cultivation. For every slave he brought in, he got 50 acres of land as "headright"; thus by buying 20 slaves, a planter was entitled to 1,000 acres. Bryan became one of the colony's richest and most powerful men because he understood every aspect of land ownership, from accumulation to development and sale. He and his two brothers may have led Oglethorpe to the site of Savannah. Their father, a South Carolinian who traded with the Indians, had by his acquisitiveness helped to provoke the Yamassee War in 1715, which left the frontier region empty of people for a decade or more. South Carolinians saw a colony to the south for defence as essential, and for it they provided laborers, arms, and soldiers. They themselves did not wish to emigrate to it – Oglethorpe's prohibition against slavery and the limits on land ownership were deterrents. The shift of allegiance in the end was due to economic slump – declining rice prices, French privateering, rising insurance, and freight charges – to Charleston's indifference and refusal to legislate for the relief of debtors, and in particular to the legalization of slavery by the Georgia Trustees in 1750, and the promise of free land to attract settlers. From 1755, after acquiring the colony from the trustees, the king selected some of the leading slaveholding immigrants to be members of the colony's executive council. One of these was Jonathan Bryan. He served on it until expelled for patriot activities in 1770. The council regulated Georgia's land system and controlled its distribution: in the colonial period as a whole it handed out one million acres. The skills of the white pioneers in Georgia, who became its first families, were, as they had been in Tidewater Virginia a century before, those of physical strength and stamina, ability in map reading and surveying, shrewdness in judging location – rice needed steady supplies of fresh water, and rivers that gave access to the sea – political influence, patronage, the readiness to commit a labor force of cowboys and fieldhands, sawyers and carpenters, to clear forests and drain swamps, and not least, to know how to market the crop that the colony grew.

When in the 1770s, all the other councillors stayed loyal to the Crown (though their sons were almost always patriot), Bryan became a patriot. Not that he saw any community of interest with the theorists or merchants of the north. By that time, with a large family to endow, he was interested not only in his extensive holdings in South Carolina and Georgia, but in the land ceded by Spain beyond the Altamaha River; and in Florida too, where Britain had forbidden settlement under the Proclamation Act of 1763. He had already left one colony for another. His loyalty was to his land, and the prospect of more, to his purse, and to his property and his pride in it.

Georgia was the first of the southern states to ratify the Constitution in 1788; it assumed its present boundaries in 1802.

7

The Colonial Golden Age

1 HOW 'GOLDEN' THE AGE?

It took the Chesapeake colonies more than a decade before they learned to export what actually grew on local soil, and what proved to be the most effective complementary product of all, tobacco. As we have seen, the workforce was supplied by indentured laborers who after a 3- to 7-year spell of engagement to a master were entitled to freedom, plus a lump sum or landholdings of their own. Thus arose a unique economy, to which the only parallel was indeed the sugar economy of Brazil, equally riparian; but Virginia's tobacco demanded neither the skills nor the capital of Brazil. At the end of its second decade of existence, half of Virginia's population consisted of white male indentured servants; it was fortified by the "headright" system, whereby those responsible for the importation of a servant received 50 acres of land. Almost from its origins, Virginia's economy was more riparian and Iberian than English.

Nor was the English model binding in politics. The colony survived the starving times not by democracy or by liberalism but by vigorous and enlightened despotism, when the right leader was found — after trial and error. It survived thanks to John Smith, not to Edwin Sandys. When the time came that tried the soul as well as the body — in 1608–10, and again in 1776 — it was not summer patriots but dictators that were needed; and miraculously, then as later, found. Throughout the colonial period, everything would turn as much on the quality of the royal governors sent out as on the public spirit of the burgesses.

Yet the remarkable feature in the story of Virginia's origins is that, out of its sufferings, and within 20 years of its first ships reaching the Capes, it had attained a General Assembly. Its language became the rhetoric that heralded 1776. It owed much of its origin to an Englishman, Edwin Sandys, who went to the Tower as a dangerous liberal. But, on the floor of its debating assembly, it began to rehearse the arguments for controlling the purse and for curbing the king's vice-roy (and in 1634 "thrusting him out") before these became the familiar political issues in England itself.

Despite the brevity of its history, this was already a diverse and class-conscious society. The interior decoration of colonial houses differed according to region and social status. In New England the farmer's house contained furniture, kitchen utensils, and tableware that were home-made and functional, and ornamental, if at all, only incidentally. The Boston merchant and shipowner could afford silver plate, imported linens, and carved woodwork. The homes of the richer southern planters in the eighteenth century were lavishly, even extravagantly, furnished, frequently with objects brought from Europe.

There could, however, be no great diversity in food and drink. Rural householders had to be self-sustaining, relying for the most part on the produce of their own fields, or fish from the rivers. Because of the lack of refrigeration the winter diet tended to be monotonous, relying as it did upon salt meat and fish. The New England farmer had to buy his salt, molasses, spice, tea, coffee, and rum. Cane sugar was a luxury to most of the rural folk, who sweetened their meals sometimes with maple sugar or honey but generally with molasses. Baking, churning and preserving, like weaving, were tasks for individuals in their own homes. The ordinary New England diet included salt pork, fish, baked beans, and Indian pudding; hoecake and baked pumpkins were popular features of the breakfast menu. Punch, beer, and cider were consumed in amazing quantities by New Englanders, and while the wealthier also drank imported Madeira, claret, port, and other wines, the poorer people managed to buy rum, most of it distilled in New England. According to one contemporary judgment, the rum was "so bad and unwholesome that it is not improperly called 'kill-devil'." In the South, according to resources, ham and succotash, cornbread and, at breakfast, hominy grits, were familiar – though the latter was not always especially welcome. For the poor – as Benjamin Franklin could remember of his childhood – breakfast and supper might be simply bread and milk. For him, membership of a rising gentry was marked when his wife surprised him at breakfast:

it was lucky for me that I had one as much dispos'd to industry and frugality as my self. She assisted me chearfully in my business, folding and stitching pamphlets, tending shop, purchasing old linen rags for the papermakers etc. etc. We kept no idle servants, our table was plain and simple, our furniture of the cheapest. For instance, my breakfast was for a long time bread and milk (no tea) and I ate it out of a twopenny earthen porringer with a pewter spoon. But mark how luxury will enter families, and make a progress, in spite of principle. Being call'd one morning to breakfast, I found it in a china bowl with a spoon of silver. They had been bought for me without my knowledge by my wife, and had cost her the enormous sum of three and twenty shillings, for which she had no other excuse or apology to make, but that she thought *her* husband deserv'd a silver spoon and china bowl as well as any of his neighbors. This was the first appearance of plate and china in our house, which afterwards in a course of years as our wealth increas'd augmented gradually to several hundred pounds in value.[1]

The popular rural drinks were cider, grog, milk punch or "cherry bounce," a combination of cherry wine and rum; farmers made their own beer, mead, brandy, and table wine; with brandy and rum as mixes, the South cultivated some potent brews, to which it gave exotic names like "bumbos," "slings," or "flips." And not only among Scots-Irish, whiskey was an all-but-universal beverage. James Madison, a scholarly and sober-minded man, regularly took a pint of whiskey for breakfast.

Urban fare was more sophisticated. Beef, mutton, and pork were staples; turkey, cod, salmon, oysters, and lobsters were so cheap that it was considered poor taste to serve them at a fashionable dinner. Bread was expensive, but of poor – and varied – quality; cheese usually both expensive and inferior. By the eighteenth century, tea and coffee were in use. Chocolate was fashionable in society, and city ladies on visits would carry their own tea-cups, saucers, and spoons. A traveller in Annapolis noticed a new dish served at the governor's house: "syllabub", which he diagnosed as ice-cream served with strawberries and milk: it was a favorite dish of Thomas Jefferson. At that level, madeira and rum punch were the fashionable brews. Not until the early eighteenth century were knives and forks common, although seventeenth-century notables like John Winthrop had their own personal sets. Country people were still apt to deride the table fork as an instrument "to make hay with our mouths."

For some 50 years colonial America has been seen as the "Golden Age" for women, despite the trials of the early decades, despite an

---

[1] Franklin *The Autobiography of Benjamin Franklin* ed. L. W. Labaree (New Haven, Yale University Press, 1964), p. 145.

aggressively male Puritan theology, despite the religious legal role of the paterfamilias, and the absence of the convent and of the cult of the Virgin. The high sex ratio gave women, it was said, a bargaining power in the marriage market, where their presence was seen as essential to a household's survival. This was especially so in Virginia and the Chesapeake, where male immigrants vastly outnumbered female, where mortality rates were high, where widowhood was frequent, where many widows were left with wealth as well as offspring, and few stayed widows for long. In colder and healthier New England, where marriages lasted longer and produced more children than in the South, and where the Church was more vigilant, marriages were longer-lasting and family stability more striking than in Old England; and, in the seventeenth century at least, divorce was all but nonexistent.

In colonial America, a women's work was done in the household and/or on the farm and her role was determined by her husband. Male dominance was further enhanced by intestacy laws as well as by wills that favored the eldest son, and by the legal authority of father over children and of master over servants and slaves. As population, and with it prosperity, grew, women's role did not alter much. Better quality household goods became available – but even in mid-eighteenth-century Massachusetts perhaps only half the households owned spinning-wheels or butter churns. Few had looms and wheels for wool or flax; but there was much inter-household barter in cheese and butter for woollens. And in the cities women found new roles as nurses or seamstresses, as shopkeepers, waitresses, or teachers. In the South, a wife became controller of house slaves and chief of a large domestic staff, a combination of factory overseer and community midwife, to say nothing of her role – often demanding and lengthy – as hostess. And in the North, as church membership declined, women's role and numbers in congregations grew steadily; religious and familial roles became closely linked. In all the colonies, but most of all in New England, the family was strengthened by strong laws punishing sexual offenses.

Women then as now were doctors, nurses, and soothmakers too; they were more willing than male physicians to borrow treatments from the Indians and black slaves. Women's "cookbooks," both the manuscript books kept by individuals and the printed books that might be purchased, contain recipes for medical remedies as well as for foods, including salves for sores, soothing syrups for sore throats, and even mixtures that it was fondly hoped would ward off such major killers as tuberculosis. Martha Washington, who had lost several relatives to that disease, prescribed "Capon Ale" as a cure: this was a combination of chicken soup and strong ale, no doubt more welcome to a dying patient than spices or leeches.

2 SLAVERY

In New York, and in the plantation South, a large labor force was an economic imperative — and for its first 80 years Virginia's labor force consisted more of indentured whites than slaves. By 1700, however, one-third of its population of some 60,000 was of indentured servants and slaves; of these, the slaves numbered some 6,000 — that is, 1 in 10 of its total population was black. The first blacks to arrive in British North America had been landed in Virginia in 1619; there were 19 of them, prisoners on a Dutch man-of-war. Their status was unclear. But in 1661, when the Virginia Assembly decided that children should follow the condition of their mothers, slavery as such was recognized and became hereditary. Its expansion was remorseless. The reason was simple, even frightening: the headright system ensured that land could be claimed in respect of all individuals imported, including slaves, and shipmasters could supply black people on the spot in return for tobacco and other produce. Moreover, in 1698 the Royal African Company had its monopoly cancelled. By 1700, slaves in Virginia had become the chief basis of the acquisition of title to land, and private enterprise flourished in the slave traffic. In 1700 the governor of Virginia reported that a slaver direct from Guinea had sold about 230 blacks in the York River area at the highest prices yet fetched: "There were as many buyers as negros, and I think that, if 2000 were imported, there would be substantial buyers for them." Acting governor Edmund Jenings in 1710 reported that practically no white servant had been brought in for decades. Within the next decade, Virginia's slave population doubled. By 1750 some 45,000 had reached Virginia: around 30 percent of the colony's total population, but nearer 50 percent in the Tidewater area between the York and the James River. The story of the growth of slavery was even more dramatic in South Carolina, where many of the early settlers were from Barbados, and brought their slaves with them. An economy of rice cultivation, followed by indigo, developed, and as slave numbers grew, so did land acquisition, the plantation system — and the rigor of the slave codes.[2]

---

[2] Warren M. Billings (ed.), *The Old Dominion in the Seventeenth Century: A documentary history of Virginia 1606–1689* (Chapel Hill, NC, University of

"Bondage is hoarse, and may not speak aloud." The effort to reconstruct the black experience from the ink and paper remnants left by the wealthier white men has been described as "a creative act," calling for "the skills of archaeologist, cultural anthropologist, historical demographer," and "perhaps most importantly, novelist." The answer for the most recent generation of historians has been to use the records of criminal courts, tax and census collectors, overseers of poor relief, and newspaper editors to assemble a collective portrait, composed of demographic and economic data; and to produce, firmly, a quantifier's history.

Twenty percent of the slaves died on the Atlantic crossing, on the "Middle Passage" – for they were now coming direct from Africa, from the infamous Guinea coast, Sierra Leone, and the Bight of Biafra, not now via the Caribbean. Many of them came first to South Carolina and were then shipped on. Probably another 20 percent died after their arrival, during the "seasoning." Family life was a rarity, since males outnumbered females by at least two to one. As their numbers grew, so also did fear of them; and with fear, savagery. One "unhappy effect of owning many Negroes," wrote William Byrd, "is the necessity of being severe. Numbers make them insolent, and then foul means must do, what fair will not." [3]

Virginia codified its slave laws in 1705 (and its suffrage with it; only freeholders could vote, and not blacks, women, or Catholic recusants). By that time, quite small landowners were committed to slavery as an institution. In 1716, two-thirds of the taxpayers in Virginia's Lancaster County were slave-holders, though three-quarters of these had four blacks or fewer (only four planters had more than 20, though one of these, Robert Carter, may have owned over 120.) From 1691, Virginian law, which had previously borne hard on the practice, outlawed interracial sexual liaison completely as "abominable mixture." Up to 1676, there had been more free blacks in Virginia than at any time before Emancipation: race prejudice and legal discrimination were absent, and there appears to have been little psychological prejudice. There were even black slave-owners. This system changed, partly because of Bacon's Rebellion,

---

North Carolina Press, 1975), p. 210; Warren M. Billings, John E. Selby, and Thad W. Tate, *Colonial Virginia, a History* (New York, KTO Press, 1986), p. 123; Alan Kulikoff, *Tobacco and Slaves: The development of Southern cultures in the Chesapeake 1680–1800* (Chapel Hill, NC, IEAHC, University of North Carolina Press, 1986).

[3] Thomas P. Slaughter, "From slavery to Freedom, a review essay," *Pennsylvania Magazine of History and Biography*, 113.1 (Jan. 1989), p. 89 and its footnotes.

Plate 12   Landing Negroes at Jamestown from a Dutch Man o'War.
(The Mansell Collection, London.)

which was seen as a rising of slaves and servants, and which frightened the large landowners; and partly from the enormous expansion of the slave trade from the Caribbean and then Africa that took place in and after 1690. With this, the number of blacks bred fear, then repression, and then legal discrimination. Meanwhile, emancipation was frowned on. A Virginian law of 1699 required the exportation of every African freeman within six months of his emancipation, on penalty to the planter of a levy upon his own property.

Doctor John Brickell, writing of North Carolina in the 1730s, was explicit.

There are great numbers of them born here, which prove more industrious, honest, and better slaves than any brought from Guinea; this is particularly owing to their education amongst the Christians, which very much polishes and refines them from their barbarous and stubborn natures that they are most commonly endued with. I have frequently seen them whipt to that degree, that large pieces of their skin have been hanging down their backs; yet I never observed one of them shed a tear, which plainly shows them to be a people of very harsh and stubborn dispositions.

There are several laws made against them in this province to keep them in subjection, and particularly one, viz, that if a Negroe cut or wound his master or a christian with any unlawful weapon, such as a sword, scymiter, or even a knife, and there is blood-shed, if it is known amongst the planters, they immediately meet and order him to be hanged, which is always performed by another Negroe, and generally the planters bring most of their Negroes with them to behold their fellow Negroe suffer, to deter them from the like vile practice. This law may seem to be too harsh amongst us, to put a man to death for blood-shed only, yet if the severest laws were not strictly put in execution against these people, they would soon overcome the christians in this and most of the other provinces in the hands of the English.

Notwithstanding the many severe laws in force against them, yet they sometimes rise and rebel against their master and planters, and do a great deal of mischief, being both treacherous and cruel in their natures, so that mild laws would be of no use against them when any favourable opportunity offered of executing their barbarities upon the Christians, as hath been too well experienced in Virginia, and other places, where they have rebelled and destroyed many families ...

It frequently happens, when these women have no children by the first husband, after being a year or two cohabiting together, the planters oblige them to take a second, third, fourth, fifth, or more husbands or bedfellows; a fruitful woman amongst them being very much valued by the planters, and a numerous issue esteemed the greatest riches in this country. The children all go with the mother, and are the property of the planter to whom she belongs. And though they have no other ceremony in their Marriages than I have represented, yet they seem to be jealously inclined, and fight most desperately amongst themselves when they rival each other, which they commonly do.

There are abundance of them given to theft, and frequently steal from each other, and sometimes from the Christians, especially rum, with which they entertain their wives and mistresses at night, but are often detected and punished for it.[4]

A traveller in Boston in 1687, commenting on the scarcity of white labor there, alleged that every household, "however small may be its Means," had one or two blacks. But the governor reported in 1708 that of 550 blacks in Massachusetts altogether, 400 were in Boston. A Massachusetts Act of 1705 "for the Better Preventing of a Spurious and Mixt Issue," imposed a duty of £4 a head on all blacks imported.

The wife of a Boston merchant, Sarah Kemble Knight, who travelled through Connecticut in 1704, wrote sharply that the people there were "too Indulgent (especially the farmers) to their slaves: sufering too great familiarity from them, permitting them to sit at Table and eat with them, (as they say to save time), and into the dish goes the black hoof as freely as the white hand." Benjamin Franklin in Philadelphia advertised slave sales in his *Gazette*, and when he went to England in 1757 took two slaves with him. When one ran away, and the lady to whom he offered his services reported the event to Franklin, he urged her to keep him, hoping that he would be more useful to her than he ever had been to him.

At first planters opposed the Christianization of their African slaves, fearing that it might lead to emancipation; but their misgivings were relieved by the hard-headed bishop of London, who assured them that, for the Negro, Christianity and slavery were perfectly compatible. Indirectly and unwillingly, the Negro was also influential in causing toil to be looked upon in the South as degrading; in contrast to the more characteristically American tradition of the dignity of labor, there developed in Southern minds a strong tendency to think of work as something befitting only an "inferior" race. Slavery was not unknown in the Northern colonies, but there the economic system, as well as the more democratic atmosphere, acted as a moderating force.

The Negroes brought their own culture from Africa; their dances, worksongs, religious music, and superstitious lore were transplanted

[4] John Brickell, MD, *The Natural History of North Carolina* (1740), pp. 272–5.

virtually intact to the New World, where they became a notable cultural influence. They brought their own skills also. South Carolina and Georgia rice plantations relied heavily on the technical knowledge of the slaves from the "Rice Coast" of West Africa, where sluices, banks, and ditches for the cultivation of wet rice were centuries old. Its best evidence is in the Gullah spoken in the Sea Islands off the Carolina/Georgia coast, and the West African words that survive. Eighteenth-century slave society, however, was not now mainly foreign-born. By 1740 only 17 percent of adult blacks in Virginia had arrived within the last decade; and the sex ratio was almost in balance. As plantations increased in size, the blacks on them lived in small villages, unlike whites living in distinctly separate and often widely scattered farms. The concentration of black settlement and closer ties of kinship bred an identifiable African-American culture, with its own American music and its revivalist religion – distinct, and to many whites as alarming as it was economically essential. And with improving conditions for the enslaved by mid-century came, paradoxically, increases in escape attempts.

Slavery became an issue in 1776, if only because the word was used by the colonists to describe the nature of their relationship with Britain, as in the Fairfax Resolves of 1774. It was, as to Jefferson when he drew up his first draft of the Declaration of Independence, easy if erroneous to ascribe to George III responsibility for bringing slaves across the Atlantic. But by that time, notably among the Memmonites and Quakers in Pennsylvania, and also at the instigation of Judge Samuel Sewall in Boston (*The Selling of Joseph*, 1701), there was already a considerable anti-slavery literature. The blacks, it was held, had an "equal Right unto Liberty" as the whites.

The first organization for blacks in the US – the African Society – was, like the first Anti-Slavery Society, founded in Philadelphia in 1787. (New York had its Manumission Society in the same year). Its two leading spirits, Absalem Jones and Richard Allen, intended it to give mutual aid to members in sickness, and to care for widows and fatherless children. When the yellow fever epidemic ravaged Philadelphia in 1790, blacks seemed to be less prone to it, and it was they who searched for the stricken, carried them to Stephen Girard's improvised hospital at Bush Hill, and buried the dead, white and black.

Prohibition of the slave trade came more easily in the North than the South, though enforcement was never easy. The trade was banned by Pennsylvania in 1773, and by Rhode Island and Connecticut a year later. After Independence a number of Northern states adopted measures to facilitate voluntary manumission: Delaware, New Jersey, and New York, followed, when they became states, by Kentucky and Tennessee. During the years of the War of Independence, all the Northern states except New York and New Jersey took steps to abolish slavery. Thanks to the inclusion in the Massachusetts constitution of 1780 of a declaration that all individuals were "born free and equal," a series of court decisions effectively destroyed slavery in Massachusetts.[5]

Of the population of the colonies as a whole in 1713, New England had approximately 110,000, the Middle Colonies (New York, New Jersey, Pennsylvania, and Delaware) some 73,000, and the South 157,000: some 350,000 in all, of which approximately 1 in 10 was black. In the eighteenth century there was a great increase, by which the total population doubled itself roughly every 20 years. Although immigration was appreciable, the increase was mainly due to the multiplication of the pioneer stocks in an environment which offered cheap land, a healthy climate and good trading facilities. By 1776 it was over 2.57 million, of whom half a million were blacks, and 100,000 or less were Native Americans. By 1790, at the first census, it was 3,929,214 of whom 757,208 were Negroes (two out of three of them in the Chesapeake colonies); and by that time there were only 1,500 Indians, of all tribes, in all Pennsylvania.

While recent research has demonstrated that there were indeed poor and disadvantaged in colonial America, it has not been able to rebut the emphasis of all contemporary foreign observers, as of Americans who had seen Europe themselves, that the British North American colonies were, as William Allen had said, "the best poor man's country in the world." And as the eighteenth century wore on, the economy of British America became more prosperous, not less. Led by a growing demand for colonial exports, linked to an expanding commercial empire, protected and promoted by a strong imperial system, and endowed with an abundance of natural resources, the colonies prospered. Except in the area of defense, they were "able to operate without a considerable metropolitan subsidy." Moreover, with "the obvious and crucial exceptions of black slaves and native Americans, groups whose members paid a frightful price for white society's well-being," this prosperity was "widely shared." The years just before the American revolution were a "Golden Age," in which free white colonists were better off not only than their predecessors in the colonies or than most of their contemporaries

[5] Elizabeth Donnan (ed.) *Documents Illustrative of the History of the Slave Trade to America* (1930; repr. New York, Octagon Books, 1965), vol. III, pp. 17–26; Carl Bridenbaugh, *Cities in the Wilderness* (New York, Ronald, 1938), p. 49.

elsewhere in the world, but also than their descendants were to be again for some time to come.[6]

This development was the product of pull-and-push: for the first century the pull of external markets and of the shape given by the Navigation Acts, for the second the push of mounting population pressures. Trade, overwhelmingly the Atlantic trade, was dominant. At the beginning of the eighteenth century, the colonial economy represented only 4 percent of that of the mother-country; on the eve of Independence it was one-third. By that time too its population constituted one-third of that of Britain. As Franklin recognized, if this growth of numbers and output continued, "the empire on this side" would surpass "the empire on that side."

3   EDUCATION

The Scots-Irish made three distinct contributions to colonial America: they settled the frontier; they founded the Presbyterian Kirk for it; and they built its schools. Most of these were church schools where little was taught beyond the rudiments – reading, writing, arithmetic, and spelling. The Bible was the usual daily reader, and the Shorter Catechism was recited by all the school every Saturday morning. These early schools were rough log-cabins, with benches and tables made of split logs. Pens were made of goose quills, but there were no blackboards, slates, or pencils.

If religion was basic, so was civic virtue. Without it, the republic would not survive. Such was a constant theme of John Adams and James Madison; so too with David Ramsay, the South Carolina physician and the Revolution's first historian, who lamented the "declension of our public virtue." Liberty and independence had given rise to "Pride, Luxury, dissipation and a long train of unsuitable vices."[7]

Jefferson, keen to produce an aristocracy of the talented, outlined in his *Notes on the State of Virginia* a system of local district schools, and of county grammar schools, headed by the College of William and Mary. At each stage in an individual's growth, there was no pretense of the equality of bodies or of minds; the purpose was that the "best geniuses will be raked from the rubbish." His life-long but

[6] John McCusker and Russell R. Menard, *The Economy of British America 1607–1789* (Chapel Hill, NC, University of North Carolina Press, 1985), pp. 51, 8.
[7] David Ramsay, *History of the American Revolution* [1790], ed. Lester H. Cohen (Liberty Fund, Indianapolis, 1985).

unattained objective was the creation of a Federal University as the crown of the system; his last years were spent in planning and building what is still the most beautiful campus in the world, the University of Virginia in Charlottesville. And only the best-equipped would rule: "That form of government is the best which provides the most effectually for a pure selection of ... natural aristoi, into the offices of government."[8] The most important educational influence on Jefferson was his teacher at William and Mary, William Small, an Aberdonian, who taught mathematics and natural philosophy (i.e. physics), but who did not stay long in Williamsburg. He was not the only Scot, however, who left his imprint on the shaping of colonial education. Scottish influence was the strongest of all.

The first of the schools of higher grade to be established by the Scots-Irish was the "Log College," founded in 1726 by the Rev. William Tennent, Sr, at Neshaminy, 20 miles north of Philadelphia. This school was the first institution founded by American Presbyterians designed to educate young men for the ministry. Its founder was Irish-born, a cousin of James Logan, a graduate of Edinburgh University in 1695, and a minister in the Established Church of Ireland. It was not in any sense a college (it had no charter and gave no degrees), but an academy, in which Greek, Latin, and the "arts and sciences" were taught, along with theology. Tennent taught all the classes himself, and preached on Sunday, and he earned the title of "Hell-fire Tennent." He and his son Gilbert were leaders in the Great Awakening, the religious fervour that swept the frontier, and revivalists with an emotional zeal that gave Presbyterianism its "New Side" or "New Light" character.

A contemporary description of Gilbert Tennent in the pulpit conveys the character and power of such preaching at the peak of the Great Awakening: "He seemed to have no regard to please the eyes of his hearers with agreeable gesture, nor their ears with delivery, nor their fancy with language; but to aim directly at their hearts and consciences, to lay open their ruinous delusions, show them their numerous secret, hypocritical shifts in religion, and drive them out of every deceitful refuge wherein they made themselves easy, with the form of godliness without the power." The responses to Tennent's preaching are legendary. Members of a congregation would weep, sob, and cry out in terror, falling to their knees and calling for salvation. And his younger brothers, John and William, literally sank

---

[8] Letter to John Adams, October 28, 1813, in Saul Padover (ed.), *The Complete Jefferson* (New York, Sloane and Pearce 1943), p. 283.

into comas – with William actually pronounced dead by a physician and prepared for burial – before reviving to report the indescribable beauty of the conversion experience.[9]

Despite this, the College, which was supported entirely by fees paid by its students, had distinguished alumni, one of whom, Samuel Finley, became president of Princeton, and another of whom, John Blair, "held the fort" until Witherspoon came. The Log College was the germ from which Princeton (then known as the College of New Jersey) developed.

Princeton – decisively Presbyterian and Scottish in character – was set up to provide a non-denominational higher education, in which ministerial training, however prominent, would be incidental. Yale was to some extent the model as regards instruction and textbooks; and the English dissenting academies, with their pronounced trend towards the natural sciences, as well as their evangelical tone, were a source of inspiration. But the College languished for 20 years under five presidents, whose short incumbencies were a prime cause of weakness. Of these the first three – Jonathan Dickinson, Aaron Burr and Jonathan Edwards – were New Englanders and Yale graduates, while the next two, Samuel Davies and Samuel Finley, were "Log College men;" stability and, with it, renown came under the sixth president, John Witherspoon, imported from Scotland in 1768.

Yet it was set on course by Witherspoon's predecessors, before he was induced to leave Paisley; and that course was as a national institution. Of its 338 students in its first 20 years, only 89 came from New Jersey, at a time when 90 percent of Harvard men came from Massachusetts, 75 percent of Yale men from Connecticut and almost all William and Mary students were Virginians. There are many reasons for this. The College of New Jersey was a product of the Great Awakening, and there moved to it "New Light" Congregationalists dissatisfied with Harvard and Yale, and "New Side" Presbyterians from the Middle Colonies. Its central location made it easily accessible – as a fleeing Continental Congress was to find during the British advance on Philadelphia a little later. It was readier to admit students to Advanced Standing than were Harvard or Yale, and its tuition and residence costs were lower than theirs. And, as

[9] Thomas Prince, Jr, *The Christian History, Containing Accounts of the Revival and Propagation of Religion in Great Britain and America &c. for the Years 1744–5*, vol. II (Boston, S. Kneeland and T. Green, 1745), p. 385, cited in Lawrence A. Cremin, *American Education: The colonial experience 1607–1783* (New York, Harper and Row, 1970), p. 317.

the young and ailing James Madison would have added, its climate was bracing, whereas that of Williamsburg was malaria-ish.

Unlike Harvard and Yale, Princeton's students were not conspicuously younger than today's: the average age of graduation was 20–21. And the overwhelming number did graduate: of Princeton's 338, only 25 seem not to have done so, at a time when almost half of Oxford's students left without a degree, and almost no-one at William and Mary graduated. The school was – to use today's jargon – "pre-professional;" of the 338, 158 became clergymen (97 Presbyterian and 41 Congregational, including among the latter the distinguished missionary to the Oneida and the Seneca, Samuel Kirkland); 44 became medical men, including that distinguished and cantankerous friend of all mankind, Benjamin Rush; and 49 became lawyers, including Tapping Reeve, Oliver Ellsworth, and Luther Martin. It could almost be claimed that the Great Compromise of 1787, whereby in the Constitution representation in the Senate was by states and in the House of Representatives by population, was a product of the Princeton Class, of 1766: nine members of the Continental Congress were Princeton men.

The extraordinary role that these men played in the life of their times was due not only to their industry and ability, but to their remarkable geographic dispersal. Not many went back to their place of origin. They were to be found in all the states, notably on the frontier and in the West Indies, where Hugh Knox was to play a decisive role when he advised the precocious West Indian, Alexander Hamilton, to go north, young man. Clearly Princeton (like contemporary Edinburgh, though for more obvious reasons) was Whig: only 8 of the 338 became Loyalists, and not one of them was born in Britain – whereas a Harvard man might boast (or according to taste, regret) that of the 1,224 Harvard alumni living in 1775, no fewer than 196 took the British side. By contrast, 88 of these 338 Princeton men fought for the United States, 21 served in the Continental Congress, 4 became senators, 2 became governors, two became Supreme Court justices, and one a chief justice. One of Witherspoon's students, Aaron Burr Jr, became a vice-president, and another, James Madison, became the fourth president of the United States. Moreover, it bred institutions: no less than ten colleges were founded by Nassau Hall graduates and modeled on Princeton.[10]

---

[10] Washington College, Maryland (1782); Hampden-Sydney College, Virginia (1783); the University of Georgia (1785), the University of North Carolina (1789), Washington (1806) and Jefferson (1802) Colleges, situated only seven miles apart in western Pennsylvania, on the site of "log schools" dating back to the 1780s,

Princeton was not, of course, first chronologically. Harvard had been founded as a Congregational College in 1636, as a result of John Harvard's legacy. Had plans worked out for Henrico University and College, Virginia would have been first – but the Indian massacre of 1622 ended its dream. Near the end of the seventeenth century, in 1693, the Anglican College of William and Mary had been established in Virginia; and in 1701 Connecticut legislation had provided for the establishment of Yale University. The most noteworthy feature of America's educational history was the growth of a tax-supported public school system, free to all. To New England goes much of the credit for this contribution.

Harvard's total staff throughout the eighteenth century was a president, a professor of mathematics, and four tutors, and by the time of the Revolution its enrolment was about 180; Yale had 170, and Princeton 100. Franklin's father wisely decided not to put him in for Harvard, partly because it was too expensive, partly because of "the mean living many so educated were afterwards able to obtain." And Franklin's Silence Dogood has little that is kind to say about it. Her contemporary portrait is frank:

Riches and Poverty kept the gate, and Poverty rejected those whom Riches did not recommend. Within the temple Learning sat on a high throne reached by difficult steps. Most of the worshippers contented themselves to sit at the foot with Madam Idleness and her maid Ignorance ... "Every beetle-skull seemed well satisfied with his own portion of learning, though perhaps he was e'en just as ignorant as ever." Once out of the temple, "some I perceived took to merchandising, others to travelling, some to one thing, some to another, and some to nothing; and many of them from henceforth, for want of patrimony, lived as poor as church mice, being unable to dig and ashamed to beg, and to live by their wits it was impossible ..."[11]

Puritanism had one other major effect. If it needed colleges for its supply of teachers of the Word, it needed schools to feed those colleges. Male literacy ran at the rate of 60 percent in 1660, rose to 70 percent in 1710 and reached 85 percent in 1760 (though it

---

and united as Washington and Jefferson in 1865; and, in what is now Tennessee, Davidson Academy (1785), which eventually grew into the University of Nashville; Tusculum College, at Greeneville (1794); Blount College (1794), which finally became the University of Tennessee, and Newark College, the germ of the University of Delaware.

[11] *The Papers of Benjamin Franklin*, ed. L. W. Labaree, vol. I, (Newhaven, Yale University Press, 1959), p. 16.

was much lower for women). In Virginia 60 percent of the population could read in 1710, and this proportion held until the 1790s. [12]

In the South, the farms and plantations were so widely separated that community schools like those in the more compact settlements were impossible. Perhaps some still agreed with Governor Berkeley: "I thank God there are no free schools nor printing [in Virginia], and I hope we shall not have these [for a] hundred years." [13] Planters sometimes joined with their nearest neighbors and hired tutors to teach all the children within reach. The children of wealthy planters were sent to England for schooling, but this ceased in 1776, in part because with the end of entail it became impossible to afford it. "But why send an American youth to England for education?" – so Jefferson rationalized the consequences of his philosophy – "If he goes to England he learns drinking, horse-racing and boxing. These are the peculiarities of English education."

William and Mary itself was Scotsman James Blair's achievement. Blair was an Anglican clergyman, a student at Marischal College, Aberdeen, and a graduate of Edinburgh, whom the Bishop of London sent over as his commissary, and who for over half a century remained the head of the established Church in Virginia, and a powerful figure in Virginia politics. He it was who instituted far-reaching reforms in the clergy, securing for them better salaries, filling vacant parishes with men of piety and ability, and insisting upon a better observance of the liturgy. When he returned to the colony after securing a charter for the College and a grant of money from the Crown – £2,000 sterling, plus 20,000 acres of land plus the revenue of 1d per lb on Virginia's and Maryland's tobacco exports – he brought with him plans for the main building drawn by Sir Christopher Wren. Blair himself was president of the College for many years. Blair made himself a power in the colony, chiefly through the influence of the great English prelates. He quarreled with three successive governors and his power was such that it was they who were removed, not him. The planter aristocracy were inclined to snub him as an upstart, but they did so at their peril, for he won victory after victory over them. In the end, after he had married a

[12] Kenneth Lockridge, *Literacy in Colonial New England* (New York, Norton, 974).

[13] Or recalled Thomas Hobbes, who likened England's universities, and particularly one of them, to the wooden horse that destroyed Troy. Berkeley to the Commissioners of Trade and Plantations, in William Waller Hening (ed.), *The Statutes at Large; Being a collection of all the laws of Virginia, from the first session of the legislature, in the year 1619* (Richmond, 1819–23), II.517.

Virginia lady of good family, Sarah Harrison, the First Families of Virginia took him to their hearts. He failed to reform the Church. Perhaps in the end he had ceased to want to. He died, aged 87, and as William Gooch wrote, he left £10,000; to the great comfort of his nephew, his heir;

A rupture he has had above 40 years concealed from everybody but one friend, mortified and killed him. If his belly had been as sound as his head and breast, he might have lived many years longer.[14]

Blair's college, like Samuel Johnson's King's College, NY (later Columbia), moved steadily from Tory to Whig in sentiment. The most enterprising of the colonies in the educational sphere, however, was Pennsylvania, for Quaker as well as Presbyterian reasons. The first school, begun in 1683, taught reading, writing, and the keeping of accounts. Thereafter, in some fashion, every Quaker community provided for the elementary teaching of its children. In spirit, this early Quaker development owed more to the frontier than to the urban East, and reflected the origin of the Society of Friends as an English Civil War and dissenting creed, which, like the Ranters, the Millenarians, and the Anabaptists, derided the professional clergy, preached a religion of the poor, and prayed for inspiration and the "Inner Light;" it did not depend on doctrine or even on learning. Universities, to the Digger leader Gerrard Winstanley, were but "standing ponds of stinking waters;" a liberal education did not in itself wrestle with man's addiction to sin. "Much reading," wrote William Penn, "is an oppression of the mind, and extinguishes the natural candle, which is the reason for so many senseless scholars in the World." "The Lord opened up to me that being bred at Oxford or Cambridge was not enough to fit and qualify men to be ministers of God," said the Quakers' founder, George Fox.[15]

More advanced training – in classical languages, history, literature – was offered at the Friends Public School, which still exists in Philadelphia as the William Penn Charter School. The school was free to the poor, but parents who could were required to pay for tuition for their children.

The intellectual and cultural development of Pennsylvania came almost a century after the founding of Harvard, and reflected the

[14] For Blair, see D. E. Motley, *Life of Commissary James Blair* (Baltimore, Johns Hopkins University Press, 1901), and Cremin, *American Education*, pp. 334–8.
[15] William W. Sweet, *Religion in Colonial America* (New York, Scribner's, 1953), p. 161; Cremin, *American Education*, p. 305.

vigorous personalities of four men; it too owed much to Scotland. One of these was James Logan, the Scots-Irish Quaker, secretary of the colony, at whose fine library young Benjamin Franklin found the latest scientific works. There is no doubt, however, that Franklin himself contributed more than any other single citizen to the stimulation of intellectual activity in Philadelphia. He was instrumental in creating institutions which made a permanent cultural contribution, not only to Philadelphia, but to all the colonies. As a result of his endeavors, a public academy was founded which developed later into the University of Pennsylvania. As in his essays, the Silence Dogood Papers, written when he was 16, so later, he scorned Harvard snobberies and its collegiate undergraduate character; he preferred that the College of Philadelphia be "utilitarian rather than cultural." It should teach mathematics, geography, history, logic, and natural and moral philosophy. It should be an education for citizenship, and should lead to mercantile and civic success and usefulness. In this Franklin was following the utilitarian educational values of early Quakerism. His secular and scientific spirit explains the emphasis laid on English studies, the aim of providing a practical preparation for citizenship, and its avoidance of any sectarianism or religious discrimination. Through Whitefield he had been impressed by what he had heard of the schools for Dissenters at Northampton, England, where the teaching of English was placed on equal footing with that of the classics. In his *Proposals* of 1749 Franklin made his case, though he recognized the extent of the existing preference for what he called ornamental rather than useful training. By 1750 £15,000 had been raised by private subscriptions, public lotteries, and city grants, and classes began in the Academy in 1751. Four years later, it was chartered as the College of Philadelphia. It consisted of two departments, the English School, which was the heart of Franklin's proposals, and the Latin School, to which he had in effect consented for the increased support its presence might bring to the whole.

Ironically enough, it was Franklin himself who was largely responsible for the two remarkable appointments that contributed most to this overdevelopment of the classical curriculum. Both of them were Scots. Francis Alison, Presbyterian divine and the finest classical scholar in America, took charge of the institution upon the death of David Martin in 1752, moving from New London to do so. The appointment a year later of the ardent and aggressive Anglican William Smith as rector finally cemented the supremacy of the classics. He, more than anyone else, Franklin later charged, shifted emphasis from the English to the Latin School, which after 1755 was taken under the wing of the College of Philadelphia, and served as a feeder to it. Yet in fact Smith was as much the founder of what grew into the University of Pennsylvania as Franklin himself, and, despite their later quarrels, deserves as much credit as Old Dr Doubleface. And, like many Scots (in those days), he equated godliness with a knowledge of Latin and Greek.

Smith was a force second only to Franklin in the intellectual life of the city. In 1757 he established *The American Magazine and Monthly Chronicle*, the only literary periodical in America that enjoyed financial success before the Revolution, and served as editor for many years. He raised no less than £17,000 for the College when he visited Britain ten years later. But in all his zeal and energy he was arrogant, ill-tempered when opposed, something of an intriguer. John Adams, no kind diarist about anybody, described him as "soft, polite, insinuating, adulating, sensible, learned, industrious, indefatigable; he has art enough, and refinement upon art, to make impressions." From the day of his appointment he intrigued, both openly and in secret, to bring the College completely under Anglican control. As a result, he found it impossible to keep out of local politics. As early as 1756 Benjamin Franklin wrote in exasperation to Whitefield that he wished Smith would "learn to mind Party-writing and Party-Politicks less, and his proper Business more." As the years passed the haughtiness, and the avarice, increased; so did the profanity and the addiction to strong drink.[16]

There were signs, then, of cultural as well as political ferment at work in Franklin's Philadelphia. This was evident in the group in the next generation that gathered around Rittenhouse, the Peales and the Bartrams, artists and geologists, of whom Franklin, and later Jefferson, were the leading spirits. Charles Brockden Brown of Philadelphia appeared as the first professional novelist and man of letters in the country, publishing *Wieland* in 1798, and following this in rapid succession with *Ormand*, *Edgar Huntley*, *Arthur Mervyn*, *Jane Talbot*, and *Clara Howard*, all works of a Gothic and macabre character. In journalism, a field in which the Scots-Irish were later to excel, John Dunlap founded *The Pennsylvania Packet or General Advertiser* in 1771, a journal which appeared in 1784 as the first daily newspaper in the United States under the name of *The Pennsylvania Packet and General Advertiser*. Another eminent Scots-

---

[16] John Adams to Abigail, in L. H. Butterfield (ed.), *The Book of Abigail and John, Selected Letters* (Cambridge, MA, Harvard University Press, 1975)), p. 125; Franklin to George Whitefield, July 2, 1756, Franklin, *Papers*, ed. Labaree, vol. VI (1963), p. 468.

Irishman of this era was David Ramsay, a native of Lancaster County, Pennsylvania, who later removed to South Carolina. Ramsay was the author of a *History of South Carolina*, *History of the Revolution in South Carolina*, *History of the American Revolution*, and *Life of Washington*, winning fame as one of the most distinguished historians of his time.

One other aspect of Scottish influence must be mentioned: the Edinburgh Medical School. Here again, indirectly, Franklin was the link. In 1761 he visited Scotland, and the first outgrowth of his Scottish tour was the advent of the brilliant succession of American medical students who went to Edinburgh University, largely at his suggestion, including John Morgan, destined to be founder of the medical school of the University of Pennsylvania. Edinburgh became the academic Mecca for transatlantic medical students, just as the Middle Temple in London already was for practitioners of the law. Oxford and Cambridge were ineligible: at least in form they required a profession of Anglicanism, i.e. Episcopalianism, in students and Fellows.

From 1749, when John Moultrie of South Carolina was made a Doctor of Medicine of the University of Edinburgh, to the close of the century, no fewer than 117 Americans received the medical degree of that institution alone; while uncounted others, like Thomas Parke, Samuel Powel Griffiths, and Benjamin Smith Barton, studied there. By the 1780s nearly 500 students of medicine were in the city — John R. B. Rodgers in the spring of 1785 said that Dr Munro had 399 in his anatomy class alone — and of this number there were always 15 or 20 Americans, usually two or three of them from Philadelphia.

At the beginning of the American Revolution, all the Scottish graduates in America, except Dr Bard of New York who remained true to the Crown, enlisted in the patriot army. From the student body, if not from the faculty, they imbibed more than a knowledge of anatomy and pharmacy. Yet a singular destiny attended their military careers. Potts, broken in spirit and body by his unappreciated services with the Northern Army at Ticonderoga, came back to a premature death in Reading. Rush resigned his commission in 1778 after a series of quarrels with his departmental chiefs — the evidence of a pride in his own talents that was to mark his long career. Shippen was court-martialed for alleged irregularities in his military hospital. Morgan was displaced through the intrigues of an ignoble cabal in the Congress. Perhaps the aggrieved professors at the Edinburgh Medical School saw in these calamities the visitations of a Calvinistic deity outraged at the traitorous misapplication to Revolutionary purposes of knowledge obtained in a guid Scots college?

Reduced to individuals, this could have been the story of Commissary Blair in Virginia, of William Smith in Pennsylvania, and of John Witherspoon in New Jersey – two of them, be it noted, Anglicans, and two of them (the same two) Aberdonians. It is in fact a Presbyterian and a Scottish story. The British Army in the Revolution burned Presbyterian churches as "sedition-shops," and consigned to the flames, as texts of rebellion, all Bibles with Scottish versions of the Psalms. Moreover, if there was one decisive influence on Benjamin Franklin in Britain, it was the liberal dissenting critical spirit of his Scottish friends – royal physician Sir John Pringle, Lord Kames, Adam Smith, David Hume, Principal Robertson, and his friend and printer William Strahan, whom he called "Straney." If some of these men were themselves, of course, largely Tories, the climate of opinion in which they moved was critical, dissenting, and challenging. As much as the Puritans, the Presbyterians saw society as shaped by God's purposes, and of that mission they saw themselves as the leading crusaders. Hume was pro-American; Kames had much sympathy; Smith favoured free trade and an experiment in federalism; Boswell even differed from Johnson on America. "Orthodox" or "Evangelical" Church opinion was pro-American; the Rev. Charles Nisbet of Montrose followed his friend Witherspoon to America in 1785, to become president of Dickinson College. Political Scotland, the Scotland of Bute, Dundas and Lord Adam Gordon, was solidly Tory. Most of its Edinburgh and Aberdeen academics, aware of the need for butter on their bread, were the same, including Principal Robertson. But the mood among the students they taught was Radical and dissenting, and for this one other name must be mentioned; Francis Hutcheson, graduate of and professor at Glasgow University. He had a host of friends and followers in America, as in Scotland. He was propounding in Glasgow a theory of the right of resistance to tyranny 40 years before 1776. His works appear in Smith's plans for the College of Philadelphia, and Francis Alison was dictating to students passages from Hutcheson in 1759 and 1760. His writings became set books at Yale. And he lectured not in Latin but in English – a point Franklin noted, and which his own university copied.

The ideas behind Independence came at long remove from the English Civil War of the seventeenth century, as expressed by Locke and Milton, Sidney and Harrington, and by the Scot Thomas Gordon in alliance with the West Country squire John Trenchard, whose *Independent Whig* and *Cato's Letters* were read keenly in the colonies.

They had been voiced too by the Protestant Dissenting Deputies, the powerful eighteenth-century nonconformist lobby, and not least by Scots who had only been constitutionally linked to England in 1707, and were still questioners of the merits – and the nature – of the Union. Each country, Scotland and America, was – to use Adam Ferguson's imagery – in transition from a "rude" to a "polished" state. Each developed New Towns – Edinburgh, Boston, Philadelphia – with clubs and learned societies, and a sophisticated understanding of men's environment. In the shadow of Newton, the Scottish philosophers, with their secular proclivities, developed new sciences that would now be called "social," as well as new skills in medicine. When Franklin paid his visits to France in the 1760s, he was following in Adam Smith's and David Hume's footsteps. Moreover, the Clyde valley and Glasgow were growing, less because of the Union of the Parliaments than because of the tobacco weed, and in economic terms looked west rather than south. Thus America was in the foreground of all Scottish political debate, and vice-versa. The transatlantic ties were closer than ever. Witherspoon spoke a language almost identical with that of Jefferson:

> If they [the laws] are found to be pernicious and destructive of the ends of the union, they [the people] may certainly break up the society, recall their obligation, and resettle the whole upon a better footing ... But this is only when it becomes manifestly more advantageous to unsettle the government altogether, than to submit to tyranny.[17]

The language of liberty, however, was not Scots, whether Gaelic or Lallans, but Latin – or even Greek. Moreover, it was a special Latin: the language and the texts of Cicero and Sallust, of Tacitus and Plutarch, writing when the great days of the republic were already gone, and contrasting the corruption and conspiracies they saw around them with the glories of a virtuous past. This was thus a Latin and a republic obviously suited to parallel, and to warn of, the decline of Britain, a language of lamentation and nostalgia. The writing of all the founders was dotted with classical allusions, with references and proper names from republican – not imperial – Rome. Half the signatories of the Declaration of Independence had received a college education; were familiar, that is, with the history and languages of Greece and Rome – even if Jefferson was

---

[17] Martha L. L. Stohlman, *John Witherspoon: Parson, politician, patriot* (Philadelphia, Westminster Press, 1976), p. 75; Cremin, *American Education*, p. 465.

exaggerating when he said that American farmers were "the only farmers who can read Homer." Samuel Adams, "the Cato of New England," looked forward to the establishment of a "Christian Sparta" in Boston, and provided his Sons of Liberty with Latin slogans: *vis unita fortior* (Power is made stronger by unity). As Candidus in the *Boston Gazette* he warned that the principle embodied in the murder of Caligula "may prove as destructive to men who take the lead in a Commonwealth as to absolute monarchs." When Alexander Hamilton and Gouverneur Morris devised a code to keep their exchanges secret, Washington was "Scaevolo", Jefferson "Scipio" and Madison "Tarquin." When Washington himself, no classical scholar, ordered busts for his library at Mount Vernon they were of Sallust, Terence, Horace, and Erasmus; and he had Addison's *Cato* performed for his troops in their grim winter siege at Valley Forge.

Madison's language – like that of many of his colleagues – was Latin as much as English. His references in *The Federalist Papers* are frequently to the classics, not least to Polybius – the leading authority on the city–states of Ancient Greece, and as much an advocate of a system of checks and balances as was Montesquieu. For the debates in the Constitutional Convention in 1787 Madison had alongside him a specially prepared lexicon of "the beauties and defects of the ancient republics."

To sum up, the influence of Calvinism was profound. Of the nine colleges founded before the coming of Independence, five can be ascribed to Calvinism: the Congregationalists founded Harvard, Yale, and Dartmouth; the Presbyterians Princeton; and the Dutch Reformed, Rutgers; the Anglicans founded William and Mary, and King's College in New York (now Columbia); and the Baptists, Brown in Rhode Island. Harvard had offshoots of its own: Amherst, Williams and Bowdoin. Only Franklin's brainchild in Philadelphia came by another route, even if the Anglicans and the proprietary party took it over.

The Churches exercised censorship also. In Puritan New England and in Quaker Pennsylvania, for example, opposition to stage plays and other "frivolous entertainments" hampered the development of theaters until late in the colonial period. Although the Puritans showed a distrust of musical instruments for religious services even they sang psalms, and some of the German religious groups, notably Moravians in Bethlehem, Pennsylvania, and Salem, North Carolina, emphasized music in their worship.

Of the 207 institutions of higher learning in America founded before the Civil War, all save 27 (founded by state and municipal governments) were founded by religious groups. Of these 180 religiously founded institutions, 65, or about a third, were founded by the heirs of Calvinism; 49 by Presbyterians; 21 by Congregationalists; 4 by the German Reformed Church; and 1 by the Dutch Reformed Church. One must remember that Congregationalists on the frontier outside New England tended to become Presbyterians — that is, bureaucratically rather than class dominated. In settlement after settlement Presbyterian ministers founded academies, many of which grew into colleges, in order "to prepare the men who should feed the flock of God," as the Congregationalist-Presbyterian founders of Western Reserve University once put it. No wonder that by 1851 "two-thirds of the colleges in the land were directly or indirectly under the control of the Presbyterian Church." [18]

4 THE ENLIGHTENMENT

The Enlightenment reached the North American colonies in the eighteenth century, and had similar transforming effects there as in Europe. The beginnings, however, had came in the previous century. After its founding in London in 1662, the Royal Society enlisted correspondents in the colonies, and there were at least 25 American Fellows in the period before the Revolution. The first of these was John Winthrop, Jr, who was elected in 1663 for his interests in botany, chemistry, metallurgy, astronomy, and medicine. He disseminated scientific knowledge by lending books from his library, and his secret medical powder, "rubila," was in great demand for its supposed curative powers. Gershom Bulkeley of Glastonbury, Connecticut, a preacher turned physician, established his own laboratory in about 1666. In the South, William Byrd had scientific treatises in his excellent library, was elected to the Royal Society, and contributed a paper on an albino Negro.

Puritan preachers, fascinated by Newton's theories, made an effort to show the glory of God in the natural universe. The spacious firmament on high, in all its majesty, could proclaim its great original. In 1721 Cotton Mather in his *Christian Philosopher* argued

---

[18] Ronald G. Tewksbury, *The Founding of American Colleges and Universities before the Civil War* (New York, Archon, 1965), p. 92. Cf. E. Digby Baltzell, *Puritan Boston and Quaker Philadelphia* (Boston, Beacon Press, 1979), p. 4n. But it is worth stressing that even the Great Awakening, in all its hysteria, left an educational legacy: Vanderbilt, Emory, and Duke Universities all began as Methodist foundations.

that scientific research was required to unfold the mystery of God's creation; science was the instrument, not the enemy, of theology. A member of the Royal Society, Mather sent in voluminous reports on everything from snakes to rainbows, and demonstrated his own scientific faith by advocating inoculation for smallpox during the epidemic in Boston in 1721, and by writing the earliest known account of plant hybridization.

Natural history occupied the attention of many colonial observers. Perhaps the most famous were John Bartram (1699–1777) and his son William (1739–1823), Philadelphia Quakers, whose botanical garden on the Schuylkill River attracted the attention of botanists on both sides of the Atlantic. John Bartram was in frequent communication with naturalists in Europe and supplied them with specimens collected on his numerous expeditions to other colonies. The Swedish scientist Linnaeus called Bartram the greatest "natural botanist" of his day. The American correspondents of Peter Collinson, the Quaker merchant in London, are an index of the importance of New World botanists – John Parke Custis in Williamsburg; Dr John Mitchell the mapmaker and Fellow of the Royal Society; John Clayton the clerk of Gloucester County, Virginia, also Fellow, for his publication *Flora Virginica* of 1739; William Byrd II; Governor Francis Fauquier, another Fellow and a sponsor of Jefferson; and not least, of course, Benjamin Franklin.

The most versatile and gifted product of the colonial period was undoubtedly Benjamin Franklin, who, after one year's schooling in Boston, and a vigorous apprenticeship to printing and writing in his brother's shop with its "Honest Wags," ran away, to make Philadelphia his workshop, sounding-board, and pulpit. In 1727 he founded the Junto, a society concerned with investigation and self-improvement. In 1744 he helped organize the American Philosophical Society, dedicated to the "promotion of useful knowledge" but equally concerned with mathematics and "pure science." He set up a laboratory in his house, and after a series of experiments in electricity characteristically made a practical suggestion – the use of lightning rods to protect buildings. His treatise *Experiments and Observations on Electricity*, "made at Philadelphia in America by Mr Benjamin Franklin", was published in London in 1751. After its translation into French, German, and Italian, Franklin was hailed as an authentic American genius. This publication preceded by a year the famous experiment in which Franklin attracted lightning from the clouds with a kite. When he went to Paris as negotiator, ambassador, diplomat, and manufacturer of the alliance of 1778, his task was the easier because his reputation as a scientist from a wilderness preceded him.

"In his shrewdness, versatility, self-reliance, wit, as also in his lack of the deeper reverence and imagination," Franklin, "more than any other man who has yet lived, represents the full American character." "His strength lay in his temperance, justice and courage – eminently the pagan virtues." The verdict, damning with much praise, is that of Paul Elmer More; it could equally be that of Franklin's contemporary William Smith, of Thomas Carlyle, or of D. H. Lawrence. And, by contrast, "the lonely introverted, God-intoxicated soul of Jonathan Edwards stands as a solemn witness to depths of understanding in his countrymen which Dr Franklin's keen wit had no means of fathoming."[19]

The contrast between two Puritan-raised New Englanders born within three years of each other is familiar. One was the man of Reason and of the Market Street, who believed in putting knowledge to use: lightning rods, "the causes and cure of smokey chimneys," bifocal lenses, the handling of men in assemblies and persuading them to civic projects – a library, a hospital, a college, fire insurance, and street lighting. To the news-gatherer, pamphleteer, and editor, public office came naturally: burgess, colonial agent to England, and envoy to France. The other was the man of Revelation, the precocious Yale-trained son, grandson, and great-grandson of Congregational ministers, who never went abroad, never held public office, never did military service. In 1727 Edwards joined his grandfather, 82-year-old Solomon Stoddard, in his rural pulpit in Northampton, a small community of some 200 families which was held to be the largest congregation outside Boston. Two years later, on his grandfather's death (he had served as pastor for 65 years), he replaced him. Scandalized by what he saw as the licentiousness of the young, he wrote a series of philosophical works that applied eighteenth-century physical and psychological theories not to attack Calvinism but to reinforce it. Along with the itinerant Methodist preacher George Whitefield, and Gilbert Tennent in the Middle Colonies, he preached spell-binding sermons. When in July 1741 he preached to the theme "Sinners in the hands of an angry God" at Enfield, half his congregation writhed in agony at his feet, and children swooned in fear of "hell-fire and brimstone." It was, said Edwards, "a wonderful pouring out of the spirit of God."

The Great Awakening brought to the frontier a new religious style, evangelical pietism: the reiteration is of sin and redemption by the gift of grace, God is a Being of wrath but – unheralded – also

---

[19] Paul Elmer More, *Shelburne Essays* (Boston, Houghton Mifflin, repr. of 1922), vol IV, p. 152; *Benjamin Franklin* (Boston, Houghton Mifflin, 1900), pp. 2, 39, 63.

one of mercy, and the physical agony of conversion is evidence of the coming of his felicity. Edwards was dismissed by his own congregation, who deplored religion disguised as emotionalism; he then in 1751 became a missionary to the Indians in Stockbridge; in 1757, on the death of his son-in-law, Rev. Aaron Burr, he succeeded him as president of the College of New Jersey, only to die of smallpox in March 1758, shortly after being inoculated. In Franklin's age of reason, when everything was becoming open to analysis and explanation, Edwards dwelt on mystery, miracle, prophecy, and the depravity of men. Salvation was in God's hands, not man's. But perversely, he died a victim of modern science.

In their remarkable careers, so vividly different, the two men represent the two streams into which Puritanism flowed: Reason *versus* Revelation. The mystic was also the scholar: 13 hours a day of reading was Edwards's assignment to himself. Each wrote voluminously, each wrote an *Autobiography* (though Edwards called his a Personal Narrative), each, in very different ways, needed to confess. The contrast is total when Edwards's intense agonies of spirit are set against Franklin's wrestling with his own torments in his totally secular world, in Market Street, Philadelphia, Craven Street, London, or the salons of Paris, seeking "moral perfection" by calendaring 13 virtues, checking off all infractions, and admitting (at least to some of) his *errata*. Edwards, when he was 19, similarly drew up 70 Resolutions, which he charged himself to read once a week. But in contrast, Franklin did not torment himself too much because, as he reflected, "Self-Denial was not the essence of Virtue." Yet he could echo Edwards's gloomy view of human nature, and his doctrine that the core of virtue is benevolence; he saw poverty as a result of indolence, an individual not a social responsibility; at the Constitutional Convention in 1787 he proposed a salary-less chief magistrate for the new republic because, he said, the two strongest impulses in men are love of power and love of money, and to unite both power and money in the presidency would attract the greedy and the power-mad. Of all the Founding Fathers, his origins were the humblest, and he became the champion of unrestricted manhood suffrage, annual parliaments, and a unicameral legislature. He was unorthodox but not irreligious: he drew up a liturgy for his own private use (his *Articles of Belief* and *Acts of Religion*), which would climax in the singing of Milton's "Hymn to the Creator," and the reading of some book "discoursing on and exciting to Moral Virtue;" in 1773 he collaborated with Lord Le Despencer in revising the Anglican Book of Common Prayer; though not a regular church-goer, he gave financial support first to the Presbyterian, then to the

Episcopal, Church in Philadelphia, where he had a pew from 1760 until his death; "the Catholics", said John Adams, "thought him almost a Catholic, the Church of England claimed him as one of them; the Presbyterians thought him half a Presbyterian, and the Friends believed him a wet Quaker." He was none of these, but as a man of affairs, he cultivated all of them for his causes, which were usually also theirs. He had become in fact a Deist, who believed in God and immortality, but accepted neither the divinity of Christ nor the superiority of Christianity to other religions. His attitude was not that of a theologian but of a politician. Religion was useful to the state by inculcating morality; and "the best service toward God is doing good to men." He was not far from being the Unitarian who would be a feature of Boston in the next generation.

Tho' I seldom attended any Public Worship, I had still an opinion of its Propriety, and of its Utility when rightly conducted and I regularly paid my annual Subscription for the support of the only Presbyterian Minister or Meeting we had in Philadelphia. [20]

He was ready to accept the politician's view of religious faith, the view of that other Man of Reason, Gibbon, that, to the believer, all religions are equally true, to the philosopher equally false, to the statesman, equally useful.

The difference with Edwards lay as much in style as in substance. Franklin's writing was for Market Street – terse, shrewd and at times bawdy, for "squeamish stomachs cannot eat without pickles;" his favorite literary modes are the proverbs, the adages, the tall tales – many of them shamelessly annexed and rarely acknowledged ("Why should I give my readers bad lines of my own, when good ones of other people's are so plenty?") – or at best the Socratic dialogue. For him the Enlightenment meant the power of the mind expressed through the pen. Edwards, by contrast, stood in a pulpit or wrote in a study, and his vehicle was sustained philosophical exposition by a brilliant scholar, a student of Newton and Locke who was as good a scientist as Mather. He ranged as widely as Franklin: the nature of light waves, the saltness of the sea, the cause of the impact on the earth of the streams of particles that were discharged by heavenly bodies. For a treatise on the mind he listed 56 subjects for study, covering every branch of psychology. Yet when he wrote his *History of the Work of Redemption* (published in 1774), his is a

[20] Franklin, *Autobiography*, ed. Labaree, p. 147.

free retelling of Scripture, with miraculous events reported as if historical, with Adam and Eve, Cain and Abel, Noah and Moses, and the Bible cited as absolute and sufficient source. He ends with the end of time, the end of history, and the overthrow of Satan — who much of the time comes to him dressed as the popes. History ends for him with the triumph of the Hanoverians over papist France and Jacobite Britain. It is, in Peter Gay's words, "a thoroughly traditional book, and the tradition is the tradition of Augustine."[21] He was shy, solitary, unbending in his convictions, and utterly inept in handling people. He said of himself that he was "fitted for no other business but study."

When George Whitefield was driven to preach in the fields because he was denied permission to use their churches by many ministers in Philadelphia, Franklin set about raising funds to erect a building "about the size of Westminster Hall ... for the use of any preacher of any religious persuasion who might desire to say something to the people of Philadelphia ... so that even if the Mufti of Constantinople were to send a missionary to preach Mahometanism to us, he would find a pulpit at his service." He was as concerned with measuring the carrying power of Whitefield's voice as with listening to his message. When Whitefield thanked him for his offer of hospitality and told Franklin that "if I made that kind offer for Christ's sake, I should not miss of a reward," he replied, "Don't let me be mistaken; it was not for Christ's sake, but for your sake."[22]

If Edwards the theologian was "the last mediaeval American — at least among intellectuals",[23] Franklin the journalist, politician, and diplomat was an Arminian, and the last Anglo-American. The dream of a city on a hill faded as the secular world flourished. The Puritan, and the transatlantic and imperial, age was over.

---

[21] Peter Gay, *A Loss of Mastery: Puritan historians in colonial America* (Berkeley, CA, University of California Press, 1966), p. 64.

[22] Franklin, *Autobiography*, ed. Labaree, pt 3, p. 178; cf. *The Papers of Benjamin Franklin*, ed. Labaree, vol. II, 202–4.

[23] Gay, *A Loss of Mastery*, p. 116.

8

Why, Then, Independence?

Very few contemporaries in 1763 foresaw or predicted the likelihood of independence for the British Colonies. Of course, some French observers did hope for trouble. "Colonies are like fruits which cling to the tree only till they ripen." This was Turgot's view, but he was, as a Frenchman, inevitably wishing the worst to happen to Britain. Franklin – the most balanced and shrewd of observers – certainly foresaw a world in which the weight of population and of economic power would lie across the Atlantic, though he did not then want it to be a future of separate states. Franklin in the 1760s was an "Old England man" – as were the vast majority of Americans. They – colonists in America as well as British at home – were proud of victory in 1763. There was nothing automatic or inevitable about American independence; there is indeed nothing inevitable in history unless men and women will it so. To the argument that distance, population growth, and nationalism would sooner or later have made separation inevitable, one can but reply that (a) such thinking is nonhistorical – we can but deal with facts not suppositions; and (b) the same factors did not make Canada, in 1775 or later, fight a war for independence from Britain, despite American overtures to do so, and the Canadian-British relationship proved quite different from the US–British, because of the wills, and the diplomatic skill, of generations of political leaders. Enough to say that what led to the separation was due to men, and not to mysterious ineluctable "forces." In the real world it is never as easy as determinists like to think.

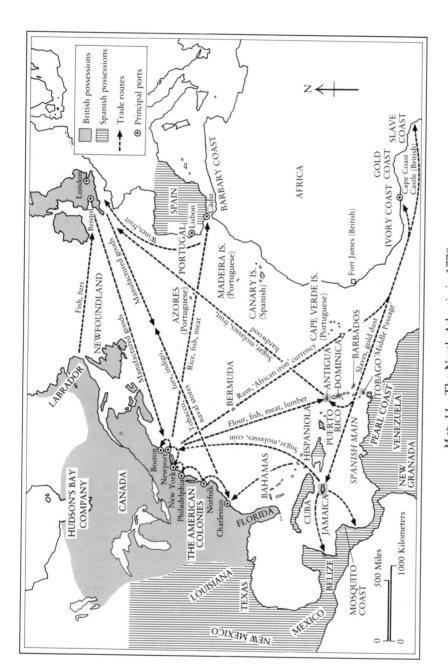

Map 11 The North Atlantic in 1770.

1 THE FRENCH AND INDIAN WAR
(1756–1763) AND THE FRONTIER STRUGGLE

The colonial war, though it did not quite end in 1763 – Pontiac was still to rebel – had not begun in 1756. In 1754–5 Washington had clashed with the French fort-builders in the Ohio country. When the preceding conflict in Europe, the War of the Austrian Succession (known in North America as "King George's War") ended in 1748, the treaty that concluded it saw the transfer back to France of Louisbourg, on Cape Breton Island, won with such colonial effort in 1745–6. So in 1748 there had been no frontier peace, and no reduction in British military involvement overseas: despite a nominal peace a garrison of 4,000 men costing on average about £95,000 a year was established in Nova Scotia, and the base set up at Halifax became the home of the Royal Naval squadron in North Atlantic waters. If individual acquisitions were to be, it seemed, so casually returned, the only course was total conquest of Canada; and Anglo-French war in (and for?) North America seemed a costly constant. The war that "ended" in 1763 was the fourth round in the Anglo-French struggle in the eighteenth century, and it proved to be a major step on the road to American independence: it provided a potential native military leader and one or two subordinates; it displayed Britain's strategical skills; it brought an uneasy peace to the Indian frontier, with the French now absentees; it confirmed the alliance of Britain with the Iroquois Confederacy, over which after 1763 it exercised wardship; and it made plain the importance of the St Lawrence, the control of which won the war, and of command of the sea – until the autumn of 1781, in every crisis Britain had complete command of the American approaches, and of the Atlantic. But few in 1763 foresaw the consequence: 1776.

The British colonies had been from the outset colonies of settlement, of *peuplement*; they had some 1½ million people, including Germans and Dutch, and by 1748 were all but self-sufficient in agriculture; they were – despite the Navigation Acts – developing a profitable and illegal foreign trade with the Caribbean, and beginning to develop a small-scale iron industry. In comparison, the French settlements had only some 60,000 people, almost entirely French, living in little more than primitive frontier posts, with an uncertain subsistence agriculture to support them; their profits came from beaver pelts and furs, and French-made trinkets were the sought-after currency among their Indian allies. The British settlements, though vulnerable along a long 1,000-mile frontier, were sheltered from

French and Indian raids by the Alleghenies, and were more compact
and self-contained than the much longer 2,000-mile area of French
exploration. The French had established the remote Illinois posts of
Fort St Louis and Fort Crevecoeur, Fort Miami on the Maumee and
Fort Vincennes on the Wabash, and, on the Mississippi, the fur-posts
of Cahokia and Kaskaskia; their flags flew in Fort Prudhomme,
Natchez, and New Orleans – all of them scattered forts, dependent
on river and forest trail for supplies, and on the uncertain and always
mercenary amity of the Indian tribes. Each French province – New
France (or Canada) and Louisiana – had its own governor and its
own intendant, the latter as financier exercising a check on the
former. Decisions were taken in Paris, not in Quebec or Montreal.

The best account of the French and Indian War, or, as L. H.
Gipson called it, the Great War for the Empire, is in the pages of
Francis Parkman's volume, *Mantcolm and Wolfe*, first published in
1841.[1] The world Parkman sought to describe was that of primitive Nature, of a continent as yet untamed; his concern was not
with the character of the white civilization on the frontier but rather
with the theme of civilization *versus* the frontier. The men who
were able to control this savage environment were, in his telling, great
men. This is not to say that Parkman's is a simplistic and personal
view of the historical process. He saw Nature, geography, and a certain "incarnate will and energy" as great and creative forces. Indeed,
in this book Wolfe hardly emerges as a "great man" in the accepted
sense. Parkman shows graphically that Wolfe's victory on the Heights
of Abraham in 1759 was in large measure the result of a series of
coincidences – by, among others, the chance that an obscure French
captain, whose task was to guard the path up the cliff, had sent his
men home the day before the landing. Without these, New France
"might have lived a little longer and the fruitless heroism of Wolfe
would have passed, with countless other heroisms, into oblivion." The
greatness lies not in victory but in the grandeur with which Nature,
and its inevitable conquest over man, is faced and fought. The am-
bush and defeat of Braddock and his 200 men at the Monongahela
in 1755 was as much at the hands of the forest and the Indian as
at the hands of Beaujeu, the French commander. And the victory
of Forbes in 1758 – like that of Amherst on Lake George and the
Hudson – was due to the unglamorous but remorseless destruction
of the forest itself. Not for the first nor the last time would it be
true to say that an army built a highway and they called it war;

---

[1] There are many editions. I have used the London (Eyre and Spottiswoode)
edition of 1964.

Fort Duquesne (Pittsburgh) was won not by the rifle but by the axe. And when Forbes's army of British regulars, with Washington and his Virginians leading its advance columns, reached the fort in 1758, they found it already abandoned, a smoking ruin. The wilderness had been the Indians' real ally. Now – and remorselessly over the centuries – it was at last to be destroyed. The long struggle on the North American continent, the effort to control the forest and the Indian as well as the French, is seen as an integral part of a great war for the Empire. Parkman's history is unashamedly a history of conflict, and perhaps only in our own time has it once again become acceptable to write of wars without omitting battles. Here Parkman is at his most graphic; Washington *versus* Jumonville at Great Meadows; Braddock's march and his disaster at the Monongahela in 1755; Montcalm's victories at Oswego and Fort William Henry; the capture of Louisbourg; Wolfe's climbing of the Heights of Abraham on the St Lawrence to give battle at Quebec; and, running through his account, a very modern secondary figure, an unheroic hero, Robert Rogers of the Rangers, more woodsman than soldier, part smuggler, part commando leader. His 180 frontiersmen-turned-marines fought, in 1758, "the battle on snowshores," and lost 130 of their number:

The best of them were commonly employed on Lake George; and nothing can surpass the adventurous hardihood of their lives. Summer and winter, day and night, were alike to them. Embarked in whaleboats or birch canoes, they glided under the silent moon or in the languid glare of a breathless August day, when islands floated in dreamy haze, and the hot air was thick with odors of the pine; or in the bright October; when the jay screamed from the woods, squirrels gathered their winter hoard, and congregated blackbirds chattered farewell to their summer haunts; when gay mountains basked in light, maples dropped leaves of rustling gold, sumachs glowed like rubies under the dark green of the unchanging spruce, and mossed rocks with all their painted plumage lay double in the watery mirror; that festal evening of the year, when jocund Nature disrobes herself, to wake again refreshed in the joy of her undying spring. Or, in the tomb-like silence of the winter forest, with breath frozen on his beard, the ranger strode on snow-shoes over the spotless drifts, and, like Dürer's knight, a ghastly death stalked ever at his side. There were those among them for whom this stern life had a fascination that made all other existence tame. ...

Month after month the great continent lay wrapped in snow. Far along the edge of the western wilderness men kept watch and ward in lonely blockhouses, or scoured the forest on the track of prowling war-parties. The provincials in garrison at Forts Edward, William Henry, and Oswego dragged out the dreary winter; while bands of New England rangers, muffled

Plate 13 The French and Indian War.
(The Mansell Collection, London).

against the piercing cold, caps of fur on their heads, hatchets in their belts, and guns in their mittened hands, glided on skates along the gleaming ice-floor of Lake George, to spy out the secrets of Ticonderoga, or seize some careless sentry to tell them tidings of the foe. Thus the petty war went on; but the big war was frozen into torpor, ready, like a hibernating bear, to wake again with the birds, the bees, and the flowers. [2]

Despite his rhetoric, Parkman catches, as does no other historian, the harshness and the beauty of the country, and its colour: the land trenched between mountain ranges still leafless and gray ... Ticonderoga, with the flag of the Bourbons like a flickering white speck waving on its ramparts ... On the left the mountain wilderness of the Adirondacks, like a stormy sea congealed." His awareness of geography becomes the key to historical explanation. Only in Lord Howe, killed by chance in 1758 in the attack on Fort Ti, did

[2] Parkman, *Montcalm and Wolfe*, p. 305 and chs 13 and 26. Cf. Lawrence H. Gipson, *The British Empire before the American Revolution*, 15 vols (New York, Knopf, 1968); Arthur Pound, *Johnson of the Mohawks* (New York, Macmillan, 1930); Douglas Southall Freeman, *George Washington, a Biography*, 7 vols (New York, Scribner's, 1948–57), vol. I, *The Young Washington*; and S. E. Morison, "The young man Washington," in *By Land and By Sea* (New York, Knopf, Borzoi Books, 1954), pp. 161–80.

Britain contrive to produce a leader with the stature of the French General Montcalm. Howe sought to train and equip British regulars to fight in the forest and to use it as an ally. It was Wolfe and his second-in-command, William Howe, the younger brother of George Augustus, who realized the need to use the country's advantages, and to train light infantry to do so. The war was won by the axe — and by using mastery of the sea to sidestep the forest. This could be done by a naval assault on Louisbourg, Quebec, and Montreal. When Montreal fell in 1760 there was no longer any point in controlling Lake Champlain. By 1760 it was the mastery of the great river that made the forest vulnerable.

The French had certain advantages. Their system of unified colonial control made for a relatively high level of military efficiency. They had a standing army in America, in forts along the St Lawrence, and at key places in the West; and they had strong and numerous Indian allies. Against these advantages must be weighed one grave weakness: New France was far too large for its population to defend. Being fundamentally a nonagricultural colony, its organization was based on an atomized fur industry and on missions to the Indians. The settled population was small, only about 60,000, and was widely spread. By contrast, the outstanding weakness of the British colonies was the lack of a unified control. A number of plans were proposed to remedy this, but no formal coordination had been established.

In the War itself there were four theaters of operation:

1 The northeast, involving the French in present-day New Brunswick vs. the British in Nova Scotia.
2 The Champlain corridor between the St Lawrence and Hudson valleys. The French held the northern half and were based at Crown Point; Britain held the southern part, from Schenectady to the sea. This natural invasion route was important in every North American war until 1815.
3 The interior, from Lake Erie to the headwaters of the Ohio River. This was particularly attractive to the French because it provided the shortest inland route from Quebec to New Orleans.
4 The West Indies, where the proximity of both French and British naval and privateering bases made sea trade perilous to the richly laden ships of both nations, and where concentration of wealth allowed great damage to be inflicted quickly.

After the end of King George's War (1739–1748) there was no relaxation of Anglo-French tension. In 1749 the governor of Canada formally claimed the upper Ohio valley. In the same year the British Crown chartered the Ohio Company to settle the area. In 1753 Lt Gov. Robert Dinwiddie of Virginia sent George Washington, a young land-surveyor, to investigate French expansion into the Ohio valley. The French built Fort Duquesne (Pittsburgh) in 1754; on July 4, they forced Washington to surrender Fort Necessity, near Fort Duquesne. The Albany Congress met in June and July; commissioners from New England, New York, Maryland, and Pennsylvania gathered to discuss Indian affairs. On July 10, Franklin's Plan of Colonial Union was accepted at Albany but was later rejected by the colonies. It would have united the colonies under a president-general appointed by the king; a council of delegates from the colonies would have had power to legislate, tax, raise armies, and deal with Indians, with veto power reserved for the president-general and king. By July 1755, the British had gained control of the Bay of Fundy and proceeded to expel the French Acadians in order to prevent a revolt (the subject of Longfellow's *Evangeline*); General Edward Braddock and 2,000 British troops, accompanied by Washington and Virginian militia, were ambushed and defeated by French and Indians near Fort Duquesne; Braddock was killed in the battle. In the Battle of Lake George on September 8, however, New Englanders under William Johnson defeated the French and Indians.

In June, 1757, William Pitt, the British Secretary of State, started an all-out campaign to win the war. Despite this, the French General Montcalm captured Fort William Henry on Lake George in August, and in September, the British failed to take Louisbourg, commanding the approach to the St Lawrence. Montcalm also repulsed a British attack on Ticonderoga (July 1758) and inflicted severe British losses. On July 26, 1758, Generals Jeffrey Amherst and James Wolfe, with about 10,000 troops, finally took Louisbourg. The war began to turn in favor of the British as they captured Fort Frontenac in August and took Fort Duquesne from the French. In July 1759, the British captured Fort Niagara, and the French blew up Ticonderoga and Crown Point.

General Wolfe landed troops near Quebec in 1759, and in early September, 4,500 of his troops climbed the cliffs west of Quebec to the Heights of Abraham. In the battle that followed, the French were badly beaten, and Wolfe and Montcalm were both killed. On September 18, the French surrendered Quebec; a year later, they surrendered all of Canada.

Like all those colonial clashes, this was part of a world war. With minor exceptions, the war in its early phases went badly for the British in every theater except India. Defeats were suffered in America by General Braddock's rashly deployed column, by British colonial forces at Niagara, Crown Point, Louisbourg, Oswego, and Fort William Henry. In the Mediterranean, Minorca was lost. On the continent of Europe, the English monarch's German kingdom of Hanover was held by the French.

But when William Pitt was brought into the London ministry in 1757 there came a transformation. Thereafter, it was "Mr Pitt's War," and he played a role in it similar to that of Winston Churchill in World War II. Leaving domestic government to the power-hungry but incompetent duke of Newcastle, who had mismanaged affairs thus far, he took personal direction of the military and naval efforts, and was as much responsible for the ultimate victory as any one man could well be. Pitt established unity of control. He did not carry on the war through his war and navy offices, or through a chief of staff and a chief of naval operations. He personally issued orders in his own name. Such direct communication, plus the urgent tone of every order, had a healthy effect on responsible officers overseas. After he took over authority, the war went well because Pitt, a vigorous and eloquent man, was precise in his orders, imaginative and farseeing — and because he chose commanders on their merits.

In the end Pitt's plans, policies, and the men he chose as leaders brought a brilliant succession of victories: Fort Duquesne, Louisbourg, Goree, Guadeloupe, Quebec, Quiberon, Martinique, Montreal, Havana, Manila, Masulipatam, Wanderwash, Pondicherry. The march of triumph in America lasted two years. In 1758 General John Forbes forced a way through Pennsylvania to Fort Duquesne, and Lord Amherst reduced Louisbourg. In the Insular Campaign of 1759 an amphibious force under the co-command of Barrington and Moore conquered Guadeloupe and its satellite islands.

By the Treaty of Paris, which brought the war to a formal close in 1763, France gave all her possessions in North America to Britain except two fishing islands south of Newfoundland and the two sugar islands of Martinique and Guadeloupe. The lands west of the Mississippi River were ceded by France to Spain as compensation for losing East and West Florida to the British. Most of occupied India, too, was kept by Britain.

The British Empire now became the foremost world power: its interests now lay clearly in territorial imperialism rather than commercial mercantilism. Its North American colonists, now free from French if not from Indian threats, could now look west and south with optimism; but they would best be prepared if they had their muskets — or preferably their rifles — near at hand. In the eighteenth as in the twentieth century, war not peace was the constant.

The British colonies in North America after the Treaty of Paris were not limited to 13, nor to the Atlantic seaboard. They now stretched from the Hudson Bay Territory, Newfoundland, Nova Scotia, and

Quebec down to East and West Florida, across into the islands of the Caribbean, from Bermuda to Jamaica, from Dominica and St Vincent to Grenada. It was primarily with the Caribbean in mind that the Navigation Acts were first conceived – to London, Barbados and Jamaica were the jewels in the imperial crown. Britain also controlled Belize and the Mosquito Coast. Although France retained the sugar islands of Guadeloupe and Martinique – which some contemporary observers thought more valuable than empty Canada – and Cayenne in French Guiana, and although Spain obtained Louisiana and the "Isle of Orleans" from France, and Cuba was returned to Spain by Britain, it was Britain that now dominated the mainland and the Caribbean.

The mainland colonies extended for 1,600 miles along the coast, and in 1763 hardly reached more than 100 miles inland. At either extremity there was a military or a naval outpost: Newfoundland was a tiny settlement of 6,000 but its numbers were doubled in the summer as the Grand Banks were swept for cod and mackerel; Florida, won from Spain in 1763, was seen as a frontier against the Spanish-controlled West, and against Spain's Indian allies, the Creeks, the Choctaws, and the Cherokees. To the acquisitions of 1713 – the Hudson Bay Territory, Newfoundland, and Nova Scotia – there was added in 1763 the vast province of Quebec. Nova Scotia had been given a representative assembly in 1758, and by 1775 its population reached 20,000. Quebec was, of course, firmly French in character, unready yet for representative government, with only 19 Protestant families living outside Quebec and Montreal.

Britain, by the Proclamation Line of October 1763, declared the lands west of the Appalachians Indian Territory, and appointed two superintendents to ensure no encroachment on Indian lands by pioneering and greedy colonists – John Stuart in the south, Sir William Johnson in his great house, Johnson Hall, in the Mohawk valley, for the north. Each was to have deputies and interpreters residing with the tribes, to ensure peaceful and fair trading. Their role was that of benevolent despots, judges, diplomats and soldiers, their calendars dotted with pow-wows marked by frequent treaty-making and re-making, and by elaborate ritual and the endless giving of gifts.[3]

North and south of the Indian reserve three new provinces were set up: Quebec, East Florida, and West Florida. The last covered the southern half of the present states of Mississippi and Alabama,

---

[3] J. R. Allen, *John Stuart and the Southern Colonial Frontier* (Ann Arbor, University of Michigan Press, 1944); Arthur Pound, *Johnson of the Mohawks* (New York, Macmillan, 1930); and James T. Flexner, *Mohawk Baronet: Sir William Johnson of New York* (New York, Harper and Row, 1959).

Louisiana east of the Mississippi, and most of the western panhandle of modern Florida: i.e. the lands west of the Chattahoochee,
the Apalachicola rivers and east of New Orleans, north to the 31st
latitude. It would open up trade with the Illinois settlements, with
Mexico, and with Creeks and Choctaws. East Florida included all
of the present peninsula except its northwestern strip. The two
new southern states were to be transformed from a frontier zone into
regular civil administrations similar to the older colonies, and to
each a governor was appointed. General James Grant, the governor
of East Florida, had served in the Indian War in South Carolina,
and won the reputation of being a liberal towards the Indians. George
Johnstone, an ex-naval officer, became governor of West Florida.
Each was expected to bring an elected assembly into existence as
soon as possible. Each was an officer who at least knew the services
and the lie of the land; each, as it happened, was a good-natured
Scot. The land would be distributed either in township grants of
up to 20,000 acres, bestowed by the Privy Council in London and
thus known as "mandamus" grants, or in family grants made by
the governor and council in Florida.

A vigorous pamphleteering took place in Britain, notably in the
Annual Registers and particularly in the *Scots Magazine*, adver-
tising the available land, particularly in East Florida, and its suit-
ability for the production of staples for exports: cotton and indigo,
silk, wine, and naval stores. Abetting this, William Knox, with
five years' experience as official landowner in Georgia, and acting
as agent both for Georgia and East Florida, was "selling" the prospects among officials. Clearly, the great proprietary estates of Lord
Baltimore, of William Penn, and of Lord Fairfax in Virginia, were
still seen as models by the land-hungry peers or MPs – as had been
the case, originally, in the Carolinas. They were fed by exotic descriptions of jungles of live oaks and towering pines, of cypress
swamps and great lakes, tales that were in fact little embroidered.
Lord Adam Gordon, the younger son of the duke of Gordon, reported that London was "Florida-mad," and organized the East
Florida Society of some 40 merchants, meeting at the Shakespeare's
Head tavern in Covent Garden. Sir Archibald Grant of Monymusk
in the Aberdeenshire Highlands concluded that "America will, at
a period, I don't presume to say when, be the grand seat of Empire and all its concomitants." They were but echoing Benjamin
Franklin's view of empire in 1763.[4]

---

[4] Bernard Bailyn, *Voyagers to the West* (New York, Knopf, 1986), p. 436; Gipson,
The British Empire before the American Revolution, vol. IX, pp. 192–4; Cecil

Plans and dreams – and access to power to obtain approval for them – were one thing; the reality of settling East Florida's mangrove swamps and pine barrens with hard-working and fit people another. The British recruits, particularly those brought out by Denys Rolle, MP for Barnstaple, to settle on the St John's River in East Florida, were almost entirely ex-convicts, and proved – unsurprisingly – unreliable. No more successful, though as exotic as the peninsula itself, was the New Smyrna settlement of Dr Andrew Turnbull, an Edinburgh physician and naturalist who was a protégé of Lord Shelburne; he had lived in Smyrna in Anatolia and had a glamorous Greek wife. In 1768 he took with him to Mosquito Inlet, 75 miles south of St Augustine, a motley assembly of Mani mountain Greeks and northern Italians, Corsicans, Minorcans, and Agean islanders – some 1400 men, women, and children in all, crowded in eight ships; over 100 died at sea in a grim three-month voyage. Bewildered and a prey to heat, mosquitoes and snakes, to disease and starvation, driven ruthlessly and to rebellion by overseers whom they could not understand, the swamps were slowly cleared of palmettos and tangle; some crops of indigo were available for export – but not quickly enough; 300 died in the first six months, and half of the total settlement within another year. Within a decade the village reverted to jungle. In numbers, the New Smyrna peasant pilgrims matched the 460 Puritan migrants of 1630. The contrast between them, however, was total. It took a generation, or more, to realize that the pattern here would be not family farms worked by British whites but semi-tropical plantations worked by black slaves.

Between 1764 and 1774 Britain made 242 grants of land in East Florida (2.8 million acres in all), 41 of land in West Florida and 82 for Nova Scotia (mainly to Scots or Yorkshiremen.) In the end, 1.4 million acres of East Florida were surveyed, and 114 titles to ownership confirmed. All but 16 were, and remained, absentees and speculators only. By the end of the British colony's existence 20 years later, only the 50 miles south and west of St Augustine had been settled, and there were no more than 300 white men. East Florida

---

Johnson, *British West Florida 1763–83* (New Haven, Yale University Press, 1943); Charles Loch Mowat, *East Florida as a British Province 1763–1784* (Berkeley, University of California Press, 1943). Thanks to his travels there and his descriptions of what he saw, the naturalist John Bartram of the Schuylkill valley greatly stirred the imagination of the poet Samuel Coleridge; here Xanadu was born. Not that all were so lyrical. Sir Alexander Grant, business man, MP and kinsman of Grant of Monymusk, denounced proprietary grants: "*imperium in imperio*," he said, "is a solecism in government," and wanted all such abandoned.

did not develop, and the reasons for Britain's sole failure as a mother-country are clear, as Henry Laurens in Charleston had foreseen: no roads, no ports, no markets, no adequate navigation, the fertile land isolated among sandy pine-barrens and marshy swamps, no workforce, no settlements and therefore no rents or taxes, and Indians ever-restless in their reserve across the St John's River. Unlike Massachusetts, the planners stayed at home, as close to Crown and Court as possible. The list of applicants is, nevertheless, a roll-call of great names.

13 members of titled families, 11 baronets or knights, 2 prime ministers (working through proxy applicants) a chancellor of the exchequer, the lord lieutenant of Ireland, the solicitor general, the secretaries to the Treasury, barracks master general, one of the King's physicians, the London agent of the colonies of Georgia and East Florida, the deputy paymaster of the army in Germany (who had returned home from the War with £400,000 in profits), 21 officers of the army and navy, 5 lesser government officials, several MPs, 4 physicians and 49 merchants, almost all of them government contractors. ... Lord Dartmouth's record total of 1,000,000 acres in East Florida was the assemblage of five-separate grants of 20,000 acres each, to himself and his four sons; the Earl of Tyrone and his two sons together received 60,000 acres.[5]

By contrast, West Florida's is a less colourful, more pedestrian, and perhaps therefore more successful story; only some 40 grants of land were made in the 1760s, averaging less than 10,000 acres each; there was rich black alluvial soil available, especially north of Natchez along the Mississippi; and given that the Spanish were now in possession of the trans-Mississippi West and of the "Isle of Orleans," which lay at the river mouth on both sides of the river, there was a defensive and military role to be played by the colony, which took over the run-down Spanish forts at Mobile and Pensacola, justifying British government support. There came a trickle, then a stream, of immigrants, to discover and exploit the colony's potential wealth of timber and corn, hemp and fruit, and later rice and tobacco, indigo and cotton. The peopling of West Florida was in family clusters, mainly from the older colonies, and notably from the back-country from western New York down to the French-Broad Holston country of the Carolinas, and not least from western Connecticut in the form of the Military Adventurers who had during the Seven years' War campaigned in the Caribbean. Unlike the

[5] Bailyn, *Voyagers to the West*, p. 440.

motley and unskilled peasants sought for East Florida, those who moved south along the great river and to the Gulf ports were farmers and carpenters, coppersmiths and blacksmiths – and entrepreneurs with their own capital. On the outbreak of the War of Independence, the colony had some 5,000 settlers, 25 percent of whom were slaves, living for the most part as close as they could get to the Mississippi.

A feature of colonial research over the last generation has been a concentration less on colonies than on smaller units – towns or provinces.[6] Alongside this emphasis, and sometimes in conflict with it, has been a new-style macroeconomic approach: students of the transatlantic economy have been prompt to see a fur zone (Hudson Bay to the Mississippi), a fish zone (from Newfoundland to Massachusetts,) a cereal zone (New York to northwestern Virginia), a tobacco zone (from Tidewater Maryland to north-central North Carolina), and a rice and indigo zone (from the lower Cape Fear River to Georgia), rather than colonies or towns.[7]

2 THE OLD COLONIAL SYSTEM – *CUI BONO?*

Given the surge in imperial and patriotic pride fed by the French and Indian War – in America as in Britain – there was no reason why in 1763 Independence should be foreseen. Neither in America nor in Britain did the notion of a Raj, in the nineteenth- and twentieth-century sense, exist, when a popular daily press could blow hot air on any embers of resentment, or on any mini-crisis waiting for fuel to whip up flames. Crises were few; a long frontier war was over, a new demesne was won. An occasional pamphlet or a bitter speech might be talked about; but in both countries the political nation was small; crises were occasional only. Prophets of future storms were rare. Lord Adam Gordon, after an extensive tour from Florida to

[6] Philip J. Greven, Jr, *Four Generations: Population, land and family in colonial Andover, Mass.* (Ithaca, NY, Cornell University Press, 1970); John Demos, *A Little Commonwealth: Family life in Plymouth Colony* (New York, Oxford University Press, 1970); Kenneth A. Lockridge, *A New England Town; the first hundred years: Dedham, Mass. 1636–1736* (New York, Norton, 1970); Gary B. Nash, *The Urban Crucible; Social change, political consciousness and the origins of the American Revolution* (Cambridge, MA, Harvard University Press, 1979); Jessica Kross, *The Evolution of an American Town: Newton, New York, 1642–1775* (Philadelphia, Temple University Press, 1983).
[7] Jacob M. Price, "The Transatlantic economy" in Jack P. Greene and J. R. Pole (eds), *Colonial British America: Essays in the new history of the early modern era* (Baltimore, Johns Hopkins University Press, 1984), p. 23.

the Mohawk valley, vehemently criticized the "leveling" spirit he found in Boston; but this was unusual. For the colonies of mainland North America were English (after 1707, British) foundations, reflecting Old World values and institutions. Britain saw its American Empire as maritime – it had 8,000 ships at sea, and 70,000 sailors – and its purposes as mercantile. Its raw material – sugar and rice, tobacco and timber, furs and fish – precisely because they could not be produced as easily, or at all, at home, were its *raisons d'être*; and in exchange the colonies were given military and naval protection and trading bounties, and bought the manufactures, the cambrics, the necessities, the luxuries they needed.

The British Empire, like other empires, was founded for the mother-country's profit, not her glory. Without this motive, the Empire would not have existed. The mercantile system – product of the Navigation Acts of 1651, 1660, and 1663, and later – saw the colonies as forming with the mother-country a self-sufficient commercial empire. The carrying trade between them was confined to British (or, later, American-built) ships. Certain enumerated commodities – sugar, tobacco, indigo, and wool, said the Act of 1660; naval stores, particularly the great masts from New England for Britain's ships of the line, rice, copper, and furs were added later – were to be shipped only to Britain or to a British colony; and, said the Act of 1663, all European exports to the colonies were to be shipped via Britain. This meant assured markets and some measure of centralized marketing. American manufactures were prohibited. But, however restricted this may now appear, the system was much less harsh than the contemporary mercantilism of France and Spain, and it was in fact by no means unfavorable to the colonists. Landholding – perhaps the most significant feature of the American economy – was not directly regulated. Throughout the colonies, and especially striking in New Jersey, Pennsylvania, and Virginia, were some 250 ironworks, blast furnaces, and forges, producing approximately one-seventh of the world's iron supplies. They were scattered, and transportation costs were high, but their basic source, timber, was abundant. And there were, of course, no restrictions on non-enumerated goods, so that the Middle Colonies had a flourishing trade with Southern Europe, exporting wheat, corn, and flour.

American tobacco was given a monopoly of the British market, and the British government waged a persistent campaign to stamp out the production of the plant in the British Isles. As tobacco exhausted the soil, so estates spread further west along the rivers; and in exchange for their tobacco, the planters imported curtains and clothes, ploughs and coaches, books, ornaments, and gracious living.

They were heavily in debt to British, especially Glasgow, merchants. Tobacco constituted 80 percent of all Scottish imports in the decade before 1776. This was the legacy of the Act of Union of 1707: in 1706 Glasgow imported 1.5 million pounds of tobacco per year, which grew to 10 million in 1743, 21 million in 1752, and 71 million (its all-time high) in 1771 (falling to 7 million in 1775, 300,000 pounds in 1776). The merchants lived in Glasgow, whose street-names still recall them – "the Tobacco Lords," "the Virginia Dons," many of them had served a spell in the Chesapeake estuary. More accurately, it was a Chesapeake–Clyde trade, with few ships able to get beyond Greenock or Port Glasgow. A century later the widening of the river would bring the trade upstream when "Glasgow made the Clyde, and the Clyde made Glasgow."[8]

Sugar and coffee enjoyed a similar monopoly. The production of naval stores in the colonies was rewarded with bounties. Britain spent large sums of money for the defense of the colonies, and provided protection on the high seas. While American vessels flew the British flag they had little to fear from the Barbary pirates or the buccaneers of the West Indies. Moreover, when goods on the enumerated list were re-exported from Britain, drawbacks were paid on the import duties. As for European goods, the colonists would probably have bought them from Britain anyway, for Britain manufactured most articles more cheaply than the Continental countries. The Acts fostering the British merchant marine were definitely advantageous to the New England shipbuilding industry. Of 7,694 vessels engaged in the Atlantic trade in 1775, 2,342 were American-built. English credits fostered colonial trade. In each of the years between 1768 and 1772, shipping earnings – most of them earned by New England and the Middle Colonies – were over £600,000, second only to tobacco. All in all, many aspects of British mercantilism favored the Americans; and much of the unfavorable legislation was not enforced, partly because it could not be, given the West Indian and American coastline, partly because the home government did not always try to enforce it, partly because the French Wars made enforcement difficult, and partly because the customs officers were hampered by the charter privileges of the colonists.

[8] Thomas Devine, *The Tobacco Lords* (Edinburgh, John Donald, 1975); T. H. Breen, *The Mentality of the Great Tidewater Planters on the eve of Revolution* (Princeton, Princeton University Press, 1985); Jacob Price, "The rise of Glasgow in the Chesapeake tobacco trade 1707–1775," *William & Mary Quarterly*, 11 (1954), 179–99.

The section of British America which least fitted into the imperial system was New England. Because of geology and geography, New England could produce none of the staples (tobacco, wool, rice) which Britain desired; cotton, despite its importance, was not yet a significant colonial export. Soil and climate compelled the New England colonists to turn to fishing and commerce, pursuits in which they competed with the mother-country. Having no commodities except timber to send to Britain in exchange for manufactures, New England tried to encourage local industry and to develop the carrying trade with the West Indies. The islands of the West Indies confined their production to sugar, and imported all their other needs. From the New England traders they purchased barrels, lumber, peas, beans, shoes, and, above all else, quantities of inferior fish which was fed to the slaves. In return, the New England merchants obtained sugar and molasses, which were converted into rum, which in turn was sold to the Indians for furs, and to the African slave markets for slaves. Thus was born the famous three-cornered trade of molasses, rum, and slaves – although recent research stresses that shuttles rather than triangular voyages were the usual pattern, and, as a market for colonial exports, Africa was of small significance. It was, of course, the major supplier of slave labor, but it was British rather than colonial shippers who dominated the slave trade.

Unfortunately for British imperialism, the British West Indies were not large enough to absorb the products of the middle and northern colonies, or to produce enough molasses. The colonial trader had to sell his surplus lumber, fish, and grain to the French West Indies, which were eager to sell molasses at any price. The economic decline of the British West Indies drove British planters and sugar interests to demand the cessation of trade between the foreign sugar islands and the American colonies. As a result of their plea, Parliament passed the Molasses Act of 1733, which put a prohibitive duty on the sugar and molasses from the French and Spanish West Indies. Had this law been enforced, it would have ruined the New England colonies, for whom the West Indies trade was essential. Fortunately, little attempt was made to enforce it, and illicit trade grew steadily, even during the Seven Years' War. Yankee traders carrying so-called "flags of truce" kept the French islands supplied with food and on their return voyages smuggled vast quantities of molasses into Boston, Newport, and Providence. Nevertheless, once laws were to be enforced, New England had much less reason to like the Navigation Acts than had the South. They had accepted them now, however, for three generations.

Moreover, the end in 1763 of the fourth round in the "Great War for the Empire" brought slump after boom. During the war, the mother-country sent not only troops with spending power, but more and more credit. During the war, Glasgow houses extended more and more liberal terms in their trade with the tobacco colonies, with chains of stores to supply credit and dry goods to smaller planters. By the 1760s the debts were heavy. In 1766 Barlow Trecothick, trader, MP and lord mayor of London, calculated that the London merchants were due £2,900,000, those of Bristol £800,000, and those of Glasgow £500,000. After 1763 retrenchment, not easy money, became the rule. The same curbs hit the West Indian islands; the sugar planters were unable to cover the rising costs of provisions like flour and bread, and to allow exporters a respectable profit, with savage impact on the port cities and on New England farmers. And as the end of the War in 1763 led to unemployment, decreased demand, and overextended credits in Britain itself, home businesses tightened the screws on colonial debtors.[9]

This empire of trade regulation was buttressed not only by the work of enforcement agencies like the Customs Service, or occasionally by the Admiralty or the Army, but by the indirect Empire: of schooling in England or in Scotland, of land-surveyors with experience of more than one colony (like Governor Dinwiddie of Virginia), the role of Dissenting Deputies, of the Society for the Propagation of the Gospel, of the role of the Bishop of London with his American "base" in Williamsburg, of the Royal Society, of which John Winthrop Jr, and Benjamin Franklin were Fellows. Until the separation came in 1775, no one had been a more lyrical Old England Man than transatlantic agent, scientist, journalist and post office supervisor, Benjamin Franklin. His affection for the Old Country from whom he and his family after all got post-office jobs, is a constant theme in his correspondence.

3   THE WEST AND THE INDIANS

There was one other area that strengthened the ties with Britain, but bred forces that put it at risk. The colonial boundaries were moving slowly inland, and were menaced by fierce and unpredictable Indian tribes from whom Britain gave protection. The Iroquois of New York might be friendly, but the Creeks and Choctaws and Cherokees of Georgia and the Southwest were not; there was an

---

[9] For Trecothick, see British Museum, Add. MS 33030, f. 215. Cf. Marc Egnal, *A Mighty Empire: the origins of the American Revolution* (Ithaca, NY, Cornell University Press, 1988), pp. 126–9.

ugly war with the last in 1759–61; and in 1763, angered by the French withdrawal, the prospect of British rule and still more by the prospect of land-grabbing by white settlers, the Ottawas west of Fort Pitt rose under Pontiac; Seneca and Shawnee in western Virginia, Huron, Erie, and Potawatomi, scattered along the Canadian boundary, rose too. They were defeated in 1764 by Colonel Henry Bouquet, but not before they had captured every western post except Detroit and Fort Pitt, and had killed some 200 settlers and traders. Moreover, they were defeated, once again, by British regulars obligingly paid for by the home government – not by any intercolonial army. This seemed a vulnerable, a sharply divided, and a very dependent world. Significantly, Fort Duquesne, when finally acquired, had been renamed Fort Pitt, not Fort Washington.[10]

To meet and placate the Indian threat to the frontier communities, the British government in October 1763 proclaimed that the land west of the Appalachians was an Indian reserve, in which white settlement was forbidden and in which Indian traders were to be licensed. The intention was not to put a permanent curb on white expansion, but to ensure that it was gradual and controlled, and not to leave the Indians at the mercy of unscrupulous traders and still more unscrupulous land speculators. This liberal measure was largely the work of Lord Shelburne, president of the Board of Trade; it was designed not only to reassure the Indians but to guarantee the fur trade; it had the further effect of confining the settlers to the tidewater and piedmont areas, and thus it was hoped to discourage not only the westward movement but the growth of colonial manufactures. What was welcome to the Indians, however, was anathema to the whites. Land settlers and frontiersmen saw in the Proclamation a barrier to be overturned or to be ignored; it was an obstacle in their path to the good bottom land of the western river valleys; it was also an obstacle to profit and, they said, an infringement of the "sea to sea" clauses of colonial charters, which permitted steady expansion westwards. Many prominent colonists, like Washington at Mount Vernon or Franklin in London, seeking a charter for his Vandalia project in the Ohio valley, resented interference with their plans; in Washington's case he ignored the checks altogether; his agent, Crawford, was buying land far beyond the Proclamation Line, and he was buying up the land-grants made to war veterans by grateful colonial governments. (Crawford was scalped by Indians in 1768.) The Proclamation did not affect actual settlers

[10] Francis Jennings, *Empire of Fortune: Crowns, colonies and tribes in the Seven Years' War in America* (New York, Norton, 1988).

who had not yet in any numbers reached the crest of the Appalachians. It did limit the large investors, who planned to buy land beyond the line and hold it for a future rise in value. These men were the most influential in Southern society, where slaves and land were the planter's major forms of investment. Moreover, the machinery for regulating Indian trade, and the military posts established in the West to halt further Indian rebellions, imposed a heavy financial burden on Britain. The British national debt stood at £133 million in 1763, an increase of £60 million in eight years, the extra cost of colonial defense would be crippling. The time had come for a new policy. It was thorough and thoughtful, as one would expect from George Grenville, the new prime minister, with what Burke called his "rage for regulation and restriction." He was a pedant, and hard to move. He would by his firmness set his government on the road to war.[11]

4 THE PATRIOT KING

While the Great War for empire was still in progress, George III (1760–1820) the grandson of George II, had succeeded to the British throne. He was the first member of the House of Hanover who was really English, and he said that he "gloried in the name of Briton." Like his grandfather and his great-grandfather, George I, he was also Elector of Hanover, and thus perforce involved in European affairs, prone to see France as enemy. Unlike them, his succession to the throne had been easy: with the defeat of Bonnie Prince Charlie at Culloden in 1746, Jacobite threats had been ended. The training he had received from his mother, Augusta, the product of a small German court and hard, reserved, and tortuous, gave him the German idea of absolutism, under which a king should rule as well as reign. There is little reason to doubt her supposed constant admonitions to him, "George, be king." Her views were reinforced by those of his tutor, the earl of Bute, who used as a text Bolingbroke's *Idea of A Patriot King*. His mother also instilled in him a personal moral code far different from that practiced by the first two Georges – or, for that matter, by many prominent politicians of the time. His home life was decorous, there were no mistresses to cause trouble.

---

[11] Edmund Burke, *The Works of Edmund Burke*, 6 vols (London, Bell, 1893), I. 265; Michael Kammen, *Empire and Interest: The American colonies and the politics of mercantilism* (Philadelphia, Lippincott, 1970); and Philip Lawson, *George Grenville: A political life* (Oxford, Oxford University Press, 1984).

He was a cultured man, a lover of and collector of paintings; and he was only 22.

The new ruler was determined to build up the royal authority that had suffered so much under his two predecessors. In so doing, however, he was wise enough not to rely upon dictatorial actions or royal prerogative, mindful of what had happened to Charles I and James II. Instead, he decided to use the existing system to his own advantage: to build up his own party supporters by appointments to sinecures, by avowed vote-buying at elections, by the lavish creation of peerages, and by thoughtful generosity.

No faction was large, and no factional leader could count on more than a handful of faithful followers. Moreover, there was a constant shifting of support from one faction to another.[12] The Old Whigs, led by the duke of Newcastle (First Lord of the Treasury 1757–62), the marquis of Rockingham (prime minister 1765–6), Edmund Burke and Charles James Fox, were supporters of parliamentary supremacy and the 1688 "Revolution," and sypmpathizers with the American cause. William Pitt, later earl of Chatham, together with the earl of Shelburne (prime minister 1782–3), Earl Temple (Pitt's brother-in-law), and Earl Camden, believed that Parliament could legislate on American affairs but not impose direct taxes; they saw the empire as a great trading system, and opposed the Stamp Act. The faction known as "the king's Friends", headed by Lord North (prime minister 1770–82) and the earl of Bute (prime minister 1762–3), favored royal leadership in government; they were mainly Tories, independents and Scottish MPs. There were also office-seekers at a price – including the duke of Bedford, George Grenville (prime minister 1763–5), and Henry Fox.

5 THE STAMP ACT

After the cessation of hostilities against the French in 1763, 6,000 British troops, in some 15 regiments, were scattered across an

[12] Sir Lewis Namier, *England in the Age of the American Revolution*, 2nd edn (New York, St Martin's Press, 1961), and *The Structure of Politics at the Accession of George III*, 2nd edn (New York, St Martin's Press, 1957); Charles R. Ritcheson, *British Politics and the American Revolution* (Norman, University of Oklahoma Press, 1954); Richard Pares, *King George III and the Politicians* (New York, Oxford University Press, 1953); Bernard Donoughue, *British Politics and the American Revolution: The Path to War 1773–75* (New York, St Martin's Press, 1964); George H. Guttridge, *English Whiggism and the American Revolution* (University of California Publications in History, XXVIII, 2nd edn, Berkeley, University of California Press, 1963).

unmapped continent, from Pensacola, Mobile, and St Augustine in the Floridas to Niagara and Fort Pitt in the northwest. Prime minister Grenville planned to station a standing army permanently in America, to guard the western settlements not only against Indians but against any resumption of French attacks, and considered it fair that the colonists should meet one-third of its cost. He also sought to enforce the Navigation Acts more strictly, and in 1764 the Sugar Act was passed, the duty on sugar and molasses was reduced so that it would be easier to collect. The laws had to be enforced. In order to raise revenue to meet part of the costs of defense, it was proposed that a Stamp Act should be passed, imposing a duty on newspapers and pamphlets, on passports, on cards and dice, on liquor, licenses, and wills, and on legal documents. Moreover, all these duties would be payable in sterling, not in the paper currency and foreign coins, the bills of exchange and direct barter, to which colonists were accustomed – and which were treated with suspicion by Britain; and the Act would be enforced in Vice-Admiralty Courts, where penalties were savage. The revenue raised would pay for officials, and for troops.

There was equity as well as logic in Grenville's proposal. In Britain the land tax kept the price of bread high, and bread riots were frequent. Yet some colonies – the Carolinas – paid no tax at all; and some – like Connecticut and Georgia – received parliamentary grants to cover the costs of the French and Indian War.

Moreover, the revenue of £60,000 per year which the measure was expected to raise would be spent entirely and exclusively in America – even though the colonists saw it as but the beginning of a policy of freeing colonial governors from their financial dependence on colonial assemblies. Benjamin Franklin, always prompt as a philosopher and still an "Old England Man," counselled his countrymen that "Idleness and pride tax with a heavier hand than kings and parliaments. If we can get rid of the former we may easily bear the latter." [13] Moreover, the Stamp Act was a device that had been used in Britain since 1694. The taxes to be raised by it were much less onerous than those imposed in Britain; colonial opinion was fully canvassed in advance, and the colonial agents fully consulted, but no alternative plan was put up by them. Indeed, from the speed with which some distinguished colonial figures, such as George Mercer of Virginia and Jared Ingersoll of Connecticut, accepted the posts

---

[13] To Charles Thomson, merchant in Philadelphia, July 11, 1765, in *The Papers of Benjamin Franklin*, ed. L. W. Labaree, vol. XII (New Haven, Yale University Press, 1968), p. 208.

of Stamp distributors, no-one could have anticipated the approaching crisis.

In fact, colonial opposition was instant, and it was all but uniform. In the Virginia House of Burgesses Patrick Henry, the outspoken frontier lawyer, presented series of resolutions attacking the Act and the king. "If this be treason," he said, "make the most of it." In Boston, Sam Adams organized the Sons of Liberty to prevent the sale of stamps by threats of direct action against those using them. Eastern merchants boycotted British goods. And delegates from nine colonies met in City Hall, New York, in the so-called Stamp Act Congress, demanding the repeal of the Act and issuing a Declaration of Rights. This claimed that as colonists were not represented in Parliament they could not be taxed by it without their consent.

Parliament, not for the first or the last time, bent before the storm. Without accepting the principle of "no taxation without representation" – since over 90 percent of the home population was as much disfranchised as the Americans – and without any abrogation of sovereignty – indeed, a Declaratory Act was passed asserting that Parliament had complete authority to make laws binding the colonists "in all cases whatsoever" – the government, headed now by the marquis of Rockingham, repealed the Stamp Act in February 1766. This was partly due to Franklin's skillful pleading at the Bar of the House; still more to the economic consequences of the boycott. The colonists felt that they had won round one of the struggle, and celebrated with bonfires, and the erection in New York of statues to the king and Mr Pitt. But neither the mood, nor the statues, lasted long.[14]

6   RIOTS AND REBELLION

The colonists' choice of heroes – Rockingham, the liberal; Mr Pitt, the war leader; John Wilkes, who repeatedly refused to be unseated by the House of Commons – was significant. Grenville, with a lawyer's logic, had thought it both lawful and expedient to tax;

---

[14] For the repeal of the Stamp Act, see *The Papers of Benjamin Franklin*, ed. Labaree, vol. XIII (1969), pp. 124–60; Verner W. Crane, "Benjamin Franklin and the Stamp Act" (Colonial Society of Massachusetts, *Publications*, vol. 32, 1937), pp. 56–77; Peter D. G. Thomas, *British Politics and the Stamp Act Crisis: The first phase of the American Revolution 1763–1767* (Oxford, Oxford University Press, 1975). Cf E. S. and H. M. Morgan, *The Stamp Act Crisis: Prologue to Revolution* (Chapel Hill, NC, University of North Carolina Press, 1953).

Rockingham, a wealthy Yorkshire landowner and one of the earliest of British party leaders, thought it lawful but not expedient; the earl of Chatham, as Pitt became in 1766, thought it neither lawful nor expedient. Chatham was a man of pride and imagination, though he was in fact the greatest imperialist of all; but from the government he headed from 1766 to 1768, he was a frequent absentee, due in theory to gout, but in fact to temperament. In 1767 his Chancellor of the Exchequer, Charles Townshend ("Champagne Charlie"), sought to honor a rashly given pledge to reduce the land tax at home by raising an American revenue, not from taxes, but from duties on certain imports: tea, glass, paper, and paint. Such trade levies, he believed, it was legitimate for Parliament to impose. With the revenue he would pay the salaries of colonial governors and judges, and free them thereby from colonial control. Further, Vice-Admiralty Courts to stop smuggling would be strengthened in power and increased in number.

These measures proved to be as unwelcome as the Stamp Act. John Dickinson in his *Letters of a Pennsylvania Farmer* distinguished between Acts intended to raise revenue, which he saw as illegal, and those intended to regulate trade, which he accepted as valid; by this standard the Townshend duties were plainly unconstitutional. At this point, indeed, the colonists began to abandon the distinction between internal and external taxes altogether, and to take the primitive, purist, but very popular line that all taxes, however imposed, are bad, and that that government is best which taxes least. The Massachusetts General Court issued a circular letter – the work of Sam Adams, James Otis, and Joseph Hawley – appealing to the other colonies for common action, and asserting that only Americans could tax Americans; Governor Bernard branded it as seditious, but seven colonies gave it endorsement. When John Hancock's sloop *Liberty* was seized for smuggling in 1768, a riot followed in which the over-efficient customs officials were mobbed and had to take refuge in Castle William, on an island in Boston harbor. The Boston garrison was strengthened by two regiments of infantry, the 14th and 29th, in an atmosphere that Thomas Hutchinson described as frankly revolutionary. Reports to Parliament on the Boston situation in 1769 led both Houses to resolve that "wicked and designing men" were responsible and should be visited with "condign punishment." The reports confirmed that Welbore Ellis had warned Governor Bernard on his appointment in 1760 that Massachusetts people were "difficult to manage." Boston, said General Gage in 1768, was in the grip of "a Kind of Democratical Despotism." When in 1775 John Adams, Samuel's more sober and legally qualified cousin, commented that "a democratical despotism is a contradiction in terms," he knew that he was allowing hope to triumph over experience.

To Samuel Adams in Boston the situation was certainly explosive. By 1770 the movement was led not by the merchants of Philadelphia or New York, who were now cautious and not a little frightened of the forces they had unleashed, but by the Sons of Liberty in New York and by the Samuel Adams machine, operating from "the Green Dragon" in Boston. To them, the presence of British redcoats – the "lobsterbacks" – was both inflammation and pretext. In New York, in January 1770, soldiers and civilians clashed round a Liberty Pole; there was blood, but no fatalities, in "The Battle of Golden Hill." In March in Boston the taunting and snowballing of soldiers, first by schoolboys and then by citizens, led to shots being fired, and five Bostonians – one of them a Negro, Crispus Attucks – were killed; the event went into history as the Boston Massacre. The soldiers were acquitted after a skillful and courageous defense by their counsel, John Adams; but their presence was proving to be not a safeguard but an irritant, and they were more often the victims than the masters of the local situation. After 1770 they were carefully confined to Castle William; and the British government repealed the Townshend duties except for the penny a pound on tea, retained, like the Declaratory Act, to assert a principle that was increasingly being seen to be only a form of words. Ironically, even that decision was taken in Cabinet by a single vote, that of the new prime minister, Lord North; had it not been taken, there might well have been no facility in 1773 to aid the East India Company's tea trade – and the history of the world might have been different. So round two went also to the colonies; once again, under whatever cloak, the government retreated; and now the cause had martyrs too. For revolutions these are more essential than issues; easier to identify, and to dramatize.

7 "TYRANNY" AND "TEA DEUM"

Between rounds two and three there came an interlude, a return of prosperity and a reaction against the radicals. The merchants abandoned their boycott, and Sam Adams lost control of the Massachusetts Assembly. Yet this was the period when he worked hardest to keep the cause alive, by pamphlets under a host of *noms-de-plume* and by the organization of the "committees of correspondence." Governor Hutchinson described the Boston Committee as composed of "deacons," "atheist," and "blackhearted fellows whom one would not wish to meet in the dark." But they began to emerge in each colony, to constitute an unelected but nevertheless representative body of those with grievances, and to provide a basis for inter-colonial action should the crisis ever come. Crowds, rarely spontane-ous, and committees, with agenda and resolutions carefully phrased in advance, played a major part in these years. Although there is no evidence that the colonists had serious grievances, Sam Adams's great achievement was to maintain a feeling of unrest and to pro-duce a machine for action.

Nor did Josiah Quincy, Joseph Hawley, Isaac Sears, Tom Paine, and Alexander McDougall counsel moderation. Behind these men were the machines of persuasion, the local committees of cor-respondence, the clubs and merchants' groups and working men's societies in every colony, the Sons of Liberty, the Sons of Neptune, the Mohawk River Indians, the Philadelphia Patriotic Society, and other groups. Their festivals, said John Adams, "tinge the minds of the people and impregnate them with the sentiments of liberty." [15] Alongside these, in 1775 there were 42 newspapers published in America, almost all of them Whig, and countless broadsides and pamphlets; all these saw themselves as the special targets of the Stamp Act and the Townshend duties on paper, the aggrieved victims of British tyranny. And their themes were echoed from every Con-gregational and Presbyterian pulpit. [16]

Alarmed at the near-bankruptcy of the East India Company, the British Government allowed it to send tea to America, granted it a drawback of all duties paid on tea re-exported to the colonies, and allowed its direct sale rather than via English merchants. This made it cheaper even than smuggled tea, and would certainly have hit hard at smuggling, and at the profits of those, like John Hancock, who traded in smuggled tea. Thus the Revolution, round three, began, oddly enough, with a mass protest against cheaper tea.

In December 1773, three tea-cargo ships reached Boston. Sam Adams addressed a large crowd – estimated at 7,000 – on the evils of drinking cheap and legal tea, and from this meeting a group moved on to the docks, disguised as Indians. There they consigned 342 tea chests to the bottom of the harbor, stoving them in as they did so. And Boston was not alone. Nine days later a ship reached the Delaware, with some 700 chests of tea. Seeing a hostile crowd as a

[15] John Adams, *Diary*, August 14, 1769, *The Adams Papers, The Diary and Autobiography of John Adams*, ed. L. H. Butterfield (Cambridge, MA, Harvard University Press, 1961–), vol. I, p. 341.

[16] A. M. Schlesinger, Sr, *Prelude to Independence: The newspaper war on Britain 1764–1778* (New York, Knopf, 1966).

Plate 14 The Boston Tea Party, December 16, 1773. Boston citizens disguised as Indians boarded the tea vessels and threw their valuable cargo into the harbor, in front of a crowd of people. The effect was inflammatory: radicals were delighted, merchants repelled by such extremism, and in London Parliament closed the port. (The Mansell Collection, London.)

welcoming committee, the captain decided to sail back to England, his cargo still intact. In the following April, a similar crowd in New York stove in the tea cargo. Only in Charlestown was any tea landed — and there it stayed unsold for three years. The Tea Party was not confined to the City of the Saints. But the events in Boston were difficult to justify, and were indeed condemned by all responsible colonial opinion, including John Adams and Franklin, and by many merchants. And this time Parliament proved uncompliant. Since 1769 it had been considering an inquiry into Massachusetts; the rendezvous of the navy had already been moved from Halifax to Boston. Half-measures would no longer suffice.

In the spring of 1774 the "Intolerable" or "Coercive Acts" were passed. The port of Boston was closed until the lost tea was paid for. Massachusetts' charter was annulled, and the governor's council became appointed by the king. The Quartering Act was re-enacted, so the troops could be quartered in Boston and in occupied as well as empty dwellings. Officers or soldiers accused of crimes were to be sent to Britain for trial. And, not least, the Quebec Act was passed. This was not intended as a punitive measure, and was planned beforehand, but it was seen as such in the colonies. It killed all hopes of the erection of new colonies in the northwest by transferring to the province of Quebec the lands — and the fur trade — between the Ohio and the Mississippi, in which Virginia, Pennsylvania, Connecticut, and Massachusetts held interests; and it gave to it — even more ominously, as Boston saw it — French civil law and the Roman Catholic religion. The regime provided for it was centralized, in keeping with the customs of the province, and there was to be no jury trial. This was a liberal and intelligent measure, drafts for which had existed since 1763. But liberally-minded MPs — Chatham and Burke, Barré and Fox — attacked it as pro-French, autocratic and wicked, and the vehemence of their attacks confirmed colonial suspicions. The timing, as distinct from the merits, of the measure, was unfortunate. There were fears now, in Chatham's phrase, of "popery and arbitrary power;" the enemy was no longer merely tyranny but popery — and prelacy too. "The sight of lawn sleeves", said John Adams, "was more terrible than ten thousand Mohawks."

There were now two firm positions. "The die is cast," said the king; "The colonists must either triumph or submit." Joseph Reed put it differently in a letter from the first Continental Congress to Lord Dartmouth: "The people are generally ripe for the execution of any plan the Congress advises, should be it war itself."

8 THE FIRST CONTINENTAL CONGRESS

The Intolerable Acts marked the end of the stages of economic and commercial grievance. The issues now were clearly political, and were seen as such in the colonies. Resolutions of sympathy and supplies of food reached Boston. When royal governors dissolved assemblies that were loud in their expression of support of Massachusetts, the members promptly formed themselves into extra-legal provincial congresses. Indeed, in Virginia the call to the First Continental Congress went out from the Raleigh Tavern, just across the street from the Williamsburg Capitol. Revolutionary spirit is often alcoholic, and sometimes no more than that. It is no less inflammatory.

At the suggestion of the Virginia Burgesses, colonial representatives were summoned to meet in Philadelphia on September 5, 1774, "to consult upon the present unhappy state of the Colonies." This meeting was the first Continental Congress, an extra-legal body chosen by provincial congresses, or popular conventions, and instructed by them. This meant that the Patriot party, which favored extra-legal action, was in control of the situation, and that extreme conservatives who would have nothing to do with resistance to

British laws were not represented. Otherwise the membership of the Congress was a fair cross-section of American opinion – both extreme and moderate. Every colony save Georgia sent at least one delegate, and the total number of 55 was large enough for diversity of opinion, but small enough for genuine debate and effective action. Behind the figures gathered together in Philadelphia there were deeper forces at work; recurrent rioting, and the organizations (the Sons of Liberty, the Mohawk River Indians, the Peep O'Day Boys) to further it; a rich assortment of newspapers, gazettes, and *courants*, all but two or three of them patriotic in emphasis; and commitees of correspondence, who now kept in touch with each other, colony by colony. The "patriot" forces consolidated themselves. They included defenders of high principle, like Jefferson, and defenders of smuggling profits, like John Hancock; the propertied, who thought all taxes wicked, and the propertyless, who had no taxes to pay and nothing to lose in any riot. Behind them were the more legal agencies, not least the Boston town meeting and the proud but liberal lead of the Virginia House of Burgesses. The federal alliance of all these made smooth the transfer of power from London to the colonial capitals.

But however variously, nobly and/or selfishly supported it might be, there was also emerging a body of doctrine. It had been expressed by a succession of writers – by Otis and by Daniel Dulany, by John Dickinson in Pennsylvania, by Patrick Henry and George Mason with their Resolves in Virginia, by Richard Bland in his *Inquiry into the Rights of the British Colonies*, and not least by Sam Adams and Ben Franklin as professionals, and under a variety of names. Protesting at first against an internal tax, the colonists had come in the end to a total denial of Parliament's right to tax them without their own consent.

A body of constitutional doctrine; agencies for riot and rebellion; a number of leaders: was this then a "national" movement, was it yet an American revolution? The answer in 1774 is clearly *no*. In the colonial scene sectionalism was still more striking than unity. The First Continental Congress, a coming together of ambassadors, was marked by an anxious process of mutual exploration, of each other and of each other's sections. It had, said John Rudledge, "no coercive or legislative authority." It was a machine for allowing the colonies to "resent in one body," as a Virginian put it. It was still negative, not positive. But from firmness in 1775 the Congress moved, albeit reluctantly, to independence in 1776.

9　THE WAR OF INDEPENDENCE

The War began, as all wars do, by inadvertence. Few wanted Independence – a "Hobgoblin of so frightful Mien," said John Adams, that few would "look it in the face." As late as August 1775, Jefferson still sought "dependence on Great Britain, properly limited." No call for separation was voiced in the Second Continental Congress when it met in Philadelphia in May 1775, even when George Washington accepted the commission of commander-in-chief on June 16, 1775. He was to take command to oppose, not the king but the "Ministerial" and "Parliamentary" army, phrases with striking echoes of England in 1640. As late as January 1776 the king's health was still toasted in Washington's mess. He did not want the command. He wrote to his wife on 18 June:

I have used every endeavour in my power to avoid it, not only from my unwillingness to part with you and the family, but from a consciousness of its being a trust too great for my capacity, and that I should enjoy more real happiness in one month with you at home than I have the most distant prospect of finding abroad, if my stay were to be seven times seven year. But it has been a kind of destiny that has thrown me upon this service ... It was utterly out of character to such censure as would have reflected dishonor upon myself, and have given pain to my friends. This, I am sure, could not, and ought not to be pleasing to you, and must have lessened me considerably in my own esteem. I shall rely, therefore, confidently on that Providence which has heretofore preserved and been bountiful to me, not doubting but that I shall return safe to you in the fall.[17]

To Burwell Bassett, his brother-in-law, he put it more objectively: "I can answer but for three things, a firm belief in the justice of our cause, close attention to the prosecution of it, and the strictest integrity." And to the frontier lawyer and fellow-Virginian Patrick Henry, more trenchantly, and with a sharp gambler's sense of the risks he ran: "Remember, Mr Henry, what I now tell you: from the day I enter upon the command of the American armies, I date my fall, and the ruin of my reputation."[18]

The self-deprecation was a feature of the man; it was part of the Virginia code, no doubt – but Washington had small taste for

[17] Douglas Southall Freeman, *George Washington, a Biography*, 7 vols (New York, Scribner's, 1948–57), vol. III, p. 453.
[18] *Ibid.*, p. 454.

failure, and as a poor boy on the make he had not been able to take risks. There were other possibilities for the post: Artemas Ward, then 47, the ailing commander of Massachusetts troops; Charles Lee, then 45, the eccentric and profane, but at least European-experienced former British regular officer; Lee's former colleague in the British forces, Horatio Gates, an associate of Washington in the Braddock campaign in 1755, and now, after Washington's persuasions, a near-neighbor in a Virginian retirement. Not least among those who became the "also-rans" was the man in charge in the early clashes in New England, who was spurring American forces to the occupation of Charlestown and Bunker Hill: Old Put," Israel Putnam, at 58 a local homespun hero of the French and Indian Wars, only semiliterate but a fiery barrel of energy, genial, popular, and keen to be so. The choice, made a long way from the fields of skirmishing, was easier than it might appear. To John Adams, leading Massachusetts delegate in the Congress and a "fixer" then and later, it seemed wise that a Southerner should lead what had thus far been a Massachusetts "show;" and the Virginian Washington, heavily muscled, standing six feet two and straight as an Indian, with experience of frontier war 20 years before, had some knowledge of the camp and of politics; and, not least, he looked the part, was reputedly the owner of 35,000 acres and the best horseman in Virginia, and refused to take pay for his services (though he was meticulous in keeping account over the eight years of what was due him in expenses).

In fact, the commander-in-chief looked and acted as, and was selected because he was, if not in origin, a natural aristocrat. He used a handsome coach, imported from London; he dressed like a wealthy squire, which he was, in a handsome uniform of dark blue faced with buff, set off by brass buttons; on formal occasions he wore a sword, and this was taken as an index of his politics. But he was taciturn: cool in action, a colleague remembered, "like a Bishop at his prayers." On occasion, however, he could be explosive. When he inspected his Boston forces in July 1775 he found them frightening – though not to any enemy: less than 50 cannon, hardly any powder, few trained gunners or engineers, little pay, and no order at all. Local militia from New Hampshire, Connecticut, and Rhode Island as well as Massachusetts, they were responding spontaneously to the events at Lexington and Concord; as militia, they elected their own officers, and some refused to serve with "strangers" from other parts of New England. Washington saw his first – and no easy – task as imposing discipline on what he called "a mixed multitude of people." One of his first and surprising orders was that "No person

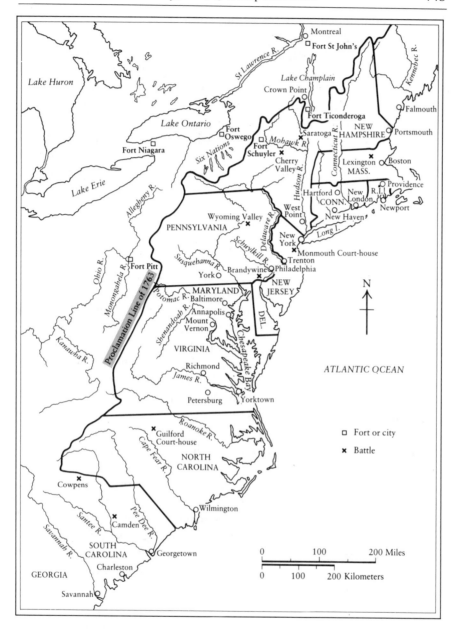

Map 12 Where the War was fought.

whatever belonging to the Army, is to be inoculated for the smallpox. He will be seen as an enemy and traitor to his country."
Though he himself carried the scars of the smallpox that had hit
him when young, and had insisted three months before on a terrified

Martha being inoculated, he could not risk the possible effects of a massive inoculation on his small and untrained force. His was a rough and miserable beginning to what proved to be an eight-year saga. He had to cajole Congress in securing uniform standards of pay, terms for re-enlistment, appointments, and demotion. In all that time he would only once be able to pay a call at Mount Vernon. In the course of it, the commander-in-chief did not change much; but the longer he lasted – to use Nathaniel Greene's phrase of all of them – the better he grew, and he grew into a legend, a legend that helped make a nation. To survive was in the end to conquer.

Lexington and Concord

Already, however, the shot had been fired that, in Emerson's words, was "heard around the world." Alarmed by the reports that the Provincial Congress was collecting stores at Concord, and under orders from home to seize the ringleaders of rebellion, General Gage, now military governor of Massachusetts, decided to raid the store-house and perhaps by a show of force to avert the incipient revolution. A British force of about 800 grenadiers and light infantrymen was ferried from Boston to Charlestown on the night of April 18, 1775, and set off on a night march for Concord, 18 miles away. Before it reached Lexington, William Dawes and Paul Revere and young Dr Prescott, whom they met *en route*, had roused the minutemen, and at dawn on April 19, 70 militia were drawn up on Lexington Green. No one knows who gave the order to fire, but in the skirmish that followed 8 militia men were killed and 10 wounded. The British troops pushed on to Concord and destroyed those stores not already removed; then, after a fight at Concord bridge, they began their long march back to Boston, sniped at all the way. They reached Boston only with the help of reinforcements under Lord Percy, and lost 273 men, three times as many as the colonists. The colonial militia, reinforced from all New England, closed in around the city and began a siege.[19]

---

[19] In fact, Paul Revere fell off his horse and was captured when trying to escape from British scouts after warning Hancock and Adams in Buckman's Tavern in Lexington. He had met Prescott – a local doctor, son and grandson of doctors – and told him his news. Prescott was returning home to Concord after visiting his girlfriend; it was his 24th birthday; he it was who warned the minutemen at Concord to hide their military stores; he died two years later in a British jail.

By the rude bridge that arched the flood,
Their flag to April's breeze unfurled,
Here once the embattled farmers stood,
And fired the shot heard round the world...

On this green bank, by this soft stream
We set to-day a votive stone;
That memory may their deed redeem,
When, like our sires, our sons are gone.

(R. W. Emerson, *The Concord Hymn*, April 19, 1836)

Within a week, some 30,000 militia had gathered round the city of the saints. Paul Revere and couriers like him carried the news to other colonies, and it was embroidered as it traveled with stories of rape, looting, and scalping. Indeed, later and ultra-patriotic American historians like George Bancroft and the poet Henry Wadsworth Longfellow were to write superb pieces of purple prose and poetry about Lexington and Concord: superb, if not always quite true.

What is certainly fact and not fancy is that the two leaders, John Hancock and Sam Adams, were at Lexington on their way to the Second Continental Congress in Philadelphia. On reaching it, they were now acclaimed as heroes. Sixty-five delegates attended, from all the Thirteen Colonies; many of them now knew each other after their meeting in the First Continental Congress nine months before; all had been chosen by radical and extra-legal conventions. The colonies, it was resolved, should be put in a state of defense. Congress assumed responsibility for the army around Boston, and imposed a quota on each colony sufficient to raise a Continental Line of 20,000 men. Benjamin Franklin, freshly returned from his ten years in London, found "all America from one End of the 12 United Provinces to the other, busily employed in learning the Use of Arms ... the Unanimity is amazing."

Even so, few in Philadelphia wanted a total break. But now shots were being fired with disturbing frequency, and events were – as in all wars – outrunning the strategists and the politicians. On May 10, Ethan Allen, never an easy man to discipline even when later he was in a British jail, and Benedict Arnold, the most combative American soldier of the war and not yet a traitor, led 300 Green Mountain Boys to capture the totally unprepared Fort Ticonderoga and Crown Point at the head of Lake George, seize some valuable artillery, and cut off British invasion routes from Canada. Allen, always good at self-advertisement, claimed that he summoned the half-sleeping British commander at Ticonderoga to surrender "in the name of the great Jehovah, and the Continental Congress," two authorities he himself never fully recognized. The New York folk version of the summons is less eloquent: "Come out," he shouted, "You damned old rat." As he told it himself:

The sun seemed to rise that morning with a superior luster; and Ticonderoga and its dependencies smiled on its conquerors, who tossed about the flowing bowl, and wished success to Congress and the Liberty and Freedom of America.[20]

On June 5, the impulsive British governor of Virginia, Lord Dunmore, took refuge on HMS *Fowey*, and for the next few months attacked Virginian coastal towns, destroying Norfolk and putting out abortive and foolish appeals to the slaves to rise in rebellion, to the alarm and anger of all Virginians. He sailed home in despair in July 1776: this was government by abnegation.

Bunker Hill

One day before Washington took up his commission in Philadelphia, the first major battle occurred. A Patriot force of 1,500 men, led by General Israel Putnam and Colonel William Prescott, set out to occupy Bunker Hill in Charlestown, commanding the port of Boston. By mistake they occupied the neighboring Breed's Hill, and dug themselves in. Next day they were shelled from British ships, but they were not driven off until three frontal assaults had been made by British troops under William Howe. Even then, they retired largely from a lack of ammunition. The American casualties were 449, of whom 145 were killed and missing; the British casualties were over 1,000, of whom 226 were killed. One-eighth of the British officers killed in the Revolutionary War fell on Breed's Hill, and almost half the British troops engaged were casualties. Well might Gage write to Lord Dartmouth, in giving an account of the battle: "the rebels are not the despicable rabble too many have supposed them to be, and I find it owing to a military spirit encouraged amongst them for a few years past, joined with an uncommon degree of zeal and enthusiasm."[21]

---

[20] Ethan Allen, *A Narrative of Col. Ethan Allen's Captivity* (4th edn, Burlington, Vt, 1846), p. 14.
[21] Gage to Lord Dartmouth, *Correspondence of General Thomas Gage*, ed. M. Carter, 2 vols (New Haven, Yale University Press, 1931–3), vol. I, p. 46.

The British held on to Boston until March 1776, by which time the burly Boston bookseller Henry Knox had brought, on sleds through the snows, the heavy cannons and mortars from Fort Ticonderoga and, from Dorchester Heights, trained them on the city and the anchorage. Howe, who had replaced Gage as commander-in-chief, evacuated his forces, and taking over 1,000 Loyalists with him, sailed away to Halifax, Nova Scotia, effectively the main naval base and strategic rear headquarters of the War. The date – to Irish rejoicing – was March 17, St Patrick's Day. Washington reported to Congress his first success; not only the enemy's withdrawal, but the booty he had won – cannon and cod, wheat and oats, powder and tools. The first round was, much to their own surprise, unquestionably won by the Americans.

Like Wellington afterwards, the commander-in-chief thought little of his troops, and with that general's similar bluntness said so, his Virginian control for once breaking down. He was, indeed, later to regret his comment on the Yankees as "an exceedingly dirty and nasty people." He was a firm disciplinarian. He deplored the extent to which officers curried favor with their men – he found one Connecticut captain of horse shaving a private soldier on the parade-ground near headquarters. He was convinced that sharp distinctions of rank were imperative; he wore a light blue ribbon across his breast, his generals pink, his aides green; officers were to wear cockades in their hats. Offenses, from cardplaying to "desertion" (absence without leave), were met by flogging – anything from 100 to 300 lashes, sometimes "to be well washed with salt and water after he has received his last fifty." In 1781 Washington was to recommend that court martials be allowed to increase the number of lashes to 500. Desertion in the modern sense was punishable by the death sentence. There were no illusions here, and no sentimentality. He knew the "dirty mercenary spirit" of his troops, and dealt with it not by democratic exhortations or the "humanitarianism" of the Revolution, but by discipline. He knew, too, the military limitations of his men;

Place them behind a parapet, a breast-work, stone wall or anything that will afford them shelter, and from their knowledge of a firelock they will give a good account of their enemy; but ... they will not march boldly up to a work, nor stand exposed in a plain.[22]

[22] Washington to Joseph Reed, November 28, 1775, in John C. Fitzpatrick (ed.), *The Writings of George Washington*, 39 vols (Washington, DC, 1931–44), vol. IV, p. 124.

His efforts were not made any easier by the arrival in camp in late July of the riflemen recruited by Congress in June: 9 companies from Pennsylvania, 3 more than were called for, and 2 each from Maryland and Virginia. Glad though Washington was to see them, especially Daniel Morgan's Virginians, who had marched 600 miles in 21 days, the "shirtmen" were hard to control. They were out to catch "lobsters," as they called the redcoats, and they appeared likely, by their fondness for sharpshooting, to use up the puny supply of powder and to encourage too many raids in retaliation. Nevertheless, their accurate fire and frontier training put fear into the British – "Never had the British Army so ungenerous an enemy," was one participant's view; "they send their riflemen, five or six at a time, who conceal themselves behind trees, &c., till an opportunity presents itself of taking a shot at our advance sentries which done they immediately retreat. What an unfair method of carrying on a war!" [23]

Through the next 12 months the attempt was made by the Continental Congress to hold out offers of conciliation. A month after Bunker Hill the Olive Branch petition, drawn up by the conservative and cautious John Dickinson, was sent to George III. It pledged continuing loyalty and pleaded for a repeal of the unjust laws of the 1760s. The king totally and ungraciously ignored it. Accompanying it, however, was the more radical "Declaration of the Causes and Necessity of Taking Up Arms": "Our cause is just. Our union is perfect ... being with one mind resolved to die free men rather than live slaves." Both at home and in America the mood hardened. Britain began to raise mercenaries first by appealing for 20,000 troops – happily unsuccessfully – to Catherine of Russia, then by hiring Germans, the so-called and inaccurately named Hessians – for the 30,000 of them who in the end saw service in North America came from all over Germany. As Ambrose Serle, Lord Howe's secretary, recognized, they "inflamed the Americans more than two or three British Armies ... the dread, which the rebels have of these Hessians, is inconceivable: they almost run at their name. Indeed, they spare nobody but glean all away like an Army of Locusts." [24] The colonies were declared by Britain to be in rebellion, their ships

---

[23] Charles Stedman, *The history of the Origin, Progress and Termination of the American War*, 2 vols (London, 1794), I. 154.

[24] Ambrose Serle, *The American Journal of Ambrose Serle, Secretary to Lord Howe 1776–1778*, ed. Edward Tatum, Jr (San Marino, CA, The Huntington Library, 1940). Cf. Charles Francis Adams, "The contemporary opinion of the Howes" (Massachusetts Historical Society, *Proceedings*, XLIV), pp. 118–20.

and cargoes liable to seizure. Petitions flooded in on Congress urging outright independence. In January 1776, in his famous and widely circulated 50-page tract *Common Sense*, Tom Paine decried the inconsistency of protesting loyalty to a king while engaging in war against his ministers: "Every thing that is right or reasonable pleads for separation. The blood of the slain, the weeping voice of nature cries, 'Tis Time to Part'." Paine for the first time put the blame squarely and vehemently not on Parliament but on the king, "the royal brute," "a hardened, sullen-tempered Pharaoh;" the voice now was openly republican, defiant – and, in British eyes, traitorous. One honest man, Paine declared, was worth more to society "than all the crowned ruffians that ever lived." The arguments now were no longer only economic, financial and constitutional. George III was seen as tyrant, and Americans were called on to oppose "not only the tyranny but the tyrant."

Freedom hath been hunted round the globe. Asia and Africa have long expelled her. Europe regards her like a stranger, and England hath given her warnings to depart. O! receive the fugitive, and prepare an asylum for mankind.

America had offered Paine himself an asylum only 15 months before: a failed English tax man, a failed tobacconist, a failed corset-maker, and a failed husband; indeed, a twice-failed husband, since his second wife paid him to leave her home. He had never been a journalist, but reached Philadelphia with aid and an open letter of support from that friend of all mankind, Benjamin Franklin. "It was," he said, after Lexington and Concord, "the cause of America made me an author." He made a fortune from his tract, but he gave half the profits to buy mittens for the American expedition against Quebec. But to Charles Lee and some 100,000 more he had "genius in his eyes."

A hundred thousand copies of Paine's tract were sold. *Common Sense* is the link between the "Declaration of the Causes of Taking Up Arms" of July 1775 and Jefferson's Declaration of Independence of July 1776. Massachusetts, North Carolina, and Virginia had by May 1776 instructed their delegates to support, or even to propose, independence.[25]

---

[25] Eric Foner, *Tom Paine and Revolutionary America* (New York, Oxford University Press, 1976); Alfred Owen Aldridge, *Man of Reason: Life of Thomas Paine* (London, Cresset Press, 1960).

Common Sense moved even Washington, no theorist, to approval and endorsement – "sound doctrine and unanswerable reasoning." "I would tell them," he wrote Joseph Reed in February, "that if nothing else could satisfy a tyrant and his diabolical ministry, we are determined to shake off all connections with a state so unjust and unnatural. This I would tell them, not under covert but in words as clear as the sun in its meridian brightness."[26] On June 24, 1776 Congress passed the Allegiance and Treason Resolves, defining the king as an enemy. R. H. Lee had introduced in Congress on June 7 his resolution that "these United Colonies are, and of right ought to be, free and independent States." It was a matter of right, no doubt, but it was also a matter of strategy; local – to bring pressure on hesitant states; and international – to win foreign aid. Independence was not a matter of theory, Lee argued, but the only means by which foreign alliances could be obtained. On July 2, Congress approved Lee's resolution, and two days later adopted Jefferson's draft of a Declaration of Independence. It listened also to the reading of a letter from Washington dated June 30:

When I had the honor of addressing you yesterday, I had only been informed of the arrival of forty-five of the (British) fleet in the morning. Since that time I have received authentic intelligence ... that one hundred and ten sail came in before night that were counted, and that more were seen about dusk in the offing. I have no doubt but that the whole that sailed from Halifax are now at the Hook.

The initiative in the War had moved from Philadelphia to Cambridge, then to New York, from a civilian-ridden Congress organized into 80 committees (with John Adams a member of almost every one of them) to Washington's headquarters. Fair or otherwise, the appearance of the shirtmen from the South alongside the loosely gathered New England companies of farmers and fishermen indicated that a continent, not a city, was in arms.[27]

The Declaration of Independence

The goals now were separation and republicanism. Congress no longer claimed "the rights of Englishmen" but "natural rights." When Thomas Jefferson, at the behest of Congress, drafted the

---

[26] Washington to Joseph Reed, February 8, 1776, in *Writings*, ed. Fitzpatrick, vol. X, p. 145.
[27] Freeman, *George Washington*, vol. III, p. 451.

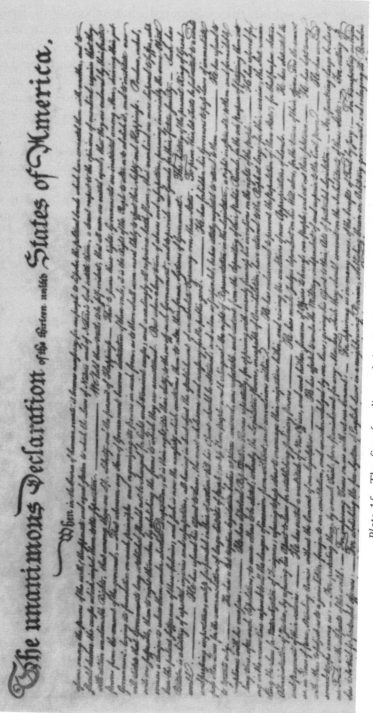

Plate 15 The first few lines of the Declaration of Independence.
(From a facsimile in the Mansell Collection, London.)

Declaration of Independence, he claimed that thus far the American people had voluntarily associated themselves with Britain, had voluntarily acknowledged the same king. This king, by his arbitrary acts — and 27 specific charges were listed — had forfeited this allegiance. There was no reference to Acts of trade, or to Parliament, at all. And this statement of fact, for a candid world, was prefaced with as noble a testament of faith in liberty and in man's capacity for it as has ever been penned:

We hold these truths to be self-evident, that all men are created equal; that they are endowed by their creator with certain unalienable rights; that among these are life, liberty and the pursuit of happiness. That, to secure these rights, governments are instituted among men, deriving their just powers from the consent of the governed; that, whenever any form of government becomes destructive of these ends, it is the right of the people to alter or to abolish it, and to institute new government, laying its foundation on such principles, organizing its powers in such form, as to them shall seem most likely to effect their safety and happiness.[28]

The Fourteenth Colony

It was now war on other fronts than New England's. A war at sea was planned. Coastal vessels were armed and manned by soldiers bred to the sea — Glover's Essex County Regiment from Massachusetts. The *Hannah*, under Captain Nicholson Broughton, the *Lee*, under Captain John Manley, and four others were instructed to capture supplies without engaging British warships. The *Lee* captured the brig *Nancy* in November, and when Gates saw her papers he said he could not have made out a better shopping list: small arms, musket shot, flints, and a brass mortar weighing 2,700 lb.

---

[28] The *Gentleman's Magazine* in London in September 1776 offered a comment that was also a rebuttals:

We hold, they say, these truths to be self-evident; That all men are created equal. In what are they created equal? Is it in size, strength, understanding, figure, moral or civil accomplishments, or situation of life? Every plough-man knows that they are not created equal in any of these. All men, it is true, are equally created, but what is this to the purpose? It certainly is no reason why the Americans should turn rebels because the people of Great Britain are their fellow creatures, i.e. are created as well as themselves. It may be a reason why they should not rebel, but most indisputably is none why they should. They therefore have introduced their self-evident truths, either through ignorance, or by design, with a self-evident falsehood; since I will defy any American rebel, or any of their patriotic retainers here in England, to point out to me any two men, throughout the whole World, of whom it may with truth be said that they are created equal.

The major offensive, however, was the plan to liberate Canada. It was believed to be lightly held – "The whole number of regulars in Canada," said Governor Trumbull of Connecticut, "does not exceed 700;" and it was thought ready, in Washington's phrase, "to run to the same goal" as the other United Colonies, "the only link wanting in the great continental chain of union." He prodded Schuyler to action in a letter of August 20, 1775, and the New Yorker, along with Brigadier Richard Montgomery, undertook an offensive from Ticonderoga and Crown Point, which had been taken so easily in May. They were to capture Fort St John's, Fort Chambly, and Montreal in succession, and then move down the St Lawrence to Quebec. Schuyler, as addicted to caution as Trumbull was to optimism, said his force of 1,700 men would be too few to use against Quebec, after garrisoning his line of march; after all, there were Indians as well as British to be faced. Washington undertook to dispatch a force of 1,000–1,200 to make a diversion which would baffle the British commander in Canada, General Sir Guy Carleton. This force would proceed along a little-known route, through the forests of Maine, up the Kennebec River, over the Dead River portages, and down the Chaudière, and would emerge on the St Lawrence opposite Quebec. To command it Washington chose Benedict Arnold, a swarthy and quarrelsome, but bold and energetic, Massachusetts colonel. Arnold, who had helped Allen to seize Ticonderoga but had won little credit, had all summer wished to attack Canada. With three companies of riflemen, one of them Daniel Morgan's Virginians, and a battalion of infantry, largely volunteers, with a wordy proclamation urging on the Canadians the value of an "indissoluble union," and with instructions to treat Catholic churches with particular respect, he was off in haste on September 17.

Montgomery's column advanced rapidly. Fort St John's, however, with 500 men, held out for eight weeks before it fell on November 3. On November 13 Montreal was occupied without opposition, though General Carleton got away downriver to Quebec, disguised as a trapper.

Arnold's expedition, however, had been a saga of endurance over "the terrible carrying place" on the Maine-Canada divide. His men had been held together only by the wills of Arnold and of Morgan – "whose appearance gave the idea history has left us of Belisarius." They lived on boiled candles and roasted moccasins until they reached the Chaudière. Colonel Enos, commanding the rear party, sent his supplies forward, but withdrew with his own men – to be court-martialed by Washington on his return to Cambridge. With his force reduced to 600 men, Arnold failed in an attempt to seize Quebec quickly, being repulsed by Colonel Allen Maclean and his Royal Highland Emigrants, and waited for Montgomery to come to the rescue with cannon, gunpowder, and warm clothing.

When Montgomery did join him, however, their numbers were dwindling. The men, miserably clothed for a winter campaign, refused to overstay their dates of enlistment. Writing to Washington on November 22, 1775; Schuyler reported that 300 of Montgomery's men had marched away, too feeble to do military duty until given their discharge, when they "instantly acquired health," and set off on a 200-mile march home "with the greatest alacrity." Nothing," he said, "can surpass the impatience of the troops from the New England colonies to get to their firesides."

On New Year's Eve Montgomery attempted a night attack through 4 ft snowdrifts. Neither of the American feints was successful, and the snow rendered the rebel firelocks useless — Montgomery was killed, by the last shot fired by a drunken sailor; Arnold was carried off the field with a ball through his leg; Morgan and 370 others were made prisoners. The wrecked army was ravaged by a smallpox epidemic — claiming one in four of his men — that was "ten times more terrible than Britons, Canadians and Indians together," — but it continued the siege through the long Canadian winter.

Round two, the war in Canada, was then a victory for Britain, thanks mainly to its liberalism three years before in passing the Quebec Act. Canada was to stay stubbornly loyal. But the victory had a dramatic personal consequence. Washington recognized that the prospects of possessing Canada were now "almost over." Arnold retreated slowly southwards, contesting the Lake Champlain waterway. If the British were to control this route, in 1776 and again in 1777 they would be able to enter New York from the Hudson valley as well as from the sea, and isolate New England. Arnold improvised a naval force of galleys and gunboats, built in haste of green wood. He was outnumbered and beaten again at Valcour Island in October 1776, and his "navy" destroyed; but he had thwarted Carleton's efforts to join up with Howe in New York at least until 1777. Had he not done so, there would have been no surrender at Saratoga, and probably no French alliance. Moreover, his efforts had diverted British supplies and men from New York to the St Lawrence. He had thus weakened Howe and delayed his attempt to regain control of the Middle States, and he had eased the pressure on Washington. Once again, however, Arnold won no plaudits, except from Washington, for his skill and dash. First Thomas, then Gates, had been given command of the Northern forces. Arnold's accounts were in disorder, and for a time he was under arrest. His bitterness grew dangerously with his failure to win recognition.

New York

From the outset, however, General Howe and his brother, the popular Admiral Lord Howe, had fully appreciated the central importance of New York, "the grand Magazine of America." Its splendid harbor could shelter the British fleet, on which, for supplies and equipment, the army would be almost totally dependent. All but surrounded by water, the city was unusually vulnerable to naval assaults. The Hudson River gave easy access to the interior as far as Albany, and thence eastward along the Mohawk into Iroquois country. This was British in sympathy, thanks to the role and skill of the British Superintendent to the Northern Indians, Sir William Johnson, who had from his headquarters at Johnson Hall until his death in 1774 dominated the New York interior. North from Albany the Hudson–Lake Champlain route allowed supplies to reach New York from Canada, and, by using it, New England could be isolated and the rebellion, it was thought, halted. Moreover, as a center of trade and traffic, New York City was Loyalist in spirit; of the *vans* and *velts* of the Hudson valley, the Van Cortlands and Schuylers provided Patriot leaders, but the Phillipses and Morrises were Loyalist.

While the Congress in Philadelphia debated and finally agreed on independence, Sir William Howe and his brother led into the Narrows the largest armada ever assembled in North American waters, and put ashore in Staten Island 30,000 British and German troops. To oppose them, Washington led 18,000 men, ill-trained and ill-equipped, many of them militia who had never smelled gunpowder.

The battle for New York City – round three of the struggle – was unquestionably a British victory. On August 27, Howe landed unopposed on Long Island, outflanked the American positions and drove the Patriots back to their fortifications on Brooklyn Heights opposite Manhattan; the American losses totalled 1,500 men, the British 300. Chastened by his experience the year before at Bunker Hill, Howe refused a frontal attack and began a siege, pushing Washington back on the East River. Washington rescued his men in a night operation, assisted by darkness and a storm, and moved across the river to occupy New York City itself. Moving slowly, and in almost leisurely and parade-ground fashion, Howe drove him north after engagements at Harlem Heights and White Plains. Washington then took his main force across the Huson at Peekskill and left to General Nathaniel Greene the decision whether or not to withdraw.

The indecision allowed British troops time to storm and capture
the only half-completed Fort Washington on the eastern bank (close
to the present George Washington Memorial Bridge); over 3,000
men were taken prisoner, and cannon and supplies captured. "I
feel mad, vexed, sick and sorry," wrote Greene to Knox. It was his
sole error of judgment in the war. Had Howe struck half-an-hour
earlier, he would have captured both Greene and Washington. As
the redcoats crossed the river in steady but slow pursuit, Washington
abandoned Fort Lee and withdrew his force of now less than 5,000
in disarray across the Jerseys, across the Delaware, and into Pennsylvania. It was an ignominious story: a series of routs, with
Washington at Kip's Bay beating his troops with his cane and half-
demented in his efforts to make them stand their ground. The retreat
he described himself as "disgraceful and dastardly." The British had
taken New York and controlled most of New Jersey in less than three
months' campaigning, and with few casualties; New York City remained in their hands throughout the war. Washington's orders to
both Lee and Greene, though clear enough, had not been sufficiently
peremptory. His tactical positions were often exposed and vulnerable. He had critics in Congress, Richard Henry Lee among them,
critics among his fellow-generals like Gates and Charles Lee, critics
even on his own headquarters staff. His secretary, Joseph Reed, and
General Charles Lee, in a correspondence Washington came upon
by accident, joined in deploring "an indecisive Mind."

The Crisis

The outlook in December was vastly different from that in March.
Congress reasoned that when the Delaware River froze, Philadelphia, too, would fall to the British, and it prudently moved to
Baltimore, giving Washington full powers to act. The British swarmed
across New Jersey to Trenton and Bordentown – and garrisoned
them, with unfortunate political results, with German troops. Howe
offered pardons to all who would submit, and 3,000 accepted. The
American cause looked hopeless: "the heat of the rebellion is now
really broken," wrote Ambrose Serle, Howe's secretary; Washington's
numbers were now down to 3,000 and more would leave on January
1. Tom Paine's pamphlet *The Crisis*, written during the retreat,
began with the words:

These are the times that try men's souls. The summer soldier and the
sunshine patriot will, in this crisis, shrink from the service of their country;
but he that stands it *now* deserves the love and thanks of man and woman.

Even in this chronicle of disaster, however, there was some slight encouragement. Washington crossed the ice-choked Delaware River on Christmas night 1776, with 2,000 men, and struck at the Hessian post at Trenton. Leutze's famous portrait of the crossing – painted 70 years later and using the Rhine as background – is not likely to have been faithful to the original; Washington is unlikely to have stood tall, upright, and commanding, gazing calmly and intrepidly forwards into the teeth of a piercing north wind, nor is the boat behind him likely to have had a mounted rider sitting on his horse nonchalantly in mid-stream. In fact, two of his supporting groups failed to make the crossing at all. But the Hessian commander, appropriately saluting the Christmas spirit, was happily befuddled and fell mortally wounded, and 1,000 of his men were captured; Washington's casualties were exactly three, one of them future president, James Monroe. Not satisfied with this, and while Cornwallis with 8,000 men was chasing "the old fox," three days later Washington struck the British garrison at Princeton, and drove it from the town with heavy casualties (between 250 and 350; 40 Americans dead, 100 wounded). When he took up winter quarters at Morristown, Washington had done much by these two quick blows to redeem his failure in New York. And Howe, after ample opportunities, had failed to capture him.

1777 was the turning point of the war. From the outset the British strategy depended on the central importance of the Hudson valley. From it could come a liberating army from Canada, which "Gentleman" Johnny Burgoyne – MP and playwright, adventurer and egotist – would gladly lead, for fame mattered to him even more than fortune; "the old gamester," was Gates's view of him. Carleton wanted to complete in 1777 what he had almost succeeded in doing the year before, to free Canada from the threat of American invasion, and to reinforce Howe by land – to do so by sea would leave Canada exposed, and the anxious wait for Burgoyne's reinforcements during Quebec's siege in 1776 was too recent a memory – and, by compelling Washington to divide up his puny army still further, to facilitate Howe's own movements. Howe, for his part, wanted to tie Washington down in New York, and believed that only a small force was needed to go north to Albany; a third force, backed by Indians, would advance from the west into the Mohawk and form yet one more supporting column for Burgoyne. This would allow Howe with the main force to take Philadelphia. He could always then go north to cooperate with Burgoyne, in the unlikely event that such support from him would be necessary. All the British commanders save Clinton were richly endowed with the adrenalin of over-confidence.

In July 1777 Howe sailed for the Chesapeake with an armada of 260 ships and 15,000 men – to Washington's surprise and bewilderment. By the time he had grasped that Howe's intentions were to move on Philadelphia, he had already sent north to oppose Burgoyne all the men he could spare, including the leaders Morgan, Lincoln, and Arnold, who were to do so much to win the day at Saratoga.

On September 11, 1777, Howe defeated Washington on the Brandywine creek; American casualties were over 1,000 out of 10,000 men engaged. Ten days later at Paoli, 300 of Wayne's 1,500 men were casualties in a British bayonet charge. Howe occupied Philadelphia on September 27, and the Continental Congress fled to Lancaster. The British spent a happy and well-fed winter in Philadelphia, a city they found curiously and suddenly rich in Loyalist sentiment. They celebrated with parties, balls, and good sport by day and night: a number of officers had to sell their commissions to pay their gambling debts, and returned home. A splendid fete, described as a "Mischianza," was organized for Sir William: a regatta followed by a medieval tournament, and culminating in a display of fireworks. It was, said the cynics, the only gunpowder Howe had smelt for nine months. In sharp contrast, Washington's now partly barefoot force were encamped at Valley Forge, 20 miles away. For them it was the most agonizing experience of the long seven years of war.

Washington described Valley Forge as "a dreary kind of place, and uncomfortably provided." His men lived in shabby tents until they felled trees to make logs for cabins – but there were few nails or tools for building them. Half of them were without blankets, nearly half without shoes. "All my men," reported Colonel Livingston, "except eighteen are unfit for duty for want of shoes, stockings and shirts, breeches and coats ... and ... we are becoming exceedingly lousy." Sullivan reported his officers "so naked they were ashamed to be seen." Even the deserters could hardly leave camp for lack of decent covering. While the British ate good beef and butter from rich Pennsylvania "Dutch" larders, the Americans drank soup "full of burnt leaves and dirt, enough to make a Hector spew." "Poor food – hard lodging – cold weather – fatigue – nasty clothes – nasty cookery – vomit half my time – smoked out of my senses – the Devil's in't – I can't endure it," wrote the surgeon Albigence Waldo.

But they did endure: they grew as tough and determined as they were lean, and after the arrival of the Prussian Baron Friedrich Wilhelm von Steuben they were better drilled than ever before. Washington's greatest achievement as commander was to keep an army in being and to train it at Valley Forge. He always declared afterwards that Howe could still have won the war had he attacked at that point; but so long as he endured, Washington prevented the British from dominating the central colonies, and threatened them both in New York and Philadelphia.

Saratoga

Already, however, the tide had in fact turned. For if round five, the campaign for Philadelphia, was – like the campaign for New York a year before – a British victory, as most such set-piece battles proved to be, round six, fought in the narrow defiles of the Hudson valley, proved to be decisive. It brings into the story a colorful figure: Major-General "Gentleman Johnny" Burgoyne. In February 1777, Burgoyne had presented to the king, and to Lord George Germain, Secretary of State for the Colonies, a plan, his "Thoughts for conducting the war from the side of Canada" – a decisive scheme, though not an original one. The colonies should be cut off from each other, and New England isolated by a powerful thrust from Canada down the Lake Champlain–Hudson valley route, supported by a secondary effort eastward from Lake Erie up the Mohawk. Meeting at Albany, the combined force would join with a full-scale converging thrust by Howe up the Hudson from New York. King George's troops would be united in the very heartland of the insurrection, and Boston, the hotbed of the troubles, would be isolated.

However attractive on paper, the plan was over-optimistic about the numbers and response of the Loyalists, and minimized the logistical problems – the transport of heavily burdened troops and their guns through congested narrow rocky defiles, commanded by Indians and with many forested obstacles. Moreover, Howe had an alternative plan for ending the war, and was already engaged on it: the occupation of Philadelphia. Germain may have appreciated that these two plans were irreconcilable, in that Howe could not be in two places at the same time. In any event, he gave no direct order to Howe to cooperate with Burgoyne, though Howe does seem to have known of Burgoyne's plan to advance from Albany from Canada; being a confident man, he may have hoped to get there from a now submissive Philadelphia before the end of Burgoyne's campaign.

Indeed, the failure began with the personal rivalries of the commanders in their failure to understand each other, and their different personalities: Howe was a competent, hitherto successful, infantryman, but lacking in imagination, and believing that a display of force would bring surrender; Burgoyne, with the reputation of a playwright, was an MP, and a moderate on the American question, with experience as a successful soldier in Portugal in the Seven Years' War.

In any event, Burgoyne, an optimist and full of braggadocio, set off from St John's in the summer of 1777 with 7,000 men, including some 3,000 Hessians under General von Riedesel, fully equipped with 42 field guns and massive stores, aided – or hindered? – by Indian allies, naval frigates, and some 400 women camp-followers. Some of them were wives of officers; the majority were companions, licit or merely attached, of the troops, and were often described and dressed as "washerwomen." Their services were needed, for it was a long journey. In July Burgoyne recaptured Ticonderoga, at the southern end of Lake Champlain. Here he was to have been met by a diversionary force of 1,600 British and Iroquois Indians under Colonel Barry St Leger and the Mohawk chief Brant, moving down the St Lawrence from Oswego and then along the Mohawk. This column, however, while besieging Fort Stanwix, was checked at Oriskany by a band of frontier Germans under General Herkimer, and when a second American army under Arnold approached, St Leger retreated to Oswego and Montreal; his Indian allies deserted what seemed to be the losing cause, and Burgoyne was left to fend for himself.

Burgoyne spent a month collecting supplies. He sent two large foraging parties into Vermont, but they were attacked at Bennington by John Stark and the Green Mountain Boys, and all 1,000 of them were killed or captured. These successes brought the New England militia, almost as volatile in their allegiance as the Indians, to Gates's colours; in the end, in the Hudson Valley he had 12,000 militia and 5,000 Continentals. But Burgoyne had 6,000 mouths to feed, an army overloaded with baggage and with wives, and his transport was wearing out. Congress did not help the American cause by shuffling the command between Gates and Schuyler – there were five changes in command between the two in 15 months. Gates was, in October 1777, the chosen of Congress and the chosen of Fortune. Whether or not he personally deserved the victory, as a professionally trained soldier and former colleague of Washington's, he won the confidence of the Yankee militia, as Schuyler, a wealthy New York landowner, did not; he had able subordinates – Morgan of Virginia with his riflemen, sent to his aid by Washington; Benjamin Lincoln of Massachusetts; and Arnold, brash and as jealous as ever; and he disposed his forces ably in strongly entrenched positions at Saratoga.

Burgoyne attempted twice to attack Gates's forces – unsuccessfully (September 19, October 7). Only a quick retreat could have saved his army, and this he did not attempt, in the hope that General

Henry Clinton might come from his headquarters in New York. The Baroness von Riedesel, wife of the commander of the Brunswick troops with Burgoyne, has left in her *Memoirs* a vivid description of the plight of the dwindling, stranded, and hungry army, and a vividly hostile description of its chief, spending half the nights singing and drinking, "and amusing himself with the wife of a commissary, who was his mistress, and who, as well as he, loved champagne." On October 14, 20 miles away from his target, Albany, he offered to negotiate, and the "Convention of Saratoga" was signed on October 17.[29]

Saratoga was not a total disaster, and it was, nominally at least, a convention not a surrender. A band played "Yankee Doodle", and toasts were drunk to King George and to General Washington. The Anglo-German troops, now numbering 5,000, were to abandon arms and material, march to Boston, and embark on British transports on condition that they did not again serve in America. These were easy terms won from Gates by "Gentleman Johnny," the skillful playwright, when his soldierly qualities had failed him; but it was the arms that Gates wanted, for Clinton was now pushing north, and Gates's own militia were leaving him already. The "Convention Army," as it came to be known, did not, however, reach Britain until after the war. Congress found a series of excuses to reject Gates's terms, and the army was shuttled back and forth between Virginia and Massachusetts, becoming the first prisoner and internment problem in American history. When they finally sailed for Europe in 1783, 1,500 chose to stay behind.

Nevertheless, Saratoga transformed the war. A large British army had been destroyed; the Americans had again decisively denied the Hudson valley to the British, and, in particular, the victory made France an active ally. For two years, through Beaumarchais, dramatist turned agent, and his fictitious company, Hortalez et Compagnie, trading nominally with the West Indies, supplies had been reaching America secretly and illicitly. The weapons of the American forces at Saratoga had been largely supplied by France. But sympathetic though it was, not even Benjamin Franklin's popularity could induce the French Court to declare war until there was evidence of a chance of American victory. That was provided – or held to be provided – by Saratoga. In fact, it was less victory in the field that turned the tide than the French foreign minister Vergennes's fears of the British conciliation proposals, on which Franklin and

[29] Max M. Mintz, *The Generals of Saratoga, John Burgoyne and Horatio Gates* (New Haven, Yale University Press, 1990).

Beaumarchais played. These peace proposals, presented by Lord North to Parliament in November 1777, hung fire over the Christmas season, and were not approved until February 17, 1778. By then, it was too late. On February 6, 1778, political and commercial treaties were signed by which France recognized the independence of the revolting colonies and agreed to make war upon Britain until American independence was won. Neither side was to make a separate peace without the consent of the other.

In April 1779, Spain came in as an ally of France – though not an ally of America – and for her own good reasons: to regain Gibraltar and the Floridas. The Dutch gave financial aid to the American cause, and by 1780 were at war with Britain over questions of neutral rights at sea. Britain also faced the League of Armed Neutrality, which by 1783 all the major and many of the minor states of Europe had joined. Britain's political and trading rivals in Europe were using the situation to their advantage; the colonial war had become worldwide. America by her treaties had become entangled in the affairs of Europe – in ways so embarrassing that she deplored entangling alliances for the next 170 years; and Britain, facing again her European foes, began to consider the independence of America, a price that it might be cheap to pay. With France in the field, the American war, as again in 1812, became a sideshow.

The character of the struggle in America was thus transformed. French and Spanish and Dutch money and ships of war came to American aid, and volunteers too, from all over Europe: the young marquis de Lafayette, enthusiastic, lovable and ambitious for "glory;" Louis Alexander Berthier, later one of Napoleon's marshals; the Baron Johann de Kalb, whose original mission was to persuade Congress to replace Washington as commander by his patron, the Comte de Broglie; the Pole Casimir Pulaski, who, like Baron Johann de Kalb, was to die serving America; Thaddeus Kosciusko, who organized the defenses of Saratoga and West Point, and was to Gates what Lafayette was to Washington, aide and admirer; and the Prussian drill-captain Baron von Steuben, whose rank Franklin inflated to that of general, who drilled Washington's men at Valley Forge. The aid was welcome, the men, the ships, and the money. Not only welcome but timely, for there was no jingoism left in Washington's army in the winter of 1777. Indeed, by February 1778, there was hardly an army left at all.

The surrender of Saratoga, the awareness of the possibility now of defeat, if not by Washington's puny army, then, in the end, by the impossibility of disciplining a vast and untamed continent, the entry of France and the need to direct 8,000 men to hold the West

Indies sugar islands: with all these factors the War was now widened and transformed. The threat from the old enemy, it is true, brought back into service men like Sir Jeffry Amherst and Admiral Keppel, who had refused thus far to take up arms against Americans. But the American War was now too expensive. A peace commission went out in the summer of 1778 under the Earl of Carlisle and offered terms which three years earlier might well have averted the clash altogether – the removal of standing armies in peacetime, the renunciation of the right to tax, the amending of colonial charters only at the request of colonial assemblies, and recognition of Congress. But in 1778 such terms were scorned, because now – unlike 1775 – bloodshed had bred the wish for total independence. As Tom Paine had noted, to many Americans Britain was no longer the mother-country; and thousands of Loyalists had fled. Moreover, there was a real possibility of an actual French invasion of the home islands. In the exploits of John Paul Jones, who raided his native area, the Solway, in 1779, and made Brest a major centre from which to terrorize Britain's shipping lanes, the threat was made all too real and personal. Franklin drew up plans, and instructed John Paul Jones as admiral, and Lafayette as likely commander, of an invading force. Privateers had been menace enough already, but mainly in New England waters. Jones in his first year at sea captured 16 British ships. From now on the French navy played a key role in the war. The French and Spanish put 120 ships of the line into the War; they besieged Gibraltar for the next four years; the Spanish threatened Jamaica, and in 1780 took Mobile and Pensacola. In July 1778 Comte d'Estaing arrived with 12 ships of the line in Delaware Bay, turned and unsuccessfully attacked Newport, Rhode Island, and wintered in the West Indies: a marauding and unpredictable enemy threatening Britain's Atlantic supply lines. Britain's problems of communication and administration were sharply worsened. French and Dutch bankers now supplied badly needed funds. In North America itself a new British strategy had to be devised. It looked to new areas – and it took uglier forms.

Fearing a Franco-American joint attack, Clinton, who had replaced Howe, withdrew his forces from Philadelphia back to the one reliable British base, New York. From it at least his forces could be dispersed to all the danger points: Florida, the West Indies, Halifax, or the St Lawrence. In the course of the retreat, the British rearguard withstood a half-hearted attack at Monmouth Court House (June 1778); the failure of this attack Washington blamed on General Charles Lee, his erratic and unbalanced ex-British second-in-command, till then part Polonius, part Iago, a brilliant and experienced, but egocentric and untrustworthy, officer. He was court-martialed and dismissed. By 1779 Washington's reputation, despite a steady succession of defeats, and the clumsy intrigues of the "Conway Cabal," was proving resistant both to the criticism of Congress and of fellow-officers. Total integrity and dedication, almost superhuman self-control, a strong physique (despite a constant preoccupation with illnesses and a conviction that death would come early), a remarkable capacity for survival, and the stubbornness bred of a Virginian identification of his own "fame" with his country's cause — these were proving to be the bedrock on which the survival of an army, and with it of a nation, were founded. He was always conscious of his role as the first servant of a civilian state. After 1779 the criticisms died away; he was now seen and described as *Pater Patriae*. The first such reference appears in Pennsylvania in 1779 in a German almanac: he is "Des Landes Vater." His career was the triumph, not of intellect, but of character and of courage.

Treason

However, the reality in America was still grim; senior officers — Schuyler and Sullivan, Monroe and Hamilton — resigned their commissions. There was worse: not merely the Conway Cabal, seeking to replace Washington as commander-in-chief by Horatio Gates, the victor of Saratoga, but treason itself.

Benedict Arnold, the Connecticut drug merchant, with conspicuous successes at the capture of Fort Ticonderoga (May 1775), in Quebec (December 1775), at Valcour Island (October 1776), and not least at Saratoga (October 1777), was made restless by what seemed lack of recognition. Commanding the forces that garrisoned Philadelphia in 1778–9, and marrying an attractive wealthy girl, Peggy Shippen, he incurred heavy debts, and in 1779 was court-martialled for what he said were minor fiscal irregularities. He began an intrigue with the British to turn over to them the strategic American fort at West Point on the Hudson, to the command of which he was soon to move. The agent he employed was a Loyalist merchant who talked to Major John André, aide-de-camp to the British commander-in-chief, General Henry Clinton. Had the fort been surrendered, Clinton would have controlled the Hudson valley and would have been in a position to isolate New England. In September 1780, André, while returning from a final rendezvous with Arnold, then in command at West Point, and wearing civilian clothes that made him technically a spy, was captured and found to be carrying incriminating papers that revealed the plot. He was tried, found guilty and executed – later to be interred as a national hero in Westminster Abbey. Benedict Arnold was now seen as a traitor by the Americans; he fled to the British Army, and was appointed a brigadier-general. Although he led British raiding parties in Virginia in December 1780, he was unsuccessful; in 1781 he went to Britain. Arguably the ablest battle commander on either side, he ended his career in poverty and disgrace.[30]

The Western Strategy

There was another theatre of war besides the Hudson valley or New York; a wild and indeterminate 1,000-mile line of mountains and valleys, little known back East, and all but unmapped. In the West, the clashes between Indians jealous of their hunting grounds and whites greedy for land had preceded 1776 and did not stop in 1783. The frontier from the St Lawrence to the pine-barrens of Georgia was and had been all but impossible for Britain to control from London. So it was from Philadelphia, from whose Quaker pacifism and mercantile tastes it was quite alien. The "men of the western waters," proud, isolated, rough, and self-contained, were always in their own fashions at loggerheads with the East. This tended to make the West Loyalist country, especially so among the Iroquois in the Mohawk valley – although one Iroquois tribe, the Oneida, under the influence of the missionary Samuel Kirkland, was Patriot in sympathy. Further south, in the frontier country of North Carolina, there was a long history of violence; the Regulator associations had come into being as vigilance societies in protest against the corruption of the Tidewater, the high taxes, the exorbitant fees of lawyers, and the lack of adequate representation of the West in colonial assemblies. All they sought was "justice and good order." In 1771 the Regulators had been defeated by the militia at the battle of the Alamance, and some of their ringleaders were hanged. In 1776 the Carolina frontier rose again, this time flying Loyalist banners. They did so in order to march to the lower reaches of the Cape Fear River, in the firm expectation of support by British regulars under Clinton from Boston, and the fleet under Vice-Admiral Sir Peter Parker – a support that did not come in time. Some 1,500 Loyalists, mainly Scots and Scots-Irish, assembled at Moore's Creek Bridge, and were indeed inspected, and addressed in Gaelic, by Flora

[30] Carl Van Doren, *The Secret History of the American Revolution* (New York, Viking Books, 1941); Willard Sterne Randall, *Benedict Arnold, Patriot and Traitor* (New York, William Morrow, 1990).

MacDonald riding a milk-white charger — the same Flora MacDonald who 30 years before had abetted Bonnie Prince Charlie in his escape back to France after the Battle of Culloden. They were defeated by the Patriots in a 3-minute engagement, and nearly 850 of them were taken prisoner, including Flora MacDonald's husband Alan. The British force that might have helped kept prudently to the coast, and was in any case eight weeks late. This frontier stayed uneasily quiet for the next three years.

The real threat in the West came from the Indians, who could strike at settlements quickly without warning, who used tomahawks mercilessly, and who were often in British pay, with whiskey and trinkets as currency. In 1776 and again in 1778 there were attacks by the Cherokee in the Carolinas, especially against the Watauga settlement, and counter-attacks in kind. Scalping was not just an Indian practice. Further north, in 1778 some of the worst savagery of the war occurred in the Wyoming valley and Cherry valley massacres at the hands of the Six Nations of the Iroquois, equipped from the British post at Niagara. Alarmed at the reports that the British commander at Detroit, Colonel Henry Hamilton ("the Hair Buyer"), encouraged the Indians by offering to buy Patriot scalps, Governor Patrick Henry and the Virginia legislature in 1778 sent out George Rogers Clark with 175 militia and frontiersmen to seize British forts in the Northwest, in that region which since 1774 had been technically part of the Province of Quebec. By the summer of 1778 Clark, by floating down the Ohio to Fort Mossac in Illinois and then moving overland, had made himself master of the old French towns of Kaskaskia and Cahowkia and proclaimed the region part of Virginia as Illinois County. The French *habitants* cared little about America's Revolution, but were impressed at the news of the Franco-American alliance. Hamilton struck back in December and fortified himself in Vincennes. Early in 1779, after a gruelling march of 200 miles in the dead of winter across flooded prairies of ice and snow, Clark and his men captured Vincennes and its commander.

I expect you shall immediately surrender yourself with your garrison prisoners at discretion. If any of the stores be destroyed or any letters or papers burned, you may expect no mercy, for by Heavens you shall be treated as a murtherer.

Clark had won the Northwest for the Patriots, but neither he nor his men got a cent of pay. Indeed, in retrospect this least-known area of the war was in fact much the most significant. A tiny unpaid Virginian column of less than 200 men won for the United States a northwest empire larger than the combined area of contemporary France and Prussia. Indeed, by contrast, Frederick the Great fought 16 major battles involving half a million men during the Seven Years' War, and in the end not an acre of German ground changed hands. Savage and sanguinary fighting continued in this vast and uncharted no man's land for the next four years.

The Southern Strategy

The War of Independence came to an end in the area that had been, in terms of grand strategy, thus far largely neglected, the South. From the beginning there was in London and in Europe a belief that the American rebellion was only a Yankee affair, Yankee and a legacy of Dissent. The Hessians were struck by the character of the armies and the people they met. Thus the letter-book of Captain Johann Heinrichs:

Call this war, dearest friend, by whatsoever name you may, only call it not an American Rebellion, it is nothing more or less than an Irish-Scotch Presbyterian Rebellion. Those true Americans who take the greatest part therein, are the famous Quakers. The most celebrated, the first ones in entire Pennsylvania and Philadelphia and Boston are, properly speaking, the heads of the Rebellion. I am not allowed to write to you explicitly, just how the matter developed, but you can guess at what I have omitted, and you will hit it pretty fairly ...

For the first you must assume two Rebellions proper. The former was fomenting fifty years ago. It was the result of a state projected upon false principles, whose citizens consisted of seemingly hypocritical pious impostors, and downright cheats. These hypocrites are the Quakers. I cannot tell you all of the infamy I hold these people capable of; for I can think of nothing more abominable, than to practise, under the guise of Religion — malice, envy, yea even ambition (thirst of power). ... By means of such cabals these manifest cheats contrived to attract the Germans who have settled here.

The second rebellion is that which originated amongst the rebels during the past campaign, namely that for Independence ... just as Congress consists of Scoundrels, so the Army consists of people, warmed up in part by the war party ... This is the army proper of the enemy, numbering about 12,000 men. The remainder substitutes and Militia, of whom ten or twenty thousand are mobile at times, these fight only for the Province in which they dwell, and have been unable to resolve joining the Army and go into another province.[31]

[31] "Letter-Book of Captain Johann Heinrichs," *Pennsylvania Magazine of History and Biography*, 22 (1898), pp. 137–9. The diary of Captain Heinrichs, together

If New England could be cut off at the Hudson, or if the unnatural alliance of Massachusetts and Virginia could be broken, the sources of sedition would be blocked. Some governors, notably Josiah Martin of North Carolina, Lord William Campbell of South Carolina, and Sir James Wright of Georgia, encouraged these rosy views. An expedition commanded by Sir Peter Parker and General Clinton sailed south in 1776, intended for Charleston – the news of which had produced the abortive rising at Moore's Creek Bridge. It did not reach Charleston until June. Under Colonel William Moultrie, gallantly defending a fort on Sullivan's Island of soft and green palmetto logs, which proved happily absorbent of British shells – the state seal of South Carolina still permanently salutes the occasion – the South Carolinians repulsed a British landing force on June 28, 1776.

In 1778, with the Hudson valley campaign now an unhappy memory, and the Middle Colonies, it seemed, permanently lost, the British returned to their Southern strategy. The Loyalists here were thought to be numerous; this was tobacco and rice country, the staple crops of the Navigation system; Under-Secretary of State William Knox had his own estates in Georgia; the Indians were militant. In December 1778 a British force captured Savannah, and held it in October 1779 against an amphibious force led by General Benjamin Lincoln and d'Estaing. After his failure, Lincoln took refuge in Charleston, was besieged there by a British force of 14,000 led by Clinton and Cornwallis, and in 1780 had to surrender it with 5,000 men. This was Saratoga in reverse; in the South the war seemed far from over.

The only American columns were of irregulars and partisans, fighting now an ugly guerrilla war, and showing that Indians had no monopoly of savagery. They were led in the West by John Sevier and Isaac Shelby, in the Carolina lowlands by Andrew Pickens, Thomas Sumter, and Francis Marion, "the swamp fox." "There was scarce an inhabitant between the Santee and the Pee Dee that was not in arms against us," said Cornwallis.[32] Congress sent south Horatio Gates, the hero of Saratoga, and still, in the eyes of a few,

---

with other Hessian accounts and some letters, can be found in Bernhard A. Uhlendorf (ed.), *The Siege of Charleston* (University of Michigan Publications in History and Political Science, XII, Ann Arbor, 1938).

[32] Lt Colonel Banastre Tarleton, *A History of the Campaigns of 1780 and 1781* (London, 1787), p. 200, cited in Samuel Griffiths, *The Defense of The Public Liberty: Britain, America and the struggle for independence from 1760 to the surrender at Yorktown in 1781* (London, Jonathan Cape, 1977), p. 610.

the real hero of the War. In August 1780, however, he was routed at Camden, South Carolina, in what was the most crushing defeat of the whole war, and one which totally destroyed his reputation. Gates retreated precipitately, leaving North Carolina exposed, and was replaced by Nathaniel Greene, Washington's quartermaster. The defeat at Camden rid Washington of his only rival. Never happy as a quartermaster, Greene was ready to fight the war in the South on the Washington model, and indeed, unlike Gates, was "subject to the control of the Commander-in-Chief." The army was now co-ordinated. Under Greene, the object now became not to win battles but to avoid defeats, to draw Cornwallis away from Charleston and his naval supply route, to use "Lighthorse Harry" Lee's cavalry to counter Lt Colonel Tarleton's, and to attack isolated units with guerrillas.

Tarleton was defeated at Cowpens in January 1781. Cornwallis reached the Dan, on the boundaries of southwestern Virginia, and fought a pitched battle at Guilford Court House, a British victory of the sort that ruins an army – "A pledge", said Tarleton, "of ultimate defeat." It was now a war of chase and maneuver, a "country dance" with the British led at last by a commander – Cornwallis – who sought decisions. He took his army to Wilmington, and in April 1781, to Clinton's consternation, marched into Virginia to secure reinforcements.

In the previous two years there had been four raids into Virginia up the tidal rivers, one of them led by Arnold; Richmond, and Petersburg, with its stores of tobacco, and some plantation homes, had been burnt. Virginia's waterways made it vulnerable to inva-sion, but little had been done to prepare its defenses; its governor, Jefferson, was happier as a theorist than as an executive. And it offered tempting booty. Cornwallis drove into Richmond, and Tarle-ton's cavalry almost captured Governor Jefferson at Charlottesville: he rode down one side of his little mountain as Tarleton galloped up the other. Lafayette took up the game of dodging and parrying. Cornwallis moved towards the sea to be near the British fleet, and to maintain communications more easily with Clinton in New York City; in July he set up defenses on the Yorktown peninsula.

The idea of bottling up the British in Virginia had presented itself already, and Washington had lost his temper when it failed against Arnold, through what he thought the lethargy of the French. In 1781 he had some 5,000 Continentals in New York, and he was joined by Rochambeau with some 5,000 French, brought from Newport. In July they pressed the new French naval commander in the West Indies, the Comte de Grasse, to sail for the Chesapeake and to attempt a combined operation. When he agreed, Washington and Rochambeau began to move their forces southwards to trap Cornwallis (August 17). Though they tried to hide their intentions from Clinton, he informed Cornwallis (September 2) that Virginia was the probable target. The Virginian major, St George Tucker, exulted: "We shall have a Burgoyneade in Virginia."

Washington did not find it so easy to exult. He marched his men through Philadelphia and their numbers raised a dust "like a smothering snowstorm;" but alongside the French regiments they were unkempt and ill-disciplined, and they had not been paid for months. It was only the news of de Grasse's arrival off the Chesapeake that enabled Robert Morris to pay them, and this he did by borrowing a month's pay from Rochambeau himself. To confirm that the Fates were smiling on American efforts, the *Resolve* reached Boston with two million livres from France, and the casks of coins were dragged over New England and New Jersey roads to Philadelphia. Washington was in his own country now, seeing familiar orchards and fields golden with the finest crops for seven years. He paused at Mount Vernon before taking command at Williamsburg on September 15.

Even then his difficulties were not over, and de Grasse gave him more trouble than Cornwallis. With 40 ships of the line, de Grasse defeated a relieving force under Admiral Graves on September 5, and wanted to continue the struggle at sea. He had no taste for the passive role in a war of sieges – and wanted to return to the West Indies. A conference was held on his flagship, *Ville de Paris*, which seven months later was to be a riddled hulk at the Battle of the Saints; de Grasse finally gave way to Washington's pleas, but he still refused to station frigates above Cornwallis's position, and left him therefore a thin and desperate chance of escape. But Rochambeau had received valuable siege artillery; a storm crippled the British fleet, which withdrew for refitting to New York; continuing gales prevented attempts at supply forces; and Cornwallis, outnumbered by two to one (15,000 French and Americans versus 8,000 British), and only dimly aware of the naval battle off the Virginia Capes, was bottled up in Chesapeake Bay.

The Yorktown siege lasted three weeks (September 28–October 19, 1781). American and French engineers dug trenches ever closer, but were thwarted by British redoubts. Washington decided to capture these by surprise night-time bayonet raids. They were taken on October 14 – one of them, no. 10, by a force led by Lt Colonel Alexander Hamilton, Washington's former aide-de-camp. Surrender now was inevitable; Cornwallis requested talks on the terms.

Washington refused to consider a convention like that at Saratoga, and gave identical terms to those offered by Clinton to Lincoln at Charleston in 1780: total surrender. Lincoln was appointed to receive Cornwallis's sword, but the latter pleaded illness, and the surrender on October 19 was formally made by General O'Hara.[33]

There is a vivid account of events at the surrender as seen from the trenches by a participant, Sarah Osborn. She was a cook and a washerwoman, and had served since 1780 – the widow of one soldier, the wife of another. She exchanged quips with Washington, when she said that it would not do for the men to fight and starve too. Cornwallis she saw after the surrender – "a man of diminutive appearance and having cross eyes." The evidence comes from depositions made by survivors, when in 1832 Congress decided to grant a pension to every survivor of the revolutionary armies who had served for at least six months. Each applicant had to swear to the truth of his or her deposition at a local court-house. Sarah Osborn made her claim in 1837, when she was 98 years old. She was awarded her two pensions. Her third husband had carelessly not enlisted.[34]

It was a total surrender. The British garrison marched out, colors cased, the bands not being allowed to play any American or French marches, as was permitted when full honors of war were granted. One of the marches played was an English tune, "The World Turned Upside Down." Cornwallis surrendered 7,200 soldiers and 804 seamen; his casualties had been 156 killed and 320 wounded. The Americans losses were 53 killed and 65 wounded; 60 Frenchmen had been killed and 193 wounded.

On the morning of Cornwallis's surrender, Clinton sailed from New York with a relief force of 7,000 men, convoyed by Graves's reinforced fleet of 27 ships of the line. They arrived off Chesapeake Bay on October 24, five days late, and Clinton then learned of Cornwallis's surrender. He and Graves decided to avoid another battle

---

[33] William B. Willcox, "The British road to Yorktown, a study in divided command," *American Historical Review*, 52 (1946), pp. 1–35.

[34] John C. Dann (ed.) *The Revolution Remembered: Eyewitness accounts of the War for Independence* (Chicago, University of Chicago Press, 1980), pp. 240–50.

For an analysis of the movements of Cornwallis and of the "guerrilla" war against him, see Don Higginbotham, "Reflections on the War of Independence," in Ronald D. Hoffman and Peter J. Albert (eds), *Arms and Independence: The military character of the American Revolution* (US Capitol Historical Society, University of Virginia Press, 1984), pp. 1–24.

with de Grasse's superior fleet — now 36 ships of the line — and they
returned to New York.

Yorktown was decisive. The struggle did not end at once, but there
was little more serious combat. French assistance had been vital,
especially at sea. But the end came because of Washington's grasp
of the strategic situation, his speed and decisiveness, and his skill
in handling his French allies on land and at sea.

10   THE TREATY OF PARIS

By the terms of the Treaty of Paris, Britain recognized the independence of the United States and accepted the Mississippi River as
the western boundary. The navigation of the river was to be open
to British and Americans, as were fishing rights off Newfoundland.
The boundaries to the North and South were ill-defined and were
to be matter thereafter for long and acrimonious debate. Canniness
triumphed in Paris and in the colonies; the new United States won
by diplomacy far more than they were entitled to by force of arms.

With the surrender of Cornwallis at Yorktown, the war was virtually over. The king was with difficulty dissuaded from abdicating.
Lord North resigned in March 1782 when Shelburne became, first,
secretary of state and then, on Rockingham's death in July, prime
minister. Shelburne opposed the idea of independence, but not for
long. With the Scottish merchant Richard Oswald (who had made his
money in the slave trade) as his emissary in Paris, negotiations were
opened with the American envoys — John Adams, John Jay, and
Benjamin Franklin — in April 1782, and concluded in November.
Franklin broke his word in concluding a separate peace without
French participants, but in the thick air of spying and counterspying
in Paris it was hardly possible for the French foreign minister,
Vergennes, a long-experienced diplomat and spymaster, to be un-
aware of what was happening. Congress agreed to recommend to
the individual states that they indemnify the Loyalists and pay their
debts in Britain — but this was easy to say, hard to implement. In
the end only Pennsylvania indemnified the Loyalist sufferers, but
Britain itself was generous with land grants in Canada, and with
£3 million in compensation to them. Brant's Iroquois, Britain's major
ally, were generously treated with land grants in and near what
is now Brantford, Ontario. Spain regained the Floridas, for what
value they might be to her, but not Gibraltar. The Loyalists were the
losers, since many Southerners had taken refuge in what became
Britain's last mainland colonies south of the Canadian line. France

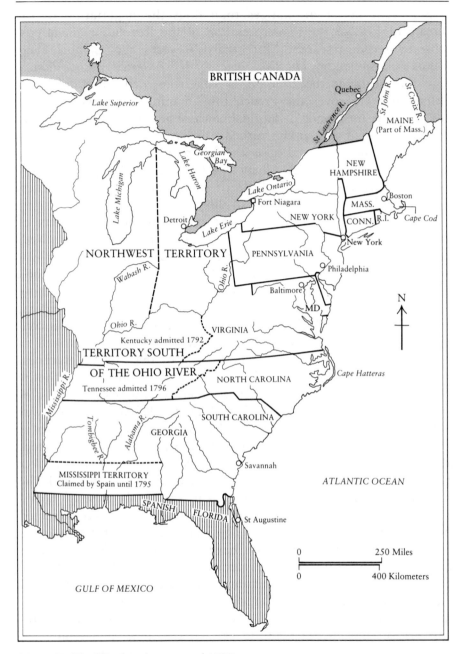

Map 13 The US after the peace of 1783.

won some West Indian islands – and a huge debt, the full interest on which would be six years in falling due. For the Americans, who had caused the war, it was a total triumph.

No event better dramatizes than does the negotiation of the Treaty of 1782–3 the reinterpretation of the Revolution made possible by recent research. More than 30 years ago, Samuel Flagg Bemis's classic study, *The Diplomacy of the American Revolution*,[35] saw the treaty as the triumph of American virtue not only over Britain but also over the French foreign minister, Vergennes, and his wily ally, the Conde de Floridablanca of Spain. John Adams, John Jay, and Benjamin Franklin turned European rivalries to America's advantage, and produced a series of American diplomatic victories beginning with the French Alliance of 1778 and ending triumphantly with the Treaty of Paris of 1783. It was, Bemis said, "the greatest victory in the annals of American diplomacy."

Recent students of diplomatic history add to Bemis's mastery of the Spanish archives a sharp awareness of the personalities involved, and of the fact that events in America were but part of a wider war involving most of the great states in Europe, and that the War took place within a system of balance-of-power politics familiar to those who negotiated in the rue des Petits Augustins; they write as realists, free from Woodrow Wilson-like moral judgments, and from his conviction that virtue always triumphs over vice. Franklin as well as Vergennes knew his way down both sides of the street. Vergennes, it appears, was not panicked into forming an alliance with the United States by fear of an Anglo-American rapprochement after the Battle of Saratoga. He had already decided to enter the war when French naval preparations had been completed, and did so as planned. Nor was he the evil genius that Adams and Jay suspected. Rather, during the peace process, he played the role of honest broker between his allies. If in 1782 he seemed anxious to settle with the British at America's expense, the reason was not because he hoped to cripple the new republic. Vergennes's interest in peace stemmed not from nefarious schemes to deprivethe United States of gains the new nation might otherwise have achieved, but from concerns about the growing threat of Russian expansionism in eastern Europe, France's own sad financial situation, and the deterioration of French naval power. The realist in Vergennes was also the cynic: originally, like Shelburne, he sought a Yankee state, with the Southern states still British; he did not want to see a large, new, and republican regime poised on the North Atlantic, where France still had tiny fishing-base islands, and hopes of a restored and French Quebec. Not so: thanks to Franklin's obduracy, he conceded a united America.

Recent research also emphasizes two aspects hitherto minimized.

---

[35] Bloomington, Ind., University of Indiana Press, 1957.

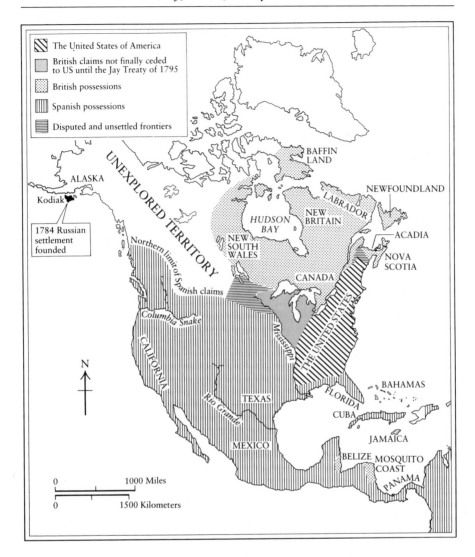

Map 14 The terms of the Treaty of Paris. By the Treaty of Paris of September 3, 1783, Britain recognized the independence of the United States, withdrew all military and naval forces, agreed to fix the boundary of Canada by negotiation, and returned Florida to Spain.

One is the importance of Spain's role. Given the essentially amoral quality of eighteenth-century diplomacy, there was nothing evil or even unusual about Spanish policy. Moreover, Spain advanced the American cause in tangible ways. France's involvement in the war was predicated on Spain's. Spanish forces cleared the Mississippi valley and the Floridas of British troops, and the attempted invasion of England in 1779, although a debacle, forced the British to keep much of their fleet close to home for the remainder of the war, limiting their ability to control North American waters. The other aspect that has been emphasized is that of the "ifs" basic to all diplomatic assessments. In the early 1770s, France proposed an alliance with Britain against the Russian threat in eastern Europe, only to be rebuffed. Had the alliance materialized, the French later would probably never have come to America's aid. Britain also failed to take advantage of the opportunity to forge an alliance with the Russians that would have forced the French to think twice about an American pact. When Spain demanded the return of Gibraltar by Great Britain as the price of neutrality, London declined, even though British policy-makers had concluded that the Rock was more a liability than an advantage. Since Spain's involvement in the war was vital to France, this was a dreadful blunder. Finally, the British decision to declare war on the Dutch because they refused to abandon their trade in naval stores with France was also a mistake. The French navy was not dependent on those stores. Moreover, Dutch participation in the war forced the British to stretch their own naval forces too far. The French admiral, Comte de Grasse, was able to control the waters around Yorktown in 1781 because Admiral Rodney and his fleet were engaged in pillaging the Dutch island of St Eustatius.

Driven by their almost paranoid suspicions of Franklin, of Shelburne, and of Vergennes, the American diplomatists Jay and Adams, who between them dominated American participation in the peace negotiations, mishandled their assignments. Moreover, in the process they lost the opportunity to achieve a treaty that would have been silent on the Loyalist and debt questions and would have given the United States a far more advantageous boundary than the one finally agreed upon. The envoys never really understood Shelburne's purposes, and appear not to have realized even after the fall of the North ministry that a war-weary Britain was unprepared to continue military operations in North America.

If not dominion, then trade, Shelburne held; the empire of trade would continue, whatever flag flew. Despite mercantilism, the Americans hoped to persuade Shelburne's government to allow them to trade freely inside the British empire after the War, i.e. to eat their cake as before while enjoying new dishes of their own. But Shelburne stayed in office only long enough to get the Treaty through the House of Commons, and even then negotiations were helped on their way only because Parliament was in recess; Parliament and diplomacy never walk smoothly together. When Shelburne fell, so did his Adam Smithian liberal dream of a new economic order. He was always a

Chathamite, preferring the study to the hurly-burly of Westminster.

This is to say that, although American policy-makers deplored balance-of-power politics in the early days of their Revolutionary struggle, they hoped to counter its influence in international affairs. In practice, Franklin and Oswald were hard-headed men who learnt to use the old diplomatic system — and just happened also to be patient, old-fashioned, and old friends. It was no mere chance that Franklin the American negotiator had lived for 20 years in Craven Street, London — a small edition of Market Street, Philadelphia — and that his old London cronies, the Old Whigs, were his fellow-spirits, fellow-journalists, addicted to Dissent, and many of them his old Scots and convivialists of Fleet Street and the Strand; and that Oswald, the Scots-born British negotiator, had had in his heyday a plantation in South Carolina. Oswald was more than a mere intermediary. He told Franklin what he thought would be acceptable. He played down Shelburne's preference for an America divided into North and South, and moderated a number of Shelburne's assertions — for example, that he would never give up the Loyalists (a point on which Franklin felt especially strongly), that British ships should be allowed to trade with every port in America as in the past, and that America must end all connection with France. It was Oswald's free trade sentiments that brought him close to Franklin: if America were independent, British trade would profit. It was commercial empire, not territorial jurisdiction, that mattered to the liberals.

In his Journal entry of May 6, 1782, Oswald set down his private opinion on the subject. Had he been an American, he declared, he would have insisted for the sake of future peace that all the settled parts of the continent, including Canada, Nova Scotia, Newfoundland, and East Florida, must "be brought under the cover of one and the same political constitution." This was the major step: from partition and from the loose ties of continuing political association to, now, independence. As for the Thirteen Colonies:

The more these States extend themselves in Population and Cultivation, the better it will be for England. While they have such immense expansion of vacant Lands behind them to be taken into Appropriation at almost no expense, they will never become Manufacturers. ... the States will, therefore, for Centuries to come, continue extending themselves backwards, and according as they produce, they will consume and be in a condition to pay for the material of consumption ... so that a Nation who has a free and safe access to their Ports ... will never fail to profit by their Correspondence.[36]

[36] Richard Oswald, Journal, Public Record Office, FO 95/511, no. 4 and no. 7; Vincent T. Harlow, *The Founding of the Second British Empire, 1763–1793,*

More than this, recent writers have gone far to weaken, if not destroy, the long-held thesis that the American Revolution bred, ten years on, the French Revolution. The events across the Atlantic had in fact few direct effects on the Old World. British politics did change during the postwar era. The power of Parliament grew, special interest groups became more influential, and a new political consciousness developed in outlying areas of Britain; but few of these innovations can be attributed to the impact of the American Revolution. In France, those with experience of America played a small part in France in 1789, and afterwards. Only in Spain's western hemispheric empire does the ratification of the Treaty of Paris seem to have played an important role. From the moment of its signing, the Creoles in South America thought of themselves not as Spaniards but as Americans. The treaty of 1783 was a major step on the road to Latin American revolution, but to revolution nowhere else.[37]

11 HOW AND WHY?

In a popularly written but thoroughly researched study of the War, *The Story of the Continental Army 1775–83*, Lynn Montross gives some interesting facts.[38] He calculates that 234,782 men fought for Washington. This figure compares well with the even more probing analysis in Howard Peckham's *The Toll of Independence*,[39] who puts the total of Americans "in service at one time or another" at 200,000. These figures do not distinguish between continental and militia service, nor do they take account of the fact that one man might re-enlist on a number of occasions. Washington, of course,

2 vols (London, Longman's, 1952–64), vol I, pp. 245–6; Richard B. Morris, *The Peacemakers: The Great Powers and American Independence* (New York, Harper and Row, 1965), pp. 248–81.

[37] James T. Hutson, *John Adams and the Diplomacy of the American Revolution* (Lexington, University Press of Kentucky, 1980); Jonathan Dull, *A Diplomatic History of the American Revolution* (New Haven, Yale University Press, 1985); idem, *Franklin the Diplomat: The French mission, Transactions of the American Philosophical Society* (1982); Ronald Hoffman and Peter J. Albert (eds), *Peace and the Peacemakers: The Treaty of 1783* (University of Virginia for the US Capitol Historical Society, 1986); Prosser Gifford (ed.), *The Treaty of Paris (1783) in a Changing States System* (Maryland Universities Press of America for the Woodrow Wilson International Center for Scholars, 1985).

[38] New York, Barnes and Noble, 1967; originally published as *Rag Tag and Bobtail* (New York, Harper and Row, 1952).

[39] Chicago, University of Chicago Press, 1974.

rarely had more than a small section of these under his command, and at Valley Forge he was down to 2,000.

Britain put 32,000 men ashore in New York in 1776; its total force by 1782 – across the world, in what then was a world war – was 150,000, of which perhaps 50,000 were at any one time in North America, though never at one place. British forces usually outnumbered the particular American force against them by two to one (though not of course at Saratoga, nor at Yorktown). Britain also spent £4,500,000 to obtain the services of some 30,000 Hessians (four times the total of the French loan to the Patriots).

There were, calculates Peckham, 1,331 military engagements (some 60 major battles) and 215 naval engagements. The grand total of American battle casualties was 6,824 killed, 8,445 wounded, 18,152 captured, 1,426 missing and 100 deserted. There were probably over 25,000 deaths from all causes, including disease, in camp and among the prisoners – 12½ percent or 1 in 8 of the participants, almost as high as those (13 percent) suffered by Union troops in the Civil War.

The American victory in the War was, then, more costly in lives than is usually assumed. It was also unexpected, and still appears puzzling. It had about it what Washington called the "marks of fiction." As he wrote at the end of the war to Nathaniel Greene, the future historian would find it hard to believe "that such a force as Great Britain has employed for eight years in this country could be baffled in their plan of subjugating it, by numbers infinitely less, composed of men oftentimes half starved, always in rags, without pay, and experiencing every species of distress which human nature is capable of undergoing." [40]

Britain seemed at the outset to have all the advantages: professionally trained armies and experienced commanders, an overwhelming advantage in manpower on land and sea, and great resources. That disparity was especially striking in the early days: American supplies had to be tightly rationed from the start, with a daily allowance of only 9 musket rounds per man against 60 for each redcoat. This disadvantage was, however, offset by the American rifleman's superior marksmanship ("Who could fail to hit men when trained to catch rabbits?") and by the skill of the English-born Philadelphia merchant Robert Morris and his trading house of Willing and Morris, and of the Providence firm of Brown Hopkins Jenakes and Bowen, in seeking out arms and gunpowder from the West Indies and Europe – at a steady 2½ percent commission.

[40] *Writings*, ed. Fitzpatrick, vol: XXIV, p. 408.

Whatever Britain's original superiority in organization and supplies, there was as much uncertainty in the direction of the War from London as there had been political uncertainty before it broke out. The reputation of Lord George Germain, the colonial secretary, had not recovered from the charge of cowardice at Minden, for which he had been court-martialed — if largely for political reasons; he was an efficient administrator, compelled, however, to rely heavily on the discretion of his commanders 3,000 miles away. Despite the size of the British army, the task of disciplining a still unmapped continent and of controlling it from the sea defied all numbers, as Gage had recognized at the outset, all numbers of troops sent from home should be at least quadrupled. It was the continent, with its vast forests, its mountains and rocky defiles, its wide estuaries and bridgeless rivers, that won the war; the elephant defied the whale.

There was some ineptness in Whitehall. If Lord Sandwich at the Admiralty was industrious and able — however profligate in private life — the ships of the line were in poor condition, timber supplies low, and many of the crews inexperienced; 1,243 seamen died in battle between 1776 and 1780, 18,500 died of disease, and 42,000 deserted. There was even more ineptness in the field. The Howe brothers, skillful though they were in their elements, were second cousins of George III and were charged or charged themselves to play the role of conciliators as well as commanders; they never struck home, as they could have done in New York and the Jerseys in 1776. One cynical English view of General Howe was that he should be raised to the peerage as Baron "Delay Warr." Clinton's *Narrative* of his campaigns reveals a shy and dilatory man, his moods alternating between timidity and aggressive confidence. Burgoyne was an ineffective commander, who paid the price at Saratoga of culpable over-confidence. Cornwallis marred a decisiveness that brought false hopes in London by his recklessness in invading Virginia, and farther south by condoning pillage and plunder that fostered a guerrilla war; the campaign in the Carolinas was fought in country ill-suited to war, and was won by the Patriots in a score of small engagements marked by heavy losses. Carleton came to full command too late; his nobility impressed many Americans; his skill kept Canada loyal. Only Carleton condemned the plundering raids of Indians, of Tories, and of British regulars, which were in the end a matter of approved and unfortunate British strategy.

The British put a pathetic faith in the Loyalists, although by 1780 it had become clear that they were effective only when there was a regular corps near by. The employment of Hessians was unwise.

They caused trouble in the Jerseys, they themselves resented the pride and arrogance of the English regular officers, and they showed little adaptation to American conditions. General Haldimand, writing to Clinton from Quebec in 1779, thought "the Germans were unfit by nature and education for the American service." Of 30,000 Hessians, only 17,000 returned home: some 7,000 died, some 5,000 deserted. Not all the deserters had an easy time of it. One worked for four years for nothing, and when, in 1782, he protested, he was promptly jailed. In the end, Isaac Clinkerfoose married a Pennsylvanian woman and settled down as a farm laborer. Life for most people in the eighteenth century was hard, and especially so if they had no luck.

Yet arguably no British commander could have won the war. Adjutant General Harvey saw with sharp clarity in June 1775: "it is impossible to conquer America ... with our British army" it was like driving a hammer into a bin of corn — the biggest risk was that the hammer would get lost. At one point or another, Britain held Boston, New York, Newport, Philadelphia, and Charleston — all to no avail. The country was utterly different from the Europe in which the art of war had been practiced: forested, humid, intersected by malarial creeks and swamps, short of roads and bridges. There were, as a result, some remarkable military disasters. In the war as a whole there were 14 actions in which the defeated force was either captured entire or destroyed, and in 9 of these the better supplied, better disciplined British army was the victim: Moore's Creek, Trenton, Bennington, Saratoga, Vincennes, Stony Point, King's Mountain, Cowpens, Yorktown. Three of these, Trenton, Saratoga, and Yorktown, were psychological or military turning-points, and two of them were won by Washington. In these nine engagements, the British losses, exceeding 20,000, were sufficiently serious to be decisive in a war waged on a small scale

Unlike the British, Washington's army was civilian and unprofessional. Recruited haphazardly, rarely numbering more than 10,000 after 1775, as many as two-thirds might be local militia and undependable — "the Long Faces". They "come in," said Washington, "you cannot tell how; go, you cannot tell when; and act, you cannot tell where; consume your provisions, exhaust your stores and leave you at last at the critical moment."

His army was short of everything; Franklin proposed in the beginning that the Pennsylvania troops be equipped with bows and arrows, Indian style. His advice was ignored: but rear ranks were issued with 12 ft iron shafts for use as spears. Problems of supply and clothing were not overcome until 1782, even with French aid;

even then, there was never enough clothing for the men to be "deloused;" pay was short, winters appalling. So with tactics, and maneuvers. It took three years before the appropriate drill was devised and before officers as well as men were persuaded by Steuben to learn it; it took longer for cavalry and artillery to be used skillfully. Washington deplored the desertions and the cowardice of his men, especially at the beginning; but much more than this, he deplored the lack of able officers: "Our men," agreed Greene, "are infinitely better than the officers." But the officers emerged: "Lighthorse Harry" and his cavalry, Morgan and his riflemen, John Glover and his marines, Greene and Knox, Wayne and Stirling.

Washington's most useful resource was that over which he had least direct control; those whom he called "our rascally privateersmen." The US soon had 136 ships, which outnumbered the British fleet by 4 to 1. The privateers were self-financed, captured British ships and their cargoes, and did well out of the war: witness Elias Hasket Derby of Salem, the Cabots of Boston, Robert Morris, George Washington himself, and his friend and bookseller-turned-artillery officer, Henry Knox, who said that he looked not to the war but to privateering as his device to ensure that he could be "lazy for life."

It is true that Washington never defeated the main British army in the open; he was more successful as administrator than as trainer of men; at times he was hesitant and too deferential to his fellow-generals. He lacked Lee's flair and Arnold's dash; but he also lacked their faults. Though tactically he was never more than an amateur, yet he made distinct contributions to the art of war: the use of light infantry and skirmishers; the employment of riflemen; the fondness for maneuver rather than sieges, and particularly for maneuver at night (sometimes forced upon him); the effort at combined operations. For one with so little experience, he was daring and surprisingly resilient, "much bolder in spirit," says Freeman, "than circumstances permitted him to be in strategy." This strategy was inevitably defensive, and there was no glory to be won — or volunteers to be enlisted — in a policy of retreat, a war of posts; no glory, much criticism, and a recurring, humiliating sense of failure. Yet to survive was in the end to conquer; as Greene expressed it in the South in 1781: "Don't you think that we bear beating very well, and that ... the more we are beat, the better we grow?"

Distance and geography; inefficiency in Whitehall and — despite repeated copybook victories — hesitation in the field; and in the end the entry of France, so that the center of the struggle moved back to Europe; a French invasion of the home islands was all too likely in 1779, as planned by Franklin, John Paul Jones, and Lafayette; it was this change in the center of gravity that was decisive, not the scale of the French contribution. France had, of course, been aiding the colonists tacitly with money, and on a small scale with volunteers, from the beginning; not from love of America, and certainly not from love of democracy (a suspect cause in Bourbon eyes) but as part of a long-cherished plan of the French foreign minister, the Duc de Choiseul, and of his successor, Vergennes, for revenge on Britain. France greatly assisted the Americans with subsidies and supplies (to the value of some $8 million in all), but it did this before and after 1778. Vergennes's motives were more commercial than territorial. When France deemed it safe to declare war — after Saratoga — it intervened as a sea power. Its objectives were West Indian sugar islands rather than American independence, and it gave that cause, in fact, small assistance. France put some 9,000 troops into America. The important contribution was Rochambeau's force of 5,000 which arrived in 1780, well disciplined, well dressed, and psychologically of great importance. But the American war could still have been won without the formal intervention of French troops.

For Britain, however, the entry of France was decisive. This was the long-awaited and much-feared step. The first result was an attempt at concessions to America. North's Conciliatory Propositions of February 1778 made a number of surrenders, especially of the right to tax. The Coercive Acts were withdrawn and a commission was sent to Philadelphia empowered to offer anything short of independence. The hope was held out of a return to the *status quo* of 1763. But Congress refused to negotiate except on a basis of independence and a withdrawal of British forces.

The entry of France produced a national war effort in Britain that the war against the colonies had not quite aroused, high though feelings had risen by 1778. It totally transformed British strategy. Until 1778 Britain could blockade American ports and attack the coast where it chose. With France and Spain, Holland and the League of Armed Neutrality at war with Britain by 1780, the British grip on the Atlantic and on the American coast was imperiled. Invasion of Britain became a real threat; in 1779 a Franco-Spanish armada was dispersed only by a gale in the Channel. John Paul Jones, part freebooter, part hero, but in any guise material for legend, fought his greatest battle off Flamborough Head within sight of the Yorkshire coast. Gibraltar was besieged, India threatened, and West Indian islands lost. Not for the first time, America was to profit from European discord and from Britain's agonizing dilemma.

Benjamin Franklin's greatest achievement was not so much to make France an active ally as to widen the struggle into a world war, in such a way that at its height the original belligerent could quietly make peace without consulting its ally. As Franklin saw, the war France fought was never quite the same war as America's; and, never unduly concerned over protocol, he was content to withdraw when he could.

The war was lost by the British rather than won by the Americans, and it was lost to the terrain rather than to the enemy. They won, it is true, every pitched battle in the war. Where these battles were ordered affairs the British won easily, on copybook lines: Bunker Hill, Brooklyn Heights, Brandywine, Camden, Guilford Court House. But they were expensive victories. And the surrenders were disastrous. At Saratoga 5,000 men, and at Yorktown 7,000, stacked their arms. Moreover, despite the cost, there were not enough battles to end the war; the enemy disappeared, the conquest of territory and towns – New York, Philadelphia, Charleston – brought no advantage. Washington could speak of withdrawing intact if necessary across the Alleghenies. In the end, unless the British numbers were unlimited, the supplies constant, the lines of communication unbroken, it was the land that would win.

These are enough to explain British failure, and would have been enough to allow "a new nation conceived in liberty and dedicated to the proposition that all men are created equal" to come into being. Lincoln's words of 70 years later, however, are not an accurate description of the new nation in 1783. It was not yet a nation, but 13 distinct and separate states, some of which had fought their own wars, and some of which continued for years to fight trade wars with each other. Recent research suggests that only 1 in 5 of Americans were Patriots, and that at least 80,000 (1 in 30 of the whole), and perhaps more, left it heartbroken during or after the struggle. Its militia came and went. It too was badly directed by Congress, which had more than once to move lest it fall into enemy hands.

Recent historians, no doubt because 1976 was the year of the bicentenary and a year therefore of jubilo, have emphasized the "isms" for which the Patriots fought: freedom, opportunity – and the rights of men. There were certainly some who were fighting for a cause greater than the patch of ground they belonged to. Indeed, many knew more patches of ground than they had ever known before. No doubt such notions were unfamiliar on the other side – to the Hessians, fighting for pay; the Indians, fighting for cash and trinkets, and by their own peculiar code of honor; the ill-paid British regulars, fighting a long way away from home because they were offered no other job. But freedom is an elusive concept; as we now know, between the thoughtful Loyalist and the thoughtful Patriot there was no sharp divide on doctrine: both were Old Whigs at heart. To both sides, opportunity had to be balanced by responsibility. Freedom in the eighteenth century could never entirely exclude some measure of deference to one's betters, even in the New World, and some approximate idea of hierarchy. The American world was richer in opportunity, the ladder easier to climb than the British, but that such ideas induced in ill-educated men a sense of a Great Cause is hard to credit. Social stratification, and not just because of color, still counted.

Yet in compiling a balance sheet, one cannot exclude the subtle part played by conviction and by ideology, by the repetition of the ideas drawn from the struggle against the Stuarts, by the insistence in sermons and pamphlets that the struggle was one against "Tyranny;" and that there was a Great Conspiracy to undermine American freedom. That it was untrue did not matter – men can fight and die for illusions more readily than for realities. There was, moreover, a new note being struck in the New World. "Men must see the reason and the use of any action or movement," said Timothy Pickering. "'Tis the boast" of European commanders "that their men are mere mechanics ... God forbid that my countrymen should be degraded ... standing armies are composed of very different men. These serve only for their pay." Von Steuben found it also: "The genius of this nation is not in the least to be compared with that of the Prussians, Austrians or French. You say to your soldier 'Do this', he doeth it; but I am obliged to say 'This is the reason why you ought to do it' and then he does it." This rationalism – what in Missouri is called "Show me" – along with their general political views, they would enshrine in a charter. The Virginia Bill of Rights declared among other things that the militia was a "noble palladium of Liberty" and "the proper natural and safe defense of a free state." What was also being fought for were the "Liberties Privileges and Immunities" of a people who now felt themselves to be – however wrongly in British eyes and by the statutes of a British Parliament – in nature free. The war was fought out between two rival and contradictory notions of freedom and order. And only success in battle – however won – could decide it.[41]

It was America that won the War: a land of mountains and of wide estuaries, of defiles, rocks, and swamps was hard to conquer

---

[41] D. Echeverria, *Mirage in the West* (Princeton, NJ, Princeton University Press, 1957), p. 86.

from a few seaports. It was helped by foreign aid. It remains a controversial matter: could Washington's army have done it alone? It is possible, but it remains an unhistorical question. Franklin manufactured a French alliance in 1778, and a treaty of peace in November 1782. Without the – very brief – French command of the sea off Yorktown, and Rochambeau's well-dressed and well-fed legions, it could have been a longer and might have been a very different War.

This, and one man's patience. It was Washington who kept an army in being, not least at Valley Forge; who survived the intrigues of critics who were, at one point in 1777, also conspirators; who gave to the cause part of his own fortune and all of his own integrity. The war was won by Washington's skill in the field, and by Franklin's skill in the long intrigues in Paris that led to the treaty of peace.

12 THE LEGACY

Within one decade of Yorktown, Alexander Hamilton, the first secretary of the Treasury, was to recommend the imposition of taxes far more burdensome than any devised by George Grenville or Lord North, and with much greater likelihood of their being collectable. In this sense, this war – like most wars – was fought in vain. But by 1789 it was accepted that taxation at least required representation, and at least the taxes were levied by Americans on themselves. Moreover, if in 1783 political independence was won, at the end of the War Americans remained linked to Britain by close ties of trade and culture; and quite a few of them regretted the forcible parting of the ways. The break was never total. John Adams, as American ambassador, was received at Court by George III in 1786. The moving frontier which in 1783 reached the Mississippi, and was soon to go far beyond it, remained culturally English and, in its own strange way, English-speaking.

The War, however rich its paradoxes, nevertheless marks the beginning of the story of a new nation, and opens a new republican and secular chapter in world history. Metaphorically at least, the shots fired at Lexington Green and Concord Bridge have echoed round the world. The statues that are grouped outside the White House in what is significantly called Lafayette Square – statues commemorating heroic revolutionary leaders like Kosciusko and von Steuben, Lafayette and Rochambeau – are a reminder of those many volunteers from Europe who then saw in the struggle for

American independence a symbol and a portent of the struggle of other nations, then and since, to be free. It is impossible indeed to find limits to the consequences for the world that have followed from the events that took place on the narrow Atlantic seaboard in the years from 1763 to 1783.

The War of American Independence was the first successful struggle in modern history of a colony against its mother-country. It was waged on land and sea, and along the fringe of a 1,000-mile-long unmapped and savage frontier, from the Great Lakes to Kaskaskia on the Mississippi, from Anticosti to Savannah. It was therefore in its extent and also in its character a Great War, a struggle of a distant and divided colonial territory against a great maritime empire, which by its end had developed into a reopened chapter in an older European and world conflict of the British *versus* the French.

It was also a civil war, with families divided among themselves, and brother fighting brother. It was rich in suffering and exiles. There were, per head of population, many more emigrés from Revolutionary America between 1776 and 1783, and after it, than from Revolutionary France a decade later. It was indeed a rehearsal of the struggle that took place later in Paris: a number of French leaders, many of them as volunteers, some of them as adventurers, saw action in North America; and Lafayette in 1789 and 1790 sought to play the role of the Washington of France (with singular lack of his mentor's skill, and none of his success). When he sent to Washington the key of the demolished Bastille, he did so, as he said, "as a tribute which I owe ... as a Missionary of Liberty to its Patriarch."

It was, however, a struggle for independence from Britain, rather than for social revolution. Compared to the *levée en masse* of 1792, the struggle was less obviously ideological; Jefferson's rhetoric of revolution was strikingly cooler than Danton's, even though his Declaration of Independence is a superb statement of the liberal credo. The Loyalist emigrés were numerous, and they drained the colonial establishment of its natural leaders; but they came from all classes, not just from the aristocracy or the Church. The American War was not of Nobs *versus* Mobs.

It was, until the Vietnam War, the longest war in American history. It was one of the first guerrilla wars. It saw some of the first examples of planned invasions from the sea, of what would in World War II be called Combined Ops. It led to new military tactics; Sir John Moore (of later Corunna fame) claimed that he had learnt in the War of American Independence the importance of the rifle, of fire power, and of mobility. The Virginia and Kentucky riflemen were described as "the most fatal widow-and-orphan makers in the world." The War was marked by few pitched battles, almost all of which were – paradoxically – won by the ultimate loser, Britain. The American army of 1776 was the first people's army to fight and win a modern war.

In the revolutionary years, ca.700,000 men were of military age (18–60 as it was then construed) in the colonies. Some 230,000 were listed on muster rolls, but of them some are duplicated because of re-enlistment in order to obtain more than one bounty. The colonies, however, never had more than 90,000 in the field at any one point; and some thousands of men also served in the navy and as privateers. This was thus a tremendous experience for a large and scattered population, in a war fought more as 13 wars, state by state, across which marched the continental army chasing or being chased by an enemy (British and Hessian) army. The War was not just an instrument of policy or a sequence of military operations, but, in John Shy's words, "a social process of political education." [42]

The continentals, both officers and privates, were recruited from all callings of American civilian life, and they remained essentially civilian in their outlook even after some of them had learned to fight like professionals. It was this civilian character of the revolutionary army that was both its strength and weakness, and it was only those generals who recognized this fact, and adapted their tactics and discipline to it, who were eventually able to forge American manpower into a weapon of victory. Yet, though the new nation came to birth out of war, bloodshed and treason, it remained almost until our own day strikingly civilian-minded in character, hostile – like seventeenth-century Britain – to standing armies, proud of and intent on the right of the individual citizen to possess and bear arms, but in essence (and outside the South) non-belligerent. The twentieth century, here as in so much else, worked a change for the worse. The path from Yorktown to Saigon was a long and sad one.

13 THE SIGNIFICANCE OF THE WAR

For many in our own generation, this event-oriented view of the War has not been a sufficient explanation; on it, and its social

---

[42] John Shy, *A People Numerous and Armed: Reflections on the military struggle for American independence* (London, Oxford University Press, 1976); Charles Royston, *A Revolutionary People at War* (Chapel Hill, NC, IEACH, University of North Carolina Press, 1979); Hoffman and Albert, *Arms and Independence*.

consequences, there has been an explosion of interpretive writing. The War is no longer seen merely as an imperial, military, and naval struggle, but as the "cradle of a nation's birth, a new nation" "conceived in liberty and dedicated to the proposition that all men are created equal" (Lincoln's words at Gettysburg in 1863, recalling Jefferson's Declaration of 1776); a nation, too, that was – unlike its origins in 1607, 1620, and 1630 – secular and tolerant. Since its preachers and pamphleteers were fanned by the memories, and the reading and rereading, of the tracts and tales of England's own civil war of the 1640s, and by their classical republican and oppositionist ideology, it saw itself as fighting against tyranny, and was prompt to sniff it in every tainted Atlantic breeze. Moreover, as each successive crisis showed, Britain was following continental Europe in moving from the liberty of a free constitution into autocracy: witness the Stamp Act, the Townshend Duties, the Boston Massacre, and ultimately and overwhelmingly the Coercive Acts: the total sum added up to malevolence, and the purpose, finally revealed in 1775, was the replacement of civil by military authority. What has mattered to the last generation of historians of the Revolution is the evidence in the pamphlets that they read of "an integrated group of attitudes and ideas" (in Bernard Bailyn's words), that when tyranny is abroad, submission is a crime. It was not to be explained by British declarations, or even actions, but by American responses, and thus by understanding the ideologies, and the opinions, of the people at the receiving end; it became psychological and intellectual warfare. In turn, this raises another question. Do books and tracts cause revolutions? Do the ideas of scholars and pamphleteers call out mobs and enlist armies – in America in 1776, France in 1789, China in 1911 or 1949? But perhaps they do, as in Russia in 1917, if the time is ripe and opportunity knocks, even if the ground is ill-chosen (as Lenin recognized) and proves to be (in the very long run) too stony. [43]

About the examination of the causes of any violent overthrow of authority there is another preliminary "philosophic" problem: is a revolution caused by discontent? The colonies were in a fortunate position in 1763, with the French threat removed. They certainly enjoyed more freedom and less inequality than the citizens of Old

---

[43] Bernard Bailyn (ed.), *Pamphlets of the American Revolution* (Cambridge, MA, Belknap Press of Harvard University Press, 1965), Introduction, citing Andrew Eliot's pamphlet, p. 59. Compare also Bailyn's *The Ideological Origins of the American Revolution* (Cambridge, MA, Harvard University Press, 1967), ch. 4.

World countries: land was abundant and cheap; and food supplies plentiful. What disputes there had been with the mother-country were few and transient. Before 1775 few voices had called for independence. But the colonists — or the small number of the vocal among them — did not necessarily see their position as fortunate; nor, if they did, did they give Great Britain the credit for it. They were developing the country themselves, and their own assemblies with it; after a certain stage, they were beginning to generate their own desires and ambitions, not necessarily the same as those of Great Britain. Paradoxically, therefore, discontent could arise from prosperity, and prosperity could be strength rather than weakness. Moreover, they and their immigrant ancestors, though the majority of them had probably arrived as indentured servants, had become adventurers in the course of crossing and surviving the sea; they were accustomed to hardship and hard work, and well-endowed with courage, stamina, and endurance.

It is difficult to assess how much weight to give to economic factors. The generation of Charles Beard and Carl Becker in the 1920s and 1930s put great emphasis on them.[44] The Becker-Beard approach was carried on most sophisticatedly in the work of Merrill Jensen.[45] Élisha P. Douglass, *Rebels and Democrats: The struggle for equal political rights and majority rule during the American Revolution*,[46] summarizes many of the points of controversy and offers his own arguments for an "abortive" internal revolution.

The oppressive taxation, the irksome Trade and Navigation Laws, at least in New England, the drain on colonial finance and the opportunity to be rid of debtors and creditors were certainly important. But it is to be remembered that Franklin as late as 1775 was willing to try to get the Trade and Navigation Acts re-enacted in each colony, if Great Britain would only drop her claim to taxation;

---

[44] See Charles Beard, *The Economic Interpretation of the Constitution* (New York, Macmillan, 1913), chs 2–5. The major statements of the Becker-Beard approach are well known: Carl L. Becker, *The History of Political Parties in the Province of New York 1760–1776* (Madison, University of Wisconsin, 1909); J. F. Jameson, *The American Revolution as a Social Movement* (Princeton, NJ, Princeton University Press, 1940); L. M. Hacker, "The first American Revolution," *Columbia University Quarterly*, 27 (1935)

[45] Particularly in *The Articles of Confederation: An interpretation of the social-constitutional history of the American Revolution, 1774–1781* (Madison, University of Wisconsin, 1948). For an interesting review of his earlier position by Jensen himself, see his article "Democracy and the American Revolution," *Huntington Library Quarterly*, 20 (1956–7), pp. 321–41.

[46] Chapel Hill, NC, University of North Carolina Press, 1955.

that the Declaration of Rights of 1774 allowed for Great Britain's right to external taxation for regulation of trade; and that Washington always denied that "independence" was simply a device for refusing to honor debts. [47]

L. A. Harper and O. M. Dickerson suggest that the Navigation Acts *per se* were no great impediment to colonial trade, but they produce new evidence of one source of irritation: the corruption of British enforcing agents, the custom revenue collectors ("customs racketeers" is Dickerson's phrase) and the customary problems of bureaucracy and petty tyrannies. [48]

It was certainly a struggle in North America, in Carl Becker's phrase of two generations ago, not only for home rule, but over who should rule at home. Loyalist estates were confiscated. Quit-rents, primogeniture, and entail disappeared in those colonies/states where they still survived. Jefferson took as much pride in revising the laws of Virginia, and in drafting the Statute of Virginia for Religious Freedom, as he had in his authorship of the Declaration of Independence. The Declaration, with its eloquent second paragraph, and its long indictment of the errors of George III, was a lawyer's statement, a follow-up to Jefferson's *Summary View* of two years before, and to John Dickinson's writing of eight years before; its language – "self-evident" instead of "sacred and undeniable," "the pursuit of happiness" rather than Locke's "property" – revealing the impact on him less of Locke's *Two Treatises of Government* than of the Scottish school of Hutcheson, Thomas Reid, and David Hume, which he owed to William Small, his tutor at William and Mary College, whom he always held to have been the most influential mind he met. In the real world the colonial establishment was overthrown, since the Loyalists who went into exile to Canada or to Britain – though drawn from all sections and social groups – were overwhelmingly the governing classes, Customs and Admiralty officers, judges and Anglican clergymen, the wealthy merchants and "the friends of government" who had now for four generations been the visible sign of the mother-country in residence overseas. What

---

[47] The single work which most directly challenges the Becker-Beard approach is Robert E. Brown's *Middle-Class Democracy and the Revolution in Massachusetts, 1691–1780* (Ithaca, NY, Cornell University Press, 1955). A convenient summary of the "Brown thesis" is in his article "Democracy in colonial Massachusetts," *New England Quarterly*, 25 (1952), pp. 291–313.

[48] L. A. Harper, *The English Navigation Laws* (New York, Columbia University Press, 1939), and O. M. Dickerson, *The Navigation Acts and the American Revolution* (Philadelphia, University of Pennsylvania Press, 1951).

emerged was a society not yet "democratic," but much more open than that of contemporary Britain, and with new men at the top. If few of them were fighting for social justice, and if upcountry farmers and seaboard merchants, urban artisans and urban elites differed profoundly over what they wanted, many of them were hoping for social betterment, and in any case, when the shooting war began, too many of them had a stake in the future, and now ran too big a risk, to hold back.[49]

But was the Opposition ideology, born of criticism of Walpole's commercial-maritime policies, and inheriting the English Civil War themes and vocabulary of almost a century before, relevant to America, the new rich and vast land of opportunity? Moreover, if some areas did not gain as much as others from the Navigation Acts system, there is little evidence of an alliance of the sections — until the leading men met each other in Philadelphia in 1774. The "Regulator" country of backwoods North Carolina, with all its grievances, was distant and distinct from the tenant riots of the Hudson valley. Add the personalities of individuals — "When tyranny was abroad," wrote Andrew Elliot in 1765, "submission is a crime."

It is hard not to agree with Burke that as the rumor mills in printshops and saloon crowds generated their slogans, each side became imprisoned in its own imagery. "The Americans," he wrote in 1769, "have made a discovery, or think they have made one, that we mean to oppress them. We have made a discovery, or think we have made one, that they intend to rise in rebellion against us ... we know not how to advance, they know not how to retreat ... some party must give way."[50]

What evidence there was pointed to the clash of section *with* section, not in alliance *vs* the propertied: witness New Yorkers *vs* New Englanders over land claims in the Green Mountains of present-day Vermont, northeastern Pennsylvanians *vs* immigrants from Connecticut on the upper Susquehanna, other Pennsylvanians clashing with intruders from Virginia in the new settlements on the Ohio, Tidewater *vs* mountain men in North Carolina.

While the seven-year War was a unifying, Federalist-inspiring and — perhaps — a sharply secular experience for those involved, it was not only a war fought by 13 states in uneasy alliance, but by many more sections. Outside Boston, New England was fairly solidly Whig; small towns strong in a sense of community. By

---

[49] Garry Wills, *Inventing America: Jefferson's Declaration of Independence* (New York, Doubleday, 1978).

[50] Edmund Burke, "On the present state of the nation," *Works*, I.395.

contrast, the Delaware-Maryland peninsula, English-settled and tobacco land, was strong in Loyalism. If New York City, the British base, was perforce Tory, the state was a mosaic: Queen's County, on western Long Island near New York City, was Dutch-settled and Tory; Suffolk County, the eastern part of the island and settled largely from Connecticut, the reverse. The clash along the patroonships on the Hudson was determined by the rivalry of the barons. Along the Mohawk, the line is clear: older settlers – usually Presbyterian, German or Scots-Irish – were prevailingly Patriots, the newer, usually Anglicans or Highland Scots, tending to Loyalism. And here there were no man's lands also: notably Bergen County, New Jersey, and Westchester County on the Hudson, just north of New York City. Only in the South, coming in late as a theater of war, and when the central government was near-bankrupt, and where the war was fought mainly as a series of guerrilla clashes, was there savagery – as in the use of Catawba Indians as trackers, to flush out Loyalists taking refuge in the swamps. In response, Banastre Tarleton, Cornwallis's handsome and dashing cavalry leader, fought a ruthless war, and left a bitter legacy behind. His campaigns were of small help to a state that was probably the most thoroughly Loyalist of all.

To summarize, and thus to distort: the War was a colonial war for Independence;[51] it was also a social revolution over who should rule – and lose – at home;[52] and it was an intellectual and ideological struggle too.[53] For many of today's (and yesterday's?) historians this has been the most interesting and challenging theme of all, perhaps because it is the area in which, had they themselves lived in 1776, they feel that they would have been most sympathetic? A distinctive "school" of thinking about the Revolution emerged in the 1960s – legacy of and reflecting the contemporary concerns with Vietnam, the end of segregation, and the wave of liberal causes. Broadly, "the New Past" or "the New Left" looked afresh at class

[51] Thomas C. Barrow, "The American Revolution as a colonial war of liberation," *William and Mary Quarterly*, 25 (Jan. 1968), pp. 452–64; cf. Cecilia M. Kenyon, "Republicanism and radicalism in the American Revolution: an old-fashioned interpretation," ibid., 19 (Apr. 1962), 163–82.

[52] Jensen, *Articles of Confederation; The New Nation* (New York, Knopf, 1950); *The Founding of a Nation: A history of the American Revolution 1763–1776* (New York, Oxford University Press, 1968); Jackson Turner Main, "Government by the people: the American Revolution and the democratization of the legislatures," *William & Mary Quarterly*, 23 (July 1966), pp. 391–407.

[53] See Bailyn, *Ideological Origins of the American Revolution*, and *The Origins of American Politics* (New York, Knopf, 1968); and Gordon Wood, *The Radicalism of the American Revolution* (New York, Knopf, 1992).

conflict, and saw proof of it abundantly.[54] Theirs was history "from the bottom up." It was, in a measure, forecast by Edmund Morgan's searching probe in an address in 1956: "The American Revolution: Revisions in need of revision."[55]

There are many other themes and subthemes in so rich a vein of historian's gold.[56] All this writing, whether contemporary or of the eighteenth century, is persuasive and analytic. The eighteenth century, all of it, has to be judged critically according to one's judgment of its veracity or its own degree of self-illusion, bearing in mind that those called – by themselves or by others – to be pamphleteers were highly literate, scholarly and probably quite unrepresentative men. Did their writing "cause" the deeds, or were they just putting a gloss on the events – sometimes in retrospect?

[54] Staughton Lynd, *Class Conflict, Slavery and the United States Constitution* (Indianapolis, Bobbs Merrill, 1968 edn); Barton J. Bernstein, *Towards a New Past: Dissenting essays in American history* (New York, Random House, 1968); and Alfred J. Young (ed.), *The American Revolution* (De Kalb, Northern Illinois University Press, 1976).

[55] Printed in Edmund Morgan (ed.), *The American Revolution* (Englewood Cliffs, NJ, Prentice-Hall, 1965).

[56] Ian R. Christie and Benjamin Labaree, *Empire or Independence 1760–1776: A British-American dialogue on the coming of the American Revolution* (New York, Norton, 1976); Pauline Maier, *The Old Revolutionaries: Political lives in the age of Samuel Adams* (New York, Knopf, 1980); Michael Kammen, *A Season of Youth: The American Revolution and the historical imagination* (New York, Knopf, 1978); and, not least for its bibliography, Edward Countryman, *The American Revolution* (New York, Hill and Wang, 1985). Cf. also the various essays in Don Higginbotham, *War and Society in Revolutionary America: The wider dimensions of conflict* (Columbia, University of South Carolina Press, 1988), and his essay on guerrilla war in Hoffman and Albert, *Arms and Independence*, "Reflections on the War of Independence."

L'Envoi

The mainland colonies south of Quebec won their independence. They owed their success to the impossibility of a sea-power, with only a few toeholds on a rocky and indented coast, overcoming Nature. The thickly forested land, intersected by broad rivers or narrow rock-infested defiles, was the enemy of all invaders. It had taken a century and a half to master. The French gave assistance too, though not intending that all 13 colonies should become independent, and hoping that they might in the process regain Canada and the St Lawrence valley. With access to the Mississippi, they could block British ex-colonists from access to the Father of Waters, to New Orleans, and to the lands beyond. They neither foresaw nor welcomed the prospect of 13 totally independent republics.

Britain's other disadvantage was her failure to tap and to marshal Loyalist sentiment. For this had been a civil war. Although 1 in 4 of all the Americans in 1776 stayed loyal to George III, and some 40 Loyalist regiments were in name enlisted, they were not enough. The Board of Associated Loyalists was successful neither as recruiting agency nor as drill-master. In the course of the war and after, many Loyalists chose a reluctant exile; thousands took refuge in Florida, moving there with what they could carry and with small bands of slaves, only to find in 1783 that Florida too became independent. For many it proved but a staging post *en route* to more permanent exile in the West Indies or in the icy wastes of New Brunswick or Quebec. Many of them became the Founding Fathers – and Mothers – of British Canada, the United Empire Loyalists. They never needed a war to acquire independence; but they waited almost a century before they won dominion status.

The war, once won, gave a new significance to the Declaration of Independence. The war had not been won because of Jefferson's golden prose, nor from a philosopher's bench, but by Washington's skill as commander-in-chief, and by Franklin's blarney and shrewdness in obtaining French military and naval support, and French and Dutch loans. Along with Lafayette and John Paul Jones, he had in 1779 planned an invasion of the British Isles. As in 1558, as again in 1804, as again in 1940–1, the plans were not fruitful. The Channel winds blew, and the home islands were indeed a "fortress built by Nature for herself/Against infection and the hand of war" (*Richard II*, II.i). The Channel was moat indeed; and Ireland was always near-enemy as well as neighbor. Moreover, the prospect of a French invasion made France, not the colonists, Britain's major enemy; by 1783 the colonists could have their freedom if it permitted troops and ships to be recalled to check the potential invader in his home ports.

More in retrospect than at the time did Jefferson's prose receive the credit. The choice of author could easily have been John Dickinson, who had, in the previous decade, already written much along similar lines. But he had hesitated over independence. Tom Paine's *Common Sense* was a more resounding battle-cry and an open attack – as Jefferson's was not – on "the royal brute". Franklin, a man of many parts, had more training and skill as a journalist than either of them; but it is often said that he was not chosen as author of the Declaration, lest he put a joke in it. His best services were performed, in any case, in Paris.

From seven years of war, from the discipline of service, and from the experience of combat often far away from home, came an awareness of a new society that shared common values and – more or less – a common language, extending for 1,500 miles from the bluffs on the Bay of Fundy south to Florida's swamps, and inland for some 150 miles or more. A new nation, and a republic, came into being. Its secret weapon was its extent, and its method of organizing – and marketing – it. The Land Ordinance of 1785 by the Continental Congress established the method by which federally owned land was to be divided and sold. New regions were surveyed into square townships, to be further subdivided into 36 one-square-mile (640 acre) sections and sold at public auction. Proceeds of the sale of section 16 in each township were to be devoted to "the maintenance of public schools." This ordinance, much amended in detail, imposed the checkerboard pattern that still marks most of the land west of the Appalachians. The Northwest Ordinances of 1787 provided a system of government for western territories. At the very start of the nation's independent existence, it established the principle that as the country grew, new states should be admitted "on an equal footing with the original States in all respects whatsoever." This rejection of the concept of colonial dependency made orderly expansion of the country possible. Slavery was also banned, but since the original ordinance applied only to the region between the Mississippi and Ohio rivers and the Great Lakes, this part of the system was not always included when the ordinance was extended to cover territories farther west. These ordinances of 1785 and their later modifications made land available in relatively small units and at prices that large numbers of individuals could afford.

Yet, if independent and self-governing in politics, and rich in land and resources, the new country was still English-speaking, bound by language and ties of family and trade to its mother-country. That mother-country's long 23 years of war with France would give the new country freedom from renewal of war, and a peace in which it could be left free to flourish and expand. By 1815 its independence was established; now it was fact, not controversy. The Atlantic gave it immunity from a war-addicted Europe. It was a republic that could grow into an empire, and owed no loyalty now except to the notions of rationalism, enlightenment, and industry. Now it was sufficient to itself alone.

Chronologies

1509	Sebastian Cabot reached (what he claimed as) Hudson Bay.
1513	Juan Ponce de Leon explored the Florida coasts.
1513	Vasco de Balboa crossed the isthmus of Panama and reached the Pacific.
1519–21	Conquest of Mexico by Hernando Cortés.
1524	Esteban Gomez sailed from Nova Scotia to Florida, thus completing Spanish exploration of the east coasts of North and South America.
1524	Giovanni da Verrazano, seeking a route to the Indies, entered the harbor of what is now New York and established French claim to North America.
1528	Panfilo de Narvaez landed at Tampa with 400 settlers, and marched north to Tallahassee. They were shipwrecked, and almost all were lost on the way back to Mexico. In 1536, a lone survivor returned to Mexico.
1534–43	Jacques Cartier claimed Newfoundland and Prince Edward Island for France. He then entered the estuary of the St Lawrence River in 1535 and went on to the site of Quebec; he wintered there and returned to France in the spring. By 1540, France was able to control fishing off Newfoundland. Cartier again reached Quebec in 1541. His voyages helped establish French trade with the Indians, which began two years later.
1533	Fortuno Ximenes discovered Lower California.
1535	Spain established the vice-royalty system, in which New Spain was ruled by a vice-roy and a provincial governor.
1539–42	Hernando de Soto brought 600 soldiers to Tampa and journeyed to North Carolina. He later explored west to Mobile, discovered the Mississippi River near the site of Memphis, and explored west to Oklahoma, where he died of fever.
1576–8	Martin Frobisher of England reached Baffin Land and Frobisher Bay in search of the so-called Northwest Passage to the Orient, and sailed through Hudson Strait.
1577–80	Sir Francis Drake sailed to plunder Spanish shipping in the Pacific. He reached San Francisco Bay and claimed it for England. After failing to find the western, end of the Northwest Passage (1579–80), he crossed the Pacific, arriving in England on September 26, 1580, with great amounts of plunder taken from Spanish shipping.
1585–7	John Davis made three voyages to find the Northwest Passage.

1539	Francisco de Ulloa sailed into the Gulf of California.
1540–2	Francisco de Coronado explored New Mexico, Texas, and Kansas in search of the legendary treasures of the Seven Cities of Cibola.
1542	Juan Cabrillo sailed north along the California coast, and discovered San Diego and Monterey.
1551	The University of Mexico was founded as the Royal and Pontifical University of St Paul.
1562	In competition with Spain, Jean Ribaut established an unsuccessful French Huguenot colony at Port Royal, near Charleston. Two years later, René de Laudonnière settled a French Huguenot colony at St John's River, Florida.
1565	Pedro Menendez de Aviles of Spain was ordered to drive the French from Florida; he left Cádiz in June with 2,600 soldiers and sailors; Ribaut went to Florida to reinforce Laudonnière. Menendez founded St Augustine in September and directed the Spanish massacre of almost the entire French settlement.
1566–7	Menendez established settlements at Charlotte Bay, Tampa Bay, Miami, and elsewhere.
1566–72	Jesuit missions were established in Florida.
1574	Spain abandoned west coast posts.
1595–1606	Franciscan missions were established in present-day Georgia; these were later abandoned, but the missions in Florida were retained.
1598	Don Juan de Onate founded San Juan near the site of Sante Fe and claimed New Mexico for Spain.
1600	By this time there were over 150,000 settlers in New Spain.
1602–3	San Diego and Monterey were rediscovered.
1609	Santa Fe was founded. From then until 1769, there was little additional Spanish expansion into New Mexico and California except where missions were founded.
1769–70	San Diego and Monterey were occupied as missions, and the Spanish discovered San Francisco. In the period until 1823, the Franciscans — initially under the leadership of Junipero Serra (d.1784) — established 21 missions in California, the first at San Diego, the last at Sonoma.

CHRISTOPHER COLUMBUS

Note: The calendar in 1492

At the time of Columbus's voyages of discovery, the Christian world used the Julian calendar, and had been doing so for nearly 1,500 years. By 1492 the astronomical year was out of phase with the calendar because each year was 11 minutes and 14 seconds too long. A year had been set at 365.25 days rather than 365.242199 days. These errors had accumulated to nine days, so all Columbian dates need this number of days added to bring them into line with modern calendars.

Pope Gregory XIII proclaimed a new calendar which was adopted by the Catholic world in 1582. England, with her conservative resistance to change, clung to the past for more than a century and a half until 1752 (by which time the error had grown to 11 days), confusing historians as well as the general reader.

Curiously, Columbus Day is still celebrated on the Old Style (OS) rather than the New Style (NS) date of October 21.

1451	Christopher Columbus was born in Genoa, Italy, the son of Domenico Columbus and his wife Susannah Fontanarosa. The precise date may be disputed, but Genoa is now generally accepted as his birthplace, despite the claims of other competing towns throughout Europe.
1464	Christopher probably began his maritime career at about 13, making short trading trips. His formal education has not been documented but it is believed he learnt the rudiments of reading, writing, spelling and drawing or painting from the local friars, as was the custom.
1470	First documentary evidence naming Christopher and his father, dated 22 September and headlined Genoa.
1474–5	Columbus served aboard a ship trading as far east as Chios, an island off Turkey in the Aegean and at the time a Genoese possession.
1475 or 1476	Columbus became involved in a corsair enterprise off Tunisia in an attempt to capture an Aragonese ship.
1476	Columbus voyaged to England, but *en route* the Genoese ship in which he served, which formed part of a convoy, was intercepted by a French corsair squadron. Columbus's ship was sunk but he survived by swimming ashore near Cape St Vincent, August 13.
1477	Columbus arrived in England in December 1476. He spent the winter and the spring of 1477 there, and embarked at Bristol in a ship bound for Iceland. That summer/autumn he returned to Lisbon, Portugal, and settled there.

1478	Columbus made a trading voyage to Madeira, commissioned by the influential Paola di Negro. The deal went wrong and in the following year Columbus testified in Genoa in a lawsuit, August 25, 1479.
1479	September/October is the preferred date for the marriage of Columbus to Felipa Moniz Perestrello, daughter of the governor of Porto Santo.
1480–2	First son, Diego, was born. Columbus made trading voyages to the Canaries and Azores.
1482–3	He sailed to Guinea, the Gold Coast and Cape Verde Islands. Returned to Lisbon. He had by now formulated his plan to sail to the west to discover the islands of Japan and the Indies.
1483–4	King John II of Portugal rejected Columbus's plans.
1485	Henry VII ascended the English throne. Columbus's wife, Felipa, was dead by now. Practically destitute, Columbus moved with Diego to Palos and La Rábida.
1486	In January, Columbus presented his plans to the Catholic Sovereigns. While a commission scrutinised his plans throughout 1487 he lived for months in Córdoba and came to know Beatrice Enriquez de Harana.
1487	In August, the plans were rejected.
1488	A son, Ferdinand, was born to the unmarried Beatrice and Columbus.
1489–91	Columbus sought sponsorship from the wealthy Andalusian dukes and King John of Portugal.
1492	Surrender of the Moors at Granada completed the reconquest of the Iberian peninsula. After more rejections, King Ferdinand and Queen Isabella finally approved Columbus's Capitulations. In May, fitting out of the expedition started at Palos. On August 3, *Santa Maria*, *Pinta* and *Niña* sailed on the first stage of the first voyage of discovery. On September 8, the ocean crossing began, and on October 12, at 2 am, land was sighted. Columbus landed at dawn on the island of Guanahani in the Bahamas group. During October/December he discovered Cuba and Hispaniola, and on December 24–25, *Santa Maria* was shipwrecked.
1493	The return voyage started on January 16, and on March 4 Columbus arrived at the estuary of the Tagus, then went on to Lisbon. At the end of April the Discoverer was received in Barcelona by the Catholic Sovereigns.
	On September 25, the second voyage of discovery began from Cádiz. The voyage lasted till June 11, 1496 — nearly

	three years. It included the discovery of countless islands, and in June 1495 the sending home of five shiploads of Indians — the start of the slave trade.

1496   June 11, Columbus arrived at Cádiz. In October finance was allocated for the third voyage.

1498   Columbus's father died in February. On May 30, the third voyage of discovery began. On July 31, Columbus arrived at the island of Trinidad, and the following day he sighted the mainland of South America.

1499   Rebellion in Hispaniola. The discoverer Alonso de Ojeda sailed (with Amerigo Vespucci aboard) and discovered Venezuela.

1500   Columbus was arrested and returned to Cádiz. He was soon freed and returned to favor.

1502   In May, Columbus started on his fourth voyage from Cádiz. He followed the coastline of today's Panama, Costa Rica, Nicaragua and Honduras.

1503   He reached Jamaica.

1504   November 7, the fourth voyage ended when Columbus landed at Sanlucar de Barrameda. On November 26 Queen Isabella died.

1506   Christopher Columbus died at Valladolid.

1542   Columbus's remains were exhumed and taken to Hispaniola

1898   His remains were taken to Seville Cathedral.

THE TIDEWATER, 1584–1624

1584   Sir Walter Ralegh sent out a colonial expedition to North Carolina. From this came a settlement of 100 at Roanoke Island, NC, that was abandoned in 1586 because of unrest among the Indians.

1587   The "Lost Colony" of Roanoke was established under Ralegh's patent on Roanoke Island, with John White as governor and 150 settlers. Virginia Dare was the first white child born in English America. White, who had gone to England for supplies, returned in 1591 to find the settlers had vanished, presumably killed in an attack by Indians.

1606   In April, James I authorized patents for two joint-stock companies to colonize the New World; the Virginia Company of London received a grant of land between the 34th and 41st latitudes north, and the Virginia Company of Plymouth was to settle further north. Three ships of the London company, carrying 120 settlers, sailed for Virginia in December and landed at Jamestown in May 1607. Indians, disease, famine, and internal dissension plagued the colony for several years.

1608   Captain John Smith effectively ruled the colony, but he was almost executed by the settlers, and left Virginia in 1609.

1609   A new charter gave control to a council chosen by the company. A governor and councillors replaced the old ruling council. Soon after, 400 new colonists arrived.

1609–10   Famine reduced the population from 500 to 60.

1610   A new governor, Thomas, Lord De La Warr, arrived and tried to establish order.

1612   The "Dale Code" of governor Sir Thomas Dale (1611–12, 1614–16) imposed a severe regime to check continuing disorder. The code was given up in 1619.

1612   John Rolfe started tobacco cultivation.

1619–23   The company gave 44 land patents to subsidiary corporations.

1619   A Dutch vessel brought the first 21 Negroes from Africa to Virginia as indentured servants.

1619   General Assembly, the first in the New World, met in Jamestown in August with governor, council, and 22 burgesses from 11 towns, hundreds, and plantations present. It eventually became bicameral.

1622   Indians massacred 347 settlers, and another 500 died of disease the following year, leaving a population in 1624 of 1,275. From then on Virginia followed a policy of unremitting warfare against the Indians.

1624   Virginia became a royal colony when financial instability and the high death rate led to annulment of the charter. The government remained the same except that the governor was now appointed by the Crown, not the company. Sir Francis Wyatt continued as first royal governor until 1626, when Sir George Yeardley replaced him.

THE ENGLISH SETTLEMENTS, 1600–1660

1558–1603   Queen Elizabeth followed an anti-Spanish policy with raids on the Spanish treasure fleet until 1603.

1584   Sir Walter Ralegh sent out colonial expedition to North Carolina.

1588   Defeat of the Spanish Armada.

1603–25   King James I began a policy of mercantilism in which he sought to establish a favorable balance of trade. Colonies would provide raw materials and markets for home manufacturing.

1606 The Virginia Company was established. The earliest colonies were corporate, as in Massachusetts Bay, or proprietary, as in Maryland. In America, Virginia was the only royal colony until 1679.

1620 Mayflower Compact; Pilgrims reached Plymouth.

1621 William Bradford elected governor of Plymouth settlement.

1622 Indians massacred Virginian settlers.

1624 Virginia became royal colony. Captain John Smith wrote his *General Historie of Virginia*.

1625–49 King Charles I struggled with Parliament over the powers of the Crown.

1630 Massachusetts Bay Company settled at Boston.

1632 Charles I made a proprietary grant of Maryland to the Calvert family.

1634–41 Commission for Foreign Plantations aided the Privy Council in its administration of the colonies.

1641 The Body of Liberties made Massachusetts Bay a commonwealth.

1642–9 Civil war in England between king and Parliament; victory for parliamentary forces.

1642–52 First administration of Virginia by royalist governor, Sir William Berkeley, who gained from the Indians the lands between the York and the James Rivers.

1647–9 A radical army group in England, the Levellers, favored social equality, direct democracy through one representative body, and complete manhood suffrage, ideas that later had great influence on the American radicals (1763–76).

1649 Charles I was tried by the army and beheaded on January 30. This began the period of the Commonwealth, ostensibly government by Parliament, which continued under Oliver Cromwell until 1653. A Declaration of Parliament brought all colonies under its control; the Council of State set up a committee to handle trade and plantations.

1651 First Navigation Act, aimed at driving Dutch ships out of the colonial market. No goods from Asia, Africa, or America could be imported into England, Ireland, or the colonies, except on English ships.

1652–4 First Dutch War, mostly on the seas.

1653–8	The Protectorate: rule by the Puritans under Oliver Cromwell. After Cromwell's death in 1658, his son was unable to continue the Protectorate.
1660	Restoration of the monarchy under Charles II (1660–85). Berkeley reinstated by Charles II.

THE NEW ENGLAND COLONIES

Puritanism originated in England in the 1560s when a group of men sought to "purify" the Church of England of bishops, church courts and other remnants of Catholicism. The English Crown, which under Henry VIII had renounced Catholicism, was hostile to Puritanism and tried to establish conformity to Anglican practices. By 1600 the Puritans were divided into two groups: Congregationalists, who were organized as small independent churches made up only of true believers, and Presbyterians, who wanted a central authority and accepted all comers into the faith. Congregationalists were of two types: the Separatists or Pilgrims, who left the Anglican Church and went to Plymouth, and the Puritans, who wished to remain within the Church of England (but did not) and settled at Massachusetts Bay. Whatever the group, Congregational Puritans believed in the extreme power of God in the predestination of man to heaven or hell and in the teachings of the Bible. They believed also that a church member must have a religious experience in which God told him that he was saved.

Plymouth

1606	James I gave Plymouth Company rights to settle between the 38th and 45th parallels. Its first expedition built a temporary fort at the mouth of the Kennebec River (1607), but the colony was unsuccessful.
1608	Separatists from the Church of England (henceforth called Pilgrims) moved to Holland to avoid religious persecution.
1614	Captain John Smith explored the northeastern coast of present-day Unites States and named it New England.
1619	The Pilgrims set up a joint-stock company with a Virginia Company patent to settle near Jamestown.
1620	In July, 35 Pilgrims under William Brewster left Holland for England in the *Speedwell*. In August, they joined other English Separatists (and non-Pilgrims) in Plymouth and set forth for America on the *Speedwell* and the *Mayflower*, but returned to port when the *Speedwell* sprang a leak. The *Mayflower* sailed for the New World on September 16; Brewster led the Pilgrims, and Captain Myles Standish sailed as military leader. On November 9, the *Mayflower* entered Cape Cod Bay, far north of its destination.

Since the patent from the Virginia Company was inoperative in the north, and since they were afraid that the non-Pilgrims would rebel, the Pilgrims persuaded 41 adults aboard to sign the Mayflower Compact on November 21. The signers agreed to follow laws "for the generall goode of the colonie." In December, an exploring party landed at Plymouth; on the 26th, the *Mayflower* anchored at Plymouth, and settlers went ashore.

1621   Over half the settlers died of disease during the first winter. In March, a treaty was made with the Wampanoag Indians, and in April, William Bradford was elected governor. He was annually re-elected (except for five years) until his death in 1657. The government consisted of an annual assembly (the General Court) composed of governor, assistants, and all freemen (those granted the right to vote). The Council for New England (the Plymouth Company reorganized to include land between the 40th and 48th parallels) granted the Pilgrims a patent to settle at Plymouth on June 1.

1623   The Pilgrims granted each family a parcel of land.

1626   The Company in London sold all rights to the settlers, who divided up the remaining land, Eight Pilgrims, including Bradford, took over the debts of the colony. Colony and corporation were merged but Plymouth never received a royal charter.

1636   Representative system of government began. The General Court consisted of two deputies from each town, together with the governor and his assistants.

1691   Massachusetts Bay Colony absorbed the Plymouth Colony.

Massachusetts Bay

1626   The Council for New England set up a fishing post at Cape Ann, north of Boston.

1628   The New England Company received a patent from the Council for New England for land from three miles south of the Charles River to three miles north of the Merrimack River and sent 40 settlers to Salem.

1629   A royal charter merged the New England Company with the Massachusetts Bay Company (March 14), which sent its first group of settlers to Salem in July. Religious and economic difficulties led John Winthrop, Richard Saltonstall, and others of the Massachusetts Bay Company, most of them Puritans, to decide to migrate to the New World, provided the charter and government of the Company went with them (the Cambridge Agreement). The Company agreed, and Winthrop was elected governor.

1630   From March to October, over 1000 settlers sailed for Salem in 17 ships and then founded Boston, Charlestown, and Watertown.

The 12 freemen (company stockholders eligible to vote), consisting of governor, deputy governor, and assistants, ruled.

1631   On May 28, the number of freemen (which came to mean landowners who could vote) was raised from 12 to 130, but only church members could be freemen. The governor was still elected by the assistants, who were chosen by the freemen. Direct election of the governor by all freemen began a year later.

1634   Each town gained the right to send deputies to the meeting of the General Court, which passed all laws for the colony.

1635   Rev. Roger Williams was banished in September from Massachusetts Bay for preaching his belief in the separation of Church and State.

1636   The antinomian views of Mrs Anne Hutchinson and other Bostonians threatened orthodoxy.

1637   John Winthrop was re-elected governor and continued to serve almost every year to 1649.

1638   Winthrop ignored a privy council order in April to give up the charter. The English civil war prevented further action.

1641   The Body of Liberties made Massachusetts Bay a Commonwealth or independent republic, dominated by the church.

1644   The General Court became bicameral with a House of Deputies and a House of Assistants.

1646   Rev. John Eliot began to convert the Indians in eastern Massachusetts to Christianity.

1656   Massachusetts Bay banished two Quakers for religious nonconformity.

1658   Massachusetts established the death penalty for banished Quakers who returned, and had hanged four by 1661.

1664   Four royal commissioners sent to investigate the governing of New England demanded that landowners be given the vote, that laws against the Crown be repudiated, that all Churches be recognized. Plymouth, Connecticut, and Rhode Island agreed with the commissioners but Massachusetts refused to comply. No action was taken against Massachusetts.

1669   Massachusetts annexed Maine.

1676   Royal agent Edward Randolph accused Massachusetts of denying residents the right of appeal to the privy council and of failing to enforce the Navigation Acts.

1684   The charter of Massachusetts Bay was annulled by the Crown because of Randolph's charges.

1686   In December, the Dominion of New England, with Sir Edmund Andros as governor, assumed authority over New England. In the period 1687–8, Andros irritated New Englanders by requiring Congregationalists to share churches with Anglicans, by trying to appropriate town land for the Crown, and by limiting town meetings to one a year. Rev. John Wise of Ipswich, Mass., denounced Andros for taxation without representation. News of the Glorious Revolution reached Boston in April, 1689, and a mob forced Andros to surrender, charged him with misgovernment, and sent him to England for trial.

1691   Massachusetts became a royal province (October 17), with a governor appointed by the Crown, with property rather than religion as a qualification for voting, and with royal veto power over all legislation. Plymouth was absorbed into Massachusetts.

New Hampshire and Maine

1622   The Council for New England granted Sir Ferdinando Gorges and John Mason the land between the Merrimack and the Kennebec Rivers.

1623–4 Settlers arrived at Great Bay, New Hampshire (including Portsmouth) and at the Saco River and Casco Bay in Maine.

1629   New Hampshire and Maine were divided at the Piscataqua River.

1641–58 Many New Hampshire and Maine towns put themselves under the jurisdiction of Massachusetts because of the threat from Indian attacks.

1679   New Hampshire became a separate royal province and in 1692 was separated from the Dominion of New England. From 1698 to 1741 New Hampshire shared a governor with Massachusetts, getting its own governor, Benning Wentworth, in 1741.

Connecticut

1631   Lord Say and Sele and others received a patent from the Crown for Connecticut.

1633   The Dutch laid claim to the area and built Fort Good Hope (Hartford); in the same year, a party from Plymouth traveled the Connecticut River valley from its mouth north to Windsor.

1634   Settlers from Massachusetts Bay established Wethersfield and, in 1635, Hartford.

1635   Connecticut patent holders sent John Winthrop Jr to settle at Saybrook, at the mouth of the Connecticut River.

1636–7 The Pequot Indians attacked Wethersfield and other settlements, and were finally subdued by a combined force from Massachusetts, Plymouth, and Connecticut colonies.

1637	In May, settlers in Hartford, Windsor, and Wethersfield founded what became the colony of Connecticut with a representative general court for the population of 800. In the same year, Rev. John Davenport and Theophilus Eaton sailed from England and founded New Haven.
1639	Hartford, Wethersfield, and Windsor agreed to the Fundamental Orders, which called for the governor and magistrates to be elected by "admitted inhabitants" (Trinitarian householders).
1643	Colony of New Haven was formed and was joined by two other towns.
1662	Connecticut requested from the Crown and received a charter granting it autonomy under the Fundamental Orders and allowing it to absorb New Haven.

Rhode Island

1636	Roger Williams and his followers founded the relatively democratic colony of Providence.
1638	Anne Hutchinson, after her expulsion from Massachusetts Bay, settled Portsmouth.
1640	Newport, founded 1639, united with Portsmouth.
1647	Providence, Newport, and Portsmouth formed the colony of Rhode Island. Governor and both houses of the legislature were elected annually by freeholders.
1663	Charles II granted Rhode Island a charter but allowed it to continue under its old independent rule. A statement was added about religious toleration, and Rhode Island continued to operate under this charter until 1842.

RESTORATION AND ADMINISTRATION, 1660–1767

1660	Restoration of the monarchy in England under Charles II.
1660–75	Committee for Trade and Plantations of the Privy Council set up to administer colonies.
1660	Second Navigation Act: no goods could enter or leave English colonies except on English ships (including colonial ships). Enumerated articles (tobacco and sugar included) could be shipped from the colonies only to England or other colonies,
1663	Third Navigation Act: most colonial imports from Europe had to travel on English ships and pass through England. (These Acts encouraged shipbuilding but tended to hurt the tobacco trade.)

1673	Fourth Navigation Act: duties were to be collected on enumerated articles at the port of departure to prevent evasion of duties. Customs Commissioners were appointed to enforce Acts.
1675–96	The Lords of Trade, a committee of the Privy Council, was put in charge of colonies.
1681–5	Tension between king and Parliament rose over the rights of the Crown. Charles II ruled without Parliament until his death in 1685.
1685–8	Anti-Parliament and pro-Catholic policies of Charles II's successor James II led to the Glorious Revolution of 1688. James II fled England in December: he was succeeded by his son-in-law, William of Orange, and his daughter Mary, ruling jointly.
1689	Bill of Rights required free election of Parliament and Parliament's consent to taxation.
	John Locke's *Two Treatises on Civil Government* defended the sovereignty of the people and their right of revolution.
1696– 1782	Board of Trade and Plantations was established to supervise the colonies.
1696	A further Navigation Act tightened the enforcement of earlier Acts and set up vice-admiralty courts in the colonies with jurisdiction over cases involving violations of the trade laws. These courts were unpopular because they did not use juries.
1699	Wool Act forbade the export of wool products from any colony in an effort to protect British producers from competition.
1701	Act of Settlement made royal ministers responsible to Parliament.
1702	Queen Anne succeeded William of Orange.
1705–74	Under various Acts, bounties were paid for tar, hemp, turpentine, and indigo.
1714	George of Hanover became George I of England.
1727	Accession of George II.
1732	Hat Act put restrictions on colonial manufacture of hats.
1733	Molasses Act put a high duty on rum (9d./gal.) and molasses (6d./gal.) imported from foreign West Indies to the mainland of North America. It was not enforceable.
1750	Iron Act forbade construction of slitting and other iron mills in the colonies and allowed colonial pig and bar iron into England duty-free.

1751	Money Act prohibited New England colonies from setting up land banks or issuing bills of credit (paper money) as legal tender.
1760	Accession of George III.
1767	Non-enumerated goods destined for Europe north of Cape Finisterre had to be shipped to Britain first. By about 1763, Parliament controlled trade, while the colonial assemblies controlled taxation, appointed lower officials, raised troops, and maintained their rights as Englishmen.

THE MAKING OF INDEPENDENCE, 1763–1790

1763	Peace of Paris: Britain acquired Canada. British national debt £133 million.
	George III's Proclamation on October 7 closed to colonists all land south of Quebec, north of Florida and west of the Appalachian divide.
1764	Sugar Act: reduced tax on sugar and molasses imported from foreign West Indies.
1765	Stamp Act to raise revenue for defense met with fierce colonial opposition.
1766	Repeal of Stamp Act.
1767	Charles Townshend, Chancellor of the Exchequer, imposed import duties on tea, glass, paints, oil, lead, and paper.
1769	Virginia House of Burgesses rejects Parliament's right to tax.
1770	Boston "Massacre": British troops kill five when crowd attacks them. Townshend Act repealed taxes except that on tea – as a symbol of Parliament's right to tax.
1773	Boston Tea Party.
1774	Coercive Acts: Boston port to be closed until tea paid for. First Continental Congress.
1775	Fighting at Lexington and Concord; Second Continental Congress assembles; Battle of Bunker Hill. "Olive Branch" Petition.
1776	Thomas Paine, *Common Sense*; Congress agrees to Declaration of Independence, July 4.
1777	Saratoga: surrender of General Burgoyne to General Gates.
1778	Franco-American alliance.
1781	Articles of Confederation proclaimed; surrender of British at Yorktown on October 14.
1782	H. St John de Crevecoeur, *Letters from an American Farmer*.

1783	Articles of Peace ratified (Treaty of Paris).
1785	Ordinance passed for sale of western lands.
1787	Constitutional Convention meets in Philadelphia; Northwest Ordinance provides for government of Old Northwest.
1787–8	Alexander Hamilton, James Madison, and John Jay write *The Federalist Essays*.
1788	Constitution ratified.
1789	George Washington elected first US president.
1790	First US census shows population of 3.9 million.

Bibliographies

Each major American publishing house now has its own major text-book surveying the history of the United States, sometimes 2-volume "standard" works. Each such text has its own daunting and catholic bibliography. It is not my purpose to rival these, least of all since there are two standard bibliographies. The first of these, itself in two volumes, is the *Harvard Guide to American History*, edited by Frank Freidel with the assistance of Richard K. Showman (Cambridge, MA, Belknap Press of Harvard University Press, 2nd edn revised, 1974). It does not, however, cite the publishers of the volumes it lists, and much has been written in the last 20 years. Supplementing this Harvard Guide is a set of 24 volumes in paperback, under the general title *The Goldentree Bibliographies in American History*, general editor Arthur S. Link (New York, Meredith corporation, 1969). These are much easier to handle, each being in format a 100-page large pamphlet, listing titles by themes and topics, and citing relevant articles in periodicals. Those I have found most useful are:

Alden T. Vaughan, *The American Colonies in the Seventeenth Century*
Jack P. Greene, *The American Colonies in the Eighteenth Century 1689–1763*
John Shy, *The American Revolution*
E. James Ferguson, *The Confederation and the Constitution, 1781–1801*
John Hope Franklin, *American Negro History*
Fletcher M. Green, *The Old South*
Don E. Fehrenbacher, *Manifest Destiny and the Coming of the Civil War 1841–1860*
Norman A. Graebner, *American Diplomatic History Before 1890*
Edwin A. Miles, *American Nationalism and Sectionalism, 1801–1841*
Gerald N. Grob, *American Social History Before 1860*
Alpheus T. Mason, *American Constitutional Development*
George Rogers Taylor, *American Economic History Before 1860*
David Donald, *The Nation in Crisis, 1861–1877*

What follows is only one man's guide to the field; the books are grouped according to the topics referred to in my survey, with comments where appropriate.

INTRODUCTION

For the European discoveries, and the view that Columbus was *primus inter pares*, see S. E. Morison, *The European Discovery of America: The northern voyages* AD *500–1600* (New York, Oxford University Press, 1971) – a companion volume to his *The European Discovery of America: The southern voyages* AD *1492–1616* (New York, Oxford University Press, 1974), together abridged in one volume as *The Great Explorers* (New York, Oxford University Press, 1978); Morison's superb 2-volume *Admiral of the Ocean Sea: A life of Christopher Columbus* (New York, Oxford University Press, 1942), and his 1-volume life, *Christopher Columbus, Mariner* (Boston, Little Brown, 1955). Cf. also Morison's "Letters on the Harvard Columbus Expedition," in his *By Land and Sea* (New York, Knopf, 1954), and, with Mauricio Obregon, *The Caribbean as Columbus Saw It* (Boston, Little Brown, 1964), esp. chs 9 and 10; and his *Journals and Other Documents on the Life and Voyages of Christopher Columbus* (New York, Oxford University Press, 1963).

Compare Italy's leading expert on Columbus, Paolo Taviani, *Christopher Columbus, the Grand Design* (London, Orbis, 1985), who finds him unskillful only in his handling of people; and for a continuous story drawing on Columbus's own writings, see J. M. Cohen (ed. and trans.), *The Four Voyages of Christopher Columbus* (London, Cresset Books, 1969), and Gianni Granzotto, *Christopher Columbus, the Dream and the Obsession* (London, Collins Grafton, 1988), notably for the study of Columbus's character, and for the story of the first voyage. For the first landing and its locale, see Robert H. Fuson's (ed. and trans.), *The Log of Christopher Columbus* (Ashford Press, Southampton, 1987), and "A theoretical reconstruction of the first Atlantic crossing of Christopher Columbus," *Proceedings of the Association of American Geographers*, 8 (1976), pp. 155–9. For England's role, see D. B. Quinn's *England and the Discovery of America* (London, Allen and Unwin, 1973), and W. P. Cumming, R. A. Skelton and D. B. Quinn, *The Discovery of North America* (London, Elek, 1971); and for sparkling but meticulous surveys of many enterprises, G. V. Scammell, *The World Encompassed: The first European maritime empires* c. *800–1650* (London and New York, Methuen, 1981), and D. W. Meinig, *The Shaping of America* (Yale University Press, New Haven, Conn., 1986). The savage side of the story is well portrayed in De Las Casas, *Devastation of the Indies* (New York, Seabury Press, 1974). Although respecting Columbus's skill as seaman, Hans Koning, *Columbus: His enterprise* (New York, Monthly Review Press, 1976), is a sustained critic of Columbus's barbarism towards the Indians; the book has recently been reissued by the Latin American Bureau, with an afterword by a Bolivian activist for Indian rights, Domitila Chungara. There are also three excellent 1-volume biographies: Ernle Bradford, *Christopher Columbus* (London, Michael Joseph, 1973); Felipe Fernandez-Arnesto, *Columbus* (Oxford, Oxford University Press, 1991): and David Thomas, *Christopher Columbus, Master of the Atlantic* (London, Deutsch, 1991). For a masterly survey of recent literature, see John Larner, "The certainty of Columbus: some recent studies," *History*, 73 no. 237 (Feb. 1988), pp. 3–23; and also his article "North American hero? Christopher Columbus 1702–2002," *Proceedings of the American Philosophical Society*, 137 no. 1 (March 1993), pp. 46–63.

The best brief accounts of the Norse voyages and of the discovery of L'Anse aux Meadows is by the discoverer himself, Helge Ingstad, in his chapters in Geoffrey Ashe (ed.), *The Quest for America* (London, Pall Mall Press, 1971), pp. 96–114 and 175–98. For the fuller story, see Anne Stine Ingstad (vol. I) and Helge Ingstad (vol. II), *The Norse Discovery of America* (Oslo, Norwegian University Press, 1985, distributed by Oxford University Press); and F. Pohl, *Atlantic Crossings before Columbus* (New York, Norton, 1961). Cf. also Helge Ingstad, *Westward to Vinland* (New York, St Martin's Press, 1969). For a useful summary, see also D. B. Quinn, *North America from Earliest Discovery to First Settlements: The Norse voyages to 1612,* (New York, Harper and Row, 1977), pp. 21–40, and its bibliography; and Scammell, *The World Encompassed*, pp. 1–37. Gwyn Jones, *A History of the Vikings* (London, Oxford University Press, 1968) is valuable background. For the Vinland map, see Helen Wallis *et al.*, "The strange case of the Vinland map," *Geographical Journal*, 140 (1974), pp. 183–214.

1 THE ADMIRAL WHO RARELY PUT TO SEA:
RALEGH AND ROANOKE

The standard work on which a generation of students has been raised is C. M. Andrews, *The Colonial Period of American History*, 4 vols, (New Haven, Yale University Press, 1934–8); cf. Richard R. Johnson, "Charles McLean Andrews and the invention of American colonial history," *William & Mary Quarterly*, 43 (1986), pp. 519–41. There are also a number of outstanding studies by some outstanding and voluble scholars: Daniel J. Boorstin, *The Americans: The colonial experience* (London, Pelican Books, 1958); Nicholas Canny and Anthony Pagden (eds), *Colonial Identity in the Atlantic World 1500–1800* (Princeton, NJ, Princeton University Press, 1987); David D. Hall, John M. Murrin and Thad W. Tate (eds), *Saints and Revolutionaries: Essays on early American history* (New York, Norton, 1984); Jack P. Greene and J. R. Pole (eds), *Colonial British America: Essays in the new history of the early modern era* (Baltimore, Johns Hopkins University Press, 1984); Milton M. Klein and Jacob E. Cooke (gen. eds), *A History of the American Colonies* (New York, Scribner's).

A number of distinguished contemporary scholars have specialized in studies of the approaches to and landings on the east coast. David B. Quinn has been described as the Richard Hakluyt of today: D. B. Quinn (ed.), *New American World: A documentary history of North America to 1612*, 5 vols (Arno Press and Hector Bye, 1979); D. B. Quinn, *The Hakluyt Handbook*, 2 vols (London, Hakluyt Society, 1974); *Sir Walter Raleigh* (London, English Universities Press, 1955); *England and the Discovery of America, 1481–1620* (London, Allen and Unwin, 1973); *North America from Earliest Discovery to First Settlements: The Norse voyages to 1612* (New York, Harper and Row, 1977); *Set Fair for Roanoke: Voyages and colonies 1584–1606* (Chapel Hill, NC, University of North Carolina Press, 1985); and D. B. Quinn and A. N. Ryan, *England's Sea Empire 1550–1642* (London, Allen and Unwin, 1983).

There are other valuable studies: Kenneth R. Andrews, *Trade, Plunder, and Settlement: Maritime enterprise and the genesis of the British empire, 1480–1630* (Cambridge, Cambridge University Press, 1984); Hugh Honour, *The New Golden Land: European images of America from the discoveries to the present time* (New York, Pantheon, 1975); Gwyn Jones, *The Norse Atlantic Saga: Being the Norse voyages of discovery and settlement to Iceland, Greenland, America* (rev. edn, London, Oxford University Press, 1986); Karen Ordahl Kupperman, *Roanoke: The abandoned colony* (Totowa, NJ, Rowan and Allanheld, 1984); C. J. Marcus, *The Conquest of the North Atlantic* (New York, Oxford University Press, 1981); P. J. Marshall and Glyndwr Williams, *The Great Map of Mankind: Perceptions of new worlds in the Age of Enlightenment* (Cambridge, MA, Harvard University Press, 1982); S. E. Morison, *The European Discovery of America*, 2 vols (New York, Oxford University Press, 1971 and 1974); J. H. Parry, *The Age of Reconnaissance: Discovery, exploration and settlement 1450–1650* (Cleveland, World, 1963); J. H. Parry, *The Discovery of South America* (New York, Taplinger, 1979); Erik Wahlgren, *The Vikings and America* (New York, Thames and Hudson, 1986); James A. Wlilliamson, *The Age of Drake*, 5th edn (London, A. and C. Black, 1965).

For Spain, see Charles Gibson, *Spain in America* (New York, Harper and Row, 1966); Kenneth R. Andrews, *The Spanish Caribbean: Trade and plunder, 1530–1630* (New Haven, Yale University Press, 1978), and *Trade, Plunder and Settlement: Maritime enterprise and the genesis of the British Empire 1480–1630* (Cambridge, Cambridge University Press, 1984); K. R. Andrews, N. P. Canny and P. E. H. Hart (eds), *The Westward Enterprise: English activities in Ireland, the Atlantic and America 1480–1630* (Detroit, Wayne State University Press, 1979); J. H. Elliott, *The Old World and the New 1492–1650* (Cambridge, Cambridge University Press, 1970); Mario Gongora, *Studies in the Colonial History of Spanish America*, trans. Richard Southern (Cambridge, Cambridge University Press, 1975).

Also paradoxically, the best account of Verrazzano's journey is in Hakluyt's translation; the French sources are thin. See also Lawrence

C. Wroth, *The Voyages of Giovanni da Verrazzano 1524–28* (Yale University Press, 1970), esp. pp. 165–8. Verrazzano was fortunate – like Columbus – to have a brother (Girolamo) who was a cartographer. According to Hakluyt, a copy of their map was presented by one or other of them to Henry VIII of England. On Cartier, H. P. Biggar is still the best authority: *The Voyages of Jacques Cartier* (Ottawa, 1924) and *Precursors of Jacques Cartier, 1497–1534* (Ottawa, 1911). But the "feel" of the sea, and the menace of the fog, ice and storms of the northern waters, still comes through most vividly in Morison's *The European Discovery of America*.

For Raleigh himself, see Stephen J. Greenblatt, *Sir Walter Ralegh, The Renaissance Man and his Roles* (New Haven, Yale University Press, 1973); and Stephen Coote, *A Play of Passion: The life of Sir Walter Ralegh* (London, Macmillan, 1993).

For the image of America in Europe see Honour, *The New Golden Land*; Howard Mumford Jones, *O Strange New World: American culture, the formative years* (New York, Viking, 1964); and for France, see W. J. Eccles, *France in America* (New York, Harper and Row, 1972).

2   THE FIRST ENGLISH SETTLEMENTS

For Jamestown, see Philip L. Barbour (ed.), *The Jamestown Voyages 1607–9*, 2 vols (Cambridge, Cambridge University Press, 1969); Carl Bridenbaugh, *Vexed and Troubled Englishmen 1590–1642* (New York, Oxford University Press, 1968), and C. M. Andrews, *The Colonial Period of American History*, 4 vols (New Haven, Yale University Press, 1934–8), vol. I (1939), pp. 98–150.

On John Smith, see Philip L. Barbour, *The Three Worlds of Captain John Smith* (New York, Houghton Mifflin, 1964), and (ed.), *The Complete Works of Captain John Smith (1580–1631)*, 3 vols (Chapel Hill, NC, IEAHC, 1986); Karen Ordahl Kupperman (ed.), *Captain John Smith: A select edition of his writings* (Chapel Hill, NC, IEAHC, University of North Carolina Press, 1988); Alden T. Vaughan, *American Genesis: Captain John Smith and the founding of Virginia* (Library of American Biography, Little Brown, 1975); and Kevin J. Hayes (compiler), *Captain John Smith, A Reference Guide* (Boston, G. K. Hall, 1991).

The best recent survey of the First Americans is in two review essays. H. C. Porter's "Reflections on the ethnohistory of early colonial North America," *Journal of American Studies* 16.2 (1982), pp. 243–54, stresses the "new view" that has obtained since the civil rights struggles of the 1960s and the Vietnam War. Words like "civilized" and "advanced," "primitive" and "barbarous," are now taboo; to recent writers, cultural parity obtains between white men and red; Indian diplomacy, especially that of Powhatan or of the Mohawks, seems as worthy of study, and as skillful, as that of Talleyrand. If Porter is detached, compare James Axtell,

"The ethnohistory of early America," *William & Mary Quarterly*, 35.1 (1978), pp. 110–44, who dates the change of attitude to 1946, with the creation by Congress of the Indian Claims Commission, and to 1954, with the foundation of the journal *Ethnohistory*. He stresses the fluctuating frontiers in the first century of colonial history, and the cultural clashes along them, and identifies the areas that still call for an ethno-historical reassessment. He buttresses his masterly and critical analysis with a massive bibliography.

The Iroquois story has been the most amply "covered" by historians. It is now clear that their "confederacy" was much looser in structure than earlier historians, notably Lewis Morgan and Parkman, believed, and that the wars of the Iroquois were more often of Seneca with Mohawk and each with Onondaga than with the French. What made the Iroquois important, and powerful, for a longer span of time than any others, was their location where the Ottawa and the St Lawrence routes met the Hudson-Mohawk, and their role as regular traders with white men.

For the origins and history, Henry Rowe-Schoolcraft, *Legends of the American Indians* (Minerva, Geneva, 1980), and Thomas Page, *The Civilization of the American Indians* (Minerva, Geneva 1979), are valuable sources for Indian legends, abetted by the Museum of the American Indian, The Heye Foundation, New York. See too Angie Debo, *A History of the Indians of the United States* (Norman, University of Oklahoma Press, 1970); Harold E. Driver, *Indians of North America*, 2nd edn (Chicago, University of Chicago Press, 1969), John Collier, *Indians of the Americas: the long hope* (New York, Norton, 1947); Dee Brown, *Bury My Heart at Wounded Knee: An Indian history of the American West* (London, Pan Books, 1972); Virginia I. Armstrong (Compiler), *I Have Spoken: American History through the voices of the Indians* (Chicago, Swallow Press, 1971); Alvin M. Josephy, Jr, *The Patriot Chiefs* (New York, Viking Press, 1969); Frances Svensson, *The Ethnics in American Politics: American Indians* (Minneapolis, Burgess Publishing Co., 1973).

The best studies of European-Indian relations include: James Axtell, *The European and the Indian: Essays in the ethnohistory of colonial North America* (New York, Knopf, 1978 and 1981), which has a valuable section of notes on the sources of many of the ideas he discusses. See also his *The Invasion Within: The contest of cultures in colonial North America* (New York, Oxford University Press, 1983), the first of a 3-volume project. Also Richard Drinnan, *Facing West: The metaphysics of Indian-hating and empire building* (Minneapolis, Minnesota, 1980); George T. Hunt, *The Wars of the Iroquois* (Madison, University of Wisconsin Press, 1960), offering a fresh view of the Iroquois; Wilbur R. Jacobs, *Dispossessing the American Indians: Indians and whites on the colonial frontier* (New York, Scribner's, 1972) – perhaps an overstatement of the Indian side of the case?; Robert F. Berkhofer, Jr, *Salvation and the Savage: An analysis of Protestant missions and American Indian response, 1787–1862* (University of Kentucky Press, 1965; repr. New York, Atheneum, 1972); Cornelius

J. Jaenen, *Friend and Foe: Aspects of French-Amerindian cultural contact in the sixteenth and seventeenth centuries* (New York, Columbia University Press, 1976); Francis Jennings, *The Invasion of America: Indians, colonisation and the cant of conquest* (Chapel Hill, NC, University of North Carolina Press, 1975), robustly written, and with a "strong aversion toward the Puritan gentry;" Karen Ordahl Kupperman, *Settling with the Indians: The meeting of English and Indian cultures in America, 1580–1640* (Totowa, NJ, Rowman and Littlefield, 1980); Gary B. Nash, *Red, White and Black: The peoples of early America* (Englewood Cliffs, NJ, Prentice-Hall, 1974), notable for telling the colonial story as much from a red and a black as from a white viewpoint, and not least for its superb bibliographical essay; Gary B. Nash and Richard Weiss (eds), *The Great Fear: Race in the mind of America* (New York, Holt, Rinehart, 1970); Richard Slotkin, *Regeneration Through Violence: The mythology of the American Frontier, 1600–1860* (Middletown, Conn., Wesleyan University Press, 1973); J. M. Smith (ed.), *Seventeenth Century America: Essays in colonial America* (Chapel Hill, NC, University of North Carolina Press, 1959), esp. for Nancy Oestreich Lurie's "Indian cultural adjustment to European civilization." See also Barbara Graymont, *The Iroquois in the American Revolution* (Syracuse, NY, Syracuse University Press, 1972). One of the best recent studies of Indian-white relations is William C. Sturtevant (ed.), *Handbook of North American Indians*, vol. IV, *History of Indian White Relations*, ed. Wilcomb E. Washburn (Washington, DC, Smithsonian Institution, 1988). It was largely the legacy of the work of the Indian Claims Commission; it is wide-ranging over political and military clashes and reflects the viewpoint of the 1980s. The other valuable recent studies are James H. Merrell, *The Indians' New World: Catawbas and their neighbors, from European contact through the era of removal* (Chapel Hill, IEAHC, 1989); and Helen C. Rountree, *The Powhatan Indians of Virginia* (Norman, University of Oklahoma, 1989).

For specific events and personalities, see: Bruce G. Trigger, *The Children of Aataentsic: A history of the Huron people to 1660*, 2 vols (Montreal, McGill-Queen's University Press, 1976); Anthony Wallace, *The Death and Rebirth of the Seneca* (Seneca, NY, Knopf, 1970), and *Teedyoung, King of the Delawares* (Philadelphia, University of Pennsylvania Press, 1949); Wilcomb E. Washburn, *The Indian in America* (New York, Harper and Row, 1975); Allen W. Trelease, *Indian Affairs in Colonial New York: The seventeenth century* (Port Washington, NY, Kennikat Press, 1971); Howard Peckham, *Pontiac and the Indian Uprising* (Princeton, NJ, Princeton University Press, 1947); Arthur Pound's splendid if now dated *Johnson and the Mohawks* (New York, Macmillan, 1930), and James T. Flexner, *Mohawk Baronet: Sir William Johnson of New York* (New York, Harper and Row, 1959); Nicholas B. Wainwright, *George Croghan: Wilderness diplomat* (Chapel Hill, NC, University of North Carolina Press, 1959); Paul Wallace, *Conrad Weiser 1696–1760, Friend of Colonist and Mohawk* (Philadelphia, University of Pennsylvania Press, 1945); William

A. Brophy and Sophie D. Aberle, *The Indian: America's unfinished business*, Report of the Commission on the Rights, Liberties and Responsibilities of the American Indian (Norman, University of Oklahoma Press, 1969); Felix S. Cohen (ed.), *Handbook of Federal Indian Law* (Albuquerque, University of New Mexico Press, 1971; Facsimile of 1942 edn); Council on Interracial Books for Children (comp. and ed.), *Chronicles of American Indian Protest* (Greenwich, Conn., Fawcett Publications, 1971); Vine Deloria, Jr, *Custer Died for Your Sins: An Indian manifesto* (New York, Macmillan, 1969); idem, *Of Utmost Good Faith* (San Francisco, Straight Arrow Books, 1971); idem, *We Talk, You Listen: New tribes, new turf* (New York, Macmillan, 1970); D'Arcy McNickle, *Native American Tribalism: Indian Survivals and Renewals* (New York, published for the Institute of Race Relations by Oxford University Press, 1973); D'Arcy McNickle and Harold E. Fey, *Indians and Other Americans: Two ways of life meet*, rev. edn (New York, Harper and Row, 1970); Stan Steiner, *The New Indians* (New York, Harper and Row, 1968); and D'Arcy McNickle, *They Came Here First* (Harper and Row, Perennial Paperback, 1975). Finally, Carl Wildman (compiler), *Atlas of the North American Indian* (New York, Facts on File Publication, 1985), and Francis Paul Prucha, *Atlas of American Indian Affairs* (Lincoln, Nebr., University of Nebraska Press, 1990), are both useful background.

For recent comments, see Reginald Horsman, *Expansion and American Indian Policy* (East Lansing, Michigan State University Press, 1967), and his *Race and Manifest Destiny: The origins of American racial Anglo-Saxonism* (Cambridge, MA, Harvard University Press, 1981); Robert F. Berkhofer, Jr, *The White Man's Indian: Images of the American Indian from Columbus to the Present* (New York, Knopf, 1978). In *The Indian Population of New England in the Seventeenth Century* (Berkeley, CA, University of California Press, 1976), the late Sherburne F. Cook doubled all earlier estimates of Indian numbers in New England,

3 THE PURITAN DREAM

For seventeenth-century American Puritanism, the two basic sources are William Bradford's *Of Plimouth Plantation* (best edn, ed. S. E. Morison, New York, Knopf, 1952), an expression of Puritan piety in the form of a biblical exodus from a tyranny or as an Errand into the Wilderness; and John Winthrop's address on "The Modell of Christian Charity" on the *Arbella*, as an expression of the Puritan social ideal. In the first and second generations after "History" as a discipline established itself in the USA in the 1890s, it became fashionable to "debunk" the Puritans as strait-laced and doom-laden, given to tyrannizing over other creeds, even those not dissimilar from their own. The word became synonymous with a killjoy, a prohibitionist, a prude haunted by the fear that some one might be enjoying him or herself, opposed – in Macaulay's words – to bear-baiting not because it was cruel to the bear but because it gave pleasure to the spectators. In the mid-twentieth century, a number of more dedicated scholars have pointed to the complexities and diversities of Puritanism. Their preoccupation was with the life of the mind, with thought and theology. Among these are: Perry Miller, *Orthodoxy in Massachusetts* (Cambridge, MA, Harvard University Press, 1933); *The New England Mind: The 17th century* (New York, Macmillan, 1939); and *The New England Mind: From colony to province* (Cambridge, MA, Harvard University Press, 1953); Perry Miller and Thomas H. Johnson (eds), *The Puritans: A source-book of their writings*, 2 vols (New York, Harper and Row, 1963), Perry Miller, *Jonathan Edwards: A profile* (New York, Macmillan, 1940), and *Roger Williams, his Contribution to the American Tradition* (Indianapolis, Bobbs-Merrill, 1953). See also William Haller, *The Rise of Puritanism 1570–1643* (New York, Columbia University Press, 1938), and *Liberty and Reformation in the Puritan Revolution* (New York, Columbia University Press, 1955).

In 1985 A. Heimert and A. Delbanco (eds) produced *The Puritans in America: A narrative history* (Cambridge, MA, Harvard University Press, 1985), designed to succeed rather than replace the Miller and Johnson anthology, which was organized thematically. The editors stress how much the intellectual development of New England was prefigured in the arguments of the first generation of settlement, and how constant the themes were of "the burden of doubt" as to their own reading of God's will, and their "relentless introspection." Add Perry Miller's collection of essays *Errand into the Wilderness* (Cambridge, MA, Belknap Press of Harvard University Press, 1956); P. B. Perry, *Puritanism and Democracy* (New York, Vanguard Press, 1944), esp. chs 4 and 5 (for the Puritan creeds), and 9 (for its analyses of "Temptation" and "Salvation"); and notably Edmund S. Morgan, (ed.), *Puritan Political Ideas* (Indianapolis, Bobbs-Merrill, 1965) and *The Puritan Dilemma: The story of John Winthrop* (Boston, Little Brown, 1958), the latter valuable for Winthrop's political career. Loren Baritz, *City on a Hill* (New York, John Wiley, 1964) is valuable for Winthrop's political ideas. Compare also Andrew Delbanco, *The Puritan Ordeal* (Cambridge, MA, Harvard University Press, 1989); S. E. Morison, *Builders of the Bay Colony* (Boston, Houghton Mifflin, 1958); Darrett Rutman, *Winthrop's Boston: Portrait of a Puritan town 1630–1689* (Chapel Hill, NC, IEAHC, 1965) and his exchanges with George Selement and David Hall in *William & Mary Quarterly*, 41.1 (1984), pp. 33–61; also Rutman's *American Puritanism, Faith and Practice* (Philadelphia, Lippincott, 1970); David D. Hall, *The Faithful Shepherd: A history of the New England ministry in the seventeenth century* (Chapel Hill, NC, IEAHC, 1972), and Religion and society: problems and reconsiderations," in Jack P. Greene and J. R. Pole (eds), *Colonial British America* (Baltimore, Johns Hopkins University Press, 1984), pp. 317–44; Michael McGiffert (ed.) *God's Plot: Paradoxes of Puritan piety, being the autobiography and journal of Thomas Shephard* (Amherst, 1972); and Emery

Battis, *Saints and Sectaries: Anne Hutchinson and the Antinomian Controversy in the Massachusetts Bay Colony* (Chapel Hill, NC, IEAHC, 1962). David D. Hall has edited two documentary surveys, *The Antinomian Controversy 1636–1638*, 2nd edn (Durham, NC, Duke University Press, 1990) and *Witchhunting in Seventeenth-Century New England: A documentary history (1638–1692)* (Boston, Northeastern University Press, 1991). Michael McGiffert surveyed "American Puritan Studies in the 1960s" in *William & Mary Quarterly*, 27 (1970), pp. 36–67, and David Hall provided a similar valuable essay, "On Common Ground: The coherence of American Puritan studies," *William & Mary Quarterly*, 44.2 (Apr. 1987), pp. 193–229.

If there are themes running through these studies, they are of man as a transgressor in Eden, born a sinner into a sinful world, only to be saved by a gift of grace that he could not earn except by his own efforts of will and by Christian living, and not always then. The words that haunt Puritan prose are predestination, sin, and grace. For the vast majority of them, submission and prayer mattered; and, for the literate, the Good Book was usually a family's only reading matter. Their leaders, usually Cambridge-educated, wanted a still-more-reformed Church, simpler in form and devoid of ceremony; they sought reform of Church, not State — until without the reform of the latter the former proved impossible. They did not yet use the language of politics, or the jargon words "fair," "justice," "rights." They were more addicted to the phrases of the Bible and the world of John Holland: it was "never merry world in England since gentlemen came up" (*Henry VI, Part Two*).

Carl Bridenbaugh described Perry Miller's *The New England Mind* as "a Sybilline Book for students of American History, Literature and Thought" (*American Historical Review*, 45 (1939–40), p. 889); but George Selement has shown that Miller drew mainly on six clergy, two of them Increase and Cotton Mather, and that Puritanism was not quite the unchanging monolith of Miller's contriving: "Perry Miller: a note on his sources," (*William & Mary Quarterly*, 31 (1974, p. 453); cf. Andrew Delbanco, "The Puritan Errand re-viewed," *Journal of American Studies*, 18 (1984), pp. 345–60.

S. E. Morison, *The Intellectual Life of Colonial New England* (Ithaca, NY, Cornell University Press, 1965) and *Builders of the Bay Colony* and Caroline Robbins, *The Eighteenth-Century Commonwealthman* (Cambridge, Harvard University Press, 1959), are valuable for the carry-over of Puritan ideas into the framework of American history. The post-Perry Miller generations (Miller died in 1963) have been secular and social rather than intellectual in their emphases, although some excellent studies, such as Harry Stout's *The New England Soul* (Oxford, Oxford University Press, 1986), see the importance of preaching and of preachers as key forces in a secular world. Not all who heard the Word understood its provenance: cf. Teresa Toulouse, *The Art of Prophesying* (Athens, University of Georgia, 1987); and see Alan Simpson, "How democratic was Roger Williams?"

in *William & Mary Quarterly*, 3rd ser., 13 (1956), pp. 53–67, for a new look at the classic case of Puritan persecution. For the social aspects and impact of Puritanism see Larzer Ziff, *Puritanism in America: New culture in a new world* (New York, Viking, 1973), and the whole issue of the *William & Mary Quarterly* for July 1974, entitled "Religion and Society" (31.4). See also Edward Arber, *The Story of the Pilgrim Fathers 1606–1623, As told by Themselves, their Friends and their Enemies* (Boston, Houghton Mifflin, 1897), a fascinating, anecdotal, but untidy collection, and George Willison, *The Pilgrim Reader* (New York, Doubleday, 1953), the most "handle-able" and the best organized of the collections, with a condensed version of the story in his *Saints and Strangers* (London, Heinemann, 1966). For Salem, see John Putnam Demos, *Entertaining Satan: Witchcraft and the culture of early New England* (New York, Oxford University Press, 1982), and Hall, *Witchhunting in Seventeenth-Century New England*. As befits a scholar of literature, Ziff sees the later, like the contemporary, influence of Puritanism, as being due to the economic chaos and social collapse that marks its origin. His post-Marxian point of view is perhaps closer to that of Roger Williams than to that of Perry Miller: Puritanism for him is an expression of "democratic capitalism;" the colonists' motivation was less Christian charity than to "conquer and subdue."

Among the many colonial histories two are especially valuable: C. M. Andrews, *The Colonial Period in American History*, 4 vols (New Haven, Yale University Press, 1934–8), esp. for the settlements of the first colonies in vol. I, chs 13–21; and R. C. Simmons, *The American Colonies* (London, Longman, 1976), with its superb bibliographical essay. Simmons's essay "The Massachusetts Charter of 1691" is also valuable, in H. C. Allen and R. Thompson (eds), *Contrast and Connection* (London, Bell, 1976), pp. 66–87. See also J. M. Smith (ed.), *Seventeenth Century America* (Chapel Hill, NC, IEAHC, University of North Carolina Press, 1959); Morgan, *The Puritan Dilemma*; Richard Dunn, *Puritans and Yankees, the Winthrop Dynasty of New England 1630–1717* (Princeton, NJ, Princeton University Press, 1962) and Rutman, *Winthrop's Boston*. Cf. also J. R. Greene, *Great Britain and the American Colonies 1606–1763* (New York, Harper and Row, 1970), and *New England and the English Civil Wars 1630–1670* by Francis J. Bremer (New York, Garland, 1989). For the world from which they came, see Wallace Notestein's classic, *The English People on the Eve of Colonisation?* (London, Hamish Hamilton, 1954); Carl Bridenbaugh, *Vexed and Troubled Englishmen* (New York, Oxford University Press, 1968); Peter Laslett, *The World We Have Lost* (London, Methuen, 1971); K. G. Davies, *The North Atlantic World in the Seventeenth Century* (Minneapolis, University of Minnesota Press, 1974); and David Hackett Fischer's controversial *Albion's Seed: Four British Folkways in America* (New York, Oxford University Press, 1989) and the later references to it.

For the West Indies, see Christopher Hill, *The Intellectual Origins of the English Revolution* (Oxford, Oxford University Press, 1965), 208–11;

Roger Howell, *Sir Philip Sidney, the Shepherd Knight* (Boston, Little Brown, 1968); George H. Williams (ed.), *Thomas Hooker, Writings in England and Holland* (Cambridge, MA, Harvard University Press, 1975), p. 244; Williams to Winthrop in *Winthrop Papers, Massachusetts Historical Society Collections*, 4th ser. VI, pp. 289–91, and (for Davenport's views) p. 203; Delbanco, "The Puritan Errand re-viewed," pp. 343–60; and Karen Ordahl Kupperman, "Errand to the Indies," *William & Mary Quarterly*, 45.1 (Jan. 1988), pp. 70–99.

For Hugh Peter, see the life *The Strenuous Puritan 1598–1660* by Raymond P. Stearns (Urbana, University of Illinois Press, 1954). Cf. Angus Calder, *The Revolutionary Empire* (New York, Dutton, 1981), pp. 235–6.

The best study of the events of 1689–92 in Maryland is Lois Green Carr and David William Jordan, *Maryland's Revolution of Government 1689–1692* (Ithaca, NY, Cornell University Press, 1974). Cf. also Paul G. E. Clemens, *The Atlantic Economy and Colonial Maryland: From tobacco to grain* (Ithaca, NY, Cornell University Press, 1980); Allan Kulikoff, *Tobacco and Slaves: The development of southern cultures in the Chesapeake 1680–1800* (Chapel Hill, NC, IEAHC, University of North Carolina Press, 1986); and two excellent articles; David W. Jordan, "Political stability and the emergence of a native elite in Maryland," in Thad Tate and David L. Ammerman, *The Chesapeake in the Seventeenth Century, Essays on Anglo-American Society* (Chapel Hill, NC, IEAHC, 1979), pp. 243–73; and Ronald Hoffman, "Marylando-Hibernus: Charles Carroll the Settler, 1660–1720," *William & Mary Quarterly*, 45.2 (Apr. 1988), 207–36. For background, Richard Walsh and William Lloyd Fox (eds), *Maryland: A history 1632–1974* (Baltimore, Johns Hopkins University Press, 1974); for the origins, Andrews, *The Colonial Period of American History*, vol. II, pp. 275–83.

Some contemporary selected writings include: John Smith, *A True Relation of ... Virginia* (1608); Roger Williams, *The Bloudy Tenet of Persecution* (1644), which attacked Congregational theology; William Bradford, *History of Plimouth Plantation* (written *c.*1630–48, published in 1856); John Winthrop's *Journal* (1649, published in 1790); Cotton Mather, *The Wonders of the Invisible World* (1693), which defended the witchcraft trials; his *Magnalia Christi Americana* (1702) provided a theological interpretation of New England's history; Robert Beverley, *The History and Present State of Virginia* (1705, ed. Louis Wright, Chapel Hill, NC, IEAHC, University of North Carolina Press, 1947). John Wise, *The Churches' Quarrel Espoused* (1710), which supported democratic Congregationalism.

4 THE RESTORATION

For the English background, see G. N. Clark (gen. ed.), *The Oxford History of England, esp. The Early Stuarts 1603–1660* by Godfrey Davies

(Oxford, Oxford University Press, 1937), and for the later period *The Later Stuarts 1660–1714* by Sir George Clark himself, (Oxford, Oxford University Press, 2nd edn, 1955). For the Restoration period, essential is David Ogg, *England in the Reign of Charles II*, 2 vols (Oxford, Oxford University Press, 1934). For a vivid portrait of the royal personalities, see J. P. Kenyon, *The Stuarts* (London, Batsford, 1958), and for the Cromwellians, see Christopher Hill, *Puritanism and Revolution* (London, Secker and Warburg, 1958).

For the colonies themselves, see C. M. Andrews, *The Colonial Period of American History*, 4 vols ((New Haven, Yale University Press, 1934–8); George A. Billias and Alden T. Vaughan (eds), *Perspectives on Early American History: Essays in honor of Richard B. Morris* (New York: Harper and Row, 1973); Daniel J. Boorstin, *The Americans: The colonial experience* (New York, Random House, 1958); Nicholas Canny and Anthony Pagden (eds), *Colonial Identity in the Atlantic World, 1500–1800* (Princeton, NJ, Princeton University Press, 1987); Milton M. Klein and Jacob E. Cooke (gen. eds), *A History of the American Colonies*, esp. Warren M. Billings, John E. Selby, and Thad W. Tate, *Colonial Virginia: A history* (White Plains, NY, KTO, 1986); Joseph E. Illick, *Colonial Pennsylvania: A history* (New York, Scribner's, 1976); Michael Kammen, *Colonial New York: A history* (New York, Scribner's, 1975); Benjamin W. Labaree, *Colonial Massachusetts: A history* (Millwood, NY, KTO, 1979); Aubrey C. Land, *Colonial Maryland: A history* (Millwood, NY, KTO, 1981); Hugh T. Lefler and William S. Powell, *Colonial North Carolina: A history* (New York, Scribner's, 1973); John E. Pomfret, *Colonial New Jersey: A history* (New York, Scribner's, 1973); Robert J. Taylor, *Colonial Connecticut: A history* (Millwood, NY, KTO, 1979); Robert M. Weir, *Colonial South Carolina: A history* (Millwood, NY, KTO, 1983); also David S. Lovejoy, *The Glorious Revolution in America* (New York, Harper and Row, 1972); and Gary B. Nash, *Red, White, and Black: The peoples of early America* (Englewood Cliffs, NJ, Prentice-Hall, 1974).

Jon Butler, in a number of wide-ranging essays, has mapped out many of the most interesting questions and issues: see his "Magic, astrology, and the early American religious heritage, 1600–1760," *American Historical Review*, 84 (1979), pp. 317–46; "Enthusiasm described and decried: the Great Awakening as interpretive fiction," *Journal of American History*, 69 (1982–3), pp. 303–25; and "The future of American religious history: prospectus, agenda, transatlantic problematique," *William & Mary Quarterly*, 3rd ser., 42 (1985), pp. 167–83. See also David D. Hall, "Religion and society: problems and reconsiderations," in Jack P. Greene and J. R. Pole (eds), *Colonial British America, Essays in the new history of the early modern era* (Baltimore, Johns Hopkins University Press, 1984), pp. 317–44. For Puritanism, see David D. Hall, *"On common ground: the coherence of American Puritan studies,"* *William & Mary Quarterly*, 3rd ser., 44 (1987), pp. 193–29. For an excellent recent general study of early American religion, see Patricia U. Bonomi, *Under the Cope of Heaven: Religion, society, and politics in colonial America* (New York, Oxford University Press, 1986); Carl Bridenbaugh, *Mitre and Sceptre: Transatlantic faiths, ideas, personalities, and politics, 1689–1775* (New York, Oxford University Press, 1962); John Putnam Demos, *Entertaining Satan: Witchcraft and the culture of early New England* (New York, Oxford University Press, 1982); David D. Hall, *The Faithful Shepherd: A history of the New England ministry in the seventeenth century* (Chapel Hill, NC, IEAHC, 1972); Joseph Haroutunian, *Piety versus Moralism: The passing of the New England theology* (New York, Holt, 1932).

The best analysis of Salem's witchcraft epidemic is Paul Boyer and Stephen Nissenbaum, *Salem Possessed* (Cambridge, MA, Harvard University Press, 1974), since it places it in its social context, as a drama of family disputes. Because based on careful research in local records, it even overshadows Arthur Miller's *The Crucible*. See also Thomas J. Holmes, *Increase Mather*, a bibliography, 2 vols (Cambridge, MA, Harvard University Press, 1931), and *Cotton Mather*, a bibliography of his work, 3 vols (Cambridge, MA, Harvard University Press, 1940); Perry Miller, *The New England Mind, from Colony to Province* (Cambridge, MA, Harvard University Press, 1953), esp. chs 2 and 3, and for his view that the intellectual life of New England up to 1720 "can be written as though no such thing" as the witchcraft trials "ever happened" (p. 191). It should also be set in the balance sheet that in his *Essay concerning Human Understanding* (1690), John Locke gave witchcraft credence, as did the jurist Sir William Blackstone in his *Commentaries* (1765–9), and that in the sixteenth and seventeenth centuries 30,000 accused witches were executed in Britain (by hanging in England and by burning in Scotland), 75,000 in France, and 100,000 in Germany. By contrast, only 32 executions for witchcraft took place in the New England colonies, and of them only 4 in Boston itself (cf. A. B. Tourtellot, *Benjamin Franklin: The shaping of genius, the Boston years* (Garden City, NY, Doubleday, 1977), p. 77.

For George Downing, see John H. Beresford, *The Godfather of Downing Street* (London, Cobden-Sanderson, 1925). For the Winthrops, see Richard S. Dunn, *Puritans and Yankees: The Winthrop dynasty of New England, 1630–1717* (Princeton, NJ, Princeton University Press, 1962); and Edmund S. Morgan, *The Puritan Dilemma: The story of John Winthrop* (Boston, Little Brown, 1958). For the Mathers, Robert Middlekauff, *The Mathers, Three Generations of Puritan Intellectuals 1596–1728* (Oxford University Press, 1971); Kenneth Silverman, *The Life and Times of Cotton Mather* (New York, Harper and Row, 1984). For William Blathwayt, see G. A. Jacobson, *William Blathwayt* (New Haven, Yale University Press, 1933).

5 THE EMPIRE OF THE NORTH ATLANTIC
IN THE SEVENTEENTH CENTURY

For seventeenth- and eighteenth-century Anglo-American relations, C. M. Andrews's *The Colonial Period of American History*, 4 vols, (New Haven, Yale University Press, 1934–8) is still indispensable. It now needs supplementing from the 21 volumes of K. G. Davies's *Documents of the American Revolution* (Dublin, Irish Academic Press, 1977), and his Sarah Tryphena Phillips Lecture at the British Academy, "The end of British administration in the North American colonies," read March 12, 1975. L. W. Labaree, *Royal Government in America* (New Haven, Yale University Press, 1930), and *Royal Instructions to British Colonial Governors 1670–1776*, 2 vols (New Haven, Yale University Press, 1935), provide a definitive study of the governors and of their clashes with their colonial assemblies. For personal details of and sources for the study of each of them, see J. W. Raimo, *Biographical Directory of American Colonial and Revolutionary Governors 1607–1789* (Westport, Conn., Meckler Books, 1980). Compare with Andrews the first three volumes of Lawrence Gipson's massive 15-volume *The British Empire before the American Revolution*, 2nd edn (New York, Knopf, 1959–60), and his Harmsworth Inaugural Lecture at Oxford, published as *The British Empire before the American Revolution: Its strength and its weakness* (Oxford, Oxford University Press, 1952), esp. p. 23. The work of Andrews, and of Gipson and Labaree (both his students), is marked by its London orientation, product of years of research in the Public Record Office.

The best single volume on *The Glorious Revolution in America* is the survey with that title by David Lovejoy (New York, Harper Torchbooks, 1974).

The best introduction to Connecticut and Rhode Island is in the volume (originally lectures) by C. M. Andrews, *Our Earliest Colonial Settlements* (New York University Press, 1933.) To buttress this, read each of the volumes in the series *A History of the American Colonies* (gen. eds, Milton M. Klein and Jacob E. Cooke): Robert J. Taylor, *Colonial Connecticut* (New York, Scribner's, 1976) and Sydney V. James, *Colonial Rhode Island* (New York, Scribner's, 1978).

For New York, see Milton Klein, *The Politics of Diversity* (Port Washington, NY, Kennikat Press, 1974); Patricia U. Bonomi, *A Factious People: Politics and society in colonial New York* (New York, Columbia University Press, 1971); Edward Countryman, *A People in Revolution: American revolution and political society in New York 1760–80* (Baltimore, Johns Hopkins University Press, 1981); Esmond Wright, "The New York Loyalists: a cross-section of colonial society," in Robert A. East and Jacob Judd (eds), *The Loyalist Americans: A focus on Greater New York* (Tarrytown, NY, Philipsburg Foundation, Sleepy Hollow, 1975); Pauline Maier, "Isaac Sears and the business of revolution," in her *The Old Revolu-*

tionaries: Political lives in the age of Samuel Adams (New York, Knopf, 1980); and Catherine Snell Crary, "Forfeited Loyalist lands in the western district of New York – Albany and Tryon Counties," *New York History*, 35 (1954), pp. 239–58.

For Lewis Morris, see Eugene R. Sheridan, *Lewis Morris 1671–1746: A study in early American politics* (Syracuse, NY, Syracuse University Press, 1981); for Gouverneur Morris, see Max M. Mintz, *Gouverneur Morris and the American Revolution* (Norman, University of Oklahoma Press, 1970). For another unrelated Morris, more important than any of those, who was born in Liverpool and orphaned, but prospered with Thomas Willing in the Philadelphia trade, see *Robert Morris: Revolutionary Financier*, with an *Analysis of his Earlier Career* (Philadelphia, University of Pennsylvania, 1954).

For Boston, see Samuel Sewall, *Diary, Collections of the Massachusetts Historical Society*, 5th ser., vol. 6, p. 73 (also ed. Thomas M. Halsey, 2 vols, New York, Farrar, Straus and Giroux, 1973); Walter Whitehill, *Boston: A topographical history* (2nd edn, Cambridge, MA, Harvard University Press, 1968), pp. 22–46; A. B. Tourtellot, *Benjamin Franklin: The shaping of a genius, the Boston years* (Garden City, NY, Doubleday, 1977), p. 57; S. E. Morison, *Builders of the Bay Colony* (Boston, Houghton Mifflin, 1958), p. 95; cf. Edmund Morgan, *The Puritan Dilemma* (Boston, Little Brown, 1958), and, of course, Benjamin Franklin, *The Autobiography of Benjamin Franklin*, ed. L. W. Labaree, (New Haven, Yale University Press, 1964), p. 75.

For Philadelphia, see Gottlieb Mittelberger, *Journey to Pennsylvania*, ed. and trans. Oscar Handlin and John Clive (Cambridge, MA, Harvard University Press, 1960); Carl Bridenbaugh, (ed.), *Gentleman's Progress* (Chapel Hill, NC, University of North Carolina Press, 1948); Martin P. Snyder, *City of Independence* (New York, Praeger, 1975).

Each of the middle and southern colonies has been fortunate in that its history has been well surveyed in the Scribner's (now KTO Press), series edited by Milton Klein of the University of Tennessee and Jacob Cooke of Lafayette College. Each discusses recent interpretations, religion and architecture, food and "culture," as well as politics, and each has a valuable bibliography. Especially notable are the volumes on *Colonial Virginia* by Warren Billings, John E. Selby, and Thad W. Tate (White Plains, NY, KTO Press, 1986); on *Colonial North Carolina* by Hugh Lefler and William S. Powell (New York, Scribner's, 1973), notable for the references to the Lost Colony of Roanoke; and on *Colonial South Carolina* by Robert M. Weir (Millwood, NY, KTO Press, 1983). They bring out colonial diversities, but also the frequency of clashes with Britain, even if on many, often quite distinct, themes.

New Jersey's history has been told frequently: Samuel Smith in 1765 through William A. Whitehead in the mid-nineteenth century, E. P. Tanner and E. J. Fisher working under Professor Herbert L. Osgood in the 1900s, Irving Kull in the 1930s, Donald Kemmerer and Nelson Burr, Wheaton

Lane, Leonard Lundin, and others in the Princeton University Series in the 1940s, and still more recently John Pomfret and Richard McCormick for the New Jersey Historical Series. Its most recent chronicler is Dr John Pomfret, former president of the College of William and Mary, director emeritus of the Huntington Library, and historian of New Jersey's seventeenth-century proprietary era. His volume in the Scribner's/KTO series is catholic in range, and vividly written: *Colonial New Jersey* (New York, Scribner's, 1973).

For Virginia and its Northern Neck, see Douglas Southall Freeman's *George Washington: The young Washington* (New York, Scribner's, 1949), vol I, pp. 462–87. See also *The Journal and Letters of Philip Vickers Fithian 1773–4*, ed. H. D. Farish, (Colonial Williamsburg, 1945) and L. B. Wright, *The First Gentlemen of Virginia*, (Huntington Library, CA, 1940).

The most detailed and vivid contemporary accounts of Virginia in the late seventeenth century are Robert Beverley's *The History and Present State of Virginia* (1705; ed. Louis B. Wright, and published by the University of North Carolina Press in 1947 as the first volume published on behalf of the Institute of Early American History and Culture [IEAHC] formed in Williamsburg in 1943), written by the son of the former clerk of the House of Burgesses, who, though at the outset a vehement supporter of Governor Berkeley, after Bacon's Rebellion became the conscience and the protesting voice of the colony against the claims of proprietors, of governors, or of the Crown – the son echoed his father's voice; and *The Present State of Virginia, and the College* by Henry Hartwell, James Blair, and Edward Chilton, originally written at the request of the recently constituted Board of Trade in London, and in fact an indirect attack on Governor Andros; it was printed in 1697, and edited by H. D. Farish for Colonial Williamsburg in 1940.

For John Pynchon, see the pathbreaking *The Pynchon Papers*, ed. Carl Bridenbaugh, collected by Juliette Tomlinson, 2 vols (Boston, Colonial Society of Massachusetts Publications, 1982). On Bacon's Rebellion, Wilcomb E. Washburn, *The Governor and the Rebel: A history of Bacon's Rebellion in Virginia* (Chapel Hill, NC, and New York, Oxford University Press, 1954), is favorable to the governor; T. J. Wertenbaker's older *Torchbearer of the Revolution* (Princeton, NJ, Princeton University Press, 1940) is the reverse: to him, the governor was an autocrat. Compare Robert Beverley's critical contemporary view of Bacon in his *The History and Present State*, pp. 78–85, and David Lovejoy's article in Alison Gilbert Olson and Richard Maxwell Brown (eds), *Anglo-American Political Relations 1665–1775* (New Brunswick, Rutgers University Press, 1970). Bernard Bailyn's article on "Politics and social structure in Virginia," in J. M. Smith (ed.), *Seventeenth-Century America Essays in colonial history* (Chapel Hill, NC, IEAHC, University of North Carolina Press, 1959), is valuable as a background for understanding Bacon.

For North Carolina, in addition to William Byrd's secret *History of the Dividing Line*, which did not appear in print until 1844, see A. Roger

Ekirch, "Poor Carolina": Politics and society in colonial North Carolina 1729–1776 (Chapel Hill, NC, University of North Carolina Press, 1981), and Lefler and Powell's *Colonial North Carolina*. For South Carolina, see Weir, *Colonial South Carolina*, and cf. M. Eugene Sirmans, *Colonial South Carolina: A political history 1663–1763* (Chapel Hill, NC, IEAHC, University of North Carolina Press, 1966).

For New France, see Andrew Hill Clark, *Acadia: The geography of early Nova Scotia to 1760* (Madison, University of Wisconsin Press, 1968); Olive Patricia Dickason, *The Myth of the Savage and the Beginnings of French Colonialism in the Americas* (Edmonton, University of Alberta Press, 1984); W. J. Eccles, *Canada under Louis XIV, 1663–1701* (New York, Oxford University Press, 1964); *The Canadian Frontier, 1534–1760* (New York, Holt, Rinehart and Winston, 1969); *Essays on New France* (Toronto, Oxford University Press, 1987); and *France in America* (New York, Harper and Row, 1972); Gustave Lanctot, *A History of Canada*, trans. Josephine Hambleton and Margaret M. Cameron, 3 vols (Cambridge, MA, Harvard University Press, 1963–5; George A. Rawlyk, *Nova Scotia's Massachusetts: A study of Massachusetts–Nova Scotia relations, 1630–1784* (Montreal, McGill-Queen's University Press, 1973).

The standard edition of the *Jesuit Relations* is that edited by Reuben G. Thwaites, *The Jesuit Relations and Allied Documents*, 73 vols (Cleveland, Ohio, Burrows, 1896–1901). The volumes were published annually, beginning in 1632 and continuing until 1673. They were collections of the reports of missionaries in the field to their superior at Quebec, edited by him for publication, and forwarded to the provincial of the order in Paris, who did the final editing. The volumes had a wide circulation among the elite. They constitute what is probably the most important single source for the history of Canada during the period of company government. For a useful evaluation, see Charles W. Colby "The Jesuit Relations," *American Historical Review*, 7, (1901–2), pp. 36–55. For the effect of the *Relations* on opinion in Europe, see G. Chinard, *L'Amérique et le rêve exotique* (Paris, Hachette, 1913). A selection of the *Relations* has been edited by Edna Kenton: *Black Gown and Redskins* (New York, Longmans, 1956).

6 THE EIGHTEENTH CENTURY:
FROM THE ST LAWRENCE TO SAVANNAH

For a fresh view of the diversity of the British empire in America in the mid-eighteenth century, see Bernard Bailyn and Philip D. Morgan (eds), *Strangers within the Realm* (Williamsburg, IEAHC, 1991); and Bernard Bailyn, *The Peopling of British North America* (New York, Knopf, 1986).

There is a considerable research literature on the "indentured" who crossed the Atlantic for a century or more in such numbers. Mildred Campbell, "Social origins of some early Americans," in J. M. Smith (ed.),

Seventeenth Century America (Chapel Hill, NC, IEAHC, University of North Carolina Press, 1959), contends that farmers and skilled workers probably outnumbered "laborers." David W. Galenson, in "Middling people or common sort, the social origins of some early Americans re-examined, with a rebuttal by Mildred Campbell," *William and Mary Quarterly*, 35.3 (July 1978), pp. 499–540, queries the statistics and the categories, and holds that the vast majority came from the "common sort." Perhaps both would agree with the view of Hector St John de Crevecoeur, *Letters from an American Farmer* (1782), Letter III, 75, that "the rich stay in Europe, it is only the middling and the poor that emigrate." See also Peter Laslett, *The World We Have Lost* (London, Methuen, 1971), p. 38. Three valuable studies are Abbot Emerson Smith, *Colonists in Bondage: White servitude and convict labor in colonial America: an economic analysis* (Chapel Hill, NC, IEAHC, 1947; repr. Cambridge, Cambridge University Press, 1981); Stephen Innes (ed.), *Work and Labor in Early America* (Chapel Hill, NC, IEAHC, 1988); and David W. Galenson, *White Servitude in Colonial America, an Economic History* (Cambridge, Cambridge University Press, 1981). For "the standard of living" see the discussion held at the 1987 Organization of American Historians, and the papers subsequently published in the Forum section of *William & Mary Quarterly*, 41.1 (Jan. 1988), pp. 116–70, notably John J. McCusker's summary. For the convicts especially, see A. Roger Ekirch, *Bound for America: The transportation of British convicts to the colonies 1718–75* (Oxford, Clarendon Press, 1987).

David Hackett Fischer, in the first volume of a cultural history modeled on the work of the Annales school in France, *Albion's Seed: Four British folkways in America* (New York, Oxford University Press, 1989), argues that North America was settled during the seventeenth/eighteenth centuries by four successive waves of English-speaking immigrants; but his work has had a very mixed reception. This is not surprising in view of his totally English-centered portrait: Dutch and German, French, Indian, and African cultural contributions are ignored, at a time when the fashion is the reverse. It was especially brave to minimize so deliberately the African and the slave contribution to Southern culture, speech, and crafts. For the debate Fisher's book occasioned, see in particular *William & Mary Quarterly*, 48 (Apr. 1991), Forum, pp. 224–308, and ibid. (Oct. 1991), pp. 515–30, 598–611, in which the author replies to his critics. For other views on immigrants and immigration, see David Cressy, *Coming Over: Migration and communication between England and New England in the seventeenth century* (Cambridge, Cambridge University Press, 1987); David Grayson Allen, *In English Ways: The movement of societies and the transferal of English local law and custom in Massachusetts Bay in the seventeenth century* (Chapel Hill, NC, IEAHC, University of North Carolina Press, 1981); Frank Thistlethwaite, *Dorset Pilgrims: The story of Westcountry Pilgrims who went to New England in the seventeenth century* (London, Barrie and Jenkins, 1989).

For architecture, see Carl Bridenbaugh, *Peter Harrison: First American Architect* (Chapel Hill, NC, University of North Carolina, 1949) and *The Colonial Craftsman* (New York, New York University Press, 1950); Louis B. Wright, *The First Gentlemen of Virginia* (Huntington Library, 1940); A. Cummings, *The Framed Houses of Massachusetts Bay 1625–1725* (Cambridge, MA, Belknap Press of for Harvard University Press, 1979); *The Correspondence of the Three William Byrds of Westover, Virginia 1684–1776*, ed. Marion Tinling, 2 vols (Charlottesville, University Press of Virginia, 1977); Eleanor Berman, *Thomas Jefferson Among the Arts* (New York Philosophical Library, 1947); and Robert Beverley, *The History and Present State of Virginia* (1705), ed. Louis. B. Wright (Chapel Hill, NC, IEAHC, University of North Carolina Press, 1947), p. 295.

The best studies of the Chesapeake economy, and of tobacco's dominance in it, are A. P. Middleton's vividly detailed *Tobacco Coast: A maritime history of Chesapeake Bay in the Colonial Era* (Newport, Newport News Mariner's Museum, 1953), and Allan Kulikoff, *Tobacco and Slaves: The development of Southern cultures in the Chesapeake 1680–1800* (Chapel Hill, NC, University of North Carolina Press, 1986). For plantation society in general, see Thad W. Tate and David L. Ammerman (eds), *The Chesapeake in the Seventeenth Century: Essays on Anglo-American Society* (Chapel Hill, NC, IEAHC, University of North Carolina Press, 1979), Aubrey C. Land (ed.), *Bases of a Plantation Society* (New York, Harper and Row, 1969), and *Colonial Maryland: A History* (Millwood, NY, KTO Press, 1981). A new importance has recently been given to the Chesapeake by Jack Greene in *Pursuits of Happiness: The social development of early modern British colonies and the formation of American culture* (Chapel Hill, NC, IEAHC, 1988). He sees the Chesapeake as a social extension of Old England, unlike the quite untypical regions to its north and south. The two best surveys of the tobacco trade are Tom Devine's *The Tobacco Lords* (Edinburgh, John Donald, 1975), and Jacob M. Price, *France and the Chesapeake*, 2 vols, (Ann Arbor, University of Michigan Press, 1972). There are also a number of excellent articles: Jacob M. Price, "The rise of Glasgow in the Chesapeake tobacco trade 1707–75," *William & Mary Quarterly*, 11 (Apr. 1954), pp. 179–99; Emory G. Evans, "Planter indebtedness and the coming of the Revolution in Virginia," *William & Mary Quarterly*, 3rd ser., 19 (1962), pp. 62–110, and "Private indebtedness and the Revolution in Virginia," ibid., 28 (1971), pp. 112–40; Marc Egnal, and Joseph A. Ernest, "An Economic interpretation of American revolution," ibid., 29 (1972), pp. 202–32; Thad W. Tate, "The coming of the Revolution in Virginia: Britain's challenge to Virginia's ruling class 1763–1776," ibid., 19 (1962), pp. 5–60; David W. Jordan, " 'God's Candle' within government: Quakers and politics in early Maryland," ibid., 39.4 (Oct. 1982), pp. 628–54; and Russell R. Menard, "From servant to freeholder: status mobility and property accumulation in seventeenth-century Maryland," ibid., 28.1 (Jan. 1973), pp. 37–64, showing how for most indentured servants in the early decades –

unless they were skilled and literate – the Chesapeake was not rich in opportunity.

For other planters, see Richard B. Davis (ed.), *William Fitzhugh and his Chesapeake World* (Chapel Hill, NC, University of North Carolina Press, 1963), Joseph Gurn, *Charles Carroll of Carrollton 1737–1832* (New York, Kennedy, 1932), and Ronald Hoffman, " 'Marylando-Hibernus,' Charles Carroll The Settler 1660–1720," in *William & Mary Quarterly*, (Apr. 1988), pp. 207–36. For an alternative crop, see David Klingamen, "The significance of grain in the development of the tobacco colonies," *Journal of Economic History* (June 1969), 268–78. And for rice and indigo, see Lelia Sellers, *Charleston Business on the eve of the American Revolution* (Chapel Hill, NC, University of North Carolina Press, 1934); Peter H. Wood, *Black Majority: Negroes in colonial South Carolina from 1670 through the Stono Rebellion* (New York, Knopf, 1974); and David Coon, "Eliza Lucas Pinckney and the re-introduction of indigo culture in South Carolina," in *Journal of Southern History* (Feb. 1976), pp. 61–76.

The history of Philadelphia is bound up less with William Penn than with his secretary James Logan. Going to Philadelphia in 1699 at the age of 25 as secretary to William Penn, he was by the time of his death, 52 years later, one of the three or four most considerable men in colonial America, rich, learned, powerful, and respected, if not universally loved. He is well described in F. R. Tolles's biography, *James Logan and the Culture of Provincial America* (Boston, Little Brown, 1957). Logan foresaw American independence: "America in the succession of Ages may also put on another Face: the danger will be missed only if the Colonies are treated with Tenderness and Humanity and not considered only as Slavishly Subservient to the Interest of the Country they came from." Cf. Joseph E. Johnson (ed.), "A Quaker imperialist's view of the British colonies in America 1732," which contains Logan's "State of the British Plantations," *Pennsylvania Magazine of History and Biography*, 40 (1936), pp. 97–130; and Roy N. Lokken, "The social thought of James Logan," *William & Mary Quarterly*, 27.1 (1970), pp. 68–89. For Penn himself, see William W. Comfort, *William Penn 1644–1718* (Philadelphia, University of Pennsylvania, 1944). See also Carl and Jessica Bridenbaugh, *Rebels and Gentlemen; Philadelphia in the age of Franklin* (New York, Oxford University Press). Some cautions to Bridenbaugh's picture of the city's growth are offered by Gary Nash and Billy G. Smith, "The population of eighteenth-century Philadelphia," *Pennsylvania Magazine of History and Biography*, 99 (July 1975), pp. 362–8; Gary B. Nash, *The Urban Crucible* (Cambridge, MA, Harvard University Press, 1979); and John K. Alexander, "The Philadelphia numbers game: an analysis of Philadelphia's eighteenth-century population," *Pennsylvania Magazine of History and Biography*, 98 (1974), pp. 314–34. S. B. Warner, *A Private City: Philadelphia in three periods of its growth* (Philadelphia, University of Pennsylvania Press, 1968), pp. 410–11, calculated the population in 1776 at 23,000, not the 40,000 formerly assumed.

The best recent colonial survey of Georgia is Kenneth Coleman's *Colonial Georgia, a History* (New York, Scribner's, 1976); cf. Rodney Baine and Phinizy Spalding (eds), Oglethorpe's *Some Account of the Design of the Trustees for establishing Colonys in America* (Athens, GA, University of Georgia Press, 1990). The best study of Oglethorpe is still Amos Ettinger, *James Edward Oglethorpe: Imperial idealist* (Oxford, Oxford University Press, 1936), but it now needs supplementing from Phinizy Spalding and Harvey H. Jackson (eds), *Oglethorpe in Perspective: Georgia's founder after two hundred years* (Tuscaloosa, University of Alabama Press, 1989); and P. Spalding, "James Oglethorpe: a bibliographical survey," *Georgia Historical Quarterly*, 56 (Fall 1972), pp. 332–48, and *Oglethorpe in America* (Chicago, University of Chicago Press, 1977).

For slavery in the southern colonies, see Julia Floyd Smith, *Slavery and Rice Culture in Low-Country Georgia, 1750–1860* (Knoxville, Tenn., 1985), pp. 4–5, 10–11, 20–1, 24. On the origins of rice cultivation in the Deep South see Daniel C. Littlefield, *Rice and Slaves: Ethnicity and the slave trade in Colonial South Carolina* (Baton Rouge, 1981), and articles by Harvey H. Jackson, "The Carolina Connection: Jonathan Bryan, his brothers, and the founding of Georgia 1733–1752," *Georgia Historical Quarterly*, 68 (1984), pp. 147–72, and "Hugh Bryan and the Evangelical Movement in colonial South Carolina", *Wlliam & Mary Quarterly*, 3rd ser. 43 (1986), pp. 594–614; Alan Gallay, "The origins of slaveholders' paternalism: George Whitefield, the Bryan family and the Great Awakening in the South," *Journal of Southern History*, 53 (1987), pp. 369–94, and his "Jonathan Bryan's plantation empire: land, politics and the formation of a ruling class in colonial Georgia," *William & Mary Quarterly*, 45.2 (April, 1988), pp. 253–79.

For kith and kin, see J. M. Sosin, *English America and the Restoration Monarchy of Charles II: Transatlantic Politics, Commerce and Kinship* (Lincoln, Neb., University of Nebraska Press, 1981); Alison Gilbert Olson, *Anglo-American Politics 1660–1775: The relationship between parties in England and colonial America* (New York, Oxford University Press, 1973); Michael Kammen, *Empire and Interest: The American colonies and the politics of mercantilism* (Philadelphia, Lippincott, 1970).

For the First Families of Virginia, see Thomas J. Wertenbaker, *The Golden Age of Colonial Culture* (Ithaca, Cornell University Press, 1961); Michael Kraus, *Intercolonial Aspects of American Culture* (New York, Columbia University Press, 1928); Louis B. Wright, *The First Families of Virginia* (San Marino, CA, Huntington Library, 1940); Charles S. Sydnor, *Political Leadership in Eighteenth-Century Virginia* (Oxford, Clarendon Press, 1951); Kenneth Silverman, *A Cultural History of the American Revolution 1763–1789* (New York, Crowell, 1976); J. A. Schultz, *Thomas Pownall, British Defender of American Liberty* (Glendale, CA, A. H. Clark, 1951); Jackson T. Main, *The Social Structure of Revolutionary America* (Princeton, NJ, Princeton University Press, 1965). Cf. the studies of individual governors in John A. Schutz, *William Shirley, King's Governor* of Massachusetts (Chapel Hill, NC, IEAHC, 1961), and William W. Abbot, *The Royal Governors of Georgia 1754–1775* (Chapel Hill, NC, IEAHC, 1959).

For the latter part of the eighteenth century there are various competent "institutional" studies, if now dated: A. H. Basye, *The Lords Commissioners of Trade and Plantations 1748–82* (New Haven, Yale University Press, 1925), Margaret M. Spector, *The American Department of the British Government* (New York, Columbia University Studies 466, 1940); and Francis Wickwire, *British Sub-Ministers and Colonial America 1763–83* (Princeton, NJ, Princeton University Press, 1966). Wickwire's invention of the alien word "sub-minister" weakens the book in that it blurs the functions of the officials he describes: they were under-secretaries or permanent civil servants, not elected Members of Parliament.

More recent studies attempt to translate transatlantic institutions and administration into people and issues, economic as well as political; see Olson, *Anglo-American Politics 1660–1775*, and Alison Gilbert Olson and Richard Maxwell Brown (eds), *Anglo-American Political Relations 1675–1775* (New Brunswick, NJ, Rutgers University Press, 1970), in particular the essays by Stanley Katz on the James De Lancey family interests in New York and London; by Thomas Barrow on the "Old Colonial System"; by John Shy on Thomas Pownall and Henry Ellis; and the valuable bibliographical essay by Joseph E. Illick. A fresh, indeed controversial, thesis of what he calls "garrison government," which may be more relevant after 1681 than before it, is presented in Stephen Saunders Webb's *The Governors-General: The English army and the definition of the empire 1569–1681* (Chapel Hill, NC, IEAHC, 1979), and his *1676: The end of American Independence* (New York, Knopf, 1984).

On the colonial economy in the late seventeenth and eighteenth centuries, John McCusker has become the major authority: *Money and Exchange in Europe and America 1600–1775: A handbook* (Chapel Hill, NC, University of North Carolina Press, 1978); McCusker and Russell R. Menard, *The Economy of British America 1607–1789* (Chapel Hill, NC, University of North Carolina Press, 1985), and Hoffman, McCusker, Menard and Albert (eds), *The Economy of Early America, The Revolutionary Period* (Charlottesville, University of Virginia Press, 1988).

Among a number of studies of the colonial agents are: Michael Kammen, *A Rope of Sand* (Ithaca, NY, Cornell University Press, 1968); Ross J. S. Hoffman, *Edmund Burke, New York Agent* (Philadelphia, American Philosophical Society, 1956); Carl Cone, *Burke and the Nature of Politics: The age of the American Revolution* (Lexington, KY, University of Kentucky, 1957); William Sachse, *The Colonial American in Britain* (Madison, University of Wisconson Press, 1956); and J. M. Sosin, *Agents and Merchants: British colonial policy and the origins of the American Revolution 1763–1775* (Lincoln, Neb., University of Nebraska, 1965), and the comment on it by Michael Kammen in *William & Mary Quarterly*, 23 (1966), pp. 492–5. There are many biographies of Benjamin Franklin, the latest my own, *Franklin of Philadelphia* (Cambridge, MA, Harvard University Press, 1986), as well as his own *Autobiography*, ed. L. W. Labaree (New Haven, Yale University Press, 1964).

7 THE COLONIAL GOLDEN AGE

Bernard Bailyn and Philip D. Morgan (eds), *Strangers within the Realm* (Chapel Hill, NC, IEAHC, 1991), sees the British empire less as a London-centered but liberal regime than as a congerie of distinct ethnic group – Native Americans, African-Americans, Scots-Irish, Dutch, and Germans, with the "Reluctant Creoles" of the West Indies. Contrast the "institutional" views of Andrews, Gipson, and Davies.

For population, see Benjamin Franklin, "Observations concerning the increase of mankind," in *The Papers of Benjamin Franklin*, ed. L. W. Labaree, vol. IV, (New Haven, Yale University Press, 1961), pp. 225–34; J. Potter, "The growth of population in America 1700–1860," in D. V. Glass and D. E. C. Eversley (eds), *Population in Historical Demography* (London, Edward Arnold, 1963), pp. 631–88; and Robert V. Wells, *The Population of the British Colonies in America before 1776: A survey of census data* (Princeton, NJ, Princeton University Press, 1975).

On the position of women, see Mary Ritter Beard, *Women as a Force in History* (New York, Macmillan, 1946); but also Roger Thompson, *Women in Stuart England and America: A comparative study* (London, Routledge and Kegan Paul, 1974) and Mary Beth Norton, *Liberty's Daughters: The Revolutionary experience of American women, 1750–1800* (Boston, Little Brown, 1980), and not least the latter's article "The evolution of white women's experience in early America," *American Historical Review*, 89 (June 1984), pp. 593–623. Cf. also Joy Day Buel and Richard Buel, Jr, *The Way of Duty: A woman and her family in Revolutionary America* (New York, Norton, 1984); Linda K. Kerber, *Women of the Republic: Intellect and ideology in Revolutionary America* (Chapel Hill, NC, IEAHC, 1980); and *William & Mary Quarterly*, 48.1 (Jan. 1991), special number on *Studies in Gender*.

Over the past generation perhaps no field of historical inquiry has generated more vital, more controversial, and more consistently excellent scholarship than that of slavery. Among the more important surveys of this field are Ira Berlin, "Time, space, and the evolution of Afro-American society on British mainland North America," *American Historical Review*, 85 (1980), pp. 44–78; Peter H. Wood, "'I Did the Best I Could for My Day': the study of early black history during the Second Reconstruction, 1960 to 1976," *William & Mary Quarterly*, 3rd ser., 35 (1978), pp. 185–225; T. H. Breen, "Creative adaptations: peoples and cultures," in Jack P. Greene and J. R. Pole (eds), *Colonial British America: Essays in the new history of the early modern era* (Baltimore, Johns Hopkins University Press, 1984), pp. 195–232; Ira Berlin and Ronald Hoffman (eds), *Slavery and freedom in the age of the American Revolution: Perspectives on the American Revolution* (Charlottesville, United States Capitol Historical Society, University Press of Virginia, 1983); T. H. Breen and Stephen Innes, *"Myne Owne Ground": race and freedom on Virginia's eastern shore, 1640–1676* (New York, Oxford University Press, 1980); Philip D. Curtin, *The Atlantic Slave Trade: A census* (Madison, University of Wisconsin Press, 1969); David Brion Davis, *The Problem of Slavery in the Age of Revolution, 1770–1823* (Ithaca, NY, Cornell University Press, 1975), *The Problem of Slavery in Western Culture* (Ithaca, NY, Cornell University Press, 1966), and *Slavery and Human Progress* (New York, Oxford University Press, 1984); James W. St G. Walker, *The Black Loyalists: The search for a promised land in Nova Scotia and Sierra Leone, 1783–1870* (New York, Dalhousie University Press, Holmes and Meier, 1976); Betty Wood, *Slavery in Colonial Georgia, 1730–1775* (Athens, GA, University of Georgia Press, 1984); Peter H. Wood, *Black Majority: Negroes in colonial South Carolina from 1670 through the Stono Rebellion* (New York, Knopf, 1974); Lorenzo J. Greene, *The Negro in Colonial New England, 1620–1776* (New York, Columbia University Press, 1942); Winthrop D. Jordan, *White over Black: American attitudes toward the Negro, 1550–1812* (Chapel Hill, IEAHC, University of North Carolina Press, 1968); Allan Kulikoff, *Tobacco and Slaves: The development of Southern cultures in the Chesapeake, 1680–1800* (Chapel Hill, NC, IEAHC, University of North Carolina Press, 1986); Duncan J. MacLeod, *Slavery, Race, and the American Revolution* (Cambridge, Cambridge University Press, 1974); and Edmund S. Morgan, *American Slavery, American Freedom: The ordeal of colonial Virginia* (New York, Norton, 1975).

The magisterial study of education is Lawrence A. Cremin, *American Education: The colonial experience 1607–1783* (New York, Harper and Row, 1970), with its massive bibliographical essay. It can be supplemented by the works of piety: Clifford K. Shipton, *Biographical Sketches of those who attended Harvard College (Sibley's Harvard Graduates)* (Cambridge, MA, Harvard University Press, 1933–62), and James McLachlan (though himself a Columbia man), *Princetonians 1748–1768: biographical dictionary* (Princeton, NJ, Princeton University Press, 1976); Martha Lou Lemmon Stohlman, *John Witherspoon: Person, politician, patriot* (Philadelphia, Westminster Press, 1976), and the valuable edition of Witherspoon's letters, *John Witherspoon Comes to America*, ed. L. H. Butterfield (Princeton, Princeton University Library, 1953), which traces his doubts and his hopes. Young Billy Patterson, a future associate justice of the Supreme Court, greeted the news of Witherspoon's coming by writing to his chum John McPherson; "Mercy on me: We shall be overrun with Scotchmen, the worst vermin under heaven." Cf. the study of Quaker, Anglican, Puritan, and Moravian Churches in the papers presented at the Sesquicentennial Symposium at Moravian College in Bethlehem, printed as a special issue of the quarterly, *Pennsylvania History*

XXV (no. 3, July 1958); and Howard Miller, *The Revolutionary College: American Presbyterian higher education 1707–1837* (New York, New York University Press, 1976). S. E. Morison, *The Founding of Harvard College* (Cambridge, MA, Harvard University Press, 1935), and *Harvard College in the Seventeenth Century*, 2 vols (Harvard University Press, 1936), are the master's tributes to *alma mater*. See also "The Gentlemen's Library in early Virginia," *Huntington Library Quarterly*, (1937); H. L. Ganter, "William Small, Jefferson's beloved teacher," *William & Mary Quarterly*, 3rd ser., 2 (1946); P. J. Anderson, "Aberdeen influence on American universities," *Aberdeen University Review*, 5 (1917–18).

For the Scottish contribution to American independence, see Caroline Robbins, *The Eighteenth-Century Commonwealthman* (Cambridge, MA, Harvard University Press, 1961), and J. Clive and Bernard Bailyn, "England's cultural provinces: Scotland and America," *William & Mary Quarterly*, 11 (1954); Bernard Bailyn, *Education in the Forming of America Society: Needs and opportunities for study* (Chapel Hill, NC, IEAHC, 1960) was a seminal study, as was his (ed.) *Pamphlets of American Revolution*, vol. I (Cambridge, MA, Harvard University Press, 1965) esp. its introductory essay, "The transforming radicalism of the American Revolution."

The best account of the shaping of student attitudes at colonial colleges is in David Robson, *Educating Republicans: The college in the era of the American Revolution 1750–1800* (Westport, Greenwood, Conn., 1985), and in two articles by Louis Tucker of the Massachusetts Historical Society, *Connecticut's Seminary of Sedition: Yale College* (Chester, Conn., 1974), and "Centers of sedition: colonial colleges and the American Revolution," (Massachusetts Historical Society, *Proceedings*, XCI, 1979), pp. 16–34. The best study of New England is James Axtell, *The School upon a Hill: Education and society in colonial New England* (New Haven, Yale University Press, 1974). For Franklin's world, see Carl and Jessica Bridenbaugh, *Rebels and Gentlemen: Philadelphia in the age of Franklin* (New York, Oxford University Press, 1962), esp. ch. 2, and Esmond Wright, *Franklin of Philadelphia* (Cambridge, MA, Harvard University Press, 1986). For Edwards, see Perry Miller, *Jonathan Edwards* (New York, Macmillan, 1940), Alfred O. Aldridge, *Jonathan Edwards* (New York, Macmillan, 1964) and David Levin (ed), *Jonathan Edwards: A profile* (New York, Hill and Wang, 1969). Cf. also Edmund Morgan, *Visible Saints: The history of a Puritan idea* (New York, New York University Press, 1963); Alan Heimert, *Religion and the American Mind: From the Great Awakening to the Revolution* (Cambridge, MA, Harvard University Press, 1966); and Nathan O. Hatch and Harry S. Stout (eds), *Jonathan Edwards and the American Experience* (New York, Oxford University Press, 1988).

For background on the Enlightenment in America, consult Henry F. May, *The Enlightenment in America* (New York, Oxford University Press, 1976), and Adrienne Koch (ed.), *The American Enlightenment* (New York, Braziller, 1965); also Norman Fiering, *Jonathan Edward's Moral Thought and its British Context* (Chapel Hill, NC, IEAHC, 1981).

8 WHY, THEN, INDEPENDENCE?

As is inevitable, controversy among historians still surrounds the causes of the War. Oliver M. Dickerson, *The Navigation Acts and the American Revolution* (Philadelphia, University of Pennsylvania Press, 1951), and Lawrence A. Harper, *The English Navigation Laws* (New York, Columbia University Press, 1939), come to opposite conclusions regarding the effect of British trade policies. The colonial fear of episcopacy is a main theme in Carl Bridenbaugh, *Mitre and Sceptre: Transatlantic faiths, ideas, personalities, 1689–1775* (New York, Oxford University Press, 1962). L. W. Labaree, *Royal Government in America* (New Haven, Yale University Press, 1930), should be compared with Jack P. Greene, *The Quest for Power 1689–1776* (Chapel Hill, NC, IEAHC, 1963), and both with S. Saunders Webb, *The Governors General: The English colonies and the definition of the empire, 1569–1689* (Chapel Hill, NC, IEAHC, University of North Carolina Press, 1979). Kenneth Coleman, *The American Revolution in Georgia* (New York, Scribner's, 1958), and Davis S. Lovejoy, *Rhode Island and the American Revolution* (Providence, Brown University Press, 1958), are two examples of good regional studies by authors who do not feel that class conflict played a major part in bringing about the revolution.

For some historians, fundamental political and constitutional theories were at issue. See Bernard Bailyn, "Political experience and Enlightenment ideas in eighteenth-century America," *American Historical Review*, 67 (Jan. 1962), pp. 339–51, and the same author's *The Ideological Origins of the American Revolution* (Cambridge, MA, Harvard University Press, 1967). See also H. Trevor Colbourn, *The Lamp of Experience* (Chapel Hill, NC, IEAHC, University of North Carolina Press, 1965). For a delightful sketch of the political rivalries ripening into an intellectual companionship, see Merrill D. Peterson, *Adams and Jefferson: A revolutionary dialogue* (Oxford, Oxford University Press, 1976).

General introductions

For events up to the outbreak of the War and as a general introduction, see John C. Miller, *The Origins of the American Revolution* (New York, Oxford University Press, 1945; rev. 1959 and 1966, Stanford, Stanford University Press); Pauline Maier, *From Resistance to Revolution: Colonial radicals and the development of American opposition to Britain 1765–1776* (London, Routledge and Kegan Paul, 1973); L. H. Gipson, *The Coming of the Revolution 1763–1775* (New York, Harper and Row, Harper Torchbooks, 1954); and my own studies, *Fabric of Freedom 1763–1800* (London, Macmillan, 1964; 2nd edn 1978), and *Causes and Consequences of the American Revolution* (Chicago, Quadrangle Books, 1966), in both of which are fuller bibliographies.

For the Boston Tea Party, see Benjamin Labaree, *The Boston Tea Party* (New York, Oxford University Press, 1964). There is an admirable essay on the Boston caucus by Alan and Katherine Day in *Journal of American Studies* (published by Cambridge University Press for the British Association for American Studies in 1971), vol. 5.

On the propaganda that led up to the outbreak of war, see Philip Davidson *Propaganda and the American Revolution* (Chapel Hill, NC, University of North Carolina Press, 1941); John C. Miller, *Samuel Adams, Pioneer in Propaganda* (1936; republished Stanford, Stanford University Press, 1960); A. J. Schlesinger, Sr., *Prelude to Independence: The newspaper war on Britain 1764–1768* (New York, Knopf, 1966); and Sydney Pomerantz, "Patriot newspapers and the American Revolution," in R. B. Morris (ed.), *The Era of the American Revolution* (New York, Columbia University Press, 1939; New York, Harper and Row, Harper Torchbooks, 1964).

General surveys of the War of Independence

There are many readable popular general surveys of the War. Among them are Richard Ketchum, *The Winter Soldiers: George Washington and the way to Independence* (London, Macdonald, 1973); Michael Pearson, *Those Damned Rebels* (London, Heinemann, 1972); and Reginald Hargreaves, *The Bloody Backs; British servicemen in North America 1655–1783* (London, Hart Davis, 1968).

There are a number of other studies, in appearance as popular as the above, which are based on very thorough research and are likely to be found more useful. Among them are Lynn Montross, *The Story of the Continental Army 1775–83* (New York, Barnes and Noble, 1967), originally published as *Rag Tag and Bobtail* (New York, Harper and Row, 1952); Howard H. Peckham, *The War for Independence; A military history* (Chicago, University of Chicago, The Chicago History of American Civilization, 1958); and Harrison Bird, *The March to Saratoga: General Burgoyne and the American Campaign 1777* (London, Oxford University Press, 1963), a follow-up to the same author's *A Battle for a Continent: The French and Indian War 1754–63* (Oxford University Press, 1965), and his *Navies in the Mountains: Battles on the waters of Lake Champlain and Lake George, 1609–1814* (London, Oxford University Press, 1962). J. R. Alden, *The American Revolution, 1775–1783* (New York, The New American Nation Series, Harper and Row, 1954), is a good survey of the War.

For readable extracts, however, one could well begin either with George F. Scheer and Hugh E. Rankin (eds), *Rebels and Redcoats: The living story of the American Revolution* (Cleveland, Ohio, World, 1957), or Samuel E. Morison and H. S. Commager, *The Spirit of '76*, 2 vols (Indianapolis, Bobbs Merrill, 1958), or William P. Cumming and Hugh Rankin, *The Fate of a Nation: The American Revolution through contemporary eyes* (London, Phaidon, 1975).

If, however, one single secondary source had to be cited for introductory reading for the War of American Independence, my own choice would rest between Don Higginbotham, *The War of American Independence* (New York, Macmillan, 1971) and Robert Middlekauff, *The Glorious Cause* (New York, Oxford University Press, 1982). In the same category of excellence, however, should be added John Shy, *Towards Lexington* (Princeton, NJ, Princeton University Press, 1965), and his *A People Numerous and Armed: Reflections on the military struggle for American Independence* (London, Oxford University Press, 1976).

There are a number of interesting older secondary studies and/or biographies. On the early stages of the war, see Alan French, *The Day of Lexington and Concord* (Boston, Little Brown, 1925), *General Gage's Informers* (Ann Arbor, University of Michigan Press, 1932), and *The First Year of the American Revolution* (Boston, Houghton Mifflin, 1934). Compare with Alan French the study by A. B. Tourtelot, *Lexington and Concord: The beginning of the War of the American Revolution* (Norton, 1959; originally published as *William Diamond's Drum*). Tourtelot's study is now in paperback, as are T. J. Fleming's *The Story of Bunker Hill* (London, Collier Books, 1962), and James T. Flexner, *The Benedict Arnold Case* (London, Collier Books, 1962; originally entitled *The Traitor and the Spy*).

Alan Valentine published a biography of Lord George Germain (New York, Oxford University Press, 1962), which was critically received. A superior study of this controversial figure is by Gerald Brown, *The American Secretary: The colonial policy of Lord George German 1775–78* (Ann Arbor, University of Michigan Press, 1964). There was some skepticism about the approach of W. B. Willcox in his study, *Portrait of a General: Sir Henry Clinton and the War of American Independence* (New York, Knopf, 1954), because of its psychological interpretation. Compare Willcox and Frederick Wyatt's article, "Sir Henry Clinton: a psychological exploration in history", in *William & Mary Quarterly*, 16 (1959), pp. 3–26.

J. R. Alden has written two very useful biographies: *General Charles Lee: Traitor or patriot?* (Baton Rouge, Louisiana State University Press, 1951); and *General Gage in America* (Baton Rouge, Louisiana State University Press, 1948). The Hon. Piers Mackesy's *The War for America 1775–1783* (London, Longman, 1964), written from a British point of view, is both readable and scholarly. The serious student of the War, however, will soon need to consult the views of the commanders in the field, notably the commander-in-chief: Washington's *The Writings of George Washington*, ed. John C. Fitzpatrick, were published in 39 vols (Washington, DC, 1931–44); his role in the War has been chronicled almost day by day in Douglas Southall Freeman's *George Washington, a Biography*, 7 vols (New York, Scribner's, 1948–57); vols III, IV, and V are indispensable for the War. Washington is being edited again in a project at the University of Virginia. For shorter treatments, see James

T. Flexner, *George Washington*, 4 vols, (Boston, Little Brown, 1965–72); Marcus Cunliffe, *George Washington, Man and Monument* (London, Collins, 1958); and Esmond Wright, *Washington and the American Revolution* (London, English Universities Press, 1957).

The War in the West

Nor should it be forgotten that there was a war being fought in the West. It was a war as much against the Indians as against the British, since the Iroquois had long been Britain's allies. There are interesting studies of some fascinating figures in it: J. R. Alden, *John Stuart and the Southern Colonial Frontier* (Ann Arbor, University of Michigan Press, 1944); Arthur Pound, *Johnson of the Mohawks* (New York, Macmillan, 1930); and J. W. Lydekker, *The Faithful Mohawks* (Cambridge, Cambridge University Press, 1938). T. P. Abernethy's *Western Lands and the American Revolution* (New York, Appleton-Century, 1937) is a detailed and difficult but valuable book. There is a concise and readable paperback by Jack M. Sosin, *The Revolutionary Frontier 1763–83* (Lincoln, Nebr., University of Nebraska Press and New York Holt, Rinehart and Winston, 1967). For the effect of the War on its participants, and on the civilian population, see the writings of John Shy, especially his *A People Numerous and Armed*, and his essay, and those of Rowland Berthoff and John M. Murrin, in Stephen G. Kurtz and James H. Hutson (eds), *Essays on the American Revolution* (Chapel Hill, NC, University of North Carolina Press, 1973). Cf. Thomas C. Barrow, "The American Revolution as a colonial war of liberation," *William & Mary Quarterly*, 25 (Jan. 1968), pp. 452–64; Charles Royston, *A Revolutionary People at War* (Chapel Hill, NC, IEAHC, University of North Carolina Press, 1979); Ronald D. Hoffman and Peter J. Albert (eds), *Arms and Independence: The military character of the American Revolution* (US Capitol Historical Society, University of Virginia Press, 1984). In the same volume, Don Higginbotham analyses the movements of Cornwallis and the "guerrilla" war against him: "Reflections on the War of Independence," pp. 1–24.

The Loyalists

A number of new studies are now appearing on the Loyalists, largely under the stimulus of the programme for Loyalist Studies Publications under the general direction of Professor Robert East in the City University of New York. Andrew Oliver published a new edition of *The Diary of Samuel Curwen* (Cambridge, MA, Belknap Press of Harvard University Press, 1973); note also Bernard Bailyn, *The Ordeal of Thomas Hutchinson* (Cambridge, MA, Harvard University Press, 1974). Other titles on the Loyalists include Wallace Brown, *The King's Friends* (Providence, RI, Brown University Press, 1965), and *The Good Americans* (New York,

Morrow Paperbacks, 1969); Mary Beth Norton, *The British-Americans* (Boston, Little Brown, 1972); Robert Calhoon, *The Loyalists in Revolutionary America 1760–81* (New York, Harcourt Brace Jovanovich, 1973); J. Gregory Palmer (ed.), *A Bibliography of Loyalist Source Material in the United States, Canada and Great Britain* (Westport, CT, Meckler Books, 1982); and Robert Stansbury Lambert's splendid study of the *South Carolina Loyalists in the American Revolution* (Columbia, University of South Carolina Press, 1987), calculating that 16,000 people in the state were Loyalists (22 percent of the population), and Robert Calhoon's essay, "The Re-integration of the Loyalists and the disaffected," in Jack P. Greene (ed.), *The American Revolution, its Character and Limits* (New York, New York University Press, 1987); cf. also Paul Smith, *Loyalists and Redcoats* (Chapel Hill, NC, IHEAC, University of North Carolina Press, 1964), and Esmond Wright (ed.), *A Tug of Loyalties* (London, Athlone Press, 1974), and idem (ed.), *Red, White and True Blue, The Loyalists in the Revolution* (New York, AMS Press, 1976). Loyalist dilemmas have also been described with much sympathy in a number of short sketches: Catherine Fennelly, "Governor William Franklin of New Jersey," *William & Mary Quarterly*, 6 (1949); E. H. Baldwin, "Joseph Galloway" (Colonial Society of Massachusetts, *Publications*, XXXIV, 1942). Leonard Labaree's essay, "The nature of American Loyalism," *Proceedings of the American Antiquarian Society*, n.s. 54 (1944), is also worth noting, as is Anne Y. Zimmer, *Jonathan Boucher, Loyalist in Exile* (Detroit, Wayne State University Press, 1978).

Economic, social, constitutional aspects

An interesting study of the impact of American affairs on British parliamentary politics is Peter Brown, *The Chathamites: A study in the relationship between personalities and ideas in the second half of the eighteenth century* (London, Macmillan, 1967), especially for the sketches of Shelburne, Isaac Barre, and Jonathan Shipley.

For the Navigation Acts, see Harper, *The English Navigation Laws*, and Dickerson, *The Navigation Acts and the American Revolution*; and for the place of New England in the trading pattern of the Navigation System, see J. F. Shepherd and G. M. Walton, *Shipping, Maritime Trade and the Economic Development of Colonial North America* (Cambridge, Cambridge University Press, 1972), and Michael Kammen, *Empire and Interest: The American colonies and the politics of mercantilism* (Philadelphia, Lippincott, 1970). For the Southern trade, see Thomas Devine, *The Tobacco Lords* (Edinburgh, John Donald, 1975); Jacob M. Price, *France and the Chesapeake: A history of the French tobacco monopoly 1674–1791* (Ann Arbor, University of Michigan Press, 1973), and Alan Kulikoff, *Tobacco and Slaves* (Chapel Hill, NC, University of North Carolina Press, 1986).

The most persuasive exposition of the argument that the Americans were struggling for "the rights of Englishmen" and ready to see in George

III a reincarnation of a wicked Charles I, and that they were engaged in a constitutional struggle against unconstitutional acts, is that of Bernard Bailyn in his brilliant introductory essay to vol. I of *Pamphlets of the American Revolution 1750–76* (Cambridge, MA, Harvard University Press, 1965), entitled "The Transforming radicalism of the American Revolution," reprinted in 1967 as *The Ideological Origins of the American Revolution* (Cambridge, MA, Harvard University Press). In his *Ordeal of Thomas Hutchinson*, Bailyn contends that "while the surface was that of the age of Walpole – hard, cynical, unsentimental, pragmatic, venal – below were the passions of an age of ideology" (p. 32). A similar preoccupation with the reading, language and psychology of the leading colonial politicians and editors occurs in Douglas Adair, *Fame and the Founding Fathers* (New York, Norton, 1974); Colbourn, *The Lamp of Experience*; Caroline Robbins, *The Eighteenth-Century Commonwealthman* (Cambridge, MA, Harvard University Press, 1959); and Gordon S. Wood, *The Creation of the American Republic 1776–87* (Chapel Hill, NC, University of North Carolina Press, 1969). See too Gordon S. Wood, "A Note on mobs in the American Revolution," *William & Mary Quarterly*, 3rd ser., 23 (1966), pp. 635–42. Of interest, too, is Wood's effort to graft Bernard Bailyn's "intellectual" view of the Revolution onto the older socioeconomic approach in "Rhetoric and reality in the American Revolution," *ibid.*, pp. 3–32. For another approach, see Jackson T. Main, "Government by the people: the American Revolution and the democratization of the legislatures," *ibid.*, 391–407; and Staughton Lynd, *Anti-Federalism in Dutchess County, New York* (Chicago, University of Chicago Press, 1962).

It is difficult to assess the importance of economic factors. Charles Beard and Carl Becker laid heavy emphasis on them: see Charles Beard, *The Economic Interpretation of the Constitution* (New York, Macmillan, 1913); Carl L. Becker, *The History of Political Parties in the Province of New York 1760–1776* (Madison, University of Wisconsin, 1909); and also J. F. Jameson, *The American Revolution as a Social Movement* (Princeton, NJ, Princeton University Press, 1940); L. M. Hacker, "The first American Revolution," *Columbia University Quarterly*, 27 (1935). The Becker-Beard approach was followed up by Merrill Jensen, *The Articles of Confederation: An interpretation of the social-constitutional history of the American Revolution, 1774–1781* (Madison, University of Wisconsin, 1948). For an interesting review of his earlier position by Jensen himself, see his article "Democracy and the American Revolution," *Huntington Library Quarterly*, 20 (1956–7), pp. 321–41. The Becker-Beard approach is challenged by Robert E. Brown, *Middle-Class Democracy and the Revolution in Massachusetts, 1691–1780* (Ithaca, NY, Cornell University Press, 1955), which is summarized in his article "Democracy in colonial Massachusetts," *New England Quarterly*, 25 (1952), pp. 291–313. On the controversy, see Elisha P. Douglass, *Rebels and Democrats: The struggle for equal political rights and majority rule during the American Revolution* (Chapel Hill, NC, University of North Carolina Press, 1955).

Recent titles of interest on the role of women are Linda K. Kerber, *Women of the Republic: Intellect and ideology in Revolutionary America* (Chapel Hill, NC, University of North Carolina Press, 1980); Mary Beth Norton, *Liberty's Daughters, the Revolutionary Experience of American Women 1750–1800* (Little Brown, 1980), and her article, "The evolution of white women's experience in early America," *American Historical Review*, 89 (1984), pp. 593–619. The *Pennsylvania Magazine of History and Biography*, 115.2 (Apr. 1991), is devoted to the theme "Women in the Revolutionary Era."

The freshest writing on the transforming radicalism of the war experience, and on its productive impact on altering a classical ideology into what became today's constitutionalism, is in two studies by Gordon Wood, *The Creation of the American Republic 1776–1787* (Chapel Hill, NC, IEAHC, University of North Carolina Press, 1969), and his *The Radicalism of the American Revolution* (New York, Knopf, 1991). Cf. for a more familiar left-wing view Dick Hoerder, *Crowd Action in Revolutionary Massachusetts 1765–1800* (New York, Academic Press, 1977) and two articles of Jesse Lemisch, "Jack Tar in the streets: merchant seamen in the politics of revolutionary America," *William & Mary Quarterly*, 25 (1968), pp. 371–407, and "The American Revolution from the bottom up," in Barton J. Bernstein (ed.) *Towards a New Past: Dissenting essays in American history* (New York, Random House, 1968).

Fiction

It should not be forgotten that there are some pieces of fiction which are still good reading. Robert Graves's *Sergeant Lamb of the 9th* (London, Penguin, 1950), is admirable research history presented as fiction, and so is Kenneth Roberts's *Oliver Wiswell* (many editions), an admirable pro-Loyalist portrait, and *Arundel*, the story of Benedict Arnold's expedition against Quebec. See also Walter D. Edmond's *Drums Along the Mohawk* (Bantam Books, 1936; 1956), and not least the novels of James Fenimore Cooper, especially *The Spy* (many editions), in which the hero is secretly in the intelligence service of "Mr Harper" (George Washington). As history, but with many of the qualities of fiction, note Catherine Crary, "The Tory and the Spy: the double life of James Rivington," in *William & Mary Quarterly*, 16.1 (Jan. 1959), pp. 61–72; Lewis Einstein, *Divided Loyalties* (London, Cobden Sanderson, 1933); and Carl Van Doren's *Secret History of the Revolution* (New York, Viking Press, 1941).

Quick reference

For quick and factual reference, see the admirable handbooks of Colonel Mark M. Boatner III, *Encylopedia of the American Revolution* (New York, McKay, 1966), and *Landmarks of the American Revolution* (Stackpole

Books, Harrisburg, PA, 1973). There are also two valuable compendia edited in recent years by Jack P. Greene and J. R. Pole: *The Blackwell's Encyclopedia of the American Revolution* (Oxford, Blackwell, 1991), and *Colonial British America: Essays in the new history of the early modern era* (Baltimore, Johns Hopkins University Press, 1984).

Index

Index by Meg Davies